Beginning Java EE 5

From Novice to Professional

Kevin Mukhar and Chris Zelenak
with James L. Weaver and Jim Crume

Apress®

Beginning Java EE 5: From Novice to Professional

ISBN (pbk): 1-59059-470-3

Printed and bound in the United States of America 9 8 7 6 5 4 3 2 1

Lead Editor: Steve Anglin
Technical Reviewer: Dilip Thomas
Editorial Board: Steve Anglin, Dan Appleman, Ewan Buckingham, Gary Cornell, Tony Davis, Jason Gilmore, Jonathan Hassell, Chris Mills, Dominic Shakeshaft, Jim Sumser
Project Manager: Sofia Marchant
Copy Edit Manager: Nicole LeClerc
Copy Editors: Marilyn Smith, Ami Knox, Nicole LeClerc
Assistant Production Director: Kari Brooks-Copony
Production Editor: Laura Cheu
Compositor: Susan Glinert Stevens
Proofreader: Elizabeth Berry
Indexer: Broccoli Information Management
Artist: Kinetic Publishing Services, LLC
Cover Designer: Kurt Krames
Manufacturing Director: Tom Debolski

Distributed to the book trade worldwide by Springer-Verlag New York, Inc., 233 Spring Street, 6th Floor, New York, NY 10013. Phone 1-800-SPRINGER, fax 201-348-4505, e-mail orders-ny@springer-sbm.com, or visit http://www.springeronline.com.

For information on translations, please contact Apress directly at 2560 Ninth Street, Suite 219, Berkeley, CA 94710. Phone 510-549-5930, fax 510-549-5939, e-mail info@apress.com, or visit http://www.apress.com.

The source code for this book is available to readers at http://www.apress.com in the Source Code section.

Contents at a Glance

Contents

About the Authors

KEVIN MUKHAR is a software developer from Colorado Springs, Colorado. For the past seven years, he has worked on various software systems using different Java Enterprise technologies. He has coauthored several other books, including *Beginning Java Databases: JDBC, SQL, J2EE, EJB, JSP, XML* (Wrox, 2001; ISBN 1-86100-437-0) and *The Ultimate Palm Robot* (Osborne/McGraw-Hill, 2003; ISBN 0-07-222880-6). In addition to developing software during the day, he is working on a master's degree in computer science. His web page is `http://home.earthlink.net/~kmukhar/`.

CHRIS ZELENAK is a programmer at Learning Assistant Technologies, where he helps in the development of server-side Cocoon and Rails applications, Java and .NET client applications, and rampant devil's advocacy. He recently graduated from the Computer Science department of Indiana Wesleyan University, and is writing this introduction.

JIM WEAVER is a founding partner of Learning Assistant Technologies (`www.lat-inc.com`), a company that specializes in learning and medical software development.

JIM CRUME (`jcrume@fusionalliance.com`) is a Java architect with Fusion Alliance, an Indianapolis-based consulting company that specializes in web applications development. Jim has spent many years as a consultant, and he specializes in architecting and developing web-based systems. For the past seven years, Jim has worked on many software systems using J2EE technologies.

About the Technical Reviewer

DILIP THOMAS is an open source enthusiast who keeps a close watch on LAMP technologies, open standards, and the full range of Apache Jakarta projects. He is coauthor of *PHP MySQL Website Programming: Problem – Design – Solution* (Apress, 2003; ISBN 1-59059-150-X) and a technical reviewer/editor on several open source/open standard book projects. Dilip is an editorial director at Software & Support Verlag GmbH.

Dilip resides in Bangalore with his beautiful wife, Indu, and several hundred books and journals. You can reach him via e-mail at `dilip.thomas@gmail.com`.

Acknowledgments

The thing that excites me most about programming is the ability to make ideas come alive through software. I enjoy writing software that makes someone's job better or easier. And I enjoy sharing what I know with other programmers. That's why I'm grateful to the editors at Apress for letting me contribute to this book. I hope that what we've written in this book will help you do your job a little bit better or easier.

This edition has been in the works for over a year, and during that year, my wife and I have experienced a lot of changes and challenges. I'd like to thank the many people who helped throughout that year: Tom and Marg Gimmy, the doctors and nurses at Harrogate Health Center, Dave and Kris Johnson, my family, Anne's family, the doctors and nurses at University of Chicago Hospital, Dr. Maria Augusteijn, Dr. Richard Meinig, Dr. Brian Toolan, Dawn Girard, Don Haase, Tedd Dawson, Judy French, Sondra Wenzel, Jenn Masamitsu, the fall semester CS330 class at UCCS, and all the folks at Apress.

Finally, this book is dedicated to my wife, Anne, and my daughter, Christine.

Kevin Mukhar

I would not have been able to finish this book without the expert assistance of Jim Crume, whose fast provision of code and sharp wit were necessary encouragements to my revisions. Kevin Mukhar also deserves my thanks, for being gracious enough to allow a fledgling writer to help in this book's revision. I would also like to thank (and thank, and thank) the people at Apress, who showed an astronomic amount of patience with the work in preparing this book, most notably Laura Brown (who departed partway through to welcome her son, Ian Daniel Brown, into the world), Steve Anglin, Sofia Marchant, Dilip Thomas, Marilyn Smith, and Laura Cheu. The patience of my seemingly worldwide network of friends and family has been incredibly appreciated, and I wish I could name you all and do you justice: Michelle and Derek, Becky and John from CARE Auto Auction, Russell and Boggstown, Chorna, AJ, Keith and my brother Matt—you all seemed to show up just when I needed you. Most important, I'd like to acknowledge my parents, John and Lynn Zelenak, whom no compliment could truly do justice. Jim Weaver, your trust allowed me to assist in revising this edition and also make a good friend in the process.

Chris Zelenak

This book is dedicated to my wife, Julie; daughters, Lori and Kelli; "son," Marty; and grandson, Kaleb James. Thanks for your constant love and support. It is also dedicated to the memory of Ken Prater, who we miss dearly. Thanks to Merrill and Barbara Bishir, Marilyn Prater, and Walter Weaver for being such wonderful examples. Thanks also to Laura Lee and Steve Brown, Jill Weaver, Shari and Doug Beam, Wade and Dawn Weaver, Dan and David Wright, Jerry and Cheryl Bishir, and Pastor Steve and Cheri Colter. Special thanks go to Chris Zelenak for his tireless effort on this book, and to Apress for their encouragement. Isaiah 26:3.

Jim Weaver

This book is dedicated to my wife, who loves me for who I am; my son Chris and his wife Michelle; and my daughter Liz, who all gave up my time for this project. Again, thanks can't even come close. I love you all! Joshua 24:15.

Jim Crume

Introduction

We, the authors, have read a lot of books on designing and developing software—some better than others—and have spent a lot of time and money in the process. We had some very specific thoughts as we put this book together. The authors of this book are software engineers first. Like you, we have more projects than time to do them in, and we understand that you don't have time to waste when it comes to learning new technologies. We hope the result of our efforts here is a book that you will pick up frequently, highlight, bookmark, and consider a valued addition to your development resources.

First and foremost, the focus of this book is on the practical aspects of getting started with developing distributed software for Java Platform, Enterprise Edition (Java EE). Enterprise Java is a broad and deep subject, and getting started can be like taking a drink from a fire hose. We wanted to put together a practical approach to getting started and spend most of our time talking about the topics that you'll use 90% (or more) of the time. We are serving up meat and potatoes here.

When we pick up a book on software development, we like to have the option of reading straight through or skipping around and picking and choosing the topics that we're interested in at a given time. As an introduction to Java EE, you'll learn the most if you first read through each chapter in order. Later, as you go back to particular sections, you'll find it easy to locate specific concepts to refresh your memory and then skip around in the book. We hope that we've done a good job of making each topic stand on its own and provided examples that are straightforward and relevant.

Like Java Platform, Standard Edition, Java EE consists of several packages that contain classes and interfaces that define the framework. You're already familiar with J2SE, and you gained your expertise by taking the J2SE framework one topic at a time. We'll take Java EE the same way—one topic at a time.

Part of the allure of programming is the breakneck speed with which software components are designed, developed, and made available to users. Java EE 5 could be said to be the poster child for such qualities, as its specification is going through the final steps of development and review at the same time this book is being published. The book you hold in your hands right now attempts to provide a good picture of the specification using the JBoss advance implementation to demonstrate the Java EE features. But the funny thing about specifications in development is that they often change. (Trust us on that one.) The topics presented in the book have been consciously written to present those concepts that are not likely to change. That's no guarantee, however, so we strongly recommend that you visit the book's page on the Apress site (`www.apress.com/book/bookDisplay.html?bID=420`) in case changes or alterations become available. If you'd like to stay abreast of changes made to the specification, keep a close eye on the Java EE 5 specification development page (`http://jcp.org/en/jsr/detail?id=244`), the JBoss website (`www.jboss.com/developers/index`), and the TheServerSide.com site (`www.theserverside.com`).

Who This Book Is For

This book is mainly aimed at people who already have knowledge of standard Java and have been developing small, client-side applications for the desktop. If you have read and absorbed the information contained in an entry-level book such as *Ivor Horton's Beginning Java 2* (Wrox, 2004; ISBN 0-7645-6874-4), then you will be well placed to begin your journey to developing server-side applications using Java EE.

We assume that you know how to use your development environment to compile class files and create JAR files. If you are a vi and command-line lover, we assume you know how to set a classpath and use javac to compile files. If you use an integrated development environment (IDE), we assume you know how to use your IDE to create and compile projects, and deploy those projects. Maybe you use the Jakarta Ant build system; in that case, we assume you can create and run your own Ant build scripts to compile, package, and deploy applications. Whatever system you use, we assume you are comfortable with the process of writing and compiling code.

If you are coming from another object-oriented language, such as C++ or C#, and you wish to begin developing enterprise-level applications with Java, then you will also benefit greatly from this book. The coding concepts, principles, and constructs are similar—you just need to watch out for the syntax differences and, obviously, the different code architecture for the different technology areas of Java EE.

What This Book Covers

This book will take you from having a good grip of the basic Java language to being able to create reusable and scaleable components of Java EE, such as JavaServer Pages (JSP) pages, Enterprise JavaBeans (EJBs), and web services.

The sections that follow present a rundown of what you can expect to see as you work through the book.

Chapter 1: Java EE Essentials

This chapter lays out a road map of what Java EE is and how it is used as an application foundation. You'll get an introduction to the primary components of Java EE and how they fit together.

Chapter 2: Getting Started

Having your machine configured correctly is essential if you want to be able to run the sample code presented in this book. This chapter walks through the installation, configuration, and testing of the core components of Java EE.

Chapter 3: JavaServer Pages

This chapter presents an introduction to the world of server-side web programming using JSP pages. This chapter covers how to write simple JSP pages, covering the fundamentals of the technology and how JSP pages can be useful in your web applications.

Chapter 4: Advanced JSP Topics

In this chapter, we continue our coverage of JSP basics and look at some more advanced features of the technology, such as the expression language, custom actions, and the JSP Standard Tag Library.

Chapter 5: JavaServer Faces

This chapter is an introduction to JavaServer Faces (JSF), a framework for creating component-based user interfaces. You'll learn how to use JSF with JSP pages to create feature-rich user interfaces.

Chapter 6: Servlets

Here we cover another frequently used component in Java EE web applications: Servlets. Servlets are designed to be extensions to servers and to extend the capabilities of servers and provide dynamic behavior.

Chapter 7: Working with Databases

At some point when you're developing a Java EE application, you'll likely need to store and manipulate data in a data source. This is where JDBC comes in.

Chapter 8: Advanced Topics in JDBC

After learning the basic data access functionality in the previous chapter, you'll delve deeper into JDBC in this chapter, which covers prepared statements and stored procedures, transactions, and locking.

Chapter 9: EJB Fundamentals and Session Beans

In this part of the book, we begin to examine a feature of Java EE dedicated to expressing the business logic of an application: Enterprise JavaBeans (EJBs). This chapter mainly focuses on an overview of the EJB technology and looks at session beans in detail.

Chapter 10: EJB Entity Beans

This second chapter on EJBs discusses another type of EJB, entity beans, and how they relate to and fit in with other types of beans. We cover two different types of persistence and take a look at the EJB Query Language (EJB QL).

Chapter 11: EJB Relationships, EJB QL, and JDBC

Creating container-managed relationships and combining the use of JDBC and EJBs are the two topics of this chapter. We also build on the EJB QL foundation from the previous chapter by looking at EJB QL select methods.

Chapter 12: Design Patterns and EJB

In this chapter of the book, we look at what design patterns are, how they can be applied to EJB applications, and what benefits they offer.

Chapter 13: Message-Driven Beans

In the final EJB chapter of the book, we examine message-driven beans (MDBs). MDBs provide a way for your web application to respond to external events.

Chapter 14: Web Services and JAX-WS

The last chapter in the book covers concepts of enabling distributed applications via the magic of web services. We examine web services fundamentals, guidelines, and good practices, and other issues that you should be aware of when creating web services.

Appendix A: Tomcat: Who Needs Java EE 5?

This appendix briefly lists some alternates to running a full application server such as JBoss. It also provides instructions on how to obtain, install, and run the Tomcat web container, which is used in Chapters 3 through 8.

Appendix B: SQL and EJB QL

This appendix provides a brief introduction to the Structured Query Language (SQL) and the Enterprise JavaBeans Query Language (EJB QL), two techniques for accessing data that you can use in Java EE programming. We use SQL in Chapters 7 and 8, and we use both SQL and EJB QL in Chapters 10 and 11.

Appendix C: Java EE Glossary

This appendix features a list of significant Java EE terms and their definitions.

What You Need to Use This Book

The prerequisite system and software requirements for this are not very extensive. Since you already have a background in Java, you no doubt have a version of the J2SE SDK installed on your machine already.

In this book, we've used the latest version of the Standard Edition SDK, which is J2SE 5 at the time of this writing. Throughout the book, we use Microsoft Windows as our operating system, but since Java adheres to the "write once, run anywhere" philosophy, you can use another platform such as Solaris or Linux without any major changes to the code you see.

The other software you'll need is a web container and application server of some kind. In this book, we used the latest release of the Tomcat web container and the JBoss application server. At the time we wrote this book, JBoss was the only application server that supported the EJB 3.0 specification. We used Tomcat stand-alone in Chapters 3 through 8, since the examples in these chapters did not need all the features of JBoss. However, since JBoss uses Tomcat as its web container, you should be able to run all the examples in this book with just the JBoss application server.

Alternatively, you could use any application server that supports the Java EE 5 specification and the various specifications for the other Java EE technologies. We wrote all the code examples in this book to comply with the latest specifications, and we refrained from using features that are Tomcat or JBoss specific. All of the examples should run in any Java EE application server without needing to be changed. However, the deployment steps may vary by application server. For more information, please consult your application server's documentation.

Style Conventions

We have used certain layout conventions and font styles in this book that are designed to help you to differentiate between the various kinds of information. This section outlines the styles used, with an explanation of what they mean.

As you might expect, we present code in two different ways: code used inline with text and code that is displayed on its own. When we need to mention keywords and other coding specifics within the text (e.g., in discussion relating to an `if...else` construct or the `beans` package) we use the single-width font as shown in the parentheses in this sentence. If we want to show a more substantial block of code, we display it like this:

Listing 9-2. *SimpleSessionBean.java*

```
package beans;

import javax.ejb.Stateless;

@Stateless
public class SimpleSessionBean implements SimpleSession {
  public String getEchoString(String clientString) {
    return clientString + " - from session bean";
  }
}
```

If the code is a complete listing that is part of an example, the code will include a caption with a listing number and source name as just shown. In cases where we are presenting a snippet of code, we simply list the code.

Sometimes you will need to type in commands on the command line, which we display using the following style:

```
> set classpath=.;%Java EE_HOME%\lib\j2ee.jar
> javac -d . client/*.java
```

We show the prompt using a > symbol and then the commands you need to type.

■Note Advice, hints, and background information come in this type of font offset by borders. Important pieces of information also come in this format. Depending on the type of information, we preface the text with the word Note, Tip, or Caution. Notes consist of incidental information of one type or another that defines, explains, or elaborates upon the main discussion. Tips will make your programming easier. For instance, a Tip might point out another way to use a certain feature that's not obvious from the main discussion. Cautions indicate a potential hazard. For example, a Caution might be a method that if misused could crash your application server.

Bullets appear indented, with each new bullet marked as follows:

- **Important Words** are in a bold font.
- Words that appear on the screen, or in menus like `File` or `Window`, are in a monospaced font.

Downloading the Code for This Book

Visit the Apress web page for the book at `www.apress.com/book/bookDisplay.html?bID=420`, and then click on the Source Code link (in the "Book Extras" area on the right side of the page) to obtain all the code for the book.

A Note About URLs in XML Files

A major feature of Java Platform, Enterprise Edition 5 (Java EE 5) is the use of XML files to configure web applications and web components. As you will see throughout this book, the elements in these XML files often have attributes that have a uniform resource locator (URL) as their value. For example, one XML file you will see over and over again is called the *deployment descriptor*, and its top-level element looks something like this:

```
<web-app xmlns="http://java.sun.com/xml/ns/javaee"
        xmlns:xsi="http://www.w3.org/2001/XMLSchema-instance"
        xsi:schemaLocation="http://java.sun.com/xml/ns/javaee/web-app_2_5.xsd"
        version="2.5">
```

We have spared no expense to ensure that the URLs used in the book are correct. We have hired scores of authors, editors, reviewers, proofreaders, and occasional random programmers from off the street to check and recheck every URL. Despite our best efforts, though, there is the potential for a problem.

As we mentioned, we wanted this book to be filled with practical information of value to you. Part of making this book useful is ensuring that it is available to you when the technology is available. As of the time of this writing, however, Sun has not finalized the specifications underlying the technologies in this book. It is entirely possible that the specifications will change between the time we publish the book and when you read the book. This affects not only the URLs in XML files, but the entire book as well.

So, as you start testing the examples in this book or experimenting with JSPs, Servlets, and EJBs, you should check both the documentation for your application server and the specification supported by your application server, to ensure you are using the correct format for XML files in your web application.

What to Do If You Encounter Problems

Despite all our best efforts, and despite this book's numerous sharp-eyed editors, there is a possibility that errors managed to sneak through. It has been known to happen.

If you are having problems with any of the text or code examples, the first place to go for corrections is the web page for the book (`www.apress.com/book/bookDisplay.html?bID=420`). If any errata have been identified, you will find a link for Corrections on the book's web page. If you click this link, you will find a page that lists known errors with the code or book text, and corrections for those problems.

If you can't find your problem listed on the Corrections page, you will find a link to Submit Errata on the main book page. If you've double-checked and triple-checked your problem and still can't get the code to work or the text to make sense, use the Submit Errata link to send us a description of the problem. We can't promise a speedy response, but we do see all submissions and post responses to the Corrections page after we've had a chance to check out the problem.

CHAPTER 1

Java EE Essentials

The word *enterprise* has magical powers in computer programming circles. It can increase the price of a product by an order of magnitude and double the potential salary of an experienced consultant. Your application may be free of bugs, and cleanly coded using all the latest techniques and tools, but is it enterprise-ready? What exactly is the magic ingredient that makes enterprise development qualitatively different from run-of-the-mill development?

Enterprise applications solve business problems. This usually involves the safe storage, retrieval, and manipulation of business data: customer invoices, mortgage applications, flight bookings, and so on. They might have multiple user interfaces: a web interface for consumers and a graphical user interface (GUI) application running on computers in the branch offices, for example. Enterprise applications must deal with communication between remote systems, coordinate data in multiple stores, and ensure the system always follows the rules laid down by the business. If any part of the system crashes, the business loses part of its ability to function and starts to lose money. If the business grows, the application needs to grow with it. All this adds up to what characterizes enterprise applications: robustness in the face of complexity.

When we set out to build a GUI application, we don't start by working out how to draw pixels on the screen and build our own code to track the user's mouse around the screen; we rely on a GUI library, like Swing, to do that for us. Similarly, when we set out to create the components of a full-scale enterprise solution, we would be crazy to start from scratch.

Enterprise programmers build their applications on top of systems called *application servers*. Just as GUI toolkits provide services of use to GUI applications, application servers provide services of use to enterprise applications—things like communication facilities to talk to other computers, management of database connections, the ability to serve web pages, and management of transactions.

Just as Java provides a uniform way to program GUI applications on any underlying operating system, Java also provides a uniform way to program enterprise applications on any underlying application server. The set of libraries developed by Sun Microsystems and the Java Community Process that represent this uniform application server application programming interface (API) is what we call the Java Platform, Enterprise Edition 5 (Java EE 5), and it is the subject of this book.

This chapter provides a high-level introduction to Java EE. In this chapter, you will learn:

- Why you would want to use Java EE
- What the benefits of a multitier application architecture are
- How Java EE provides vendor independence and scalability

- What the main Java EE features and concepts are
- How to use common Java EE architectures

So, without further ado, let's get started!

What Is Java EE?

Since you're reading this book, you obviously have some interest in Java EE, and you probably have some notion of what you're getting into. For many fledgling Java EE developers, Java EE equates to Enterprise JavaBeans (EJBs). However, Java EE is a great deal more than just EJBs.

While perhaps an oversimplification, Java EE is a suite of specifications for APIs, a distributed computing architecture, and definitions for packaging of distributable components for deployment. It's a collection of standardized components, containers, and services for creating and deploying distributed applications within a well-defined distributed computing architecture. Sun's Java web site says, " Java Platform, Enterprise Edition 5 (Java EE 5) defines the standard for developing component-based multitier enterprise applications."

As its name implies, Java EE is targeted at large-scale business systems. Software that functions at this level doesn't run on a single PC—it requires significantly more computing power and throughput than that. For this reason, the software needs to be partitioned into functional pieces and deployed on the appropriate hardware platforms. That is the essence of distributed computing. Java EE provides a collection of standardized components that facilitate software deployment, standard interfaces that define how the various software modules interconnect, and standard services that define how the different software modules communicate.

How Java EE Relates to J2SE

Java EE isn't a replacement for the Java 2 Standard Edition (J2SE). J2SE provides the essential language framework on which Java EE builds. It is the core on which Java EE is based. As you'll see, Java EE consists of several layers, and J2SE is right at the base of that pyramid for each component of Java EE.

As a Java developer, you've probably already learned how to build user interfaces with the Swing or Abstract Window Toolkit (AWT) components. You'll still be using those to build the user interfaces for your Java EE applications, as well as HTML-based user interfaces. Since J2SE is at the core of Java EE, everything that you've learned so far remains useful and relevant.

In addition, Java EE provides another API for creating user interfaces. This API is named JavaServer Faces (JSF) and is one of the newest Java EE technologies. You'll also see that the Java EE platform provides the most significant benefit in developing the middle-tier portion of your application—that's the business logic and the connections to back-end data sources. You'll use familiar J2SE components and APIs in conjunction with the Java EE components and APIs to build that part of your applications.

Why Java EE?

Java EE defines a number of services that, to someone developing enterprise-class applications, are as essential as electricity and running water. Life is simple when you simply turn the faucet and water starts running, or flip the switch and lights come on. If you have ever been involved with building a house, you know that there is a great deal of effort, time, and expense in building the infrastructure of plumbing and wiring, which is then so nicely hidden behind freshly painted walls. At the points where that infrastructure is exposed, there are standard interfaces for controlling (water faucets and light switches, for example) and connecting (power sockets, lamp sockets, and hose bibs, for example) to the infrastructure.

Suppose, though, that the wiring and plumbing in your home wasn't already there. You would need to put in your own plumbing and electricity. Without standard components and interfaces, you would need to fabricate your own pipes, wiring, and so on. It would be terrifically expensive and an awful lot of work.

Similarly, there is a great deal of infrastructure required to write enterprise-class applications. There are a bunch of different system-level capabilities that you need in order to write distributed applications that are scalable, robust, secure, and maintainable. Some vital pieces of that infrastructure include security, database access, and transaction control. Security ensures that users are who they claim to be and can access only the parts of the application that they're entitled to access. Database access is also a fundamental component so that your application can store and retrieve data. Transaction support is required to make sure that the right data is updated at the right time. If you're not familiar with some of these concepts, don't worry—you'll be introduced to them one at a time throughout this book.

Putting in a distributed computing infrastructure—the plumbing and wiring of an architecture that supports enterprise applications—is no simple feat. That's why Java EE-based architectures are so compelling; the hard system-level infrastructure is already in place.

But why not custom build (or pay someone to custom build) an infrastructure that is designed around your particular application? Well, for starters, it would take a fantastic amount of time, money, and effort. And even if you were to build up that infrastructure, it would be different from anyone else's infrastructure, so you wouldn't be able to share components or interoperate with anyone else's distributed computing model. That's a lot of work for something that sounds like a dead end. And if you were lucky enough to find a vendor that could sell you a software infrastructure, you would need to worry about being locked into that single vendor's implementation, and not being able to switch vendors at some point in the future.

The good news is, no surprise, that Java EE defines a set of containers, connectors, and components that fill that gap. Java EE not only fills the gap, but it's based on well-known, published specifications. That means that applications written for Java EE will run on any number of Java EE-compliant implementations. The reference implementation supplied with the Java EE Software Development Kit from Sun (Java EE SDK) provides a working model that we'll use throughout this book, since it's the implementation that Sun has built from the specification and is freely available. In the next chapter, you'll get an introduction to installing and testing the Java EE SDK.

Multitier Architecture

One of the recurring themes that you'll run into with Java EE is the notion of supporting applications that are partitioned into several levels, or *tiers*. That is an architectural cornerstone of Java EE and merits a little explanation. If you are already familiar with *n*-tier application architectures, feel free to skip ahead. Otherwise, the overview presented here will be a good introduction or review that will help lay the foundation for understanding the rationale behind much of Java EE's design and the services it provides.

If you think about a software application composition, you can break it down into three fundamental concerns, or logical layers:

- The first area of concern is displaying stuff to the user and collecting data from the user. That user interface layer is often called the *presentation layer*, since its job is to present stuff to the user and provide a means for the user to present stuff to the software system. The presentation layer includes the part of the software that creates and controls the user interface and validates the user's actions.
- Underlying the presentation layer is the logic that makes the application work and handles the important processing. The process in a payroll application to multiply the hours worked by the salary to determine how much to pay someone is one example of this kind of logic. This logical layer is called the *business rules layer*, or more informally the *middle tier*.
- All nontrivial business applications need to read and store data, and the part of the software that is responsible for reading and writing data—from whatever source that might be—forms the *data access layer*.

Single-Tier Systems

Simple software applications are written to run on a single computer, as illustrated in Figure 1-1. All of the services provided by the application—the user interface, the persistent data access, and the logic that processes the data input by the user and reads from storage—all exist on the same physical machine and are often lumped together into the application. That monolithic architecture is called *single tier*, because all of the logical application services—the presentation, the business rules, and the data access layers—exist in a single computing layer.

Single-tier systems are relatively easy to manage, and data consistency is simple because data is stored in only one single location. However, they also have some disadvantages. Single-tier systems do not scale to handle multiple users, and they do not provide an easy means of sharing data across an enterprise. Think of the word processor on your personal computer: It does an excellent job of helping you to create documents, but the application can be used by only a single person. Also, while you can share documents with other people, only one person can work on the document at a time.

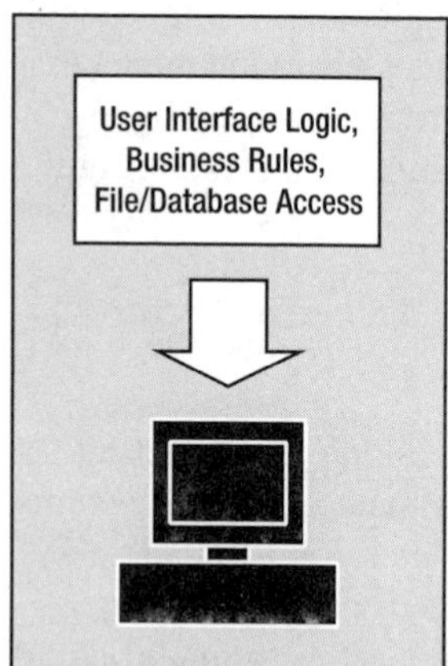

Figure 1-1. *In the traditional computer application, all of the functionality of the application exists on the user's computer.*

Client/Server (Two-Tier) Architecture

More significant applications may take advantage of a database server and access persistent data by sending SQL commands to a database server to save and retrieve data. In this case, the database runs as a separate process from the application, or even on a different machine than the machine that runs the rest of the program. As illustrated in Figure 1-2, the components for data access are segregated from the rest of the application logic. The rationale for this approach is to centralize data to allow multiple users to simultaneously work with a common database, and to provide the ability for a central database server to share some of the load associated with running the application. This architecture is usually referred to as *client/server* and includes any architecture where a client communicates with a server, whether that server provides data access or some other service.

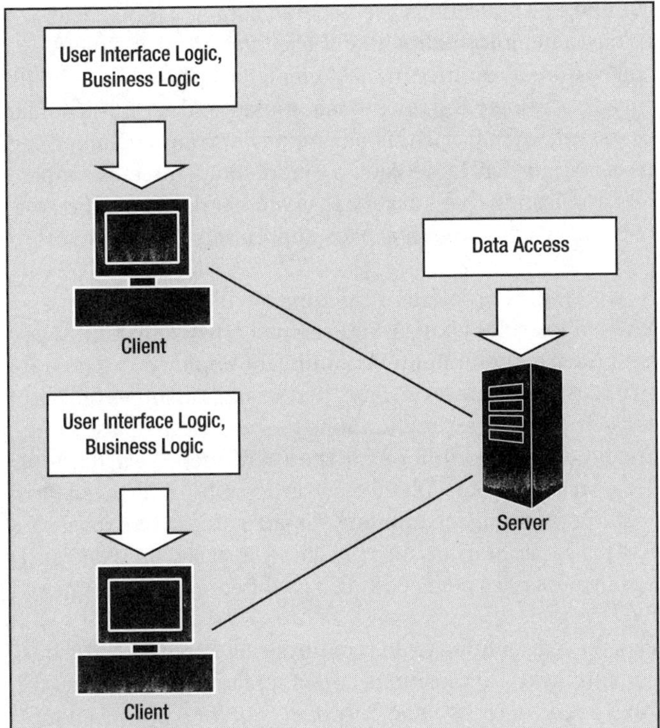

Figure 1-2. *In a client/server architecture, an application client accesses services from another process to do its job.*

It's convenient and more meaningful to conceptualize the division of the responsibility into layers, or tiers. Figure 1-3 shows the client/server software architecture in two tiers.

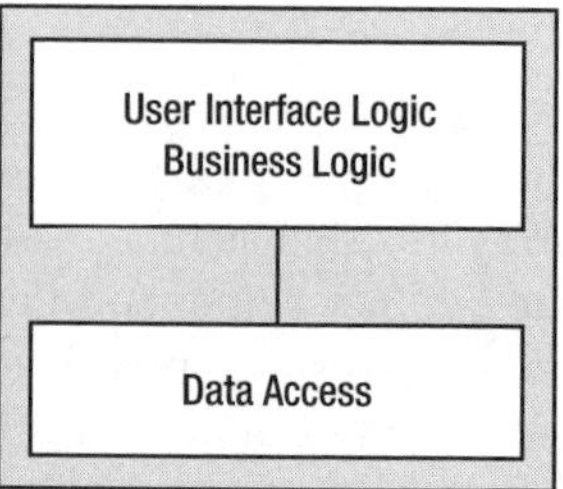

Figure 1-3. *The client/server architecture shown in a layer, or tier, diagram*

One of the disadvantages of two-tier architecture is that the logic that manipulates the data and applies specific application rules concerning the data is lumped into the application itself. This poses a problem when multiple applications use a shared database. Consider, for example, a database that contains customer information that is used for order fulfillment, invoicing, promotions, and general customer resource management. Each one of those applications would need to be built with all of the logic and rules to manipulate and access customer data. For example, there might be a standard policy within a company that any customer whose account is more than 90 days overdue will be subject to a credit hold. It seems simple enough to build that rule into every application that's accessing customer data, but when the policy changes to reflect a credit hold at 60 days, updating each application becomes a real mess.

You might be tempted to try to solve this problem by building a reusable library that encapsulates the business rules. When the rules change, you can just replace that library, rebuild the application, and redistribute it to the computers running the application. There are some fundamental problems with that strategy, however. First, that strategy assumes that all of the applications have been created using the same programming language, run on the same platform, or at least have some strategy for gluing the library to the application. Next, the applications may need to be recompiled or reassembled with the new library. Moreover, even if the library is a drop-in replacement without requiring recompiling, it's still going to be a royal pain to make sure that each installation of the application has the right library installed simultaneously (it wouldn't do to have conflicting business rules being enforced by different applications at the same time).

In order to get out of that mess, the logical thing to do is to physically separate those business rules out from the computers running the applications onto a separate server so that the software that runs the business rules needs to be updated only once, not for each computer that runs the application.

N-Tier Architecture

Figure 1-4 shows a third tier added to the two-tier client/server model. In this model, all of the business logic is extracted out of the application running at the desktop. The application at the desktop is responsible for presenting the user interface to the end user and for communicating to the business logic tier. It is no longer responsible for enforcing business rules or accessing databases. Its job is solely as the presentation layer.

■Note Bear in mind that at this point we're talking somewhat abstractly and theoretically. In a perfect world, without performance and other implications, the division of responsibility in an application would be very clear-cut. You'll see throughout this book that you must make practical, balanced implementation decisions about how responsibilities are partitioned in order to create an application that is flexible and performs well.

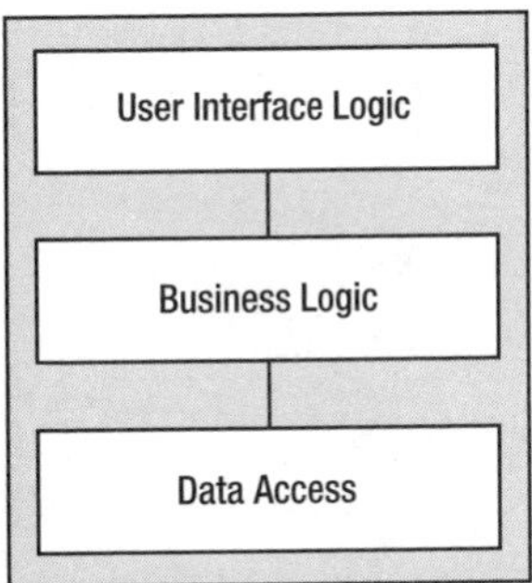

Figure 1-4. *A common enterprise architecture consists of three tiers: presentation, business, and data.*

Typically, in a deployed application, the business logic tier executes on a server apart from the workstation (you'll see shortly that this isn't absolutely required, though). The business logic tier provides the logical glue to bind the presentation to the database. Since it's running on a server, it's accessible to any number of users on the network running applications that take advantage of its business rules. As the number of users demanding those services increases, and the business logic becomes increasingly complex and processor-intensive, the server can be scaled up or more servers can be added. Scaling a single server is a lot easier and cheaper than upgrading everyone's workstations.

One of the really great things that this architecture makes possible is the ability to start to build application models where the classes defined in the business logic tier are taken directly from the application domain. The code in the business logic layer can work with classes that model things in the real world (like a `Customers` class) rather than working with complex SQL statements. By pushing implementation details into the appropriate layer, and designing applications that work with classes modeled from the real world, applications become much easier to understand and extend.

It's possible to continue the process of partitioning the application functionality into increasingly thin functional layers, as illustrated in Figure 1-5. There are some very effective application architectures based on *n*-tier architecture. The application architect is free to partition the application into as many layers as appropriate, based on the capabilities of the computing and network hardware on which the system is deployed. However, you do need to be careful about reaching a point of diminishing returns, since the performance penalty for the network communication between the layers can start to outweigh any gains in performance.

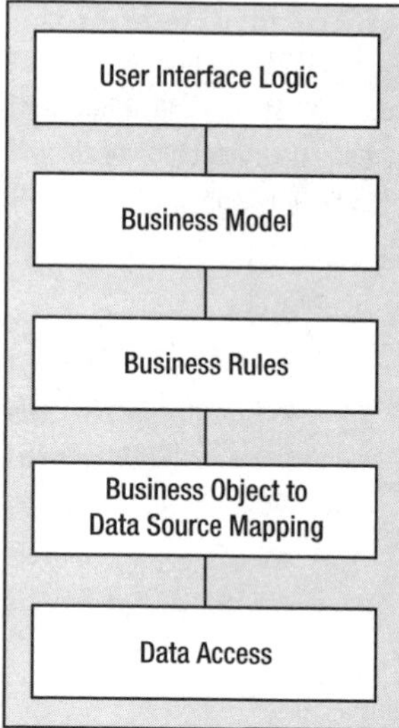

Figure 1-5. *An enterprise application is not limited to two or three tiers. The software architect can design the system to consist of any number of layers, depending on the system requirements and deployment configuration.*

In summary, *n*-tier application architecture is intended to address a number of problems, including the following:

- The high cost of maintenance when business rules change. *N*-tier applications have improved maintainability.
- Inconsistent business rule implementation between applications. *N*-tier applications provide consistency.
- Inability to share data or business rules between applications. *N*-tier applications offer interoperability.
- Inability to provide web-based front ends to line-of-business applications. *N*-tier applications are flexible.
- Poor performance and inability to scale applications to meet increased user load. *N*-tier applications are scalable.
- Inadequate or inconsistent security across applications. *N*-tier applications can be designed to be secure.

The Java EE architecture is based on the notion of *n*-tier applications. Java EE makes it very easy to build industrial-strength applications based on two, three, or more application layers, and provides all of the plumbing and wiring to make that possible.

Note that *n*-tier architecture does not demand that each of the application layers run on a separate machine. It's certainly possible to write *n*-tier applications that execute on a standalone machine, as you'll see. The merit of the application design is that the layers can be split apart and deployed on separate machines, as the application requires.

■ **Note** Labeling a particular architecture as *three-tier*, *five-tier*, and so on is almost guaranteed to spur some academic debate. Some insist that tiers are defined by the physical partitioning, so if the application components reside on client workstations, an application server, and a database server machine, it's definitively a three-tier application. Others will classify applications by the logical partitioning where the potential exists for physical partitioning. For the discussions in this chapter, we'll take the latter approach, with apologies in advance for those who subscribe to the former.

Vendor Independence

Sun Microsystems—the company that created the Java platform and plays a central role in Java technologies, including the Java EE specification—has promoted the Java platform as a solid strategy for building applications that aren't locked into a single platform. In the same way, the architects of Java EE have created it as an open specification that can be implemented by anyone. To date, there are scores of Java EE-based application servers that provide a platform for building and deploying scalable *n*-tier applications. Any application server that bills itself as Java EE-compliant must provide the same suite of services using the interfaces and specifications that Sun has made part of Java EE.

This provides the application developer with a number of choices when implementing a project, and similar choices down the road as more applications are added to an organization's suite of solutions. Building an application atop the Java EE architecture provides substantial decoupling between the application logic that you write and the other stuff—security, database access, transaction support, and so on—provided by the Java EE server..

Remember that all Java EE servers must support the same interfaces defined in the Java EE specification. That means you can design your application on one server implementation and deploy it on a different one. You can decide later that you want to change which Java EE server you use in your production environment. Moving your application over to the new production environment can be almost trivial.

Platform independence is something that you can take advantage of in your development. For example, you may be away from the office quite a bit, and use your notebook computer running Windows to do development. It's pretty easy to use that configuration to build, test, and debug (Java EE has great support for pool-side computing). When you're back in the office and happy with a particular component, you can deploy it to, say, Linux-based servers with little effort, despite the fact that those servers are running a different operating system and different Java EE implementation (after testing, of course!).

Bear in mind that each Java EE vendor provides some added value to its particular Java EE implementation. After all, if there weren't market differentiators, there would be no competition. The Java EE specification covers a lot, but there is also a lot that is not specified in Java EE. Performance, reliability, and scalability are just a few of the areas that aren't part of the Java EE specification but are areas where vendors have focused a great deal of time and attention. That added value may be ease of use in its deployment tools, highly optimized performance, support for server clustering (which makes a group of servers able to serve application clients as if it were a single super-fast, super-big server), and so on. The key point here is to keep two issues in mind:

- Your production applications can potentially benefit from capabilities not supported in the Sun Java EE reference implementation. Just because your application's performance stinks on the reference implementation running on your laptop doesn't mean that Java EE is inherently slow.
- Any vendor-specific capabilities that you take advantage of in your production applications may impact the vendor independence of your application.

Scalability

Defining throughput and performance requirements is a vital step in requirements definition. Even the best of us get caught off-guard sometimes, though. Things can happen down the road—an unanticipated number of users using a system at the same time, increased loading on hardware, unsatisfactory availability in the event of server failure, and so on—that can throw a monkey wrench into the works.

The Java EE architecture provides a lot of flexibility to accommodate changes as the requirements for throughput, performance, and capacity change. The *n*-tier application architecture allows software developers to apply additional computing power where it's needed. Partitioning applications into tiers also enables refactoring of specific pain points without impacting adjacent application components.

Clustering, connection pooling, and failover will become familiar terms to you as you build Java EE applications. Several providers of Java EE application servers have worked diligently to come up with innovative ways to improve application performance, throughput, and availability—each with its own special approach within the Java EE framework.

Features and Concepts in Java EE

Getting your arms around the whole of Java EE will take some time, study, and patience. You'll need to understand a lot of concepts to get started, and these concepts will be the foundation of more concepts to follow. The journey through Java EE will be a bit of an alphabet soup of acronyms, but hang tough—you'll catch on, and we'll do our best on our end to help you make sense of it. Here, we'll provide an overview of some important Java EE features and concepts.

Java EE Clients and Servers

Up to this point, we've been using terms like *client* and *server* somewhat loosely. These terms represent fairly specific concepts in the world of distributed computing and Java EE.

A Java EE client can be a console (text) application written in Java, or a GUI application written using the Java Foundation Classes (JFC) and Swing or AWT. These types of clients are often called *fat clients* because they tend to have a fair amount of supporting code for the user interface.

Java EE clients may also be web-based clients; that is, clients that live inside a browser. Because these clients offload much of their processing to supporting servers, they have very little in the way of supporting code. This type of client is often called a *thin client.* A thin client may be a purely HTML-based interface, a JavaScript-enriched page, or one that contains a fairly simple applet where a slightly richer user interface is needed.

It would be an oversimplification to describe the application logic called by the Java EE clients as the "server," although it is true that, from the perspective of the developer of the client-side code, that illusion is in no small way the magic of what the Java EE platform provides. In fact, the Java EE application server is the actual server that connects the client application to the business logic.

The server-side components created by the application developer can be in the form of web components and business components. Web components come in the form of JSPs or Servlets. Business components, in the world of Java EE, are EJBs.

These server-side components rely on the Java EE framework. Java EE provides support for the server-side components in the form of *containers.*

Containers

Containers are a central theme in the Java EE architecture. Earlier in this chapter, we talked about application infrastructure in terms of the plumbing and electricity that a house provides for its inhabitants. Containers are like the rooms in the house. People and things exist in the rooms, and interface with the infrastructure through well-defined interfaces. In an application server, web and business components exist inside containers and interface with the Java EE infrastructure through well-defined interfaces.

In the same way that application developers can partition application logic into tiers of specific functionality, the designers of Java EE have partitioned the infrastructure logic into logical tiers. They have done the work of writing the application support infrastructure—things that you would otherwise need to build yourself. These include security, data access, transaction handling, naming, resource location, and the guts of network communications that connect the client to the server. Java EE provides a set of interfaces that allow you to plug your application logic into that infrastructure and access those services.

Think of containers as playing a role much like a video gaming console into which you plug game cartridges. As shown in Figure 1-6, the gaming console provides a point of interface for the game—a suite of services that lets the game be accessed by the user and allows the game to interact with the user. The game cartridge needs to be concerned only with itself; it doesn't need to concern itself with how the game is displayed to the user, what sort of controller is being used, or even if the household electricity is 120VAC or 220VAC. The console provides a container that abstracts all of that stuff out for the game, allowing the game programmer to focus solely on the game and not worry about the infrastructure.

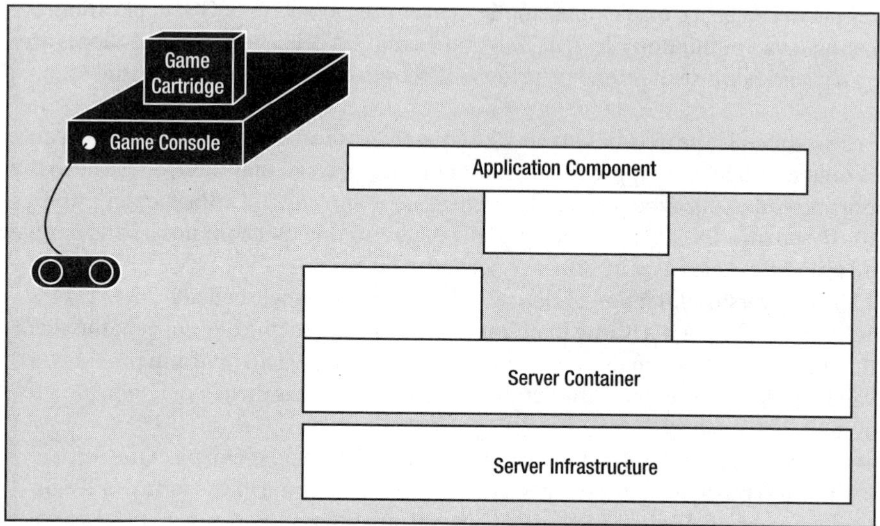

Figure 1-6. *The container provides an environment for components and an interface between the components and the services of the server.*

If you've ever created an applet, you're already familiar with the concept of containers. Most web browsers provide a container for applet components, as illustrated in Figure 1-7. The browser's container for applets provides an environment for the applet. The browser and the container know how to interact with any applet because all applets implement the `java.applet.Applet` class interface. When you develop applets, you are relieved of the burden of interfacing with a web browser, and are free to spend your time and effort on the applet logic. You do not need to be concerned with the issues associated with making your application appear to be an integral part of the web browsers.

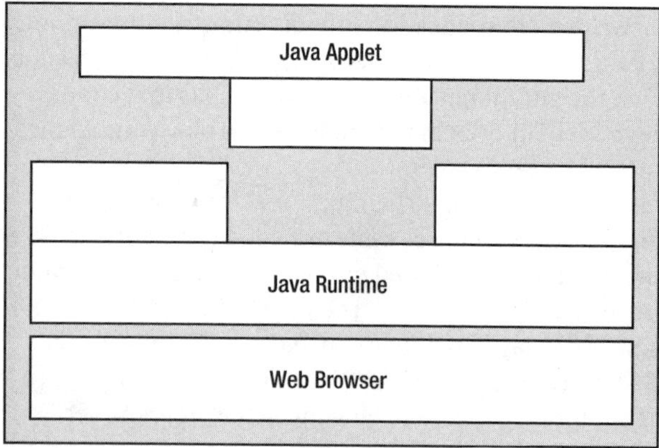

Figure 1-7. *Browsers don't directly access applets. Instead, the applet runs in a container inside the browser. The container provides an environment for the applet and acts as an interface between the browser and the applet.*

Java EE provides server-side containers for the same reason: To provide a well-defined interface, along with a host of services that allow application developers to focus on the business problems they're trying to solve, without worrying about the plumbing and electricity. Containers handle all of the mundane details involved with starting up services on the server side, activating the application logic, and cleaning up the component.

Java EE and the Java platform provide containers for web components and business components. These containers—like the gaming console analogy presented earlier in the chapter—provide an environment and interface for components that conform to the container's established interfaces. The containers defined in Java EE include a container for Servlets, JSPs, and EJBs.

Java Servlets

You are no doubt familiar with accessing simple, static HTML pages using a browser that sends a request to a web server, which, in turn, sends back a web page that's stored at the server, as illustrated in Figure 1-8. In that role, the web server is simply being used as a virtual librarian that returns a document based on a request.

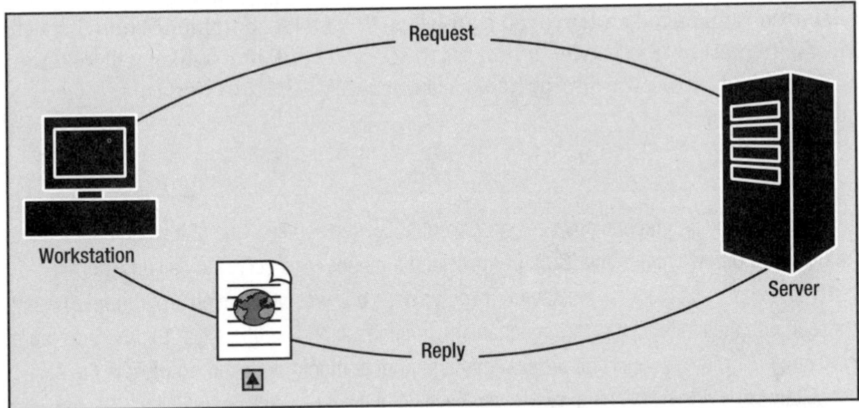

Figure 1-8. *A web browser running on a workstation sends a request to a web server. The server identifies the web page specified in the request and returns that web page to the browser.*

That model of serving up static web pages doesn't provide for dynamically generated content, though. For example, suppose that the web client wants the server to return a list of HTML documents based on some query criteria. In that case, some means of generating HTML on the fly and returning it to the client is needed, as illustrated in Figure 1-9.

Servlets are one of the technologies developed to enhance servers. A Servlet is a Java component implementing the `javax.servlet.Servlet` interface. It is invoked as a result of a client request for that particular Servlet. The Servlet model is fairly generic and not necessarily bound to the Web and HTTP, but all of the Servlets that you'll encounter will fall into that category. The web server receives a request for a given Servlet in the form of an HTTP query. The web server, in turn, invokes the Servlet and passes back the results to the requesting client. The Servlet can be passed parameters from the requesting web client. The Servlet is free to perform whatever computations it cares to, and returns results to the client in the form of HTML.

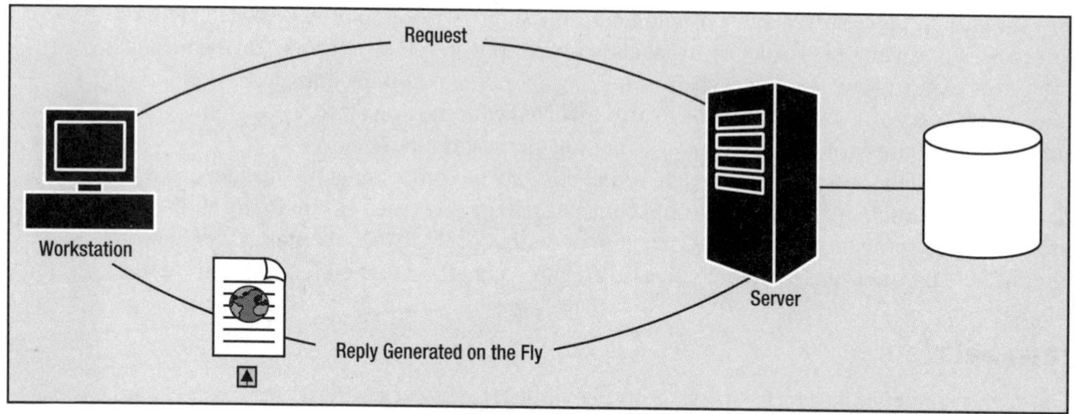

Figure 1-9. *Web servers can be supplemented by other processes that perform data access or some other processing. This other processing is then converted into an HTML web page and sent back to the client. Thus, web servers that were designed to serve static content can be enhanced to provide dynamic content.*

The Servlet itself is managed and invoked by the Java EE Servlet container. When the web server receives the request for the Servlet, it notifies the Servlet container, which will load the Servlet as necessary, and invoke the appropriate `javax.servlet.Servlet` interface service method to satisfy the request.

■ **Note** Servlets were not the first technology designed to enhance web servers. One of the earlier solutions is known as the Common Gateway Interface (CGI). CGI provided a means for a server to call an external process that performed additional work for the server. If you've done any web application programming using CGI, you'll be familiar with the limitations of that mechanism, including lack of portability (CGI programs were often written in C) and no intrinsic support for session management (a much-overused example is the ability to maintain a list of items in a virtual shopping cart). If you have not done any development using CGI, consider yourself lucky and take our word for it—life with Java EE is a whole lot better!

Java Servlets are portable, and as you will see in later chapters, the Servlet containers provide support for session management that allows you to write complex web-based applications. Servlets can also incorporate JavaBean components (which share little more than a name with Enterprise JavaBeans) that provide an additional degree of application compartmentalization. Servlets are covered in detail in Chapter 6.

JavaServer Pages (JSPs)

JSPs, like Servlets, are concerned with dynamically generated web content. These two web components—Servlets and JSPs—comprise a huge percentage of the content of real-world Java EE applications.

Building Servlets involves building Java components that emit HTML. In a lot of cases, that works out well. However, that approach isn't very accessible for people who spend their time on the visual side of building web applications and don't necessarily care to know much about software development. Enter JSP. JSP pages are HTML-based text documents with chunks of Java code called *scriptlets* embedded into the HTML document.

When JSPs are deployed, something remarkable happens: The contents of the JSP are rolled inside out, like a sock, and a Servlet is created based on the embedded tags and Java code scriptlets, as shown in Figure 1-10. This happens pretty much invisibly. If you care to, you can dig under the covers and see how it works (which makes learning about Servlets all the more worthwhile).

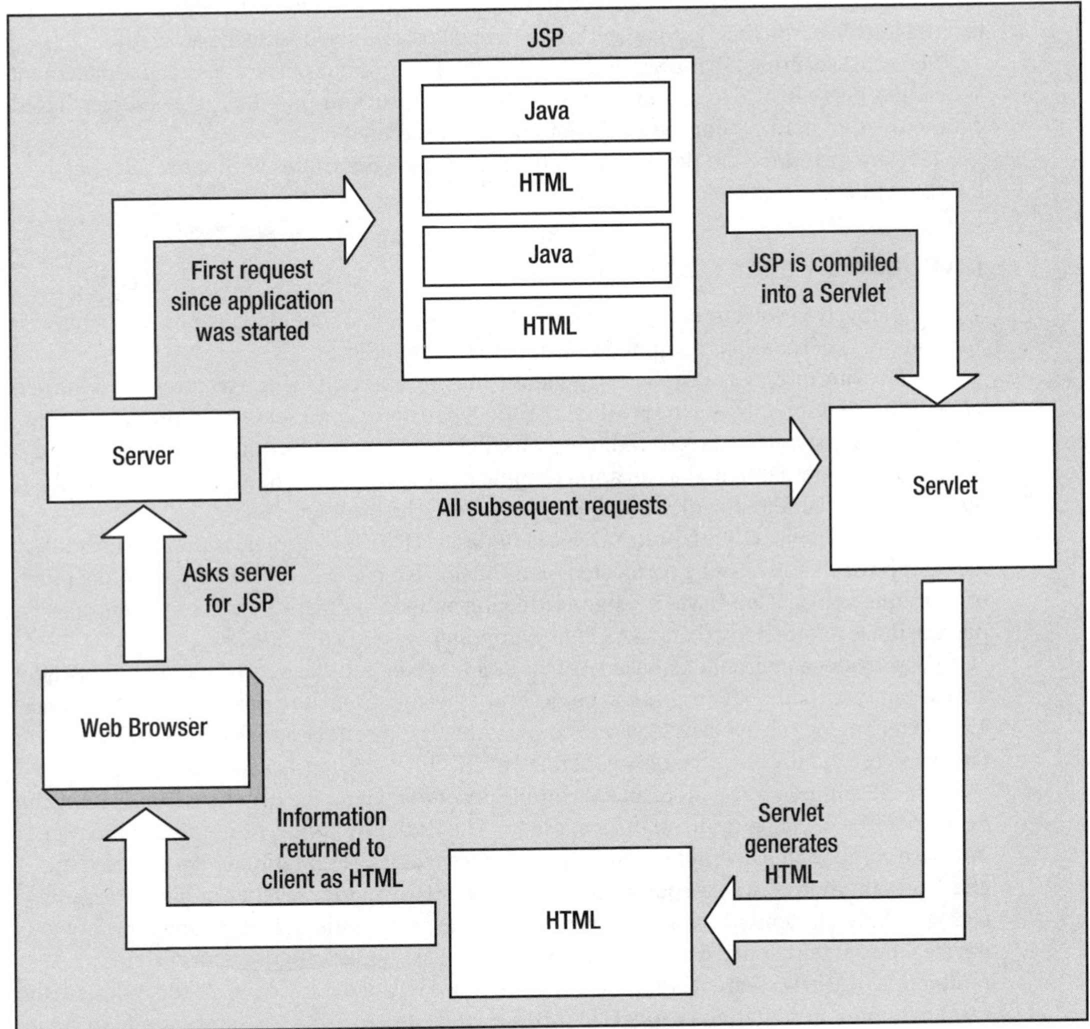

Figure 1-10. *When a web server receives a request for a JSP, it passes the request to the JSP container (not shown). If the JSP page has not been translated, the container translates the JSP into a Java Servlet source file, and then compiles the source file into a class. The Servlet class is loaded and the request is passed to the class. The Servlet processes the request and returns the result to the client. All subsequent requests are routed directly to the Servlet class, without the need to translate or compile again.*

You may have had some exposure to JavaScript, which is a Java-like scripting language that can be included within a web page, and is executed by the web browser when a page containing JavaScript code is sent to the browser. JSP is a little like that, but the code is compiled and executed at the *server*, and the resulting HTML is fed back to the requesting client. JSP pages are lightweight and fast (after the initial compilation to the Servlet), and they provide a lot of scalability for web-based applications.

Developers can create both static and dynamic content in a JSP page. Because content based on HTML, XML, and so on forms the basis of a JSP page, a nontechnical person can create and update that portion of a page. A more technical Java developer can create the snippets of Java code that will interface with data sources, perform calculations, and so on—the dynamic stuff.

Since an executing JSP is a Servlet, JSP provides the same support for session management as Servlets. JSPs can also load and call methods of JavaBean components, access server-based data sources, or perform complex calculations at the server.

JSPs are introduced in detail in Chapter 3. Chapter 4 continues with more advanced JSP concepts.

JavaServer Faces (JSF)

JSF is a relatively new technology that attempts to provide a robust, rich user interface for web applications. JSF is used in conjunction with Servlets and JSPs.

When using just JSPs or Servlets to generate the presentation, your user interface is limited to what can be implemented in HTML. HTML does provide a good set of user interface components, such as lists, check boxes, radio buttons, fields, labels, and buttons. Alternatively, the client might be implemented as an applet. Applets can provide a rich user interface, but they do require the client to download and execute code in the browser.

The main drawback with both Servlet-generated HTML and applets is that the user interface components still must be connected to the business logic. When using this solution, much of your time as a developer will be spent retrieving and validating request parameters, and passing those parameters to business logic components.

JSF provides a component-based API for building user interfaces. The components in JSF are user interface components that can be easily put together to create a server-side user interface. The JSF technology also makes it easy to connect the user interface components to application data sources, and to connect client-generated events to event handlers on the server.

The JSF components handle all the complexity of managing the user interface, leaving the developer free to concentrate on business logic. The flexibility comes from the fact the user interface components do not directly generate any specific presentation code. Creating the client presentation code is the job of custom renderers. With the correct renderer, the same user interface components could be used to generate presentation code for any arbitrary device. Thus, if the client's device changed, you would simply configure your system to use a renderer for the new client, without needing to change any of the JSF code. At the moment, the most common presentation format is HTML, and JSF comes with a custom renderer to create HTML user interfaces. JSF technology is covered in Chapter 5.

JDBC

If you've done anything at all on the Web other than simple surfing, you've probably used a database. Of course, that database has been hidden behind a fancy user interface, but you've used one nonetheless.

Have you searched for books or other products at `www.amazon.com` or `www.costco.com` or any other online store? The information about the products for sale is kept in some kind of database.

Have you searched for web sites on `www.google.com` or `www.yahoo.com` or any other search engine? Information about web pages and the data in them is kept is some kind of database.

Have you looked for information about public laws (`thomas.loc.gov`), driving directions (`www.mapquest.com`), or satellite imagery (`www.terraserver.com`)? This information is kept in some kind of database.

The examples can go on and on. The point should be clear though: Almost any type of nontrivial application will use a database of some kind. In the previous sentence, the term *database* is used in its loosest most general meaning as a collection of some data. That database could be anything from a text file of information for very simple applications to full-blown, enterprise-level relational or object databases for very complex systems. It could also include other data-storage systems, such as directories.

Most Java EE applications will include some kind of data-storage solution. Most often, that data-storage solution will be a relational database server of some kind. The database server may be an integral part of the application server, or it may be an application separate from the application server.

In any case, your application components need some means to communicate with the data-storage system. That is the job of JDBC. JDBC is a set of common APIs and system-specific libraries for communicating with a data-storage system. By communicating with the data-storage system through the common APIs, you can concentrate on the data, without needing to learn custom syntax for the particular data-storage system; that job is left to the system-specific library.

Most JDBC applications are used to communicate with a relational database. In a relational database, data is stored, conceptually, in tables. Each row in a table represents a set of data—a customer record, product information, a web site listing, and so on. And each column in the table represents a piece of data in that set. Tables can be linked by creating a *relation* between tables, thus it's called a *relational* database. For example, a database might have a table of customer information and a table of information about orders. It makes no sense to repeat customer information for each order, so the orders table would include a customer ID that corresponds to a similar piece of data in the customers table, thus relating every order to a customer.

While JDBC is used most often with relational databases, it can be used with any data-storage system, as long as someone has created a system-specific library for that data-storage system. Using JDBC in Java EE applications is covered in Chapters 7 and 8.

EJBs

EJBs are to Java EE what Mickey Mouse is to Disney—they represent the flagship technology of the platform. When Java EE is mentioned, EJBs are what immediately comes to mind. We mentioned earlier that Java EE is a whole lot more than EJB, but we don't mean to trivialize EJBs; the attention that the technology gets is certainly merited.

In order to better understand what EJBs are and do, it helps to start out with Java's Remote Method Invocation (RMI). If you're not already familiar with RMI, or if you need a quick overview or a refresher, you may want to refer to `http://java.sun.com/rmi`.

RMI is Java's native means of allowing a Java object to run on one computer and have its methods called by another object running on a separate computer across a network. In order to create a remote object with RMI, you first design an interface that extends the `java.rmi.Remote` interface. This interface defines the operations that you want to expose on your remote object. The next step is to design the remote object as a Java class that implements the interface you've defined. This class extends the `java.rmi.server.UnicastRemoteObject` class, which provides the necessary network communications between this object and the objects that call it. Finally, you write an application that creates an instance of this class and registers that instance with the RMI registry.

The RMI registry is a simple lookup service that provides a means to associate a name with an object, analogous to the way a phone directory associates a name to a phone number. The same registry service is used by the client application, which requests a named object from the registry. Once it receives a local reference to the remote object, it can call the methods of the object; however, rather than executing the method on the client's computer, the method call is passed across the network and executed on the machine where the remote object resides.

What RMI provides is a bare-bones client/server implementation. It provides the basic stuff: a registry for lookup, the guts of network communication for invoking operations and passing parameters to and from remote objects, and a basic mechanism for managing access to system resources as a safeguard against malicious code running on a remote computer.

However, RMI is lightweight. It's not designed to satisfy the requirements of enterprise-class distributed applications. It lacks the essential infrastructure that enterprise-class applications rely on, such as security, data access, transaction management, and scalability. While it supplies base classes that provide networking, it doesn't provide a framework for an application server that hosts your server-side business components and scales along with your application. You must write the client and the server applications. This is where EJBs come into the picture.

EJBs are Java components that implement business logic. This allows the business logic of an application (or suite of applications) to be compartmentalized into EJBs and kept separate from the front-end applications that use that business logic.

The Java EE architecture includes a server that is a container for EJBs. The EJB container loads the bean as needed, invokes the exposed operations, applies security rules, and provides the transaction support for the bean. If it sounds to you like the EJB container does a lot of work, you're right—the container provides all of the necessary plumbing and wiring needed for enterprise applications.

As you'll see in Chapter 9, building EJBs follows the same basic steps as creating an RMI object. You create an interface that exposes the operations or services provided by the EJB. You then create a class that implements the interface. When you deploy an EJB to an application server, the EJB is associated with a name in a registry. Clients can look up the EJB in the registry, and then remotely call the methods of the EJB. Since the EJB container provides all of the enterprise plumbing, you get to spend more time building your application and less time messing around with trying to shoehorn in services like security and transaction support.

EJBs come in a few different flavors: session beans, entity beans, and message beans. *Session beans,* as the name implies, live only as long as the conversation, or session, between the client application and the bean lasts. The session bean's primary reason for being is to provide application services, defined and designed by the application developer, to client applications. Depending on the design, a session bean may maintain state during the session or may be stateless. With a *stateful* EJB, when a subsequent request comes from a client, the values of the internal member variables have the same values they had when the previous request ended, so that the EJB can maintain a conversation with the client. A *stateless* EJB provides business rules through its exposed operations but doesn't provide any sense of state; that responsibility is delegated to the client.

Entity beans represent business objects—such as customers, invoices, and products—in the application domain. These business objects are persisted so they can be stored and retrieved at will. The Java EE architecture provides a lot of flexibility for the persistence model. You can defer all of the work of storing and retrieving the bean's state information to the container, as shown in Figure 1-11. This is known as *container-managed persistence.*

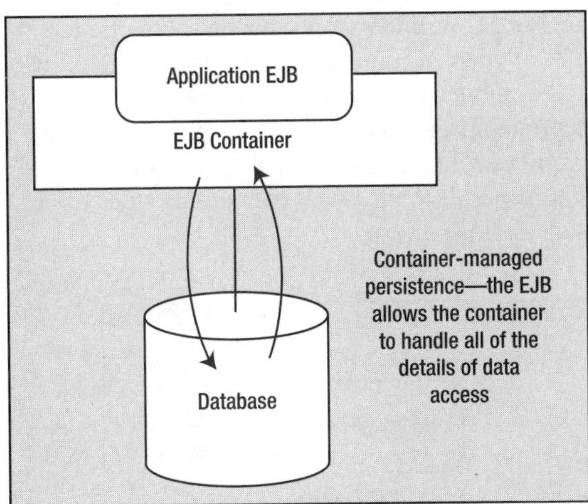

Figure 1-11. *In container-managed persistence, the EJB container is responsible for all actions required to save the state of the EJB to some persistent store, usually a database.*

Alternatively, the Java EE architecture allows you to have complete control over how the EJB is persisted (which is very useful when you're dealing with interfacing your Java EE system to a legacy application!). This is known as *bean-managed persistence* and is illustrated in Figure 1-12.

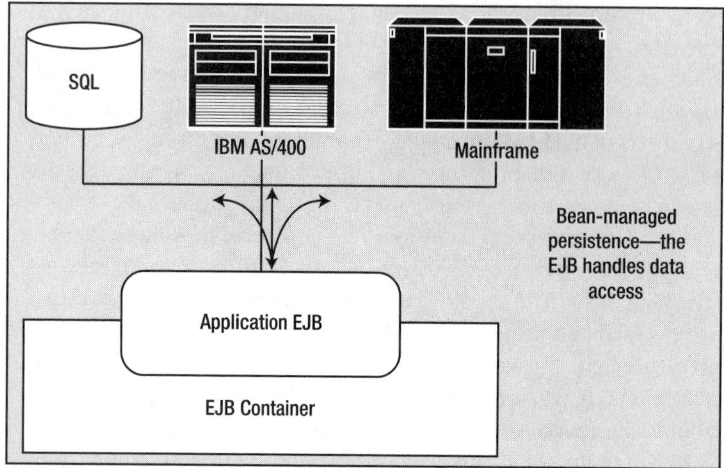

Figure 1-12. *With bean-managed persistence, the developer must manage all aspects of persisting the state of the EJB.*

The third type of EJB, the *message bean*, provides a component model for services that listen to Message Service messages, as illustrated in Figure 1-13. The Java EE platform includes a message queue that allows applications to post messages to a queue, as well as to *subscribe* to queues that get messages. The advantage of this particular way of doing things is that the sender and the receiver of the message don't need to know anything about each other. They need to know only about the message queue itself. This differs from a client/server model, where a client must know the server so that it can make a connection and a specific request, and the server sends the response directly to the client. One example of using a message queue is an automated stock trading system. Stock prices are sent as messages to a message queue, and components that are interested in stock prices consume those messages. With message-driven EJBs, it is possible to create an EJB that responds to messages concerning stock prices and makes automatic trading decisions based on those messages.

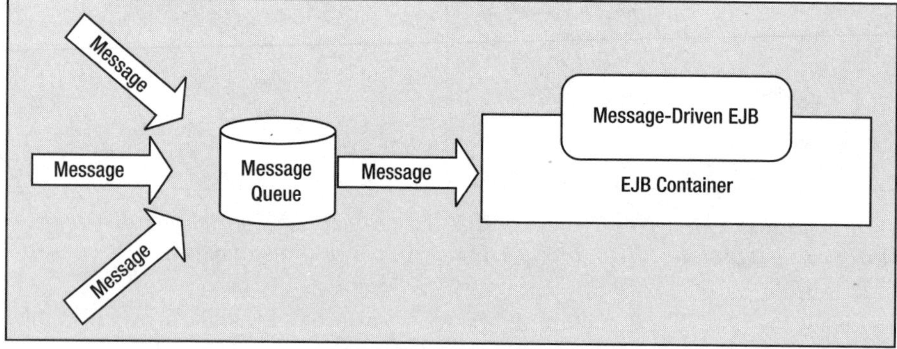

Figure 1-13. *A message queue allows senders and receivers of messages to remain unaware of each other. Senders of messages can send the message to a queue, knowing that something will get the message, but not knowing exactly what receives the message or when it will be received. Receivers can subscribe to queues and get the messages they are interested in, without needing to know who sent the message.*

You will learn a lot about the ins and outs of using session and entity beans in Chapters 9 through 12. Your Java EE applications will typically be comprised of both session and entity beans. Message beans are covered in Chapter 14. They're not used as frequently as the other flavors in most applications, but they're still pretty darn cool!

XML Support

Extensible Markup Language (XML) is a significant cornerstone for building enterprise systems that provide interoperability and are resilient in the face of changes. There are several key technologies in Java EE that rely on XML for configuration and integration with other services.

Java EE provides a number of APIs for developers working with XML. Java API for XML Processing (JAXP) provides support for generating and parsing XML with both the Document Object Model (DOM), which is a tree-oriented model, and the Simple API for XML (SAX), which is a stream-based, event-driven processing model.

The Java API for XML Binding (JAXB) provides support for mapping XML to and from Java classes. It provides a compiler and a framework for performing the mapping, so you don't need to write custom code to perform those transformations.

The Java API for XML Registries (JAXR), Java API for XML Messaging (JAXM), and Java API for XML-based Remote Procedure Calls (JAX-RPC) round out the XML API provisions. These sets of APIs provide support for SOAP and web services (discussed in the following section).

This book assumes that you are familiar with XML basics. If you need a refresher on XML, you might want to review the Sun Java XML tutorial at `http://java.sun.com/xml/tutorial_intro.html`.

Web Services

The World Wide Web is becoming an increasingly prevalent backbone of business applications. The endpoints that provide web applications with server-side business rules are considered *web services*. The World Wide Web Consortium (W3C), in an effort to unify how web services are published, discovered, and accessed, has sought to provide more concrete definitions for web services. Here's a definition from the Web Services Architecture, Working Group Note 11 (`www.w3.org/TR/ws-arch`):

> *A Web service is a software system designed to support interoperable machine-to-machine interaction over a network. It has an interface described in a machine-processable format (specifically WSDL). Other systems interact with the Web service in a manner prescribed by its description using SOAP messages, typically conveyed using HTTP with an XML serialization in conjunction with other Web-related standards.*

This definition contains some specific requirements:

- A web service allows one computer to request some service from another machine.
- Service descriptions are machine-processible.
- Systems access a service using XML messages sent over HTTP.

The W3C has established the Web Service Description Language (WSDL) as the XML format that is used by web services to describe their services and how clients access those services. In order to call those services, clients need to be able to get their hands on those definitions. XML registries provide the ability to publish service descriptions, search for services, and obtain the WSDL information describing the specifics of a given service.

There are a number of overlapping XML registry service specifications, including ebXML and Universal Description, Discovery, and Integration (UDDI). The JAXR API provides an implementation-independent API for accessing those XML registries.

Simple Object Access Protocol (SOAP) is the *lingua franca* used by web services and their clients for invocation, parameter passing, and obtaining results. SOAP defines the XML message standards and data mapping required for a client application to call a web service and pass it parameters. The JAX-RPC API provides an easy-to-use developer interface that masks the complex underlying plumbing.

Not surprisingly, the Java EE architecture provides a container that hosts web services, and a component model for easily deploying web services. Chapters 15 and 16 in this book cover SOAP and web services.

Transaction Support

One of the basic requirements of enterprise applications is the ability to allow multiple users of multiple applications to simultaneously access shared databases and to absolutely ensure the integrity of that data across those systems. Maintaining data consistency is no simple thing.

Suppose that your application was responsible for processing bank deposits, transfers, and withdrawals. Your application is processing a transfer request from one account to another. That process seems pretty straightforward: deduct the requested amount from one account and add that same amount to the other account. Suppose, however, that immediately after deducting the sum from the source account, something went horribly wrong—perhaps a server failed or a network link was severed—and it became impossible to add the transfer to the target account. At that point, the data's integrity has been compromised (and worse yet, someone's money is now missing).

Transactions can help to address this sort of problem. A transaction represents a set of activities that collectively will either succeed and be made permanent, or fail and be discarded. In the situation of a bank account transfer, you could define the transaction boundaries to start as the transfer amount is withdrawn from the source account, and end after the target account is updated successfully. When the transaction had been made successfully, the changes are committed. Any failure inside the transaction boundary would result in the changes being rolled back and the account balances restored back to the original values that existed before the start of the transaction.

Java EE—and the EJB in particular—provides substantial transaction support. The EJB container provides built-in support for managing transactions, and allows the developer to specify and modify transaction boundaries without changing code. Where more complex transaction control is required, the EJB can take over the transaction control from the container and perform fine-grained or highly customized transaction handling.

You'll find an introduction to transactions, in the context of database transactions with JDBC, in Chapter 8.

Security

Security is a vital component in enterprise applications, and Java EE provides built-in security mechanisms that are far more secure than homegrown security solutions that are typically added as an afterthought.

Java EE allows application resources to be configured for anonymous access where security isn't a concern. Where there are system resources that need to be secured, however, it provides authentication (making sure your users really are who they say they are) and authorization (matching up users with the privileges they are granted).

Authorization in Java EE is based on roles of users of applications. You can classify the roles of users who will be using your application, and authorize access to application components based on those roles. Java EE provides support for declarative security that is specified when the application is deployed, as well as programmatic security that allows you to build fine-grained security into the Java code.

■ **Note** If you're interested in learning more about Java EE-specific security, refer to a book devoted to Java security. One such book is *Hacking Exposed J2EE & Java*, by Art Taylor, Brian Buege, and Randy Layman (Osborne/McGraw Hill, 2002; ISBN 0-07-222565-3).

Sample Java EE Architectures

There is no such thing as a single software architecture that fits all applications, but there are some common architectural patterns that reappear frequently enough to merit attention.

As we explained earlier in the chapter, Java EE provides a platform that enables developers to easily create *n*-tier (multitier) applications in a number of different configurations. The basic n-tier architecture can have any number of components in each tier, and any combination between tiers.

Here, we will briefly review some architectures that you're likely to run into as you examine and develop Java EE-based systems. Each one of these has its own merits and strong points. We present them here to illustrate that there are a number of ways to put together applications and as a short "field guide" for identifying these architectures as you spot them in the wild.

Application Client with EJB

Figure 1-14 shows an architecture where an application client composes the presentation tier and communicates with an EJB in the business tier.

The client application is built as a stand-alone (JFC/Swing or console) application. The application relies on business rules implemented as EJBs running on a separate machine.

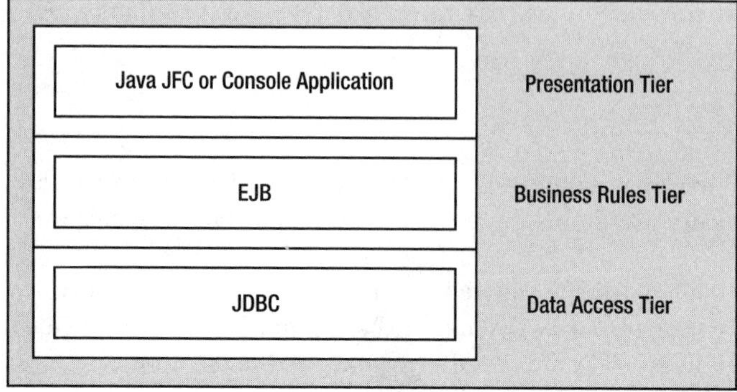

Figure 1-14. *An application client can be implemented as a normal Java application based on Swing or AWT, or even as a console application. The client communicates with EJBs in the business tier.*

JSP Client with EJB

Figure 1-15 shows an architecture based on JSPs. JSPs on the server interface with the business layer in response to requests. The response is generated as a web page, which is sent to the client's web browser.

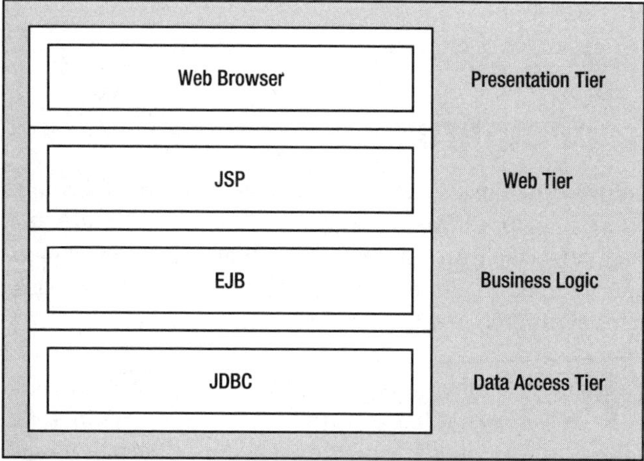

Figure 1-15. *In this architecture, the application client is a web page in a browser. The web page is generated by a JSP that communicates with the business layer.*

The client in this architecture is a web browser. JSPs access business rules and generate content for the browser.

Applet Client with JSP and Database

Figure 1-16 shows an architecture similar to the one shown in Figure 1-15. In this case, the client is a Java applet that resides entirely in the presentation tier and communicates with the business layer. Although the business layer could be an EJB, as in the previous example, in this example, the business layer is constructed from JSPs.

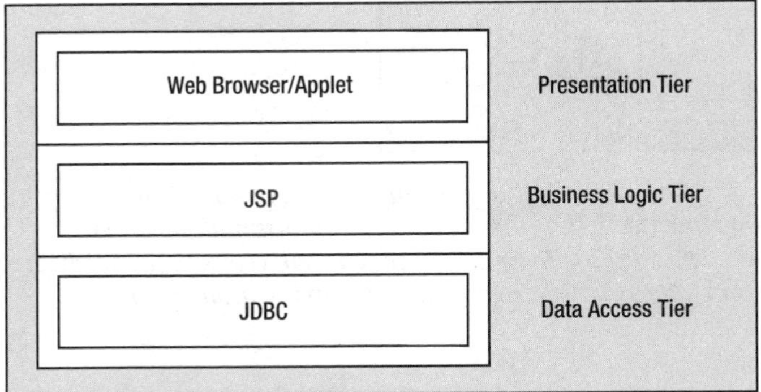

Figure 1-16. *An applet in the presentation layer can communicate over the network with JSPs (or Servlets) in the business layer.*

The Java applet is used within a web page to provide a more interactive, dynamic user interface for the user. That applet accesses additional content from JSPs. Even though JSPs are normally used to generate HTML web pages, a JSP could consist of only business logic. The JSPs access data from a database using the JDBC API.

Web Services for Application Integration

Even though Java EE is Java-based, a web application architecture is not limited solely to Java components. An obvious example is the data tier, where many enterprise-level databases are implemented in a high-level language such as C or C++. Similarly, components in a tier can be implemented in languages other than Java, as long as they provide a well-defined interface that allows for interprocess communication. In the example shown in Figure 1-17, a client application implemented in C# accesses data from a web service implemented in Java.

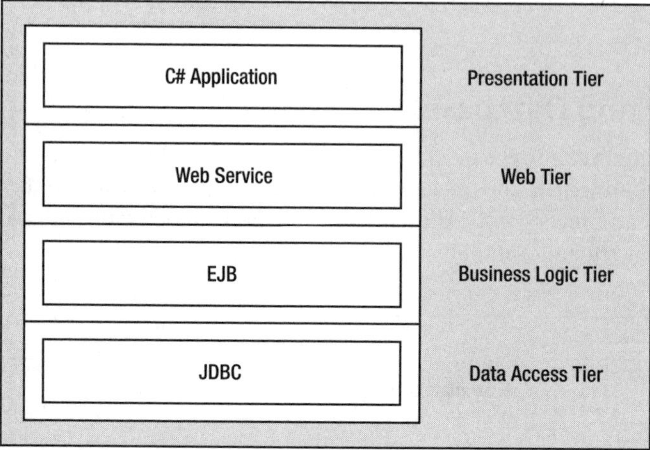

Figure 1-17. *The web service interface provides a well-defined interface between clients and web services. It allows clients to be implemented in any language that supports making HTTP requests to a server. For example, clients written in C# can format a web service request, which can be serviced by an EJB written in Java and running in a Java EE application server.*

Summary

In this opening chapter, we provided an overview of Java EE and how all the various bits fit together to enable you to create powerful business components. We first looked at what Java EE is and tackled the obvious issue of moving from creating desktop applications with J2SE to building enterprise-level applications and dynamic, data-driven web sites using Java EE. We covered how the two relate to each other and how they differ from each other, as well as looking at how applications are built using Java EE.

Java EE provides a platform for developing and deploying multitiered, distributed applications that are designed to be maintainable, scalable, and portable. Just as an office building requires a lot of hidden infrastructure of plumbing, electricity, and telecommunications, large-scale applications require a great deal of support infrastructure. This infrastructure includes database access, transaction support, and security. Java EE provides that infrastructure and allows you to focus on your applications.

Building distributed applications (software with components that run as separate processes, or on separate computers) allows you to partition the software into layers of responsibility, or *tiers*. Distributed applications are commonly partitioned into three primary tiers: presentation, business rules, and data access. Partitioning applications into distinct tiers makes the software more maintainable and provides opportunities for scaling up applications as the demand on those applications increases.

Java EE architecture is based on the idea of building applications around multiple tiers of responsibility. The application developer creates components, which are hosted by the Java EE containers. Containers play a central theme in the Java EE architecture.

Servlets are one type of Java EE web component. They are Java classes that are hosted within, and invoked by the Java EE server by requests made to, a web server. These Servlets respond to those requests by dynamically generating HTML, which is then returned to the requesting client.

JSPs are very similar in concept to Servlets, but differ in that the Java code is embedded within an HTML document. The Java EE server then compiles that HTML document into a Servlet, and that Servlet generates HTML in response to client requests.

JSF is a Java EE technology designed to create full and rich user interfaces. Standard user interface components are created on the server and connected to business logic components. Custom renderers take the components and create the actual user interface.

JDBC is a technology that enables an application to communicate with a data-storage system. Most often that is a relational database that stores data in tables that are linked through logical relations between tables. JDBC provides a common interface that allows you to communicate with the database through a standard interface without needing to learn the syntax of a particular database.

EJBs are the centerpiece of Java EE and are the component model for building the business rules logic in a Java EE application. EJBs can be designed to maintain state during a conversation with a client, or can be stateless. They can also be designed to be short-lived and ephemeral, or can be persisted for later recall. EJBs can also be designed to listen to message queues and respond to specific messages. Java EE is about a lot more than EJBs, although EJBs do play a prominent role.

The Java EE platform provides a number of services beyond the component hosting of Servlets, JSPs, and EJBs. Fundamental services include support for XML, web services, transactions, and security.

Extensive support for XML is a core component of Java EE. Support for both document-based and stream-based parsing of XML documents forms the foundation of XML support. Additional APIs provide XML registry service, remote procedure call invocation via XML, and XML-based messaging support.

Web services, which rely heavily on XML, provide support for describing, registering, finding, and invoking object services over the Web. Java EE provides support for publishing and accessing Java EE components as web services.

Transaction support is required in order to ensure data integrity for distributed database systems. This allows complex, multiple-step updates to databases to be treated as a single step with provisions to make the entire process committed upon success, or completely undone by rolling back on a failure. Java EE provides intrinsic support for distributed database transactions.

Java EE provides configurable security to ensure that sensitive systems are afforded appropriate protection. Security is provided in the form of authentication and authorization.

After reading this chapter, you should know:

- Containers provide an environment and infrastructure for executing Java EE components.
- Servlets and JSPs provide server-side processing and are used to create the presentation layer of a Java EE system.
- JSF provides user interface components that make it easy to create flexible user interfaces and connect user interface widgets to business objects.
- JDBC is an interface to database systems that allows developers to easily read and persist business data.
- EJBs represent business objects in a Java EE application. EJBs come in various categories, including stateful session beans, stateless session beans, entity beans, and message-driven beans.

- Java EE systems can be used to develop service-oriented architectures or web services systems. A web service architecture is one that provides machine-to-machine services over a network using a well-defined protocol.
- Some of the essential architectural patterns used in Java EE applications include an application client with EJBs, a JSP client with EJBs, an applet client with JSPs and a database, and web services used for application integration.

That's it for your first taste of how Java EE works and why it is so popular. In the next chapter, you'll see the steps required to set up your environment and make it ready for developing powerful Java EE applications.

CHAPTER 2

■ ■ ■

Getting Started

Since this is a book for developers by developers, you'll get the most out of the material covered here by running the examples and experimenting. In this chapter, you'll make sure that you've properly installed the JBoss application server and walk through the steps of setting up the environment and writing a simple application. This is vital to ensuring that you don't encounter needless frustration as you work through the examples. You'll also get a taste of the essential steps of creating a Java EE application, what those steps do, and why they're needed.

Even if you already have your environment set up, it's a good idea to read through the development steps in this chapter not only to ensure that your environment is set up correctly, but also to gain some essential insights into the fundamentals of building a Java EE application.

In this chapter, you will learn the following:

- The prerequisites for installing the JBoss application server
- How to configure your system to run enterprise Java applications
- How to construct, deploy, and run a simple JSP application

Note The installation files for the JBoss application server are available from the JBoss website (`www.jboss.org/products/jbossas/downloads`). You'll need to download version 4.0.3 or higher of the JBoss application server to get started using Java EE 5. To install and run the server, you'll also need the J2SE SDK from the Sun website at `http://java.sun.com`. The URL for J2SE 5 SDK is `http://java.sun.com/j2se/1.5.0/download.jsp`.

Installing JBoss

Installing the JBoss application server couldn't be much easier. As you saw in Chapter 1, the JBoss application server is based on Java Platform, Standard Edition (J2SE), so you need to have that installed before following the steps described in this chapter. Also, you'll need to ensure that you have the Java Development Kit (JDK) for J2SE 5 (or later) installed. If you have an earlier JDK, you need to update it. If you're not certain which version of Standard Edition you have, you can find out by opening a command prompt window and entering the following command:

```
> java -version
```

If you have installed the J2SE SDK correctly, a block of text will appear informing you of the version number for your J2SE SDK installation (see Figure 2-1). You should install the correct version of the J2SE SDK if this number isn't 1.5.0 or higher.

```
C:\WINDOWS\system32\cmd.exe

C:\>java -version
java version "1.5.0"
Java(TM) 2 Runtime Environment, Standard Edition (build 1.5.0-b64)
Java HotSpot(TM) Client VM (build 1.5.0-b64, mixed mode, sharing)
```

Figure 2-1. *Checking the J2SE SDK version number*

Once you've checked that you have the correct software installed, installing JBoss is a breeze. Simply decompress the JBoss archive you've downloaded to some memorable location such as `C:\jboss`. Since you're a tough developer who wouldn't even dream of using a GUI installer, there are some steps you'll need to take before continuing; you'll need to extract the files manually, and you'll need to create an environment variable called `JBOSS_HOME` before you can successfully run the application server.

■ **Note** *Environment variables* are used by the Windows operating system as a shortcut to selected directories on your system. You can set either user-specific environment variables or (provided you're logged in as a user with administrative rights) systemwide environment variables. Once you set an environment variable for your Java installation, you'll find it much quicker and easier to compile and run your Java applications from the command line, as you'll see shortly.

Once the installation is complete, it's time to set up the environment variables you'll need to run the examples in this book. You can check and set these from the ystem Properties dialog box (see Figure 2-2). To access this dialog box, from the Control Panel choose the System applet. Select the Advanced tab and click the Environment Variables button.

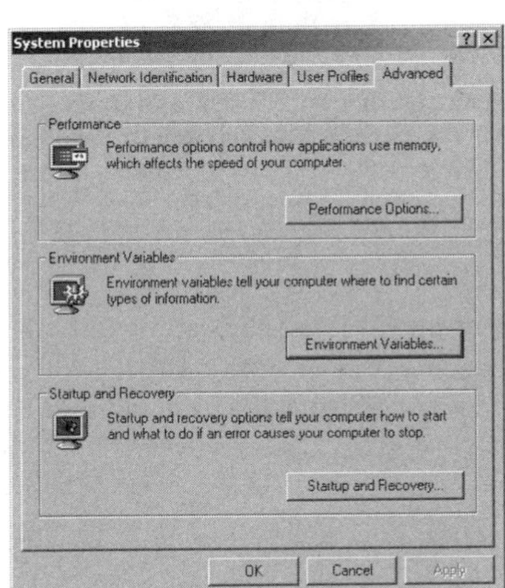

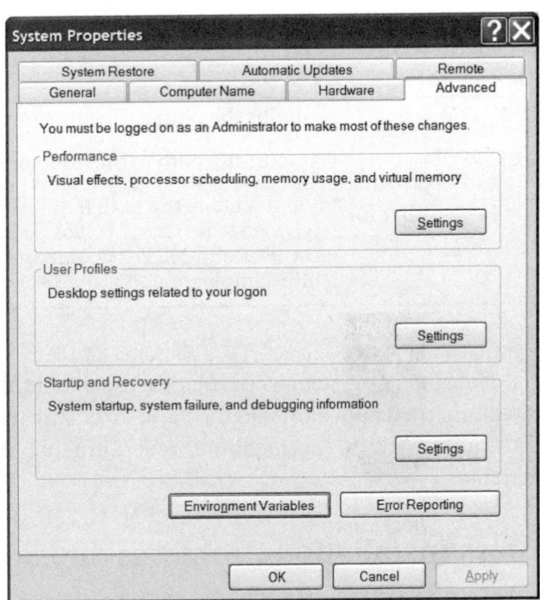

Figure 2-2. *System Properties dialog box in Windows 2000 (left) and Windows XP (right)*

When you click the Environment Variables button, a dialog box appears that allows you to check and set the values for environment variables (see Figure 2-3).

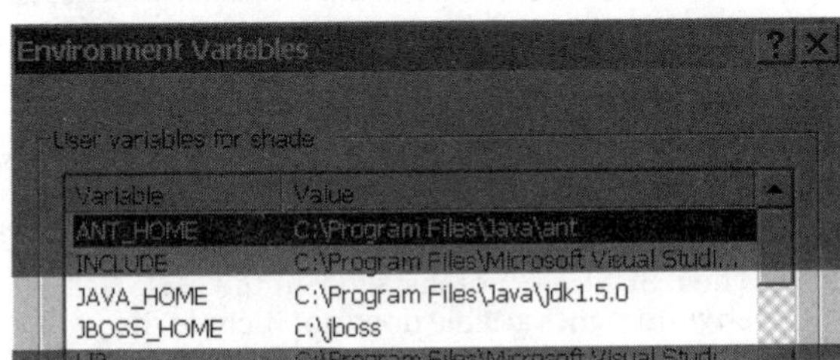

Figure 2-3. *Checking and setting the environment variables*

Make sure that the environment variables listed in Table 2-1 are set either in your local user variables or in the system variables. If they don't already appear in the list, you can add them by clicking the New button. If they need to be modified, edit them by clicking the Edit button. Click OK when you've finished.

Table 2-1. *Environment Variable Descriptions*

Variable	Description
`JAVA_HOME`	Contains the path to the directory where J2SE is installed (e.g., `C:\j2sdk5`).
`JBOSS_HOME`	Contains the path to the directory where JBoss is installed (e.g., `C:\jboss`).
`PATH`	Should include the path to the `\bin` directories of the J2SE SDK and JBoss (e.g., `C:\j2sdk5\bin;c:\JBoss\bin;...`). You can alternatively use the `JAVA_HOME` and `JBOSS_HOME` environment variables in your path to make things a little simpler (e.g., `%JAVA_HOME%\bin;%JBOSS_HOME%\bin;...`).

Note that the system will search for executable files using the `PATH` variable, starting with the directories that appear first in the path. To ensure that there aren't other versions of the J2SE or JBoss interfering on this machine, make sure that these new entries go at the front of the `PATH` variable.

JBoss Installation Problems and Solutions

Table 2-2 outlines some possible problems you might encounter when running through the previous steps to install JBoss, as well as their solutions.

Table 2-2. *Installation Troubleshooting*

Problem	Solution
Java version is lower than 1.5	Obtain and install the latest version of the J2SE SDK. You may want to uninstall the older version before installing the newer version. (You don't have to, but unless you have a compelling reason to keep the older version around, it's just dead weight.)
`java -version` returns the following message: 'java' is not recognized as an internal or external command, operable program or batch file.	The J2SE SDK is not installed, or the `JAVA_HOME` environment variable does not include the path to the J2SE SDK installation directory. Check the `JAVA_HOME` variable and correct the problem, or reinstall the J2SE SDK.

Testing the JBoss Installation

If everything went according to plan, your system should be set up and ready to use. In this section, we'll walk through some quick tests to ensure that you're ready to run the code in this book.

Starting the Server

The first step in verifying that your installation is working correctly is to start the JBoss server. The server is launched from the command line (you can also create a shortcut to make this process easier for you) using the following command (also shown in Figure 2-4):

```
>%JBOSS_HOME%\bin\run -c all
```

```
C:\WINDOWS\system32\cmd.exe

C:\>%JBOSS_HOME%\bin\run -c all
```

Figure 2-4. *JBoss startup command*

Once you've done this, you will see a large number of messages flash across the command window. This will continue for a short time, until you arrive at a screen that looks much like Figure 2-5.

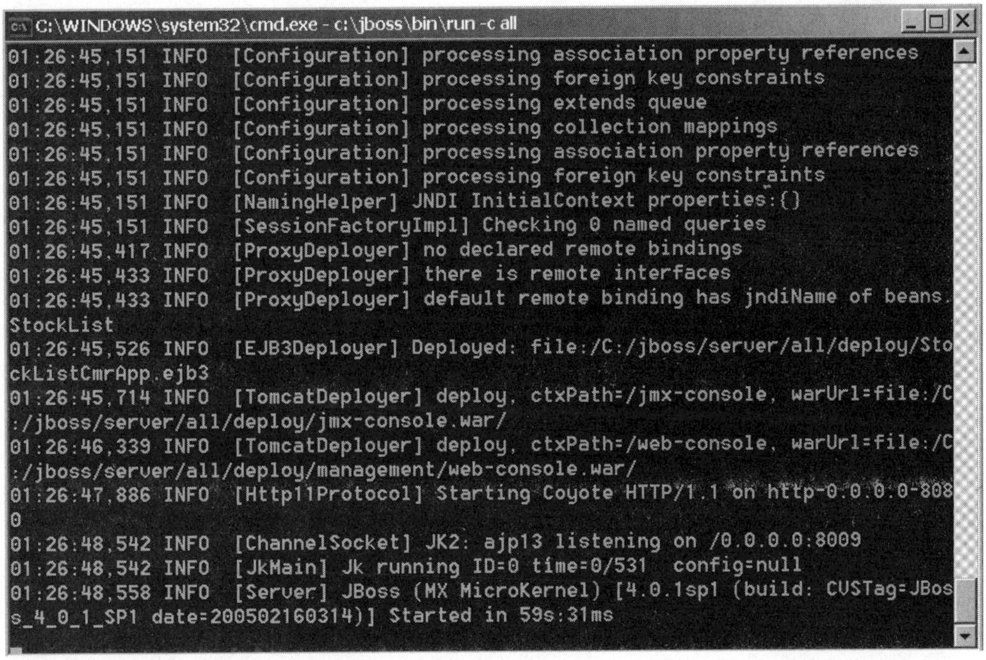

```
C:\WINDOWS\system32\cmd.exe - c:\jboss\bin\run -c all
01:26:45,151 INFO  [Configuration] processing association property references
01:26:45,151 INFO  [Configuration] processing foreign key constraints
01:26:45,151 INFO  [Configuration] processing extends queue
01:26:45,151 INFO  [Configuration] processing collection mappings
01:26:45,151 INFO  [Configuration] processing association property references
01:26:45,151 INFO  [Configuration] processing foreign key constraints
01:26:45,151 INFO  [NamingHelper] JNDI InitialContext properties:{}
01:26:45,151 INFO  [SessionFactoryImpl] Checking 0 named queries
01:26:45,417 INFO  [ProxyDeployer] no declared remote bindings
01:26:45,433 INFO  [ProxyDeployer] there is remote interfaces
01:26:45,433 INFO  [ProxyDeployer] default remote binding has jndiName of beans.
StockList
01:26:45,526 INFO  [EJB3Deployer] Deployed: file:/C:/jboss/server/all/deploy/Sto
ckListCmrApp.ejb3
01:26:45,714 INFO  [TomcatDeployer] deploy, ctxPath=/jmx-console, warUrl=file:/C
:/jboss/server/all/deploy/jmx-console.war/
01:26:46,339 INFO  [TomcatDeployer] deploy, ctxPath=/web-console, warUrl=file:/C
:/jboss/server/all/deploy/management/web-console.war/
01:26:47,886 INFO  [Http11Protocol] Starting Coyote HTTP/1.1 on http-0.0.0.0-808
0
01:26:48,542 INFO  [ChannelSocket] JK2: ajp13 listening on /0.0.0.0:8009
01:26:48,542 INFO  [JkMain] Jk running ID=0 time=0/531  config=null
01:26:48,558 INFO  [Server] JBoss (MX MicroKernel) [4.0.1sp1 (build: CVSTag=JBos
s_4_0_1_SP1 date=200502160314)] Started in 59s:31ms
```

Figure 2-5. *Application server output*

At this point, the JBoss server is started. Open a browser, and go to the following URL:

```
http://localhost:8080
```

The web browser should display the default JBoss web page, as shown in Figure 2-6. Pat yourself on the back for a job well done. Let's go shred a little code for a final test.

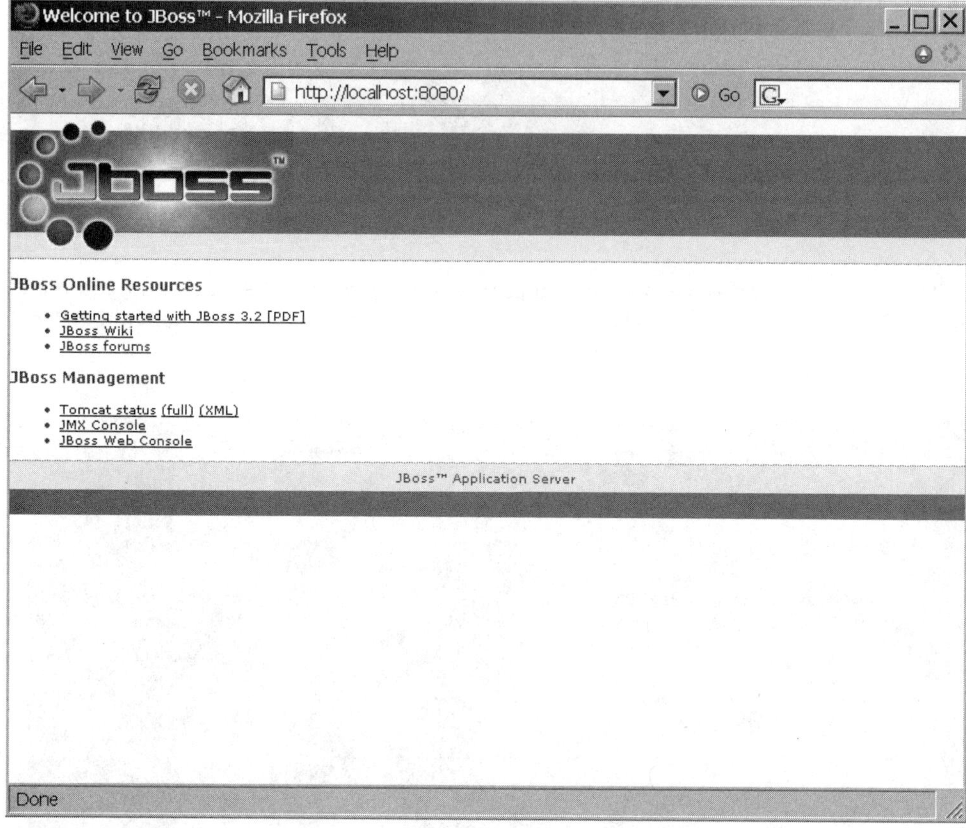

Figure 2-6. *The JBoss default web page is displayed when the server first runs.*

JBoss Server Installation Problem and Solution

Table 2-3 shows a potential problem you might come up against when running through the previous steps to test your JBoss application server installation, as well as its solution.

Table 2-3. *Startup Troubleshooting*

Problem	Solution
The web browser reports "Page cannot be displayed" when trying to open the URL `http://localhost:8080`	Make certain that there aren't any errors reported when you start the JBoss server. If you see messages indicating that the server couldn't start because TCP ports were in use by other processes, you may have either another web server using port 8080 or another instance of the JBoss server running. Also, make certain that you've specified the port 8080 in the URL (this is the default port used by JBoss).

Compiling and Deploying a JSP Page

As a final test, we're going to walk through the process of creating and deploying a JavaServer Pages (JSP) page. This procedure, which consists of the following steps, will confirm that the Java EE server is working properly and give you your first taste of building, deploying, and testing a Java EE application:

1. Create a working directory. This will give you a sandbox where you can create and edit the application files.
2. Create a text file for the JSP page. This will be a text file of HTML with snippets of Java code, which will be compiled by the Java EE server into a Servlet.
3. Package the files you create into a Web Archive (WAR). The WAR is a JAR file that bundles all of the application components into a single file for easy deployment.
4. Package the WAR into an Enterprise Archive (EAR), along with some deployment instructions for the JBoss server.
5. Copy the EAR to the JBoss server deployment directory. Once this is done, the application is available and ready to be run.
6. Test the application.

So, let's get started!

Creating the Example Application

Here are the steps to follow to create the example application:

1. Create a directory on your machine that will be your sandbox for this exercise. We'll use `C:\BJEE5\Ch02` in this example.
2. Create a new file called `index.jsp` in that directory using your favorite text editor. Here's the code for that file:

```
<%--
    file: index.jsp
    desc: Test installation of Java EE SDK 5
--%>
<html>
<head>
  <title>Hello World - test the Java EE SDK installation
  </title>
</head>
<body>
<%
  for (int i = 1; i < 5; i++)
  {
%>
```

```
        <h<%=i%>>Hello World</h<%=i%>>
<%
  }
%>
</body>
</html>
```

3. Create a subdirectory called META-INF, and in this directory create a file called application.xml. This file contains settings used to identify your application and the resources it depends on to JBoss, and to configure how users will access said resources. Create this file with the following contents:

```
<?xml version="1.0"?>
 <application>
     <display-name>Hello Java EE World!</display-name>
      <module>
         <web>
             <web-uri>web-app.war</web-uri>
             <context-root>/hello</context-root>
         </web>
      </module>
 </application>
```

4. You need to create a new WAR and EAR file. The WAR file will contain the web components of the Java EE application, along with a descriptor or "table of contents" that describes what is in the archive. Web applications frequently consist of many more files than this simple application, and the WAR is a convenient means of bundling up all of those files into a single file for deployment. Likewise, an EAR file is a collection of WAR files, JAR files, and resources that are all meant to operate within the context of a single application. To create these files, open a command-line window, change your current directory to the folder you created for this example (e.g., cd\BJEE5\Ch02), and type the following two commands:

```
>jar cf web-app.war index.jsp
>jar cf helloworld.ear web-app.war META-INF
```

5. Copy the resultant EAR file, helloworld.ear, to your JBoss server deployment directory (C:\jboss\server\all\deploy) and start JBoss from the command line with the command shown in Figure 2-7.

6. It's time to test your first JSP page. Start a web browser and open the following URL:

```
http://localhost:8080/hello
```

After a couple of seconds, you should see the web page shown in Figure 2-8. Congratulations! Your first JSP page is a success.

```
C:\WINDOWS\system32\cmd.exe - c:\jboss\bin\run -c all

C:\>%JBOSS_HOME%\bin\run -c all
===============================================================================

  JBoss Bootstrap Environment

  JBOSS_HOME: c:\jboss\bin\\..

  JAVA: C:\Program Files\Java\jdk1.5.0\bin\java

  JAVA_OPTS:  -Dprogram.name=run.bat -Xms128m -Xmx512m

  CLASSPATH: C:\Program Files\Java\jdk1.5.0\lib\tools.jar;c:\jboss\bin\\run.jar

===============================================================================

01:25:48,761 INFO  [Server] Starting JBoss (MX MicroKernel)...
01:25:48,776 INFO  [Server] Release ID: JBoss [Zion] 4.0.1sp1 (build: CVSTag=JBo
ss_4_0_1_SP1 date=200502160314)
01:25:48,776 INFO  [Server] Home Dir: C:\jboss
01:25:48,776 INFO  [Server] Home URL: file:/C:/jboss/
01:25:48,776 INFO  [Server] Library URL: file:/C:/jboss/lib/
01:25:48,776 INFO  [Server] Patch URL: null
01:25:48,776 INFO  [Server] Server Name: all
01:25:48,776 INFO  [Server] Server Home Dir: C:\jboss\server\all
```

Figure 2-7. *Command-line results for this chapter's JSP example*

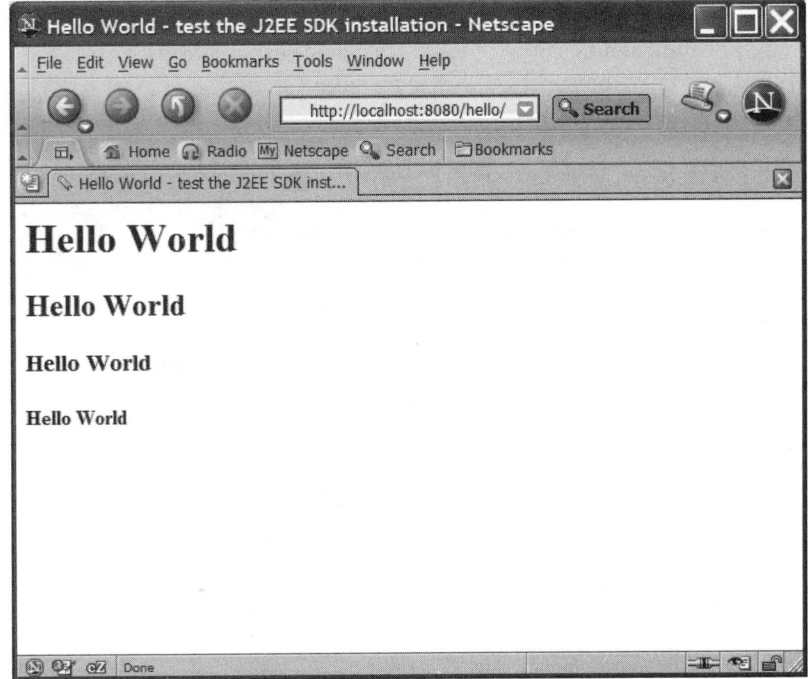

Figure 2-8. *Onscreen results for this chapter's JSP example*

Learning to Say “Hello”

The JSP file that you created is a text file that consists of HTML and embedded snippets of code. Notice that in this file are tags with enclosed Java code, as we discussed in Chapter 1:

```
<%--
    file: index.jsp
    desc: Test installation of JBoss for Beginning Java EE 5
--%>
<html>
<head>
  <title>Hello World - test the Java EE SDK installation
  </title>
</head>
<body>
<%
  for (int i = 1; i < 5; i++)
  {
%>
   <h<%=i%>>Hello World</h<%=i%>>
<%
  }
%>
</body>
</html>
```

When the JSP page is compiled into a Servlet, that Servlet code expands the JSP page’s code snippets and HTML into code that writes HTML to an output stream:

```
out.write("\n\n");
out.write("<html>\n");
out.write("<head>\n");
out.write("  <title>Hello World - test the Java EE SDK installation");
out.write("  </title>\n");
out.write("</head>\n");
out.write("<body>\n");
for (int i = 1; i < 5; i++)
{
  out.write("\n   ");
  out.write("<h");
  out.write(String.valueOf(i));
  out.write(">Hello World");
  out.write("</h");
  out.write(String.valueOf(i));
  out.write(">\n");
}
out.write("</body>\n");
out.write("</html>\n");
```

That code, when executed, will write the following HTML code to the stream that is sent back to the requesting browser:

```
<html>
<head>
  <title>Hello Hello World - test the Java EE SDK installation
  </title>
</head>
<body>

   <h1>Hello World</h1>

   <h2>Hello World</h2>

   <h3>Hello World</h3>

   <h4>Hello World</h4>

</body>
</html>
```

That's how the JSP code works. The process of packaging and deployment has a few more steps. Let's dig in a bit and see what's happening.

To deploy a Java EE application to a server, it has to be bundled up into an archive (i.e., a single file that packages up all the requisite files). The WAR has to contain the components you've created for the application (the JSP file) as well as other (optional) support files. Those support files include a deployment descriptor that tells the server what's contained in the WAR and how to run it, a manifest for the archive that acts as an application table of contents, and a file containing deployment information specific to the JBoss server (see Figure 2-9).

Once those contents have been assembled into a WAR file, that WAR can then be deployed to the Java EE server, or it can be repackaged inside an EAR. Packaging the WAR inside an EAR allows logic that doesn't necessarily belong inside the WAR file to coexist with the web application.

Once the archive has been copied to the server's deployment directory, the server reads the deployment descriptor to determine how to unbundle the contents. In the case of this application, it sees that the EAR contains a WAR. Once it has extracted the JSP page you created from the WAR file, it compiles that JSP page into a Servlet.

To run the application once it is deployed, you have to request the JSP page by requesting a URL with your web browser. Notice that the URL consists of the protocol (`http`), the server name (`localhost`), the root context of the application (`hello`), and the requested resource (`index.jsp`), as shown in Figure 2-10.

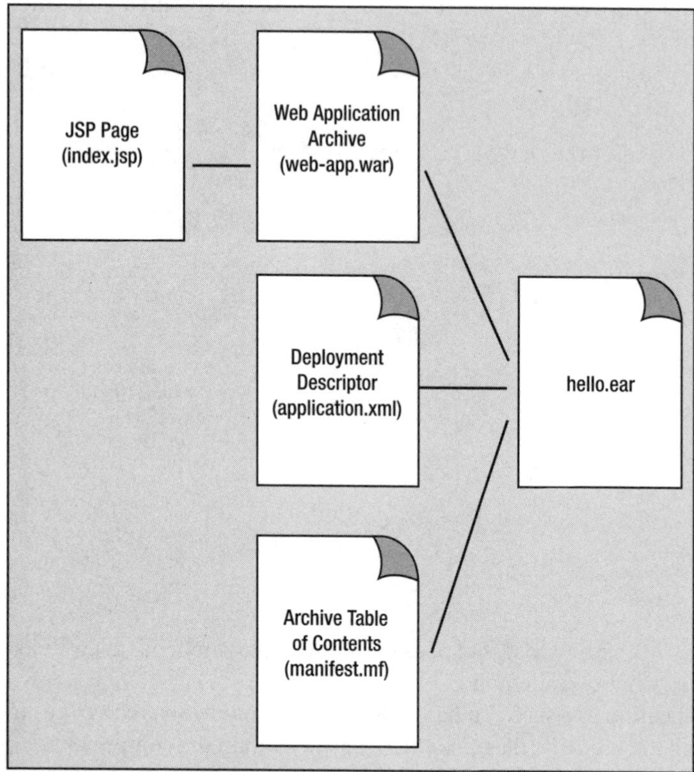

Figure 2-9. *The basic high-level model for the JSP example*

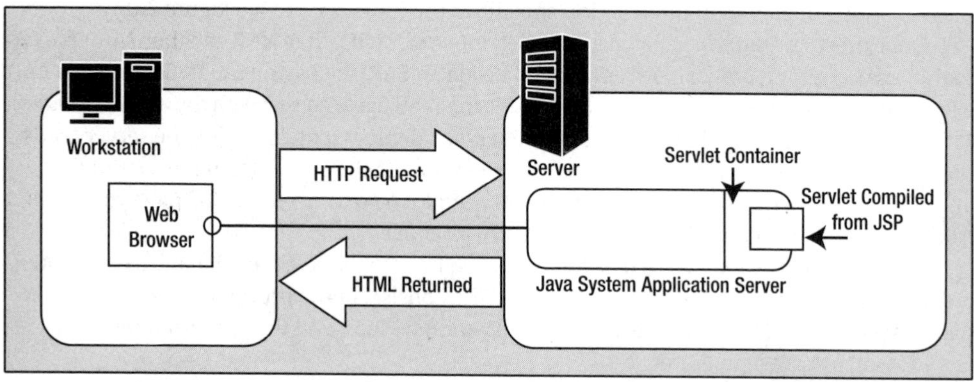

Figure 2-10. *The flow of execution for client requests from the JSP application*

The server receives the incoming HTTP request and uses the deployment information to invoke the appropriate Servlet in a Servlet container. The Servlet writes HTML to an output stream, which is returned to the web browser by the server.

Application Creation Problems and Solutions

Table 2-4 lists some common problems you may encounter during application creation and how to fix them.

Table 2-4. *Deployment Troubleshooting*

Problem	Solution
The verifier reports errors.	Carefully retrace your steps and ensure that you followed the steps correctly as described in this section.
When testing the JSP page, the web browser reports "Page cannot be displayed" when it tries to open the URL `http://localhost:8080`.	Make certain that there weren't any errors reported when you started the Java EE server. Ensure that you've specified the port 8080 in the URL (this is the default port used by the Java EE server).
When testing the JSP page, JBoss reports a compilation error in the web browser.	Double-check the code in `index.jsp`. If you've mistyped something, the server won't be able to compile the JSP page. The message in the web browser should give you a hint about where to look.

Summary

In this chapter, we described how to get the Java EE SDK installed and to verify that the installation was successful. You got your first taste of creating and running a Java EE application, and you looked at some of the core concepts involved in building Java EE applications.

After reading this chapter, you should know:

- JavaServer Pages (JSP) consist of HTML with embedded snippets of Java code. A JSP page is compiled into a Servlet by the Java EE server which, when executed, emits HTML back to the requesting client.
- Web Archives (WARs) are deployment components that contain the web components of a Java EE application. The WAR contains the components themselves (such as JSP pages), and the deployment descriptor that defines the contents of the WAR. The WAR can also contain server-specific deployment information.
- Enterprise Archives (EARs) make up high-level groupings of application components. WAR files, JAR files, deployment instructions, and application resources can all be encapsulated within an EAR file.

At this point in the book, you should now be familiar with the following procedures:

- How to install and configure the JBoss application server
- How to start and stop the JBoss server
- The essential steps of building a Java EE application:

1. Create the application components.
2. Bundle the components into an archive.
3. Verify the contents of the archive to catch problems before deploying.
4. Copy the archive to the JBoss server deployment directory.
5. Test the application.

If you've been able to get through this chapter, you're more than ready to dive into more detail. The next chapter will take you deeper into the details of JSP pages. You'll learn the essential structure of JSP pages and how to enable users to interact with your JSP pages.

CHAPTER 3

■ ■ ■

JavaServer Pages

In the previous chapters, you received a brief introduction to Java EE and got a chance to build a very simple JSP page. In this chapter, we'll start to take a much more detailed look at JSP.

JSP pages are components in a web or Java EE application that consist of HTML and Java code. You might ask, "What's so different about that? I've been putting JavaScript into my HTML for years." The difference is that JavaScript runs on the client, whereas the code in a JSP page runs on the server. JavaScript can affect only the particular page in which it is embedded and has access to only data within the client's environment. Code in a JSP can access data across the entire web application and can use server-side resources such as databases, directories, and other application components.

As components in a Java EE application, JSP pages run on a server and respond to requests from clients. These clients are usually users accessing the web application through a web browser. The protocol used by clients to call the JSP pages in the Java EE application is HTTP—the same protocol used by browsers to get HTML pages from a web server. In this chapter, we'll concentrate on the basics of creating JSP pages. We'll look at the underlying HTTP protocol in Chapter 6.

In this chapter, you will learn:

- How to write a JSP page
- How to use directive, scripting, and action elements
- How to access the implicit objects of the page
- How servers translate and compile JSP pages
- How to handle errors and exceptions
- How to forward and include pages from a JSP page

Introduction to JSP

The JSP home page (`http://java.sun.com/products/jsp/`) says, "Web developers and designers use JavaServer Pages technology to rapidly develop and easily maintain information-rich, dynamic web pages that leverage existing business systems."

JSP pages can be rapidly developed and easily maintained because they are based on HTML and XML. Documents with markup such as HTML are easy to understand, and there are many automated tools for dealing with HTML and XML documents. JSP pages are dynamic because they can contain Java code, which can process the request and tailor the response based on the request. All the power of Java sits behind every JSP page.

A JSP page executes inside a JSP container. A container is a piece of software that loads and manages Java EE components—in this case, JSP pages. This container can be part of the web server, or it can run separately from the web server. You were introduced to several different containers in Chapter 2.

JSP Development

The process of developing a JSP page that can respond to client requests involves three main steps:

- **Creation:** The developer creates a JSP source file that contains HTML and embedded Java code.
- **Deployment:** The JSP is installed into a server. This can be a full Java EE server or a stand-alone JSP server.
- **Translation and compilation:** The JSP container translates the HTML and Java code into a Java code source file. This file is then compiled into a Java class that is executed by the server. The class file created from the JSP is known as the JSP page *implementation class*.

Note that the translation and compilation step can actually occur at any one of several times, even though it's listed last here. Because the JSP contains Java code, at some point, the page is translated and compiled into a Java class. This can happen before the page is loaded to a server, or it can happen at the time the client makes a request. You can translate and compile the JSP prior to deployment, and deploy the class file directly. Compiling first allows you to catch and fix syntax errors in your code prior to deployment. Alternatively, the JSP container can compile the JSP when it is deployed to the server. Finally, the usual process is that when the first request is made for the JSP, the server translates and compiles the JSP. This is known as translation at request time.

Basic JSP Lifecycle

Once compilation is complete, the JSP lifecycle has these phases:

- **Loading and instantiation:** The server finds or creates the JSP page implementation class for the JSP page and loads it into the JVM. After the class is loaded, the JVM creates an instance of the class. This can occur immediately after loading, or it can occur when the first request is made.
- **Initialization:** The JSP page object is initialized. If you need to execute code during initialization, you can add a method to the page that will be called during initialization.
- **Request processing:** The page object responds to requests. Note that a single object instance will process all requests. After performing its processing, a response is returned to the client. The response consists solely of HTML tags or other data; none of the Java source code is sent to the client.

- **End of life:** The server stops sending requests to the JSP. After all current requests are finished processing, any instances of the class are released. This usually occurs when the server is being shut down, but can also occur at other times, such as when the server needs to conserve resources, when it detects an updated JSP source file, or when it needs to terminate the instance for other reasons. If you need code to execute and perform any cleanup actions, you can implement a method that will be called before the class instance is released, as discussed in the "Handling JSP Initialization and End of Life" section later in this chapter.

In Chapter 6, you will see that the Servlet lifecycle is the same as the JSP lifecycle. This is because the JSP is translated into a Servlet; the JSP page implementation class is a Servlet class. Figure 3-1 shows the request processing phase of the JSP lifecycle.

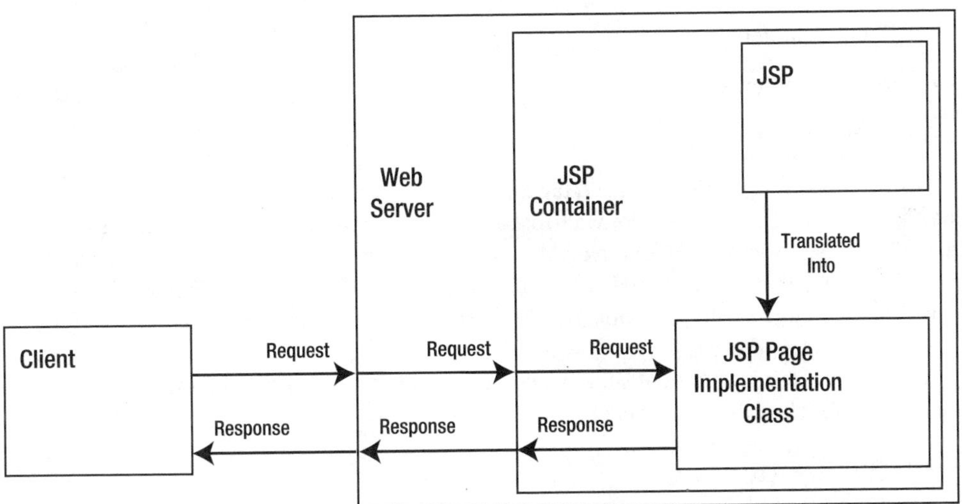

Figure 3-1. *A JSP source file is compiled into a JSP page implementation class. When the server receives a request for the JSP, the request is sent to the container, which passes the request to the correct JSP. The response follows the reverse path.*

When a client sends a request for a JSP, the web server gives the request to the JSP container, and the JSP container determines which JSP page implementation class should handle the request. The JSP container then calls a method of the JSP page implementation class, which processes the request and returns a response through the container and web server to the client. In general, this process is referred to simply as "A request is sent to a JSP."

JSP Elements

So, now that you've seen how JSP pages work, let's look at what they contain, before we move on to how you go about writing them. Take a look at the following line of JSP code:

```
<html><body><p>Hello, World!</p></body></html>
```

Admittedly, this is not a very good JSP example. However, these HTML tags do form a correct and valid JSP file. You could save this line in a file named `HelloWorld.jsp` and install it into a web application, and the server would access it as a JSP resource. The point is that JSP pages tend to look a lot like HTML pages.

The reason this example is not a very good one is that it isn't dynamic in any way. If your JSP pages don't contain Java code, you might as well just make them static HTML pages. JSP pages are intended to have dynamic behavior; they are supposed to change in response to specific client requests. You give the page dynamic behavior by embedding Java code into the page. You can think of JSP pages as web pages with bits of Java embedded in them.

However, you can't just write Java code in the page wherever you want. You need some way to tell the JSP translator which bits are code and which bits are regular HTML. To do this, the JSP specification defines HTML-like or XML tags that enclose the code in the JSP. Those tags come in three categories:

- Directive elements
- Scripting elements
- Action elements

The original JSP specification used tag formats for these elements that were not compatible with XML; that is, they were not well-formed according to the XML specification. Starting with the JSP 1.2 specification, alternative XML-compliant versions of all the tags were introduced. The XML-compliant tags can be used only in a JSP page that conforms to the XML specification. You will see both formats in this book, with the original style referred to as *JSP style* and the newer style referred to as *XML style*.

Along with these tag elements, JSP pages can include comments and template data. Now we will look at each of these page elements.

Directive Elements

Directive elements provide information to the JSP container about the page. Three directives are available: `page`, `include`, and `taglib`. We will discuss `page` and `include` here, deferring discussion of `taglib` to the next chapter. A single JSP page can have multiple instances of the `page` and `include` directives.

Page Directives

The `page` directive is used to specify page attributes. The `page` directive's JSP-style form is:

```
<%@ page attributes %>
```

The white space following `<%@` and before `%>` is optional.

The `page` directive's XML-style form is:

```
<jsp:directive.page attributes />
```

As with all HTML attributes, attributes must be name/value pairs, with an equal sign (`=`) separating the name from the value and the value in quotes. You can find the complete list of attributes and their meanings in the JSP specification, which you can download from `http://java.sun.com/products/jsp`. Table 3-1 shows the attributes you are most likely to use as you start developing JSP pages.

Table 3-1. *Common Page Directive Attributes*

Attribute	Description
`import`	Lists the Java packages to be imported into the page. Just as with a Java source file, the Java code embedded in a JSP page must import the packages of the classes used with the code. Multiple package statements are delimited by commas; for example, `import="java.io.*,java.util.*"`.
`session`	Whether the page participates in a session. The valid values are `true` or `false`. The default value is `true`. If `true`, the page participates in a session; if `false`, then it does not, and cannot access any session information. Sessions are covered later in the chapter, in the "The session Object" section.
`isThreadSafe`	Whether the container can pass requests concurrently to the page. The valid values are `true` or `false`. The default is `true`. If `true`, the container can use the JSP for multiple concurrent request threads. If `false`, the container must pass the requests one at a time in order of receipt. Page authors must also ensure that access to shared resources is properly synchronized.
`info`	An arbitrary string. This can have any value. It is provided so that the JSP can provide a management tool with information about its contents, purpose, name, and so on.
`errorPage`	The URL of the web page that should be sent to the client if an error occurs in a page. The default URL is implementation-dependent. When you do not provide a URL, the container can use its own default.
`isErrorPage`	Whether the current page is an error page. The default is `false`.
`contentType`	Defines the content type of the page. The content type can appear as a simple type specification, or as a type specification and a character set (charset). The default value is `text/html` for JSP-style JSP tags and `text/xml` for XML-style JSP tags. When including the charset, the syntax for the attribute is `contentType="text/html;charset=char_set_identifier"`. White space can follow the semicolon in the attribute value. Charsets indicate how written characters are encoded, so that pages can support languages that use different scripts. You can find information about charsets at `http://www.w3.org/TR/REC-html40/charset.html`.
`pageEncoding`	The charset of the current page. The default is ISO-8859-1 (Latin script) for JSP-style and UTF-8 (an 8-bit Unicode encoding) for XML-style tags.

Include Directives

The `include` directive is used to include another page within the current page. The `include` directive's JSP-style form is:

```
<%@ include attributes %>
```

And its XML-style form is:

```
<jsp:directive.include attributes />
```

You might typically include a standard header or footer with the include directive, but it can actually be any content. You would use this when you have standard data that you want to include in multiple JSP pages. The file that contains the standard data is included when the page is translated into its Java form.

This directive has a single attribute named file. The file attribute specifies the name of the file to be included at the current position in the file. The included file can be any HTML or JSP page or fragment of a page. The file is specified using a URL to a file within the web application; the path is relative to the JSP file.

Scripting Elements

The scripting elements are the elements in the page that include the Java code. There are three subforms of this element: declarations, scriptlets, and expressions.

Declarations

A declaration is used to declare, and optionally define, a Java variable or a method. It works just like any declaration within a Java source code file. The declaration element's JSP-style form is:

```
<%! declaration %>
```

And its XML-style form is:

```
<jsp:declaration>declaration</jsp:declaration>
```

The declaration appears only within the translated JSP page, but not in the output to the client. For example, to declare a Vector in your JSP, you would use one of these forms:

```
<%! Vector v = new Vector(); %>
<jsp:declaration>Vector v = new Vector();</jsp:declaration>
```

This JSP fragment declares a variable v of type Vector and initializes it by calling the Vector constructor. Any variable you declare within a declaration element becomes an instance variable of the JSP page implementation class, and therefore is global to the entire page. Thus, you must take care when initializing variables with a declaration, because instance variables are not thread-safe. By default, the server can send multiple requests to the same page simultaneously. You don't want one thread to change the variable while another thread is using the variable.

You can also declare and define methods within a declaration element, as in these examples:

```
<%!
public int void countTokens(String s) {
  StringTokenizer st = new StringTokenizer(s);
  return st.countTokens();
}
%>
<jsp:declaration>
public int countTokens(String s) {
  StringTokenizer st = new StringTokenizer(s);
  return st.countTokens();
}
</jsp:declaration>
```

Any method you declare within a `declaration` element becomes an instance method of the JSP page implementation class, and thus it is global to the entire page. Variables or methods in a `declaration` element can be called by any other code in the page.

Declarations, variables, and methods inside `declaration` elements must be valid Java code; that is, they must conform to all Java syntax and semantic rules.

Scriptlets

Scriptlets contain Java code statements. The code in the scriptlet appears in the translated JSP, but not in the output to the client. The `scriptlet` element's JSP-style form is:

```
<% scriptlet code %>
```

And its XML-style form is:

```
<jsp:scriptlet>code fragment</jsp:scriptlet>
```

Any legal Java code statements can appear within a scriptlet. For example, to repeat the phrase "Hello, World!" ten times in the output page, you could use this scriptlet:

```
<%
  for (int i = 0; i < 10; i++) {
%>
Hello, World!
<%
  }
%>
```

As in this code snippet, you can freely interleave Java code and HTML and/or text data. Everything between the scriptlet markers (`<%` and `%>`) is script code; everything outside the markers is template data, which is sent to the client as written. Notice that in this example, the Java code block does not need to begin and end within the same `scriptlet` element. This allows you complete freedom to mix Java code and HTML elements as needed within the page.

■Note The scriptlet example shown here is relatively simple. As your application gets more complex and involved, you'll get more and more code mixed in with the HTML, and the page will tend to get complicated. In the next chapter, you will see how tag libraries can give the same rich behavior as in this example, but using only XML tags.

Since scriptlets can contain Java statements, the following is a legal scriptlet:

```
<%
Vector v = new Vector();
// More code...
%>
```

This looks very similar to the code snippet in the declaration section you saw earlier, which might lead you to wonder what the difference between scriptlets and declarations is, since they appear to be the same. Despite that seeming similarity, they are different in the following ways:

- Scriptlets cannot be used to define a method; only declarations can be used for that.
- Variables declared in a declaration are instance variables of the JSP page implementation class. These variables are visible to all other code statements or methods in the page.
- Variables declared in a scriptlet are local to a method in the JSP page implementation class. They are visible only within their defining code block.

Expressions

Expressions are used to output the value of a Java expression to the client. The `expression` element's JSP-style form is:

```
<%= expression %>
```

And its XML-style form is:

```
<jsp:expression>expression</jsp:expression>
```

For example, this code fragment in a JSP would result in the text, "The number of tokens in this statement is 9." being displayed in the browser:

```
The number of tokens in this statement is
   <%= countTokens("The number of tokens in this statement is n") %>.
```

This code snippet calls the hypothetical `countTokens(String)` method that was shown previously in the `declaration` element example. To count the number of tokens in the statement, a literal copy of the statement is passed to the method. In this code snippet, the method call returns an int value, which is printed to the client's browser. Here is the same expression using XML style:

```
The number of tokens in this statement is
<jsp:expression>
   countTokens("The number of tokens in this statement is n")
</jsp:expression>.
```

Any legal Java expression can be used with an `expression` element. An expression could contain a method call, as shown in the example, a literal expression such as `2 + 2`, an expression using Java variables or keywords such as `v instanceof Vector`, or any combination of these. Notice also that because declarations and scriptlets contain Java code, the lines of Java code must be terminated with a semicolon. Expressions, however, will not necessarily be legal code statements (but they will be valid expressions), so they do not need a terminating semicolon.

Action Elements

Standard actions are defined by the JSP specification (which is one reason why they are called standard). They look similar to HTML tags, but they cause the page to perform some action, hence the name. You can also create your own actions, which are known as *custom actions*. We will look at standard actions here, and you will see how to create custom actions in Chapter 4.

The JSP 2.0 specification defines the following standard actions:

- `<jsp:useBean>`
- `<jsp:setProperty>`
- `<jsp:getProperty>`
- `<jsp:param>`
- `<jsp:include>`
- `<jsp:forward>`
- `<jsp:plugin>`
- `<jsp:params>`
- `<jsp:fallback>`
- `<jsp:attribute>`
- `<jsp:body>`
- `<jsp:invoke>`
- `<jsp:doBody>`

■ **Note** Although, here, we follow the specification syntax of using *<jsp:action_name>* to identify the actions, the `jsp` prefix can be redefined in a tag library descriptor (TLD). As you will see in the next chapter, you can also define your own actions that can be used in a JSP page. The next chapter will show how to set the prefix for both standard actions and custom actions in a TLD.

In this section we will look at the `<jsp:useBean>`, `<jsp:setProperty>`, and `<jsp:getProperty>` actions. Later in the chapter, in the "Including and Forwarding from JSP Pages" section, we will cover the `<jsp:include>`, `<jsp:forward>`, and `<jsp:param>` actions.

The elements `<jsp:attribute>` and `<jsp:body>` are used with standard and custom actions. The elements `<jsp:invoke>` and `<jsp:doBody>` are valid only in tag libraries. Custom actions and tag libraries are covered in Chapter 4.

The `<jsp:plugin>`, `<jsp:params>`, and `<jsp:fallback>` elements are used to include applets or JavaBeans in the HTML page generated by a JSP page. Using these over hand-coding the HTML allows the server to create browser-specific HTML from the JSP tags. See the JSP specification for details about using these tags.

The <jsp:useBean> Action

The `<jsp:useBean>` action element makes a JavaBean available to the page. A JavaBean (which is not the same as an Enterprise JavaBean) is simply a Java class that follows certain requirements. The following two requirements are important for our purposes:

- The JavaBean class has a no-argument constructor.
- Every property of the bean that is provided for client use has a method to set the value of the parameter and a method to get the value of the parameter.

The getter and setter methods have this form:

```
public type getSomeParameter() { return someParameter; }
public boolean isSomeParameter() { return someBooleanParameter; }
public void setSomeParameter(type someParameter) {
  // Set the parameter
}
```

The name of every setter and getter uses the name of the parameter, with the first letter capitalized, appended to the token `set`, `get`, or `is`. The getter method has the form `is`*`XXX`*`()` for boolean properties; for other properties, its form is `get`*`XXX`*`()`.

The `<jsp:useBean>` element has the attributes shown in Table 3-2.

Table 3-2. *Attributes of the useBean Tag*

Attribute	Description
`id`	The name used to access the bean in the rest of the page. It must be unique. It is essentially the variable name that references the bean instance. When a `<jsp:useBean>` action is used in a scriptless page, or in the body of an action marked as scriptless, no Java scripting variables are created; instead, an Expression Language variable is created. The next chapter covers Expression Language in detail.
`scope`	The scope of the bean. Valid values are `page`, `request`, `session`, or `application`. The default is `page`. See the "JSP Scope" section later in this chapter for more information.
`class`	The fully qualified class name of the bean class.
`beanname`	The name of a bean, as expected by the `instantiate()` method of the `java.beans.Beans` class. Most often, you will use the `class` attribute, rather than `beanName`. Refer to the JavaBeans specification at `http://java.sun.com/products/javabeans` for details on how to supply a name to the `instantiate()` method.
`type`	The type to be used for the variable that references the bean. This follows Java rules, so it can be the class of the bean, any parent class of the bean, or any interface implemented by the bean or by a parent class.

The <jsp:useBean> element causes the container to try to find an existing instance of the object in the specified scope and with the specified id. If no object with the specified id is found in that scope, and a class or bean name is specified, the container will try to create a new instance of the object. You can use the class, beanName, and type attributes in these combinations:

- class: Creates an instance of the class that can be referred to by the given id.
- class, type: Creates an instance of the given class; the variable that refers to the bean will have the given type.
- beanName, type: Creates an instance of the given bean; the variable that refers to the bean will have the given type.
- type: If an object of the given type exists in the session, the id will refer to that object.

You must create a reference to a JavaBean using the <jsp:useBean> element before you can use <jsp:setProperty> or <jsp:getProperty>.

The <jsp:setProperty> Action

The <jsp:setProperty> action element sets the property for a JavaBean. It has the attributes shown in Table 3-3.

Table 3-3. *Attributes of the setProperty Tag*

Attribute	Description
name	The id of the bean as defined by the useBean action.
property	The name of the property whose value will be set. The property attribute can explicitly name a property of the bean; in which case, the setXXX() method for the property will be called. The value can also be "*"; in which case, the JSP will read all the parameters that were sent by the browser with the client's request and set the properties in the bean that have the same names as the parameters in the request.
param	The parameter name in the browser request whose value will be used to set the property. Allows the JSP to match properties and parameters with different names.
value	The value to assign to the property.

The name and property attributes are always required. The param and value elements are mutually exclusive. If neither param nor value is used, the jsp:setProperty element attempts to use the request parameter with the same name as the property attribute. You will see how request parameters are used later in this chapter, in Listing 3-9.

Suppose you have a JavaBean that holds information about a user of the system. This bean might look like this:

```
public class User {
  private String id;
  private String surname;
  public void setId(String id) { this.id = id; }
  public String getId() { return id; }
  public void setSurname(String surname) { this.surname = surname; }
  public String getSurname() { return surname; }
}
```

Here is one simple example of using the `<jsp:setProperty>` element with a literal value and an expression:

```
<jsp:useBean id="userA" class="User" />
<jsp:setProperty name="userA" property="surname" value="Smith" />
<jsp:setProperty name="userA" property="id"
                 value="<%= validateId("86753") %>" />
```

After this code in the compiled JSP executes, the `surname` property of the instance of `User` has a value of `"Smith"`, and the `id` property has whatever value is returned by the hypothetical `validateId()` expression. The JSP translator takes the elements in the example and translates them into code that creates an instance of the `User` class, and then calls the `setSurname()` and `setId()` methods of the object.

The <jsp:getProperty> Action

The `<jsp:getProperty>` element retrieves the value of a property from a JavaBean. It has the attributes shown in Table 3-4.

Table 3-4. *Attributes of the getProperty Tag*

Attribute	Description
`name`	The id of the bean
`property`	The name of the property to get

The `name` and `property` attributes are always required. When used within a JSP, the value of the property will be output as part of the response. Given the example in the previous section, you could write template data (described in the next section) that uses `<jsp:getProperty>` like this:

```
The user with id <jsp:getProperty name="userA" property="id" />
has a surname of <jsp:getProperty name="userA" property="surname" />
```

When the JSP page is translated into Java code, this will result in calls to the `getSurname()` and `getId()` methods of the object. The return values are then output with the template data to the response, so that the client sees this in his browser:

```
The user with id 86753 has a surname of Smith
```

Comments and Template Data

You can use standard HTML comments within the JSP, and those comments will appear in the page received by the client browser. Standard HTML comments have this form:

```
<!-- This comment will appear in the client's browser -->
```

You can also include JSP-specific comments that use this syntax:

```
<%-- This comment will NOT appear in the client's browser --%>
```

JSP comments will not appear in the page output to the client.

Everything that is not a directive, declaration, scriptlet, expression, action element, or JSP comment (usually all the HTML and text in the page) is termed *template data*. In other words, template data is anything that the JSP translator is ignorant about. This data is output to the client as if it had appeared within a static web page.

Creating and Deploying a JSP Web Application

Earlier, you saw an example of a JSP page that had no dynamic behavior. Now that you know about the makeup of a JSP page, we can develop a dynamic example—a welcome page to an application that manages a Frequently Asked Questions (FAQ) forum. We will go through the code, and then see how to deploy the JSP application to the Java EE reference implementation server and to a stand-alone Tomcat server.

Writing the JSP Web Application

Start by creating a directory structure to match the web application. If you are planning to deploy this application to a stand-alone Tomcat server, you can create this directory directly in the Tomcat /webapps directory. Figure 3-2 shows the directory structure with the files that will be created.

Figure 3-2. *Directory structure for the first JSP example*

As you go through the following steps and create each file, refer to this directory structure in Figure 3-2 to determine where to save each file.

Listing 3-1 is the `welcome.jsp` file. This is the first page that will be accessed by a user of the web application.

Listing 3-1. *welcome.jsp*

```
<%@ page errorPage="/WEB-INF/errorPage.jsp"
         import="java.util.Iterator,com.apress.faq.FaqCategories" %>

<html>
  <head>
    <title>Java FAQ Welcome Page</title>
  </head>

  <body>
    <h1>Java FAQ Welcome Page</h1>
    Welcome to the Java FAQ

<%! FaqCategories faqs = new FaqCategories(); %>
Click a link below for answers to the given topic.
<%
  Iterator categories = faqs.getAllCategories();
  while (categories.hasNext()) {
    String category = (String) categories.next();
%>
    <p>
    <a href="<%= replaceUnderscore(category) %>.jsp"><%= category %>
    </a></p>
<%
  }
%>

<%@ include file="/WEB-INF/footer.jspf" %>
  </body>
</html>

<%!
public String replaceUnderscore(String s) {
  return s.replace(' ','_');
}
%>
```

The `welcome.jsp` page has a JSP `include` directive to add a standard footer. Because the include file is just a fragment and not a complete JSP file, we use the convention of naming the file with a `.jspf` extension, as recommended by the JSP specification. Listing 3-2 shows the `footer.jspf` file.

Listing 3-2. *footer.jspf*

```
<hr>
Page generated on <%= (new java.util.Date()).toString() %>
```

With this simple example, we don't expect any errors to occur. In the unlikely event that one does occur, Listing 3-3 shows an error page that can be served to the client.

Listing 3-3. *errorPage.jsp*

```
<%@ page isErrorPage="true" import="java.io.PrintWriter" %>

<html>
  <head>
    <title>Error</title>
  </head>
  <body>
    <h1>Error</h1>
    There was an error somewhere.
    <%@ include file="/WEB-INF/footer.jspf" %>
  </body>
</html>
```

And finally, Listing 3-4 shows the helper file that will be used by `welcome.jsp`, `FaqCategories.java`. After entering the source, compile the file into a class file.

Listing 3-4. *FaqCategories.java*

```
package com.apress.faq;

import java.util.Iterator;
import java.util.Vector;

public class FaqCategories {
  private Vector categories = new Vector();

  public FaqCategories() {
    categories.add("Dates and Times");
    categories.add("Strings and StringBuffers");
    categories.add("Threading");
  }
  public Iterator getAllCategories() {
    return categories.iterator();
  }
}
```

The welcome.jsp file (Listing 3-1) demonstrates many of the features that have been introduced in this chapter so far. It begins with the page directive:

```
<%@ page errorPage="/WEB-INF/errorPage.jsp"
        import="java.util.Iterator, com.apress.faq.FaqCategories" %>
```

This directive has two attributes. First, an errorPage is defined, to which the browser will be redirected if an error occurs on the welcome.jsp page. The other attribute used with the page directive is the import. The page imports two Java classes: the Iterator class from the Java API and the FaqCategories class that is part of this application.

Note that the page can also use this syntax for the import:

```
<%@ page errorPage="/WEB-INF/errorPage.jsp"
        import="java.util.*, com.apress.faq.*" %>
```

This is followed by some straight HTML. Further down in the page is a declaration scripting element:

```
<%! FaqCategories faqs = new FaqCategories(); %>
```

This element declares a variable called faqs and initializes it by calling the constructor of the FaqCategories helper class. You can see that declaration elements must follow Java coding rules, including the use of a semicolon to terminate the statement.

The next JSP element in the page is a scriptlet:

```
<%
  Iterator categories = faqs.getAllCategories();
  while (categories.hasNext()) {
  String category = (String)categories.next();
%>
    <p><a href="/<%= replaceUnderscore(category) %>"><%= category %></a></p>
<%
  }
%>
```

This scriptlet gets an Iterator from the FaqCategories instance. This Iterator is used to loop through each of the categories defined in the FaqCategories class. Each category is loaded into a String variable called category, and this is used to create an HTML link. Each category is printed twice using expression elements: first within the href attribute of the <a> tag to set the page that the link refers to, and then within the body of the link. The first expression element calls the replaceUnderscore() method (defined later in the page) and prints the result; the other expression element simply prints the category value.

Notice that with the scriptlet, you must use Java syntax. However, within an expression element, you need to use only the expression itself, without a semicolon to end the statement.

At the bottom of the page, an include directive includes a standard footer:

```
<%@ include file="/WEB-INF/footer.jspf" %>
```

The last thing in the file is another declaration element:

```
<%!
public String replaceUnderscore(String s) {
  return s.replace(' ','_');
}
%>
```

This element declares the `replaceUnderscore()` method, which replaces the spaces in a string with underscores. It was called by the scriptlet earlier in the file.

The next file is `footer.jspf` (Listing 3-2). You can see that this is not a complete JSP file. This file uses an expression element to print the current date and time at the server when the page is served to the user. The file uses the extension `.jspf`, as recommended by the JSP specification, to indicate that this file is a fragment. Also, because it is a fragment and is not meant to be publicly available, we put the file into the `WEB-INF` directory. Files in this directory are not publicly available. This means that you cannot enter an address into a browser to access this file. Only code within the application can access files within the `WEB-INF` directory.

The `errorPage.jsp` file (Listing 3-3) is meant to be used when an uncaught exception occurs in the `welcome.jsp` page. It includes the standard footer. However, assuming everything in the `welcome.jsp` page is correct, it will not be called in this application. This page is not meant to be publicly available, so it also resides in the `WEB-INF` directory. Also, since `errorPage.jsp` is an error page, the `isErrorPage` attribute of the `page` directive is set to `true`. Apart from that directive, this page contains just straight HTML and an `include` directive to include the `footer.jspf` file.

The final source file is `FaqCategories.java` (Listing 3-4). This is a helper class that supplies three categories to the `welcome.jsp` page. In a real-world application, the categories would come from some persistent store such as a database or a directory. For this example, the helper class hard-codes the categories for `welcome.jsp`. The categories are stored in a `Vector` object, which is an instance member of the class. In the class constructor, the hard-coded categories are added to this `Vector`. Finally, the class defines a `getAllCategories()` method, which simply returns the `Iterator` for the `Vector`. The JSP page uses this `Iterator` to loop through each of the categories in turn.

That finishes the code for the application, but before it can actually be accessed by clients, it must be deployed to an application server. We'll look at two application servers in this chapter: the reference implementation server that comes with the Java EE SDK, and the stand-alone Tomcat server. First, let's see how to deploy the application with the Java EE server.

Deploying the Web Application in Java EE

Here are the steps for deploying the sample JSP web application in Java EE:

1. Ensure the Sun Application Server is running, and then start up the Sun Java EE Deployment Tool (introduced in Chapter 2).

2. Select File ➤ New ➤ Web Component from the menu to create a new web component. This will start the New Web Application Wizard, as shown in Figure 3-3.

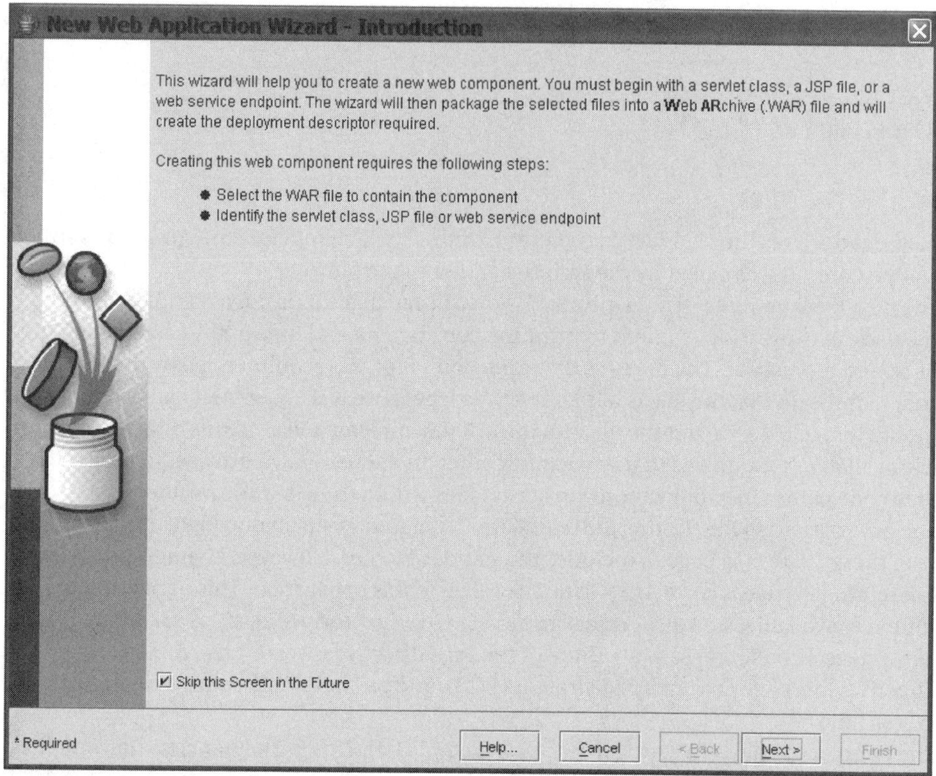

Figure 3-3. *The opening screen of the New Web Application Wizard. You can check the Skip this Screen in the Future box at the bottom of the dialog box to skip this screen the next time you run the wizard.*

3. Click the Next button to advance to the first step of the wizard, shown in Figure 3-4. Click the Edit Contents button in the Contents panel and add the application files to the web archive (WAR): `FaqCategories.class`, `errorPage.jsp`, `footer.jspf`, and `welcome.jsp`. Make sure that the `errorPage.jsp` and `footer.jspf` files appear in the correct location underneath the `WEB-INF` directory. If they do not, you can drag-and-drop them into the correct location. Note that the wizard will create several files for you, including the deployment descriptor, `web.xml`. You do not need to add `web.xml` to the application.

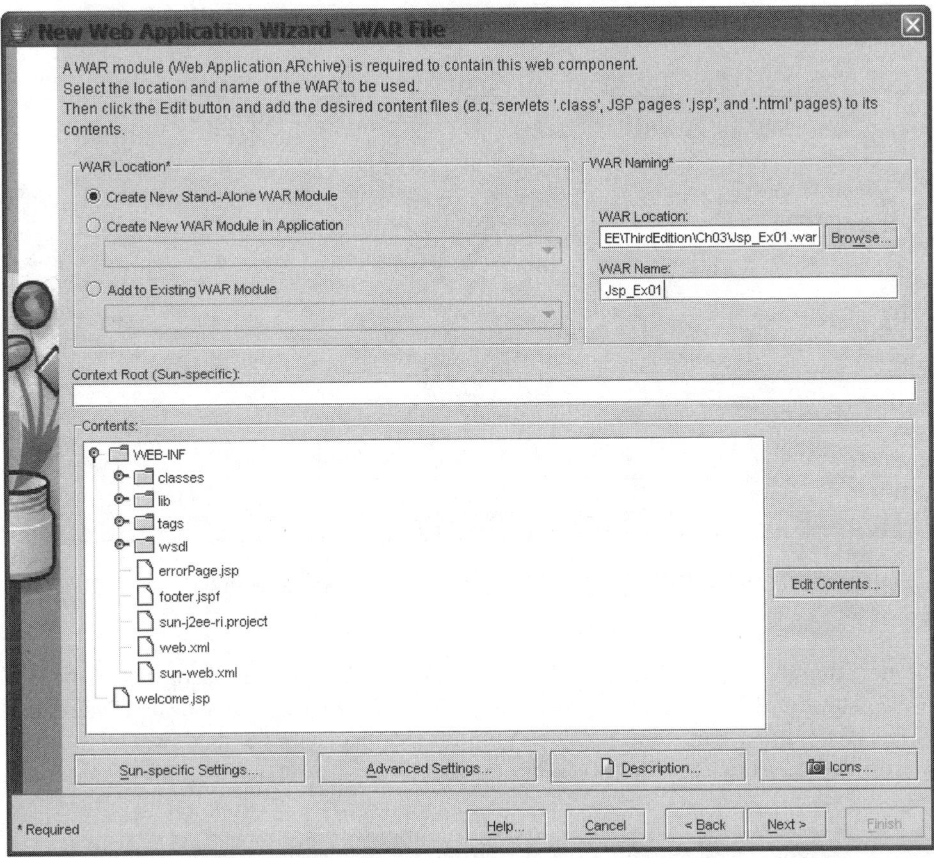

Figure 3-4. *The first page of the wizard is used to add files to the web component and name the web component.*

4. In the WAR Naming section of the first wizard step, select a location for the WAR file and a name for the file. In Figure 3-4, you can see that we selected `Jsp_Ex01`, for JSP Example 01, as the WAR name on our system, which is the name we will refer to here. Click the Next button.

5. At the next wizard step, shown in Figure 3-5, select the JSP Page radio button and click the Next button.

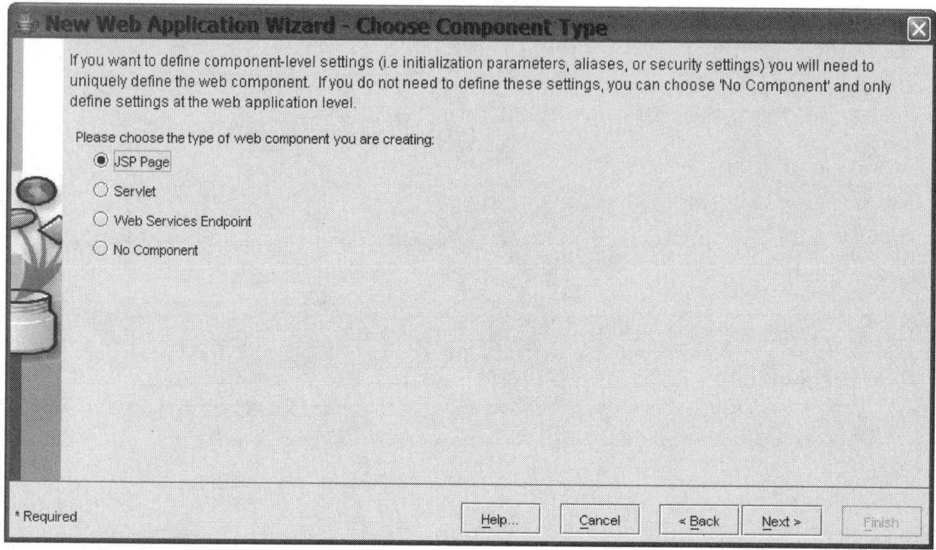

Figure 3-5. *The Choose Component Type dialog box allows you to select which type of component is being created.*

6. The next page of the wizard is the Component General Properties dialog box. In the JSP Filename drop-down box, select `/welcome.jsp` as the JSP to define, as shown in Figure 3-6. The Web Component Name and Web Component Display Name fields will be filled in automatically. Click the Finish button.

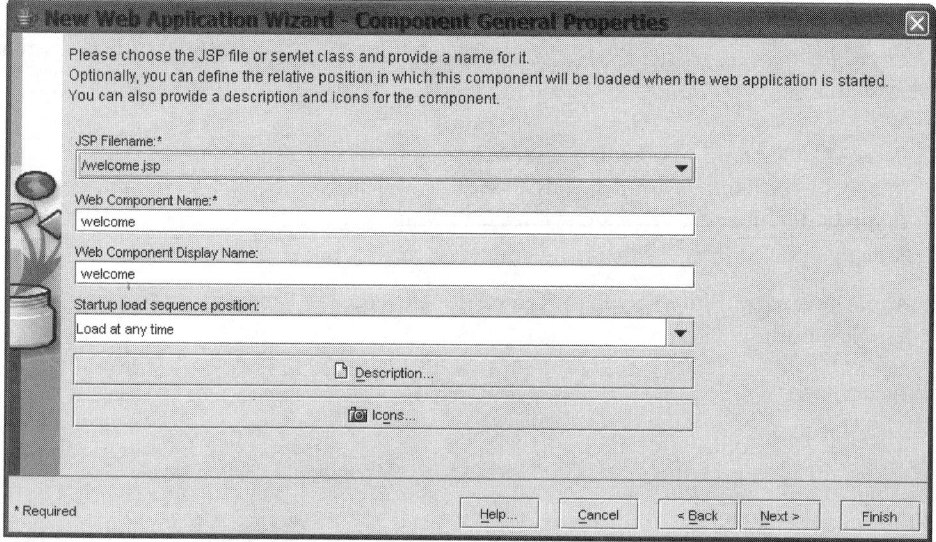

Figure 3-6. *The Component General Properties dialog box allows you to select which JSP is being configured. If your application has multiple JSPs, you can rerun the wizard multiple times and select a different JSP each time.*

7. The wizard will close and return you to the Deployment Tool. Select the WAR file (`Jsp_Ex01` in this example) in the left pane. Select the File Refs tab in the right pane. Click the Add button for Welcome files to add an entry for a Welcome File. Enter the name `welcome.jsp` in the Welcome Files field, as shown in Figure 3-7.

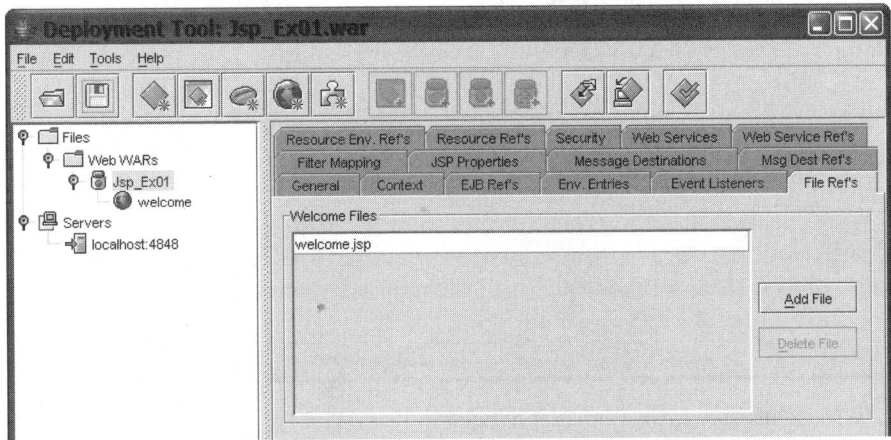

Figure 3-7. *Creating a welcome file list ensures that users will always see a valid web page, rather than a directory listing, when they access the web component.*

8. Save the WAR file.

9. Select Tools ➤ Deploy from the menu. The Deployment Tool allows you to select the server to which the web application is deployed. Most likely, you are deploying to the localhost and will not have any other servers. You may also need to enter the admin username and password for the server (we hope you wrote those down when you installed the Java EE server).

10. When you are ready, click the OK button. The Deployment Tool will deploy your web application. The Deployment Tool displays the results of the deployment in a new window.

11. When the tool is finished deploying the web component, open a browser window. Enter the appropriate address to run the application, such as `http://localhost:8080/Jsp_Ex01`. The `welcome.jsp` page will load, as shown in Figure 3-8.

■ **Note** If the welcome page does not display, first check that the server is running. If it is, you should get a valid page when you type the default URL, usually `http://localhost:8080`. If the server is running, you could have a translation or compilation problem. After we look at how to deploy the web components to Tomcat, we'll look at how to deal with translation or compilation problems.

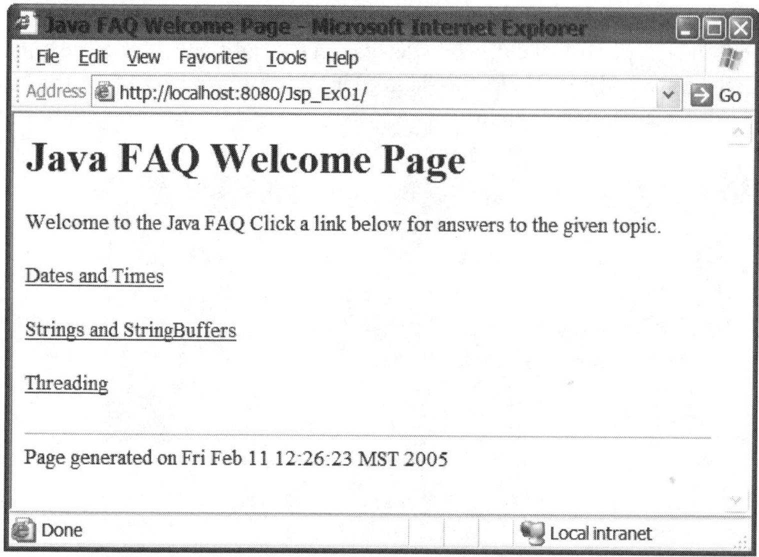

Figure 3-8. *The welcome.jsp page in a browser window*

The address and port you use in the web browser depend on where the server is located and which port it uses to listen for HTTP requests. If you installed the Java EE server to the same machine as the web browser, then you can access it using localhost, or you can use the localhost IP address 127.0.0.1 or the actual IP address of the machine. The default HTTP port for the Java EE reference implementation is 8080, so if you kept the default port setting during installation (and named your WAR file `Jsp_Ex01`), you will access the web application using the URL `http://localhost:8080/Jsp_Ex01`. If, however, you installed the Java EE server to a different machine, or selected a different port for the server to listen for HTTP requests, you will need to change the URL to use the name or IP address of that machine and the correct port for the server.

Deploying the Web Application in Tomcat

Deploying applications to a stand-alone Tomcat server is easy, but it does require you to write a special XML file, known as a *deployment descriptor*. This file is also required by the Java EE server, but the Deployment Tool creates it for you, so you don't need to write it by hand.

■ **Tip** For details on how to use Tomcat, check out *Pro Jakarta Tomcat 5*, by Matthew Moodie (Apress, 2004; ISBN 1-59059-331-6).

Deployment descriptors are XML files that contain configuration information about the entire web application. Deployment descriptors are covered in more detail in Chapter 6. Listing 3-5 is the deployment descriptor for our Java FAQ application. This file is called `web.xml` and is placed in the application's `WEB-INF` directory.

Listing 3-5. *web.xml for Java FAQ Web Component*

```
<?xml version="1.0" encoding="UTF-8"?>
<web-app version="2.5"
        xmlns="http://java.sun.com/xml/ns/javaee"
        xmlns:xsi="http://www.w3.org/2001/XMLSchema-instance"
        xsi:schemaLocation="http://java.sun.com/xml/ns/javaee
        http://java.sun.com/xml/ns/javaee/web-app_2_5.xsd">
<display-name>Jsp_Ex01</display-name>
<servlet>
  <display-name>welcome</display-name>
  <servlet-name>welcome</servlet-name>
  <jsp-file>/welcome.jsp</jsp-file>
</servlet>
<welcome-file-list>
  <welcome-file>welcome.jsp</welcome-file>
</welcome-file-list>
</web-app>
```

If the Java EE server is running, shut it down and start the Tomcat server. If you created the directory structure shown in Figure 3-2 earlier in the chapter within the Tomcat `/webapps` directory, then you are finished. If the application directory is not under the Tomcat `/webapps` directory, you can simply copy the directory structure to Tomcat `/webapps`. Alternatively, you can navigate to the top-level directory of the web application (for example, if the highest directory of the application is `/Jsp_Ex01`, you would navigate into that directory), create the web archive (WAR) file manually using the command `jar cf Jsp_Ex01.war *`, and then copy the `.war` file to the Tomcat `/webapps` directory.

Open a browser window and enter the appropriate address, such as `http://localhost:8080/Jsp_Ex01`. The `welcome.jsp` file will load, as shown earlier in Figure 3-8.

Note If the welcome page does not display, first check that the server is running. If it is, you should get a valid page when you type the default URL, usually `http://localhost:8080`. If the server is running, you could have a translation or compilation problem. The next section talks about how to handle translation or compilation problems.

Since you'll need to write a deployment descriptor for any web applications you want to deploy to a stand-alone Tomcat server, let's take a moment to look at the `web.xml` file in this example. The file begins with the standard XML declaration and the root element `<web-app>`, which includes attributes for the schema declarations, which you can use for any JSP deployment descriptors.

```
<?xml version="1.0" encoding="UTF-8"?>
<web-app version="2.5"
        xmlns="http://java.sun.com/xml/ns/javaee"
        xmlns:xsi="http://www.w3.org/2001/XMLSchema-instance"
        xsi:schemaLocation="http://java.sun.com/xml/ns/javaee
        http://java.sun.com/xml/ns/javaee/web-app_2_5.xsd">
```

Next comes the XML content of the file. There are three elements in this descriptor: a `display-name` element, a `servlet` element that provides information about the JSP, and the `welcome-file-list` element.

```
<display-name>Jsp_Ex01</display-name>
<servlet>
  <display-name>welcome</display-name>
  <servlet-name>welcome</servlet-name>
  <jsp-file>/welcome.jsp</jsp-file>
</servlet>
<welcome-file-list>
  <welcome-file>welcome.jsp</welcome-file>
</welcome-file-list>
</web-app>
```

The `display-name` element allows you to provide a user-friendly name for your web application. This name can be displayed by web application tools. For example, Tomcat has a management tool that you can link to from the main Tomcat page (`http://localhost:8080/`). If you access the management page, it will list all the deployed web components in the server using the display name to identify the web components. The Sun Java EE server has a management page that you can access at `http://localhost:4848`. Figure 3-9 shows this page, where the display name from the deployment descriptor is used as the web application name.

The `servlet` element provides information about any JSPs or Servlets that are part of the web application. As you will see later in this chapter, JSP source files are translated into Servlet files, and the JSP page implementation class is a Servlet, which is why the element is named `servlet`, rather than JSP.

The final element is `welcome-file-list`. This element lists the files that will be served to any client that simply enters the application context from a browser, rather than identifying a specific resource in the application. These files are referred to as *welcome files*. For example, an address like `http://localhost:8080/Jsp_Ex01` does not reference any resource within the web component. Anyone who enters a URL like this will be served a welcome file from the list. If multiple files are listed in the welcome file list, the server will respond with the first file that it finds in the welcome file list.

■ **Note** We will cover specific elements of the deployment descriptor as they are used, but will wait to look at deployment descriptors in more detail in Chapter 6. You can also find more information about deployment descriptors in the documentation for Tomcat, as well as in the JSP and Servlet specifications.

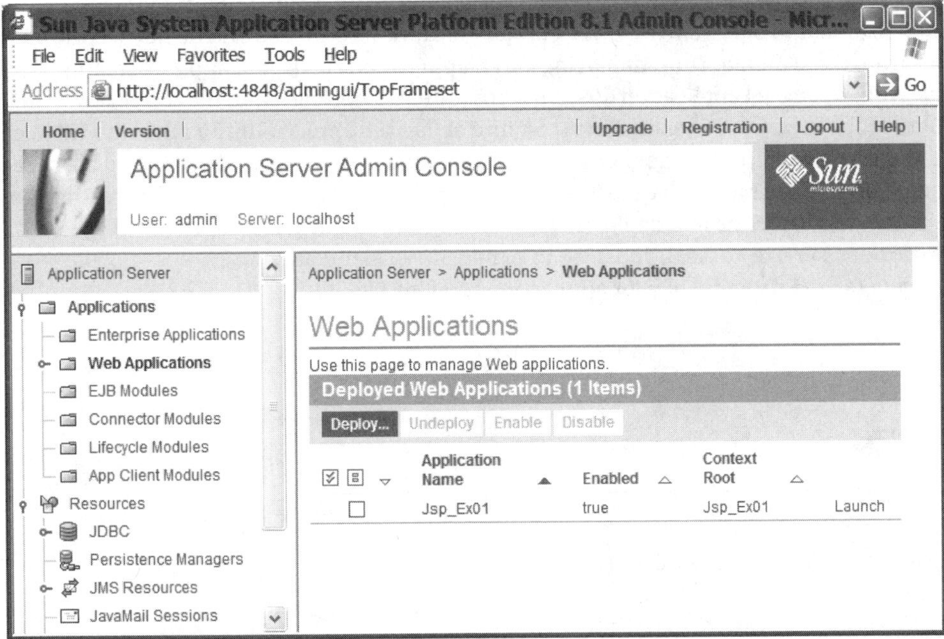

Figure 3-9. *The Web Applications page in the Sun Application Server management tool shows the web applications that have been deployed to the server. The display name field in the deployment descriptor is used to populate the Application Name field in the page.*

When you loaded the welcome page, you probably saw that the links in that page do not reference actual resources within the application. If you clicked one of the links, you probably received an HTTP 404 error in the browser. You did not see the error page, because the problem was a resource not found on the server, not an uncaught exception in the page.

■ **Caution** Starting with the Servlet 2.4 specification, elements in the deployment descriptor can occur in any order. For example, if you take the deployment descriptor in Listing 3-5, and move the `welcome-file-list` element to be the first element in the file, the web application will still work properly. However, in earlier Servlet and JSP specification versions, the elements in the deployment descriptor had to follow a particular order specified by a Document Type Definition (DTD) (JSP 1.2 and earlier) or an XML Schema (JSP 2.0), or the server would not start the application. If your server supports only Servlet 2.3 or JSP 2.0 (or earlier versions), you will need to check the specification for the correct order of deployment descriptor elements.

To actually deploy the application to Tomcat, you need to copy the files to Tomcat's `/webapps` directory. If you don't want to store the application's files directly in this directory, you can deploy the application by packaging all the files into a WAR file.

The WAR file is a convenient way to package all the files and components that make up a web application into one archive. All JSP containers know how to read and deploy web applications from the WAR file. Thus, deploying a web application can be as simple as creating the archive with the correct application directory structure and putting it into the correct directory location for the container. The directory structure of the web application, and thus the WAR, is defined in the Servlet specification. Likewise, the deployment descriptor is defined by the specification. When you use a tool like the Sun Java EE Deployment Tool, it takes care of creating the correct directory structure and deployment descriptor for you. When you're deploying to a stand-alone server like Tomcat, you need to handle these manually.

In general, the structure of your application will look like this:

```
app_context/
  public web resources
  WEB-INF/
    web.xml
    tlds/
      tld files
    lib/
      archives used by application
    classes/
      class files used in application
```

The directory at the top of the structure defines the web application context. The application context provides a separation between different web applications. Under the application context directory are the public files of the application. These will generally include the HTML and JSP pages of the application. Under the application context is the `WEB-INF` directory. This directory contains the deployment descriptor (`web.xml`) and other files that are not publicly accessible by clients of the application. There can be any number of directories under `WEB-INF`, but three common directories are `tlds`, `lib`, and `classes`. The `tlds` directory is not required, but it is commonly used for keeping tag library descriptor files (see Chapter 4). The `lib` directory is used for Java archives (`.jar` files) that are used by the web application. Finally, the `classes` directory is used for class files in the web application.

Handling Translation or Compilation Problems

The highly experienced technical team at Apress reviewed and tested all the code in this book, and of course, it's going to work perfectly for you every time—at least, it should.

However, when entering the code from this book, or when developing your own JSPs, you may occasionally come across a typo or some other error that causes the translation or compilation to fail. Here, we will give you some pointers on how to find and resolve these problems.

The JSP specification identifies many situations that will cause a translation error. For example, it says that the `page` directive can appear multiple times, but that any attribute can be specified only once. If the same attribute appears a second time, it must have a value identical to the first appearance; otherwise, a translation error occurs.

To see how this works, go back to `welcome.jsp` (Listing 3-1). Add this line of code anywhere in the file:

```
<%@ page errorPage="/WEB-INF/errorPage2.jsp" %>
```

Then redeploy the JSP application. On our Tomcat server, when we tried to load the welcome page, we saw the display shown in Figure 3-10. In this case, Tomcat has sent a nicely formatted and helpful error page. Depending on your server, you should see a similar message for translation errors on your system.

Although you can't see all of it in the figure, the first line of the stack trace looks like this:

```
org.apache.jasper.JasperException: /welcome.jsp(10,0) Page directive: ➥
illegal to have multiple occurrences of errorPage with different values ➥
(old: /WEB-INF/errorPage.jsp, new: /WEB-INF/errorPage2.jsp)
```

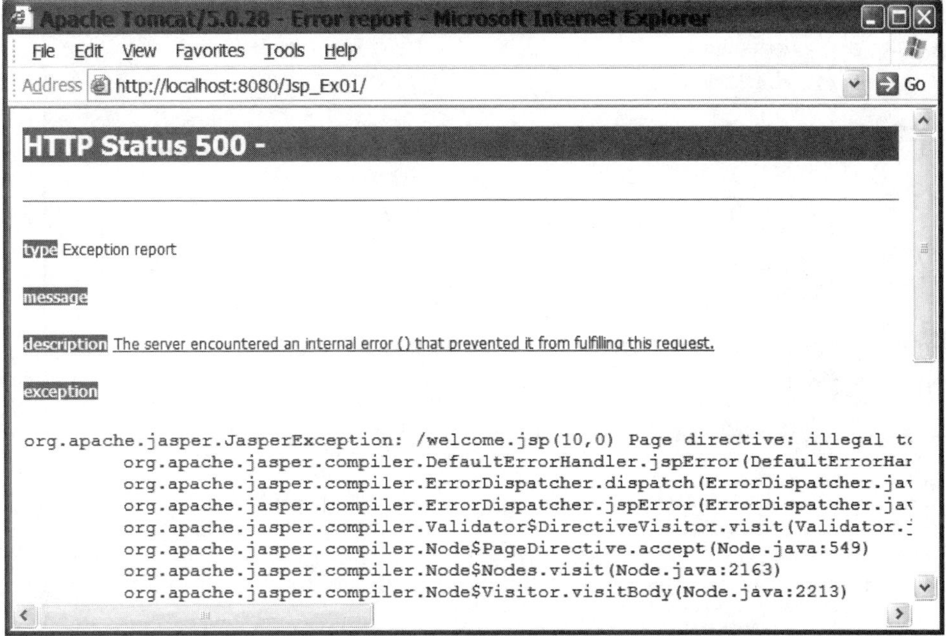

Figure 3-10. *Tomcat shows you a helpful stack trace with information about the translation problem. This makes it easy to find and fix the problem.*

As you can see, the stack trace says in which file the error occurred (`welcome.jsp`), and in which line and at which character (10,0) the error occurs. It also gives you a clear description of the error. With this information, you should be able to easily go to line 10 in the file, find the offending multiple occurrence of `errorPage`, and fix it.

Compilation problems, unfortunately, are not always so easy to find. Return to `welcome.jsp` again and remove the offending duplicate `errorPage` directive (if you added it earlier). Now add an extra curly brace, as shown here:

```
<%@ include file="/WEB-INF/footer.jspf" %>
<%
  }
%>
  </body>
</html>
```

When we deployed this broken file to Tomcat, we got the page shown in Figure 3-11. Tomcat again sends an errorPage with a nicely formatted stack trace, but this page does not indicate where in the JSP source the error occurred. In fact, it shows five errors, starting with this:

```
C:\Program Files\Apache Software Foundation\Tomcat 5.030\work\Catalina\➥
localhost\Jsp_Ex01\org\apache\jsp\welcome_jsp.java:43: 'try' without ➥
'catch' or 'finally'
    try {
    ^
```

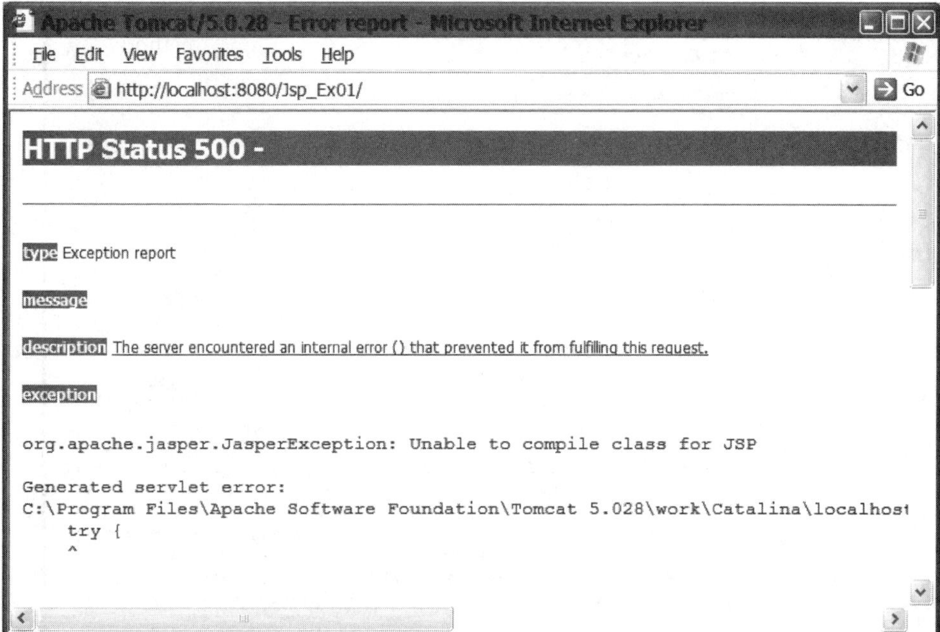

Figure 3-11. *When the server cannot compile the JSP, it sends an error page to the browser. Compilation errors can sometimes be hard to find.*

At this point, you might be really puzzled. Why in the world is Tomcat complaining about try without catch? There is no try-catch block in the JSP source. As we mentioned earlier in the chapter, the JSP source file is translated into a page implementation class. It is the source file for this class that contains the try-catch block. Once you realize that, it should be obvious in hindsight that adding an extra brace messed up the class and caused all the compilation errors. However, in the real world, you wouldn't knowingly put in an error, so even though you realize there is something wrong with the JSP, it won't necessarily be easy to find and fix.

One way to deal with this problem is to look at the translated source file. The stack trace shown in Figure 3-11 tells you where the source file, welcome_jsp.java, is located. You can open it in an editor and search for the problem there. This may or may not be easier than looking at the JSP file. In this case, the stack trace says the first error is on line 43 of the translated file, when, in fact, the real problem occurs much later in the file, at the point where the translated extra brace occurs.

Sometimes, the best way to deal with a mysterious compilation problem—one where the error message does not tell you which line of the JSP has the problem—is to go back to basic Java syntax. Check that all code lines end with a semicolon. Check that all braces match up. Check that all those little syntax problems that your fancy IDE handles automatically in a Java file are not causing you problems in your JSP file.

Handling JSP Initialization and End of Life

In the JSP lifecycle section earlier in this chapter, we mentioned that you can add methods to your JSP that will be called when the JSP is initialized and when the JSP is destroyed. These methods are declared using the declaration scripting element.

When you need to perform one-time initialization of the JSP, add this method to the JSP:

```
<%!
public void jspInit() {
  // ...perform one time initialization.
  // ...this method is called only once per JSP, not per request
}
%>
```

If you need to clean up any resources used by the JSP, add this method to the JSP:

```
<%!
public void jspDestroy() {
  // ...perform one time cleanup of resources
}
%>
```

If you don't need to perform initialization or cleanup, you do not need to add these methods to the JSP.

JSP Scope

Objects that are created as part of a JSP have a certain lifetime and may or may not be accessible to other components or objects in the web application. The lifetime and accessibility of an object is known as *scope*. In some cases, such as with the implicit objects discussed in the next section, the scope is set and cannot be changed. With other objects (JavaBeans, for example), you can set the scope of the object. There are four valid scopes:

- **Page scope:** This scope is the most restrictive. With page scope, the object is accessible only within the page in which it is defined. JavaBeans created with page scope and objects created by scriptlets are thread-safe. (Recall, though, that Java objects created by declaration elements are not thread-safe.)

- **Request scope:** With request scope, objects are available for the life of the specific request. This means that the object is available within the page in which it is created, and within pages to which the request is forwarded or included. Objects with request scope are thread-safe. Only the execution thread for a particular request can access these objects.

- **Session scope:** Objects with session scope are available to all application components that participate in the client's session. These objects are not thread-safe. If multiple requests could use the same `session` object at the same time, you must synchronize access to that object.

- **Application scope:** This is the least restrictive scope. Objects that are created with application scope are available to the entire application for the life of the application. These objects are not thread-safe, and access to them must be synchronized if there is a chance that multiple requests will attempt to change the object at the same time.

When you are developing the components in your web application, you need to carefully consider the scope of the objects. You should give your objects only as much scope as needed to be successful. It makes no sense to give application scope to an object that is used only within a single component. Likewise, an object with too much restriction may force your application to be more complicated. Carefully consider each of the objects and their use to determine the proper scope for each object.

Using Implicit Objects

Earlier, we stated that the properties of a JavaBean can be set from the parameters in the request sent by the client browser. Your JSP page can also access the client's request directly. You access the client's request through an object named `request`. In addition to the `request` object, the JSP model provides a number of other implicit objects. These objects are *implicit* because a JSP has access to and can use them without needing to explicitly declare and initialize the objects. Implicit objects are used within scriptlet and expression elements. This section will cover using the following implicit objects:

- `request`
- `response`
- `out`
- `session`
- `config`
- `exception`
- `application`

In this section, we will show the methods of these objects that you will use most often. You should consult the Javadoc for the complete list and explanation of all the available methods. Each implicit object has a given lifespan and accessibility known as scope, as discussed in the previous section.

The request Object

JSP pages are web components that respond to and process HTTP requests. The `request` implicit object represents this HTTP request. Through the `request` object, you can access the HTTP headers, the request parameters, and other information about the request. You will most often use this object to read the request parameters.

When a browser submits a request to a server, it can send information along with the request in the form of `request` parameters. These take two forms:

- **URL-encoded parameters:** These are parameters appended to the requested URL as a query string. The parameters begin with a question mark, followed by the name/value pairs of all the parameters, with each name and value delimited by an equal sign (=), and each pair delimited by an ampersand (&):

  ```
  http://www.myserver.com/path/to/resource?name1=value1&name2=value2
  ```

- **Form-encoded parameters:** These parameters are submitted as a result of a form submission. They have the same format as URL-encoded parameters, but are included with the body of the request and not appended to the requested URL.

These `request` parameters can be read through various methods of the `request` object:

```
String request.getParameter(String name);
String[] request.getParameterValues(String name);
Enumeration request.getParameterNames();
Map getParameterMap();
```

The `getParameter(String)` method returns the value of the parameter with the given name. If the named parameter has multiple values (for example, when a form submits the value of check boxes), this method returns the first value. For multivalued parameters, `getParameterValues(String)` returns all the values for the given name. The `getParameterNames()` method returns all the parameter names used in the request, and `getParameterMap()` returns all the parameters as name/value pairs.

Information can also be passed to the server using extra path information. This data is appended to the requested URL. For example, suppose `/Jsp_Ex01/MyComponent` were the context and name of a web application component; additional information could be appended to the path like this: `/Jsp_Ex01/MyComponent/extraPathInfo`. With the correct configuration, the server would send the request to `MyComponent`, and `MyComponent` would get the extra path information using this method:

```
String request.getPathInfo();
```

The `request` object has request scope. That means that the implicit `request` object is in scope until the response to the client is complete. It is an instance of `javax.servlet.HttpServletRequest`. For further information about the methods of `request`, see Chapter 6.

The response Object

The `response` object encapsulates the response to the web application client. Some of the tasks you can do using the `response` object are set headers, set cookies for the client, and send a redirect response to the client. You can perform those functions with the following methods:

```
public void addHeader(String name, String value)
public void addCookie(Cookie cookie)
public void sendRedirect(String location)
```

The `response` object is an instance of `javax.servlet.HttpServletResponse`, and it has page scope.

The out Object

The `out` implicit object is a reference to an output stream that you can use within scriptlets. Using the `out` object, the scriptlet can write data to the response that is sent to the client. For example, you could rewrite the earlier `welcome.jsp` (Listing 3-1) to use the `out` object like this:

```
<%
  Iterator categories = faqs.getAllCategories();
  while (categories.hasNext()) {
    String category = (String)categories.next();
    out.println("<p><a href=\"" + replaceUnderscore(category) + "\">" +
                category + "</a></p>");
  }
%>
```

This scriptlet would cause the same HTML to be sent to the client as was sent in the original version of `welcome.jsp`.

The `out` object is an instance of `javax.jsp.JspWriter`. It has page scope.

■ Note One of the purposes of JSP is to separate the HTML from the Java code. Therefore, the example shown here is not the best use of the `out` object.

The session Object

HTTP is a stateless protocol. As far as a web server is concerned, each client request is a new request, with nothing to connect it to previous requests. However, in web applications, a client's interaction with the application will often span many requests and responses. To join all these separate interactions into one coherent conversation between the client and application, web applications use the concept of a *session*. A session refers to the entire conversation between a client and a server.

The JSP components in a web application automatically participate in a given client's session, without needing to do anything special. Any JSP page that uses the `page` directive to set the `session` attribute to `false` does not have access to the `session` object, and thus cannot participate in the session.

Using the `session` object, the page can store information about the client or the client's interaction. Information is stored in the `session` object, just as you would store information in a `Hashtable` or a `HashMap`. This means that a JSP page can store only objects, not Java primitives, in the session. To store Java primitives, you need to use one of the wrapper classes such as `Integer` or `Boolean`. The methods for storing and retrieving session data are as follows:

```
Object setAttribute(String name, Object value);
Object getAttribute(String name);
Enumeration getAttributeNames();
void removeAttribute(String name);
```

When other components in the web application receive a request, they can access the session data that was stored by other components. They can change information in the session or add new information to it.

■ **Caution** Be aware that sessions are not inherently thread-safe. You should consider the possibility that two or more web components could access the same objects from the same session simultaneously. If this could be a problem for your application, you must synchronize access to the objects stored in the session.

Normally, you don't need to write code in your page to manage the session. The server creates the `session` object and associates client requests with a particular session. However, this association normally happens through the use of a cookie that is sent to the client. The cookie holds a session ID; when the browser sends the cookie back to the server, the server uses the session ID to associate the request to a session. When the browser does not accept cookies, the server falls back to a scheme called *URL rewriting* to maintain the session. If there is the possibility that the server will be using URL rewriting, your page needs to rewrite any embedded URLs. This is actually done with a method of the `response` object:

```
response.encodeURL(String);
response.encodeRedirectURL(String);
```

The second method is used when the URL will be sent as a redirect to the browser using the `response.sendRedirect()` method. The first method is used for all other URLs.

The `session` object has session scope, and all the objects stored in the `session` object also have session scope. The `session` object is an instance of `javax.servlet.http.HttpSession`.

The config Object

The `config` object is used to obtain JSP-specific initialization parameters. These initialization parameters are set in the deployment descriptor, but are specific to a single page. JSP initialization parameters are set in the `<servlet>` element of the deployment descriptor. This is because the page implementation class of the JSP (the Java class that is compiled from the JSP page) is a Servlet class. The `<servlet>` element with the `<init-param>` element will look something like this:

```
<servlet>
  <servlet-name>StockList</servlet-name>
  <servlet-class>web.StockListServlet</servlet-class>
  <init-param>
    <param-name>name</param-name>
    <param-value>value</param-value>
  </init-param>
</servlet>
```

See Chapter 6 for more information about how to use the <servlet> element.

If JSP initialization parameters are defined in the deployment descriptor, you can access them using this method:

```
config.getInitParameter(String name);
```

The `config` object has page scope.

The exception Object

The `exception` object is available only within error pages. It is a reference to the `java.lang.Throwable` object that caused the server to call the error page. You would use it just as you would use any other `Exception` or `Error` object in the `catch` block of a `try-catch` section of code. The `exception` object has page scope.

The application Object

The `application` object represents the web application environment. You will use this object to get application-level configuration parameters. Within the deployment descriptor, you can set application parameters using this element:

```
<webapp>
  <context-param>
    <param-name>name</param-name>
    <param-value>value</param-value>
  </context-param>
</webapp>
```

The value of the parameter can be accessed using the following method:

```
application.getInitParameter(String name);
```

The `application` object has application scope.

Using Standard Actions and Implicit Objects in JSP Pages

Let's look at an example that uses standard actions and implicit objects. This example expands on the previous example, adding a registration page to the Java FAQ application. The registration page will use a JavaBean. This example will also use the implicit `request` object to read `request` parameters.

Figure 3-12 shows the application structure for this example.

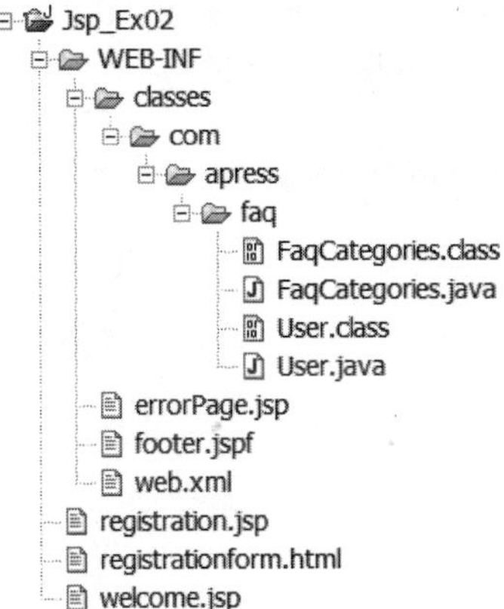

Figure 3-12. *Directory structure for the second JSP example*

Start by creating the JavaBean. This bean consists of a class called `User`, and it represents a user of our application. Listing 3-6 shows the source code for this class. After entering the source, compile it into a class file.

Listing 3-6. *User.java*

```
package com.apress.faq;

public class User {
  private String firstName;
  private String surname;
  private String loginName;
  private int age;

  public String getFirstName() { return firstName; }
  public void setFirstName(String newFirstName) {
    this.firstName = newFirstName;
  }

  public String getSurname() { return surname; }
  public void setSurname(String newSurname) {
    this.surname = newSurname;
  }

  public String getLoginName() { return loginName; }
  public void setLoginName(String newLoginName) {
    this.loginName = newLoginName;
  }
  public int getAge() { return age; }
  public void setAge(int newAge) {
    this.age = newAge;
  }
}
```

Next, modify `welcome.jsp` from the earlier example (Listing 3-1). Listing 3-7 shows the new `welcome.jsp`. This page will ask users to register, if they haven't already done so.

Listing 3-7. *Revised welcome.jsp for Using Standard Actions and Implicit Objects*

```
<%@ page errorPage="/WEB-INF/errorPage.jsp"
    import="java.util.Iterator, com.apress.faq.*" %>

<html>
  <head>
    <title>Java FAQ Welcome Page</title>
  </head>

  <body>
    <h1>Java FAQ Welcome Page</h1>

<%
  User user = (User) session.getAttribute("user");
  if (user == null) {
%>
    You are not yet registered, please
    <a href="registrationform.html">register</a>.
<%
  } else {
%>
    Welcome to the Java FAQ

<%! FaqCategories faqs = new FaqCategories(); %>
Click a link below for answers to the given topic.
<%
    Iterator categories = faqs.getAllCategories();
    while (categories.hasNext()) {
      String category = (String) categories.next();
%>
      <p>
      <a href="<%= replaceUnderscore(category) %>.jsp"><%= category %>
      </a></p>
<%
    }
%>

<%@ include file="/WEB-INF/footer.jspf" %>
<%
  }
%>
  </body>
</html>
```

```
<%!
public String replaceUnderscore(String s) {
  return s.replace(' ','_');
}
%>
```

Next, create the `registrationform.html` page that collects the user information. This source is shown in Listing 3-8.

Listing 3-8. *registrationform.html*

```
<html>
  <head>
    <title>Registration Page</title>
  </head>
  <body>
    <h1>Registration Page</h1>

    <form action="registration.jsp" method="POST">
      <table>
        <tr>
          <td align="right">First name:</td>
          <td align="left"><input type="text"
              name="firstName" length="30"/></td>
        </tr>
        <tr>
          <td align="right">Surname:</td>
          <td align="left"><input type="text"
              name="surname" length="30"/></td>
        </tr>
        <tr>
          <td align="right">Login Name:</td>
          <td align="left"><input type="text"
              name="loginName" length="30"/></td>
        </tr>
        <tr>
          <td align="right">Age:</td>
          <td align="left"><input type="text"
              name="age" length="5"/></td>
        </tr>
      </table>

      Which topics are you interested in?
      <br><input type="checkbox" name="topics"
                 value="Dates and Times">
```

```
        Dates and Times</input>
      <br><input type="checkbox" name="topics"
                value="Strings and StringBuffers">
          Strings and StringBuffers</input>
      <br><input type="checkbox" name="topics"
                value="Threading">
          Threading</input>
      <p><input type="submit" value="Submit"/></p>
    </form>
  </body>
</html>
```

This form submits to a JSP page that gathers the form data and populates the `User` bean. Listing 3-9 shows the JSP that accepts the form submission, `registration.jsp`.

Listing 3-9. *registration.jsp*

```
<html>
  <head>
    <title>Register User</title>
  </head>
  <body>
    <h1>Register User</h1>

    <jsp:useBean id="user" scope="session" class="com.apress.faq.User">
      <jsp:setProperty name="user" property="*" />
    </jsp:useBean>

    Welcome new user, these are the values you submitted:
    <p>Your first name is <%= user.getFirstName() %>.</p>
    <p>Your last name is
       <jsp:getProperty name="user" property="surname" />.</p>
    <p>Your user id is
       <jsp:getProperty name="user" property="loginName" />.</p>
    <p>Your age is
       <jsp:getProperty name="user" property="age" />.</p>
    You selected these topics:

<%
  String[] topics = request.getParameterValues("topics");
  if (topics == null) { topics = new String[] {"No topics"}; }
  for (int i = 0; i < topics.length; i++) {
%>
    <br><%= topics[i] %>
```

```
<%
  }
%>
    <p>Go to <a href="welcome.jsp">Topic List Page</a></p>
    <%@ include file="/WEB-INF/footer.jspf" %>
  </body>
</html>
```

The other files for this application remain the same as in the previous example: `errorPage.jsp` (Listing 3-3), `footer.jspf` (Listing 3-2), and `FaqCategories.java` (Listing 3-4). If you are using the Sun Deployment Tool, it will create `web.xml` for you. If you are using Tomcat, Listing 3-10 shows the deployment descriptor, `web.xml`.

Listing 3-10. *web.xml for Jsp_Ex02*

```
<?xml version='1.0' encoding='UTF-8'?>
<web-app
        version="2.5"
        xmlns="http://java.sun.com/xml/ns/javaee"
        xmlns:xsi="http://www.w3.org/2001/XMLSchema-instance"
        xsi:schemaLocation="http://java.sun.com/xml/ns/javaee
        http://java.sun.com/xml/ns/javaee/web-app_2_5.xsd"
        >
    <display-name>Jsp_Ex02</display-name>
    <servlet>
        <display-name>welcome</display-name>
        <servlet-name>welcome</servlet-name>
        <jsp-file>/welcome.jsp</jsp-file>
    </servlet>
    <servlet>
        <display-name>registration</display-name>
        <servlet-name>registration</servlet-name>
        <jsp-file>/registration.jsp</jsp-file>
    </servlet>
    <welcome-file-list>
        <welcome-file>welcome.jsp</welcome-file>
    </welcome-file-list>
</web-app>
```

Deploy this application to the server of your choice, using the same steps as you did for the first example in this chapter (outlined in the "Deploying the Web Application in Java EE" or "Deploying the Web Application in Tomcat" section). If you are using the Sun Deployment Tool, you will need to run the wizard twice. Add all the files and configure one of the JSPs the first time; the second time, all you need to do is configure the second JSP.

Enter the URL for the `welcome.jsp`. If you are connecting to your local machine on the default port, the URL is `http://localhost:8080/Jsp_Ex02`. Figure 3-13 shows the page you should see in your browser.

Figure 3-13. *The welcome page of the application asks the user to register.*

Click the register link to load the registration page, as shown in Figure 3-14.

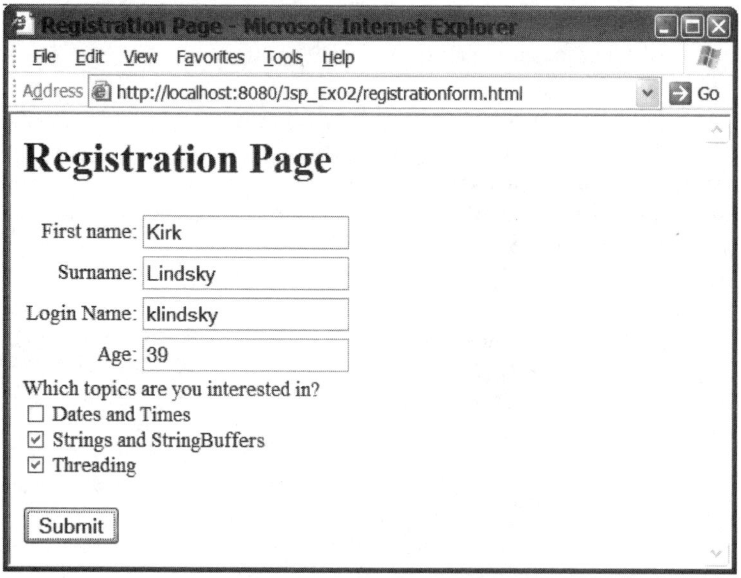

Figure 3-14. *The user enters data into the registration screen and submits it.*

Fill in the fields and check one or more of the boxes. Click the Submit button. Clicking the Submit button will cause the registration information to be passed to `registration.jsp`. That JSP will process the request and display the page shown in Figure 3-15.

Finally, click the link in this page to return to `welcome.jsp`. This time, `welcome.jsp` will display the topic list, as shown in Figure 3-16.

Figure 3-15. *The response from the registration.jsp page*

Figure 3-16. *The welcome.jsp page after the user has registered*

As in the first example in this chapter, the entry into the application is the welcome.jsp page. However, this time, the page checks for the existence of a User object in the session using this code:

```
User user = (User)session.getAttribute("user");
```

Recall that all JSP pages have access to the implicit session object, unless specified otherwise with the page directive. Using the getAttribute() method, the page attempts to get the named object from the session. Notice that getAttribute() returns a reference of type Object, which must be cast to the proper type to assign it to the user variable.

If there is no user object in the session (that is, if user is null), welcome.jsp outputs the HTML with a link for the registrationform.html page. Later, when returning to this page, the user object will exist, and the welcome page displays the topic list. The remainder of this page is unchanged.

The registrationform.html page is a standard web page with a form that submits form data to the server. The resource that it submits to is given in the <form> tag:

```
<form action="registration.jsp" method="POST">
```

The action attribute contains the URI for the server resource that should receive the data. This URI can be relative, as shown here, or absolute. The method attribute indicates which HTTP method should be used for the submission. The form includes some text fields and some check boxes. The form submits all its data to registration.jsp.

The first interesting thing about registration.jsp is the <jsp:useBean> tag shown here:

```
<jsp:useBean id="user" class="com.apress.faq.User">
  <jsp:setProperty name="user" property="*" />
</jsp:useBean>
```

This tag creates an instance of the class given by the class attribute. Throughout the rest of the page, the object can be referred to using the variable user. Enclosed within the <jsp:useBean> element is a <jsp:setProperty> element. This element uses the property="*" attribute, which causes the page to find each set*XXX* method of the given bean, and call each method with the same named parameter in the request. If you look at the User class, you will see it has four public setXXX methods: setFirstName(String), setSurname(String), setLoginName(String), and setAge(int). These methods must be matched by four request parameters. If you examine registrationform.html, you will see that it does have four form fields with the correct names: firstName, surname, loginName, and age. The value from each of these request parameters is used to set the properties of the User bean.

You may recall that the <jsp:setProperty> tag also has an attribute named param. This attribute is used when the names in the request do not match the names in the bean. For example, suppose that the web page form had a field named lastName instead of surname and that you were not allowed to change the web form or the bean. The JSP could not use the property="*" syntax, because the JSP is not able to match request parameters to bean properties in this case. The way to set the properties would be to use this syntax:

```
<jsp:useBean id="user" class="com.apress.faq.User">
```

```
  <jsp:setProperty name="user" property="surname" param="lastName"/>
</jsp:useBean>
```

Using this syntax, the page knows that it can set the bean's surname property using the value of the request parameter called lastName.

Although it is shown enclosed within the <jsp:useBean> element, you can use <jsp:setProperty> any time after the bean is created.

Also, because the bean is created with session scope, the implementation class will store the object in the session. Notice that there is no code in the JSP source file to do this. The code to store the bean in the session is generated when the JSP is translated into a class. Storing the bean in the implicit session object makes it available to every component in the application. Thus, when the welcome.jsp page is called again, it will find the bean object in the session.

Then the page prints the values of the User bean's properties. For the first property, a JSP expression is used to print the property. For the remainder of the properties, the <jsp:getProperty> element is used. The reason for doing this is simply to show different ways of printing bean properties.

```
<p>Your first name is <%= user.getFirstName() %></p>
<p>Your last name is
    <jsp:getProperty name="user" property="surname" />.</p>
```

The page then prints the remainder of the request parameters. These are the values of the check boxes that were checked in the form. The page calls the method, and then prints every element in the String array returned by the method. Notice that the web browser submits values only for the boxes that were checked. Finally, the JSP prints a link to the welcome.jsp page.

When welcome.jsp is called this time, the User object exists in the session, so the JSP outputs the topic list.

Translation and Compilation

As you develop and test JSP pages, you may have noticed that the first time you access a new page, there is some delay before the page is sent to the browser. This is a result of the server translating and compiling the page at request time. After the page has been translated and compiled, subsequent requests to the page are processed more quickly.

When a page is translated, whether at request time or earlier, it is translated into a Java source file. This Java class is known as a Servlet. As noted earlier, much of what a JSP does is based on the Servlet API, another API within Java EE. In fact, the Servlet API predates the JSP API.

Servlets were developed to allow a server's capabilities to be extended by Java code that ran inside the server. HttpServlets are Servlets that run inside an HTTP server. A Servlet accepts HTTP requests from clients and creates dynamic responses to those requests. It sends response data to the client through an OutputStream. The Servlet uses a session object to store data about a client and the client's interactions with the server. The Servlet has access to the application through a ServletContext object, and it can access Servlet parameters through a ServletConfig object. In fact, all the features of JSP pages described in this chapter are based on the Servlet model.

So, if Servlets can do everything JSP pages can do, why do you need JSPs? If a JSP page is an HTML page with bits of embedded code, a Servlet is Java code with bits of HTML. However, the larger the web application, the more HTML tends to be in the Java code. This becomes very difficult to maintain, especially if your team has web experts who are not programmers.

Servlets tend to be good at computations and processing. JSP pages tend to be good at data presentation. The JSP specification was created to make it easier for web developers to create dynamic user interfaces and web applications. By embedding Java code into JSPs, the pages can dynamically respond to user requests. Unfortunately, this leads to the opposite of the problem found with Servlets: as the web application gets larger, the more Java code tends to be embedded in the JSPs. This becomes very hard to maintain, especially if your team has programmers who are not web experts.

If only there were a way to get all the HTML out of Servlets, and all the Java code out of JSP pages. That way, programmers could work on the Servlets, and web designers could develop the JSP pages. In Chapter 4, you will see how to use Expression Language, custom actions, and tag libraries to achieve this goal.

So, although you don't need to be a Servlet expert to work with JSPs, knowing how Servlets work can help you to understand what is happening with the page. We'll look at Servlets in detail in Chapter 6. Here, we'll just take a quick look at a translated JSP to see how the JSP page is translated into code that implements a Java Servlet. (We will focus on only some of the lines that show the relationship between the JSP source and the Java source.)

Most servers will keep the translated `.java` source file in the file system, so you can examine it. For Sun's Java EE server, that location is *JAVAEE_HOME*`\domains\`*{domain}*`\ generated\jsp\j2ee-modules\`*{app name}*`\org\apache\jsp`, where *JAVAEE_HOME* is the location of the Java EE installation on your system (`/Sun/AppServer` for Windows), *{domain}* is the domain name used when you start your server (`domain1` is the default), and *{app name}* is the name of the application. For the stand-alone Tomcat server, that location is *TOMCAT_HOME*`\work\Catalina\localhost\application_context\org\apache\jsp`, where *TOMCAT_HOME* is the appropriate location of the Tomcat installation on your system.

If you have deployed the examples in this chapter, navigate to the appropriate directory and open the source file for the `welcome.jsp` page. The Java EE reference implementation and Tomcat both name the source file as `welcome_jsp.java`.

Note The example in this section is the `welcome_jsp.java` source file created by Tomcat 5.028 for the previous example. Your Java source file may differ, depending on which server you have and which source file you are viewing.

One of the first things you will notice is that the `import` attribute of the `page` directive has been turned into `import` statements:

```
package org.apache.jsp;

import javax.servlet.*;
import javax.servlet.http.*;
import javax.servlet.jsp.*;
import java.util.Iterator;
import com.apress.faq.*;
```

This is followed by the class statement:

```
public final class welcome_jsp
    extends org.apache.jasper.runtime.HttpJspBase
    implements org.apache.jasper.runtime.JspSourceDependent {
```

Notice that the class extends HttpJspBase. In Chapter 6, you will see that Servlets in a web application extend HttpServlet.

Next, you will see that the two declarations in the JSP page have been turned into a variable declaration and a public method declaration in the Java source. Note that the variable is declared as a member variable of the class, and so it is accessible from all the methods in the class:

```
FaqCategories faqs = new FaqCategories();

public String replaceUnderscore(String s) {
  return s.replace(' ','_');
}
```

The main body of the JSP is contained in the _jspService() method:

```
  public void _jspService(HttpServletRequest request,
                                      HttpServletResponse response)
        throws java.io.IOException, ServletException {

    JspFactory _jspxFactory = null;
    PageContext pageContext = null;
    HttpSession session = null;
    ServletContext application = null;
    ServletConfig config = null;
    JspWriter out = null;
    Object page = this;
    JspWriter _jspx_out = null;
    PageContext _jspx_page_context = null;
```

In the Servlet API, the analogous method is service(). This method starts by declaring the implicit objects that are used when servicing a request. Of course, they are not so implicit now that the translator has added the code to declare and initialize them.

Next is code that initializes all the implicit objects. Although we will not look at all the translated code, we do want to show one last snippet from the _jspService() method:

```
out.write("  <body>\r\n");
out.write("    <h1>Java FAQ Welcome Page</h1>\r\n");
out.write("\r\n");

User user = (User) session.getAttribute("user");
if (user == null) {

  out.write("\r\n");
  out.write("    You are not yet registered, please\r\n");
  out.write("    <a href=\"registrationform.html\">register</a>.\r\n");
```

This is part of the code that outputs the template data to the client. Notice that the translated code uses the same implicit out object that the JSP can use. Also notice that the white space from the JSP source file is preserved in the Java source file. A Servlet implementing the same page would similarly output the HTML template data using print statements. However, with a Servlet, you would need to code those statements manually. With a JSP page, it is much easier to write the template data as HTML and let the container perform the translation to Java code.

Earlier in the chapter, we stated that you could declare and define a jspInit() method and a jspDestroy() method. If you define those methods in the JSP, they will appear as additional methods in the Java source file.

Handling Errors and Exceptions

If you've typed in any of the examples in this chapter, or if you have created any JSP pages of your own, you have probably run into the situation where you had bugs in your page. Whether these bugs occur at translation time or at request time affects the response that you see in the browser when you attempt to test your page. Sometimes, you see a very ugly stack trace. Well, maybe not ugly to you, as the developer, but you don't want any of the users of your application to see anything so unfriendly.

Java web applications can deal with exceptions in a number of ways. Obviously, some exceptions can be handled as you develop the web application by adding data validation and try-catch blocks into the code. This technique avoids the exceptions. However, you need a way to deal with unexpected exceptions. Two ways to deal with unexpected exceptions are through the page directive and through the deployment descriptor.

Dealing with Exceptions through the page Directive

You have already seen how to include a page directive in your JSP page. The page directive can have an attribute named errorPage. Whenever an uncaught exception occurs in that particular page, the server sends the specified error page to the client. This allows you to use different error pages for different components in the application. The errorPage attribute looks like this:

```
<%@ page errorPage="/WEB-INF/errorPage.jsp" %>
```

The value of the errorPage attribute is the path to the error page file. The drawback is that you can specify only a single error page for all exceptions in the JSP page.

Dealing with Exceptions in the Deployment Descriptor

The deployment descriptor allows you to specify application-wide error handlers for errors in the application. This provides a way to specify different error pages for exceptions that might occur within a single page. If a given exception or HTTP error occurs anywhere in the application, the deployment descriptor identifies an error page that can be served to the client. A specific error page identified in a JSP page takes precedence over the error page identified in the deployment descriptor.

You can specify error pages for Java exceptions and for HTTP errors. Error page elements come immediately after the <welcome-file-list> element in the deployment descriptor.

To specify an error page for a Java exception, use this element in the deployment descriptor:

```
<error-page>
  <exception-type>java.lang.NumberFormatException</exception-type>
  <location>/WEB-INF/BadNumber.htmljsp</location>
</error-page>
```

To specify an error page for an HTML error, use this element:

```
<error-page>
  <error-code>404</error-code>
  <location>/WEB-INF/NoSuchPage.jsp</location>
</error-page>
```

From these two examples, you can see that the <error-page> element is relatively easy to use. The body of each <error-page> element contains two subelements.

First, there must be either an <exception-type> element or an <error-code> element. The value of <exception-type> must be the fully qualified class name of an exception that could occur in the web application. This can be any exception, not just standard Java API exceptions. The value of <error-code> must be a valid HTTP error code as defined by the HTTP specification. A complete list of the HTTP error codes can be found in the HTTP specification at http://www.w3.org/Protocols/rfc2616/rfc2616-sec10.html.

The second subelement is the <location> element. The value of this element must be the relative URL of the error page to be sent to the client when the container catches the exception specified in the <exception-type> subelement or the error code specified in the <error-code> subelement. The specification also requires that the URL begin with a leading forward slash (/). This page is located relative to the web application context. So, for example, if your web application is located at http://localhost:8080/Jsp_Ex03, the page listed in the preceding snippet for error code 404 would be located at http://localhost:8080/Jsp_Ex03/WEB-INF/NoSuchPage.jsp.

Adding Exception Handling in JSP Pages

Let's take the Java FAQ example and add error handling to it. The structure of the web application is shown in Figure 3-17.

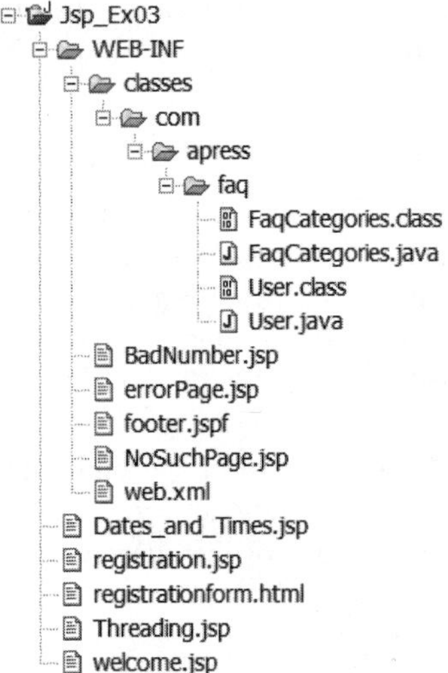

Figure 3-17. *Directory structure for the third JSP example*

As in the second example in this chapter, any files not explicitly shown here are the same as in previous examples, and you can refer to earlier listings for their source. Listing 3-11 is a new page in the Java FAQ application. The page is `Threading.jsp`, and it is located in the root directory of the application (the same directory where `welcome.jsp` is located).

Listing 3-11. *Threading.jsp*

```
<%@ page errorPage="/WEB-INF/errorPage.jsp" %>
<html>
  <head><title>Threading FAQs</title></head>
  <body>
<% Integer i = new Integer("string"); %>
  </body>
</html>
```

If you examine this JSP, you should see that it will throw a `java.lang.NumberFormatException` as soon as it is called. This is a deliberate exception.

Next, modify `errorPage.jsp` as shown in Listing 3-12.

Listing 3-12. *Revised errorPage.jsp*

```
<%@ page isErrorPage="true" import="java.io.PrintWriter" %>

<html>
  <head>
    <title>Error</title>
  </head>
  <body>
```

```
    <h1>Error</h1>
    There was an error somewhere.
    <p>Here is the stack trace
    <p><% exception.printStackTrace(new PrintWriter(out)); %>
<%@ include file="/WEB-INF/footer.jspf" %>
  </body>
</html>
```

Create the JSP `Dates_and_Times.jsp` as shown in Listing 3-13.

Listing 3-13. *Dates_and_Times.jsp*

```
<html>
  <head>
    <title>Dates and Times FAQ</title>
  </head>

  <body>
    <h1>Dates and Times FAQ</h1>
<% Integer i = new Integer("string"); %>
<%@ include file="/WEB-INF/footer.jspf"%>
  </body>
</html>
```

This JSP will also throw a `NumberFormatException` when it is called.

Now, create two JSP pages that will be used as error pages. The first is `NoSuchPage.jsp`, and it is located in the `WEB-INF` directory. It is shown in Listing 3-14.

Listing 3-14. *NoSuchPage.jsp*

```
<html>
  <head>
    <title>Resource Not Found</title>
  </head>

  <body>
  <!--
This is an html comment to ensure the page has enough characters
so that IE displays the page. See the sidebar.
123456789012345678901234567890123456789012345678901234567890
123456789012345678901234567890123456789012345678901234567890
123456789012345678901234567890123456789012345678901234567890
123456789012345678901234567890123456789012345678901234567890
123456789012345678901234567890123456789012345678901234567890
1234567890123456789012345678901234
```

```
  -->
    <h1>Resource Not Found</h1>
    You are attempting to go to a page that does not exist
    or is not available. If you entered the address by hand,
    please go to the <a href="welcome.jsp">Welcome Page</a>.

    <p>If you clicked on a link on this site, the page is
      temporarily unavailable. Try again later.
<%@ include file="/WEB-INF/footer.jspf"%>
  </body>
</html>
```

■ **Note** In Listings 3-14 and 3-15, you'll notice that each JSP has an HTML comment embedded in the page to bring the size of the JSP up to 1024 bytes. This is due to a feature of Microsoft Internet Explorer that causes Internet Explorer to display its own error page when the server sends a response page under a certain size with an HTTP status code of 500. The `errorPage.jsp` file did not need this comment because including a stack trace adds enough characters.

The second error page is shown in Listing 3-15 and is named `BadNumber.jsp`. It is also located in the `WEB-INF` directory.

Listing 3-15. *BadNumber.jsp*

```
<html>
  <head>
    <title>Invalid Number</title>
  </head>

  <body>
  <!--
This is an html comment to ensure the page has enough characters
so that IE displays the page. See the sidebar.
1234567890123456789012345678901234567890123456789012345678901234567890
1234567890123456789012345678901234567890123456789012345678901234567890
1234567890123456789012345678901234567890123456789012345678901234567890
1234567890123456789012345678901234567890123456789012345678901234567890
1234567890123456789012345678901234567890123456789012345678901234567890
1234567890123456789012345678901234567890123456789012345678901234567890
1234567890123456789012345678901234567890123456789012345678901234567890
1234567890123456789012345678901234567890123456789012345678901234567890
1234567890123456789012345
```

```
  -->
    <h1>Invalid Number</h1>
    You entered a number that is incorrect.
    Only digits are allowed. Please press the
    back button and try again.
<%@ include file="/WEB-INF/footer.jspf"%>
  </body>
</html>
</html>
```

If you are using Tomcat, create the deployment descriptor as shown in Listing 3-16.

Listing 3-16. *web.xml for Jsp_Ex03*

```
<?xml version='1.0' encoding='UTF-8'?>
<web-app
        version="2.5"
        xmlns="http://java.sun.com/xml/ns/javaee"
        xmlns:xsi="http://www.w3.org/2001/XMLSchema-instance"
        xsi:schemaLocation="http://java.sun.com/xml/ns/javaee ➥
                       http://java.sun.com/xml/ns/javaee/web-app_2_5.xsd">
    <display-name>Jsp_Ex03</display-name>
    <servlet>
        <display-name>welcome</display-name>
        <servlet-name>welcome</servlet-name>
        <jsp-file>/welcome.jsp</jsp-file>
    </servlet>
    <welcome-file-list>
        <welcome-file>welcome.jsp</welcome-file>
    </welcome-file-list>
    <error-page>
        <exception-type>java.lang.NumberFormatException</exception-type>
        <location>/WEB-INF/BadNumber.jsp</location>
    </error-page>
    <error-page>
        <error-code>404</error-code>
        <location>/WEB-INF/NoSuchPage.jsp</location>
    </error-page>
</web-app>
```

If you are using the Java EE Deployment Tool, modify the File Refs tab for the WebApp as shown in Figure 3-18. You need to add two entries to the Error Mapping list. One entry is for `java.lang.NumberFormatException`, and the resource to be called for this exception is `/WEB-INF/BadNumber.jsp`. The second entry is for HTTP error code 404, and the resource for this error is `/WEB-INF/NoSuchPage.jsp`.

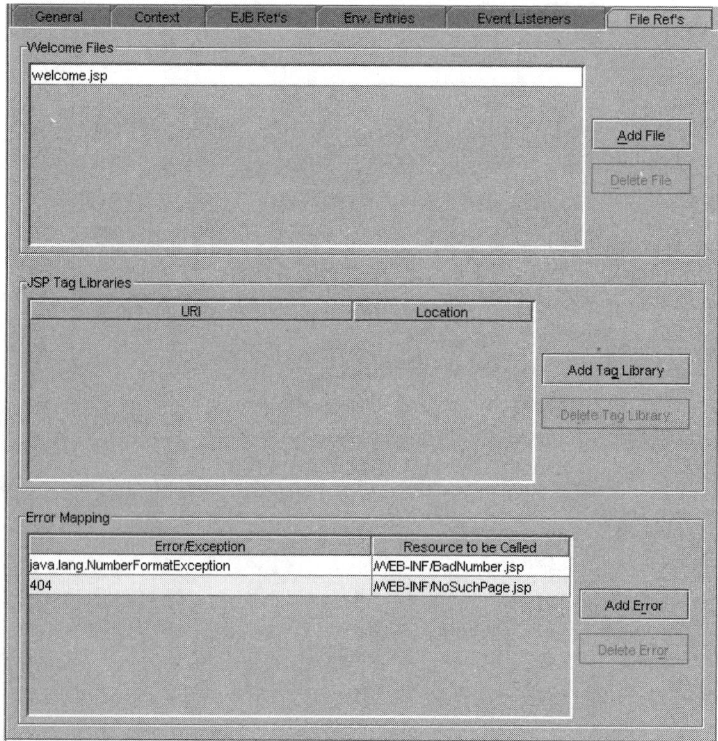

Figure 3-18. *The File Refs tab in the Java EE Deployment Tool can be used to create error page mappings for errors that occur in the web application.*

Deploy the application as described earlier in this chapter. Then open a browser and navigate through the screens until you reach the topic list page, as shown in Figure 3-19.

Click the link for Threading. The page displayed is shown in Figure 3-20.

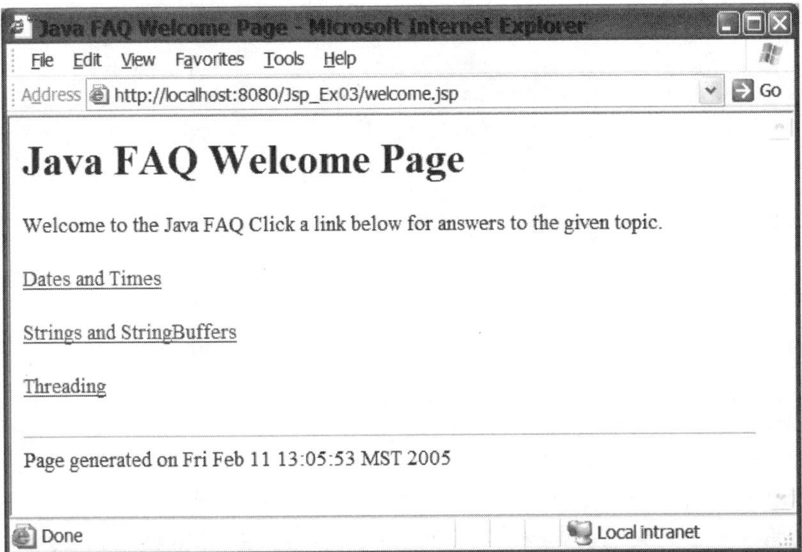

Figure 3-19. *The topic list page*

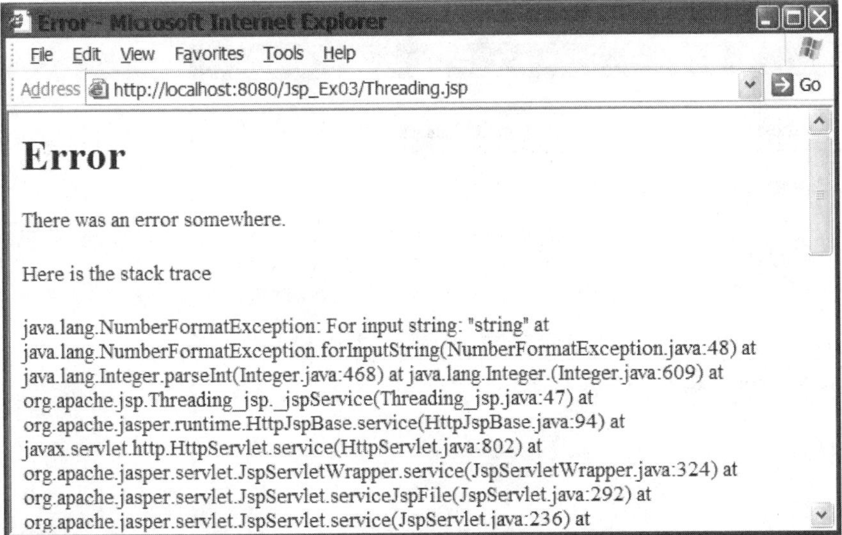

Figure 3-20. *The errorPage.jsp page is called when Threading.jsp throws an exception.*

Click the link for Dates and Times. You will see a page similar to Figure 3-21.

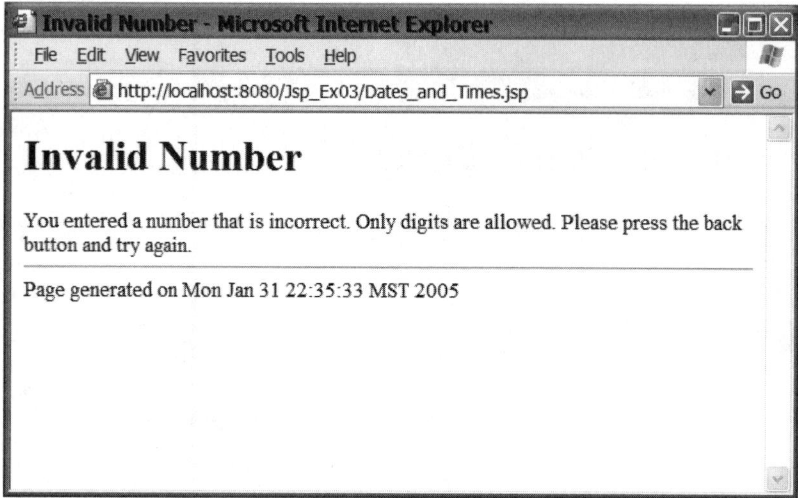

Figure 3-21. *The BadNumber.jsp page is called when Dates_and_Times.jsp throws a java.lang.NumberFormatException.*

Click the link for Strings and StringBuffers. You will see the page shown in Figure 3-22.

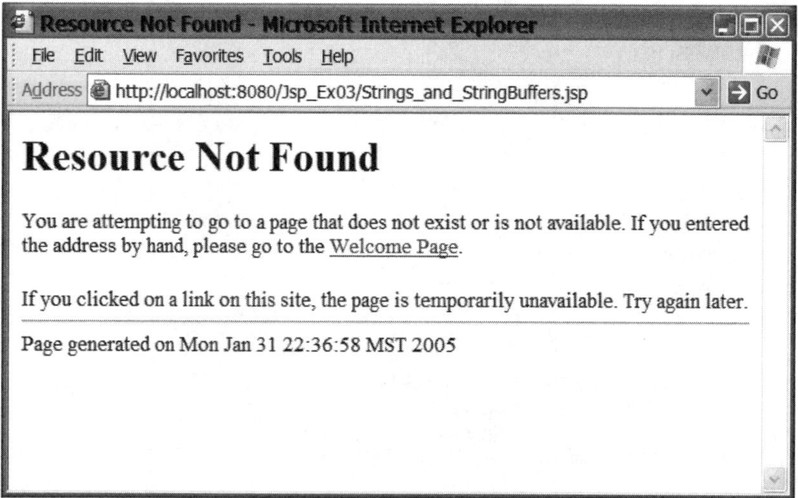

Figure 3-22. *When the String and StringBuffers page cannot be found, NoSuchPage.jsp is called.*

Three pages were added to the application, each of which causes a different error-handling mechanism to control the page flow.

The Threading.jsp page included a page directive that specified the error page. Since Threading.jsp attempts to create an Integer object with an invalid argument to the constructor, an exception is thrown, and the page does not have an error handler to catch the exception. This causes the server to call the error page specified by the page directive, and that page is sent to the client.

The error page, errorPage.jsp, has access to the implicit exception object. This is because the page includes the page directive with the isErrorPage attribute set to true. Pages that don't have this attribute do not have access to the exception object. You can use this object together with the implicit out object to print out the stack trace to the response, like this:

```
<p><% exception.printStackTrace(new PrintWriter(out)); %>
```

This works because the java.lang.Throwable interface defines a printStackTrace➥(PrintWriter) method. The PrintWriter constructor can take an OutputStream instance, which is exactly the type of the implicit out object. The method prints the stack trace to the given PrintWriter.

■ **Note** Keep in mind that you wouldn't print a stack trace in a live page meant for a user of the application. It provides no useful information for users, and just gives them a bad feeling about your application. The example here is just intended to demonstrate that you can access the implicit exception object in an error page.

The Date_and_Times.jsp also uses an Integer object to cause an exception to be thrown from the page. However, this page does not specify an error page in the page directive. In this case, the server matches the exception thrown to an exception specified in an <error-page> element in the deployment descriptor. The server sends the BadNumber.html page to the client. If the exception did not match a specification in the deployment descriptor, the server would probably have sent an HTTP 500 error to the client.

Finally, the Strings_and_StringBuffer.jsp page does not exist. This creates an HTTP 404 error in the server. Since this error code matches an error code specified in an <error-page> element in the deployment descriptor, the server sends the specified page to the client. If the error code had not matched a specification in the deployment descriptor, the server would have taken some server-specific action. Some servers, such as Tomcat, may send a server-specific page back to the client with the error; other servers might simply send the error code to the browser and let the browser decide how to display the error to the user.

IS IT A BUG OR A FEATURE?

The first edition of this book was written with J2EE SDK 1.4 Beta 1 and Tomcat 4.0 as the Servlet container. When we developed the example showing how to use error pages, it worked perfectly. When you clicked the link for a bad page, the server would respond with the correct error page.

Then Sun released new versions of the Java EE SDK and moved to Tomcat 5.0 as the Servlet container. When we tested the error page example with the new server, error pages stopped working as we expected.

We tried almost everything: We moved the pages to different locations, we played with the values of the `<error-page>` element, and we tried changing the error page JSPs to HTML pages. Nothing resolved the issue.

After thrashing around and getting nowhere, we searched for "error page not working with Tomcat 5" using Google. In the results, we found several pages that showed that others had the same problem we had seen. For example, the search results listed a page in the Apache bug database for Bug 21341 (`http://issues.apache.org/bugzilla/show_bug.cgi?id=21341`), which described the exact same problem: Error pages that worked with Tomcat 4 no longer worked with Tomcat 5. In the resolution, a developer talked about an incorrect method being invoked in the error case and provided a patch to Tomcat. Another developer responded and said that patch was probably bad. However, other bug listings claimed that there was no problem and that error page dispatching worked correctly. Based on the evidence of our example, we believed that users were right and the developers were wrong: Error page dispatching was broken.

Then we took another look at Bug 21341. Bug 21341 had a clue that we missed earlier. It said that Microsoft Internet Explorer does not show the error page if the message size is less than some number. Then we found Bug 29505 (`http://issues.apache.org/bugzilla/show_bug.cgi?id=29505`), which was even more specific information. It showed that when there was an error page returned by the application, Tomcat 4 returned HTTP status code 200, while Tomcat 5 returned status code 500. It also stated that Internet Explorer displays its internal error page if the response has less than 512 bytes.

Suddenly, it made sense! Java EE and Tomcat weren't broken; we had been bitten by an Internet Explorer bug—oops, we mean *feature*. We went back to the sample code and added an HTML comment until the error pages were displayed by Internet Explorer. On our system, it turned out that we needed the file size of the error pages to be 1024 bytes. (On another system we tested, the error pages worked when they were 512 bytes.) Now when we clicked the links to go to the example pages, Internet Explorer correctly displayed the error pages we had developed. Of course, if you are using some other web browser, you may not see this problem at all.

Including and Forwarding from JSP Pages

JSP pages have the ability to include other JSP pages or Servlets in the output that is sent to a client, or to forward the request to another JSP page or Servlet for servicing. This is accomplished through the standard actions `<jsp:include>` and `<jsp:forward>`, mentioned earlier in the chapter.

include Action

Including a JSP page or Servlet through a standard action differs from the `include` directive in the time at which the other resource is included and how the other resource is included. Recall that an `include` directive can be used in either of the following two formats, anywhere within the JSP:

```
<%@ include file="/WEB-INF/footer.jspf">
<jsp:directive.include file="/WEB-INF/footer.jspf"/>
```

When the JSP container translates the page, this directive causes the indicated file to be included in that place in the page and become part of the Java source file that is compiled into the JSP page implementation class; that is, it is included at translation time. Using the include directive, the included file does not need to be a complete and valid JSP page.

With the include standard action, the JSP file stops processing the current request and passes the request to the included file. The included file passes its output to the response. Then control of the response returns to the calling JSP, which finishes processing the response. The output of the included page or Servlet is included at request time. Components that are included via the include action must be valid JSP pages or Servlets.

The included file is not allowed to modify the headers of the response, nor to set cookies in the response.

The syntax of the include action is:

```
<jsp:include page="URL" flush="true|false">
  <jsp:param name="paramName" value="paramValue"/>
</jsp:include>
```

For the include element, the page attribute is required, and its value is the URL of the page whose output is included in the response. This URL is relative to the JSP page. The flush attribute is optional, and it indicates whether the output buffer should be flushed before the included file is called. The default value is false.

If the JSP needs to pass parameters to the included file, it does so with the <jsp:param> element. One element is used for each parameter. This element is optional. If it is included, both the name and value attributes are required. The included JSP page can access the parameters using the getParameter() and getParameterValues() methods of the request object.

forward Action

With the forward action, the current page stops processing the request and forwards the request to another web component. This other component completes the response. Execution never returns to the calling page. Unlike the include action, which can occur at any time during a response, the forward action must occur prior to writing any output to the OutputStream. In other words, the forward action must occur prior to any HTML template data in the JSP, and prior to any scriptlets or expressions that write data to the OutputStream. If any output has occurred in the calling JSP, an exception will be thrown when the forward action is encountered.

The format of the forward element is as follows:

```
<jsp:forward page="URL">
  <jsp:param name="paramName" value="paramValue"/>
</jsp:forward>
```

The meaning and use of the attributes and of the <jsp:param> element are the same as those for the include action.

Adding include and forward Actions to JSP Pages

In this last example of the chapter, you will modify the Java FAQ application to use `forward` actions to control the application flow. Figure 3-23 shows the application structure.

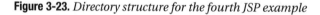

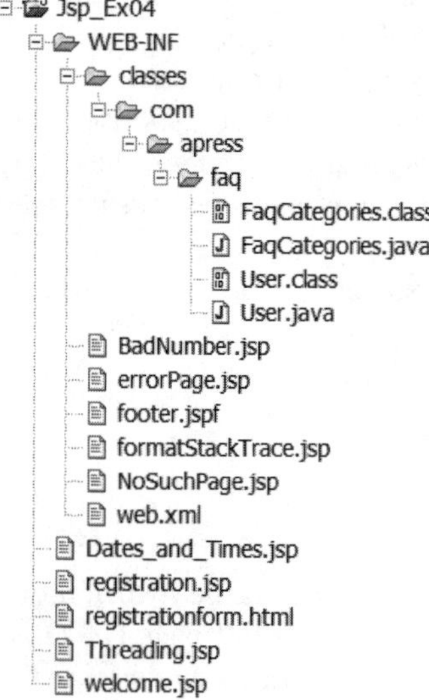

Figure 3-23. *Directory structure for the fourth JSP example*

Start by modifying `welcome.jsp` as shown in Listing 3-17.

Lisitng 3-17. *Revised welcome.jsp for Forwarding*

```
<%@ page errorPage="/WEB-INF/errorPage.jsp"
  import="java.util.Iterator, com.apress.faq.*" %>

<%
  User user = (User)session.getAttribute("user");
  String reqType = request.getParameter("reqType");
  if (user == null && reqType == null) {
%>
    <jsp:forward page="registrationform.html"/>
<%
  } else if (user == null && reqType != null) {
%>
    <jsp:forward page="registration.jsp">
        <jsp:param name="submitTime"
                   value="<%=(new java.util.Date()).toString()%>" />
    </jsp:forward>
<%
  }
%>
```

```
<html>
  <head>
    <meta name="Cache-control" content="no-cache">
    <title>Java FAQ Welcome Page</title>
  </head>

  <body>
    <h1>Java FAQ Welcome Page</h1>
    Welcome to the Java FAQ

<%! FaqCategories faqs = new FaqCategories(); %>
Click a link below for answers to the given topic.
<%
    Iterator categories = faqs.getAllCategories();
    while (categories.hasNext()) {
      String category = (String) categories.next();
%>
      <p><a href="<%= replaceUnderscore(category) %>.jsp">
         <%= category %></a></p>
<%
    }
%>

<%@ include file="/WEB-INF/footer.jspf" %>
  </body>
</html>

<%!
public String replaceUnderscore(String s) {
  return s.replace(' ','_');
}
%>
```

The next modified file is registrationform.html. Only the single line that contains the form tag needs to be modified, as shown in Listing 3-18.

Listing 3-18. *Revision to registrationForm.jsp for Forwarding*

```
<html>
  <head>
    <title>Registration Page</title>
  </head>
  <body>
    <h1>Registration Page</h1>

    <form action="welcome.jsp?reqType=register" method="POST">
      <table>
```

```
<!-- The remainder of registrationform.html is the same as before,
     so it is not shown here -->
```

A single new line of code has been added to the registration.jsp file; only the applicable snippet is shown here in Listing 3-19.

Listing 3-19. *Revision to registration.jsp for Forwarding*

```
<%    String[] topics = request.getParameterValues("topics");
      if (topics == null) { topics = new String[] {"No topics"}; }
      for (int i = 0; i < topics.length; i++) {
%>
        <br><%= topics[i] %>
<%
      }
%>
      <p>This request was submitted at
        <%= request.getParameter("submitTime") %>
      <p>Go to <a href="welcome.jsp">Topic List Page</a></p>
    <%@ include file="/WEB-INF/footer.jspf" %>
  </body>
</html>
```

Listing 3-20 shows the revised errorPage.jsp. This file now has an include action in addition to the include directive for the standard footer.

Listing 3-20. *Revised errorPage.jsp for Forwarding*

```
<%@ page isErrorPage="true" import="java.io.PrintWriter" %>

<html>
  <head>
    <title>Error</title>
  </head>
  <body>
    <h1>Error</h1>
    There was an error somewhere.
    <p>Here is the stack trace
    <p>
      <% request.setAttribute("ex", exception); %>
      <jsp:include page="formatStackTrace.jsp" />
<%@ include file="/WEB-INF/footer.jspf" %>
  </body>
</html>
```

The JSP page included by the include action in errorPage.jsp is shown in Listing 3-21. It is named formatStackTrace.jsp.

Listing 3-21. *formatStackTrace.jsp*

```
<%@ page import="java.io.PrintWriter" %>
<%
  out.println("<pre>");
  Throwable t = (Throwable) request.getAttribute("ex");
  if (t != null) {
    t.printStackTrace(new PrintWriter(out));
  }
  out.println("</pre>");
%>
```

Create the web application with these new files and the files you developed in previous examples. Deploy the application to the Java EE server or the stand-alone Tomcat server. For the Java EE server, use the same web application settings as in the previous example (Figure 3-18). For Tomcat, you can use the same deployment descriptor as in the previous example (Listing 3-16).

Open a browser and enter the appropriate address for the `welcome.jsp` page. The browser will display the registration form page. Enter some values on the registration form page, and then click the Submit button. The browser will display the registration page. Click the link in the registration page, and the browser will display the welcome page with the topic list. If the topic list is not displayed, your browser has probably cached the welcome page. Click the Refresh button to get the correct page. Click the Threading topic link. The browser will display the `errorPage.jsp` page with a nicely formatted stack trace, as shown in Figure 3-24.

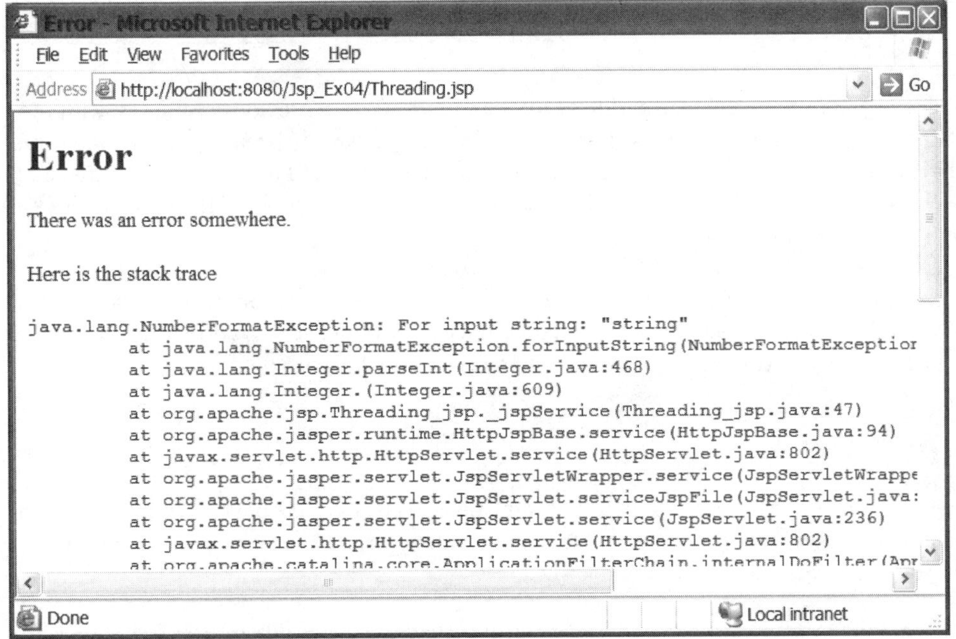

Figure 3-24. *The error page includes the output of another JSP to format the stack trace.*

The first thing the welcome.jsp page does now is to check for the existence of the user object, as previously, and for a request parameter with the name reqType. As before, the user object is put into the session by the registration.jsp; the reqType parameter will be added to the request by the registrationform.html page. If both of these are null, neither the registrationform.html page nor the registration.jsp page has been called, so the welcome.jsp page forwards the request to the registrationform.html page.

If you look at the registrationform.html, you will see that the action attribute of the <form> tag has been modified to add a request parameter to the URL. When the Submit button is clicked, the form submits to welcome.jsp. This method of submitting request parameters in the URL is known as *URL encoding*. This time, welcome.jsp finds that the user object is still null, but that the reqType parameter has a value. Since this indicates that the registrationform.html page has been visited, but the registration has not been submitted, welcome.jsp forwards the request to registration.jsp; it includes another request parameter with the request using the <jsp:param> element.

■ **Note** This flow is artificially complicated, because it probably makes more sense to have registrationform.html submit directly to registration.jsp. The main reason for submitting to welcome.jsp is to provide several different examples of the use of the <jsp:forward> action. However, there is a little justification for having all requests go through the welcome.jsp page. This is a very simple example of something known as a Model 2, or Model-View-Controller (MVC), architecture. With a Model 2 architecture, one component acts as a controller, directing the requests to the component that is set up to handle a particular request. We will look at the Model 2 architecture in more detail in Chapter 6.

The registration.jsp page performs the same actions as in previous examples, with the addition of reading the new request parameter added by welcome.jsp and displaying the value of that parameter. When you click the link, the request is again sent to welcome.jsp. This final time, both user and reqType are not null, so welcome.jsp does not forward the request, but instead completes the response itself.

Clicking the Threading topic link again calls Threading.jsp, which still causes a NumberFormatException. This time, however, errorPage.jsp includes formatStackTrace.jsp. The formatStackTrace.jsp page outputs the stack trace just as older versions of errorPage.jsp did, but it wraps it in a <pre> tag, so that the stack trace is nicely formatted.

Summary

In this chapter, we've taken a tour of many of the basic features of JSP pages. With the information in this chapter, you should be able to begin creating JSP web applications of your own. After reading this chapter, you should know:

- JSP pages consist of HTML data, also known as *template data*, and Java code. Before a JSP can process a request, it must be compiled into a page implementation class and deployed to a JSP container.

- You can specify an error page for a JSP using `<%@page errorPage=""%>`. Error pages are used to provide meaningful error information to a user when something bad happens to the web application.
- You can import Java packages for the page using `<% page import="" %>`.
- Java code is included in the page using a declaration `<%! declaration %>`, a scriptlet `<% scriptlet %>`, or an expression `<%= expression %>`. These elements allow you to mix Java code with the template data in the page.
- JavaBean instances can be created using the `<jsp:useBean>` standard action; properties of the bean can be set using `<jsp:setProperty>`; and the value of a bean's properties can be obtained using `<jsp:getProperty>`. JavaBeans are one way to encapsulate business or domain logic so that JSP pages can be used primarily for presentation.
- Various implicit objects—such as `request`, `response`, `out`, `session`, and so on—are always available to the JSP to help process a request. The `session` object is particularly useful because it enables the web application to keep track of user information, such as the contents of a user's shopping cart in an e-commerce application.
- Servers translate and compile JSPs into Java classes that behave like Servlets.
- You can specify error handlers for the entire application using the `<error-page>` element in the deployment descriptor.
- A JSP can include the output of other JSPs or Servlets in the response to clients. This is done through the `<jsp:include>` standard action.
- A JSP can forward a request to another JSP or Servlet for processing. This is done through the `<jsp:forward>` standard action.

That's quite a lot. All these features put together allow application developers to create dynamic and powerful web applications that can be used for many purposes—from chat rooms to e-commerce, and from virtual communities to business applications. However, you may have noticed that as the examples in this chapter became more dynamic and full-featured, they also tended to have more and more Java code interspersed in the JSP pages. This tends to be a problem because web page developers are often not Java developers.

What would be ideal is a way to create JSP pages that hide the Java code from the page developers. This would allow the page developer to concentrate on the format and structure of the markup, and leave Java developers free to work on only the Java code. There are several ways to do this, and you will see some of them in the next chapter, where we explore some of the new JSP features introduced in the latest version of the JSP specification.

Exercises

1. Declare an `init` and a `destroy` method in a JSP. Include some debug output so that you can see when these methods are called. Deploy the JSP and determine when these methods are called. (Depending on your container, you may not see the output from the `destroy` method.)

2. Write additional JSP pages for the Java FAQ application that allow a user to submit a question and answer a question.

3. Create a JSP web application that presents a quiz to the user. Use a JSP page to present each question one at a time to the user. Use the same page to accept the answer submitted by the user. (That is, the HTML created by the page should submit the answer to the same JSP page.) The page should determine whether or not the answer is correct, compute the current score of the user, select a graphic that illustrates the current status, and select the next question—this is all put into the response back to the client.

4. Create a JSP that echoes the request data back to the client. You can use implicit objects such as `request` and `session` to retrieve the request data.

CHAPTER 4

Advanced JSP Topics

The previous chapter introduced you to JSP and provided enough information to enable you to begin writing and using those web components. However, the previous chapter only scratched the surface of what can be done with JSP pages.

You may have noticed in the previous chapter that as the examples became more involved, the JSP source pages became littered with a lot of Java code. This is fine if the JSP developer is also a software developer, but not so good if the page developer knows little or nothing about Java. One of the design goals for JSP 2.0 was to make it easier to use without needing to learn how to program in Java. In this chapter, we'll look at some of the ways that the Java code inside the JSP page can be moved back to the realm of the software developer, leaving the page designer free to concentrate on presentation and usability.

In this chapter, you will learn:

- How to use Expression Language (EL) to simplify expressions in JSP pages
- How to create custom actions
- How to use the JSP Standard Tag Library (JSTL) in your JSP pages

---

Note Some of the material in this chapter has been in use for a while as part of earlier JSP specifications. Other material comes from the JSP 2.0 and JSP 2.1 specifications, and so is relatively new. For the examples in this chapter that rely on new JSP 2.0 features, you will need to use a server that supports JSP 2.0, such as J2EE 1.4, Java EE 5.0, Tomcat 5.0, or Tomcat 5.5. (Tomcat 5.0 is designed to run under Java 2 version 1.4; Tomcat 5.5 is designed to run under Java 2 version 5.) For JSP 2.1 and EL 2.1, you will need a server that supports JSP 2.1 and EL 2.1. For details about JSP 2.0 see the JSP 2.0 specification (`http://jcp.org/aboutJava/communityprocess/final/jsr152/`). For details about JSP 2.1 or EL 2.1, see the JSP 2.1 or EL 2.1 specification (`http://jcp.org/aboutJava/communityprocess/edr/jsr245/index.html`).

Expression Language

In the previous chapter, you saw how to create scripting elements that can be used to embed Java code in the JSP file. Scripting elements include Java declarations, scriptlets, and expressions, as in these examples:

```
<%! int a = 5; %> <%-- declaration --%>
<% while (x < 10) { out.write("x=" + x); } %> <%-- scriptlet --%>
<%= user.getFirstName() %> <%-- expression --%>
```

JSP 2.0 adds Expression Language (EL) statements to the JSP toolkit. EL statements provide a somewhat simpler syntax for performing some of the same actions as the JSP scripting elements. You can use EL statements to print the value of variables and access the fields of objects in a page. It has a rich set of mathematical, logical, relational, and other operators, and can be used to call Java functions. In short, EL makes it easy for nonprogrammers to provide dynamic behavior in JSP pages. Furthermore, you can use EL statements in scriptless JSP pages. *Scriptless JSP pages* are those pages that, for whatever reason, are not allowed to use Java declarations, scriptlets, or scripting expressions.

Note EL was added as part of JSP 2.0. Java Server Faces, which we will see in more detail in the next chapter, implemented a similar EL. JSP 2.1 unifies the two versions.

Scriptless JSPs

You can, of course, write any JSP page without using any declarations, scriptlets, or expressions. You saw an example of one such page at the beginning of the previous chapter: `HelloWorld.jsp`. That page was scriptless by choice. In other words, `HelloWorld.jsp` could have included Java declarations, scriptlets, or expressions, but we chose to write it using only standard HTML tags. You can also force a page to be scriptless; that is, you can configure your web application so that Java declarations, scriptlets, and expressions cannot be used in JSP pages. One reason for doing this is to enforce a separation between display elements and business logic.

When you have scriptless pages—pages without Java scriptlets, directives, or declarations—the dynamic behavior of JSP pages must be provided through other elements such as JavaBeans, EL statements, custom actions, and standard tag libraries. By encapsulating business logic in JavaBeans and custom actions, the page designers do not need to learn any Java code. (Using JavaBeans with JSP was discussed in the previous chapter, and you will see how to use custom actions and standard tag libraries later in this chapter.) Whether or not your application should have scriptless JSP pages is a decision you must make based on the requirements and needs of your application.

With JSP 2.0 and JSP 2.1, you mark a page as scriptless through the deployment descriptor. EL statements are disabled or enabled through the `page` directive or through the deployment descriptor. With earlier JSP versions, you can use the `page` directive to disable or enable scripting, but EL is not supported. If a page is marked as scriptless, then the presence of scriptlets, scripting expressions, and declarations in the page will cause a translation error.

Designating Scriptless Pages with JSP 2.0 or JSP 2.1

Within the `<web-app>` element of the deployment descriptor, the `<jsp-config>` element supplies configuration information for the JSP pages in a web application. Within the `<jsp-property-group>` element of `<jsp-config>`, the `<url-pattern>` identifies the JSP pages to which the configuration applies.

Under JSP 2.1, the `<scripting-invalid>` element defines whether or not scripting is enabled. The default is `false`, so scripting elements (scriptlets, declarations, and directives) are not invalid, and thus are allowed in a JSP. If you explicitly specify `true`, as follows, then scripting elements are invalid in a JSP page and will cause a translation error if they occur.

```
<jsp-config>
  <jsp-property-group>
    <url-pattern>*.jsp</url-pattern>
    <scripting-invalid>true</scripting-invalid>
  </jsp-property-group>
</jsp-config>
```

Enabling EL Statements with JSP 2.0 or JSP 2.1

EL statements are enabled or disabled through two different techniques:

- You can enable EL statements for particular pages through the `page` directive.
- You can enable EL statements for whole sets of pages using the deployment descriptor.

The `page` directive for enabling or disabling EL statements looks like this:

```
<%@ page isELIgnored="true|false" %>
```

If the value of the `isELIgnored` attribute is `true`, then EL statements in the JSP are ignored and treated as template data. If the value is `false`, then EL statements are evaluated. If you do not use the attribute, the default is `false`, and EL statements are enabled.

You can also specify EL configuration information in the deployment descriptor. EL statements are evaluated based on the value of the `<el-ignored>` element of the `<jsp-property-group>` element:

```
<jsp-config>
  <jsp-property-group>
    <url-pattern>*.jsp</url-pattern>
    <el-ignored>true</el-ignored>
  </jsp-property-group>
</jsp-config>
```

As you might guess, if the value is `true`, EL statements are ignored and treated as template data. If the value is `false`, EL statements are evaluated, and the result of evaluation is sent as part of the page output. If a JSP source page that matches a URL pattern also contains an `isELIgnored` attribute, the attribute in the `page` directive overrides the value of the `<el-ignored>` element in the deployment descriptor. If there is no `<el-ignored>` element, the default is `false`, so that EL statements are not ignored.

You can have multiple `<jsp-property-group>` elements within the `<jsp-config>` element, each with different URL patterns to match. If a resource matches more than one group, the pattern that is most specific applies.

Also, even though the `<scripting-invalid>` and `<el-ignored>` elements were shown separately, the `<jsp-property-group>` element can contain both `<scripting-invalid>` and `<el-ignored>` elements.

Designating Scriptless Pages with JSP 1.2 or Earlier

In the event you are stuck with a server that supports only JSP 1.2 or earlier, the methods for enabling scripting are slightly different. EL is not supported in JSP 1.2 or earlier.

With JSP 1.2, the page directive has an attribute for scripting. The value of the attribute can be `true` or `false`. The page directive for enabling or disabling scripting looks like this:

```
<%@ page isScriptingEnabled="true|false" %>
```

The default for `isScriptingEnabled` is `true`.

You can also enable scripting in the deployment descriptor. Where the page directive applies to a single page, the deployment descriptor can apply to whole sets of pages. For example, to enable scripting, add the following element to the deployment descriptor:

```
  <jsp-config>
    <jsp-property-group>
      <url-pattern>*.jsp</url-pattern>
      <scripting-enabled>true</scripting-enabled>
    </jsp-property-group>
  </jsp-config>
</web-app>
```

The `<scripting-enabled>` element defines whether or not scripting is enabled. The default is `true`.

You can have multiple `<jsp-property-group>` elements within the `<jsp-config>` element, each with different URL patterns to be matched. If a resource matches more than one group, the pattern that is most specific applies.

Finally, the `isScriptingEnabled` attribute of the page directive takes precedence over the `<scripting-enabled>` elements of the `<jsp-property-group>`. So, if the `<scripting-enabled>` element is set to `false`, but a page's `isScriptingEnabled` attribute is set to `true`, then scripting will be enabled for the page.

Syntax of EL Statements

The basic syntax for an EL statement is as follows:

```
${expr}
```

where *expr* is a valid expression.

If you have a server that supports EL 2.1, you can also use this syntax:

```
#{expr}
```

The EL will parse and evaluate `${expr}` and `#{expr}` in exactly the same manner. However, the JSP 2.1 specification places additional restrictions on where and how `${expr}` and `#{expr}` can be used. In general, JSP 2.1 specifies `${expr}` for expressions that are evaluated immediately and `#{expr}` for expressions whose evaluation is deferred. Because of this restriction, you can use only `${expr}` in template text. Both `${expr}` and `#{expr}` can be used to set the value of attributes in actions.

Valid expressions can include literals, operators, object references (variables), and function calls. EL statements cannot be nested, so the following expression is not valid:

```
${ 2 + ${subexpr} }
```

In the remainder of this chapter, we will use the ${} syntax for all EL statements, but remember that if you have a server that supports EL 2.1, you can also use #{} where appropriate.

Literals

The EL syntax provides for a number of literal values that can be used in expressions, as shown in Table 4-1.

Table 4-1. *Literal Values That Can Be Used in EL Statements*

Value	Description
Boolean literals	`true` or `false` values.
String literals	Any string delimited by single or double quotes. The backslash is used as an escape character for quotes and backslashes. For example, `'This string\'s value has an escaped single quote'` or `"the directory is c:\\My Documents\\apress"`. You need to escape quotes only when they are enclosed by a quote of the same kind; in other words, `'\''` or `"\""`. Therefore, this version does not need to be escaped: `"This string's value has a single quote"`.
Integer literals	Any positive or negative integer number (`-13`, `45`, `2374`, and so on).
Floating-point literals	Any positive or negative floating-point number (`-1.3E-30`, `3.14159`, `2.00000000000001`, `.45`, `.56e2`, and so on).
Null literal	A null value.

Here are some examples of simple expressions and what they evaluate to in a page:

```
${true} <%-- evaluates to true --%>
${"Single quotes inside 'double quotes' do not need to be escaped"}
  <%-- evaluates to Single quotes inside 'double quotes'
       do not need to be escaped --%>
${2*4} <%-- evaluates to 8 --%>
```

Operators

You can use most of the usual Java operators in EL statements. Table 4-2 shows the available operators.

Table 4-2. *Operators That Can Be Used in EL Statements*

Type	Operator
Arithmetic	+, -, *, /, div, %, mod
Relational	== and eq
	!= and ne
	< and lt
	> and gt
	<= and le
	>= and ge
Logical	&& and and
	|| and or
	! and not
Other	(), empty, [], . (dot)

You are probably familiar with most of the operators listed in Table 4-2. However, note that many of the operators have both symbolic and word variants (such as / and div, or < and lt). These equivalents are provided so that if your JSP page needs to be XML-compliant, you can avoid using entity references (such as < for <). Within an XML document, an EL expression for "less than" could be coded ${2 lt 3} rather than ${2 < 3}.

In the next few paragraphs, we will look at the last four "other" operators in the list: (), empty, [], and . (dot).

As with most expressions, parentheses can change the precedence of the expression:

```
${ (2 * 4) + 3 } <%-- evaluates to 11 --%>
${ 2 * (4 + 3) } <%-- evaluates to 14 --%>
```

You can use the empty operator to test for various conditions. Here is an example:

```
${empty name}
```

This expression will return true if *name* references a null object or if *name* references an empty String, List, Map, or array. Otherwise, empty returns false. The object referenced by *name* is an object stored in the page, request, session, or application implicit objects. Here is an example:

```
<% Vector vec = new Vector();                    // Create empty vector
pageContext.setAttribute("someName", vec); %> // Store vector in pageContext
${empty someName}   // Evaluates to true; notice the operator acts on the
                    // attribute name someName, not the variable name vec
```

Keep in mind that this works for any object in one of the contexts, not just objects you explicitly add using setAttribute() as shown in the example here. For example, as you will see later in this chapter, custom actions can create variables that are accessible through EL expressions. The empty operator can be applied to these variables. Another way to add objects to a context is by creating a JavaBean; JavaBeans are stored in a context based on the scope attribute of the `<jsp:useBean>` action. The point is that you can apply the `empty` operator to any object that can be referenced by name in one of the contexts.

The dot operator (`.`) and the `[]` operator are used to access the attributes of an object in the page. The left-value (`lvalue`) of the operator is interpreted to be an object in the page; the right-value (`rvalue`) is a property, key, or index. For example, if you have defined a bean in the page using the `<jsp:useBean>` standard action, you can access the properties of the bean using either notation. Given a bean with the ID `user` and with the properties `firstName` and `surname`, you could access its properties using either notation, like this:

```
${user.firstName}
${user[surname]}
```

The two notations are equivalent when accessing the properties of an object in the page. Either expression results in the page attempting to find the given object in the page and call the `getXXX()` method for the given property.

The `.` and `[]` operators can also be used for `Map`, `List`, or array values. When either operator is applied to a `Map` (such as `Hashtable` or `HashMap`), the page class attempts to access the `Map` attribute with the key given by the `rvalue`. For example, given the following:

```
${myObject[name]} <%-- myObject is a Hashtable or HashMap --%>
```

the equivalent code statement is:

```
myObject.get(name);
```

■ **Note** In many places in this chapter, you will see code that is equivalent to an EL statement. However, when the JSP is translated, the EL statement is *not* translated into that same code. We show equivalent code so that you can relate the EL statement to the code that you, as a developer, would need to write to achieve the same effect. The code generated by the JSP translator to evaluate the expression is different.

If the operator is applied to a `List` or array, the page attempts to convert the `rvalue` into an index. When the object implements `List`, the page class uses the `get(int)` method of `List` to get the value of the expression:

```
myObject.get(name);          // myObject is a List
```

When the object references an array, the `get(Object, int)` method of `Array` is used:

```
Array.get(myObject, name);   // myObject is an array
```

Object References and Implicit Objects

As you have learned, EL statements can include object references. Object references are created in numerous ways. JSP includes implicit objects that are always available to a page. These implicit objects, such as `out` or `request`, can be included as part of an EL statement. Objects that are created as part of the `useBean` standard action can be referenced in EL statements. In general, any object reference that is available in scripting statements is also available in EL statements. Through the implicit objects, the EL expression can perform many of the actions that can be performed through scriptlets and JSP expressions. The implicit objects are shown in Table 4-3.

Table 4-3. *Implicit Objects That Can Be Used in EL Statements*

Object	Description
`pageContext`	The `javax.servlet.jsp.PageContext` object for the page. Can be used to access the JSP implicit objects such as `request`, `response`, `session`, `out`, and so on. For example, `${pageContext.request}` evaluates to the `request` object for the page.
`pageScope`	A `Map` that maps page-scoped attribute names to their values. In other words, given an object, such as a bean, that has page scope in the JSP page, an EL expression can access the object with `${pageScope.`*`objectName`*`}`, and an attribute of the object can be accessed using `${pageScope.`*`objectName.attributeName`*`}`.
`requestScope`	A `Map` that maps request-scoped attribute names to their values. This object allows you to access the attributes of the `request` object.
`sessionScope`	A `Map` that maps session-scoped attribute names to their values. This object is used to access the `session` objects for the client.
`applicationScope`	A `Map` that maps application-scoped attribute names to their values. Use this object to access objects with application scope.
`param`	A `Map` that maps parameter names to a single `String` parameter value (obtained by calling `ServletRequest.getParameter(String name)`). Recall that a `request` object contains data sent by the client. The `getParameter(String)` method returns the parameter with the given name. The expression `${param.name}` is equivalent to `request.getParameter(name)`. (Note that `name` is not the literal string `'name'`, but the name of the parameter.)
`paramValues`	A `Map` that maps parameter names to a `String[]` of all values for that parameter (obtained by calling `ServletRequest.getParameterValues(String name)`). Similar to the `param` implicit object, but it retrieves a `String` array rather than a single value. For example, the expression `${paramValues.name}` is equivalent to `request.getParameterValues(name)`.
`header`	A `Map` that maps header names to a single `String` header value (obtained by calling `ServletRequest.getHeader(String name)`). Requests always contain header information such as the content type and length, cookies, the referring URL, and so on. The expression `${header.name}` is equivalent to `request.getHeader(name)`.
`headerValues`	A `Map` that maps header names to a `String[]` of all values for that header (obtained by calling `ServletRequest.getHeaders(String)`). Similar to the `header` implicit object. The expression `${headerValues.name}` is equivalent to `request.getHeaderValues(name)`.
`cookie`	A `Map` that maps cookie names to a single `Cookie` object. A client can send one or more cookies to the server with a request. The expression `${cookie.name.value}` returns the value of the first cookie with the given name. If the request contains multiple cookies with the same name, you should use `${headerValues.name}`.
`initParam`	A `Map` that maps context initialization parameter names to their `String` parameter values (obtained by calling `ServletContext.getInitParameter(String name)`). To access an initialization parameter, use `${initParam.name}`.

For example, in this code snippet, the bean has been given page scope, and it has a property named `topic`:

```
<jsp:useBean id="questions" scope="page" class="com.apress.jsp.Questions">
  <jsp:setProperty name="questions" property="topic"/>
</jsp:useBean>
${pageScope.questions.topic} <%-- Evaluates to the topic property of the
                                  bean referenced by the id 'questions' --%>
```

As another example, if you've added an object to the session, you can access it as shown here:

```
<% session.put("address", "123 Maple St."); %>
${sessionScope.address}           <%-- evaluates to 123 maple St. --%>
<%= session.get("address"); %>   <%-- equivalent scripting expression --%>
```

Attribute Values in Standard Actions

You can use EL statements of the form `${expr}` as attribute values in standard actions. (They can also be used anywhere there is template text, such as HTML or non-JSP elements, in the JSP file.) Standard actions were introduced in Chapter 3, and they include actions such as `useBean`, `setProperty`, `include`, `forward`, and so on.

EL statements can be used as an attribute value for any attribute that can accept request-time expression values, such as the page attribute of the `forward` action:

```
<jsp:forward page="${param.nextPage}" />
```

In this example, the `<jsp:forward>` action will forward the request to the URL specified by the request parameter named `nextPage`. If the request parameter does not exist, or if its value is not a valid URL, an error will occur in the page.

Table 4-4 shows the attributes the JSP 2.1 specification lists as able to accept request-time expression values.

Table 4-4. *Standard Action Attributes That Can Accept Request-Time Expression Values*

Action	Attribute
useBean	beanName
setProperty	Value
include	page
forward	page
param	value
height	plugin
width	plugin
element	name

Since the `#{expr}` syntax is used for deferred evaluation, it is not legal for the attribute value of standard actions. The `#{expr}` syntax can be used for custom actions. See the "Writing a Tag Library Descriptor" section later in this chapter for information about using `#{expr}` with custom actions.

Errors and Default Values in EL Statements

Because of their use in display-oriented JSP pages, EL statements do not throw the same exceptions that you might expect from the equivalent Java expression. The EL specification states:

> *The Expression Language has been designed with the presentation layer of web applications in mind. In that usage, experience suggests that it is most important to be able to provide as good a presentation as possible, even when there are simple errors in the page. To meet this requirement, the EL does not provide warnings, just default values and errors. Default values are type-correct values that are assigned to a subexpression when there is some problem. An error is an exception thrown (to be handled by the environment where the EL is used).*

For example, given this expression:

```
${user.surname}
```

The analogous Java expression is:

```
user.getSurname();
```

Now, if you were writing this Java code manually, and you had not defined the `user` variable or did not provide a `getSurname()` method, the compiler would warn you of this situation. Before the code was ever executed, the compiler would warn of the missing method, and you would be able to supply it. If you did not initialize the variable `user` at runtime, the code would throw a `NullPointerException`.

However, in a JSP page, many of these requirements cannot be checked until runtime. You might not realize a method was missing because compilation might not occur until the first request for the page. Similarly, you might not realize that the reference `user` had not been initialized until a page request was made. And at that point, the person who sees the error message from the server is the page client, not the developer. A translation error or compilation error at that point could result in an ugly stack trace being sent to the user of your application. However, since the JSP page is usually used for presentation, many EL expressions result in default values, rather than thrown exceptions.

For example, in the previous expression, if `user` is null, the value of the EL expression is null rather than a `NullPointerException`. With many of the operators, if either the `lvalue` or the `rvalue` is null, the default value of the expression is null, rather than a thrown exception. (Consult the EL specification for the full list of default values.) This will usually result in the user receiving some kind of response page, even though that page might have bad data in it, rather than an error page. When an EL expression does result in an exception, the exception is handled via the normal JSP exception-handling mechanisms.

JSP Pages That Use EL

At this point, you have enough information to put together a simple application that uses some of the techniques covered in this chapter. In this first example, we'll create a few JSPs that use EL expressions. Note that you must deploy this example to a server that supports JSP 2.0 or JSP 2.1. If you are trying this example with Java EE or Tomcat, you will need to use J2EE 1.4, Java EE 5.0, Tomcat 5.0, or Tomcat 5.5. The directory structure of the application is shown in Figure 4-1.

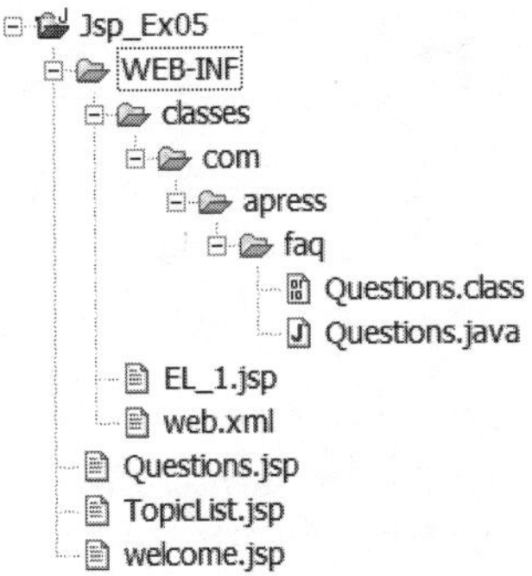

Figure 4-1. *Directory structure for the first EL example, JSP_Ex05*

■ **Note** At the time this book was written, there was no application server that supported JSP 2.1 and EL 2.1. We will run this example under J2EE 1.4 and Tomcat 5.0. By the time you read this, though, a server that supports EL 2.1 may be available. We have made every effort to follow the specifications so that this example, and the other examples in the book, will work with both JSP 2.0 and JSP 2.1, as well as EL 2.1. However, you should check `www.apress.com` to see if the source code has been updated to accommodate changes in the specification.

We will create the files `welcome.jsp`, `TopicList.jsp`, `Questions.jsp`, `EL_1.jsp`, and `Questions.java`. If you are using the Sun Deployment Tool, the `web.xml` file will be created for you. If you are deploying to Tomcat, you will need to create the `web.xml` deployment descriptor manually. The basic flow of the application is shown in Figure 4-2. (We will use this same flow for several examples in this chapter.)

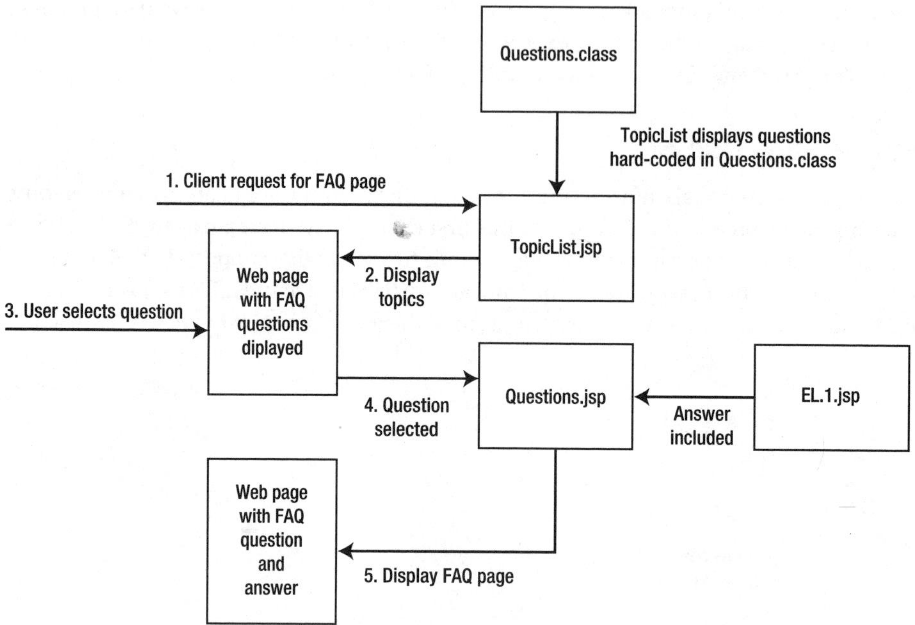

Figure 4-2. *TopicList.jsp displays a list of questions from Questions.class. When the user selects a question, the request is sent to Questions.jsp, which includes the correct answer JSP page.*

Although this example appears to build on the Java FAQ example from the previous chapter, you do not need to use any of the files from previous examples. This example does have a file named `welcome.jsp`, but it is different from the previous versions. The much simpler `welcome.jsp` is shown in Listing 4-1.

Listing 4-1. *welcome.jsp*

```
<html>
  <head>
    <title>Java FAQ Welcome Page</title>
  </head>

  <body>
    <h1>Java FAQ Welcome Page</h1>

    <p>Welcome to the Java FAQ. Click a topic to see FAQ
    questions about that topic.</p>

    <p><a href="TopicList.jsp?topic=EL">Expression Language
    </a></p>
  </body>
</html>
```

The only purpose of `welcome.jsp` is to call the topic list page with the appropriate parameter. The file `TopicList.jsp` is shown in Listing 4-2.

Listing 4-2. *TopicList.jsp*

```
<%@ page import="java.util.*" %>
<html>
  <head><title>Topic Questions</title></head>
  <body>
    <h1>Topic Questions</h1>

    <jsp:useBean id="questions" class="com.apress.faq.Questions">
      <jsp:setProperty name="questions" property="topic" />
    </jsp:useBean>

The number of questions in topic ${questions.topic} is ${questions.numQuestions}
<%
  Map topic = questions.getQuestions();
  Iterator keys = topic.keySet().iterator();
  while (keys.hasNext()) {
    String key = (String) keys.next();
    pageContext.setAttribute("key", key);
%>
<p>Question <a href="Questions.jsp?qid=${key}">
   ${key}</a>:
   ${questions.questions[key]}
<%
  }
%>
  </body>
</html>
```

The `TopicList.jsp` page displays a list of questions for a given topic. These questions are hard-coded into the `Questions.java` class, shown in Listing 4-3.

Listing 4-3. *Questions.java*

```
package com.apress.faq;

import java.util.Map;
import java.util.HashMap;
import java.util.TreeMap;

public class Questions {
  private String topic;
  private int numQuestions;
  private Map questions = new HashMap();
```

```
    public String getTopic() { return topic; }
    public void setTopic(String t) {
      topic = t;
      setNumQuestions(getQuestions().size());
    }

    public int getNumQuestions() { return numQuestions; }
    public void setNumQuestions(int n) { numQuestions = n; }

    public Map getQuestions() {
      return (Map) questions.get(topic);
    }
    public void setQuestions(Map m) { questions = m; }

    public Questions() {
      Map topic = new TreeMap()
      topic.put("EL_1", "How do I use implicit objects?");
      topic.put("EL_2", "How do I use the JSTL?");
      topic.put("EL_3", "How do I use the 'empty' operator?");
      questions.put("EL", topic);
    }
  }
```

Compile this file into `Questions.class`.

After displaying the list of questions, the user can click a link for a particular question. The request is posted to the `Questions.jsp` file, shown in Listing 4-4. (Yes, this really is the whole file!)

Listing 4-4. *Questions.jsp*

```
<jsp:include page="/WEB-INF/${param.qid}.jsp" />
```

As you can see, `Questions.jsp` simply includes the appropriate question file based on the user's selection. For this example, we will create the JSP page for only the first question (see Listing 4-5). In a later example, you will see `EL_2.jsp`. The `EL_3.jsp` page is not presented here, but it is included with the downloadable code for this book.

Listing 4-5. *EL_1.jsp*

```
<html>
  <head>
    <title>Expression Language Q1</title>
  </head>

  <body>
    <h1>Expression Language Question 1</h1>
    <h2>How do I use implicit objects?</h2>
```

```
    <p>The implicit objects are</p>
    <ul>
      <li>pageContext</li>
      <li>pageScope</li>
      <li>requestScope</li>
      <li>sessionScope</li>
      <li>applicationScope</li>
      <li>param</li>
      <li>paramValues</li>
      <li>header</li>
      <li>headerValues</li>
      <li>cookie</li>
      <li>initParam</li>
    </ul>

    <p>Implicit objects form the lvalue of an EL expression, and their
      properties are accessed using the . or [] operator. Here are some
      examples:</p>
<%-- The four lines after this comment contain special expression syntax
     needed to display a literal ${} in the output of a JSP. This is done
     by using an expression to evaluate the literal '${'. That is, the
     expression ${ '${' } evaluates to ${, and whatever follows the
     expression is treated as normal template text.
--%>
    <p>${'${'}pageContext.request.requestURI} evaluates to
       "${pageContext.request.requestURI}"</p>
    <p>${'${'}param.qid} evaluates to "${param.qid}"</p>
    <p>${'${'}header.referer} evaluates to "${header.referer}"</p>
    <p>${'${'}cookie.JSESSIONID.value} evaluates to
       ${cookie.JSESSIONID.value}</p>
  </body>
</html>
```

Deploying the FAQ Application to Tomcat

If you are deploying to Tomcat or some other stand-alone JSP container, you will need a deployment descriptor. Listing 4-6 shows a very simple `web.xml` file that will do the job.

Listing 4-6. *web.xml for Jsp_Ex05*

```
<?xml version="1.0" encoding="ISO-8859-1"?>

<web-app xmlns="http://java.sun.com/xml/ns/javaee"
    xmlns:xsi="http://www.w3.org/2001/XMLSchema-instance"
    xsi:schemaLocation="http://java.sun.com/xml/ns/javaee/web-app_2_5.xsd"
    version="2.5">
```

```
  <display-name>Jsp_Ex05 - Expression Language</display-name>
  <welcome-file-list>
    <welcome-file>welcome.jsp</welcome-file>
  </welcome-file-list>
</web-app>
```

Note that the deployment descriptor does not need to explicitly enable scripting or EL statements, because they are enabled by default. If you want to explicitly enable them, add the following to the deployment descriptor:

```
<jsp-config>
  <jsp-property-group>
    <url-pattern>*.jsp</url-pattern>
    <scripting-invalid>false</scripting-invalid>
    <el-ignored>false</el-ignored>
  </jsp-property-group>
</jsp-config>
```

If you are deploying to a stand-alone Tomcat 5.0 server, you can copy the entire directory structure into the Tomcat `/webapps` directory. Alternatively, you can create a `.war` file and place that into `/webapps`. You create the `.war` file by navigating to the top-level directory of the application (`/Jsp_Ex05` in this example) and executing this command:

```
> jar cvf Jsp_Ex05.war *
```

Deploying the FAQ Application to Java EE

If you are using the Sun Application Server, follow these steps to deploy the application:

1. Run the Deployment Tool and Create a new Web Application Archive by selecting File ➤ New ➤ Web Component from the menu.
2. Add the files `welcome.jsp`, `TopicList.jsp`, `Questions.jsp`, `EL_1.jsp`, and `Questions.class` to the WAR. Make sure you place the `EL_1.jsp` file into the `/WEB-INF` directory. Click Next.
3. Select the JSP radio button, and click Next.
4. In the next wizard step, select `TopicList.jsp` as the component to create. Click Finish.
5. Deploy the application using Tools ➤ Deploy from the menu.

Running the FAQ Application

After the application is deployed, open a web browser and enter the address `http://localhost:8080/Jsp_Ex05/welcome.jsp`. Note that because this example has not been fully implemented, the links for EL_2 and EL_3 will not work correctly. When you enter the URL, you should see a page like the one shown in Figure 4-3.

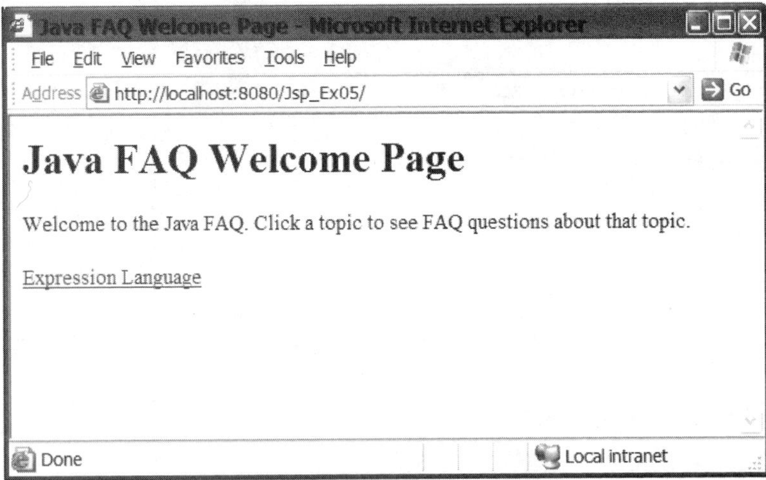

Figure 4-3. *The welcome.jsp page for the application has a link to the TopicList.jsp page. That page shows the questions for the Expression Language topic.*

When you click the Expression Language link, you will see the page shown in Figure 4-4.

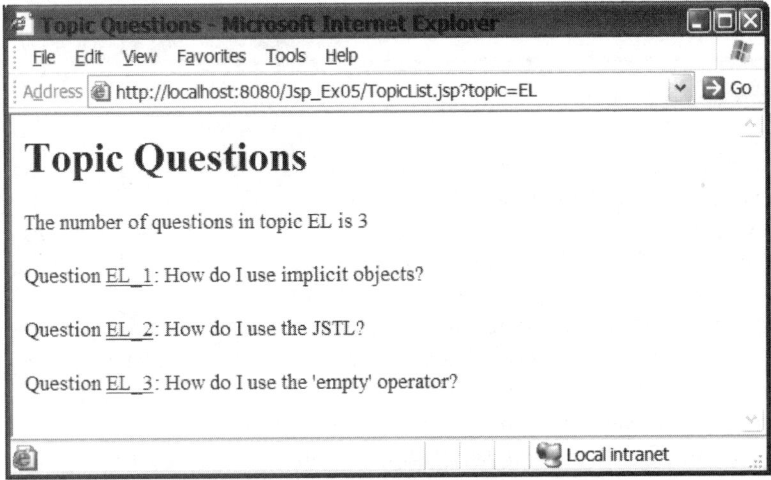

Figure 4-4. *There are three questions in the Expression Language topic. Clicking a link here will display the page for that question.*

Click the EL_1 link, and you will see the page displayed in Figure 4-5.

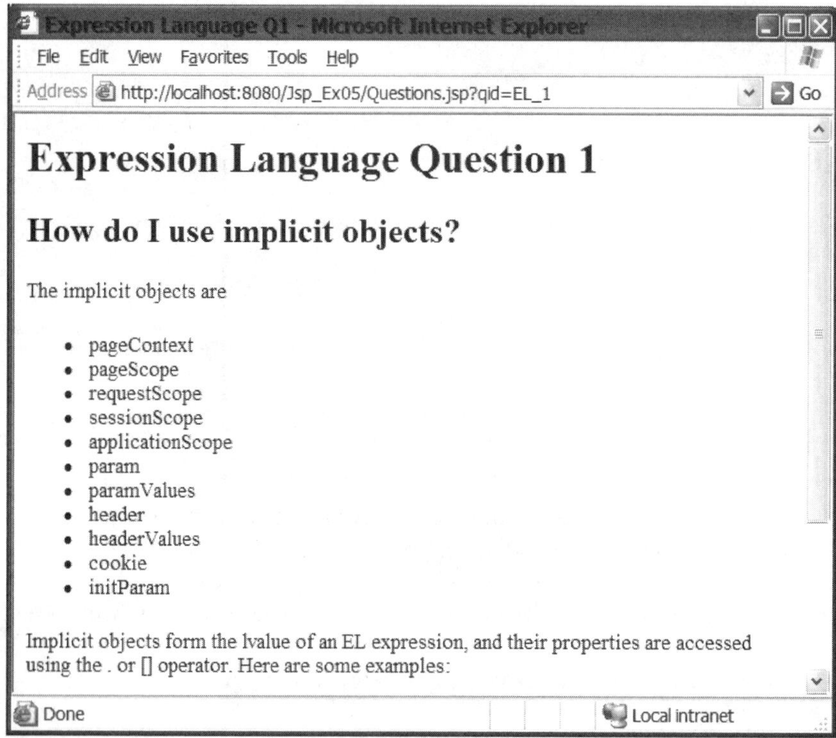

Figure 4-5. *The Questions.jsp page includes the appropriate FAQ page in its output.*

The questions that are displayed on the page for each topic are hard-coded into the `Questions` JavaBean class. This class has a field named `questions`, of type `Map`, which is used to store the set of individual questions for each topic. The questions for each topic are also stored in a `Map` keyed by the question number. The `Map` for the topic is stored in the `questions` `Map` keyed by a topic abbreviation.

The constructor for the class creates a `topic` map holding three questions, and then stores this map in the `questions` map. When the class is instantiated in the `TopicList.jsp` page, the `topic` field is set to the selected topic using the `<jsp:setProperty>` tag.

This class has standard JavaBean setter and getter methods. This means that in an EL expression, you can access the `questions` field using the dot notation:

```
${questions.questions}
```

When the EL expression is translated, it is translated into code that calls the `getQuestions()` method of the `Questions` class. The `TopicList.jsp` page also accesses the `topic` and `numQuestions` fields of the class. These are also translated into code that calls the appropriate getter methods of the class.

The `TopicList.jsp` page uses a `<useBean>` tag to instantiate an instance of the `Questions` class. The object that is created automatically has page context, so you can reference it in an EL statement using the name set by the `id` attribute in the `<jsp:useBean>` tag. That is the next thing the page does, accessing the `topic` and `numQuestions` properties using this line of code:

```
The number of questions in topic ${questions.topic}
is ${questions.numQuestions}
```

The EL expression references the bean using its id from the <jsp:useBean> action. It accesses the properties using the dot notation. The expression ${questions.topic} evaluates to the value of the topic property of the bean, which happens to be "EL". The expression ${questions.numQuestions} evaluates to the value of the numQuestions property, which is "3". Next, the page uses a scriptlet to iterate over the keys used in the Map that holds the questions. Notice that each time through the loop, the page stores the current value of the key as a pageContext attribute using the name "key". This allows another EL expression to access the current key using the expression ${key}.

Not only does the page access the value of key to create a link in the page, it uses key to access the value of the question stored by the Questions object.

Since you can access any particular value in a Map if you know the name, you can retrieve a particular question held by the Questions object like this:

```
${questions.questions[key]}
```

Because the value of key is a String that was used as the key to store a question in a Map object, the expression ${questions.questions[key]} is equivalent to this code:

```
Map m = questions.getQuestions();
String q = (String)m.get(key);
```

■ **Note** Even though the expression ${questions.questions[key]} is equivalent to the code shown, it is not translated into that code. You can see what the actual code looks like by examining the translated source file. See the "Translation and Compilation" section in Chapter 3 for information about how to find a translated source file.

The value of the expression after evaluation is simply the question string stored by the class. This is output to the response.

When you click one of the links in the page created by TopicList.jsp, the request is sent to the Questions.jsp page. This is a very simple page consisting of a single standard action, the <jsp:include> action:

```
<jsp:include page="/WEB-INF/${param.qid}.jsp" />
```

Notice that this file does not contain any template text. JSP files can consist solely of JSP elements and still be valid JSP pages. The include action uses an EL expression in the page attribute to determine which JSP page to include. It does this by using the implicit param object and the name of the parameter that is being accessed. The TopicList.jsp page outputs a link that looks like this:

```
<a href="Questions.jsp?qid=EL_1">EL_1</a>
```

This link sends the request to the Questions.jsp file with a request parameter of qid=EL_1. The Questions.jsp page can access the value of that parameter with this EL expression:

```
${param.qid}
```

We want to use this value to include the answer to the selected question in the response to the user. In this case, the answer is found in a page called EL_1.jsp in the WEB-INF directory, so the page attribute for our <jsp:include> action is set to "/WEB-INF/EL_1.jsp".

This answer page also uses EL expressions. One interesting thing to note is that the specification provides a way to have a literal ${*expr*} in the output of a page. This is done by placing the quoted expression '${' in an EL expression. The EL expression ${'${'} evaluates to ${ in the page, and the rest of the string is output without evaluation. For example, this line:

```
<p>${'${'}param.qid} evaluates to "${param.qid}"</p>
```

will generate this HTML:

```
<p>${param.qid} evaluates to "EL_1"</p>
```

The remainder of the page uses various EL expressions to show how to use some of the implicit objects available in an EL expression.

Although using EL statements in the TopicList.jsp page allowed us to eliminate some scriptlet statements, we still needed to use scriptlets to be able to iterate over the set of questions. We would also need to use scriptlets if we wanted to use a for or while loop. So, using EL statements by themselves cannot completely eliminate the need for scriptlets in JSP pages. To make pages that are truly scriptless, we need more tools. One of those other tools is custom actions, which are described in the next section.

Custom Actions and Tag Handlers

Several times in the previous chapter, we talked about removing Java code from the JSP page to further separate the display elements from the business logic. In reality, the Java code is not removed from the page, but it is hidden from the page developer.

Standard actions were introduced in the previous chapter. Standard actions are defined by the JSP specification and are actions that must be implemented by every JSP container. They provide a way to encapsulate Java code so that the page designer needs to know only the syntax of the tag. A standard action appears in a JSP page as an XML-style tag. Here is the tag for a useBean standard action with an enclosed setProperty action:

```
<jsp:useBean id="questions" class="com.apress.faq.Questions">
  <jsp:setProperty name="questions" property="topic"/>
</jsp:useBean>
```

At the start of the tag is the namespace prefix, jsp (a namespace is analogous to a Java package). This is followed by the action name. The standard action can have attributes, and some actions have bodies between the start and end tag. Tag bodies can include other tags (as shown in the example here) and/or template data. To anyone familiar with XML, this looks like a standard XML tag. But even though the tag looks like an XML tag, it is used in a JSP file, which does not need to be an XML document, and the JSP translator "sees" the tag a little differently.

The translator sees the tag as a token that is to be replaced by Java code. This Java code implements the functionality specified by the tag. Thus, the Java code is not removed from the page, but it is *encapsulated* within the tag. For example, when the JSP translator for Tomcat 5.0.28 sees the previous tag, it generates the following code:

```
com.apress.faq.Questions questions = null;
synchronized (_jspx_page_context) {
  questions = (com.apress.faq.Questions) _jspx_page_context.getAttribute(
    "questions", PageContext.PAGE_SCOPE);
  if (questions == null){questions = new com.apress.faq.Questions();
  _jspx_page_context.setAttribute("questions", questions,
    PageContext.PAGE_SCOPE);
```

Now, if the only actions you had available were the standard actions, you would still need to use Java code embedded in your JSP page. Fortunately, the JSP specification provides a way for developers to create their own actions. These actions are known as *custom actions*. Custom actions are deployed to the web application using a tag library. The mechanism for defining, implementing, deploying, and executing custom actions is known as *tag extension*. Using standard and custom actions, a web designer can build a dynamic web page without needing to know how to program in Java. Custom actions allow developers to take advantage of the power of Java—object reuse, encapsulation, and ability to debug—to provide a consistent mechanism for page designers to provide dynamic web pages.

Frequently in web application development, there are tasks that are done over and over within a web page. When you come across this type of situation, a light bulb should illuminate, and you should consider making the task into a custom action. Once you create a custom action, a JSP page can take advantage of the encapsulated functionality very easily by just referencing the custom actions using XML. Of course, it is also possible to encapsulate functionality in JavaBeans, and many page authors take that approach. So when should you use a custom action instead of a JavaBean? The answer is rather simple: JavaBeans cannot access the JSP page environment, so if you need access to the JSP page environment in a reusable piece of code, use a custom action.

How Custom Actions Work

When we use the term *custom action* (or standard action, for that matter), we are generally referring to the tag in the JSP file. Custom actions are used to create a dynamic response to a request.

Custom actions, like standard actions, can be used just like any other tag in a JSP file. They look like HTML tags in a JSP page. They can be customized through attributes passed by the caller and can access all objects in a JSP page. Custom actions can have bodies and can be nested.

Custom actions are identified by a prefix and a name:

```
<prefix:name />
```

The prefix is used to avoid conflicts between tags with the same name. The prefix is selected and used by the page developer, although the tag developer can suggest a prefix, as you will see later. The name is the name of the action. This is specified by the tag developer.

Custom actions can be empty (without a body):

```
<x:MyCustomAction />   <%-- Start and end tags combined into single tag --%>
<x:MyCustomAction></x:MyCustomAction>   <%-- Separate tags --%>
```

Or they can have bodies:

```
<x:MyCustomAction>
  Body content
</x:MyCustomAction>
```

The Java code that implements the tag can direct the page to evaluate the body or skip the body. Actions can be nested. Here is an example using the `<jsp:useBean>` and `<jsp:setProperty>` standard actions:

```
<jsp:useBean id="user" class="com.apress.faq.User">
  <jsp:setProperty name="user" property="*"/>
</jsp:useBean>
```

Also, as shown with the `<jsp:useBean>` and `<jsp:setProperty>` actions, an action can have attributes that customize the action. Actions can access the implicit objects of JSPs (`request`, `response`, and so on) and use these objects to modify the response to the client. Objects can be created by a custom action, and these objects can be accessed by other actions or scriptlets in the JSP.

The actual behavior of a custom action is provided at runtime by an instance of a Java class. This Java class is also known as a *tag handler*. Figure 4-6 shows the relationship between custom actions in a JSP page and the page implementation class for that page.

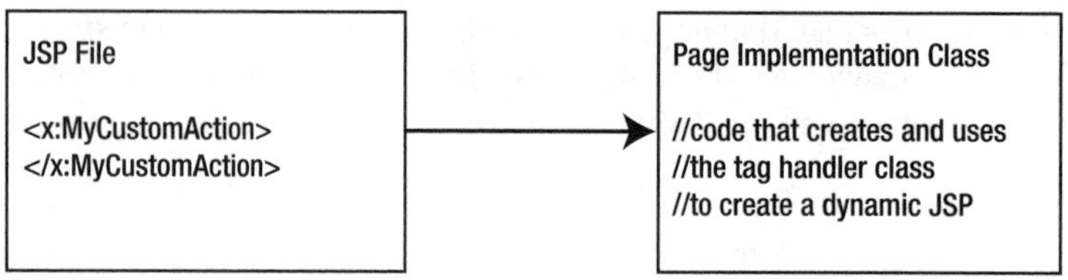

Figure 4-6. *A custom tag is translated into code in the page implementation class.*

The tag handler is the Java class that implements the behavior of a custom action. The tag handler class follows the requirements of a JavaBean, and it will implement one of the tag extension interfaces. There are several tag handler interfaces available. These interfaces are defined in the `javax.servlet.jsp.tagext` package. These interfaces will be located in some JAR file of your application server. For example, Tomcat 5.0 is the reference implementation for J2EE 1.4. So, for the stand-alone Tomcat 5.0 server or the J2EE 1.4 application server, the interface class files are located in the `jsp-api.jar` file. If you have a different application server, your JAR file will probably have a different name, but you should be able to find it easily enough by searching the JAR files used by your application server.

Table 4-5 shows the different tag handler interfaces, the specification in which they were introduced, and the Tomcat and Java EE versions that support them.

Table 4-5. *Tag Handlers Listed by the JSP Specification*

JSP Tag Handler Interfaces	JSP Specification	Reference Implementation
`Tag`, `BodyTag`	JSP 1.1	Tomcat 3, J2SDKEE 1.2
`IterationTag`	JSP 1.2	Tomcat 4, J2SDKEE 1.3
`SimpleTag`, `JspFragment`	JSP 2.0	Tomcat 5, J2EE 1.4, Java EE 5.0

As you can see in Table 4-5, JSP 1.1 has two interfaces for tag handlers: `Tag` and `BodyTag`. `Tag` handles a simple action with no iteration and no need to process the body of the tag. `BodyTag` is used when the body of the tag is processed (rather than simply output) as part of the action.

JSP 1.2 introduced the `IterationTag` to deal with iteration (JSP 1.1 used `BodyTag` to handle iteration). These three interfaces—`Tag`, `IterationTag`, and `BodyTag`—are known as *classic tag handlers*.

JSP 2.0 adds the `SimpleTag` interface to make tag handling easier, and the `JspFragment` interface to encapsulate the body content of a tag in an object. `SimpleTag` and `JspFragment` are known as *simple tag handlers*.

■ **Tip** If performance concerns are critical, we suggest that you first implement your tag handler as a simple tag, and then taking some performance metrics to see if your criteria are met before embarking on the more complicated and time-consuming path of writing a classic handler.

The tag extension mechanism of JSP 1.2 was powerful, but it was also relatively complicated to use. JSP 2.0's simple tag handlers simplify the process of developing a tag handler. They are no less capable than classic tag handlers in dealing with iteration and processing of body content. You are more likely to be using simple tag handlers than the more complicated classic tag handlers in your development, so we will look at those first.

Simple Tag Handlers

JSP 2.0 introduces the `SimpleTag` interface and a base class, `SimpleTagSupport` that implements the interface shown in Figure 4-7.

Using the `SimpleTag` interface and its associated base class significantly simplifies the process of implementing a tag handler. You can use this interface and base class to implement any tag handlers in JSP 2.0, regardless of whether the tag needs to be processed multiple times or has a body that needs to be processed.

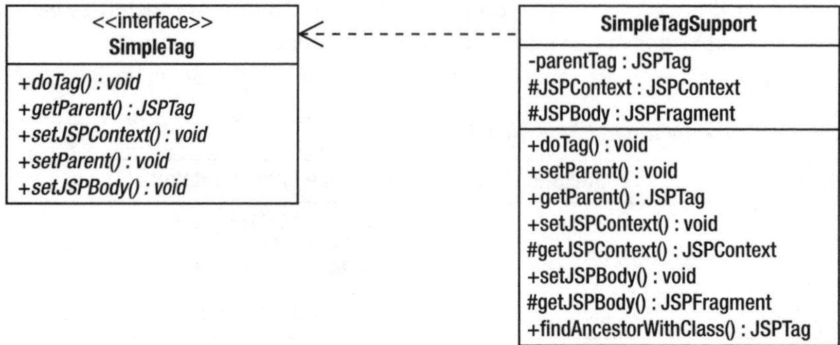

Figure 4-7. *The UML diagram for the SimpleTag interface and the SimpleTagSupport class*

To create a custom action, you create a tag handler class that extends the `SimpleTagSupport` base class, overriding the methods as necessary to provide the behavior for a custom action. Usually, all you will need to do is override the `doTag()` method. This method provides all the behavior of the custom action, including tag logic, iterations, and body evaluation. As you will see later, classic tag handlers used three methods to do everything that is done within the single `doTag()` method of `SimpleTag`.

Translating a Tag Handler

When the tag appears in a JSP source file, the translator creates code that does the following:

- Creates an instance of the tag handler by calling the zero-argument constructor of the implementation class
- Calls `setJspContext(JspContext)` to set the context for the tag handler
- Calls `setParent(JspTag)` if the tag is nested
- Initializes the tag handler attributes
- Creates a `JspFragment` object and passes the `JspFragment` object to `setJspBody(JspFragment)` if the tag has a body
- Calls the `doTag()` method

For the page implementation code to be able to create the tag handler instance and initialize its properties, all tag handlers follow the JavaBean conventions. You may recall that for our purposes, this means two things:

- The tag handler class must have a no-argument constructor.
- Properties of the class that can be used by clients must be exposed through public `setXXX()` methods to set the value and must have `getXXX()` or `isXXX()` methods to retrieve the value.

This provides a standard way for JSP containers to create instances of tag handlers and set the properties of tag handlers from attributes of the custom action element in the JSP. Each attribute in the custom action tag must correspond to a property of the tag handler that can be set using some `setXXX()` method.

After the tag handler class is created and initialized, the page class calls `doTag()`. This method is called only once for the tag. If the body content needs to be evaluated, it does that through the `JspFragment` object that was passed to the class through `setJspBody()`.

Using a JspFragment

Like `SimpleTag`, `JspFragment` is also an interface, but the implementation of the interface is left entirely to the JSP container. As a developer, you need to know only how to call a fragment to evaluate its contents. If your `SimpleTag` tag handler needs to evaluate the body of the tag, it calls the `invoke()` method of `JspFragment`:

```
public void invoke(java.io.Writer out)
```

As you can see, `invoke()` takes a single argument. If the `Writer` argument is null, the fragment will write its output to the current output stream of the client response; otherwise, the fragment will write its output to the given `Writer`. `JspFragment` objects can contain template text, JSP action elements, and EL expressions, but they cannot contain JSP scriptlets or scriptlet expressions. Variables used in EL expressions are set through context attributes, as you will see in the example later in this section.

Writing a Tag Library Descriptor

After creating one or more classes that implement a tag, you need to inform the container which tag handlers are available to the JSP pages in an application. This is done through a descriptor file called a *tag library descriptor* (TLD). The TLD is an XML-compliant document that contains information about the tag handler classes in a tag library. The tag in the JSP page must conform to the constraints described in the TLD. If the tag is not used correctly, as described by the TLD, then a translation error will occur.

A TLD for JSP 2.0 will provide information about the tag library using a `<taglib>` element, as shown in Listing 4-7.

Listing 4-7. *Sample TLD*

```
<?xml version="1.0" encoding="UTF-8" ?>

<taglib xmlns="http://java.sun.com/xml/ns/javaee"
        xmlns:xsi="http://www.w3.org/2001/XMLSchema-instance"
        xsi:schemaLocation="http://java.sun.com/xml/ns/javaee/web-jsptaglibrary_2_1.xsd"
        version="2.1">
  <tlib-version>1.0</tlib-version>
  <short-name>apress</short-name>
```

```
  <tag>
    <name>example</name>
    <tag-class>com.apress.faq.Example</tag-class>
    <body-content>empty</body-content>
    <variable>
      <name-given>script1</name-given>
    </variable>
    <variable>
      <name-from-attribute>attr1</name-from-attribute>
    </variable>
    <attribute>
      <name>attr1</name>
      <required>yes</required>
      <rtexprvalue>true</rtexprvalue>
    </attribute>
    <attribute>
      <name>attr2</name>
      <required>no</required>
      <rtexprvalue>false</rtexprevalue>
    </attribute>
  </tag>
</taglib>
```

The `<taglib>` element can have a number of subelements. The mandatory elements are shown in Table 4-6.

Table 4-6. *Mandatory Subelements of <taglib>*

Element	Meaning
`tlib-version`	The version number of the library
`short-name`	A simple default name, which may be used as the preferred prefix value in `taglib` directives
`Tag`	Information about a tag handler

The `<tag>` element has several subelements. Two subelements—`name` and `tag-class`—are mandatory. In addition, you will often need to use the optional subelements of the `<tag>` element. The `<tag>` subelements are shown in Table 4-7.

Table 4-7. *Subelements of <tag>*

Element	Meaning
`name`	The name of the tag handler (mandatory).
`tag-class`	The fully qualified class name of the tag handler class (mandatory).

Table 4-7. *Subelements of <tag>*

Element	Meaning
body-content	Whether the body of the tag can have content. Valid values are tagdependent, scriptless, or empty. The default is scriptless. If the value is empty, the tag is not allowed to have a body.
variable	Defines the scripting variables created by this tag handler and made available to the rest of the page. This element must contain one of two subelements: name-given or name-from-attribute. If name-given is used, the value of this element defines the name that other JSP elements can use to access the created scripting variable. If name-from-attribute is used, the value of the attribute with the name given by this element defines the name of the scripting variable.
attribute	Defines attributes for the tag. This element has three subelements: name, required, and rtexprvalue. The value of the name element will be the name of the attribute. The element named required is optional, and must be one of true, false, yes, or no. This indicates whether the attribute is required or optional. The default value is false (meaning the attribute is optional). The rtexprvalue element is optional, and must be one of true, false, yes, or no. The default value is false, which means that the attribute can be set only by using a static value known at compile time. If the element contains true or yes, the attribute can be set using a runtime expression.

The TLD in Listing 4-7 is for a tag library that the developer has identified as version 1.0. It relies on JSP 2.0. The suggested prefix for tags from the library is apress. However, note that page developers can use whatever prefix they desire. This is so that name conflicts between libraries with the same suggested prefix can be avoided.

The TLD defines one tag with the name example. The tag handler class for the tag is com.apress.faq.Example. The tag must have an empty body, because the value of the <body-content> element is empty.

The tag creates two objects that are made available to the rest of the page as scripting variables. The JSP page accesses the first object using the name script1 (from the <name-given> element). The second object is accessed by the name given in the attr1 attribute of the tag.

The tag takes two attributes. The attribute attr1 is required, and can be set by a runtime expression. The attribute attr2 is optional, and cannot be set at runtime from an expression.

When rtexprvalue is set to true, the attribute can take an EL expression of the form ${expr}. If the tag element also includes either <deferred-value/> or <deferred-method/> as an empty element, then the attribute can be set using an EL expression of the form #{expr}. See the JSP specification for more details about using request-time expressions to set the value of an attribute.

After creating the tag handler classes and the TLD, you need to take a few final steps before you can use the tags in a JSP page. These include properly setting up the application structure, writing the deployment descriptor, and importing the tag library into the page.

Building an Application Structure

Although some parts of the structure of a web application are not specified, locations for tag libraries and TLDs are specified. The following is an example of an application structure.

```
context-root
  META-INF/
    jar_that_contains_TLD.jar
  WEB-INF/
    lib/
      taglib.jar
    tlds/
      descriptor.tld
    classes/
      path/to/tag/handler.class
```

Tag handler classes must be placed in the /classes subdirectory of WEB-INF or in a .jar file in the /lib subdirectory of WEB-INF. TLD files must be placed under WEB-INF, although the actual location under WEB-INF is unspecified. In the example shown here, a TLD is located in the /tlds directory of WEB-INF. If a TLD is in a .jar file, it must be in the META-INF directory of the application.

Writing the Deployment Descriptor

Within the web.xml deployment descriptor, you can create a mapping from a URI to a TLD location. This is done through the <taglib> element. For example, the following element maps the URI /examples to the TLD descriptor.tld.

```
<taglib>
  <taglib-uri>/examples</taglib-uri>
  <taglib-location>/WEB-INF/tlds/descriptor.tld</taglib-location>
</taglib>
```

This mapping can then be used in the JSP files, as you will see next.

Importing a Tag Library into a Page

To use a custom action, you need to "import" the tag library into the JSP. This is done with the taglib directive. The taglib directive has this form:

```
<%@ taglib uri="URI_of_library" prefix="tag_prefix"%>
```

This element must appear in the JSP file prior to any custom action that uses a tag from the tag library.

The uri attribute is either an absolute or relative path to the TLD file. Alternately, if the web.xml deployment descriptor has a <taglib> element, you can refer to the TLD using the value of the <taglib-uri> element from web.xml. For instance, in the example in the previous section, the <taglib-uri> element contained the string /examples. This same URL can be used in the taglib directive in the JSP page:

```
<%@ taglib uri="/examples" prefix="ex"%>
```

Combined with the `<taglib>` element of the previous section, this directive would import the tag library defined by `descriptor.tld`. Within the particular JSP file that used this `taglib` directive, the custom actions would be referenced using the prefix given. For example, the previous TLD defined a tag handler named `example`. With the `taglib` directive shown here, the action would be referenced in a JSP page as follows:

```
<ex:example />
<%-- or as --%>
<ex:example></ex:example>
```

Implementing a Simple Tag Handler

Let's develop a simple tag handler class and deploy it to the Java FAQ application. In this example, we'll develop a tag handler using the simple tag handler interfaces of JSP 2.0. This tag handler will perform iteration and process the body content of the tag. When this example is complete, you will see that custom actions and simple tag handlers can make your JSP files extremely easy to develop. This example has the directory structure shown in Figure 4-8.

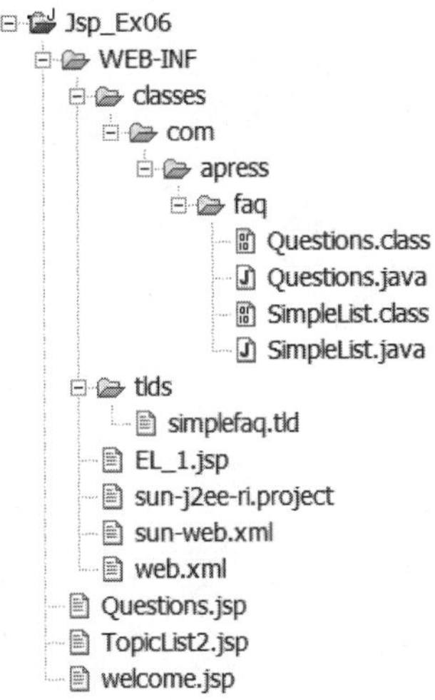

Figure 4-8. *Directory structure for the Jsp_Ex06 application*

Start with a new tag handler class that extends `SimpleTagSupport`. This file is called `SimpleList.java` (see Listing 4-8), and is located in the `/WEB-INF/classes/com/apress/faq` directory. Since this class uses the JSP API, when you compile the class, your classpath will need to include the correct libraries. If you are using Java EE, your classpath must include `javaee.jar`. If you are using Tomcat 5.0, your classpath must include `jsp-api.jar`. If you are using some other JSP container, check your documentation for the correct `.jar` file to include in the classpath.

Listing 4-8. *SimpleList.java*

```
package com.apress.faq;

import java.util.*;
import javax.servlet.jsp.tagext.*;
import javax.servlet.jsp.*;
import java.io.*;

public class SimpleList extends SimpleTagSupport {
  private String topic;
  public void setTopic(String s) { topic = s; }
  public String getTopic() { return topic; }

  public void doTag() throws JspException {
    Questions questions = new Questions();
    questions.setTopic(topic);

    // Get list of questions and the iterator for the keys
    Map qmap = questions.getQuestions();
    Iterator keys = qmap.keySet().iterator();

    while (keys.hasNext()) {
      try {
        Object key = keys.next();
        // Store the parameters for invoke()
        getJspContext().setAttribute("qid", key);
        getJspContext().setAttribute("question", qmap.get(key));
        // Process the body
        getJspBody().invoke(null);
      } catch (IOException e) {
        throw new JspException("Exception processing body");
      }
    }
  }
}
```

Now we need to create a TLD for this tag handler. The TLD is named `simplefaq.tld`, and it is shown in Listing 4-9. Save the TLD to the `/WEB-INF/tlds` directory.

Listing 4-9. *simplefaq.tld*

```
<?xml version="1.0" encoding="UTF-8" ?>

<taglib xmlns="http://java.sun.com/xml/ns/javaee"
      xmlns:xsi="http://www.w3.org/2001/XMLSchema-instance"
      xsi:schemaLocation="http://java.sun.com/xml/ns/javaee/web-jsptaglibrary_2_1.xsd"
      version="2.1">

  <tlib-version>1.0</tlib-version>
```

```
  <short-name>simplefaq</short-name>

  <tag>
    <name>simplelist</name>
    <tag-class>com.apress.faq.SimpleList</tag-class>
    <body-content>scriptless</body-content>
    <attribute>
      <name>topic</name>
      <required>yes</required>
      <rtexprvalue>true</rtexprvalue>
    </attribute>
  </tag>
</taglib>
```

If you are using Tomcat, you'll need to manually create a deployment descriptor. Listing 4-10 shows the `web.xml` deployment descriptor.

Listing 4-10. *web.xml for Jsp_Ex06*

```
<?xml version="1.0" encoding="ISO-8859-1"?>

<web-app xmlns="http://java.sun.com/xml/ns/javaee"
    xmlns:xsi="http://www.w3.org/2001/XMLSchema-instance"
    xsi:schemaLocation="http://java.sun.com/xml/ns/javaee/web-app_2_5.xsd"
    version="2.5">

  <display-name>Jsp_Ex06 - Simple Tag Handler</display-name>
  <welcome-file-list>
    <welcome-file>welcome.jsp</welcome-file>
  </welcome-file-list>
  <jsp-config>
    <taglib>
      <taglib-uri>/simplequestions</taglib-uri>
      <taglib-location>/WEB-INF/tlds/simplefaq.tld</taglib-location>
    </taglib>

    <jsp-property-group>
      <url-pattern>*.jsp</url-pattern>
      <el-ignored>false</el-ignored>
      <scripting-invalid>true</scripting-invalid>
    </jsp-property-group>
  </jsp-config>
</web-app>
```

Note that the deployment descriptor shown in Listing 4-10 declares that scripting is invalid for any JSP in this application, but that EL statements are processed.

If you are using the Java EE Deployment Tool, the mapping between the URI /simplequestions and the TLD simplefaq.tld is set in the JSP Tag Libraries section of the File Ref's tab for the web application. Figure 4-9 shows the entries to make in that tab.

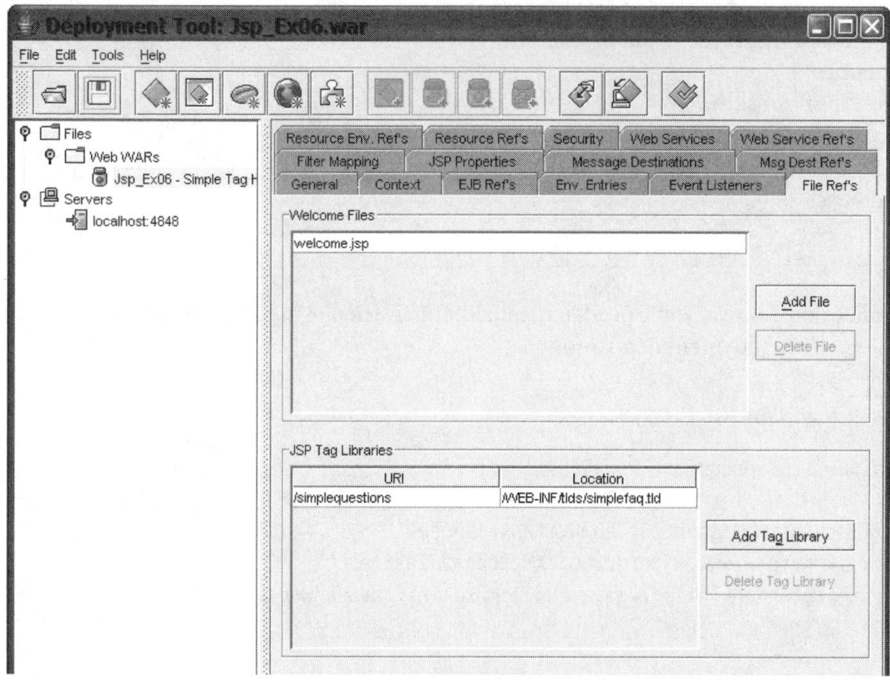

Figure 4-9. *You can use the Java EE 5 Deployment Tool to map between a coded reference and the actual tag library location.*

Now we'll create a new version of TopicList.jsp that uses this new tag. This is TopicList2.jsp, which is shown in Listing 4-11.

Listing 4-11. *TopicList2.jsp*

```
<%@ taglib uri="/simplequestions" prefix="faq"%>
<html>
  <head><title>Topic Questions 2</title></head>
  <body>
    <h1>Topic Questions 2</h1>

    <faq:simplelist topic="${param.topic}">
      <p>Question <a href="Questions.jsp?qid=${qid}">${qid}</a>
         ${question}</p>
    </faq:simplelist>
    <p>Click a link to get the answer.</p>
  </body>
</html>
```

Finally, we need to modify the welcome.jsp page. Add the welcome.jsp source from Listing 4-1 to this example and modify the anchor tag (<a>) so that it looks like this:

```
<a href="TopicList2.jsp?topic=EL">Expression Language
```

No other changes need to be made to welcome.jsp. Finally, you can directly reuse three files from the first example in this chapter: Questions.java (Listing 4-3), Questions.jsp (Listing 4-4), and EL_1.jsp (Listing 4-5).

Deploy these files to the server of your choice and access welcome.jsp from a browser using the correct URL for your server. If you are using the Sun Application Server or Tomcat, the URL will probably be http://localhost:8080/Jsp_Ex06/welcome.jsp. Don't be shocked when you see that it looks the same as the first example in this chapter (or it should, assuming everything is correct).

All the processing for a SimpleTag happens in the doTag() method. The doTag() method of the SimpleList class starts by instantiating a Questions bean and setting its topic property to the value of the topic property of our tag handler:

```
Questions questions = new Questions();
questions.setTopic(topic);
```

We can do that because the <simplelist> tag is required to have an attribute named topic. When the TopicList2.jsp page used the <simplelist> tag, it included the topic attribute with a value of EL. So, when an instance of the SimpleList class is instantiated to handle the tag, the page implementation class also sets its topic property based on the value of the topic attribute in the tag. Since the doTag() method is called after the class is instantiated, we know that the topic field has been initialized and can be used in the setTopic() method call of the Questions class.

Next, the SimpleList class creates an Iterator that will be used to step through the questions. It does this by calling the getQuestions() method to get the set of questions (which is also stored in a map). It then uses the map to get the list of keys used in the map.

```
Map qmap = questions.getQuestions();
Iterator keys = qmap.keySet().iterator();
```

The class then iterates over each question in the collection. For each question, two pieces of data used by the body of the tag are saved as attributes in the JspContext. First, the question itself is saved as an attribute value using the name "question" as the attribute name. The key value is then stored with the name "qid".

```
Object key = keys.next();
// Store the parameters for invoke()
getJspContext().setAttribute("qid", key);
getJspContext().setAttribute("question", qmap.get(key));
```

After the parameters for a single question are saved in the JspContext, the doTag() method gets a reference to the JspFragment for the tag and calls its invoke() method:

```
getJspBody().invoke(null);
```

Since null is passed as the argument, the body content is passed to the client's output response stream; that is, it is sent directly to the client.

The body of the tag consists of HTML text and EL statements that create a link to the question page for each question. The EL statements ${qid} and ${question} can be evaluated because the SimpleList class stored values for both of these names in the page context before calling the doTag() method.

Now let's look at the tag as it is used in TopicList2.jsp. This page uses the taglib directive to specify the TLD. The URI /simplequestions is mapped by the deployment descriptor to simplefaq.tld. The prefix used for the tag is faq. Notice that this is not the short-name used in the TLD. As we've mentioned several times, the page developer chooses the prefix. The name of the tag is the name given in the TLD, and the tag has a single attribute, called topic. This attribute was specified in the TLD as a required attribute that could be set using an expression. In our TopicList2.jsp page, the value of the attribute is indeed set, with the expression ${param.topic}:

```
<faq:simplelist topic="${param.topic}">
  <p>Question <a href="Questions.jsp?qid=${qid}">${qid}</a>
    ${question}</p>
</faq:simplelist>
```

The tag has a body, which is allowed by the TLD. The body content is represented by the JspFragment instance in the doTag() method. When the invoke() method is called, the body is evaluated and sent as part of the response to the client. You can see that the body of the tag includes two EL expressions. The values of these expressions come directly from the parameters that the doTag() method added to the JspContext. The doTag() method placed data into the JspContext using the names question and qid. When the EL expressions are evaluated, their value is obtained by getting the value of the attribute with the same name as the expression body.

Classic Tag Handlers

Prior to JSP 2.0, three interfaces and two implementing classes provided the basic design for tag handlers. As you will see here, using classic tag handlers is somewhat more involved than using simple tag handlers. For that reason, as we said earlier, you will probably use simple tag handlers rather than classic ones. However, you may need to use classic tag handlers for several reasons:

- You're working on a project that still uses a server that supports only JSP 1.2.
- You need to work with tag handlers that were written under JSP 1.2.
- You need the greater flexibility provided by classic tag handlers.

Figure 4-10 shows the class design for the tag extension API of JSP. The javax.servlet.jsp.tagext.Tag interface is the primary interface for classic tag handlers. It provides an interface for simple tag handler classes that do not need to manipulate their body content. IterationTag extends Tag to provide an interface for tag handlers that need to perform some iteration or looping. Finally, BodyTag extends IterationTag for tag handlers that manipulate their body content. The tag extension API includes two classes that implement these interfaces: TagSupport implements IterationTag, and BodyTagSupport implements BodyTag.

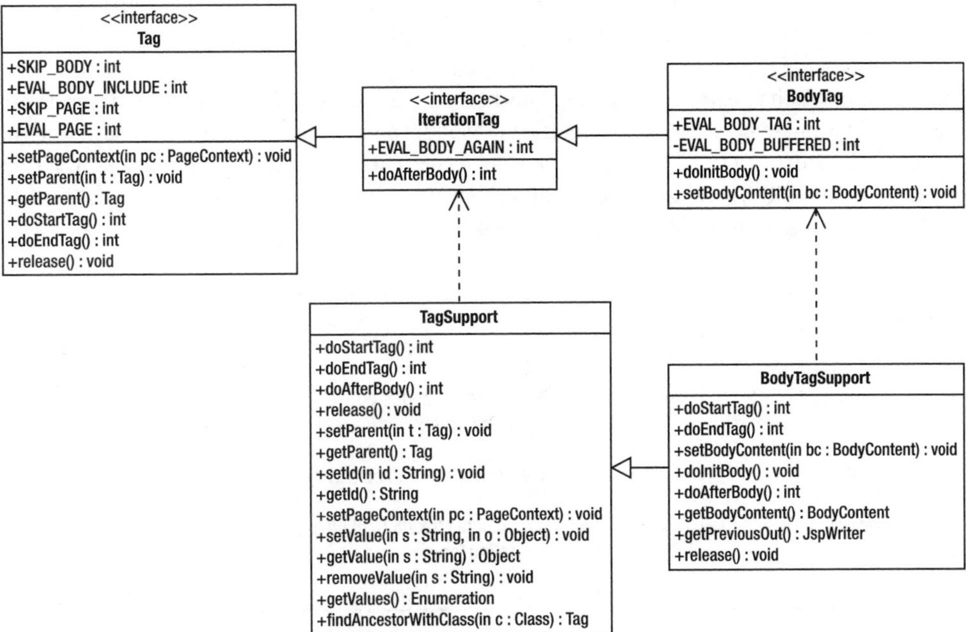

Figure 4-10. *The first interface in the classic tag hierarchy is the Tag interface. This interface is extended by IterationTag, which is extended by BodyTag. The IterationTag and BodyTag interfaces are implemented by the classes TagSupport and BodyTagSupport.*

Implementing Tag

Tag is the interface to implement when the tag handler does not need to process multiple times and does not need to manipulate its body. As an alternative to implementing the Tag interface, your tag handler can extend TagSupport (since TagSupport implements IterationTag, which extends Tag). In fact, this is the usual way you will implement a tag handler for a tag. When you extend TagSupport, you will only need to override doStartTag() or doEndTag(). So a tag handler class that has no properties will look like this:

```
public class MyTag extends TagSupport {
  public int doStartTag() { // method body }
  public int doEndTag() { // method body }
}
```

The doStartTag() method is called by the page class at the point where the start tag appears in the JSP file. When you implement a tag handler, you implement the doStartTag() method with code that you want to have executed before the body of the tag is processed. When your code is finished, it returns one of two values defined by the Tag interface. If it returns Tag.SKIP_BODY, the body of the tag, which can include template (HTML) data, JSP elements, or other tag extensions, is not evaluated.

Earlier, you saw that a TLD file contains information about the tag extensions. If the <body-content> element of the TLD has the value empty, this indicates that a tag *must* be empty, and SKIP_BODY is the only allowed return value. If your doStartTag() method returns Tag.EVAL_BODY_INCLUDE, the body of the tag is evaluated.

The doEndTag() method is called by the page class at the point where the end tag appears in the JSP file. When you implement a tag handler, you implement the doEndTag() method with code that you want to have executed after the body of the tag is processed. After your doEndTag() completes, it returns Tag.SKIP_PAGE or Tag.EVAL_PAGE. The value SKIP_PAGE indicates that the remainder of the JSP should not be evaluated; EVAL_PAGE indicates the opposite.

This execution flow is illustrated in Figure 4-11.

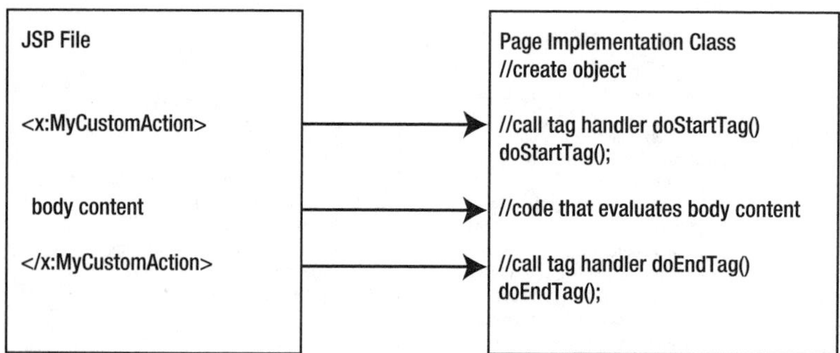

Figure 4-11. *With classic tags, when the start of a tag is encountered, the doStartTag() method is called. When the end of a tag is encountered, the doEndTag() method is called.*

Note that when extending TagSupport, you can, but do not need to, implement both doStartTag() and doEndTag(). If the tag handler does not need to perform any action prior to the body, and the tag must have an empty body, you do not need to implement doStartTag(). However, because the TagSupport implementation of doStartTag() returns SKIP_BODY, if the tag can have a body, you should implement a minimal doStartTag() that returns EVAL_BODY_INCLUDE. If the tag handler does not need to perform any action after the body, you do not need to implement doEndTag(). The TagSupport implementation of doEndTag() returns EVAL_PAGE.

Implementing IterationTag

When you need a tag handler class to iterate or loop its actions, your tag class will implement IterationTag. As with Tag, you will usually just extend TagSupport. IterationTag adds one method and one property, which are used to provide the looping behavior. Here is a tag handler class without any properties:

```
public class ListQuestions extends TagSupport {
  public int doStartTag() throws JspTagException { // method body }
  public int doAfterBody() throws JspTagException { // method body }
  public int doEndTag() throws JspTagException { // method body }
}
```

This time, the example includes the new method: doAfterBody().

Figure 4-12 illustrates the implementation class methods that correspond to the various tags in the JSP page. After calling doStartTag() and after evaluating the body of the tag, the page class calls the doAfterBody() method. The doAfterBody() method allows the tag handler class to determine whether the page class should evaluate the body another time. If so, doAfterBody() should return a value of IterationTag.EVAL_BODY_AGAIN, which indicates that the page class should evaluate the body of the tag again; if not, it returns Tag.SKIP_BODY. The page class then calls doEndTag() and proceeds as with a Tag.

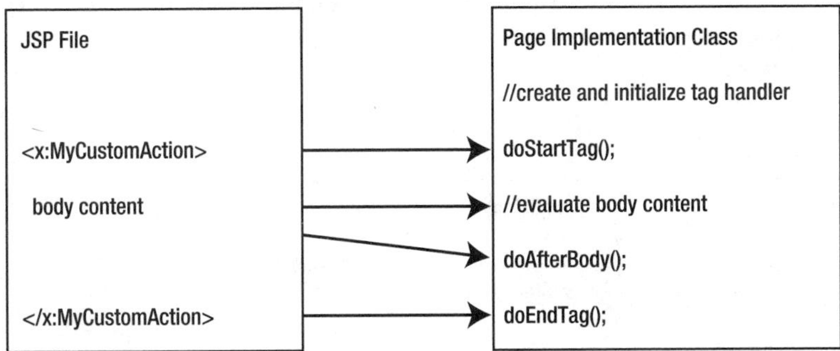

Figure 4-12. *After evaluating the body of the classic tag, the doAfterBody() method of the tag handler class is called. The return value of doAfterBody() determines whether the body of the tag is evaluated again.*

Note An additional interface that you can use with any class that implements Tag, IterationTag, or BodyTag is the TryCatchFinally interface. The TryCatchFinally interface requires that implementing classes implement two additional methods: doCatch(Throwable) and doFinally(). The container will call doCatch(Throwable) and doFinally() if an exception is thrown in any of the tag handling methods of the tag handler. See the Javadoc for details about using these methods.

Implementing BodyTag

With Tag and IterationTag, the implementing class can indicate whether the body of the tag should be evaluated by the page class; however, the tag handler classes that implement Tag or IterationTag have no way of actually manipulating the contents of the tag body. This is possible through the BodyTag interface and its implementing class, BodyTagSupport:

```
public class ListQuestionsInBody extends BodyTagSupport {
  public int doStartTag() throws JspTagException { // method body }
  public void setBodyContent(BodyContent bc) { // method body }
  public void doInitBody() { // method body }
  public int doAfterBody() throws JspTagException { // method body }
  public int doEndTag() throws JspTagException { // method body }
}
```

Figure 4-13 shows the correspondence between tags in the JSP page and the methods in the page implementation class. For the most part, the doStartTag() method is the same as for Tag or IterationTag. The difference is that the BodyTag interface defines an additional return value for the method: BodyTag.EVAL_BODY_BUFFERED. When your code returns EVAL_BODY_BUFFERED, the page class calls the setBodyContent() and doInitBody() methods. This makes the body content available to your code in the doAfterBody() and doEndTag() methods. When the return value of doStartTag() is EVAL_BODY_BUFFERED, the page class evaluates the tag body and stores the result in an instance of BodyContent. (Thus, an instance of BodyContent will not contain actions, scriptlets, and so on—only the results of those elements.) The page class then needs to pass the BodyContent instance to the tag handler so that it can manipulate the body content. It does this by calling setBodyContent(). The page class then calls doInitBody(). Inside the doInitBody() method, the tag handler class can perform any initialization that depends on the body of the tag.

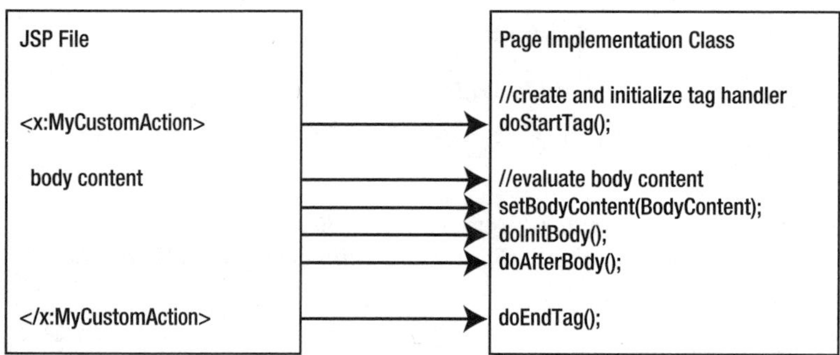

Figure 4-13. *The doInitBody() and doAfterBody() methods are called to process the body of a tag.*

Normally, you will manipulate the body content in the doAfterBody() method. However, the BodyContent object is also available to the doEndTag() method, so you can use the BodyContent object there. The BodyContent class defines various methods for getting the body content and writing the body content to an output stream. For example, this code snippet shows how to write the body content to the response:

```
public void doAfterBody() {
  // bodyContent is an instance variable of BodyTagSupport
  // Call the getEnclosingWriter() method to get the enclosing JspWriter
  Writer writer = bodyContent.getEnclosingWriter();
  // Call the writeOut(Writer) method to send the body content
  // to the writer
  bodyContent.writeOut(writer);

  if (need_to_eval_body_again) {
    return EVAL_BODY_AGAIN;
  } else {
    return SKIP_BODY;
  }
}
```

The page class will evaluate the body again if the `doAfterBody()` method returns `EVAL_BODY_AGAIN`; otherwise, if `doAfterBody()` returns `SKIP_BODY`, the page class calls `doEndTag()`.

Implementing a Classic Tag Handler with TagSupport

In our next example, we'll create a custom action using classic tag handlers to list the FAQ questions in the `TopicList.jsp` page. As with the previous tag handler example, by putting the iteration into the custom action, all the Java code will be eliminated from the JSP page and encapsulated in the tag handler. This will make the page simpler than the version introduced in the first example of the chapter. Encapsulating the Java code in beans and tag handlers also makes the page easier for page developers to develop and maintain. Figure 4-14 shows the application structure.

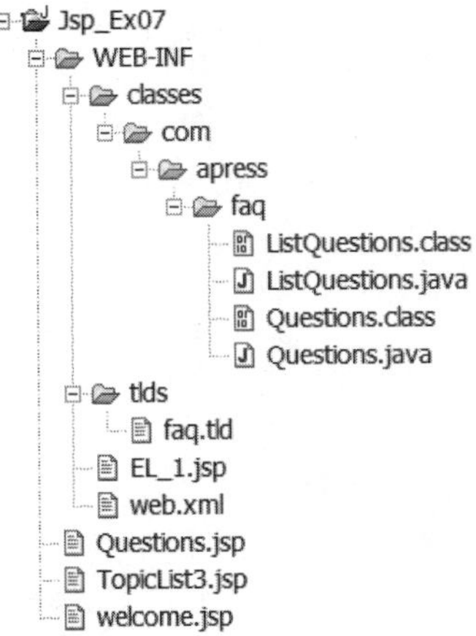

Figure 4-14. *Directory structure for the Jsp_Ex07 application*

Most of these files are the same as in the previous example. The new files are `TopicList3.jsp`, `web.xml`, `faq.tld`, and `ListQuestions.java`; you can reuse the files `Questions.class` (Listing 4-3), `Questions.jsp` (Listing 4-4), and `EL_1.jsp` (Listing 4-5). The file `welcome.jsp` (Listing 4-1) requires a simple change to be used with this example.

Listing 4-12 shows the tag handler, `ListQuestions.java`. The tag handler will need to iterate over a collection of questions, so it extends `TagSupport`. Since this class uses the JSP API, when you compile the class, your classpath will need to include the correct libraries. If you are using Java EE, your classpath must include `javaee.jar`. If you are using Tomcat 5.0, your classpath must include `jsp-api.jar`. If you are using some other JSP container, check your documentation for the correct `.jar` file to include on the classpath. Also, you will need to ensure that `Questions.class` either exists or is compiled at the same time. You can do that by using `javac *.java` (assuming the classpath is set).

Listing 4-12. *ListQuestions.java*

```
package com.apress.faq;
package com.apress.faq;

import java.util.*;
import javax.servlet.jsp.tagext.*;
import javax.servlet.jsp.*;
import java.io.*;

public class ListQuestions extends TagSupport {
  private String topic;
  /** Iterator over the question keys.
   * It is an instance variable because it is set in doStartTag()
   * and used in doAfterBody() */
  private Iterator qids;
  /** Map of questions keyed on question id.
   * It is an instance variable because it is set in doStartTag()
   * and used in doAfterBody() */
  private Map qmap;

  public void setTopic(String s) { topic = s; }

  public int doStartTag() throws JspTagException {
    Questions questions = new Questions();
    questions.setTopic(topic);

    qmap = questions.getQuestions();
    qids = qmap.keySet().iterator();
    try {
      // Write some preliminary data to the response
      pageContext.getOut().write("<h2>Questions for Topic</h2>");
      pageContext.getOut().write("\nThe number of questions in topic " +
                                 topic + " is " + qmap.size());

    } catch (IOException e) {
      throw new JspTagException("Error writing to out");
    }
    return EVAL_BODY_INCLUDE;
  }

  public int doAfterBody() throws JspTagException {
    // Create the link for a single question
    // Each time this method is called by the page class,
    // the Iterator advances to the next question
    if (qids.hasNext()) {
      String qid = (String) qids.next();
      String s = "<p>Question <a href=\"Questions.jsp?qid=" + qid +
```

```
        "\">" + qid + "</a>: " +
        qmap.get(qid) + "</p>";
      try {
        pageContext.getOut().write(s);
      } catch (IOException e) {
        throw new JspTagException("Error writing to out");
      }
      // Tell the page class to evaluate the body again
      return EVAL_BODY_AGAIN;
    } else {
      // faqs.next() was false, so no more questions
      return SKIP_BODY;
    }
  }

  public int doEndTag() throws JspTagException {
    try {
      pageContext.getOut().write("<p>Click a link to see the answer</p>");
    } catch (IOException e) {
      throw new JspTagException("Error writing to out");
    }
    return EVAL_PAGE;
  }
}
```

The TLD (faq.tld) for this tag is shown in Listing 4-13.

Listing 4-13. *faq.tld*

```
<?xml version="1.0" encoding="UTF-8" ?>

<taglib xmlns="http://java.sun.com/xml/ns/javaee"
    xmlns:xsi="http://www.w3.org/2001/XMLSchema-instance"
    xsi:schemaLocation="http://java.sun.com/xml/ns/javaee/web-jsptaglibrary_2_1.xsd"
    version="2.1">

  <tlib-version>1.0</tlib-version>
  <tag>
    <name>listFaqs</name>
    <tag-class>com.apress.faq.ListQuestions</tag-class>
    <body-content>scriptless</body-content>
    <attribute>
      <name>topic</name>
      <required>yes</required>
      <rtexprvalue>true</rtexprvalue>
    </attribute>
  </tag>
</taglib>
```

If you are deploying to Tomcat, you will need to add a `<taglib>` element to the deployment descriptor. Listing 4-14 shows the deployment descriptor `web.xml` for this example.

Listing 4-14. *web.xml for Jsp_Ex07*

```
<?xml version="1.0" encoding="ISO-8859-1"?>

<web-app xmlns="http://java.sun.com/xml/ns/javaee"
    xmlns:xsi="http://www.w3.org/2001/XMLSchema-instance"
    xsi:schemaLocation="http://java.sun.com/xml/ns/javaee/web-app_2_5.xsd"
    version="2.5">

  <display-name>Jsp_Ex07 - Classic Tag Handler</display-name>
  <welcome-file-list>
    <welcome-file>welcome.jsp</welcome-file>
  </welcome-file-list>
  <taglib>
    <taglib-uri>/questions</taglib-uri>
    <taglib-location>/WEB-INF/tlds/faq.tld</taglib-location>
  </taglib>
</web-app>
```

If you are deploying to Java EE using the Deployment Tool, you will need to set the `<taglib>` element of the deployment descriptor through the Java EE 5 Deployment Tool. This is done in the File Ref's tab of the right pane when the web application is selected in the left pane. You need to add the tag library mapping is the JSP Tag Libraries section, as shown in Figure 4-15. Enter `/questions` for the URI and `/WEB-INF/tlds/faq.tld` for the Location.

Listing 4-15 shows the JSP page. Save this as `TopicList3.jsp`.

Listing 4-15. *TopicList3.jsp*

```
<%@ taglib uri="/questions" prefix="faq"%>
<html>
  <head><title>Topic Questions</title></head>
  <body>
    <h1>Topic Questions</h1>

    <faq:listFaqs topic="${param.topic}">
    </faq:listFaqs>

  </body>
</html>
```

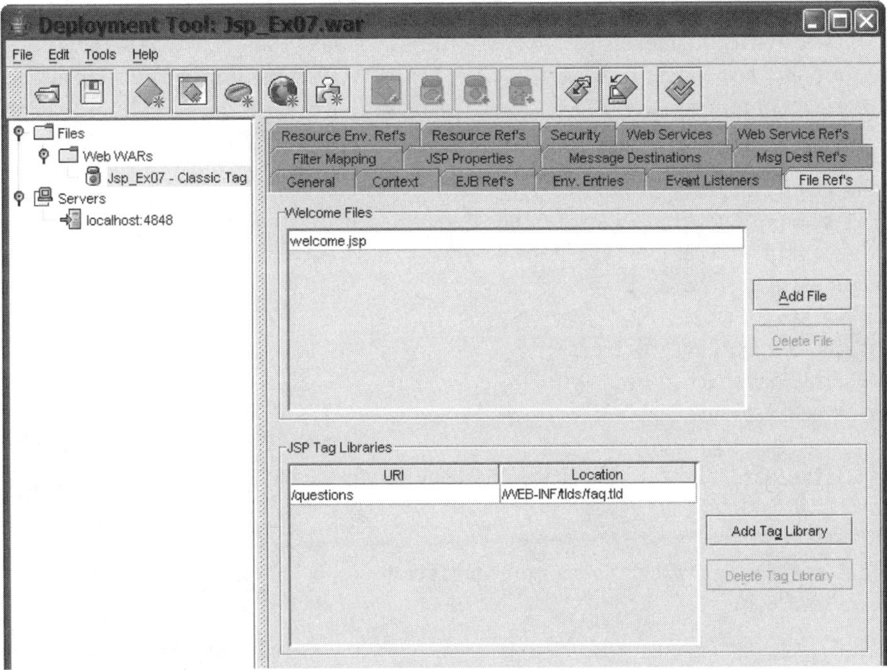

Figure 4-15. *The File Ref's tab is where JSP tag libraries are specified.*

Finally, we need to modify the `welcome.jsp` page. Add the `welcome.jsp` source from Listing 4-1 to this example and modify the anchor tag (<a>) so that it looks like this:

```
<a href="TopicList3.jsp?topic=EL">Expression Language
```

Deploy the application to your server. Open a browser window and enter the address `http://localhost:8080/Jsp_Ex07/welcome.jsp`. If everything is correct, you will see the same display as in the previous two examples in this chapter. However, even though the output from the tag handler looks the same as in previous examples, how it processes the tag is different. The tag handler class, `ListQuestions`, extends the `TagSupport` class. Since that class implements `IterationTag`, the tag handler can perform iterations, but it can't manipulate the body of the tag. Thus, the tag handler class needs to perform all the output to the response itself. `ListQuestions` provides implementations for the `doStartTag()`, `doAfterBody()`, and `doEndTag()` methods.

The `doStartTag()` creates an instance of the `Questions` class, and gets the `Map` consisting of the list of questions. It sets up an iterator for the keys used in the map and prints out some preliminary text. Notice that to do this, it gets an output stream from the `pageContext` object:

```
qmap = questions.getQuestions();
qids = qmap.keySet().iterator();
try {
  // Write some preliminary data to the response
  pageContext.getOut().write("<h2>Questions for Topic</h2>");
```

The doAfterBody() method actually uses the Iterator to create the links and text of each question. As it iterates through each question, it returns a value of EVAL_BODY_AGAIN. This signals that the page class should call doAfterBody() again. When it has iterated through all the values, doAfterBody() returns SKIP_BODY:

```
if (qids.hasNext()) {
  String qid = (String) qids.next();
  String s = "<p>Question <a href=\"Questions.jsp?qid=" + qid +
    "\">" + qid + "</a>: " +
    qmap.get(qid) + "</p>";
  try {
    pageContext.getOut().write(s);
  } catch (IOException e) {
    throw new JspTagException("Error writing to out");
  }
  // Tell the page class to evaluate the body again
  return EVAL_BODY_AGAIN;
} else {
  // faqs.next() was false, so no more questions
  return SKIP_BODY;
}
```

The TLD tells the application about the tag handler class. This TLD contains only one <tag> element. This <tag> element provides the name of the custom action, listFaq, and the name of the class that implements the action. As in the previous example, the action has one attribute named topic, which is required and can be set through an expression:

```
<tag>
  <name>listFaqs</name>
  <tag-class>com.apress.faq.ListQuestions</tag-class>
  <body-content>scriptless</body-content>
  <attribute>
    <name>topic</name>
    <required>yes</required>
    <rtexprvalue>true</rtexprvalue>
  </attribute>
</tag>
```

We also added a <taglib> element to the deployment descriptor. This <taglib> element specified that a URI of /questions referred to the TLD at /WEB-INF/tlds/faq.tld.

And now we get to the JSP page. Because all of the work is now done by the tag handler, the JSP page has become incredibly simple. Notice that there is no Java scriptlet in the page at all. At the top of the page, the tag library is imported using the taglib directive. The taglib directive specifies that the TLD is at the URI /questions. Because of the mapping in the web.xml file, this resolves to the file faq.tld.

The taglib directive specifies that the prefix for custom actions from that library should be faq. In this case, the prefix is the same as the short name, but remember that the page developer can set the prefix to any value, regardless of the short name of the library. This is the single custom action that causes the tag handler to be called:

```
<faq:listFaqs topic="${param.topic}">
</faq:listFaqs>
```

The custom action has the prefix, `faq`, followed by the tag name, and the `topic` attribute. Notice that we set this attribute using an EL expression. This is allowed because the TLD specified that the attribute could be set by a runtime expression.

So, the JSP has become much simpler, and that's good, but at what cost? The `ListQuestions` class now has HTML tags and data in it. This could become a maintenance problem. Recall that one of the reasons for JSP pages was to remove template data from code. Although it's nice that `TopicList3.jsp` is so simple, it would be better to put the presentation data back into the JSP page, and leave the tag handler to do nonpresentation tasks. Next, we'll look at how to do that through the `BodyTag` interface.

Implementing a Classic Tag Handler with BodyTagSupport

One way to move the presentation back to the JSP page and let the tag handler perform nonpresentation tasks is by extending the `BodyTagSupport` class. Figure 4-16 displays the directory structure for the latest iteration of the FAQ application.

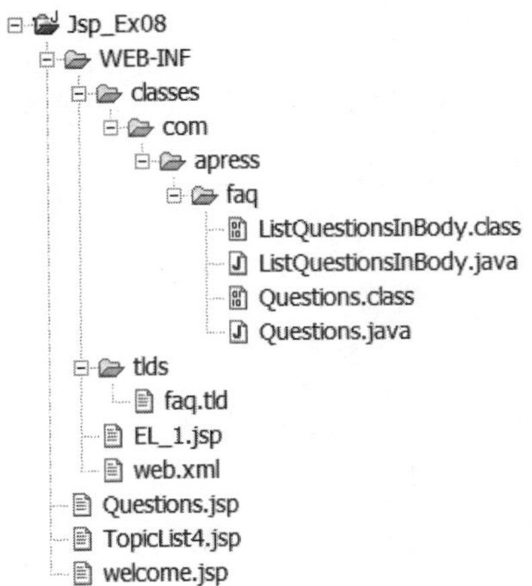

Figure 4-16. *The directory structure for the Jsp_Ex08 application*

As with previous examples, files not explicitly shown here can be reused from earlier examples in this chapter. In this example, we will create `TopciList4.jsp` and modify `welcome.jsp`. The deployment descriptor will be updated, as will `faq.tld`. The new tag handler class, `ListQuestionsInBody.java`, will extend `BodyTagSupport`.

Listing 4-16 is the final tag handler for the FAQ application. This tag handler is called `ListQuestionsInBody`. Add this class to the `/WEB-INF/classes/com.apress.faq` directory (as shown in Figure 4-16).

Listing 4-16. *ListQuestionsInBody.java*

```
package com.apress.faq;

import java.util.*;
import javax.servlet.jsp.tagext.*;
import javax.servlet.jsp.*;

public class ListQuestionsInBody extends BodyTagSupport {
  private String topic;
  private Iterator qids;
  private Map qmap;

  public void setTopic(String s) { topic = s; }

  public int doStartTag() throws JspTagException {
    Questions questions = new Questions();
    questions.setTopic(topic);
    qmap = questions.getQuestions();
    qids = qmap.keySet().iterator();

    if (qids.hasNext()) {
      Object qid = qids.next();
      setVariables(qid, qmap.get(qid));
      return EVAL_BODY_INCLUDE;
    } else {
      return SKIP_BODY;
    }
  }

  public int doAfterBody() throws JspTagException {
    if (qids.hasNext()) {
      Object key = qids.next();
      setVariables(key, qmap.get(key));
      return EVAL_BODY_BUFFERED;
    } else {
      return SKIP_BODY;
    }
  }

  public int doEndTag() throws JspTagException {
    return EVAL_PAGE;
  }
```

```
  void setVariables(Object key, Object value) {
    pageContext.setAttribute("question", value);
    pageContext.setAttribute("qid", key);
  }
}
```

We need to change the TLD so that it includes this new tag handler. Modify the `faq.tld` file as shown in Listing 4-17.

Listing 4-17. *faq.tld for Jsp_Ex08*

```
<?xml version="1.0" encoding="UTF-8" ?>

<taglib xmlns="http://java.sun.com/xml/ns/javaee"
      xmlns:xsi="http://www.w3.org/2001/XMLSchema-instance"
      xsi:schemaLocation="http://java.sun.com/xml/ns/javaee/web-jsptaglibrary_2_1.xsd"
      version="2.1">

  <tlib-version>1.0</tlib-version>

  <tag>
    <name>faqData</name>
    <tag-class>com.apress.faq.ListQuestionsInBody</tag-class>
    <body-content>scriptless</body-content>
    <variable>
      <name-given>qid</name-given>
    </variable>
    <variable>
      <name-given>question</name-given>
    </variable>
    <attribute>
      <name>topic</name>
      <required>yes</required>
      <rtexprvalue>true</rtexprvalue>
    </attribute>
  </tag>
</taglib>
```

We also need a new version of the topic list page. Listing 4-18 shows `TopicList4.jsp`.

Listing 4-18. *TopicList4.jsp*

```
<%@ taglib uri="/questions" prefix="faq"%>

<html>
  <head><title>Topic Questions 4</title></head>
  <body>
    <h1>Topic Questions 4</h1>
```

```
    <faq:faqData topic="${param.topic}">
      <p>Question <a href="Questions.jsp?qid=${qid}">${qid}</a>
        ${question}</p>
    </faq:faqData>
    <p>Click a link to get the answer.</p>
  </body>
</html>
```

Since this application uses the same initial file and the same `faq.tld` as the previous example, you could use the deployment descriptor from the previous example without any changes. However, we changed the display name to reflect that this is a new application. Listing 4-19 shows the modified deployment descriptor.

Listing 4-19. *web.xml for Jsp_Ex08*

```
<?xml version="1.0" encoding="ISO-8859-1"?>

<web-app xmlns="http://java.sun.com/xml/ns/javaee"
    xmlns:xsi="http://www.w3.org/2001/XMLSchema-instance"
    xsi:schemaLocation="http://java.sun.com/xml/ns/javaee/web-app_2_5.xsd"
    version="2.5">

  <display-name>Jsp_Ex08 - Classic Body Tag Handler</display-name>
  <welcome-file-list>
    <welcome-file>welcome.jsp</welcome-file>
  </welcome-file-list>
  <taglib>
    <taglib-uri>/questions</taglib-uri>
    <taglib-location>/WEB-INF/tlds/faq.tld</taglib-location>
  </taglib>
</web-app>
```

Finally, we need to modify the `welcome.jsp` page. Add the `welcome.jsp` source from Listing 4-1 to this example and modify the anchor tag (`<a>`) so that it looks like this:

```
<a href="TopicList4.jsp?topic=EL">Expression Language
```

No other additions or modifications are needed to the existing files in the application. After deploying the new files, enter the URL `http://localhost:8080/Jsp_Ex08/welcome.jsp`. You should see the same behavior as occurred with the previous examples. However, unlike the `ListQuestions` class, the `ListQuestionsInBody` class no longer has any template data in it and does not need to output anything to the response. All it does is process the collection of questions, exposing each one to the rest of the page through the `setVariables()` method. This method adds two attributes to the page context. This makes the variables accessible to the rest of the page. Within the page, these variables are accessed using the EL statements `${question}` and `${qid}`. To cause the body of the tag to be evaluated, `doStartTag()` returns `EVAL_BODY_INCLUDE` and `doAfterBody()` returns `EVAL_BODY_BUFFERED`. These return values cause the page class to call the `setBodyContent()` and `doInitBody()` methods of the class. Since our tag handler didn't need to do anything special with the body content, the default implementations of these methods in the parent class were sufficient.

To make the variables created by the tag handler accessible to the page, the TLD specifies that the tag handler should create two scripting variables that are then available to the rest of the page (although they are used only within the body of the tag). It did this through the <variable> element in the TLD:

```
<variable>
  <name-given>qid</name-given>
</variable>
<variable>
  <name-given>question</name-given>
</variable>
```

Each of these elements used the <name-given> element to specify the name by which the scripting variables could be accessed. These are the same names that the tag handler class must use when adding the attributes to the page context.

Finally, there is the topic page. Our new tag is called in the same way as the simple tag example, so TopicList4.jsp is simpler than the original TopicList.jsp, but not quite as simple as TopicList3.jsp. The body of the tag consists of template data and EL expressions:

```
<faq:faqData topic="${param.topic}">
  <p>Question <a href="Questions.jsp?qid=${qid}">${qid}</a>
     ${question}</p>
</faq:faqData>
```

The EL expressions access the scripting variables created by the custom action. Each time the page class evaluates the body, it gets the current values of these variables from the page context and inserts them into the response.

This allows page designers to easily change the presentation of the data without needing to edit and recompile the tag handler.

A Multitude of Custom Actions

At this point, it should be clear that you can create a rich set of behavior with very simple code that implements any of the tag handler interfaces, or more simply just by extending the tag support classes. This allows the software developers of a web application to do what they like best—coding—while providing the web page developers a set of tags that they can use to make their web pages dynamic without needing to learn how to code.

So, at this point you should be ready to go out and develop some tag handlers. You could have tag handlers for performing if-then tests and implementing switch constructs. Tag handlers for looping would also be useful. And how about some tag handlers for formatting text and numbers, and another set of tag handlers to make it easy for a JSP to communicate with a database?

Of course, if you have these great ideas, so do dozens or hundreds of other developers. All of you are out there creating tags for testing, looping, and formatting. And none of these tag handlers are compatible! What started out as an elegant solution to the problem of mixing logic and presentation has gotten ugly again.

Based on the last paragraph, you might guess that there is a solution to this problem. You're right, and that solution is the JSP Standard Tag Library, which is the subject of the next section.

JSP Standard Tag Library (JSTL)

Much of this chapter has been devoted to information about creating your own custom actions and tag libraries. However, you are not limited to using just the tags you create. You can use any tag library that is available. While there are many such libraries distributed, in this section, we will look at the JSP Standard Tag Library, or JSTL.

The JSTL grew out of the realization that with many developers creating tag libraries, many actions would be duplicated among the various libraries. Because these libraries were developed separately, the duplicated actions would probably have different names, syntaxes, and/or behaviors.

The JSTL standardizes a number of common actions. If you use one implementation of a standard tag library, switching to another standard tag library implementation should be as easy as adding the `.jar` files to your application and changing the `web.xml` file to map the `taglib-uri` to the new different TLD. In this section, we will look how to get a JSTL implementation, some of the actions in the JSTL, and using the JSTL.

Getting a JSTL Implementation

If you want to experiment with the JSTL, one place where you can get an implementation of the library is the Jakarta project. You can get a copy of the latest version at `http://jakarta.apache.org/taglibs/index.html`. At the time this was written, JSTL 1.1.2 was the current version; it is designed to run under Tomcat 5.

Using the JSTL is simple:

1. Unpack the distribution into your application. The `.jar` files containing the tag handlers should go into `/WEB-INF/lib`, and the TLDs into a directory under `/WEB-INF/`.
2. Change the `web.xml` file to map the `taglib-uri` element to the location of the TLDs.
3. Add the `taglib` directive to the pages that will use the JSTL tags.

Actions in the JSTL

The JSTL tags have been divided into four categories:

- Core actions (`c.tld`)
- XML processing (`x.tld`)
- Internationalization-capable formatting (`fmt.tld`)
- Relational database access (`sql.tld`)

If you are using the 1.1.2 or later release of the JSTL with a web container that supports JSP 2.0 or later, you will use the TLD files listed here. Since Tomcat 5 is the current reference implementation for JSP 2.1, the 1.1.2 versions of the TLD files are the ones we will use in this chapter. You should copy those TLD files into the `tld` directory of your web application.

If you have the version 1.1.2 release, you will notice that there are additional TLD files in the distribution. For example, in addition to c.tld, the 1.1.2 release includes c-1_0.tld and c-1_0-rt.tld. There are similarly named files corresponding to x.tld, fmt.tld, and sql.tld. These TLD files are included for backward-compatibility with JSTL 1.0 (hence the 1_0 part of the filename).

If you are using a web container that does not support JSP 2.0 or later, you will need to use the JSTL 1.0 versions of the TLD files. If your page uses Java scripting expressions (<%! %>, <%= %>, or <% %>), you will use the rt version of each TLD. The abbreviation rt is short for rtexprvalues, which is for runtime (or request-time) expression values. (The JSP specification uses the terms *runtime* and *request-time* interchangeably.) If your page uses EL expressions, you will use the other version. If your page uses both, you will need both TLDs. You can freely mix actions from either library in the same JSP. But remember that this applies only if your container does not support JSP 2.0 or later. The latest versions of the Java EE reference implementation use Tomcat 5, which supports JSP 2.1 as the web container.

Core Actions

The core actions provide tag handlers for manipulating variables and dealing with errors, performing tests and conditional behavior, and executing loops and iterations.

The general-purpose actions in the core category provide support for dealing with variables and errors. Table 4-8 shows the general-purpose actions with a description of how they are used.

Table 4-8. *General-Purpose Actions in the JSTL Core Category*

Tag	Meaning
<c:out value="" default="">	Sends the value to the response stream. You can specify an optional default value so that if the value attribute is set with an EL expression, and the expression is null, the default value will be output.
<c:set var="" value="">	Sets the JSP-scoped variable identified by var to the given value.
<c:set target="" property="" value="">	Sets the property of the given JavaBean or Map object to the given value.
<c:remove var="" scope="">	Removes the object identified by var from the given scope. The scope attribute is optional. If the scope is not given, each scope will be searched in the order page, request, session, application, until the object is found or all scopes are searched. If scope is given, the object is removed only if it is in the given scope. If the object is not found, an exception will be thrown.
<c:catch var="">	Encloses a block of code that might throw an exception. If the exception occurs, the block terminates but the exception is not propagated. The thrown exception can be referenced by the variable named by var.

Conditional actions, shown in Table 4-9, allow you to test expressions and evaluate tags based on the result of the test.

Table 4-9. *Conditional Actions in the JSTL Core Category*

Tag	Meaning
`<c:if test="" var="">`	Used like a standard Java `if` block. The `var` attribute is optional; if present, the result of the test is assigned to the variable identified by `var`. If the test expression evaluates to `true`, the tag is evaluated; if `false`, it is not.
`<c:choose>`, `<c:when test="">`, `<c:otherwise>`	The analog to a Java `if`...`elseif`...`else` block. The `<c:choose>` action starts and ends the block. The test in each `<c:when test="">` tag is evaluated; the first test that evaluates to `true` causes that tag to be evaluated. If no `<c:when>` action evaluates to `true`, the `<c:otherwise>` tag is evaluated.

Table 4-10 shows iterator actions, which are actions that allow you to loop over a set of values.

Table 4-10. *Iterator Actions in the JSTL Core Category*

Tag	Meaning
`<c:forEach var="" items="">`	Iterates over each item in the collection identified by `items`. Each item can be referenced by `var`. When `items` is a `Map`, the value of the item is referenced by `var.value`.
`<c:forEach var="" begin="" end="" step="">`	The tag for a `for` loop. The `step` attribute is optional.
`<c:forTokens items="" delims="">`	Iterates over the tokens in the `items` string.

Formatting Actions

Formatting actions are part of the internationalization, or I18N, library. As you might guess, they provide support for formatting output. Among the actions for setting locales and time zones, are actions for formatting numbers. Here, we'll look at two of them.

The following formatting action is for dates:

```
<fmt:formatDate value="date" [type="{time|date|both}"]
[dateStyle="{default|short|medium|long|full}"]
[timeStyle="{default|short|medium|long|full}"]
[pattern="customPattern"] [timeZone="timeZone"] [var="varName"]
[scope="{page|request|session|application}"]/>
```

With this action, only the value attribute is required. The other attributes define how to format the date. The pattern attribute can contain a custom pattern for formatting the date string.

This is a formatting action for numbers:

```
<fmt:formatNumber value="numericValue" [type="{number|currency|percent}"]
[pattern="customPattern"] [currencyCode="currencyCode"]
[currencySymbol="currencySymbol"]
[groupingUsed="{true|false}"] [maxIntegerDigits="maxIntegerDigits"]
[minIntegerDigits="minIntegerDigits"] [maxFractionDigits="maxFractionDigits"]
[minFractionDigits="minFractionDigits"] [var="varName"]
[scope="{page|request|session|application}"]/>
```

This action formats the number given by value. Various styles are possible, including currency formats and custom formatting styles. You can also use this tag without the value attribute; in which case, the number to be formatted is passed in the body of the tag.

SQL Actions

The JSTL SQL actions allow page authors to perform database queries, access query results, and perform inserts, updates, and deletes. One of the many SQL actions is <sql:query>:

```
<sql:query var="" dataSource=""> SQL Command </sql:query>
```

This action queries the database given by the dataSource attribute. The query that is performed is given in the body of the tag. The results of the query can be accessed by var.rows. You can use the <c:forEach> tag to iterate over the collection of rows.

The dataSource attribute can identify the database in two ways: use the JDBC URL to access the database or use the Java Naming and Directory Interface (JNDI) data source name to look up the database. See Chapters 7 and 8 for more information about these techniques.

Using the JSTL in a JSP

Now we will finally add another FAQ answer to the FAQ application we have been developing in this chapter. This JSP will show various uses of the JSTL. Figure 4-17 shows the structure of the web application.

For the most part, this example will reuse the files created for the example used earlier to demonstrate simple tag handlers. Start by finding the files for the simple tag handler example, Jsp_Ex06, and putting them into the directory structure shown in Figure 4-17. The new files that need to be added are EL_2.jsp and the .jar and .tld files from the JSTL.

Download the JSTL 1.1 distribution from the Jakarta web site http://jakarta.apache.org/taglibs/doc/standard-doc/intro.html. Extract the TLDs c.tld and fmt.tld into the /tlds directory you've been using for the examples in this chapter. Extract two .jar files into the lib directory: standard.jar and jstl.jar.

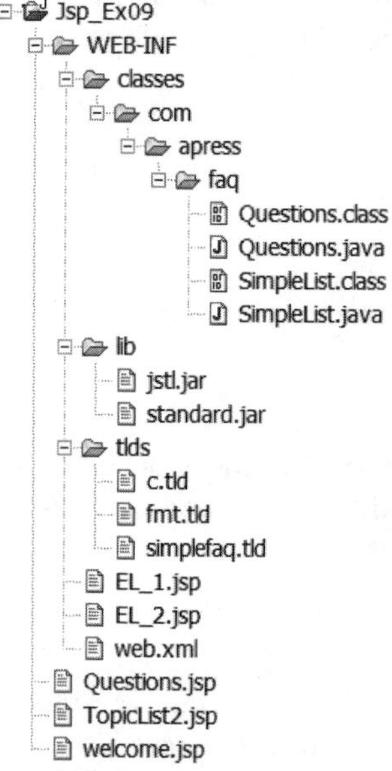

Figure 4-17. *The directory structure for the Jsp_Ex09 example application.*

Create the `EL_2.jsp` file shown in Listing 4-20. Save this file in the same place as `EL_1.jsp`.

Listing 4-20. *EL_2.jsp*

```
<%@taglib uri="http://java.sun.com/jsp/jstl/core" prefix="c"%>
<%@taglib uri="http://java.sun.com/jsp/jstl/fmt" prefix="fmt"%>
<html>
  <head>
    <title>JSTL Q2</title>
  </head>

  <body>
    <h1>JSTL Question 2</h1>
    <h2>How do I use the JSTL?</h2>

    <jsp:useBean id="questions" class="com.apress.faq.Questions"
                 scope="page">
      <jsp:setProperty name="questions" property="topic" value="EL"/>
    </jsp:useBean>

    <table border="1">
<!-- the literal JSTL tag will be in left column of table -->
<!-- the evaluated JSTL tag will be in right column of table -->
      <tr><th>tag</th><th>result</th></tr>
```

```
<!-- this tag uses c:out to send the value of an EL to the response -->
      <tr><td>&lt;c:out value="${'${'}questions.topic}"/&gt;</td>
          <td><c:out value="${questions.topic}"/></td>
      </tr>

<!-- this tag uses c:set to set the property of a JavaBean -->
    <c:set target="${questions}" property="topic" value="JSTL" />
      <tr>
        <td>&lt;c:set target="${'${'}questions}" property="topic"
                      value="JSTL"/&gt;
        </td>
        <td><c:out value="${questions.topic}"/></td>
      </tr>


<!-- this tag uses c:if to determine whether to create another row -->
      <c:if test="${questions.topic == 'EL'}">
        <tr><td>This row will not be created</td>
            <td></td>
        </tr>
      </c:if>

      <c:if test="${questions.topic == 'JSTL'}">
        <tr><td>This row was created because the c:if tag result was true</td>
            <td></td>
        </tr>
      </c:if>
    </table>

<h2>Multiplication table, 1 - 5</h2>

<!-use the forEach tag to create a table -->
    <table border="1">
      <tr><td></td><td>1</td><td>2</td><td>3</td><td>4</td><td>5</td></tr>
      <c:forEach var="i" begin="1" end="5">
        <tr><td><c:out value="${i}"/></td>
          <c:forEach var="j" begin="1" end="5">
            <td><c:out value="${i*j}"/></td>
          </c:forEach>
        </tr>
      </c:forEach>
    </table>

<h2>Formatting numbers</h2
<br>&lt;fmt:formatNumber value="23.456" type="number" /&gt; results in
    <fmt:formatNumber value="23.456" type="number" />
```

```
<br>&lt;fmt:formatNumber type="currency"&gt;23.456
    &lt;/fmt:formatNumber&gt; results in <fmt:formatNumber
    type="currency">23.456</fmt:formatNumber>
<br>&lt;fmt:formatNumber value=".23456" type="percent"/&gt; results
    in <fmt:formatNumber value=".23456" type="percent"/>
<br>&lt;fmt:formatNumber value=".23456" type="percent"
    minFractionDigits="2"/&gt; results in <fmt:formatNumber
    value=".23456" type="percent" minFractionDigits="2"/>

  </body>
</html>
```

If you are using Tomcat, modify the web.xml file as shown in Listing 4-21. If you are using the Java EE Deployment Tool, set the taglib mapping through the Deployment Tool.

Listing 4-21. *web.xml for Jsp_Ex09*

```
<?xml version="1.0" encoding="ISO-8859-1"?>

<web-app xmlns="http://java.sun.com/xml/ns/javaee"
    xmlns:xsi="http://www.w3.org/2001/XMLSchema-instance"
    xsi:schemaLocation="http://java.sun.com/xml/ns/javaee/web-app_2_5.xsd"
    version="2.5">

  <display-name>Jsp_Ex09 - JSP Standard Tag Library</display-name>

  <welcome-file-list>
    <welcome-file>welcome.jsp</welcome-file>
  </welcome-file-list>

  <jsp-config>
    <taglib>
      <taglib-uri>/simplequestions</taglib-uri>
      <taglib-location>/WEB-INF/tlds/simplefaq.tld</taglib-location>
    </taglib>

    <taglib>
        <taglib-uri>http://java.sun.com/jsp/jstl/core</taglib-uri>
        <taglib-location>/WEB-INF/tlds/c.tld</taglib-location>
    </taglib>

    <taglib>
        <taglib-uri>http://java.sun.com/jsp/jstl/fmt</taglib-uri>
        <taglib-location>/WEB-INF/tlds/fmt.tld</taglib-location>
    </taglib>
```

```
    <jsp-property-group>
      <url-pattern>*.jsp</url-pattern>
      <el-ignored>false</el-ignored>
      <scripting-invalid>true</scripting-invalid>
    </jsp-property-group>
  </jsp-config>
</web-app>
```

That should be all that's required to make the tags available. Deploy the new files and enter the URL `http://localhost:8080/Jsp_Ex09/welcome.jsp` in a browser. Click the link for EL_2, and you should see a page like the one shown in Figure 4-18.

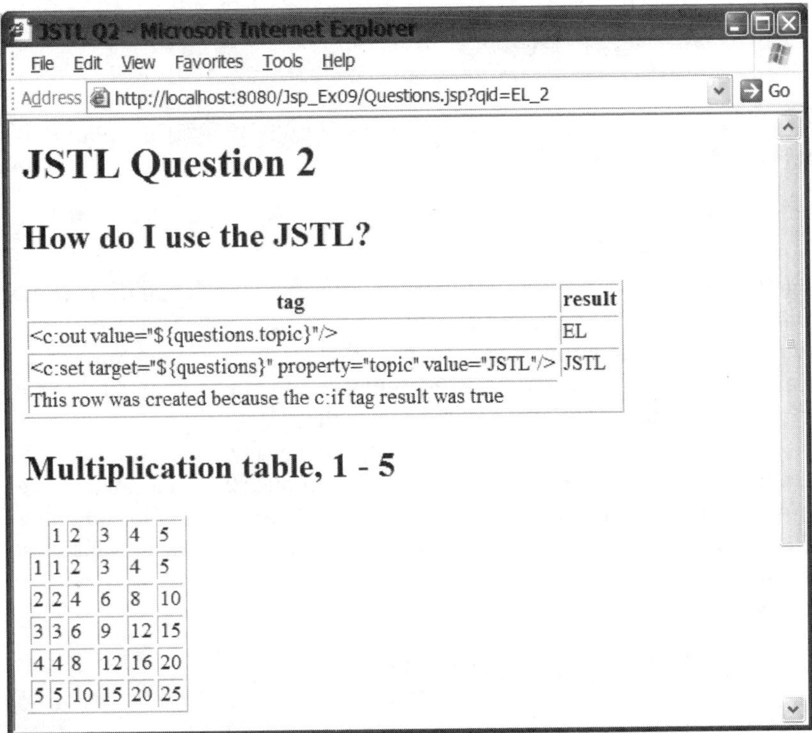

tag	result
<c:out value="${questions.topic}"/>	EL
<c:set target="${questions}" property="topic" value="JSTL"/>	JSTL
This row was created because the c:if tag result was true	

	1	2	3	4	5
1	1	2	3	4	5
2	2	4	6	8	10
3	3	6	9	12	15
4	4	8	12	16	20
5	5	10	15	20	25

Figure 4-18. *The JSTL provides many custom actions that can be used to create dynamic web pages.*

This page demonstrates a few of the JSTL tags available to you. You've seen the TLD and the `web.xml` entries several times now, so we won't cover those again here. The `EL_2.jsp` file begins by importing the tag libraries:

```
<%@ taglib uri="http://java.sun.com/jsp/jstl/core" prefix="c" %>
<%@ taglib uri="http://java.sun.com/jsp/jstl/format" prefix="fmt" %>
```

We need one taglib entry for each library we use. The EL_2.jsp uses the core and formatting libraries, so there is one taglib entry for each. The taglib entry sets the prefix for the core library to c and the prefix for the format library to fmt, following the JSTL suggestion. However, recall that you can make the prefix any value you want; the prefix is set by the page designer, not by the tag library implementer.

As we mentioned earlier, if you are forced to use the JSTL 1.0 versions of the TLD files because your web container supports only JSP 1.2, you may need two taglib entries for each library you use in the JSP page. In addition, the URL for the taglib element is slightly different. If your JSP page uses JSP scripting expressions such as scriptlets or declarations, you will use the RT version of the TLD, fmt-1_0-rt.tld, for example. If your JSP page uses EL statements, you will use the EL version of the TLD, fmt-1_0.tld, for example. So, if Listing 4-20 were being deployed to a JSP 1.2 container, the taglib entries would look like this:

```
<%@ taglib uri="http://java.sun.com/jstl/core" prefix="c" %>
<%@ taglib uri="http://java.sun.com/jstl/format" prefix="fmt" %>
```

If you then added any Java scriptlets, expressions, or declarations to the page, you would add the following taglib entries as well:

```
<%@ taglib uri="http://java.sun.com/jstl/core_rt" prefix="c_rt" %>
<%@ taglib uri="http://java.sun.com/jstl/format_rt" prefix="fmt_rt" %>
```

Comparing the URIs above to the URIs used in Listing 4-20, you can see that the JSTL 1.0 URI differs from the JSTL 1.1 URI. The JSTL 1.1 URI adds the name jsp to the URI path.

The page next creates a JavaBean from the Questions class and prints out the value of its topic property. It then sets the topic property to a different value and prints that out. Next, it uses two <c:if> tags to control the creation of another row in the table.

The next part of the page uses nested <c:forEach> tags to create a two-dimensional table and to fill the table with the result of multiplying the numbers one through five against themselves.

This example should give you a fair idea of how to get started using some of the other tags in the JSTL. There is, of course, much more information in the JSTL specification, available at the Jakarta web site and at java.sun.com.

OTHER TAG LIBRARIES

The JSTL is certainly not the only tag library available to you. There are many more commercial and free tag libraries available. Here is a short listing:

- **Struts:** The Struts tag library provides tags that are useful in building Model-View-Controller (MVC) applications. (You saw a simplistic MVC application at the end of the last chapter, and you'll see the use of MVC architecture again in the next chapter.) It is available from the Apache web site at http://struts.apache.org/.
- **Jakarta Tag Libraries:** In addition to the JSTL, the Apache Software Foundation has well over 20 different tag libraries that you can use in web applications. These libraries are listed on the Jakarta tag libraries web page at http://jakarta.apache.org/taglibs/index.html.

Continued

- **JNDI:** This library is also available from Jakarta. It provides tags for using the Java Naming and Directory Interface (JNDI) API. As you will see throughout this book, you will often use JNDI to look up resources in your web applications. More information about JNDI can be found at `http://java.sun.com/products/jndi/`. The tag library is at `http://jakarta.apache.org/taglibs/doc/jndi-doc/intro.html`.
- **BEA WebLogic Portal JSP Tag Libraries:** This tag library from BEA provides standard tags for working with BEA's web portal. For more information, see `http://edocs.beasys.com/wlac/portals/docs/tagscontents.html`.
- **Coldbeans Bar Charts:** This is one of many tag libraries available from `www.servletsuite.com/jsp.htm`. This library provides tags for creating horizontal and vertical bar charts.
- **Orion EJB:** Available at `www.orionserver.com/tags/ejbtags/`, this library provides tags for using EJBs.
- **JSPTags.com:** Not a single tag library, but a whole collection of them, can be found at `http://jsptags.com/tags/index.jsp`. If you can't find what you need here, you'll probably need to develop it yourself.

With all these resources, it should be easy to find a tag library with the functionality that you need for your web application. Once you have a tag library, using it in your web application is as easy as 1–2–3:

1. Unpack the library and add the `.jar` files to your application.
2. Change the `web.xml` file to map the URIs to the library location.
3. Add the `taglib` directive to the pages that will use the JSTL tags, and then use the tags.

Additionally, if you can't find an existing tag library with the functionality you need, you can apply what you learned about simple and classic tag handlers and write your own tag library.

Summary

So that's the nickel tour of advanced JSP topics. We spent some time getting to know the Expression Language (EL) in some detail, and we spent a lot of time with custom actions and seeing how to implement tag extensions. After that, we took a quick look at the JSP Standard Tag Library (JSTL).

By no means, though, did we cover everything on those topics. There are many other features of EL, tag extensions, and the JSTL. What we did look at, though, was the fundamental information, which will allow you to sit down and start using these technologies. After you have spent a little time writing tag extensions or EL expressions, you can start delving into the more complex material.

After having read this chapter, you should know:

- EL expressions provide a simple syntax for using expressions with attributes and template text.
- EL expressions are very Java-like in their syntax.

- Custom actions provide a way to hide the Java code from the page designer.
- Tag handlers are the Java classes that implement a custom action. You will usually extend `SimpleTagSupport`, `TagSupport`, or `BodyTagSupport` when creating a tag handler.
- Deploying a tag library is an easy, three-step procedure (copy `jar` files and `tld` files, add mapping to `web.xml`, and add a `taglib` directive and tags to the JSP page).
- The JSTL provides a library of standard tags that can be used for many basic functions.

If you want to dig deeper into JSP and other advanced topics, we recommend *Pro JSP, Third Edition*, by Simon Brown (Apress, 2003; ISBN 1-59059-225-5), and *JavaServer Pages, 3rd Edition*, by Hans Bergsten (O'Reilly, 2003; ISBN 0-59600-5636).

Exercises

1. Implement a client web page that has numerous input elements such as text fields, buttons, check boxes, radio buttons, and so on. Using only EL, create a JSP page that echoes back to the caller the request parameters from the request sent by the web page.
2. Modify `Jsp_Ex05` to include two additional topics in addition to the EL topics. Also, add a page that the user can use to select the desired topic.
3. Write two custom actions, where one action is nested inside the other action. For example, with standard actions, a `<param>` tag is nested inside a `<useBean>` tag. Do something similar with your tags.
4. When using a classic tag handler, investigate if there is any difference in how the tag handler methods are called for the two different forms of the empty tag: `<empty/>` and `<empty></empty>`. Perform the same investigation for simple tag handlers.
5. Develop a JSP that uses the `sql` tag library of the JSTL to communicate with a database. (You may want to defer this exercise until after completing Chapter 7.)
6. Use the Jakarta tag libraries (`http://jakarta.apache.org/taglibs/index.html`) to create one or more JSP pages. Here are some ideas:
   - Use the Scrape tag library to search and scrape book information from an online bookstore.
   - Use the I18N library to create a JSP that displays in two or more languages based on user preference.
   - Use the Random tag library to create a web application that simulates a dice rolling game or some other game that relies on chance.

CHAPTER 5

■ ■ ■

JavaServer Faces

JavaServer Faces (JSF), a relatively new technology in the Java EE world, is designed to further simplify web application development. JSF makes it easy to build user interface components and pages, and connect those components to business objects. It also automates the process of bean usage and page navigation.

JSF builds on the experience gained from JSP, Servlet, and various other web application frameworks. In particular, JSF builds on the Apache Struts project. This is not surprising in light of the fact that the creator of Struts is the lead specification engineer for JSF. (If you're a Struts enthusiast, you can even use JSF with Struts; see `http://struts.apache.org`.)

In this chapter, you will learn:

- Why JSF was developed and how it helps you to create dynamic user interfaces
- How to use custom tags for JSF components in JSP pages
- How to use managed beans with JSF components
- How to control page navigation
- How to convert data and validate input

Introduction to JSF

The JSF specification lists the following ways that JSF helps web application developers to create user interfaces (UIs):

- Makes it easy to construct a UI from a set of reusable UI components
- Simplifies migration of application data to and from the UI
- Helps manage UI state across server requests
- Provides a simple model for wiring client-generated events to server-side application code
- Allows custom UI components to be easily built and reused

UI development is easier because UI components are provided as reusable objects. A number of classes, corresponding to UI components, are part of the JSF specification and implementation. Rather than needing to worry about the syntax of page layout, you simply drop the UI components into your application. A custom render kit and rendering process convert the components into appropriate page layout code. The JSF implementation comes with a default render kit for HTML, but the same JSF code can be rendered by other render kits for other client systems. This means that you can use the same JSF code for a variety of client systems, and use different render kits to customize the UI for each client system.

Moving application data to and from the UI is simplified by letting the JSF implementation handle the mechanics of data transfer. You simply specify which data goes where, and the JSF implementation handles the process of moving the data from UI objects to business objects and vice versa. The JSF implementation automatically manages state across user requests, so you do not need to manage or implement any session handling.

As with data, JSF provides an easy way to manage event handling. You specify the events of interest and the business objects or classes to handle the events, and the JSF implementation takes care of calling the appropriate methods to handle any events that are generated. The JSF event-handling model is similar to models used in other UI frameworks, such as Java Swing. Specifically, this means that multiple event listeners can respond to a single event.

Finally, because JSF is based on reusable components, it provides a design that allows you to easily create and integrate your own components or third-party components into your JSF-enabled applications.

■ **Note** As with all the Java EE technologies, detailed information about the technology can be found in the JSF specification (`http://java.sun.com/j2ee/javaserverfaces`).

The Relationship Between JSF and Other Java EE Technologies

Within Java EE, technologies like JSP pages, Servlets, and EJBs are stand-alone technologies. You could, if you wanted to, create an application using just EJBs, Servlets, or JSP pages.

JSF is different because it is a *supporting* technology. You use it in conjunction with JSP pages, Servlets, or EJBs.

The primary design pattern of JSF is the Model-View-Controller (MVC) pattern. MVC separates an application architecture into three categories of components: model, view, and controller. The model is the abstraction of all the domain data in the system. It is the bank account in a banking application, or a shopping cart in an e-commerce system. The view is the visualization of the model. In a web application, the view consists of the HTML pages and the components that create the HTML pages sent to web browsers, the WAP pages sent to mobile devices, or the UI components sent to a dedicated client. The controller is the set of components that manage the communications between model and view.

As you've learned in the previous chapters, you can create UIs with JSP. In fact, as you saw, JSP was designed to make the view component of a web application easy to create and manage. It is also possible, if not as easy, to create UIs with Servlets or EJBs. Combining JSF with any of these other technologies makes UI creation—and integration of the model, view, and controller—easier by far. JSF brings a component-based model to web application development that is similar to the model that has been used in stand-alone GUI applications for years.

To use JSF with Servlets and EJBs, you use the components that make up JSF directly; that is, within your Servlet or EJB, you explicitly create instances of UI components and use the UI classes directly. However, rather than go through that here, we will focus exclusively on using JSF with JSP. The JSF implementation includes a tag library of custom tags that you can use with JSP pages to easily create JSF-enabled applications.

Request Processing Lifecycle

Regardless of whether you are using JSF with JSP pages, Servlets, or EJBs, each request/response flow that involves JSF follows a certain lifecycle. Several different kinds of request/response cycles can occur in a JSF-enabled application. You can have requests that come from a previously rendered JSF page (a JSF request) and a request that comes from a non-JSF page (a non-JSF request). Likewise, you can have JSF responses and non-JSF responses. We are concerned with these three request/response pairs:

- Non-JSF request generates JSF response
- JSF request generates JSF response
- JSF request generates non-JSF response

Of course, you can also have a non-JSF request that generates a non-JSF response. Since this does not involve JSF in any way, the JSF lifecycle does not apply.

Recall that JSP pages have a relatively simple lifecycle. A JSP page source is compiled into a page implementation class. When a web server receives a request, that request is passed to the container, which passes the request to the page class. The page class processes the request, and then writes the response back to the client. When other pages are included or the request is forwarded, or when an exception occurs, the process is a little more involved, but basically, a small set of classes processes a request and sends a response back.

When using JSF, the lifecycle is a little more involved. This is due to the fact that the core of JSF is the MVC pattern, which has several implications. User actions in JSF-generated views take place in a client that does not have a permanent connection to the server. The delivery of user actions or page events is delayed until a new connection is established. The JSF lifecycle must handle this delay between event and event processing. Also, the JSF lifecycle must ensure the view is correct before rendering the view. To ensure that the business state is never invalid, the JSF system includes a phase for validating inputs and another for updating the model only after all inputs pass validation.

■ **Note** In MVC, the presentation of data (the *view*) is separate from its representation in the system (the *model*). When the model is updated, the controller sends a message to the view, telling the view to update its presentation. When the user takes some action with the presentation, the controller sends a message to the model, telling the model to update its data. In JSF, the model is composed of business objects that are usually implemented as JavaBeans, the controller is the JSF implementation, and the UI components are the view. The MVC architecture is discussed in more detail in Chapter 6.

The JSF lifecycle has six phases, as defined by the JSF specification:

- **Restore view:** In this phase, the JSF implementation restores the objects and data structures that represent the view of the request. Of course, if this is the client's first visit to a page, the JSF implementation must create the view. When a JSF implementation creates and renders a JSF-enabled page, it creates UI objects for each view component. The components are stored in a component tree, and the state of the UI view is saved for subsequent requests. If this is a subsequent request, the previously saved UI view is retrieved for the processing of the current request.

- **Apply request values:** Any data that was sent as part of the request is passed to the appropriate UI objects that compose the view. Those objects update their state with the data values. Data can come from input fields in a web form, from cookies sent as part of the request, or from request headers. Note that this does not yet update the business objects that compose the model. It only updates the UI components with the new data.

- **Process validations:** The data that was submitted with the form is validated. As with the previous phase, this does not yet update the business objects in the application. This is because if the JSF implementation began to update the business objects as data was validated, and a piece of data failed validation, the model would be partially updated and in an invalid state.

- **Update model values:** After all validations are complete, the business objects that make up the application are updated with the validated data from the request. In addition, if any of the data needs to be converted to a different format (for example, converting a `String` to a `Date` object) to update the model, the conversion occurs in this phase. Conversion is needed when the data type of a property is not a `String` or a Java primitive.

- **Invoke application:** At this point in the lifecycle, any events that were generated during previous phases and that have not yet been handled are passed to the web application so that it can complete any other processing of the request that is required.

- **Render response:** The response UI components are rendered, and the response is sent to the client. The state of the UI components is saved so that the component tree can be restored when the client sends another request.

For a JSF-enabled application, the thread of execution for a request/response cycle can flow through each phase, in the order listed here and as shown in Figure 5-1. However, depending on the request, and what happens during the processing and response, not every request will flow through all six phases.

In Figure 5-1, you can see a number of optional paths through the lifecycle. For example, if errors occur during any of the phases, the flow of execution transfers immediately to the render response phase, skipping any remaining phases. Also, if at any point in the lifecycle the request processing is complete and a non-JSF response is to be sent to the client, the flow of execution can exit the lifecycle without completing further phases.

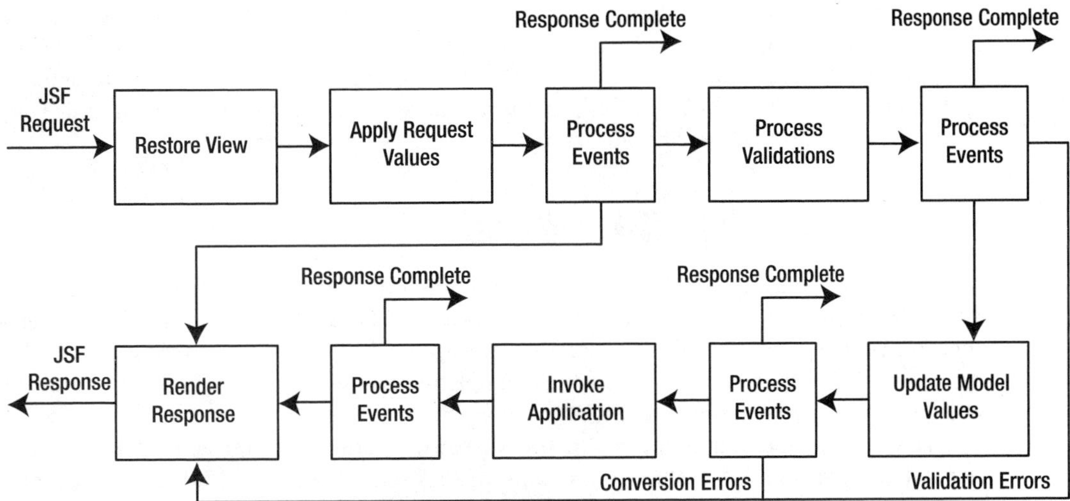

Figure 5-1. *When a request is sent to a JSF enabled application, the request can potentially encompass all six phases of the JSF lifecycle.*

Installing JSF

To run the examples in this chapter, you will need to obtain and install a copy of the JSF reference implementation, the JSP Standard Tag Library (JSTL) reference implementation, and a JSP web container or an application server that supports Servlet 2.3 and JSP 1.2 or later.

If you are running the current version of Sun's Application Server, you already have JSF and JSTL, so you do not need to take any further action.

If you are running Tomcat 5.0 or 5.5, you need to download JSF from `http://java.sun.com/j2ee/javaserverfaces/download.html` and the JSTL from `http://jakarta.apache.org/taglibs/doc/standard-doc/intro.html`. For now, simply unpack each distribution into a directory of your choice, remembering where that directory is.

There are two ways that you can make JSF and JSTL available to your web application running in Tomcat. Both involve putting the following eight JAR files, which are located in the `lib` directory of each distribution, into a location that can be accessed by the server or the web application.

- Six JSF JARs: `commons-beanutils.jar`, `commons-collections.jar`, `commons-digester.jar`, `commons-logging.jar`, `jsf-api.jar`, and `jsf-impl.jar`
- Two JSTL JARs: `jstl.jar` and `standard.jar`

If, for some reason, you want only a particular application to have access to JSF and JSTL, you can place the JAR files from these two APIs into the `WEB-INF/lib` directory of the particular web application. Then only that application will have access to those libraries. If you have another JSF application, that application would also need access to those files in its own `WEB-INF/lib` directory.

Alternatively, if you have several JSF applications, you can put the JAR files into a common location. For Tomcat, that location is `tomcat_dir/common/lib`. When the JAR files are located in the common directory, then every application in the application server has access to them. Note that if you copy the JAR files into the common directory while the server is running, you may need to restart the Tomcat server so that the new JAR files can be loaded.

Using JSF with JSP Pages

Now that you've had an introduction to JSF, let's jump right into creating and deploying a simple JSF application that shows how to use JSF with JSP. Because JSP pages are easy to implement and deploy, this example will clearly demonstrate how to use JSF in a web application. Also, the JSF specification requires that all JSF implementations support JSP pages and provide custom actions corresponding to JSF UI components.

The JSF implementation from Sun comes with two libraries of custom actions that you can use with JSP pages: HTML custom actions and core custom actions. The HTML custom actions are for components that vary based on the render kit used. These custom actions are used to create HTML elements. As shown in Table 5-1, the HTML custom actions fall into five categories or elements: input, output, selection, commands, and miscellaneous.

Table 5-1. *HTML Custom Actions*

Category	Elements	Purpose
Input	`h:inputHidden`, `h:inputSecret`, `h:inputText`, `h:inputTextarea`	Create various kinds of input elements
Output	`h:message`, `h:messages`, `h:outputFormat`, `h:outputLabel`, `h:outputLink`, `h:outputText`	Create various kinds of output elements
Selection	`h:selectBooleanCheckbox`, `h:selectManyCheckbox`, `h:selectManyListbox`, `h:selectManyMenu`, `h:selectOneListbox`, `h:selectOneMenu`, `h:selectOneRadio`	Create drop-down menus, list boxes, radio buttons, and check boxes
Commands	`h:commandButton`, `h:commandLink`	Create buttons or links that cause form submission
Miscellaneous	`h:dataTable`, `h:form`, `h:graphicImage`, `h:panelGrid`, `h:panelGroup`, `h:column`	Create various HTML elements such as tables, forms, and panels

The core custom actions create UI elements that are independent of the render kit. These actions are usually used in conjunction with the HTML actions listed in Table 5-1 to modify the behavior of those actions. Table 5-2 shows all the core custom actions, listed by category.

Table 5-2. *Core Custom Actions*

Category	Elements	Purpose
Converters	`f:convertDateTime`, `f:convertNumber`, `f:converter`	Standard converters
Listeners	`f:actionListener`, `f:valueChangeListener`	Specify a listener for a component
Miscellaneous	`f:attribute`, `f:loadBundle`, `f:param`, `f:verbatim`	Add attributes or parameters, load a resource bundle, and output verbatim HTML template text
Selection	`f:selectItem`, `f:selectItems`	Specify selection items for HTML selection elements
Validators	`f:validateDoubleRange`, `f:validateLength`, `f:validateLongRange`, `f:validator`	Standard validators
View	`f:facet`, `f:subview`, `f:view`	Create a JSF view or subview

■ Tip If you unpack the JSF implementation to your hard drive, a directory of documentation for the custom actions will be saved to the hard drive in `jsf_root/tlddocs/index.html`. This documentation is similar to the Javadoc documentation created with Java source files. For full details on using custom actions, refer to this documentation.

In this section, you will see a number of these custom tags in action. We will discuss these tags as we go along.

Creating a Simple JSF Application

Our example simulates a flight reservation system. Figure 5-2 shows the directory structure of the sample application.

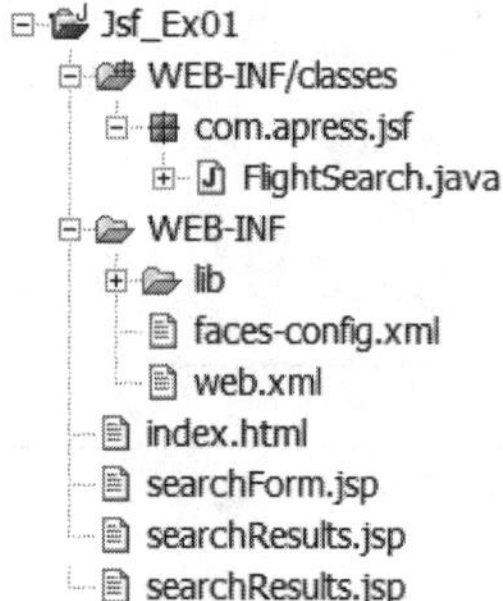

Figure 5-2. *The directory structure of the Jsf_Ex01 example*

Implementing a JavaBean

We'll start this example by showing the JavaBean class that represents the business layer of the web application. This bean will be connected to the presentation layer by the JSF system. It represents the information necessary to search for a flight in the system. The `FlightSearch` class, shown in Listing 5-1, is used to store the search parameters entered by the user. Although there are various parameters that can be used when searching for a flight, for this first example, we have chosen to include the following: origination airport, destination airport, departure date and time, and arrival date and time.

Listing 5-1. *FlightSearch.java*

```
package com.apress.jsf;

public class FlightSearch {
  String origination;
  String destination;
  String departDate;
  String departTime;
  String returnDate;
  String returnTime;

  public String getDepartDate() {
    return departDate;
  }

  public void setDepartDate(String departDate) {
    this.departDate = departDate;
  }
```

```
  public String getDepartTime() {
    return departTime;
  }

  public void setDepartTime(String departTime) {
    this.departTime = departTime;
  }

  public String getDestination() {
    return destination;
  }

  public void setDestination(String destination) {
    this.destination = destination;
  }

  public String getOrigination() {
    return origination;
  }

  public void setOrigination(String origination) {
    this.origination = origination;
  }

  public String getReturnDate() {
    return returnDate;
  }

  public void setReturnDate(String returnDate) {
    this.returnDate = returnDate;
  }

  public String getReturnTime() {
    return returnTime;
  }

  public void setReturnTime(String returnTime) {
    this.returnTime = returnTime;
  }
}
```

Looking at the class, you can see that it is a standard JavaBean. There is no explicit constructor, so the compiler provides a default no-argument constructor. There are fields for all the parameters we want to store, and methods for getting and setting each of the fields. This means that all the properties of the class are exposed as read-write properties to the web application. This will allow one part of the application to set the properties and a different part to read the properties. We'll discuss the role of JavaBeans in JSF implementations in more detail later in this chapter, in the "Using Managed Beans" section.

Before deploying this example, you will need to compile the `FlightSearch.java` source into a class file. Since this source file uses classes from only the `java.lang` package and does not use any special APIs or classes, you should be able to compile it without needing to reset your classpath. Use your IDE to compile the class, or use `javac` from the command line.

Implementing the View Components

The next part of our example is a web page to accept the user's inputs for searching for a flight. This will be a JSP page with input fields for the origination, destination, departure date and time, and return date and time. Listing 5-2 shows the initial page in our application, `searchForm.jsp`. If you created any of the examples in Chapter 3, you will recall that those examples also used input fields in an HTML page generated by a JSP page. The `searchForm.jsp` page also uses input fields, but as you will see, they are slightly different from the HTML input fields we used in Chapter 3.

Listing 5-2. *searchForm.jsp*

```
<html>
  <%@ taglib uri="http://java.sun.com/jsf/core" prefix="f" %>
  <%@ taglib uri="http://java.sun.com/jsf/html" prefix="h" %>

  <f:view>
  <head>
    <title>Freedom Airlines Online Flight Reservation System</title>
  </head>
  <body>
    <h:form>
      <h2>Search Flights</h2>
      <table>
        <tr><td colspan="4">Where and when do you want to travel?</td></tr>
        <tr>
          <td colspan="2">Leaving from:</td>
          <td colspan="2">Going to:</td>
        </tr>
        <tr>
          <td colspan="2">
            <h:inputText value="#{flight.origination}" size="35"/>
          </td>
          <td colspan="2">
            <h:inputText value="#{flight.destination}" size="35"/>
          </td>
```

```
        </tr>
        <tr>
          <td colspan="2">Departing:</td>
          <td colspan="2">Returning:</td>
        </tr>
        <tr>
          <td>
            <h:inputText value="#{flight.departDate}"/>
          </td>
          <td>
            <h:inputText value="#{flight.departTime}"/>
          </td>
          <td>
            <h:inputText value="#{flight.returnDate}"/>
          </td>
          <td>
            <h:inputText value="#{flight.returnTime}"/>
          </td>
        </tr>
      </table>
      <p>
      <h:commandButton value="Search" action="submit"/>
      </p>
    </h:form>
  </body>
  </f:view>
</html>
```

Throughout Chapter 4, we talked about ways to remove Java code from JSP pages. And as we stated at the beginning of this chapter, JSF provides another way to do this. Looking at Listing 5-2, you can see there is not a single declaration or scriptlet within the page. There are only two `taglib` directives, some standard HTML tags, and some tags that look like tags for custom actions. The tags that begin with `f:` or `h:` come from the tag libraries defined in the `taglib` directives.

As you might guess from the `taglib` directive, the tags that use the prefix `f:` provide the core JSF functionality for the page, and tags that use the prefix `h:` provide HTML elements for the page. There is one JSF tag in the page: the `view` tag. Any page that includes JSF elements must have the `view` tag as the outermost JSF tag. The rest of the JSF tags in the page create HTML elements in the page. The `form` tag creates an HTML form. The `input` tags create input text fields in the form. The `commandButton` tag creates a button in the form.

If you are familiar with HTML forms, you know that every HTML form requires an `action` attribute and can include an optional `method` attribute. The `action` attribute tells the web browser where to submit the form data. The `method` attribute tells the browser whether to submit a `GET` request or a `POST` request. The JSF tag does not use either of these attributes. The JSP specification requires that all JSF forms post to the same URL from which they were served. (If form data is submitted to the same page, how then does the application process the data and move between pages in the application? This question will be answered in Listing 5-4 and in detail in the "Controlling Page Navigation" section later in this chapter.) The specification also requires that all JSF forms use the POST method for submitting form data to web applications. Since both the method and action have mandatory values that the programmer cannot change, they do not need to be specified in the JSF tag.

Also note that the input tags have a different syntax than standard HTML for the value attribute. If you read the coverage of Expression Language (EL) in Chapter 4, you will recognize the #{} syntax as being EL syntax. With EL, an expression such as #{flight.origination} is used when the JSP page wants to access a property of an object in the page. The name to the left of the dot is the name of an object accessible by the page; the name to the right of the dot is a property of the object to be accessed. In Listing 5-1, you can see a property named origination with associated set and get methods. When this JavaBean is made available to a JSP page, that page can read or write the property when we use the #{flight.origination} expression in the page. The searchForm.jsp page uses the expression with input fields. When we submit this page to the application, the values entered into the fields will be used to set the property in the JavaBean.

In a real web application that provided an online flight reservation system, the system would search for and display flights after the user submits a request. In this example, however, we will start by simply echoing the search parameters back to the user. This is accomplished in the searchResults.jsp page, shown in Listing 5-3.

Listing 5-3. *searchResults.jsp*

```
<html>
  <%@ taglib uri="http://java.sun.com/jsf/core" prefix="f" %>
  <%@ taglib uri="http://java.sun.com/jsf/html" prefix="h" %>

  <f:view>
    <head>
      <title>Freedom Airlines Online Flight Reservation System</title>
    </head>
    <body>
      <h3>You entered these search parameters</h3>
      <p>Origination: <h:outputText value="#{flight.origination}"/>
      <p>Depart date: <h:outputText value="#{flight.departDate}"/>
      <p>Depart time: <h:outputText value="#{flight.departTime}"/>
      <p>Destination: <h:outputText value="#{flight.destination}"/>
      <p>Return date: <h:outputText value="#{flight.returnDate}"/>
      <p>Return time: <h:outputText value="#{flight.returnTime}"/>
      <p>Trip type  : <h:outputText value="#{flight.tripType}"/>
    </body>
  </f:view>
</html>
```

As with searchForm.jsp, the outermost JSF tag is the f:view tag. Within the view, the page uses h:outputText tags. The outputText tags are obviously used to output text to the page. As with the inputText tags, they use the #{object.property} syntax to access a property of an object in the page. In this case, the object is a JavaBean identified by the name flight. The outputText tag reads the property from the object and displays it in the web page generated by this JSP page.

So, now you've seen the three main parts of the web application: an input page, an output page, and a JavaBean to hold the business data. In terms of the MVC pattern, `FlightSearch` is the model, and `searchForm.jsp` and `searchResults.jsp` are the view. What we haven't shown yet is the controller. We also haven't explained how the controller knows where to find the model or the view, and how the controller knows the logic flow through the web application. In the MVC example in Chapter 3, we needed to specifically code the flow of control into the JSP pages. In the listings presented here, you can see that `searchForm.jsp` or `searchResults.jsp` do not have any information that indicates how control is transferred from page to page. Now let's see how this control is managed.

Directing Traffic in the JSF Application

Information about the view components in the web application, and information about how control flows through the application is contained in a special configuration file named `faces-config.xml`, shown in Listing 5-4. Although `faces-config.xml` can contain a lot of different information about a web application, for this example, we need it to do only two things: identify the flow of control from `searchForm.jsp` to `searchResults.jsp` and identify the JavaBean used by the application.

Listing 5-4. *faces-config.xml*

```
<?xml version="1.0"?>

<faces-config xmlns="http://java.sun.com/xml/ns/javaee"
     xmlns:xsi="http://www.w3.org/2001/XMLSchema-instance"
     xsi:schemaLocation="http://java.sun.com/xml/ns/javaee/web-facesconfig_1_2.xsd"
     version="1.2">
     <navigation-rule>
      <from-view-id>/searchForm.jsp</from-view-id>
      <navigation-case>
         <from-outcome>submit</from-outcome>
         <to-view-id>/searchResults.jsp</to-view-id>
         <redirect/>
      </navigation-case>
   </navigation-rule>

   <managed-bean>
      <managed-bean-name>flight</managed-bean-name>
      <managed-bean-class>com.apress.jsf.FlightSearch</managed-bean-class>
      <managed-bean-scope>session</managed-bean-scope>
   </managed-bean>
</faces-config>
```

The `faces-config.xml` file identifies the JavaBeans used by the web application in the `managed-bean` element. You will have a `managed-bean` element for every JavaBean used by your web application. The `managed-bean` element in Listing 5-4 contains three subelements:

- The first subelement is the name used to identify the bean in a JSP page. In Listing 5-4 the name is given as `flight`; this is why both `searchForm.jsp` and `searchResults.jsp` can access an instance of the bean using the expression `#{flight…}`.
- The second element is the fully qualified class name of the JavaBean class. This name tells the JSP container which class to load and instantiate to create an instance of the JavaBean.
- The third element identifies the scope of the object. Session scope means that the object exists for the entire interaction between the user and the application. The container must persist the object across multiple request/response cycles, until the user's session is terminated. We will look at all this in more detail in the "Using Managed Beans" section later in this chapter.

The `faces-config.xml` file is also used to tell the controller how to navigate through the application. Navigation flow is specified in `navigation-rule` elements. Our example needs only one element. In general, a `navigation-rule` element identifies the start page, a condition, and which page to navigate to when the condition occurs.

In our example, the start page is `searchForm.jsp`. If the page request is submitted with an outcome of submit, control is transferred to `searchResults.jsp`. Looking at Listing 5-2, you can see that the `commandButton` element has an action of `submit`; when the button is clicked and the form is submitted, this action matches the `from-outcome` of the `navigation-rule`.

The `navigation-rule` element also includes an empty `redirect` element. With this element, the response is created by causing the browser to redirect to the `searchResults.jsp` page, which also updates the address bar in the browser. Without this element, the response is still created correctly and sent to the browser, but the address bar of the browser will not be updated and will still display the address for the submitting page. We will look at navigation in more detail in the "Controlling Page Navigation" section later in this chapter.

We need just one final piece for our web application. In many of the examples in Chapter 3 and Chapter 4, we identified a default page to be served to users when they first access the web application. In this example, our default page will be a standard HTML page that redirects to the correct URL for a JSF application. Listing 5-5 shows `index.html`.

Listing 5-5. *index.html*

```
<html>
   <head>
      <meta http-equiv="Refresh" content= "0; URL=searchForm.faces"/>
   </head>
</html>
```

You can see that that the redirect URL is `searchForm.faces`. However, there is no component in our application named `searchForm.faces`. How then does the web application know which page to serve? All requests that are JSF requests are directed to the controller for the application, which is a Servlet supplied as part of the JSF reference implementation. As you will see when we deploy this example, we will specify that all URLs of the form `*.faces` should be sent to the controller Servlet. This Servlet then converts the `searchForm.faces` request to `searchForm.jsp`, processes the JSP page, and sends the response to the browser.

Deploying the Application to the Sun Application Server

As you've seen in the previous chapters, you can deploy applications to the Sun Application Server by using the Deployment Tool. To deploy this first JSF example, follow these general steps (for more detailed instructions on using the Deployment Tool, refer to the examples in Chapters 2, 3, and 4):

1. Create a web application in the Deployment Tool.
2. Add the files `index.html`, `searchForm.jsp`, `searchResults.jsp`, `faces-config.xml`, and `FlightSearch.class` to the application, ensuring they are in the correct location (see Figure 5-2).
3. Configure the controller Servlet `javax.faces.webapp.FacesServlet` using the name `Faces Servlet`.
4. Configure the welcome file list to include `index.html` as the welcome page.
5. Create a Servlet mapping so that all URLs that include the pattern `*.faces` are directed to the Servlet named `Faces Servlet`.
6. Save and deploy the application to the server.

Deploying the Application to the Tomcat Server

To deploy the application to the Tomcat server, start by creating an application structure like that shown in Figure 5-2. You will also need to write the `web.xml` deployment descriptor, shown in Listing 5-6.

Listing 5-6. *web.xml for Jsf_Ex01*

```
<?xml version="1.0"?>

<web-app xmlns="http://java.sun.com/xml/ns/javaee"
  xmlns:xsi="http://www.w3.org/2001/XMLSchema-instance"
  xsi:schemaLocation="http://java.sun.com/xml/ns/javaee/web-app_2_5.xsd"
  version="2.5">

  <display-name>Jsf_Ex01 - Simple JSF Application</display-name>

  <servlet>
    <servlet-name>Faces Servlet</servlet-name>
    <servlet-class>javax.faces.webapp.FacesServlet</servlet-class>
    <load-on-startup>1</load-on-startup>
  </servlet>

  <servlet-mapping>
    <servlet-name>Faces Servlet</servlet-name>
    <url-pattern>*.faces</url-pattern>
  </servlet-mapping>
```

```
  <welcome-file-list>
    <welcome-file>index.html</welcome-file>
  </welcome-file-list>
</web-app>
```

The deployment descriptor identifies the controller Servlet (`Faces Servlet`) for the application, specifies a Servlet mapping for which requests should be sent to the controller Servlet, and designates the welcome file for the application.

As explained in the "Installing JSF" section earlier in this chapter, you need to copy the JSF and JSTL JAR files into the application's `WEB-INF/lib` directory or into the Tomcat `common/lib` directory. Copy the entire directory into the Tomcat `webapps` directory, and deployment is complete.

Alternatively, after creating the directory structure, you can package all the application files into a WAR file using the Java `jar` command. Once the WAR file has been created, copy it into the Tomcat `webapps` directory. Tomcat will automatically unpack the WAR file and start the application.

Running the Application

When you have successfully deployed the application to the server, open a web browser to the address `http://localhost:8080/Jsf_Ex01`. (As always, replace `localhost` and `8080` with the correct values for your installation, and replace `Jsf_Ex01` with the correct application context name, if you created and deployed your JSF application with a different context name.)

The application starts by loading the `index.html` page, which immediately redirects to `searchForm.faces`. Because of the Servlet mapping in `web.xml`, this request is directed to the `Faces Servlet` controller. The controller knows that `searchForm.faces` is a request for the `searchForm.jsp` component. If this is the first request for `searchForm.jsp`, it is compiled by the server, and then sent to the browser, as shown in Figure 5-3.

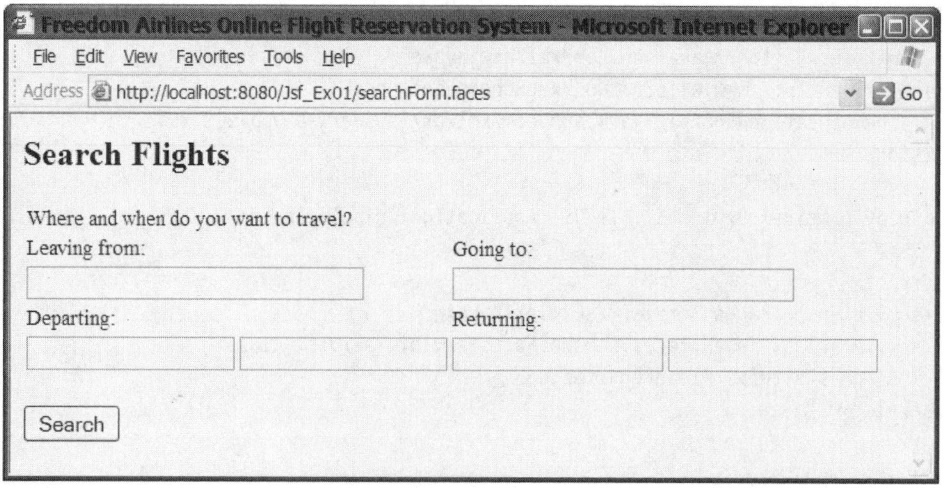

Figure 5-3. *The searchForm.jsp as sent to the browser*

If you examine the source for the page, you can see that the JSF `form` tag has been translated to an HTML `form` tag. As mentioned earlier, the method for the form is `POST` and the action is the URL for `searchForm.jsp`. Even though it appears that the form submits to the same JSP page, the controller Servlet will use the navigation rules in the `faces-config.xml` file to ensure page navigation occurs correctly. Also, each JSF input tag has been translated into an HTML input tag. Here is an extract from the HTML source showing these points:

```
<form id="_id0" method="post" action="/Jsf_Ex01/searchForm.faces"
      enctype="application/x-www-form-urlencoded">

  <h2>Search Flights</h2>
  <table>
    <tr><td colspan="4">Where and when do you want to travel?
    </td></tr>
    <tr>
      <td colspan="2">Leaving from:</td>
      <td colspan="2">Going to:</td>
    </tr>
    <tr>
      <td colspan="2">
        <input type="text" name="_id0:_id1" size="35" />
```

Enter values for each of the input fields. Since each property of the `FlightSearch` JavaBean is of the `String` type, you can enter anything you want into each text field. When you have finished entering values, click the Search button. The request is passed to the server, and the response generated by `searchResults.jsp` is sent back to the browser, as shown in Figure 5-4.

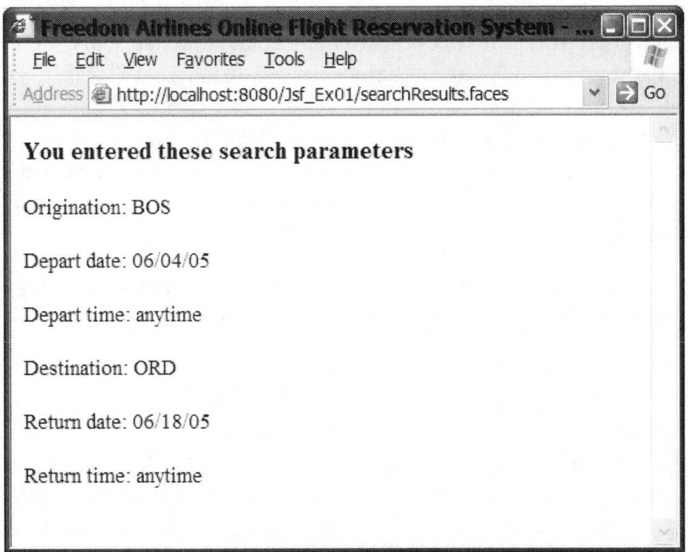

Figure 5-4. *The searchResults.jsp response from submitting the form in searchForm.jsp*

Reviewing the JSF Lifecycle for the Sample Application

The JSF_Ex01 application (Listings 5-1 through 5-6) provides examples of two different request/response processes. First, index.html causes a non-JSF request to generate a JSF response when searchForm.jsp is displayed. Then, when searchForm.jsp is submitted, this causes a JSF request to generate a JSF response.

The first request from the browser comes from a standard HTML page and does not contain any data. In the restore view phase, rather than restoring an existing view, a new component tree is created with the components from the view. This will consist of objects that represent the form and each of the input fields. These objects are stored in the component tree. Since no other processing is required, control passes to the render response phase. The UI components are rendered into HTML, and the response is sent to the client.

The lifecycle of the request and response from searchForm.jsp to searchResults.jsp follows the phases illustrated in Figure 5-1. The request from searchForm.jsp causes the component tree to be restored in the restore view phase. Next, the data passed in the form is used to update the state of the view components in the apply request values phase. The process validations phase is next, but since the values are all String types, no conversion is needed, and no validation occurs. Next, the JavaBean is updated with the values from the view in the update model values phase. Nothing occurs in the invoke application phase. Finally, in the render response phase, the view components from searchResults.jsp are translated into HTML, using the data from the JavaBean model, and the response is returned to the client.

Using Managed Beans

As noted earlier in this chapter, the primary design pattern of JSF is the MVC pattern. As you saw in the previous example, JSF custom actions and JSP pages form the view in the MVC architecture. The Faces Servlet provided by a JSF implementation is the controller. However, JSF by itself is not enough to create a working application, because you need the third leg of MVC: the model. JavaBeans provide that part of the MVC pattern. In the example, FlightSearch was the model.

JavaBeans are Java components that can be dropped into Java applications. They are simply Java classes that conform to a certain coding style (documented in the JavaBeans specification at http://java.sun.com/products/javabeans/). For our purposes, there are two aspects of the JavaBeans specification that are important:

- The JavaBean used in the web application must have a no-argument constructor. This allows the container to construct an instance of the JavaBean.
- Any property to be exposed must have a get or set method. If only a get method is present, the property is read-only. If only a set method is used, the property is write-only. If both are present, the property is read-write. The format of the set method name is the word set followed by the name of the property, with the first letter of the property name capitalized. The get method format is the word get followed by the name of the property, again with the first letter of the property name capitalized. For Boolean properties, the method is the word is followed by the name of the property.

Because JavaBeans follow a particular design, they can be used programmatically, without a developer needing to explicitly write code that uses the JavaBeans. As you saw in the previous example, by simply identifying the JavaBean to the JSF application in the JSP pages and in the configuration file, the JSF implementation was able to use the JavaBean, setting and reading its properties—you didn't need to write any explicit code.

Within the JSF implementation, JavaBeans that are used by a JSF-enabled application are referred to as *managed beans*, because the JSF implementation manages the creation and use of JavaBean objects.

Within a JSF-enabled application, managed beans appear in two contexts:

- The information needed to create and initialize the managed bean is identified within the configuration files of the application.
- The properties and methods of managed beans are referenced in JSP pages using value binding expressions or method binding expressions.

Configuring Managed Beans

You saw one method for identifying the managed bean parameters to the application in the example earlier in this chapter, where we used a file named `faces-config.xml` located in the `WEB-INF` directory of the application. However, the JSF specification identifies several other files that can contain managed bean configuration information. The specification states that configuration files will be searched for as follows:

- The JSF implementation looks for and processes files named `META-INF/faces-config.xml`. This is primarily for JSF components packaged as JAR files that are part of the application.
- The JSF implementation checks the `web.xml` deployment descriptor for a context parameter named `javax.faces.CONFIG_FILES`. If the parameter exists, the value of the parameter must be a comma-delimited list of filenames that will be processed as JSF configuration files. The filenames must be relative paths from the application root to the file, such as `WEB-INF/my-config.xml`.
- Finally, the JSF implementation processes the file `WEB-INF/faces-config.xml`, if it exists.

The configuration files are used to identify the managed beans, provide initialization parameters for the beans, and identify the navigation rules for the application (as described in the "Controlling Page Navigation" section later in this chapter). This information can be placed in a single file, as in Listing 5-4, or it can be split among multiple files. For example, you could put all the bean information into one configuration file and all the navigation information into another configuration file. These multiple files would then be listed in the `web.xml` deployment descriptor.

Identifying Managed Beans

A configuration file provides managed bean information to the application in the element of the configuration file named `managed-bean`. The `managed-bean` element declares a JavaBean that is created and populated by the JSF implementation. If the bean does not yet exist when a page that uses the bean is accessed, the JSF implementation creates the bean based on the information in the `managed-bean` element. Subsequent requests in the same session will access the existing bean.

The managed-bean element has three required subelements:

- managed-bean-name: The string used to identify the bean instance in any JSF component. For example, in Listing 5-4, the bean name was given as flight. In Listings 5-2 and 5-3, we referenced the bean instance using this name.
- managed-bean-class: The fully qualified class name of the class that provides the implementation for the bean.
- managed-bean-scope: The scope of the bean instance. We will look at scope in more depth in the "Identifying Bean Scopes" section a little later in this chapter.

The managed-bean element has a number of optional elements, including description, display-name, icon, and managed-property. The usage of the first three should be relatively obvious, so we will just look at the managed-property, which is used to initialize the properties of a managed bean.

Initializing Bean Properties

Like managed-bean, managed-property can have an optional description, display-name, and icon. It must have a nested property-name element that identifies the name of an instance variable (property) of the class with a set and get method. It can have an optional property-class element that provides the fully qualified class name of the data type of the property. If the data type is not provided, the JSF implementation will attempt to infer the type from the bean class. Finally, it can have one of several elements that initialize the value of the property: <value>, <null-value>, <list-entries>, or <map-entries>. For example, if the property of the bean is a Java primitive or a String, you can use the value element like this:

```
<property-name>myProperty</property-name>
<value>3</value>
```

If the type of the property is a Java object and not a primitive, you can also set the value to null, using this form:

```
<property-name>myProperty</property-name>
<null-value/>
```

If the type of the property is some other managed bean, you can initialize the property by referencing the other bean by the name of the bean instance. So, for example, if you have a managed bean of type MyBean, and you create an instance with the name myBean, you can initialize a property using a value binding expression that is the name of the bean:

```
<managed-bean>
   <managed-bean-name>foo</managed-bean-name>
   <managed-bean-class>com.Foo</managed-bean-class>
   <managed-bean-scope>session</managed-bean-scope>
   <managed-property>
    <value-class>com.MyBean</value-class>
    <property-name>bar</property-name>
    <value>#{myBean}</value>
   </managed-property>
```

```
    </managed-bean>
    <managed-bean>
        <managed-bean-name>myBean</managed-bean-name>
        <managed-bean-class>com.MyBean</managed-bean-class>
        <managed-bean-scope>session</managed-bean-scope>
    </managed-bean>
```

In this snippet, the bean foo has a property of name bar. The type of bar is MyBean. The value of bar is initialized by referencing the name of the MyBean object in the value binding expression #{myBean}. (We'll discuss value binding expressions in more detail in the "Using Value Binding Expressions in JSP Pages" section a little later in this chapter.)

Finally, if the type of the property is List or a subtype of List, or Map or a subtype of Map, you can initialize the List or Map in the configuration file. For example, in Listing 5-1, suppose we wanted to restrict the departTime and arriveTime properties to the values Morning, Afternoon, or Evening. We could create an additional property like this:

```
public class FlightSearch {
  List times;
  //...
}
```

We can then initialize the list like this:

```
<managed-bean>
  <managed-bean-name>flight</managed-bean-name>
  <managed-bean-class>com.apress.jsf.FlightSearch</managed-bean-class>
  <managed-bean-scope>session</managed-bean-scope>
  <managed-property>
    <property-name>times</property-name>
      <list-entries>
      <value>Morning</value>
      <value>Afternoon</value>
      <value>Evening</value>
    </list-entries>
  </managed-property>
</managed-bean>
```

The list-entries element can have an optional value-class element that provides the fully qualified class name of the objects stored in the list. If used, it appears before the value elements. When value-class is used, the JSF implementation will attempt to create objects of that type, initialize those objects with the given values, and store them in the List. You can also use the null-value element to store null values in the list.

Initializing a Map is similar. Suppose you have a property of type Map:

```
public class FlightSearch {
  Map airportNames;
  //...
}
```

You initialize the Map like this:

```
<managed-bean>
  <managed-bean-name>flight</managed-bean-name>
  <managed-bean-class>com.apress.jsf.FlightSearch</managed-bean-class>
  <managed-bean-scope>session</managed-bean-scope>
  <managed-property>
    <property-name>airportNames</property-name>
    <map-entries>
      <key-class>java.lang.String</key-class>
      <value-class>java.lang.String</value-class>
        <map-entry>
        <key>BOS</key>
        <value>Logan Internation Airport</value>
      </map-entry>
      <!-- and so on -->
    </map-entries>
  </managed-property>
</managed-bean>
```

In the element, both key-class and value-class are optional. The JSF implementation will choose appropriate classes if you do not provide either element. There can be zero or more map-entry elements, and each map-entry that appears must have a key and either a value or null-value.

Identifying Bean Scopes

When you configure a JavaBean to be used in a JSF page, you can configure it with one of four different scopes:

- **None:** Objects with this scope are not visible in any JSF page. When used in the configuration file, they indicate JavaBeans that are used by other JavaBeans in the application. Objects with none scope can use other objects with none scope.
- **Request:** Objects with this scope are visible from the start of the request until the end of the request. Request scope starts at the beginning of a request and ends when the response has been sent to the client. If the request is forwarded, the objects are visible in the forwarded page, since that page is still part of the same request/response cycle. Objects with request scope can use other objects with none, request, session, or application scope.
- **Session:** An object with session scope is visible for any request/response cycle that belongs to a session. Objects with this scope have their state persisted between requests and last until the object or the session is invalidated. Objects with session scope can use other objects with none, session, or application scope.
- **Application:** An object with application scope is visible in all request/response cycles for all clients using the application, for as long as the application is active. Objects with application scope can use other objects with none or application scope.

You may recall from Chapter 3 that JavaBeans in JSP pages have similar scopes. The difference is that JSP scope includes an additional scope: page. Since JSF requests often involve navigation between pages, objects with page scope have no value in a JSF application. For example, in the initial example in this chapter, the properties of a JavaBean were set in one JSP page, and those values were displayed in another page. If the `FlightSearch` JavaBean had been given page scope, the `searchResults.jsp` page would not have access to the `FlightSearch` JavaBean, and so would not have been able to display the data stored in the JavaBean.

Most often, you will define your JavaBeans to have session scope. However, in some cases, you may have a JavaBean that encapsulates global data. For example, you may have a JavaBean that holds information common to every page in the application; in that case, you would define the JavaBean to have application scope. JavaBeans that you use only within a single request/response will have request scope.

Using Value Binding Expressions in JSP Pages

When using JSF custom actions in your JSP pages, the JSF implementation can set or get the value of JavaBean properties, based on the tag usage. For example, Listing 5-2 includes this tag:

```
<h:inputText value="#{flight.origination}" size="35"/>
```

■ Caution The syntax in the example shown here is sufficient for Java primitive and `String` values. However, if the property is some other data type, you will probably need to supply a converter as well. See the "Converting Data" section later in this chapter for details.

This is also referred to as a *value binding expression* because it binds the value of some bean property to an attribute or property of some JSF element. When using the syntax of *`object.property`* syntax, which we call *dot notation*, the expression to the left of the dot is some object accessible to the page, and the thing to the right of the dot is some property of the object. You can also chain expressions, like this:

```
object1.object2.object3.property
```

Each expression in the chain, reading from left to right, is evaluated as an object reference, and the final expression is a property of the last object.

Another syntax you can use to write a value binding expression uses brackets to denote the property. We refer to this syntax as *bracket notation*:

```
flight["origination"]
flight['origination']
```

You would use the form with double quotes when using single quotes to delimit attribute values, and use single quotes when double quotes are used to delimit the attribute values. So, the `inputText` element could be written in either of these ways:

```
<h:inputText value="#{flight['origination']}" size="35"/>
<h:inputText value='#{flight["origination"]}' size="35"/>
```

When creating chained expressions, you can freely mix dot and bracket notation. In fact, as you will see shortly, when creating an expression to access a List or Map, mixed notation can be used to create dynamic expressions.

Getting and Setting Bean Properties

When the searchForm.jsp page is rendered, the JSF implementation calls the get method for the origination property of the FlightSearch class to get the value of the property. This value is then included in the rendering of the page. It does this for all the properties that are referenced in the page. When the page is first loaded, the properties of the FlightSearch object have no values, so the page is rendered with empty text fields.

During the processing of the request from searchForm.jsp, the values entered into the form are saved by the UI components that correspond to the UI widgets on the page. After these values are converted as necessary and validated, the JSF implementation updates the model (the FlightSearch object) by calling the set method for the property.

After the model is updated, the lifecycle advances to the render phase, and the searchResults.jsp page (Listing 5-3) is rendered. At this point, the FlightSearch object has some data, and so when the page is rendered, the JSF implementation calls the get methods for the properties that the page displays, and these values are used in the rendering and display of the page.

Notice that by using the same simple #{flight.origination} syntax, the JSF implementation calls different code depending on the current phase of the JSF lifecycle. Note also that the action does not depend on the tag type. The action taken for the h:inputText tag can be either a get or set method of the property, regardless of the fact that the JSF tag renders as an HTML input tag.

Accessing List, Array, and Map Property Types

You can also easily access bean properties that are of type List, array, and Map. You can access an element of the List or array using a value binding expression. For example, earlier we presented a possible List property added to FlightSearch:

```
public class FlightSearch {
  List times;
  //...
}
```

After the bean is initialized, we could access the first value in the list using any of the following expressions:

```
#{flight.times["1"]}
#{flight.times['1']}
#{flight.times[1]}
#{flight .times["var"]}
#{flight .times.var}
#{flight.times[var]}
```

Note For a complete list of valid expression forms, see Section 5.1.2 of the JSF specification.

As mentioned earlier, you can chain expressions together to create a value binding expression. The last expression following the dot, or inside the brackets, must evaluate to an integer or must be convertible to an integer. When updating the model, the JSF implementation will attempt to set the element at the given index. If the given index does not exist, a `PropertyNotFoundException` will occur. When reading from the model, the implementation will call the `get` method to get the element at the given index. Again, if the index does not exist, a `PropertyNotFoundException` will occur.

One difference between value binding expressions for `List` and `Map` objects is that you can use bracket notation to create dynamic value binding expressions. Suppose you had an `object` with some `intProperty` that evaluates to an integer and tried this syntax:

```
flight.times.object.intProperty
```

The expression would cause an evaluation error. The JSF implementation expects `object` to be a property of `times`, which is not the case. However, you can use a mixed form with both dot and bracket notation:

```
flight.times[object.intProperty]
```

When this expression is evaluated, the `object.intProperty` expression evaluates to an integer, which is then used to access the value stored in the `List` at that index. The same syntax can be used when accessing `Map` entries.

Again, suppose you have this `Map` property of `FlightSearch`:

```
public class FlightSearch {
  Map airportNames;
  //...
}
```

Then any of the following expressions will cause the `Map` methods `get(key)` or `set(key, value)` to be called, depending on which lifecycle phase is currently being processed.

```
flight.airportNames.key
flight.airportNames[key]
flight.airportNames["key"]
```

Using Method Binding Expressions in JSP Pages

Just as you can bind managed bean properties to expressions in the JSP page, you can also bind managed bean methods to expressions. You use method binding when setting the attribute values for actions, validators, action listeners, and value change listeners.

The syntax for method binding expressions is the same as the syntax for value binding expressions. You can use either dot or bracket notation. As with value binding expressions, every expression in the chain, except the last expression, is evaluated as an object reference.

The last expression in the chain must be a method name of a method. The method signature must follow a specific pattern, which depends on whether the method binding is used for an action, a validator, an action listener, or a value change listener.

You will see how to use method binding expressions for actions in the "Controlling Page Navigation" section later in this chapter. We will also look at method binding expressions for validators in the "Validating Input" section later in the chapter. For more information about their use with action and value changed listeners, see the JSF specification and the JSF chapter in the Java EE tutorial.

Expanding the JSF Sample Application

Let's update the first example in this chapter (Listings 5-1 through 5-6) to demonstrate some of the concepts we just discussed. For this version, we'll change the search form so that a user is required to select either a one-way trip or a round-trip. We'll also constrain the departure time and return time to be Morning, Afternoon, or Evening, as shown in Figure 5-5.

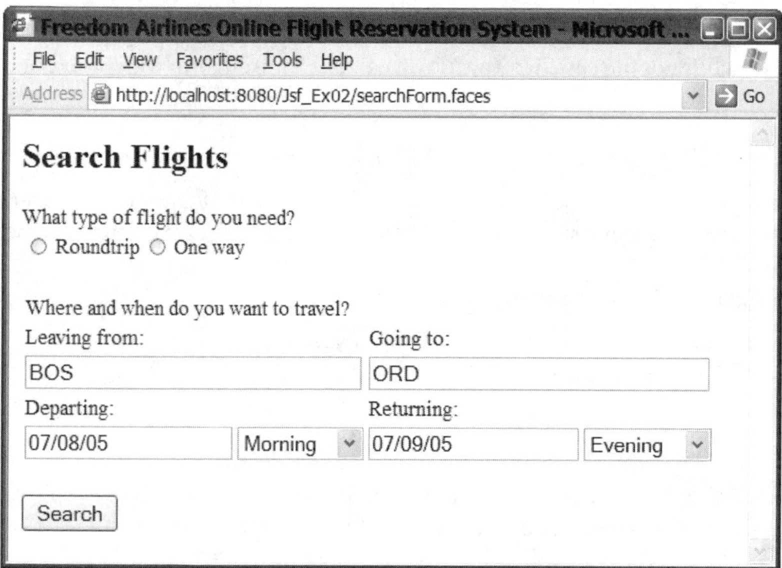

Figure 5-5. *The search form now has radio buttons for one-way or round-trip and drop-down boxes for departure and return times.*

When the user enters the search parameters, the search results page will still echo the search parameters, but will also list two matching flights (imaginary flights, since we will hard-code them into the application).

The directory structure for the Jsf_Ex02 example, shown in Figure 5-6, is similar to the one we used for the first example. The new files are FlightTypes.java, FlightTimes.java, and Flight.java.

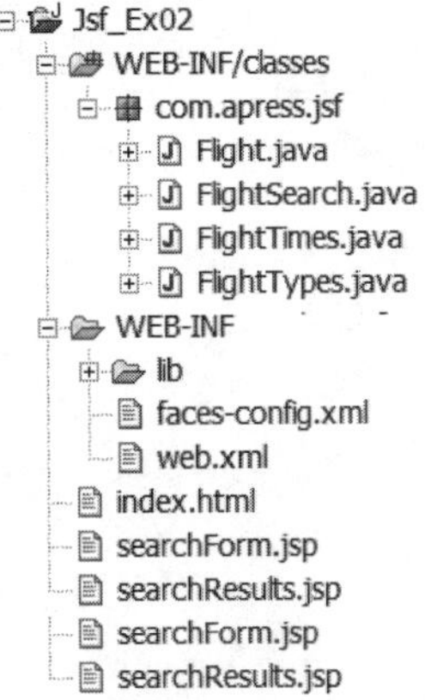

Figure 5-6. *The directory structure for Jsf_Ex02*

Listing 5-7 shows FlightTypes.java. This class is basically a data holder class with no operations. It holds the two values Roundtrip and One Way in an array of type javax.faces.SelectItem. This data type is used as part of the list-creation capability of JSF, which we will explore later when we look at the new searchForm.jsp (Listing 5-12).

Listing 5-7. *FlightTypes.java*

```
package com.apress.jsf;

import javax.faces.model.SelectItem;

public class FlightTypes {
  static SelectItem[] tripTypes = new SelectItem[] {
      new SelectItem("Roundtrip", "Roundtrip"),
      new SelectItem("One way", "One way") };

  public SelectItem[] getTripTypes() {
    return tripTypes;
  }
  public void setTripTypes(SelectItem[] tripTypes) {
    FlightTypes.tripTypes = tripTypes;
  }
}
```

Listing 5-8 shows FlightTimes.java. It is also a data holder class, this time for the departure and return time values.

Listing 5-8. *FlightTimes.java*

```
package com.apress.jsf;

import javax.faces.model.SelectItem;

public class FlightTimes {
  static SelectItem[] times = new SelectItem[] {
      new SelectItem("Anytime", "Anytime"),
      new SelectItem("Morning", "Morning"),
      new SelectItem("Afternoon", "Afternoon"),
      new SelectItem("Evening", "Evening") };

  public SelectItem[] getTimes() {
    return times;
  }
  public void setTimes(SelectItem[] times) {
    FlightTimes.times = times;
  }
}
```

Listing 5-9 shows an updated version of FlightSearch.java. This new class has two additional fields: one for trip type and one for matching flights (flights that supposedly match the search parameters). In the process of creating the FlightSearch managed bean, the matchingFlights field will be filled with two Flight objects. We will do this in the faces-config.xml file. Because we are not going to actually search for flights, each set method in this class will also update the appropriate fields in the Flight objects.

Listing 5-9. *FlightSearch.java*

```
package com.apress.jsf;

import java.util.List;
import java.util.ArrayList;

public class FlightSearch {
  String origination;
  String destination;
  String departDate;
  String departTime;
  String returnDate;
  String returnTime;
  String tripType;
  ArrayList matchingFlights = new ArrayList();
```

```
public String getDepartDate() {
  return departDate;
}
public void setDepartDate(String departDate) {
  this.departDate = departDate;
  ((Flight) matchingFlights.get(0)).setDepartDate(departDate);
  ((Flight) matchingFlights.get(1)).setDepartDate(departDate);
}
public String getDepartTime() {
  return departTime;
}
public void setDepartTime(String departTime) {
  this.departTime = departTime;
  ((Flight) matchingFlights.get(0)).setDepartTime(departTime);
  ((Flight) matchingFlights.get(1)).setDepartTime(departTime);
}
public String getDestination() {
  return destination;
}
public void setDestination(String destination) {
  this.destination = destination;
  ((Flight) matchingFlights.get(0)).setDestination(destination);
  ((Flight) matchingFlights.get(1)).setDestination(destination);
  ((Flight) matchingFlights.get(0)).setFlightNum("133");
  ((Flight) matchingFlights.get(1)).setFlightNum("233");
}
public String getOrigination() {
  return origination;
}
public void setOrigination(String origination) {
  this.origination = origination;
  ((Flight) matchingFlights.get(0)).setOrigination(origination);
  ((Flight) matchingFlights.get(1)).setOrigination(origination);
}
public String getReturnDate() {
  return returnDate;
}
public void setReturnDate(String returnDate) {
  this.returnDate = returnDate;
  ((Flight) matchingFlights.get(0)).setReturnDate(returnDate);
  ((Flight) matchingFlights.get(1)).setReturnDate(returnDate);
}
public String getReturnTime() {
  return returnTime;
}
```

```
  public void setReturnTime(String returnTime) {
    this.returnTime = returnTime;
    ((Flight) matchingFlights.get(0)).setReturnTime(returnTime);
    ((Flight) matchingFlights.get(1)).setReturnTime(returnTime);
  }
  public String getTripType() {
    return tripType;
  }
  public void setTripType(String tripType) {
    this.tripType = tripType;
  }
  public List getMatchingFlights() {
    return matchingFlights;
  }
  public void setMatchingFlights(List matchingFlights) {
    this.matchingFlights.addAll(matchingFlights);
  }
}
```

Listing 5-10 shows the `Flight.java` code. If you inspect the code in Listing 5-10, you will notice that many of the properties of the `Flight` class are identical to the fields of the `FlightSearch` class. Again, for this example, `Flight` is simply a data holder class with no significant behavior. It does, however, have a `toString()` method. This method is called by the JSF implementation when the matching flights are displayed in the search results page.

Listing 5-10. *Flight.java*

```
package com.apress.jsf;

public class Flight {
  String flightNum;
  String origination;
  String destination;
  String departDate;
  String departTime;
  String returnDate;
  String returnTime;

  public String getFlightNum() {
    return flightNum;
  }
  public void setFlightNum(String flightNum) {
    this.flightNum = flightNum;
  }
  public String getDepartDate() {
    return departDate;
  }
```

```
  public void setDepartDate(String departDate) {
    this.departDate = departDate;
  }
  public String getDepartTime() {
    return departTime;
  }
  public void setDepartTime(String departTime) {
    this.departTime = departTime;
  }
  public String getDestination() {
    return destination;
  }
  public void setDestination(String destination) {
    this.destination = destination;
  }
  public String getOrigination() {
    return origination;
  }
  public void setOrigination(String origination) {
    this.origination = origination;
  }
  public String getReturnDate() {
    return returnDate;
  }
  public void setReturnDate(String returnDate) {
    this.returnDate = returnDate;
  }
  public String getReturnTime() {
    return returnTime;
  }
  public void setReturnTime(String returnTime) {
    this.returnTime = returnTime;
  }
  public String toString() {
    return "Flight " + flightNum + " departing " + origination + " at "
        + departTime + " arriving " + destination + " 2 hours later";
  }
}
```

The `index.html` welcome page and `web.xml` deployment descriptor remain essentially unchanged for this example, so you can reuse Listing 5-5 and Listing 5-6 (if needed) for these two files. If you are using the Sun Deployment Tool, it will create `web.xml`. You may, however, want to change the `display-name` element in the deployment descriptor so that it is correct for this example.

Let's next look at the `faces-config.xml` file, shown in Listing 5-11. The navigation rule is unchanged. When the user clicks the Search button, the application will navigate to the search results form. The first significant change is in the `managed-bean` entry for the `FlightSearch` bean. The configuration file now includes an initializer for the new `matchingFlight` property of the FlightSearch bean. The matchingFlight list is initialized with two objects, given by the names flight1 and flight2. Note that the beans flight1 and flight2 are created further down in the configuration file, with a scope of none. The none scope is appropriate because these two beans are not referenced directly in any page of the application. The configuration file also initializes instances of FlightTypes and FlightTimes.

Listing 5-11. *faces-config.xml*

```
<?xml version="1.0"?>

<faces-config xmlns="http://java.sun.com/xml/ns/javaee"
      xmlns:xsi="http://www.w3.org/2001/XMLSchema-instance"
     xsi:schemaLocation="http://java.sun.com/xml/ns/javaee/web-facesconfig_1_2.xsd"
      version="1.2">
   <navigation-rule>
      <from-view-id>/searchForm.jsp</from-view-id>
      <navigation-case>
         <from-outcome>submit</from-outcome>
         <to-view-id>/searchResults.jsp</to-view-id>
         <redirect/>
      </navigation-case>
   </navigation-rule>

   <managed-bean>
      <managed-bean-name>flight</managed-bean-name>
      <managed-bean-class>com.apress.jsf.FlightSearch</managed-bean-class>
      <managed-bean-scope>session</managed-bean-scope>
      <managed-property>
       <property-name>matchingFlights</property-name>
       <list-entries>
         <value-class>com.apress.jsf.Flight</value-class>
         <value>#{flight1}</value>
         <value>#{flight2}</value>
       </list-entries>
      </managed-property>
   </managed-bean>
   <managed-bean>
      <managed-bean-name>times</managed-bean-name>
      <managed-bean-class>com.apress.jsf.FlightTimes</managed-bean-class>
      <managed-bean-scope>session</managed-bean-scope>
   </managed-bean>
   <managed-bean>
      <managed-bean-name>types</managed-bean-name>
      <managed-bean-class>com.apress.jsf.FlightTypes</managed-bean-class>
      <managed-bean-scope>session</managed-bean-scope>
   </managed-bean>
  <managed-bean>
```

```
    <managed-bean-name>flight1</managed-bean-name>
    <managed-bean-class>com.apress.jsf.Flight</managed-bean-class>
    <managed-bean-scope>none</managed-bean-scope>
  </managed-bean>
  <managed-bean>
    <managed-bean-name>flight2</managed-bean-name>
    <managed-bean-class>com.apress.jsf.Flight</managed-bean-class>
    <managed-bean-scope>none</managed-bean-scope>
  </managed-bean>
</faces-config>
```

Listing 5-12 shows the `searchForm.jsp` page. This page includes some new features. Instead of using just text fields for input, the form includes elements for creating radio buttons and drop-down menu lists: `h:selectOneRadio` and `h:selectOneMenu`. There are two ways to identify the items in these two elements. First, you can explicitly code a `selectItem` element for each element in the list. The code for that would look like this:

```
<h:selectOneRadio value="#{foo.bar}">
  <f:selectItem itemValue="Item 1"/>
  <f:selectItem itemValue="item 2"/>
</h:selectOneRadio>
```

In this code snippet, the JSF implementation creates a set of radio buttons, with one radio button for each `f:selectItem` element. The value of the `itemValue` attribute of the selected radio button is used to set the `value` attribute of the `h:selectOneRadio` element.

The second way to create a set of selection elements is to use a `selectItems` element. This is the technique we use in Listing 5-12. The `selectItems` element has an attribute named `value`, which is set by a value binding expression that returns an array of `SelectItems`. For example, in the value binding expression `#{types.tripTypes}`, the name `types` refers to a bean of type `FlightTypes` (see Listing 5-7). This object has a property named `tripTypes` of type `SelectItem[]`. When the page is rendered, the array of `SelectItems` is converted into a selection element, with one element for each item in the array. The same occurs for the two `selectOneMenu` elements.

Listing 5-12. *searchForm.jsp*

```
<html>
  <%@ taglib uri="http://java.sun.com/jsf/core" prefix="f" %>
  <%@ taglib uri="http://java.sun.com/jsf/html" prefix="h" %>

  <f:view>
  <head>
    <title>Freedom Airlines Online Flight Reservation System</title>
  </head>
```

```
<body>
  <h:form>
    <h2>Search Flights</h2>
    What type of flight do you need?
    <h:selectOneRadio layout="lineDirection"
                      value="#{flight.tripType}">
      <f:selectItems value="#{types.tripTypes}"/>
    </h:selectOneRadio>
    <p/>
    <table>
      <tr><td colspan="4">Where and when do you want to travel?</td></tr>
      <tr>
        <td colspan="2">Leaving from:</td>
        <td colspan="2">Going to:</td>
      </tr>
      <tr>
        <td colspan="2">
          <h:inputText value="#{flight.origination}" size="35"/>
        </td>
        <td colspan="2">
          <h:inputText value="#{flight.destination}" size="35"/>
        </td>
      </tr>
      <tr>
        <td colspan="2">Departing:</td>
        <td colspan="2">Returning:</td>
      </tr>
      <tr>
        <td>
          <h:inputText value="#{flight.departDate}"/>
        </td>
        <td>
          <h:selectOneMenu value="#{flight.departTime}">
            <f:selectItems value="#{times.times}"/>
          </h:selectOneMenu>
        </td>
        <td>
          <h:inputText value="#{flight.returnDate}"/>
        </td>
        <td>
          <h:selectOneMenu value="#{flight.returnTime}">
            <f:selectItems value="#{times.times}"/>
          </h:selectOneMenu>
        </td>
      </tr>
    </table>
```

```
      <p>
      <h:commandButton value="Search" action="submit"/>
      </p>
    </h:form>
  </body>
  </f:view>
</html>
```

Finally, Listing 5-13 shows an updated search results page. The only additions to this file are the new `outputText` element for trip type and the `outputText` elements for the matching flights. Note that the matching flights are displayed using the two different variations of the bracket notation for value binding expressions.

Listing 5-13. *searchResults.jsp*

```
<html>
  <%@ taglib uri="http://java.sun.com/jsf/core" prefix="f" %>
  <%@ taglib uri="http://java.sun.com/jsf/html" prefix="h" %>

  <f:view>
    <head>
      <title>Freedom Airlines Online Flight Reservation System</title>
    </head>
    <body>
          <h3>You entered these search parameters</h3>
          <br/>Trip Type  : <h:outputText value="#{flight.tripType}"/>
          <br/>Origination: <h:outputText value="#{flight.origination}"/>
          <br/>Depart date: <h:outputText value="#{flight.departDate}"/>
          <br/>Depart time: <h:outputText value="#{flight.departTime}"/>
          <br/>Destination: <h:outputText value="#{flight.destination}"/>
          <br/>Return date: <h:outputText value="#{flight.returnDate}"/>
          <br/>Return time: <h:outputText value="#{flight.returnTime}"/>
          <p/>Matching Flights
          <p/><h:outputText value="#{flight.matchingFlights[0]}"/>
          <p/><h:outputText value="#{flight.matchingFlights['1']}"/>
    </body>
  </f:view>
</html>
```

After entering all the code and compiling the Java files into classes, deploy the application to the server of your choice. When you load the search form page (see Figure 5-5), you should see the new radio buttons and drop-down menu boxes. After entering some data and clicking the Search button, you should see a results page similar to Figure 5-7.

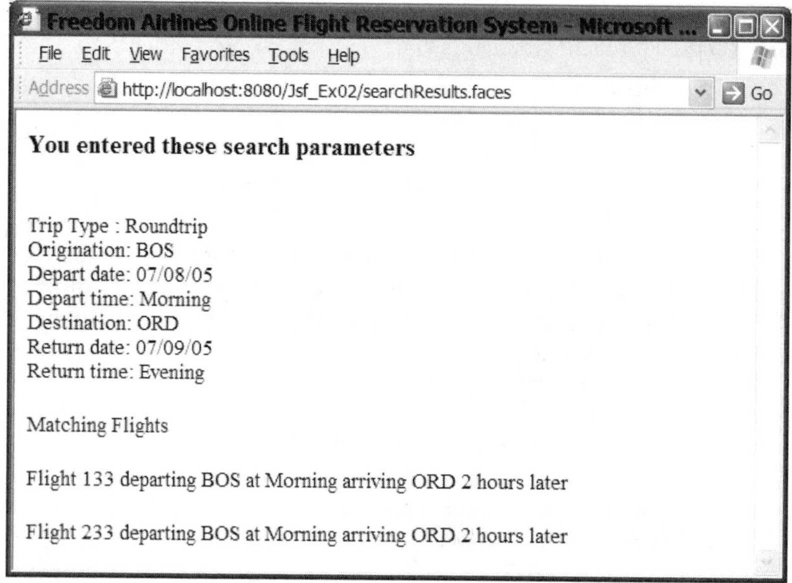

Figure 5-7. *The search results page now shows two "matching" flights.*

Controlling Page Navigation

As you saw in Listing 5-11, page navigation in your JSF application is handled by providing navigation rules in a configuration file. The navigation can specify which web component initiates the request, which web component handles the response, and which value causes navigation to follow the flow. So far, you have seen only navigation based on the hard-coded string value of an `action` attribute. You can also control navigation using value binding expressions and method binding expressions. Navigation then depends on the value of the expression.

Static and Dynamic Navigation

When you control navigation through string values of the `action` attribute, the path of navigation is known when the application is deployed. We call this *static navigation*, because the flow is statically determined and does not change. It is the same for every request.

When using static navigation, you explicitly code a value into the action attribute of a JSF custom tag. You then define navigation rules in a configuration file. The rule specifies navigation flow when the `from-outcome` of a page matches the value of the `action` attribute. When that occurs, navigation flows to the specified `to-view-id`. These elements are part of a navigation rule element in a configuration file, such as `faces-config.xml` (see Listing 5-11).

When you control navigation through value binding expressions or method binding expressions, the path of navigation is not known when the application is deployed. In fact, navigation flow can vary from request to request depending on the value of the expression. We call this *dynamic navigation*.

For dynamic navigation, you use a value binding expression or method binding expression as the value of the action attribute. With value binding expressions, the value of the property must be of type String. With method binding expressions, the method must take no parameters and return a value of type String:

```
public String methodName();
```

The String value is compared to the value specified in the navigation rule.

Navigation Rules

Two JSF custom tags are used to control page navigation in conjunction with navigation rules: commandButton and commandLink.

You specify navigation rules in a configuration file. In this chapter, we have done this in the faces-config.xml file. However, navigation rules can be in their own configuration file, which is then identified in the deployment descriptor web.xml.

The general syntax of navigation rules is as follows:

```
<navigation-rule>
  <from-view-id>/searchForm.jsp</from-view-id>
  <navigation-case>
    <from-outcome>search</from-outcome>
    <to-view-id>/searchResults.jsp</to-view-id>
  </navigation-case>
</navigation-rule>
```

The from-view-id element contains the path to the page from which navigation starts. In the configuration file, you use the correct name of the file, searchForm.jsp, as we do in Listing 5-11, rather than searchForm.faces. Note also that the path to the resource begins with a leading forward slash (/) and is the full path to the resource. So, if searchResults.jsp were in the WEB-INF/pages/results directory, you would use the path /WEB-INF/pages/results/searchForm.jsp. The from-outcome element is the string value that is compared to the value of the action attribute.

You need to specify the from-view-id only one time. This allows you to define multiple navigation-case elements that apply to one page. You use this when a page has multiple command buttons or command links.

If you have an action that applies to every page in the application, you can use a navigation-rule element without a from-view-id. For example, suppose every page in your application had a link to your privacy policy. Because the following navigation rule does not have a from-view-id, it applies to every page in the application.

```
<navigation-rule>
  <navigation-case>
    <from-outcome>privacy-policy</from-outcome>
    <to-view-id>/WEB-INF/privacy.jsp</to-view-id>
  </navigation-case>
</navigation-rule>
```

In some cases, you may have a rule that applies to some pages, but not all pages, in your application. If the pages are in a common location, you can use a wildcard to select the from-view-id:

```
<navigation-rule>
  <from-view-id>/products/*</from-view-id>
  <navigation-case>
    . . .
  </navigation-case>
</navigation-rule>
```

In this rule, the navigation case applies to every page that is served from the products directory.

Two optional elements you can use with your navigation rules are from-action and redirect. The from-action element is used in the navigation-case element. If you have a single page with multiple command actions or command links, and the command actions or links have the same value for the action attribute, you use the from-action element to distinguish between the actions. Suppose we give the FlightSearch bean two methods named search() and save(). Both methods will return the value success when used in a method binding expression. Since each returns the value success, we need some way to distinguish between a success from search() and a success from save(). You do this with the from-action element, like this:

```
<navigation-rule>
  <from-view-id>/searchForm.jsp</from-view-id>
  <navigation-case>
    <from-action>#{flight.search}</from-action>
    <from-outcome>success</from-outcome>
    <to-view-id>/searchResults.jsp</to-view-id>
  </navigation-case>
  <navigation-case>
    <from-action>#{flight.save}</from-action>
    <from-outcome>success</from-outcome>
    <to-view-id>/searchForm.jsp</to-view-id>
  </navigation-case>
</navigation-rule>
```

The other optional element is redirect. When you submit a request from a JSF form, the request is sent to the originating page. When you do not use redirect, the origination page forwards the request to the response page, so when your browser receives the response, it displays the URL of the originating page. When you use redirect, the response sent to the browser is a redirect to the response page, which gives the browser a chance to update the address to the correct responding page. With the redirect in place, both of the earlier examples show searchResults.jsp in the address bar when the response is received; without redirect, the address bar would continue to display searchForm.jsp.

Adding Dynamic Navigation to the Sample JSF Application

We can now modify the Flight Search example we have been building in this chapter to use dynamic navigation. The directory structure for this example, Jsf_Ex03, is shown in Figure 5-8. We will modify the example to simulate searching for flights that match the search criteria. In the example, the matching flights will actually be hard-coded into a JavaBean.

Figure 5-8. *Directory structure for Jsf_Ex03*

Figure 5-9 shows the search results page for this example. Notice that the page no longer echoes the search parameters. Instead, it lists flights that match the search parameters, with a link for each flight that selects the flight.

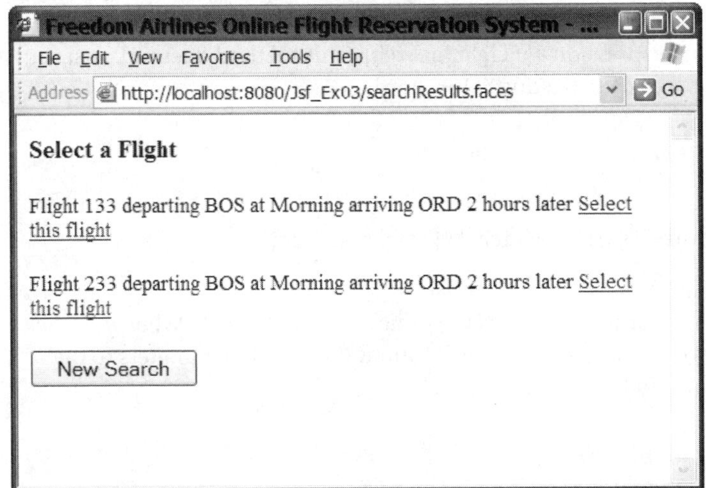

Figure 5-9. *The search results page for Jsf_Ex03 has a link to select a matching flight.*

When a link is clicked, the response page shows which flight was selected, as shown in Figure 5-10.

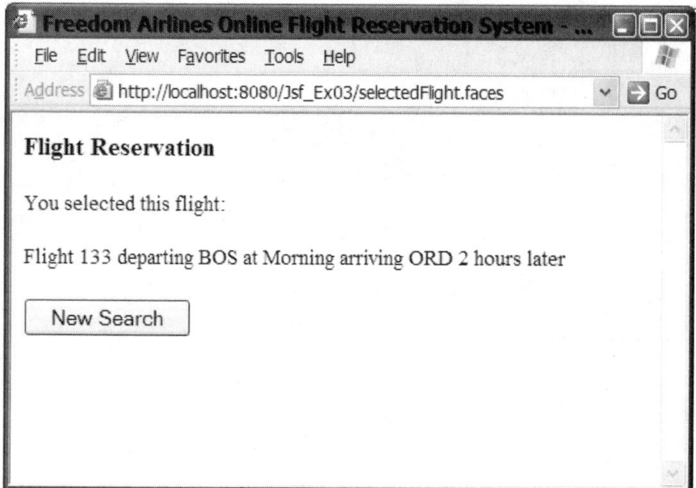

Figure 5-10. *The flight selection page shows which flight was selected.*

In this example, the files `index.html` (Listing 5-5), `web.xml` (Listing 5-6), `FlightTypes.java` (Listing 5-7), `FlightTimes.java` (Listing 5-8), and `Flight.java` (Listing 5-10) remain unchanged from the `Jsf_Ex02` example, so we will not repeat that code here.

You need to make only a single change to `searchForm.jsp`. Listing 5-14 shows the one line that is changed in the JSP page. In the `commandButton` element, we change the `action` attribute to refer to the method binding expression `#{flight.search}`. This method does not exist yet; we will add it to the `FlightSearch` class (Listing 5-19) shortly.

Listing 5-14. *searchForm.jsp Change*

```
...
      <h:commandButton value="Search" action="#{flight.search}"/>
...
```

The rest of the `searchForm.jsp` page remains the same as in Listing 5-12. When you click the Search button on the `searchForm.jsp` page, it will submit the search parameters to the `searchResults.jsp` page shown in Listing 5-15.

Listing 5-15. *searchResults.jsp for Jsf_Ex03*

```
<html>
   <%@ taglib uri="http://java.sun.com/jsf/core" prefix="f" %>
   <%@ taglib uri="http://java.sun.com/jsf/html" prefix="h" %>
```

```
  <f:view>
    <head>
      <title>Freedom Airlines Online Flight Reservation System</title>
    </head>
    <body>
      <h3>Select a Flight</h3>
      <h:form>
      <p/><h:outputText value="#{flight.matchingFlights[0]}"/>
      <h:commandLink action="#{flight.select}" value="Select this flight">
        <f:param name="flightNum"
          value="#{flight.matchingFlights[0].flightNum}" />
      </h:commandLink>
      <p/><h:outputText value="#{flight.matchingFlights[1]}"/>
      <h:commandLink action="#{flight.select}" value="Select this flight">
        <f:param name="flightNum"
          value="#{flight.matchingFlights[1].flightNum}" />
      </h:commandLink>
      <p/>
      <h:commandButton value="New Search" action="#{flight.reset}"/>
      </h:form>
    </body>
  </f:view>
</html>
```

In this new search results page, we have removed the lines that echo the search parameters. Instead, there are two similar blocks of code that print out a line of text and a link. The `outputText` elements use a value binding expression to print out an element of the `matchingFlights List` property of the `FlightSearch` object. Following the `outputText` element is a `commandLink` element. When the link created by the `commandLink` element is clicked, the JSF implementation calls the `select()` method of the `FlightSearch` class, which is specified by the method binding expression `#{flight.select}`. Like the `search()` method, `select()` is a new method. Nested within the `commandLink` element is a `param` element. It creates a name/value pair that is passed as a request parameter when the link is clicked. When we look at the `select()` method of the `FlightSearch` class, you will see how a class in the application is able to read the request parameter. Also notice in Listing 5-15 how the value binding expression to access the `flightNum` property of the `Flight` object (`#{flight.matchingFlights[0].flightNum}`) is a chained expression. As mentioned earlier in chapter, you can use both dot notation and bracket notation to create chained value binding expressions.

In this example, we need a page that will display which flight was selected by the user on the search result page. This page is `selectedFlight.jsp`, shown in Listing 5-16.

Listing 5-16. *selectedFlight.jsp*

```
<html>
  <%@ taglib uri="http://java.sun.com/jsf/core" prefix="f" %>
  <%@ taglib uri="http://java.sun.com/jsf/html" prefix="h" %>

  <f:view>
  <head>
    <title>Freedom Airlines Online Flight Reservation System</title>
  </head>
  <body>
    <h3>Flight Reservation</h3>
    <h:form>
      <p/>You selected this flight:
      <p/><h:outputText value="#{flight.matchingFlight}"/>
      <p/><h:commandButton value="New Search" action="#{flight.reset}"/>
    </h:form>
  </body>
  </f:view>
</html>
```

The last page we need to implement is the page that tells the user that no flights that match the search parameters were found. This is the `noFlights.jsp` page, shown in Listing 5-17.

Listing 5-17. *noFlights.jsp*

```
<html>
  <%@ taglib uri="http://java.sun.com/jsf/core" prefix="f" %>
  <%@ taglib uri="http://java.sun.com/jsf/html" prefix="h" %>

  <f:view>
    <head>
      <title>Freedom Airlines Online Flight Reservation System</title>
    </head>
    <body>
      <h3>Search Results</h3>
      <h:form>
      <p/>No flights that match your search parameters were found.
      <p/><h:commandButton value="New Search" action="#{flight.reset}"/>
      </h:form>
    </body>
  </f:view>
</html>
```

Each of these pages, except for the first search form page, has a New Search button, which allows the user to reset the search parameters and go back to the search form page. We need to update the `faces-config.xml` file to specify this navigation rule and the rules for moving from the search form to the other pages. Listing 5-18 shows the necessary additions and changes.

Note that the managed bean entries in the file are the same as in Listing 5-11, so we do not show them here.

Listing 5-18. *faces-config.xml Changes*

```
<?xml version="1.0"?>

<faces-config xmlns="http://java.sun.com/xml/ns/javaee"
      xmlns:xsi="http://www.w3.org/2001/XMLSchema-instance"
     xsi:schemaLocation="http://java.sun.com/xml/ns/javaee/web-facesconfig_1_2.xsd"
      version="1.2">
  <navigation-rule>
    <from-view-id>/searchForm.jsp</from-view-id>
    <navigation-case>
      <from-outcome>success</from-outcome>
      <to-view-id>/searchResults.jsp</to-view-id>
      <redirect/>
    </navigation-case>
    <navigation-case>
      <from-outcome>no flights</from-outcome>
      <to-view-id>/noFlights.jsp</to-view-id>
      <redirect/>
    </navigation-case>
  </navigation-rule>

  <navigation-rule>
    <from-view-id>/searchResults.jsp</from-view-id>
    <navigation-case>
      <from-outcome>select</from-outcome>
      <to-view-id>/selectedFlight.jsp</to-view-id>
      <redirect/>
    </navigation-case>
  </navigation-rule>

  <navigation-rule>
    <navigation-case>
      <from-action>#{flight.reset}</from-action>
      <from-outcome>success</from-outcome>
      <to-view-id>/searchForm.jsp</to-view-id>
      <redirect/>
    </navigation-case>
  </navigation-rule>

<!-- managed beans are the same as in Listing 5-11 and are not shown -->

</faces-config>
```

The navigation rule for `searchForm.jsp` now has an additional element: the Search button on the page calls the `FlightSearch` `search()` method. This returns two possible values: `success` or `no flights`. The rule specifies which page sends the response for each return value. There is a new rule for the search results page. When a link on that page is clicked, its action value causes the navigation to transfer to `selectedFlight.jsp`. Finally, there is a rule that applies to all pages, because it has no `from-view-id` element. This applies anytime the New Search button is clicked.

The final piece, presented in Listing 5-19, is `FlightSearch.java`. Much of this class is the same is in Listing 5-9, so we show only the new properties and methods.

Listing 5-19. *FlightSearch.java Changes*

```
package com.apress.jsf;

import java.util.List;
import java.util.ArrayList;
import java.util.Map;
import javax.faces.context.FacesContext;

public class FlightSearch {
  //properties:
  //origination, destination, departDate, departTime same as Listing 5-9
  //returnDate, returnTime, tripType, matchingFlights same as Listing 5-9
  String flightNum;
  Flight matchingFlight;

  //methods from Listing 5-9 not shown here

  //new methods are reset(), search(), and
  //get and set methods for flightNum and matchingFlight

  public String reset() {
    this.setDepartDate("");
    this.setDepartTime("");
    this.setDestination("");
    this.setOrigination("");
    this.setReturnDate("");
    this.setReturnTime("");
    this.setTripType("");
    return "success";
  }
  public String search() {
    if (origination.equals("BOS") && destination.equals("ORD")) {
      return "success";
    } else {
      return "no flights";
    }
  }
```

```
  public Flight getMatchingFlight() {
    for (int i = 0; i < matchingFlights.size(); i++) {
      matchingFlight = (Flight) matchingFlights.get(i);
      if (matchingFlight.flightNum.equals(flightNum)) {
        break;
      }
      matchingFlight = null;
    }
    return matchingFlight;
  }
  public void setMatchingFlight(Flight flight) {
    matchingFlight = flight;
  }
  public String getFlightNum() {
    return flightNum;
  }
  public void setFlightNum(String string) {
    flightNum = string;
  }
  public String select() {
    FacesContext context = FacesContext.getCurrentInstance();
    Map requestParams =
      context.getExternalContext().getRequestParameterMap();
    flightNum = (String) requestParams.get("flightNum");
    return "select";
  }
}
```

The `reset()` method simply resets all the properties to be empty strings and returns the value `success`. The `matchingFlights` `List` contains entries for two flights that both originate in Boston (BOS) and fly to Chicago (ORD). If the origination and destination match these values, the `search()` method returns `success`; otherwise, it returns `no flights`.

The `commandLink` element on the `searchResults.jsp` page causes the `select()` method to be called. Within this method, the code gets a reference to the context for the application, and then uses the context to get a reference to the map that holds all the request parameters. From this `Map`, the code accesses the request parameter with the name `flightNum`. Referring back to Listing 5-15, you can see that the page created a request parameter with that name. The code sets the `flightNum` property of the instance and returns the value `select`. The `flightNum` property becomes important for the `getMatchingFlight()` method.

Although most of the `get` methods simply return the current value of a property, the `getMatchingFlight()` method iterates through the `matchingFlights` list to find the flight with the same flight number as the `flightNum` property. In other words, `get` and `set` are not constrained to simply return the value of properties, but can perform processing when they are called. The `matchingFlight` property is set to this object, and it is also the return value from this method. This method is called because of the value binding expression `#{flight.matchingFlight}` in the `selectedFlight.jsp` page.

Compile the classes and deploy the application to your server. When you load the welcome page at `http://localhost:8080/Jsf_Ex03` (replacing the host, port, or name as necessary), the search form page will load, as shown earlier in Figure 5-5. If you enter BOS in the Leaving from text field and ORD in the Going to text field, and then click the Search button, the search results page will display as shown in Figure 5-9. On the search results page, clicking either link will display the `selectedFlight.jsp` page (see Figure 5-10). If you enter any other data in either the Leaving from field or Going to field and click the Search button, you should see the `noFlights.jsp` page, as shown in Figure 5-11.

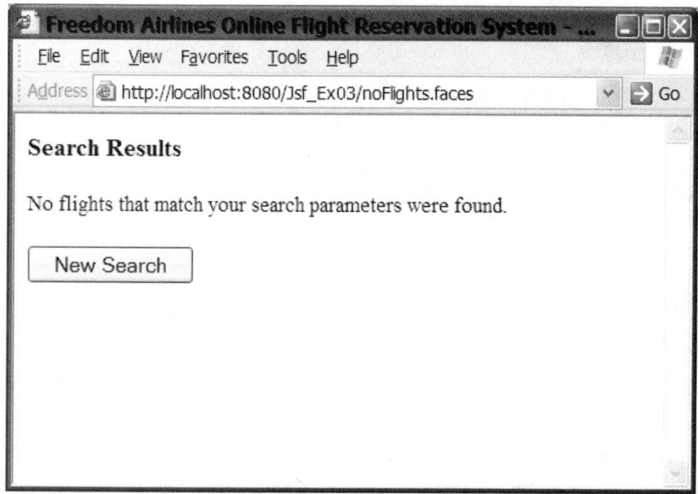

Figure 5-11. *The noFlights.jsp page is served when no flights are found.*

Accessing Context Data in Beans

Although JSF makes it easy for you to connect the view with the model without writing any code, there may be situations where you need direct access to the request data or other data of your web application. We saw such a situation in Listing 5-19. In that listing, a request parameter had been set in the JSF page, and the `FlightSearch` bean needed to access that request parameter.

JSF provides access to the request data and other data through the `FacesContext` object. As the Javadoc states, "FacesContext contains all of the per-request state information related to the processing of a single JavaServer Faces request, and the rendering of the corresponding response.... A FacesContext instance is associated with a particular request at the beginning of request processing..."

As you saw in Listing 5-19, you get access to the `FacesContext` object like this:

```
FacesContext context = FacesContext.getCurrentInstance();
```

After you have a reference to the `FacesContext` for the request, you can access all the request and application data through the `ExternalContext` object. The reference to the `ExternalContext` object is obtained through the call to the `getExternalContext()` method.

Table 5-3 shows the methods of the `ExternalContext` that return collections of request and application data. You can use these methods to access request data, session data, request header data, cookie data, and other sets of data in the application.

Table 5-3. *Request and Application Data Available Through ExternalContext*

Method	Description
`Map getApplicationMap()`	Returns a mutable `Map` representing the application scope attributes for the current application
`String getInitParameter(java.lang.String name)`	Returns the value of the specified application initialization parameter (if any)
`Map getInitParameterMap()`	Returns an immutable `Map` whose keys are the set of application initialization parameter names configured for this application, and whose values are the corresponding parameter values
`String getRemoteUser()`	Returns the login name of the user making the current request if any; otherwise, returns null
`Map getRequestCookieMap()`	Returns an immutable `Map` whose keys are the set of cookie names included in the current request, and whose values (of type `javax.servlet.http.Cookie`) are the first (or only) cookie for each cookie name returned by the underlying request
`Map getRequestHeaderMap()`	Returns an immutable `Map` whose keys are the set of request header names included in the current request, and whose values (of type `String`) are the first (or only) value for each header name returned by the underlying request
`Map getRequestHeaderValuesMap()`	Returns an immutable Map whose keys are the set of request header names included in the current request, and whose values (of type `String[]`) are all of the value for each header name returned by the underlying request
`Map getRequestMap()`	Returns a mutable `Map` representing the request scope attributes for the current application
`Map getRequestParameterMap()`	Returns an immutable `Map` whose keys are the set of request parameters names included in the current request, and whose values (of type `String`) are the first (or only) value for each parameter name returned by the underlying request
`Iterator getRequestParameterNames()`	Returns an `Iterator` over the names of all request parameters included in the current request
`Map getRequestParameterValuesMap()`	Returns an immutable `Map` whose keys are the set of request parameters names included in the current request, and whose values (of type `String[]`) are all of the values for each parameter name returned by the underlying request
`Map getSessionMap()`	Returns a mutable `Map` representing the session scope attributes for the current application

Most likely, if you are accessing request or application data in a managed bean, you will be accessing request data or session data. As you can see in Table 5-3, you access request data through the getRequestParameterMap() or getRequestParameterValuesMap() method. You can access session data through the getSessionMap() method.

Converting Data

Looking at the FlightSearch and Flight objects, we notice that it would probably make more sense for the departDate and returnDate fields to be actual Date objects rather than String objects. (To be honest, we noticed this much earlier, but did not want to address that issue until this point in the chapter.)

Modify the FlightSearch and Flight objects so that the departDate and returnDate fields are java.util.Date objects and redeploy the application. Now, bring up the search page, enter data into the fields, and click the Search button. If the application works correctly, you should see the search page again.

At this point, you should be wondering why the search page was redisplayed, especially if you entered valid data into all the input fields. The fact that the search page was redisplayed indicates that there was an error in the data.

When an error occurs in a JSF page, the JSF implementation redisplays the originating page again. In this case, the problem is that the JSF implementation does not know how to convert a string into a Date object, which is what is required for the FlightSearch object. Unfortunately, with the sample JSP pages we have deployed so far, we did not include any code to inform you of what the error is. Let's take care of that now.

Modify the searchResults.jsp page by adding an id attribute to the inputText elements and a message element following each inputText element. These changes are shown here:

```
<h:inputText id="departDate" value="#{flight.departDate}"/>
<h:message for="departDate"/>
  . . .
<h:inputText id="returnDate" value="#{flight.returnDate}"/>
<h:message for="returnDate"/>
```

The id attribute allows you to use the value of the attribute to refer to the JSF custom tag from other tags. The message element obtains a message from the component identified by the for attribute. If that component does not have a message, the message element keeps an empty string as its value. If the message component has a nonempty string value, that string is displayed when the page is rendered.

Deploy the search page with the new source, enter some data, and click the Search button again. This time, the search page is redisplayed with a message indicating the error, similar to "Conversion Error setting value '07/08/2005' for 'null Converter'," as shown in Figure 5-12.

In cases where the bean property is a Java primitive (int, float, boolean, and so on), a Java BigInteger, a Java BigDecimal, or a Java String, the JSF implementation will automatically convert the input data to the correct type. This is done with standard converters. When the bean property is a Java Date, there is a standard converter, but you need to explicitly tell the JSF implementation to perform the conversion. When the bean property is some other data type, you need to provide a converter for the data.

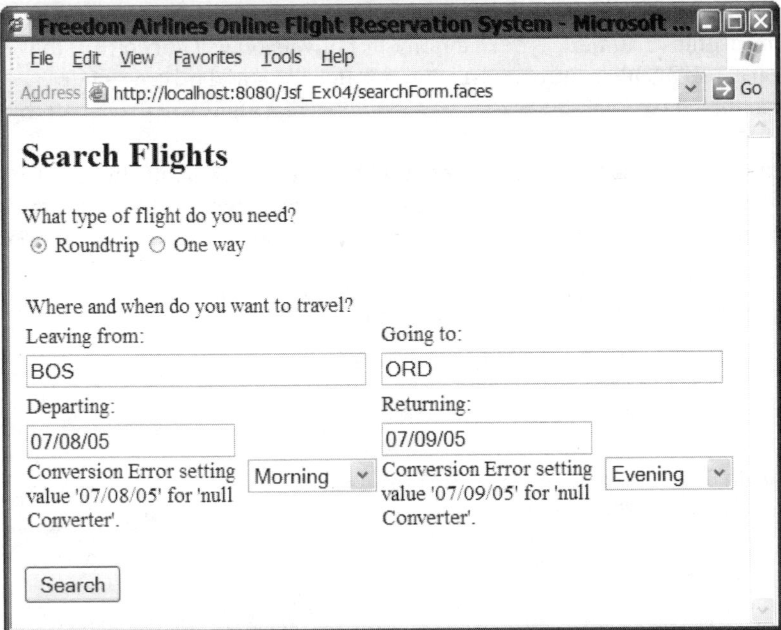

Figure 5-12. *The message element displays an error message when a UI component has an error.*

Using Standard Converters

The JSF implementation comes with two standard converters:

- `convertNumber`: Converts between strings and numbers. You can include optional attributes to format the numbers in various ways, including as currency, as integers, and as floating-point numbers.
- `convertDateTime`: Converts between strings and dates or times. You can include optional attributes to format using various styles and time zones.

To use one of these converters, you nest the converter tag inside the `inputText` tag. In general, you can nest a converter inside any of the input or output custom tags. The converter will be called by the JSF implementation in the update model values and render response phases of the JSF lifecycle. If the conversion succeeds, the lifecycle continues. If the conversion fails, the lifecycle transitions to the render response phase, where the originating page is rendered and the error message is displayed (if the page contains message tags).

■ Note You do not need to use a converter if the type of the managed bean property is a primitive type (int, double, and so on), a boolean, a `BigInteger`, a `BigDecimal`, or a `String`. You do need to use a converter if the type of the property is any other object, including `Date`.

The JSF implementation will automatically convert input values to numbers when the bean property is some primitive numeric type. If automatic conversion will not convert the number properly, you can explicitly control conversion through the standard convertNumber converter tag. For example, the convertNumber tag has attributes that allow you to convert the input value to a currency value.

The other standard converter is the convertDateTime tag. By using various attributes of this tag, you can convert dates or times, in various formats, to Date or Time properties in the managed bean. Let's modify the searchForm.jsp page to use the convertDateTime tag. The new inputText tags look like this:

```
<h:inputText id="departDate" value="#{flight.departDate}">
  <f:convertDateTime pattern="MM/dd/yy"/>
</h:inputText>
<h:message for="departDate"/>
 . . .
<h:inputText id="returnDate" value="#{flight.returnDate}">
  <f:convertDateTime pattern="MM/dd/yy"/>
</h:inputText>
<h:message for="returnDate"/>
```

The convertDateTime tag is nested in the inputText tag. The convertDateTime tag has several attributes that control the date conversion. We've used the pattern attribute to identify the pattern of the date string that will be converted. The symbols that you can use in pattern strings are the same symbols recognized by the java.text.SimpleDateFormat class. (Can you guess what the JSF implementation uses to do the conversion?) We've identified that the input value will consist of the two-digit month, followed by the two-digit day, followed by the two-digit year, with forward slashes delimiting each value. Now when you click the Search button, the JSF implementation will convert the date (assuming it follows the *MM/dd/yy* format), and the search results page will be sent to the browser.

The latest version of the Flight Search example does not provide any indication that the date is properly converted (other than displaying the search results page). Adding outputText fields to the search results page to redisplay the departure and return dates is left as an exercise to the reader.

Using Custom Converters

If you could use only the convertNumber and convertDateTime tags, your ability to create feature-rich web applications would be limited. Fortunately, as you might guess from the title of this section, you can create and use custom converters in your JSF applications.

To create a custom converter, you write a class that implements the javax.faces.convert.Converter interface. This interface has two methods:

```
Object getAsObject(javax.faces.context.FacesContext context,
   javax.faces.component.UIComponent component, java.lang.String value)
String getAsString(javax.faces.context.FacesContext context,
   javax.faces.component.UIComponent component, java.lang.Object value)
```

The `getAsObject()` method converts the `String` value (which can be null) to an instance of the supported type and returns the new instance. This method throws a `ConverterException` if the conversion fails. The `getAsString()` method converts the provided value of the supported type (which can again be null) to a `String` instance and returns the new instance. This method also throws a `ConverterException` if the conversion fails.

Note If you check the JSF Javadoc, you will see that the JSF implementation includes a number of implementations of the `javax.faces.convert.Converter` interface. These are the standard converters that handle converting input and output values to the primitive types.

Let's create an `Airport` object that will be used as the data type for the origination and destination fields of the `FlightSearch` class. We will write a converter that converts between `String` and `Airport` objects.

Listing 5-20 shows the `Airport` object. It is a simple object that holds an airport code and the name of the airport.

Listing 5-20. *Airport.java*

```
package com.apress.jsf;

public class Airport {
  String code;
  String name;
  public Airport(String code, String name) {
    this.code = code;
    this.name = name;
  }
  public String toString() {
    return code;
  }
}
```

The converter, shown in Listing 5-21, will create an `Airport` object when given a string with the airport code.

Listing 5-21. *airportconverter.java*

```
package com.apress.jsf;

import javax.faces.application.FacesMessage;
import javax.faces.component.UIComponent;
import javax.faces.context.FacesContext;
import javax.faces.convert.Converter;
import javax.faces.convert.ConverterException;
```

```
public class AirportConverter implements Converter {
  public Object getAsObject(FacesContext ctxt, UIComponent comp,
    String value) {
    Airport airport = null;
    if (value.equals("BOS")) {
      airport = new Airport("BOS", "Logan International Airport");
    }
    if (value.equals("ORD")) {
      airport = new Airport("ORD", "O'Hare International Airport");
    }
    if (airport == null) {
      FacesMessage message =
        new FacesMessage(
          FacesMessage.SEVERITY_ERROR,
          "UnrecognizedAirportCode",
          "Airport code " + value + " is not recognized");
      throw new ConverterException(message);
    }
    return airport;
  }
  public String getAsString(FacesContext ctxt, UIComponent comp,
    Object obj) {
    return obj.toString();
  }
}
```

This converter is very simple. When converting from a string to an object (the `getAsObject()` method), the code looks for either the string `"BOS"` or `"ORD"`. If either of those values is found, an `Airport` object is created. (In a real-world application, we would obviously use a more robust lookup like a database search, which would recognize all possible airport codes.) If neither string is found, the converter throws a `ConverterException` that holds a `FacesMessage` object. The `FacesMessage` object holds a summary string and a detail string, which is displayed by the `message` tag when an error occurs.

To convert an object to a `String`, the `getAsString()` method simply calls the `toString()` method of the object passed to the method. Since this object should be an instance of `Airport`, the `toString()` method of `Airport` will be called, and that will return the airport code string.

If more involved processing is needed, each method has access to the `FacesContext` of the application and the `UIComponent` of the component instance in the page that the object or string is associated with. As you saw earlier, the `FacesContext` instance can be used to get access to various maps that hold parameters from the page and request being processed.

We will add these two classes to the Flight Search application. Figure 5-13 shows the directory structure for this example. We will add the classes to the `WEB-INF` directory. After adding the classes, we need to tell the JSF implementation when to call the converter.

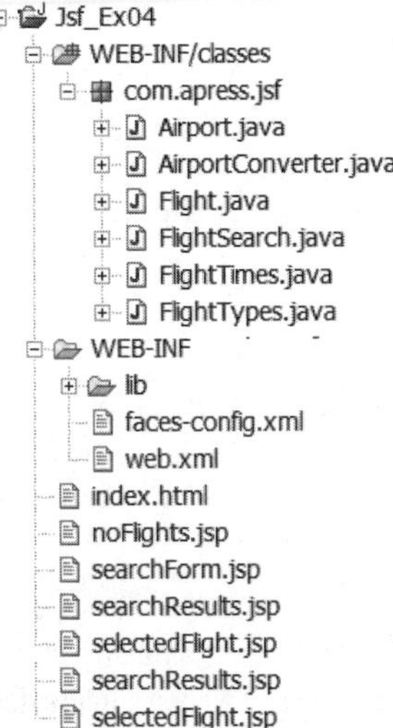

Figure 5-13. *Directory structure for Jsf_Ex04*

One way to identify a converter to the JSF implementation is to specify a `converter-id` for the converter in a configuration file, and then use that `id` in the JSP page. To do this, add this `converter` element to the `faces-config.xml` file:

```
<converter>
  <converter-id>airport.converter</converter-id>
  <converter-class>com.apress.jsf.AirportConverter</converter-class>
</converter>
```

Then, in the JSP, use the `id` in a `converter` tag like this:

```
<h:inputText value="#{flight.origination}">
  <f:converter converterId="airport.converter"/>
</h:inputText>
```

or this:

```
<h:inputText value="#{flight.origination}" converter="airport.converter"/>
```

Another way to identify a converter is to define a default converter for all properties of type `Airport`. This `converter` element in the `faces-config.xml` file does that:

```
<converter>
  <converter-for-class>com.apress.jsf.Airport</converter-for-class>
  <converter-class>com.apress.jsf.AirportConverter</converter-class>
</converter>
```

With this entry, every time you use an input or output tag that references a property of type `Airport`, like this:

```
<h:inputText value="#{flight.origination}"/>
```

the JSF implementation detects that `origination` is of type `Airport` and calls the `AirportConverter` for this element. If you use this technique, you must be sure that the converter works for all possible input strings. This is the technique we will use. Add the preceding `converter` element to the `faces-config.xml` file for this example, `Jsf_Ex04`.

■ **Note** A third way to identify the converter involves creating an object known as a *backing bean*. Interested readers should check the JSF specification for details on using backing beans.

If you have not yet done so, enter the `Airport.java` and `AirportConverter.java` source code (Listings 5-20 and 5-21) and save them in the correct directory.

In the `Flight.java` source file, change the data type of origination and destination to `Airport`, and change the `set` and `get` methods appropriately.

In the `FlightSearch.java` file, change the data type of origination and destination to `Airport`, and change the `set` and `get` methods appropriately. Change the `reset()` method to set the origination and destination to null. Also, change the `search()` method like this:

```
public String search() {
  if (origination.code.equals("BOS") &&
      destination.code.equals("ORD")) {
    return "success";
  } else {
    return "no flights";
  }
}
```

Finally, make this change to the `inputText` fields for `origination` and `destination` in the `searchForm.jsp` page:

```
  <h:inputText id="origination"
     value="#{flight.origination}" size="35"/>
  <h:message for="origination"/>
</td>
<td colspan="2">
  <h:inputText id="destination"
     value="#{flight.destination}" size="35"/>
  <h:message for="destination"/>
```

All the other files in the example remain the same as in the previous example, `Jsf_Ex03`. Compile the classes and deploy the application to the server. Unlike the previous addition of the date converter, this addition to the application will change the application's behavior. If you enter any airport code other than BOS or ORD in the origination or destination fields in the search form, the application responds with a conversion error and displays the detail string from the message generated by the converter. If you enter BOS as the origination and ORD as the destination, the application will find the matching flights. If you enter ORD as the origination and BOS as the destination, the application will return the `noFlights.jsp` page. Previously, you could enter any airport codes, and the application returned `noFlights.jsp` if the codes did not match BOS and ORD. Now, the only way to see the `noFlights.jsp` page is to enter ORD as the origination and BOS or ORD as the destination.

Validating Input

If you've worked with web applications before, you know that a lot of effort is involved in ensuring that the data entered by the user of your application is correct. JSF provides a means to simplify data validation, through the use of standard and custom validators.

Using Standard Validators

JSF provides three standard validators as part of the JSF implementation through the following custom tags:

- `validateDoubleRange`: Validates that a value is a `double`. You can include the optional attributes `minimum` and `maximum` to set minimum and maximum values.
- `validateLongRange`: Validates that a value is a `long`. You can include the optional attributes `minimum` and `maximum` to set minimum and maximum values.
- `validateLength`: Validates a string value for length. You can include the optional attributes `minimum` and `maximum` to set minimum and maximum values.

With all three validators, both of the attributes are optional. This means you could add a validator tag without either a `minimum` or `maximum` attribute. In that case, no validation will actually be performed. When you provide only a minimum, the validator checks that the value is greater than or equal to the minimum. When you provide only a maximum, the validator checks that the value is less than or equal to the maximum. When you provide both a minimum and a maximum, the validator checks that the value is greater than or equal to the minimum and less than or equal to the maximum.

One other validation you can perform in your JSF application is to require a value. The `input` and `output` tags include an optional attribute `required`. For example, the following tag would require that you enter a value in the text field:

```
<h:inputText id="origination"
   value="#{flight.origination}" size="35" required="true"/>
```

If you do not enter a value, the JSF implementation will return the originating page with a message that you did not enter a required value (assuming there is a `message` tag for the `id` `origination`).

Using Custom Validators

You create a custom validator by creating a class that implements the `javax.faces.validator.Validator` interface. All validators must implement this interface. The `Validator` interface has a single method that your class must implement:

```
void validate(javax.faces.context.FacesContext context,
    javax.faces.component.UIComponent component, java.lang.Object value)
```

In the `validate` method, if the `value` argument passes the validation check, you can simply return from the method. This signals to the JSF implementation that the value passed the validation check. If it does not pass the validation check, you throw a `javax.faces.validator.ValidatorException`. The `ValidatorException` instance includes a `FacesMessage` instance with summary and detail messages describing the validation error.

Note If you check the JSF Javadoc, you will see that the JSF implementation includes a number of implementations of the `javax.faces.validator.Validator` interface. These are the standard validators that handle validating doubles, longs, and string lengths.

Suppose we wanted to create a date validator to ensure that dates entered by the user of our Flight Search application are greater than or equal to the day after the current date, and less than one year from the current date. Listing 5-22 shows the code for this validator.

Listing 5-22. *DateValidator.java*

```
package com.apress.jsf;

import java.util.Calendar;
import java.util.Date;
import javax.faces.application.FacesMessage;
import javax.faces.component.UIComponent;
import javax.faces.context.FacesContext;
import javax.faces.validator.Validator;
import javax.faces.validator.ValidatorException;

public class DateValidator implements Validator {
  public void validate(FacesContext arg0, UIComponent arg1, Object arg2)
    throws ValidatorException {
    Calendar date = Calendar.getInstance();
    date.setTime((Date) arg2);

    Calendar tomorrow = Calendar.getInstance();
    tomorrow.set(Calendar.HOUR, 0);
    tomorrow.set(Calendar.MINUTE, 0);
    tomorrow.set(Calendar.SECOND, 0);
```

```
    Calendar oneYear = Calendar.getInstance();
    oneYear.set(Calendar.HOUR, 0);
    oneYear.set(Calendar.MINUTE, 0);
    oneYear.set(Calendar.SECOND, 0);
    oneYear.add(Calendar.YEAR, 1);

    if (date.before(tomorrow) || date.after(oneYear)) {
      FacesMessage message =
        new FacesMessage(
          FacesMessage.SEVERITY_ERROR,
          "Date Error",
          "Date must be between tomorrow and one year from today");
      throw new ValidatorException(message);
    }
  }
}
```

The code in the validate() method creates two Calendar objects: tomorrow corresponds to the day after the current date, and oneYear corresponds to one year from the current date. Then the code compares the argument passed to the validate method to see if it is between the dates represented by those two Calendar objects. If the argument is not between those two Calendar objects, a ValidatorException is thrown; if it is between those two dates, the method simply returns.

The validator is registered with the JSF implementation with the validator element in a configuration file. The validator element has two required subelements:

- validator-id: Used to create an id string that you can use in the validator tag to specify a validator instance.
- validator-class: The fully qualified class name of the validator class.

Here is an example of the element you could place in the faces-config.xml configuration file for this validator:

```
<validator>
  <validator-id>date.validator</validator-id>
  <validator-class>com.apress.jsf.DateValidator</validator-class>
</validator>
```

And in the searchForm.jsp, you could nest this validator tag in an inputText tag:

```
<h:inputText id="departDate" value="#{flight.departDate}">
  <f:convertDateTime pattern="MM/dd/yy"/>
  <f:validator validatorId="date.validator"/>
</h:inputText>
```

Notice that the value of the validatorId in the f:validator tag is the same string used in the validator-id element.

Adding this validator and deploying it with the Flight Search application is left as an exercise for the reader.

Bypassing Validation

Validation is an important aspect of your web application, because it ensures that all input values are valid before the model is updated, thereby enforcing model integrity. However, there are times when you do not want validation to occur.

For example, in various pages of the Flight Search application, we have a New Search button. If this button occurred on a page that also specified validators for any fields, we could have a problem. In the normal JSF lifecycle, the validators would be executed before the New Search button was processed. Validators are executed during the process validations phase, while command buttons are processed after the invoke application phase, which occurs after the process validations phase. By providing a New Search button, we are acknowledging that the user might want to throw away whatever values are in the page and start a new search. Thus, we would not want validations to occur when the user clicks the New Search button.

We can tell the JSF implementation to process the event from the button click after the apply request values phase (before the process validations phase) by adding an attribute named `immediate` to the `action` tag. So, for example, if we wanted the New Search button to bypass validations in a page, the tag would look like this:

```
<h:commandButton value="New Search" action="#{flight.reset}"
                 immediate="true"/>
```

Using Message Bundles

With the global nature of the web, many web applications must be internationalized. JSF provides a facility to make it easy to internationalize your web application.

To provide an internationalized version of your web application, all the text strings used in your application must be collected into a properties file that your application can load and use. Listing 5-23 shows a properties file of messages that you could use with the `searchForm.jsp` page we have developed in this chapter as part of the Flight Search application. This file holds the English language strings for the application.

Listing 5-23. *messages.properties*

```
title=Freedom Airlines Online Flight Reservation System
head=Search Flights
type=What type of flight do you need?
searchLabel=Where and when do you want to travel?
departAirport=Leaving from:
arriveAirport=Going to:
departLabel=Departing:
returnLabel=Returning:
searchButton=Search
```

Save this file somewhere in the classpath for your application. In the Flight Search example, we could save it in the `com/apress/jsf` directory. When we cause the properties file to be loaded, we will reference it by a name that includes the classpath.

The properties file is included in a JSP page with the loadBundle custom action:

```
<f:loadBundle basename="com.apress.jsf.messages" var="msgs"/>
```

The loadBundle custom action has two required attributes: basename and var. The basename attribute is the classpath qualified base name of the properties file. We reference the messages.properties file using the same package qualified name as if it were a Java class file. Notice that we do not need to provide the .properties extension of the file. When combined with locale information, the basename is the initial part of the name of the file to be loaded. A locale code is appended with an underscore, followed by the .properties extension, to create the full filename. With no locale information, the basename shown in the preceding example tells the JSF implementation to look for the file messages.properties in the directory com/apress/jsf of the application.

The var attribute is the name that you will use in the JSP to access the messages stored in the messages.properties file.

You can use these strings in your application by using a value binding expression. For example, to add the page header to the searchForm.jsp page, you would replace the original page header element:

```
<h2>Search Flights</h2>
```

with the following outputText element:

```
<h2><h:outputText value="#{msgs.head}"/></h2>
```

In elements such as commandButton, you can use the value binding expression directly in the value attribute of the commandButton element:

```
<h:commandButton value="#{msgs.searchButton}" action="#{flight.search}"/>
```

This provides two big advantages. First, if you want to change the text used in the web application, you need to change only the messages.properties message bundle. Second, and the big reason for message bundles, is that you can easily internationalize your application by providing additional message bundles for other languages. For example, you can create a second message bundle named messages_es.properties, as shown in Listing 5-24. This file holds the Spanish versions of all the strings.

Listing 5-24. *messages_es.properties*

```
title=Freedom Airlines Online Flight Reservation System
head=Busque los Vuelos
type=Qué tipo del vuelo le hace necesita?
searchLabel=Dónde y cuando le hace quiere viajar?
departAirport=La partida de:
arriveAirport=Ir a:
departLabel=Partir:
returnLabel=Volver:
searchButton=Búsqueda
```

Tip If you want to include Unicode characters with an ASCII code greater than 127, you need to encode them as escape sequences in the form `\uxxxx`. This provides the ability to support non-Western languages. And you don't need to type in these sequences by hand. The Java utility `native2ascii` can convert native characters to escape sequences for you.

You add an entry to the `faces-config.xml` file that identifies which languages your application supports. For our Flight Search application, you would add this entry to the `faces-config.xml` file:

```
<application>
  <locale-config>
    <default-locale>en</default-locale>
    <supported-locale>es</supported-locale>
  </locale-config>
</application>
```

You need to add a `supported-locale` element with a locale code for every language that your application supports. The two-letter and three-letter locale codes are listed at `http://www.loc.gov/standards/iso639-2/englangn.html`.

When a user accesses your application, and the user's browser is set to accept Spanish as the default language, your application will access strings from the `messages_es.properties` file, as shown in Figure 5-14. Note that you do not need to change the `loadBundle` tag in your JSP pages. The browser sends a header parameter that it accepts Spanish as its default language. The JSF implementation uses that parameter to determine the locale code, and then combines the `basename` attribute with the locale code `es` to determine which message bundle to load.

Adding this language bundle to the Flight Search example is left as an exercise for the reader. To see the Flight Search application with other languages, you will also need to set the language preferences of your browser. For Microsoft Internet Explorer, select Tools ➤ Internet Options ➤ Languages. If you have a different browser, you should be able to set the language preference in a similar fashion.

Caution Although we left this as the last topic for the chapter, in the real world, you would not want to leave the message bundle setup for last. Initially writing your web application with internationalization is much easier than attempting to retrofit your application with internationalization. This does not mean that you must write message bundles for every possible language up front. You should write a default message bundle, and then add other languages as needed.

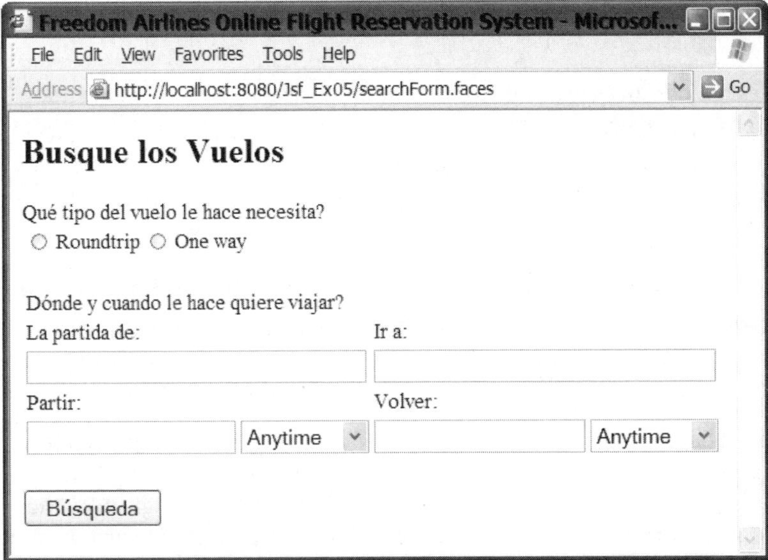

Figure 5-14. *The search form page with Spanish text*

Summary

After completing this chapter, you should know:

- JSF was developed to make it easier to create customizable UIs for web applications using a component-based system. JSF provides a set of UI components that can easily be added to web applications and connected to business objects. The components are converted into user interfaces through the use of a render kit.
- The JSF implementation comes with a set of custom actions in two tag libraries that allow you to easily integrate JSF with JSP. All JSF implementations must support JSP pages.
- Managed beans are the business objects in your JSF application. JSF makes it easy to connect managed beans with UI components. The JSF implementation handles all the work of moving data from the UI into the bean, and moving data from the bean to the UI.
- Page navigation in a JSF application is handled by adding navigation rules to a configuration file. Navigation can be controlled through value binding expressions or method binding expressions.
- Data conversion and validation is handled by converters and validators. The JSF implementation provides two standard converters: one for numbers and one for dates. The JSF implementation provides three standard validators for validating the ranges of doubles or longs and validating the length of strings.

- You can implement your own converters or validators to perform custom conversion and validation.
- Message bundles provide an easy facility for internationalizing and customizing the pages in your web application.

Exercises

1. Create an even simpler JSF application than the one given in Listings 5-1 through 5-6. Remove the `FlightSearch` JavaBean and the `searchResults.jsp` page from the application. Modify the `faces-config.xml` file so that the application consists solely of creating the display from `searchForm.jsp`. Draw the lifecycle diagram for this application.
2. Create a managed bean that uses a `Map` property to store several lists of data. Create a JSF-enabled application that accepts a key and an integer from the user, and in the response displays the value of the `List` element at that index in the `List` given by the key. Use both dot and bracket notation in the value binding expressions to explore the syntax of value binding expressions.
3. After completing Chapter 7, modify the Flight Search application to search for matching flights from a database table.
4. When the New Search button is clicked, the response page is the search form page with all the values reset to blanks. Modify the `Jsf_Ex03` example so that when the button is clicked from the `searchResults.jsp` page or the `selectedFlight.jsp` page, the search parameters are not reset. They are reset only when the user clicks the New Search button from the `noFlights.jsp` page.
5. Create a converter that converts a decimal dollar amount into cents, or converts degrees from Fahrenheit to Celsius. Create a JSF application that uses one of the converters. For example, you could have a data-entry page that accepts decimal dollars or temperature in degrees Fahrenheit, convert the value to cents or degrees Celsius, store the converted value in a managed bean, and then use a results page to display the converted value.
6. Add the date validator to the Flight Search example.
7. Add the Spanish language message bundle to the Flight Search example. (Don't forget to set the language preference in your browser to see the new messages.)

CHAPTER 6

Servlets

In Chapters 3 and 4, you learned about JSP pages, which are commonly used in Java EE web applications. Servlets are the other common component in Java EE web applications.

Servlets are server-side applications in much the same way that applets are client-side applications. An applet is a program that runs on the client side in a web browser; a Servlet is a program that runs on the server side in a web server. Like JSP pages, Servlets are Java classes that are loaded and executed by a Servlet container that can run by itself or as a component of a web server or a Java EE server. In fact, as you saw in Chapter 3, the container actually compiles the JSP page into a Servlet class that is then executed by the container. However, while JSP pages are usually HTML pages with bits of embedded Java code, Servlets are Java classes with bits of embedded HTML.

Servlets are designed to be extensions to servers and to extend the capabilities of servers. Servlets were originally intended to be able to extend any server such as a web server, an FTP server, or an SMTP (e-mail) server. However, in practice, only Servlets that respond to HTTP requests have been widely implemented. Servlets extend the capabilities of a web server and provide dynamic behavior for web applications. Servlets are designed to accept a request from a client (usually a web browser), process that request, and return a response to the client. Although all the processing can occur within the Servlet, usually helper classes or other web components such as Enterprise JavaBeans (EJBs) will perform the business logic processing, leaving the Servlet free to perform the request and response processing.

After JDBC, Servlets were the second Java EE technology invented. Since they were also developed before JSP, early Servlets had to handle display processing. This mixture of page design and code was one of the reasons JSP was introduced. When Servlets were first introduced, if you were developing a web application in Java, you were using just Servlets in the middle tier, and JDBC if you had a database. Now, of course, Servlets are just one aspect of the whole Java EE architecture.

After reading this chapter, you will be able to develop and use Servlet technology to create dynamic web applications. If you wish to dig deeper into Servlet technology or the classes and methods that are part of the Servlet API, refer to the Servlet specification at `http://java.sun.com/products/Servlet/reference/api/index.html`.

This chapter introduces Servlets and shows how to use them correctly in your web applications. In this chapter, you will learn:

- How HTTP requests are made to servers and what a response looks like
- How Servlets are designed to respond to HTTP requests
- What phases a Servlet goes through during its lifecycle

- Why you need to ensure your Servlet is thread-safe
- How to handle exceptions in your Servlet
- How to create and use sessions
- How to use filters in your web application
- What the Model-View-Controller (MVC) architecture is and how it makes applications easier to maintain

HTTP and Server Programs

Although Servlets were originally intended to work with any server, in practice, Servlets are used only with web servers. So in a Java EE application, you will be developing Servlets that respond to HTTP requests. The Servlet API provides a class named `HttpServlet` specifically for dealing with these requests. The `HttpServlet` class is designed to work closely with the HTTP protocol. The HTTP protocol defines the structure of the requests that a client sends to a web server, the format for the client to submit request parameters, and the way the server responds. `HttpServlets` use the same protocol to handle the service requests they receive and to return responses to clients. So, understanding the basics of HTTP is important to learning how to use Servlets.

Request Methods

The HTTP specification defines a number of requests that a web client, typically a browser, can make on a web server. These request types are called *methods*. Table 6-1 shows the seven methods that are defined by the HTTP specification (`http://www.ietf.org/rfc/rfc2068.txt?number=2068`).

Table 6-1. *Request Methods Defined by the HTTP Specification*

Method	Description
`GET`	Retrieves information identified by a request Uniform Resource Identifier (URI).
`POST`	Requests that the server pass the body of the request to the resource identified by the request URI for processing.
`HEAD`	Returns only the header of the response that would be returned by a `GET` request.
`PUT`	Uploads data to the server to be stored at the given request URI. The main difference between this and `POST` is that the server should not further process a `PUT` request, but simply store it at the request URI.
`DELETE`	Deletes the resource identified by the request URI.
`TRACE`	Causes the server to return the request message.
`OPTIONS`	Asks the server for information about a specific resource or about the server's capabilities in general.

When developing web applications, you will be concerned primarily with `GET` and `POST` requests, so let's take a closer look at those methods.

The GET Method

Simply stated, the GET method means that the browser sends a formatted string to the server, and the server returns the content identified by that string, known as a Uniform Resource Identifier (URI). One specific type of URI is a string that specifies the location of a resource in relation to the server, which is called a Uniform Resource Locator (URL). The resource can be a static web page or the result of a web application.

A GET request usually results when a user clicks a link in a web page or enters a URL in the address bar of the browser. However, there are other ways this can occur. For example, you can send a GET request through a telnet session or programmatically send a GET request to a server. You can even create a web page form that uses GET for its requests.

When sending a GET request, additional information can be passed to the web server. For GET requests, this information usually takes the form of request parameters that are appended to the URL. For example, when you perform a web search using the web site www.google.com, the search parameters are passed to the search engine using request parameters, as shown here:

```
http://www.google.com/search?hl=en&q=Beginning+Java+EE
```

The request parameters are prefixed by a question mark (?), the parameters are passed as name/value pairs (hl=en, q=Beginning+Java+EE), and each pair is delimited by an ampersand (&). If a request parameter includes embedded space characters, these are replaced by a plus sign (+). This format is also known as *URL encoding*.

Another way to pass parameters to a server is by appending the data as additional path information to the URL. The additional information looks like a continuation of the URL, but the web application interprets the path information as parameters. For example, suppose you had a stock brokerage application identified by the URL /stock/StockList. You could append additional information to the URL, which the StockList application would interpret as a parameter. It might look like this:

```
http://localhost:8080/stock/StockList/AddRating
```

The /AddRating part of the URL appears to be part of the URL for the web application; however, it does not identify any resource installed on the server. The resource is StockList, and the StockList application knows how to interpret the additional path information.

You can create a GET request from the command line to see the basic structure of such a request. Start by ensuring that your application server is running. Next, start a telnet client, using one of the following techniques:

Starting a telnet client on Windows: Start the HyperTerminal program (select Start ➤ All Programs ➤ Accessories ➤ Communications ➤ HyperTerminal). In the opening dialog box, enter a connection name and click OK. In the Connect To dialog box, shown in Figure 6-1, select TCP/IP from the Connect Using drop-down box. Then enter the host name or IP address and port to which you want to connect. For example, if the server on your computer is listening on port 8080, enter localhost for the host address and 8080 for the port. Click the OK button. Next, select File ➤ Properties from the menu. Select the Settings tab, and then click the ASCII Setup button. In the dialog box that opens, ensure that Echo Typed Characters Locally is selected. Click OK twice to return to the terminal window.

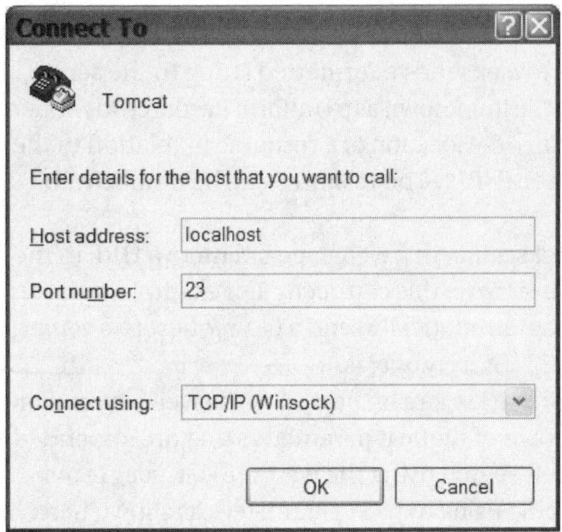

Figure 6-1. *In the HyperTerminal Connect To dialog box, select TCP/IP in the Connect Using drop-down box, and enter a valid host and port in the text fields.*

Starting a telnet client on Unix or Linux: Open a terminal or console window. Then enter **`telnet localhost 8080`** to connect to the server on the default port. You can replace `localhost` with an IP address or a host name, and the port number with the correct port for your application server, as necessary.

Now you are ready to send an HTTP request to the server. In either HyperTerminal or the telnet client, type the following command, and then enter two carriage returns:

```
GET / HTTP/1.0
```

Don't forget to press the Return key twice. The second return creates a blank line; this tells the server that the request is complete. The server should respond with the appropriate information. The following is a short excerpt of what was returned when we connected to the Sun Java System Application Server. You will get a different response if you connect to some other application server.

```
HTTP/1.1 200 OK
X-Powered-By: Servlet/2.4
ETag: W/"10335-1097261056937"
Last-Modified: Fri, 15 Apr 2005 18:44:16 GMT
Content-Type: text/html
Content-Length: 10335
Date: Sun, 17 Apr 2005 21:55:24 GMT
Server: Sun-Java-System/Application-Server
Connection: close
```

```
<!DOCTYPE HTMLPUBLIC "-//W3C//DTD HTML 4.01 Transitional//EN">
<html>
<head>
  <title>Sun Java(TM) System Application Server</title>
  <meta http-equiv="content-type" content="text/html; charset=iso-8859-1">
...remainder of response not shown...
```

Congratulations, you're now a certified web browser! Using the telnet program, you just performed the same actions that a web browser does. You sent a request to a server, and then received a response. The actual request consists of the method name (GET), followed by the relative URI of the desired resource, followed by the HTTP identifier for the HTTP version that the telnet program supports. The URI in this case is just /, which is the URI for the root resource of the server. If the server has been configured to serve a default page for this request (which both Tomcat and Java EE are), then it will send that page.

The HTTP request is terminated by a blank line. The blank line tells the server that the header is complete. Since a GET request has no body, this completes the request, and the program sends the request to the server.

A general HTTP message has this format:

```
Request-Line
Headers
<Carriage Return/Line Feed>
[ message-body ]
```

Each request begins with the request line. In our example, that was GET / HTTP/1.0. This is followed by header data. In our example, we did not use any header data. A blank line created by entering just a carriage return/line feed (CRLF) sequence signals the end of the headers. This is followed by an optional message body. Since our example was a GET request, there was no message body. POST requests have message bodies.

You can see this entire structure in the response from the server, which has the same message format as a request. The first line of the response is the status line, which consists of the HTTP version, a response code (200), and a response message (OK). This is followed by the response headers: the date, content length, and other information added by the server. The headers, whether part of the request or response, are in the format *name : value*. This is followed by the actual body of the resource. In our example, the server returns the default page for the resource /.

So, whether you are clicking a link, entering an address in a browser address bar, using telnet, or connecting to a server programmatically (using code), the request that is sent to the server must ultimately follow the format prescribed by the HTTP specification. Most of the time, however, formatting the request is handled for you automatically.

The POST Method

If the request is sent using the POST method, the request can include a message body, and the server should pass this message body to the resource in the URI for processing. POST requests are typically generated by users submitting a form through their web browser. Forms can be used with either GET or POST requests, although they are usually used with POST requests. Additionally, like GET requests, POST requests can be generated manually, using a program such as telnet, or programmatically, using classes in the java.net package.

Also, while data can be passed to the server using the same techniques as with GET requests (appending parameters or adding additional path information), a POST request usually submits data to the server in the body of a request. For example, using the hypothetical StockList application, the POST request to submit stock ratings might look like this:

```
POST /stock/servlet/StockList/AddRating HTTP/1.0
Content-type: application/x-www-form-urlencoding
Content-length: 39

analysts=3&stocks=DDC&ratings=Smashing!
```

Now, if a browser had submitted this POST request, it would pass more information than we have shown here. However, these commands are sufficient for sending data to a web application. The request starts with the method and URL, and the head of the request includes Content-type and Content-length parameters. This is followed by two pairs of CRLF characters, followed by the request data in the message-body. The message body is also terminated by two pairs of CRLF characters. In this example, the POST data consists of 39 characters, formatted using URL encoding. The data does not need to be URL-encoded, however. POST data can be in any format that the web application understands. The point is that request data for a POST request is usually included in the body of the request, rather than appended to the URL.

How a Server Responds to Requests

We already know how a server responds when the GET request is for a static HTML web page. When you enter an address or click a link, the server locates the resource identified by the URI and returns that resource as part of an HTTP message to the web browser. In the case of a web page, the browser displays the web page.

What happens, however, when the resource is a server-side program? In this case, the server needs to interpret the URI as a request for a server-side program, format the request parameters in a form the program recognizes, and pass the request to that program. In the early days of the Web, a standardized format called Common Gateway Interface (CGI) was developed for this purpose. Whenever you see a URL that has /cgi/ as part of the address, you are creating a request to a server-side program of that type. The program must interpret the request parameters, execute the appropriate processing, and return a response to the server, which returns it to the client. In the past, the server program was usually written in a language such as C or Perl, which executed in a separate process from the server. Every request caused a new process to be spawned, and when the program completed processing the request, it was terminated. This was usually resource-intensive.

Java Servlets, and specifically HttpServlets, provide some advantages over CGI programs for server-side applications. They can run in the same process as the server, so new processes don't need to be spawned for every request. Also, they are portable between servers (as long as they don't use any platform-specific code). CGI programs written and compiled in C, for example, need to be recompiled for a different operating system.

The Servlet Model and HttpServlets

Figure 6-2 presents a slightly simplified view of what happens when a client makes a request that is processed by a Servlet.

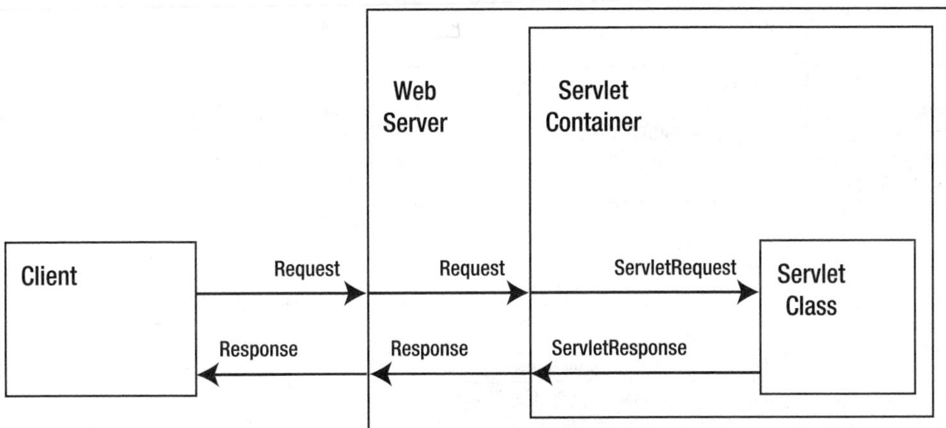

Figure 6-2. *A request for a Servlet is passed by the server to the Servlet container, which passes it to the Servlet class.*

When a client (usually, but not necessarily, a web browser) makes a request to the server, and the server determines that the request is for a Servlet resource, it passes the request to the Servlet container. The container is the program responsible for loading, initiating, calling, and releasing Servlet instances. The Servlet container takes the HTTP request; parses its request URI, the headers, and the body; and stores all of that data inside an object that implements the `javax.servlet.ServletRequest` interface. It also creates an instance of an object that implements `javax.servlet.ServletResponse`. The `response` object encapsulates the response back to the client. The container then calls a method of the Servlet class, passing the request and `response` objects. The Servlet processes the request and sends a response back to the client.

If you read the previous chapters about JSP (Chapters 3 and 4), you will realize that this request/response flow is very similar to the request/response flow for JSP pages. In fact, since JSP pages are translated into Servlets, the flow is almost identical. Is there any difference between the two? Or put another way, when should you use Servlets, and when should you use JSP pages? Here are the general guidelines:

- JSP pages are better suited for web components that contain a large amount of presentation logic and little or no business logic.

- Servlets are better suited for web components that perform processing of data or contain some business logic.

Servlets can send display data directly through the response, as shown in Figure 6-2. However, in many web applications, the Servlet will accept and process the request, using some other component to generate the response back to the client. In the next few sections, we'll look at how a Servlet receives the request and returns a response.

Basic Servlet Design

Like CGI programs, HTTP Servlets are designed to respond to `GET` and `POST` requests, along with all the other requests defined for HTTP. However, you will probably never need to respond to anything other than `GET` or `POST`. Figure 6-3 shows the classes you will use when writing Servlets.

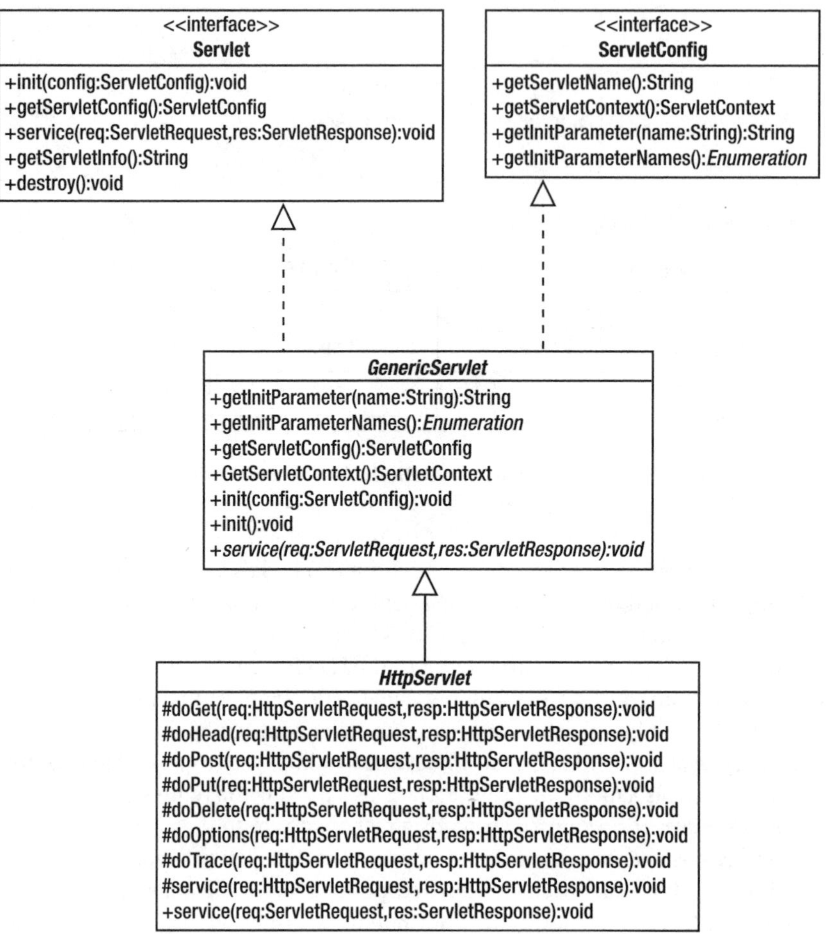

Figure 6-3. *Parent classes that provide the basic functionality of a Servlet*

When writing Servlets, you will usually extend a class named `javax.servlet.http.HttpServlet`. This is a base class that provides support for HTTP requests. The `HttpServlet` class, in turn, extends `javax.servlet.GenericServlet`, which provides some basic Servlet functionality. Finally, `GenericServlet` implements the primary Servlet API interface, `javax.servlet.Servlet`. It also implements an interface called `ServletConfig`, which allows it to provide easy access to Servlet configuration information.

Notice that `Servlet` defines only a small number of methods. You can probably guess that `init()` and `destroy()` don't handle any requests. We will look at these methods later when we discuss the Servlet lifecycle in more detail. The `getServletConfig()` and `getServletInfo()` methods don't handle requests either. That leaves only `service()` to handle requests.

The service() Method

When a Servlet container receives a request for a Servlet, the container calls the `service()` method of the Servlet. So, a Servlet that implements the `Servlet` interface must implement the `service()`

method to handle requests. However, your Servlet does not need to implement `service()`. The Servlet API provides a class named `HttpServlet`, which is a subclass of `GenericServlet`, itself a subclass of `Servlet`. As you can see in Figure 6-3, the `HttpServlet` class implements two overloaded versions of `service()`. When the Servlet container receives a request, it calls `service(ServletRequest, ServletResponse)`, which calls `service(HttpServletRequest, HttpServletResponse)`. Depending on the type of response, `HttpServlet`, then calls your Servlet to handle a specific request type: `GET`, `POST`, or one of the other HTTP request methods.

The doPost() and doGet() Methods

`HttpServlet` is intended to respond to HTTP requests, and it must handle requests for `GET`, `POST`, `HEAD`, and so on. Thus, `HttpServlet` defines additional methods. It defines a `doGet()` to handle `GET` requests, `doPost()` to handle `POST` requests, and so on; there is a `do`*`XXX`*`()` method for every HTTP method. With the exception of `doTrace()` and `doOptions()`, these methods simply return an error message to the client saying the method is not supported. You, as the developer, are expected to write your Servlet to extend `HttpServlet` and override the methods you want to support.

You will often see Servlet examples in books or tutorials that show a Servlet class that extends `HttpServlet` and overrides the `service()` method to process an HTTP request. This is acceptable for simple examples of Servlets, and you really won't have any problems if you do this in a real Java EE application. However, `HttpServlet` already implements a `service()` method, and it determines the correct `do`*`XXX`*`()` method to call for the HTTP request. In a real-world application, you should determine the HTTP methods to be supported by your Servlet and override the corresponding `do`*`XXX`*`()` method. This will almost always be `doPost()` or `doGet()`. The `doTrace()` and `doOptions()` methods are fully implemented by `HttpServlet`, so you do not need to override them in your Servlet.

When the Servlet container receives the HTTP request, it maps the URI to a Servlet. It then calls the `service()` method of the Servlet. Assuming the Servlet extends `HttpServlet`, and overrides only `doPost()` or `doGet()`, the call to `service()` will go to the `HttpServlet` parent class. The `service()` method determines which HTTP method the request used and calls the correct `do`*`XXX`*`()` method, as illustrated in Figure 6-4. If your Servlet has that method, it will be called because it overrides the same method in `HttpServlet`. Your `do`*`XXX`*`()` method processes the request, generates an HTTP response, and returns it to the client.

In Figure 6-4, note that even though `HttpServlet` and `MyServlet` are shown in separate boxes, together they constitute a single object in the system: an instance of `MyServlet`.

The actual signature of all of the `do`*`XXX`*`()` methods is as follows:

```
public void doXXX(HttpServletRequest request, HttpServletResponse response)
```

Each method—`doPost()`, `doGet()`, and so on—accepts two parameters. The `HttpServletRequest` object encapsulates the request to the server. It contains the data for the request, as well as some header information about the request. Using methods defined by the `request` object, the Servlet can access the data submitted as part of the request. The `HttpServletResponse` object encapsulates the response to the client. Using the `response` object and its methods, you can return a response to the client.

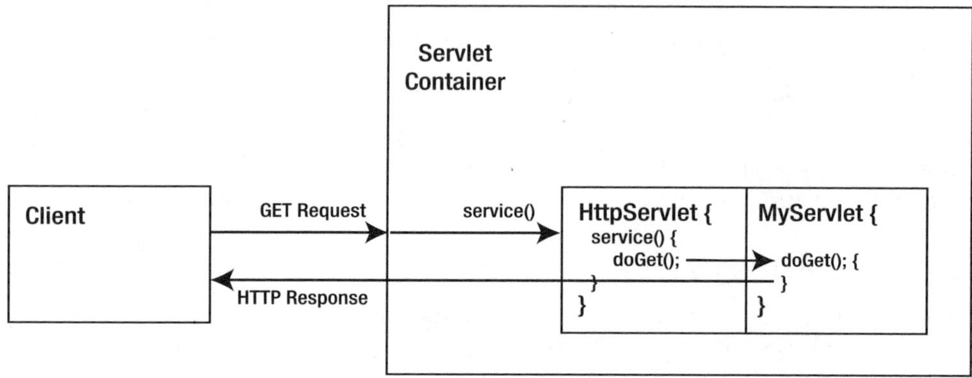

Figure 6-4. *The request is passed to the service() method of HttpServlet, which calls the correct method in the Servlet subclass.*

A Servlet That Responds to POST Requests

Since you know the basic Servlet objects at this point, let's work through a simple sample Servlet. We'll use some of the methods of `HttpServletRequest` and `HttpServletResponse`, even though they have not been introduced yet. We'll look at those methods in more detail after the example.

In this example, we'll create a Servlet that can respond to HTTP `POST` requests. Start by creating the simple Servlet shown in Listing 6-1.

Listing 6-1. *Login.java*

```
package com.apress.servlet;

import javax.servlet.http.*;
import java.io.*;

public class Login extends HttpServlet {
  public void doPost(HttpServletRequest request,
                     HttpServletResponse response)
  {
    String username = request.getParameter("username");
    try {
      response.setContentType("text/html");
      PrintWriter writer = response.getWriter();
      writer.println("<html><body>");
      writer.println("Thank you, " + username +
                     ". You are now logged into the system.");
      writer.println("</body></html>");
      writer.close();
    } catch (Exception e) {
      e.printStackTrace();
    }
  }
}
```

The Servlet can be compiled the same way as any other Java source file. You can compile it from the command line using javac, or if you are using an integrated development environment (IDE), use the IDE's compile command or menu option. You will need to include the correct Java EE library for the compilation. There are two possible libraries to choose from, depending on whether you are using the Java EE reference implementation, the Tomcat server, or JBoss. It doesn't matter which one you use. If you have the Java EE SDK, you can use the javaee.jar library; if you have Tomcat or JBoss (which uses Tomcat), you can use servlet-api.jar.

For example, if you're using the Java EE reference implementation, assuming JAVAEE_HOME is the environment variable for the location of the Java EE SDK, you could compile the Servlet with the following command line on Windows systems:

```
> javac -classpath %JAVAEEHOME%\lib\javaee.jar Login.java
```

On Linux and Unix systems, you would use this command line:

```
> javac -classpath $JAVAEEHOME/lib/javaee.jar Login.java
```

If you're using Tomcat 5, assuming CATALINA_HOME is the location of the Tomcat installation, on Windows systems, compile the Servlet with the following command:

```
> javac -classpath %CATALINA_HOME%\common\lib\servlet-api.jar Login.java
```

On Linux and Unix systems, use this command:

```
> javac -classpath $CATALINA_HOME/common/lib/servlet-api.jar Login.java
```

The Servlet in Listing 6-1 implements the doPost() method. So, to call the Servlet, you need a client that can submit a POST request. Listing 6-2 shows an HTML page (login.html) that has a form that posts to the Servlet.

Listing 6-2. *login.html*

```
<html>
  <head>
    <title>Login</title>
  </head>

  <body>
    <h1>Login</h1>

    Please enter your username and password
    <form action="Login" method="POST">
      <p>Username: <input type="text" name="username" length="40">
      <p>Password: <input type="password" name="password" length="40">
      <p><input type="submit" value="Submit">
    </form>
  </body>
</html>
```

Deploying the Login Servlet to Java EE

At this point, you are ready to deploy the Servlet. The next set of steps will show how to deploy the Servlet with the Sun Java System Application Server. These steps are virtually identical to the steps used in Chapters 3 and 4 to deploy JSP pages. If you want to deploy to Tomcat, go to the next section, "Deploying the Login Servlet to Tomcat."

1. Start the Sun Java System Application Server. For Windows, select Start ➤ All Programs ➤ Sun Microsystems ➤ Application Server ➤ Start Default Server. For Solaris or Linux, add the application server `\bin` directory to the path, and then run this script:

   ```
   asadmin start-domain domain1
   ```

2. Start the Deployment Tool. For Windows, select Start ➤ All Programs ➤ Sun Microsystems ➤ Application Server ➤ Deploytool. For Solaris or Linux, run the `deploytool` script.

3. Choose to create a new Web Application WAR. Select File ➤ New ➤ Web Component from the Deployment Tool menu. Alternatively, you can click the toolbar button for creating a new web component.

4. The New Web Application Wizard will now run. Click Next on the opening splash screen (if it is displayed).. In the War Location pane, ensure Create New Stand-Alone War Module is selected. In the War Naming pane, click the Browse button. In the Create Module File dialog box, shown in Figure 6-5, select a directory and enter a filename for the WAR file (`Servlet_Ex01` in this example). Click the Create Module File button to return to the wizard.

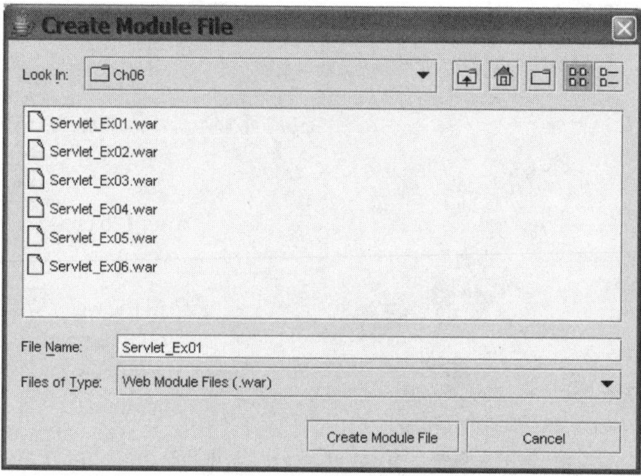

Figure 6-5. *The Create Module File dialog box allows you to enter a name for the WAR file and select the directory for this file.*

5. In the Contents pane of the wizard, shown in Figure 6-6, click the Edit Contents button and add the `login.html` and `Login.class` files to the application. Then click the Next button.

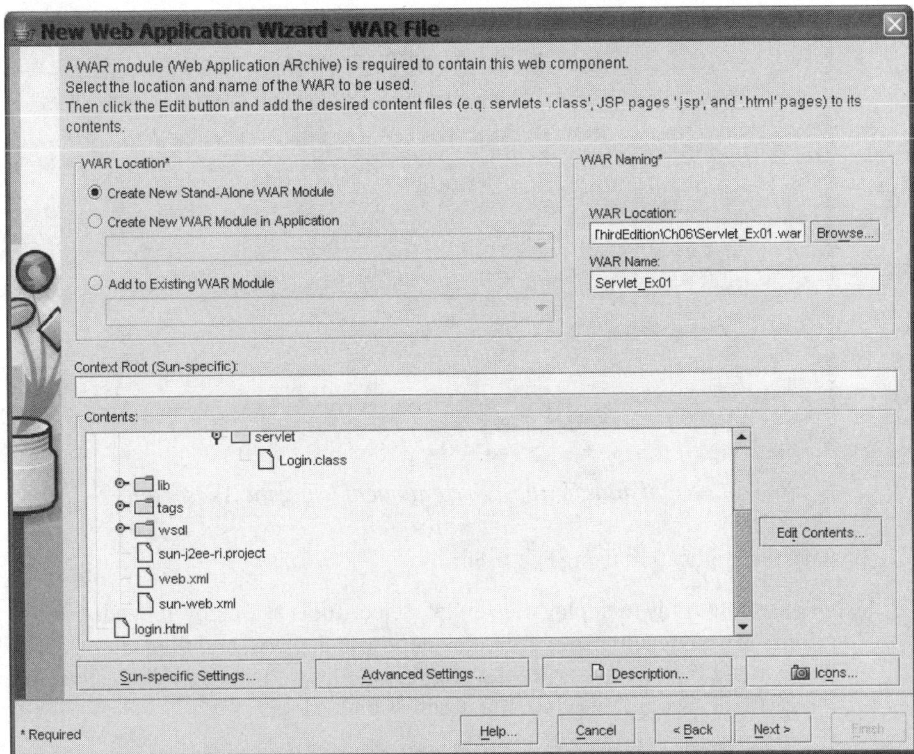

Figure 6-6. *The first page of the New Web Application Wizard is used to select the files that are part of the web component and select a name for the WAR file.*

6. The next page of the wizard allows you to select the web component to create. Servlet should already be selected, so click Next.

7. The third page of the wizard allows you to select the Servlet class and the web component name. There should be only one entry in the Servlet Class drop-down box, `com.apress.servlet.Login`, so select this. The wizard will automatically create entries for the Web Component Name and Web Component Display Name fields. Click Finish.

8. In the folder view in the left pane, select the Login WebApp, and then click the Aliases tab, as shown in Figure 6-7. Click Add to add a new alias, and enter the alias `/Login` for the Servlet.

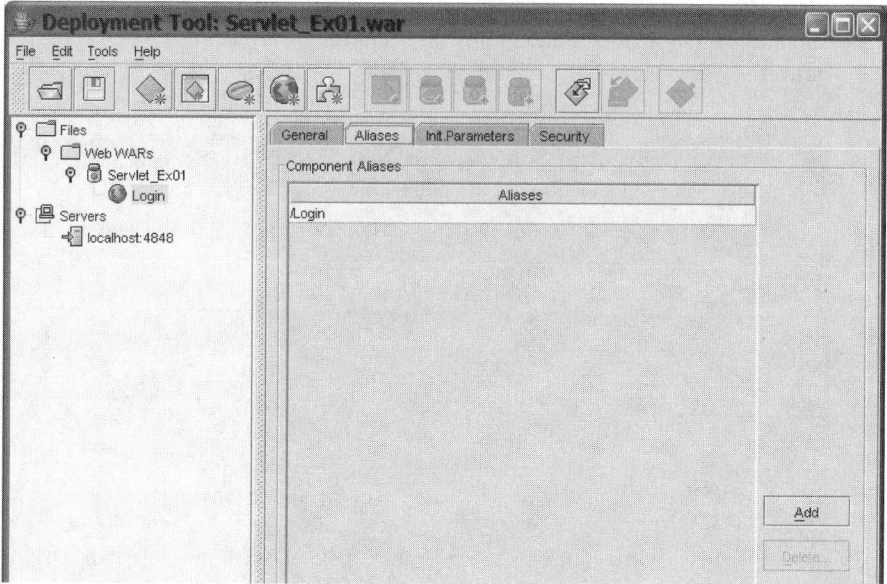

Figure 6-7. *Enter an alias for the web component using the Aliases tab.*

9. Save the application using File ➤ Save.

10. You are now ready to deploy the Servlet. Select Tools ➤ Deploy. If needed, enter the admin username and password in the deploy dialog box, and then click OK. As the deployment process proceeds, the progress is reported in a new dialog box. After the deployment is complete, close the progress dialog box.

11. Open a browser and enter the URL `http://localhost:8080/Servlet_Ex01/login.html` into the address bar. If your server is not installed on the local machine, use the actual server name or IP address in place of `localhost`; also, replace 8080 with the correct port if your application server is using a different port. The path name `Servlet_Ex01` corresponds to the WAR filename. The browser will load the login page, as shown in Figure 6-8.

12. Enter a username and password into the dialog box and click the Submit button. The Servlet will process the request and return the web page shown in Figure 6-9 to the browser.

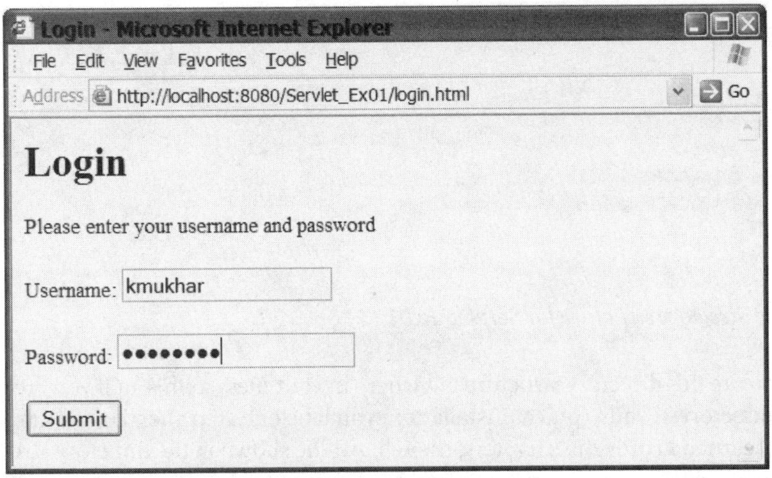

Figure 6-8. *The login.html page loaded into the browser*

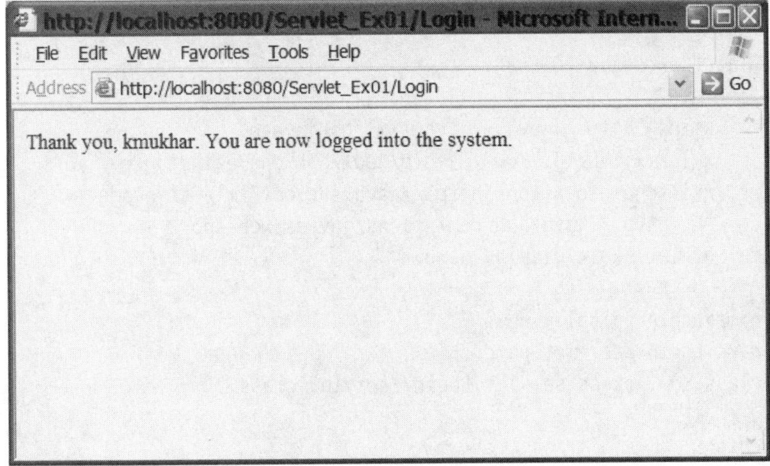

Figure 6-9. *The web page returned by the Login Servlet*

Deploying the Login Servlet to Tomcat

To deploy to Tomcat, the application needs an appropriate directory structure. Start by creating this directory structure shown in Figure 6-10 (the same directory structure created automatically by the Deployment Tool when you deploy to the Java EE server).

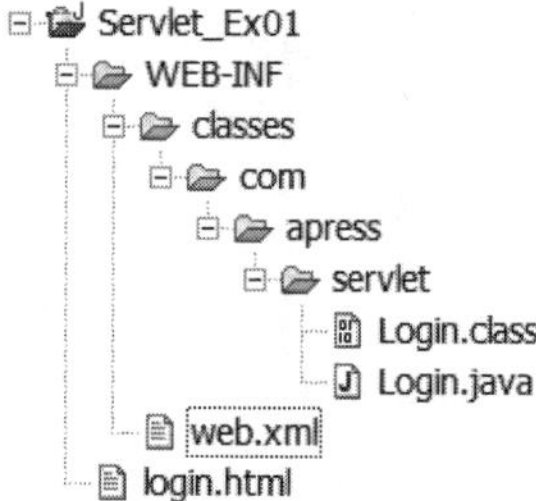

Figure 6-10. *The directory structure for Servlet_Ex01*

You can create this directory structure anywhere in your filesystem, but if you create it in the /webapps directory of your Tomcat installation, you'll be one step ahead of the game.

As you've learned in previous chapters, the web.xml file shown in the directory structure is also known as the deployment descriptor. Listing 6-3 shows the deployment descriptor (this deployment descriptor is created automatically by the Deployment Tool).

Listing 6-3. *web.xml for Servlet_Ex01*

```
<?xml version="1.0" encoding="UTF-8"?>
<web-app version="2.5"
                 xmlns="http://java.sun.com/xml/ns/javaee"
                 xmlns:xsi=http://www.w3.org/2001/XMLSchema-instance
                 xsi:schemaLocation="http://java.sun.com/xml/ns/javaee ➥
                     http://java.sun.com/xml/ns/javaee/web-app_2_5.xsd">
  <display-name>Servlet_Ex01</display-name>
  <servlet>
    <display-name>Login</display-name>
    <servlet-name>Login</servlet-name>
    <servlet-class>com.apress.servlet.Login</servlet-class>
  </servlet>
  <servlet-mapping>
    <servlet-name>Login</servlet-name>
    <url-pattern>/Login</url-pattern>
  </servlet-mapping>
</web-app>
```

If you created the directory structure in the /webapps directory of Tomcat, you can now browse to the login page. Otherwise, you need to install the application, either by copying the entire directory structure to the /webapps folder of the Tomcat installation or by creating a WAR file and copying it to Tomcat. You can navigate to the /Servlet_Ex01 directory and create the WAR file using the jar tool, as follows:

```
C:\Servlet_Ex01\>jar cf Servlet_Ex01.war *
```

If you used a different directory for your application, navigate into the root directory for your application, and then create the WAR file. Finally, copy the WAR file to the Tomcat /webapps directory.

To see the page, start the Tomcat server, if necessary, and then open a browser and enter the URL http://localhost:8080/Servlet_Ex01/login.html into the address bar. The browser will load the login page as shown in Figure 6-8. Enter a username and password, and then click the Submit button. The web browser will display a welcome message returned by the Servlet, as shown in Figure 6-9.

Let's take a quick look at the deployment descriptor for this application (Listing 6-3). It has two important elements under the <web-app> element:

```
<servlet>
  <display-name>Login</display-name>
  <servlet-name>Login</servlet-name>
  <servlet-class>com.apress.servlet.Login</servlet-class>
</servlet>
<servlet-mapping>
  <servlet-name>Login</servlet-name>
  <url-pattern>/Login</url-pattern>
</servlet-mapping>
```

The <servlet> element tells the container the class that is used for a given Servlet name, and the <servlet-mapping> element maps a URL to a Servlet name. Thus, when the Servlet container receives a URL that matches the given pattern, it will know which class to send the request to.

How the Login Servlet Works

The Login Servlet illustrates some of the main concepts you've learned. The class itself is just like any other Java class. In this case, it is a subclass of HttpServlet. As a subclass of HttpServlet, the Login class only needs to override the methods of HttpServlet that it needs to implement its behavior, or alternatively, add new methods for new behavior. In this example, Login needs to override only the doPost() method of HttpServlet.

When you click the Submit button of the login.html static web page, the web browser submits a POST request to the server. Web forms can be used to submit either GET or POST requests. The <form> tag in the web page has a method attribute that has the value POST. This tells the browser to submit a POST request to the resource indicated by the action attribute of the <form> tag. If no method attribute is used, the form defaults to the GET method.

When the server receives the POST request, it parses the URL to determine which resource to send the request to. There are two kinds of URL paths:

> **Relative paths:** These paths have no leading slash (/). The HTML in Listing 6-2 uses a relative path to identify the resource. The action attribute of the <form> tag is simply the relative address Login, and the browser converts that to the appropriate URL. When the browser converts Login to a URL, it appends it to the current application context because it is a relative path. It maps Login to a URL relative to the current page. For example, login.html was served from the URL http://localhost:8080/Servlet_Ex01/login.html. The browser appends Login to the same path as the login.html page to form the URL http://localhost:8080/Servlet_Ex01/Login.

Absolute paths: These paths begin with a slash (/). Absolute paths are formed relative to the server. If the form in `login.html` contained the absolute path `/Login`, the browser would submit the request to `http://localhost:8080/Login`. This doesn't identify a valid resource to the server, and so would result in an HTTP 404 Not Found error.

You can use either absolute or relative paths in your web pages. If you use absolute paths, you need to include the web component context as part of the path. For example, the absolute path shown in the following `<form>` tag would have caused the browser to submit the form to the correct resource:

```
<form action="/Servlet_Ex01/Login" method=POST">
```

When you deployed this Servlet, part of the deployment descriptor told the server and Servlet container how to map the request path to the Servlet class. When you use the Deployment Tool to create the web component, this mapping is created when you enter an alias for the web component. This alias is the web address for the Servlet within the web application context. Within the deployment descriptor, the mapping is specified by the `<servlet-mapping>` element.

In this example, the path element `/Servlet_Ex01` of the URL told the server to pass the request to the Servlet container. The `/Login` portion of the path maps to the `Login` Servlet, which is implemented by the `com.apress.servlet.Login` class. The Servlet container constructs instances of `HttpServletRequest` and `HttpServletResponse`, and calls the `service()` method of `Login`. Since `Login` does not implement `service()`, the parent class method is called. The `service()` method of `HttpServlet` determines that the request is a `POST` request and calls the `doPost()` method. Since `Login` does define `doPost()`, that method is used to process the request.

Within the `doPost()` method, the `Login` Servlet reads a request parameter from the `HttpServletRequest` object. The method that it uses to do this is `getParameter(String)`, which returns a `String` that has the value of the request parameter with the given name. If no such parameter exists, then null is returned. The parameter used by the Servlet is `"username"`:

```
String username = request.getParameter("username");
```

This is the same as the `name` attribute used in the web form for the `username` input field:

```
<p>Username: <input type="text" name="username" length="40">
```

There are several other methods used to retrieve the request parameters from the `request` object, as discussed in the next section.

The `Login` Servlet then uses the `response` object to return a response to the client. It starts by setting the `Content-type` of the response to `"text/html"`:

```
response.setContentType("text/html");
```

■ **Caution** The content type must be set before getting an `OutputStream` or `Writer` object from the `response` object, since the content type is used to create the `OutputStream` or `Writer`.

After setting the content type, the Servlet gets a `Writer` object from the `response` object. This `Writer` is used to send the strings that constitute the response to the client:

```
try {
  response.setContentType("text/html");
  PrintWriter writer = response.getWriter();
  writer.println("<html><body>");
  writer.println("Thank you, " + username +
                 ". You are now logged into the system");
  writer.println("</body></html>");
  writer.close();
} catch (Exception e) {
  e.printStackTrace();
}
```

Because writing to a stream can throw an `IOException`, the whole block is wrapped in a `try`...`catch` block. However, this `try`...`catch` block just prints out the stack trace for any exception thrown. While this is acceptable for this example, it is generally bad practice to ignore exceptions in the Servlet. We'll talk more about this in the "Exception Handling" section later in the chapter. You'll see the other methods of the `response` object in the "The response Object" section a bit later in the chapter.

The request Object

In the previous example, the Servlet got information from the `request` object by calling the `getParameter(String)` method:

```
String username = request.getParameter("username");
```

> **THE STRANGE CASE OF THE METHOD THAT WAS UNDEPRECATED**
>
> The `getParameter()` method is unique in that it is the only method ever undeprecated by Sun.
>
> In the second version of the Servlet specification, `getParameter(String)` was deprecated and replaced by `getParameterValues(String)`. This was done because there are several HTML elements (check boxes, multiple-selection lists, and multiple elements with the same name) that return multiple values. The `getParameter(String)` method returns only a single value. The `getParameterValues(String)` method returns a `String` array, so it can be used for multiple-value elements *and* single-value elements (by returning a single-element array).
>
> However, there are still many times when the HTML form sends a single value for a named element. While you can access array element zero in those situations, it is somewhat more syntactically cumbersome. For this reason, many developers expressed the opinion that the `getParameter(String)` method was still useful, and Sun undeprecated the method.

As you've seen, encoding and form encoding use name/value pairs to pass parameters from the browser to the server. The method `getParameter(String)` returns the `String` value for the given name in the parameter list. If no such name was submitted by the client, the method returns null.

The `ServletRequest` interface defines a few other methods for getting and using request data from the client's request:

- `public Enumeration getParameterNames()`: Returns an enumeration of all the names in the request.
- `public String[] getParameterValues(String name)`: Returns all the request parameter values for the given name.
- `public Map getParameterMap()`: Returns all the parameters stored in a `Map` object. Each parameter name is a key in the `Map`; the value returned for a name is a `String[]` array.

The `getParameterValues()` method is used when the named parameter may have multiple values. For instance, if an HTML form contains a `<select>` list that allows multiple selections, the request will contain all the selected values keyed by a single name, the name of the `<select>` list. If you call `getParameter()` on a parameter with multiple values, the value returned is the same as the first element returned by `getParameterValues()`. If you call `getParameterValues()` and the name does not exist in the request, null is returned. Also, keep in mind that web browsers only send non-null values. In other words, if an HTML form has a check box, and the user does not select the check box, neither the check box name nor value is sent in the request.

Accessing Request Metadata

You can also get information about the request using `ServletRequest` methods. Here are a few of the more useful methods:

- `public String getProtocol()`: Returns the protocol used by the request; this will usually be `"HTTP"`.
- `public String getServerName()`: Returns the host name of the server that received the request. This is useful if the server uses virtual servers.
- `public String getRemoteAddr()`: Returns the IP address of the client that made the request.
- `public String getRemoteHost()`: Returns the host name of the client that made the request.

Accessing the Raw Request Data

You can also get access to the request stream containing the unparsed request parameters. There are two methods available for accessing the request stream:

```
public BufferedReader getReader()
public ServletInputStream getInputStream()
```

You can use only one of the methods with a single request. Once you access the request input stream using one of these methods, the stream cannot be accessed again. Attempting to call either of them for the same request will result in an exception being thrown. Also, note that if you use one of these methods, the `getParameter()` and `getParameterValues()` methods may not work. Whether you can access the request stream and use the `getParameter(String)` or `getParameterValues(String)` methods is server-dependent.

Accessing Request Headers

Earlier, we looked at the format of an HTTP message. Recall that it looked like this:

```
Request-Line
Headers
<Carriage Return/Line Feed>
[ message body ]
```

The HttpServletRequest object provides a number of methods for reading the header data from the HTTP message:

```
long getDateHeader(String name)
String getHeader(String name)
Enumeration getHeaders(String name)
Enumeration getHeaderNames()
int getIntHeader(String name)
```

Two special methods are provided for getting a header value as a date or an int. Headers that are not dates or int values can be accessed using the general getHeader(String) method. The name argument passed to any of these methods should be the name of the header. Here again is part of the header portion of the response we got from the Java EE server in the first example of the chapter:

```
Last-Modified: Fri, 15 Apr 2005 18:44:16 GMT
Content-Type: text/html
Content-Length: 10335
Date: Sun, 17 Apr 2005 21:55:24 GMT
Server: Sun-Java-System/Application-Server
```

A Servlet could get the value of the Last-Modified header by calling getDateHeader ("Last-Modified"). It could get the Content-Length by calling getIntHeader("Content-Length"). A header like Server, which is neither date nor int, would be obtained by calling getHeader("Server").

Earlier in the chapter, we mentioned that browsers can append request parameters to the URL. The Servlet can obtain those parameters by calling getQueryString().

```
public String getQueryString()
```

Thus, suppose you have a request URL that looks like this:

```
http://localhost:8080/Servlet_Ex01/Login?name=Kevin
```

In this case, calling getQueryString() will return the string "name=Kevin".

We also mentioned that information could be added to the URL that looks like a continuation of the path. This extra path information can be obtained by calling getPathInfo():

```
public String getPathInfo()
```

For example, suppose you have a request URL like this:

```
http://localhost:8080/Servlet_Ex01/Login/extra/path/info
```

In this case, getPathInfo() will return "/extra/path/info".

The response Object

In the previous example, we used two methods of the response object:

```
response.setContentType("text/html");
PrintWriter writer = response.getWriter();
```

Using the Writer obtained from the response, the Servlet sent HTML data to the client browser for it to display. There is another object that can be used to send response data. You will normally use the Writer to send character data, but you can also send data to the client using an output stream obtained through this method:

```
public ServletOutputStream getOutputStream()
```

While the OutputStream object can be used for text data, its primary purpose is to send binary data to the response. The Servlet would get binary data (an image, for example) and store it in a byte array, then set the content type ("image/jpeg", perhaps), set the content length, and then write the binary data to the output stream.

The three methods just mentioned are defined by the ServletResponse interface. The HttpServletResponse interface adds methods that are useful for responding to HTTP requests. These methods allow the Servlet to add or set header data in the response:

```
void addDateHeader(String name, long date)
void addHeader(String name, String value)
void addIntHeader(String name, int value)
void setDateHeader(String name, long date)
void setHeader(String name, String value)
void setIntHeader(String name, int value)
```

The set methods are used to set a single header in the HTTP response. The add methods are used to add additional values to a header, for headers that allow multiple values. As you can tell from their names, two methods are used to set or add date headers, two methods are used to set or add int headers, and the final two methods are used for all other headers.

Deployment Descriptors

Throughout the last couple of chapters, you've seen several examples of deployment descriptors for our sample web applications contained in a file called web.xml. However, we've postponed a full coverage of deployment descriptors until now, because many of the elements involved relate to Servlets rather than to JSP pages. So, now that you know what a Servlet is, we can take a more detailed look at the deployment descriptor. This will be useful if you need to understand a deployment descriptor or manually create one.

■ **Note** Your Servlet container may have a tool that automates the process of creating the deployment descriptor. For example, the Deployment Tool that comes with Java EE can automatically create the deployment descriptor for a web application.

Because the deployment descriptor is contained in an XML file, it must conform to the XML standard. This means it should start with the XML declaration (<?xml version="1.0"?>).

```
<?xml version="1.0" encoding="UTF-8"?>
<web-app version="2.5" xmlns="http://java.sun.com/xml/ns/javaee"
            xmlns:xsi="http://www.w3.org/2001/XMLSchema-instance"
            xsi:schemaLocation="http://java.sun.com/xml/ns/javaee ➥
               http://java.sun.com/xml/ns/javaee/web-app_2_5.xsd">
</web-app>
```

The root element of the deployment descriptor is the <web-app> element. Table 6-2 shows the subelements defined by the Servlet 2.4 specification that can be used within the <web-app> element. Under the Servlet 2.4 specification, these elements can occur in any order within the deployment descriptor.

Table 6-2. *Valid Subelements for the <web-app> Element of a Deployment Descriptor*

Element	Description
context-param	Contains parameter values that are used across the application
description	A description of the web application
display-name	A name that can be used by an application management tool to represent the web application
distributable	Describes whether the web application can be distributed across servers; the default value is false
ejb-local-ref	Defines a local reference to an EJB
ejb-ref	Defines a remote reference to an EJB
env-entry	Defines the name of a resource that can be accessed through the JNDI interface
error-page	Defines the error page returned to the client when a particular error occurs
filter	Defines filter classes that are called prior to the Servlet
filter-mapping	Defines aliases for filters
icon	Contains a path to icons that can be used by a graphical tool to represent the web application
jsp-config	Defines global configuration for JSP components
listener	Defines listener classes that are called by the container when certain events occur
locale-encoding-mapping-list	Specifies a mapping between a local code and an encoding
login-config	Configures the authentication method
message-destination	Specifies a message destination
message-destination-ref	Defines a reference to a message destination within the web application

Table 6-2. *Valid Subelements for the <web-app> Element of a Deployment Descriptor (Continued)*

Element	Description
mime-mapping	Defines a mapping for the public files of the web application to MIME types
resource-env-ref	Configures an external resource that can be used by the Servlet
resource-ref	Configures an external resource that can be used by the Servlet
security-constraint	Describes the roles or users that can access the web application
security-role	Defines a security role for the application
service-ref	Defines how web components can access web services
servlet	Defines a Servlet by name and class file
servlet-mapping	Defines aliases for Servlets
session-config	Defines a timeout value for sessions
welcome-file-list	Defines the file to return to the client when no resource is specified in the URL

Caution In previous versions of the Servlet specification, the subelements under `<web-app>` were required to be in a particular order. With the latest version of the Servlet specification, this restriction has been removed. Subelements under `<web-app>` can be in any arbitrary order. If you are using a Servlet container that supports only Servlet 2.3 or earlier, you will need to use the order required by the DTD in the Servlet 2.3 specification (`www.jcp.org/aboutJava/communityprocess/final/jsr053/`): `icon`, `display-name`, `description`, `distributable`, `context-param`, `filter`, `filter-mapping`, `listener`, `servlet`, `servlet-mapping`, `session-config`, `mimemapping`, `welcome-file-list`, `error-page`, `taglib`, `resourceenv-ref`, `resource-ref`, `security-constraint`, `login-config`, `security-role`, `env-entry`, `ejb-ref`, `ejb-local-ref`.

Now, let's take a closer look at some of the most important subelements: `<context-param>`, `<servlet>`, and `<servlet-mapping>`. Later in this chapter, we'll look at a few others. In the "Filters" section, we will discuss `<filter>` and `<filter-mapping>`, and in the "Exception Handling" section, we'll discuss `<error-page>`.

The <context-param> Element

The `<context-param>` element allows you to define context parameters. These parameters specify values that are available to the entire web application context. The element is used like this:

```
<web-app>
  <context-param>
    <param-name>debug</param-name>
    <param-value>true</param-value>
  </context-param>
</web-app>
```

The deployment descriptor can contain zero or more of these elements. Each web component that has access to the Servlet context can access these parameters by name. We will show how this is done later in the chapter in Listings 6-4 and 6-6. Note that because the web.xml file is in text format, you can pass parameters to the application only as strings.

The <servlet> Element

The <servlet> element is the primary element for describing the Servlets in your web application. The <servlet> element can have the following subelements:

- <icon>
- <servlet-name>
- <display-name>
- <description>
- <servlet-class>
- <jsp-file>
- <init-param>
- <load-on-startup>
- <run-as>
- <security-role-ref>

The only required subelements are <servlet-name> and one of the subelements <servlet-class> or <jsp-file>. The <servlet-name> subelement defines a user-friendly name that can be used for the resource. The <servlet-class> or <jsp-file> subelement defines the fully qualified name of the Servlet class or JSP file. In the previous example, we used the following for the <servlet> element:

```
<servlet>
    <servlet-name>Login</servlet-name>
    <servlet-class>com.apress.servlet.Login</servlet-class>
  </servlet>
```

By defining the Servlet name as Login, and using the <servlet-mapping> element to map URLs such as /Login to the name Login, we were able to access the Servlet using the simple URL /Servlet_Ex01/Login. Okay, that's not such a big deal when the Servlet name and class name are both Login, but suppose your class name were com.mycompany.subdivision.MyServletWith➥AReallyReallyLongName. Do you really want to type that? It makes much more sense to be able to access the Servlet using SimpleName.

The `<servlet-class>` subelement told the Servlet container that all requests for `Login` should be handled by the `com.apress.servlet.Login` class.

The other subelements of `<servlet>` that you will use often are `<load-on-startup>` and `<init-param>`. The `<load-on-startup>` element, if used, contains a positive integer value that specifies that the Servlet should be loaded when the server is started. The relative order of Servlet loading is determined by the value: Servlets with lower values are loaded before Servlets with higher values, and Servlets with the same value are loaded in an arbitrary order. If the element is not present, the Servlet is loaded when the first request for the Servlet is made. Here's an example:

```
<load-on-startup>5</load-on-startup>
```

The `<init-param>` element is similar to the `<context-param>` element. The difference is that `<init-param>` defines parameters that are accessible only to the given Servlet. Here's an example:

```
<init-param>
  <param-name>debug</param-name>
  <param-value>true</param-value>
</init-param>
```

The <servlet-mapping> Element

The `<servlet-mapping>` element is used to define mappings from a particular request URI to a given Servlet name. For example, in the `Login` Servlet, we defined this mapping:

```
<servlet-mapping>
  <servlet-name>Login</servlet-name>
  <url-pattern>/Login</url-pattern>
</servlet-mapping>
```

This told the server that if it received any URI that matched the pattern `/Login`, it should pass the request to the Servlet with the name `Login`.

Servlet Lifecycle

In the previous example, we looked at a simple Servlet that processed a `POST` request. This processing encompassed just a small portion of a Servlet's lifecycle (although that's the most important portion from the client's point of view). Now, let's look at the complete lifecycle of a Servlet.

The Servlet specification defines the following four stages of a Servlet's lifecycle:

1. Loading and instantiation
2. Initialization
3. Request handling
4. End of life

These four stages are illustrated in Figure 6-11.

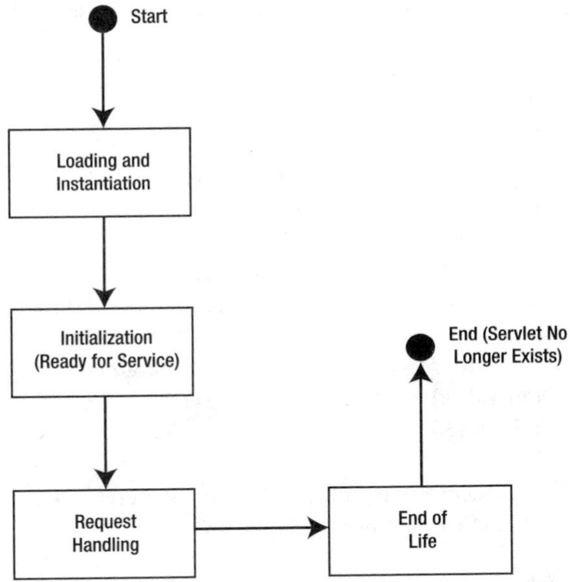

Figure 6-11. *From loading through end of life, a Servlet passes through a number of distinct phases during its lifecycle.*

Loading and Instantiation

In the first stage of the lifecycle, the Servlet class is loaded from the classpath and instantiated by the Servlet container. The method that realizes this stage is the Servlet constructor. However, unlike the other stages, you do not need to explicitly provide the method for this stage.

How does the Servlet container know which Servlets to load? It knows by reading the deployment descriptor. The Servlet container reads each `web.xml` file, and loads the Servlet classes identified in the deployment descriptor. Then the container instantiates each Servlet by calling its no-argument constructor.

Since the Servlet container dynamically loads and instantiates Servlets, it does not know about any constructors you create that might take parameters. Thus, it can call only the no-argument constructor, and it is useless for you to specify any constructor other than one that takes no arguments. Since the Java compiler provides this constructor automatically when you do not supply a constructor, there is no need for you to write any constructor at all in your Servlet. This is why your Servlet class does not need to define an explicit constructor.

If you do not provide a constructor, how does your Servlet initialize itself? This is handled in the next phase of the lifecycle, Servlet initialization.

Initialization

After the Servlet is loaded and instantiated, the Servlet must be initialized. This occurs when the container calls the `init(ServletConfig)` method. If your Servlet does not need to perform any initialization, the Servlet does not need to implement this method. The method is provided for you by the `GenericServlet` parent class. That is why the `Login` Servlet class presented earlier in the chapter did not have an `init()` method. The `init()` method allows the Servlet to read initialization parameters or configuration data, initialize external resources such as database connections, and perform other one-time activities. `GenericServlet` provides two overloaded forms of the method:

```
public void init() throws ServletException
public void init(ServletConfig) throws ServletException
```

As we mentioned in the previous “Deployment Descriptors” section, the deployment descriptor can define parameters that apply to the Servlet through the `<init-param>` element. The Servlet container reads these parameters from the `web.xml` file and stores them as name/value pairs in a `ServletConfig` object. Because the `Servlet` interface defines only `init(ServletConfig)`, this is the method the container must call. `GenericServlet` implements this method to store the `ServletConfig` reference, and then call the parameterless `init()` method that it defines. Therefore, to perform initialization, your Servlet needs to implement only the parameterless `init()` method. If you implement `init()`, your `init()` will be called by `GenericServlet`; and because the `ServletConfig` reference is already stored, your `init()` method will have access to all the initialization parameters stored in it.

If you do decide to implement `init(ServletConfig)` in your Servlet, the method in your Servlet must call the superclass `init(ServletConfig)` method:

```
public class Login extends HttpServlet {
   public void init(ServletConfig config) throws ServletException {
      super.init(config);
     // ...Remainder of init() method
  }
   //...Rest of Servlet
}
```

■ Caution If you implement `init(ServletConfig)` without calling `super.init(ServletConfig)`, the `ServletConfig` object won't be saved, and neither your Servlet nor its parent classes will be able to access the `ServletConfig` object during the remainder of the Servlet lifecycle.

The Servlet specification requires that `init(ServletConfig)` successfully complete before any requests can be serviced by the Servlet. If your code encounters a problem during `init()`, you should throw a `ServletException` or its subclass `UnavailableException`. This tells the container that there was a problem with initialization and that it should not use the Servlet for any requests. Using `UnavailableException` allows you to specify an amount of time that the Servlet is unavailable. After this time, the container could retry the call to `init()`. You can specify the unavailable time for the `UnavailableException` using this constructor:

```
public UnavailableException(String msg, int seconds)
```

The `int` parameter can be any integer: negative, zero, or positive. A negative or zero value indicates that the Servlet cannot determine when it will be available again. For example, this could occur if the Servlet determines that an outside resource is not available; obviously, the Servlet cannot estimate when the outside resource will be available. A positive value indicates that the server should try to initialize the Servlet again after that number of seconds. If you want to signal that the Servlet is permanently unavailable, use this constructor:

```
public UnavailableException(String msg)
```

After the Servlet successfully initializes, the container is allowed to use the Servlet to handle requests.

Request Handling

Earlier in the chapter, we said that the primary method defined for servicing requests during this phase of the Servlet lifecycle is the `service()` method. As each request comes to the Servlet container, the container calls the `service()` method of the appropriate Servlet to handle the request. Since you will almost always be subclassing `HttpServlet`, however, your Servlet only needs to override `doPost()` and/or `doGet()` to handle requests. Here are the signatures of those two methods:

```
protected void doGet(HttpServletRequest req, HttpServletResponse res)
    throws ServletException, IOException
protected void doPost(HttpServletRequest req, HttpServletResponse res)
    throws ServletException, IOException
```

As with `init()`, the Servlet can throw a `ServletException` or `UnavailableException` during the processing of a request. If your Servlet throws either exception, then the Servlet container is required to stop sending requests to the Servlet. For a `ServletException` or for an `UnavailableException` that indicates a permanent unavailability (it was created with no value for seconds unavailable), the Servlet container must end the Servlet's lifecycle. If the Servlet throws an `UnavailableException` with some value for seconds unavailable (as described in the previous section), the Servlet specification permits the container to keep or destroy the Servlet at its choosing. If it keeps the Servlet, it must not route any requests to the Servlet until it is again available; if it destroys the Servlet, it will presumably create a new Servlet instance when the Servlet is estimated to be available again.

End of Life

When the Servlet container needs to unload the Servlet, either because it is being shut down or for some other reason such as a `ServletException`, the Servlet container will call the `destroy()` method. However, prior to calling `destroy()`, the container must allow time for any request threads that are still processing to complete their processing. After these threads are finished processing, or after a server-defined timeout period, the container is allowed to call `destroy()`. Note that `destroy()` does not actually destroy the Servlet or cause it to be garbage-collected. It simply provides an opportunity for the Servlet to clean up any resources it used or opened. Obviously, after this method is called, the container will not send any more requests to the Servlet. The signature of the `destroy()` method is as follows:

```
public void destroy()
```

The `destroy()` method allows the Servlet to release or clean up any resources that it uses. For example, it can close database connections or files, flush any streams, or close any sockets. This method is implemented by the `GenericServlet` parent class, so if your Servlet does not need to perform any cleanup, your Servlet does not need to implement this method. After the `destroy()` method completes, the container will release its references to the Servlet instance, and the Servlet instance will be eligible for garbage collection.

Although this method is public, it is meant to be called only by the Servlet container. You should never call the `destroy()` method from within your Servlet, and you should not allow other code to call this method.

Lifecycle of the Login Servlet

Even though we did not explicitly see it, the `Login` Servlet in the previous example followed all the steps of the Servlet lifecycle. Since the deployment descriptor did not have a `<load-on-startup>` element, the Servlet was loaded when the first request for the `Login` Servlet was made. After the class was loaded, the `init()` method was called. Since the `Login.class` did not have an `init()` method, this call was handled by the `GenericServlet` class, the parent class of `HttpServlet`. After initialization completed successfully, the request was sent to the `service()` method of `HttpServlet`, which called the `doPost()` method of `Login`. When and if you stop the server, the `destroy()` method is called, again to be handled by `GenericServlet`.

Event Logging in Servlets

In addition to the methods of `GenericServlet` that were presented earlier, you will find two other methods of `GenericServlet` useful:

```
public void log(String)
public void log(String, Throwable)
```

Although you can use the poor man's debug tool (`System.out.println()`) with Servlets, `GenericServlet` provides two `log()` methods. Rather than sending their output to `System.out`, these methods write the log information to the servlet container's log. This provides a more convenient and permanent logging mechanism than `System.out.println()`. We will use these methods in the remainder of the examples in this chapter.

Multithreading in Servlets

The fact that Servlets are multithreaded may seem obvious—or maybe it doesn't. It's obvious because all Java classes are inherently multithreaded; that is, whether or not you use them as such, they have the potential to have multiple threads executing their methods. (Unless, of course, a method is marked as synchronized.) On the other hand, it's not obvious because most of the time, you don't think about multithreading when you are writing your Java classes. Think about your first `"Hello, World!"` class (or whatever you wrote as your first Java class). You probably wrote it with a single static `main()` method, in which all the processing occurred. When you ran the class, the JVM created a single thread of execution, and this thread executed the `main()` method. Even today, unless you are writing GUI applications with Swing or AWT, or web applications, most of the classes you write are usually executed by only a single thread.

With Servlets, you need to change that mindset. Since Servlets are firmly in the Web world of the HTTP protocol, where concurrent requests are the norm and not the exception, you need to plan for multiple concurrent requests being sent to your Servlet.

Listing 6-4 shows a Servlet that is not thread-safe. This is a `Calculator` Servlet, which provides a very rudimentary service for calculating the sum or difference of two numbers. In this example, you will see how a Servlet that is not thread-safe can cause problems for a web application.

Listing 6-4. *Calculator Servlet*

```
package com.apress.servlet;
import javax.servlet.http.*;
import java.io.*;
public class Calculator extends HttpServlet {
  private int result;
  private int sleepTime;
   public void init() {
    String sleep_time = getInitParameter("sleep.time");
    sleepTime = getNumber(sleep_time);
  }
   public void doPost(HttpServletRequest request,
                      HttpServletResponse response)
  {
    String value1 = request.getParameter("value1");
    int v1 = getNumber(value1);
    String value2 = request.getParameter("value2");
    int v2 = getNumber(value2);
     String op = request.getParameter("submit");
    if ("Plus".equals(op)) {
      result = v1 + v2;
    } else {
      result = v1 - v2;
    }
     try {
      Thread.sleep(sleepTime);
    } catch (Exception e) {
      log("Exception during sleep", e);
    }
     try {
      response.setContentType("text/html");
      PrintWriter writer = response.getWriter();
      writer.println("<html><body>");
      writer.println(v1 + " " + op + " " + v2 + " is " + result);
      writer.println("</body></html>");
      writer.close();
    } catch (Exception e) {
      log("Error writing output", e);
    }
  }
```

```
    private int getNumber(String s) {
      int result = 0;
      try {
        result = Integer.parseInt(s);
      } catch (NumberFormatException e) {
        log("Error parsing '" + s + "'",e);
      }
      return result;
    }
}
```

The Calculator Servlet reads two values from the request and adds or subtracts them based on a third parameter. If the parameter named submit has the value Plus, then the Servlet adds the two values; otherwise, the Servlet subtracts the second value from the first. Before printing the result, the Servlet sleeps for a short time period. That time period is set as an init parameter, which the Servlet reads in the init() method.

Listing 6-5 shows the client for this Servlet. It submits two numbers with the names value1 and value2. It also submits a string with the name "submit" and the value of "Plus" to add the two numbers or the value "Minus" to subtract the two numbers.

Listing 6-5. *calc.html*

```
<!DOCTYPE HTML PUBLIC "-//W3C//DTD HTML 4.01 Transitional//EN">
html>
  <head>
    <title>Calculator</title>
  </head>
  <body>
    <h1>Calculator</h1>
     Please enter two values
    <form action="Calc" method="POST">
      <p>Value 1: <input type="text" name="value1" length="10">
      <p>Value 2: <input type="text" name="value2" length="10">
      <p><input type="submit" name="submit" value="Plus">
         <input type="submit" name="submit" value="Minus">
    </form>
  </body>
</html>
```

You can deploy this Servlet and HTML page just as you did with the previous example in this chapter. The following sections contain instructions for deploying to the Sun Application Server and a Tomcat server.

Deploying the Calculator Servlet to Java EE

If you are using the Java EE Deployment Tool, follow these steps:

1. Use `Servlet_Ex02` as the name of the WAR file. Add the `Calculator.class` (Listing 6-4) and `calc.html` file (Listing 6-5) to the web component.

2. Select the `Calculator` Servlet in the folder pane on the left. Add an initialization parameter to the Servlet through the Init.Parameters tab, as shown in Figure 6-12. The parameter's name is `sleep.time` and the value is 5000. To add the parameter, click the Add button and enter the name in the Coded Parameter field and the value in the Value field.

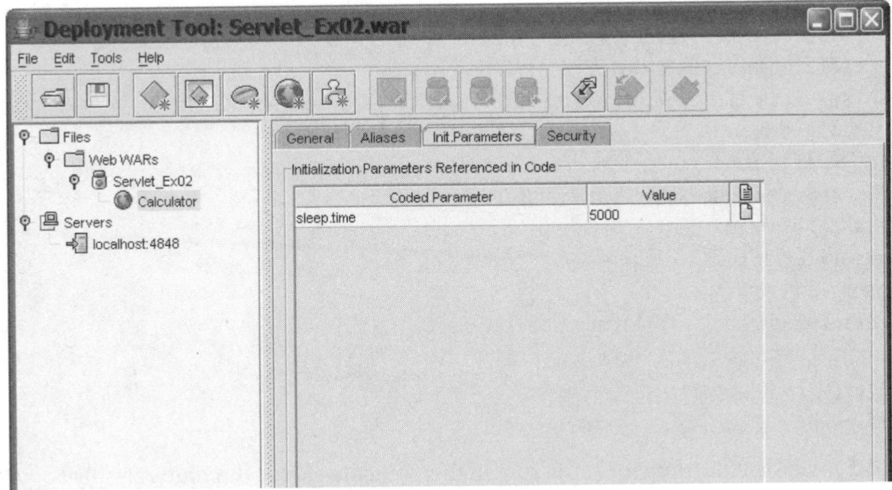

Figure 6-12. *Adding an init parameter to the Servlet*

3. Select the Aliases tab and enter the alias `Calc` for the Servlet.

Deploying the Calculator Servlet to Tomcat

If you are using a Tomcat server, create the directory structure shown in Figure 6-13.

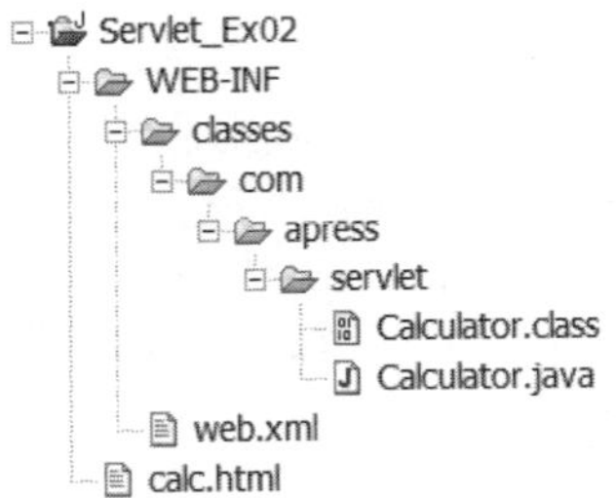

Figure 6-13. *The directory structure for Servlet_Ex02*

Listing 6-6 shows the `web.xml` for this application. In the `<servlet>` element, the Servlet name `Calculator` is associated with the `Calculator` class. This element also includes the init parameter `sleep.time`, which the Servlet reads in the `init()` method. The `<servlet-mapping>` element maps the URL pattern `/Calc` to the `Calculator` Servlet.

Listing 6-6. *web.xml for Servlet_Ex02*

```
<?xml version="1.0" encoding="UTF-8"?>
<web-app version="2.5" xmlns="http://java.sun.com/xml/ns/javaee"
         xmlns:xsi="http://www.w3.org/2001/XMLSchema-instance"
         xsi:schemaLocation="http://java.sun.com/xml/ns/javaee
                             http://java.sun.com/xml/ns/javaee/web-app_2_5.xsd">
  <display-name>Servlet Example 02</display-name>
  <servlet>
    <display-name>Servlet Example 02</display-name>
    <servlet-name>Calculator</servlet-name>
    <servlet-class>com.apress.servlet.Calculator</servlet-class>
    <init-param>
      <param-name>sleep.time</param-name>
      <param-value>5000</param-value>
    </init-param>
  </servlet>
  <servlet-mapping>
    <servlet-name>Calculator</servlet-name>
    <url-pattern>/Calc</url-pattern>
  </servlet-mapping>
</web-app>
```

If you create the directory structure in the Tomcat `webapps` directory, simply copy the Servlet class, the HTML file, and the `web.xml` file to the appropriate directory. If the directories are elsewhere, you can copy the entire directory structure and contents to `webapps`, or you can create a WAR file and copy it to `webapps`. The WAR file can be created by navigating into the top-level directory (`Servlet_Ex02/`) and running the following command:

```
C:\Servlet_Ex02\>jar cf Servlet_Ex02.war *
```

After creating the WAR file for Tomcat, copy it to the `webapps` directory, and Tomcat will deploy the web component.

■ **Note** If you have previously put a WAR file into the `webapps` directory, Tomcat will *not* redeploy the application if you copy a new version of the same WAR file into `webapps`. You need to first undeploy the application. This can be done from the Tomcat Manager page. Load the Tomcat home page (`http://localhost:8080`) and click the Tomcat Manager link. On the Tomcat Manager page, there will be an undeploy link for each web application.

Running the Calculator Servlet

To test the Servlet, open two browser windows and load the `calc.html` page into each browser. Enter values into each of the fields, but do not click either the Plus or Minus button. Figure 6-14 shows the two pages before submitting the requests to the Servlet.

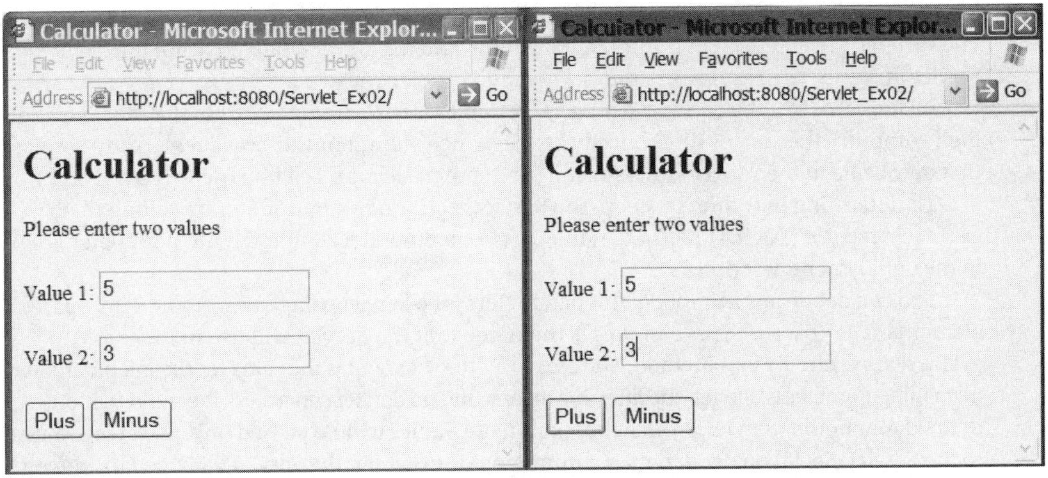

Figure 6-14. *Two windows open to the calc.html page and ready to be submitted*

After entering data into both web pages, click the Plus button in one browser; wait approximately one to two seconds, and then click the Minus button in the other browser. Figure 6-15 shows the response from the Servlet for each submission.

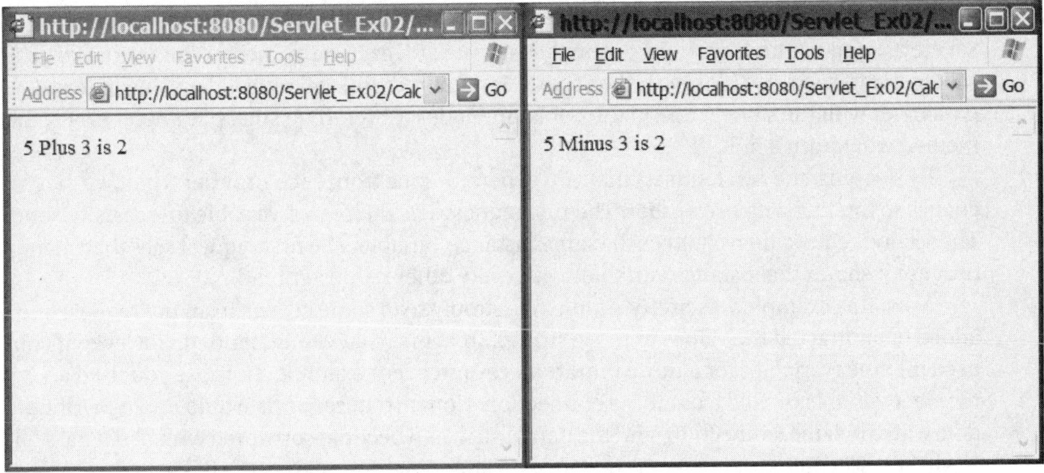

Figure 6-15. *The response from each submission*

It looks like there's a problem: one response appears to have computed the result correctly, but the other response appears to be wrong. You can easily verify that the Servlet works correctly with a single request. So what's going on when two requests are submitted at the same time?

In the `Calculator` Servlet, we've created a situation that allows multiple concurrent request threads to interfere with each other. This was done by using a member variable in the Servlet class to hold the result of the calculation. Member variables, also known as instance variables, are inherently not thread-safe. Each thread that enters a Java class has access to the same instance variables. The `Calculator` Servlet has two instance variables: `result` and `sleepTime`. The variable `sleepTime` is set during initialization, and it is never changed again during the Servlet lifecycle. The `result` variable is where the problem lies.

Inside `doPost()`, the code reads the `value1` and `value2` parameters from the request, and then computes the sum or difference based on which submit button was pressed and assigns that new value to the `result` variable. The Servlet then sleeps by calling the `Thread.sleep()`.

To determine how long to sleep, the Servlet reads an init parameter by calling the `getInitParameter(String)` method in the `init()` method. Recall that the init parameter is set in the deployment descriptor.

You can define any number of init parameters for a Servlet using one or more `<init-param>` elements. The `<param-name>` element is the name that the Servlet will use in the `getInitParameter(String)` method. The `<param-value>` element is the value for the init parameter. Each init parameter is Servlet-specific; this means that no Servlet can access the init parameters defined for another Servlet. Notice that parameter values can be passed only as `String` values to the Servlet. So, if you need to pass a number to the Servlet, the Servlet will need to convert the string to a numeric type, as the `Calculator` Servlet does.

The `getInitParameter(String)` method is defined by the `ServletConfig` interface. Your Servlet is able to call `getInitParameter(String)` because `GenericServlet` implements the `ServletConfig` interface (see Figure 6-3), and your Servlet inherits that implementation. As you may recall from the "Servlet Lifecycle" section earlier in the chapter, when the `init()` method is called, `GenericServlet` saves a copy of the `ServletConfig` object. The `GenericServlet` class implements all the required methods of the `ServletConfig` interface by delegating the method call to the `ServletConfig` object that it stored. This allows your Servlet to call the `ServletConfig` methods without explicitly using a `ServletConfig` object. When your Servlet calls `getInitParameter(String)`, the `GenericServlet` method will return the value of the parameter with the same name in the deployment descriptor. If no such parameter exists, the method will return a null.

By sleeping, the two requests that you generate—one from each browser window—have a chance to interact with each other. The first request sets the `result` variable to a certain value. The second request then changes the same instance variable. The first request sees that change because it shares the instance variables with every other request thread.

Now, this example was pretty simple. We simply read some strings from the request and added or subtracted the values in those strings. Imagine what would happen, however, if you used member variables for a more important resource. For example, suppose you used a member variable to hold a database connection. Concurrent requests would end up writing data with the same connection, and the database would become corrupted with bad data. That is why it is so important not to use instance variables for request-specific data.

How to Make Your Servlets Thread-Safe

In the `Calculator` Servlet example, you saw one way to make Servlets thread-unsafe: by using a member variable for data that was specific to a request. What you really need to know, however, is how to make your Servlet thread-safe. Here are some techniques that we recommend:

Use method variables for request-specific data. Whenever you need to access data from a request, that data should be stored in method variables, also known as local variables. These are variables defined within the scope of a method. Each thread that enters a method gets its own copy of the method variables. Thus, no thread can change the member variables of any other thread. If you need to persist data between separate requests, use a session to store that data (see the "Session Management" section later in this chapter).

Use the Servlet member variables only for data that does not change. You should do this as much as possible, but there are exceptions, as described in the next two items. Usually, you will use member variables for data that is initialized at startup and does not change for the life of the Servlet. This might be data such as lookup names for database connections (see Chapter 7), paths to other resources, paths to other web components, and so on. In the `Calculator` Servlet example, we made `sleepTime` a member variable, because this value was set at initialization and did not change during the lifetime of the Servlet.

Protect access to member variables that may be changed by a request. Occasionally, you may need to use a member variable for data that could be changed by a request. Or, you may have a context attribute that can be changed by a request. When you are using member variables or context attributes that can be changed by a request, you need to synchronize access to that data so that different threads aren't changing the data simultaneously. For example, suppose your web application allows an administrator to pause the application via a Servlet request. Information about how the application was paused needs to persist across requests and between users. So, you save the data in objects that are instance variables of the Servlet. Since you don't want two administrators trying to pause or unpause the application at the same time, you synchronize access to the objects; thus, while one administrator is pausing or unpausing the application, no other request can use those objects, and therefore cannot pause or unpause the application at the same time.

If your Servlet accesses outside resources, protect access to those resources. For example, suppose you decide to have your Servlet read and write data to a file in the filesystem. One request thread could be reading or writing to that file, while some other request thread is writing or reading the file. File access is not inherently thread-safe, so you must include code that manages synchronized access to this resource.

How Not to Make Your Servlets Thread-Safe

In addition to the preceding recommendations, you may see two other suggestions for making your Servlet thread-safe:

- Use `SingleThreadModel`
- Synchronize `doPost()`, `doGet()`, or `service()`

Do *not* follow these suggestions! They will either not solve your problem or will be too impractical for a real-world application.

Implementing the interface `SingleThreadModel` is a common, but incorrect, solution attempted by Servlet developers. `SingleThreadModel` is a marker interface. You use it like this:

```
public class MyServlet implements SingleThreadModel
```

Marker interfaces, such as `SingleThreadModel` (and other interfaces such as `Serializable` or `Clonable`), have no methods to implement. `SingleThreadModel` signals to the Servlet container that only a single thread should be allowed in the class at a time. There are various ways for the Servlet container to do this. The usual way is to create a pool of Servlet instances. The Servlet specification allows the Servlet container to create multiple instances of any Servlet that implements `SingleThreadModel`. As each request comes to the container, an instance of the Servlet from the pool is used to satisfy the request. While any request thread is executing in a Servlet instance, no other thread is allowed to execute in the same instance. However, this does not guarantee that your Servlet is thread-safe.

Remember that static member variables are shared by all instances of a Servlet; moreover, external resources, such as files, may be accessed concurrently by request threads. If your Servlet uses static member variables, outside resources, or context attributes, using `SingleThreadModel` does not make your Servlet thread-safe. You still need to synchronize access to those resources.

An even more important reason not to use `SingleThreadModel` is because it is not scalable. There is a limit to the number of Servlet instances that can be created. All those instances need to be managed. The larger the number of concurrent requests, the more unusable this solution becomes. It is always easier to create new threads than it is to create new objects. Again, we don't recommend it, but if you must use `SingleThreadModel`, you should use it only where the number of concurrent requests is relatively small (but remember that you still need to make the Servlet thread-safe).

Synchronizing methods in an attempt to make a Servlet thread-safe is even worse than attempting to use `SingleThreadModel`. If you override `service()` and make it synchronized at the same time, you have limited your Servlet to handling only a single request at a time (remember that the specification allows only a single instance of Servlet per JVM for non-`SingleThreadModel` Servlets). That may be fine while you are reading this book and you are the only client of the Servlets you write, but as soon as you move to any real-world application, this will become totally unworkable. As the number of requests increases, your clients are more and more likely to spend their time watching the little progress icon go around and around. As you probably know, it won't take much of that for users to abandon your web site. Synchronizing `doPost()` and `doGet()` is just as bad. Since the `service()` method of `HttpServlet` almost always calls `doPost()` or `doGet()`, synchronizing `doPost()` and `doGet()` has the same effect as if you had synchronized `service()`.

As we mentioned in the previous section, sometimes you must synchronize access to resources used by your Servlet. If you must synchronize code within your Servlet, you should attempt to synchronize the smallest block of code possible; the less code that is synchronized, the better your Servlet will execute.

Exception Handling

So far in this chapter, we've concentrated on how to use the various features of the Servlet API, so exception handling has consisted simply of logging the exception stack trace. In a real-world application, though, you will need to be more vigilant in the way you handle exceptions. We'll look at some techniques here.

Problems with Exception Handling

Let's begin with an example of a Servlet that doesn't perform any exception handling, as shown in Listing 6-7.

Listing 6-7. *BadServlet.java*

```
package web;
import java.io.*;
import javax.servlet.http.*;
public class BadServlet extends HttpServlet {
  public void doPost(HttpServletRequest req, HttpServletResponse res)
    throws IOException
  {
    res.setContentType("text/html");
    PrintWriter writer = res.getWriter();
    writer.println("<html><body>");
    String num = req.getParameter("number");
    Integer i = new Integer(num);
    writer.println("You entered the number " + i.intValue());
    writer.println("</body></html>");
    writer.close();
  }
}
```

Can you see the problem in the code in Listing 6-7? Listing 6-8 shows an HTML form that includes a field named `number` and calls the Servlet. Deploy the application and test various values.

Listing 6-8. *index.html*

```
<!DOCTYPE HTML PUBLIC "-//W3C//DTD HTML 4.01 Transitional//EN">
html>
  <body>
    Please enter a value
    <form action="BadServlet" method="POST">
      <p><input type="text" name="number" length="10">
      <p><input type="submit" name="submit" value="Submit">
    </form>
  </body>
</html>
```

If you entered any literal integer, the Servlet responds with a web page telling you what you entered. But what happens if you enter anything other than an integer? In this case, the `Integer` constructor throws an exception. What happens on the client side depends on the exception and the server. The user might get an ugly (from the user's point of view) stack trace, or the user might get no response from the server. Figure 6-16 shows Tomcat 5.0's response. To the client, it appears as though your application is broken (which it is). You probably should have checked the request parameters to ensure they were valid.

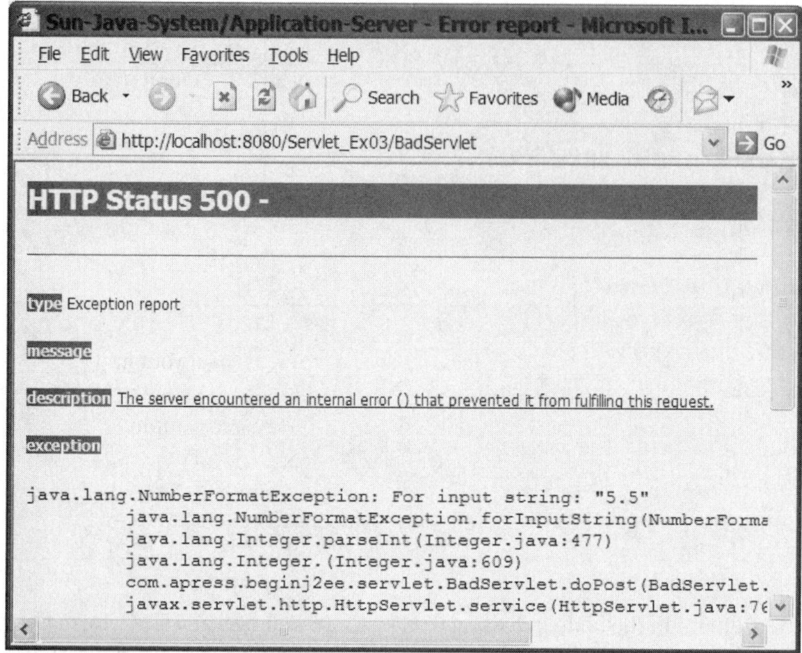

Figure 6-16. *The response from BadServlet when anything other than a literal integer is submitted in the request*

This brings up a good question: Where should data validation be done—on the client side or the server side? The answer depends in part on the requirements of your application. However, you will probably need to do data validation on both sides. You need to validate some data on the client side so that errors can be corrected prior to making the HTTP request. You need to validate on the client side to avoid a relatively expensive network communication just to tell users they did something wrong. You also need to validate data on the server side in case users bypass client-side validation.

Your Servlet also needs to attempt to provide error handling for every error that could occur. Let's look at a common attempt at error handling and why it is not the best solution. Suppose we take the example in Listing 6-8 and add a `try...catch` block, as shown in the code snippet below:

```
try {
    res.setContentType("text/html");
    PrintWriter writer = res.getWriter();
     writer.println("<html><body>");
    String num = req.getParameter("number");
    Integer i = new Integer(num);
    writer.println("You entered the number " + i.intValue());
    writer.println("</body></html>");
    writer.close();
  } catch (Exception e) {
    log("Exception in response", e);
  }
```

This looks okay, right? No, there is still a problem. What happens when the `Integer` constructor throws an exception? No output is sent back to the client, because the exception causes the thread of execution to immediately jump to the `catch` block. The client gets to stare at a blank screen.

Unless the exception is an `IOException` thrown while writing the response, you should always attempt to return some kind of response to the client. That could mean putting `try...catch` blocks around the code that you anticipate could throw exceptions or adding output statements that would be called from a `catch` block to send a response back to the client.

Error Pages

One other way to make your application more robust is to define error pages for your application. For example, given the `BadServlet` we've been using, we might create a web page or JSP that tells the user that they must enter integers only. Then we can specify that the application serve this error page whenever a `NumberFormatException` occurs. This is done with the `<error-page>` element of the deployment descriptor, as shown in Listing 6-9.

Listing 6-9. *web.xml for Servlet_Ex03*

```
<?xml version="1.0" encoding="UTF-8"?>
<web-app version="2.5"
        xmlns="http://java.sun.com/xml/ns/javaee"
        xmlns:xsi="http://www.w3.org/2001/XMLSchema-instance"
        xsi:schemaLocation="http://java.sun.com/xml/ns/javaee
        http://java.sun.com/xml/ns/javaee/web-app_2_5.xsd">

  <display-name>Servlet_Ex03</display-name>
   <servlet>
    <servlet-name>BadServlet</servlet-name>
    <servlet-class>com.apress.servlet.BadServlet</servlet-class>
  </servlet>
  <servlet-mapping>
    <servlet-name>BadServlet</servlet-name>
    <url-pattern>/BadServlet</url-pattern>
  </servlet-mapping>
   <error-page>
    <exception-type>java.lang.NumberFormatException</exception-type>
    <location>/BadNumber.html</location>
  </error-page>
</web-app>
```

Using this deployment descriptor, the `BadNumber.html` page will be sent to the client whenever the Servlet container catches a `NumberFormatException`. You can also specify error pages for HTTP error codes. The `<error-page>` element in the deployment descriptor looks like this:

```
<error-page>
    <error-code>404</error-code>
    <location>/NoSuchPage.html</location>
</error-page>
```

When a user attempts to access a page or resource that does not exist, the server generates a 404 Not Found error. Because the deployment descriptor says to send the NoSuchPage.html page whenever a 404 error occurs, this is what will be sent to the client. You can find the complete list of error codes at www.w3c.org/Protocols/HTTP/HTTPRESP.html.

You can define any number of error pages that you need for your application. If you specify an exception, the exception type needs to be the fully qualified class name of the exception. According to the Servlet specification, "The location element contains the location of the resource in the web application relative to the root of the web application. The value of the location must have a leading `/'."

■ **Note** We don't explicitly show how to deploy this example, Servlet_Ex03, in this chapter. However, a complete WAR file for this example is included with the downloadable code for this book.

The one error page you should specify for every application is for error code 500. An error code of 500 indicates an error in the server that the server was unable to deal with. This could be anything from a JSP page that cannot be compiled to an uncaught exception in a Servlet. By specifying a page to be sent to the client for a 500 error, you can be sure that if an error of this type occurs, the client will get a nicely formatted error page, rather than an ugly stack trace.

■ **Caution** As you saw in JSP_Ex03 in Chapter 3, Microsoft Internet Explorer does not always behave properly when Tomcat 5 returns an error page to the browser. When Tomcat sends a status code of 500 with an error page, Internet Explorer displays its own page rather than the error page when the error page is below a certain size (usually 512 bytes). You may need to pad your error page to ensure it meets that minimum size if any of your users have Internet Explorer. See Chapter 3 for more information.

Session Management

There's one big challenge with relying on HTTP for web applications: HTTP is a stateless protocol. Each request and response stands alone. Without session management, each time a client makes a request to a server, the server doesn't remember any information about the client. From the server's point of view, it's a brand-new user with a brand-new request, with no relation to any other request. To deal with this issue, web applications use the concept of a session.

A *session* refers to the entire interaction between a client and a server from the time of the client's first request, which generally begins the session, to the time the session is terminated.

The session could be terminated by the client's request, or the server could automatically close it after a certain period of time. A session can last for just a few minutes, or it could last days or weeks or months (if the application were willing to let a session last that long).

A web application can associate various requests into a single session by using additional information that the client sends with each request. The following are two common ways to do this:

- The application server sends a session ID as a cookie to the client. When the client makes a request, the session ID is sent back to the server, and the application server can use the ID to associate the request with a session.
- The web application embeds the session ID in the URLs in a web response. When the client clicks a link in the response web page, the URL sent to the server includes the session ID, and the web application can use the ID to associate the request with the session.

Note that when the client accepts cookies, your Servlet does not need to explicitly send the session ID to the client. However, if the client does not accept cookies, your Servlet must explicitly rewrite any URLs embedded in its web pages to include the session ID.

The Servlet API provides classes and methods for creating and managing sessions. In this section, we'll look in detail at session creation and management.

Creating and Using Sessions

Two methods of the `HttpServletRequest` object are used to access a session:

```
HttpSession getSession();
HttpSession getSession(boolean);
```

If a session already exists, then `getSession()`, `getSession(true)`, and `getSession(false)` will return the existing session. If a session does not exist, then `getSession()` and `getSession(true)` will cause one to be created by the application server. The `getSession(false)` method will return null rather than create a new session when one does not already exist. Note that you must call one of these methods before writing any data to the response. This is because the default technique for session tracking is to use cookies. Cookies are sent in the header part of an HTTP message by the application server, so they must be set in the response prior to writing any data to the response.

In addition, `HttpServletRequest` provides a few other methods for dealing with sessions:

- `String getRequestedSessionId()`: Gets the ID assigned by the server to the session.
- `boolean isRequestedSessionIdValid()`: Returns `true` if the request contains a valid session ID.
- `boolean isRequestedSessionIdFromCookie()`: Returns `true` if the session ID was sent as part of a cookie.
- `boolean isRequestedSessionIdFromURL()`: Returns `true` if the session ID was sent through URL rewriting.

Session Tracking with Cookies

All the data for the session, and all the data stored with the session, is maintained on the server. The server therefore needs some way to associate a client's request with a session on the server. The primary technique for doing this is to use cookies. When the server creates a session, it sends a session ID to the client in the form of a cookie. When the client makes another request and sends the cookie with the session ID, the server can select the correct session for the client based on the session ID.

Cookies are strings of text that a server can send to a client. The client can either accept and store the cookie or reject the cookie. Cookies should contain information relevant to the client. When the client makes a request to a given server, it sends the cookies it has from the server back with the request. (You can read the cookie specification at `www.w3.org/Protocols/rfc2109/rfc2109`).

When the client is accepting cookies, there is nothing your Servlet needs to do as far as session tracking is concerned. The Servlet container and the server handle all the session tracking for you.

Session Tracking with URL Rewriting

Some users don't like cookies. If you are working with a public web application, you can accept as fact that some users of your application will not accept the cookies sent to them by the server. When that occurs, the server resorts to another technique to track a user's session: *URL rewriting*. With this technique, the server appends the session ID to the URLs of the pages it serves. When that occurs, the Servlet does need to do something. In this case, the URLs embedded within the HTML pages of the application need to be modified for each client by rewriting the URL. This can be done with the following methods of `HttpServletResponse`:

```
encodeURL(String)
encodeRedirectURL(String)
```

These methods will rewrite the URL given by the `String` argument when the client is not accepting cookies. If the client does accept cookies, then the URLs are returned unchanged. You use `encodeRedirectURL()` for URLs that will be used with the `sendRedirect()` method of `HttpServletResponse`. Use `encodeURL()` for all other URLs.

Storing and Managing Session Data

What can you do with a session? All kinds of stuff, it turns out. Primarily, though, sessions are useful for persisting information about a client and a client's interactions with an application. If you had an e-commerce application, you could store information about the customer and the items in her shopping cart. If you were running an Internet radio station, you could use a session to record the listener's favorite music styles. Sessions store objects, so you can store anything at all in the session. Whenever your application needs to store information between requests, it can use a session to store the information.

To store and manage data, the `HttpSession` interface defines a number of methods. The methods you will probably use most often are those for setting and getting attributes from the session. You would store information in the session using the `setAttribute(String, Object)` method. Since the session is common to the entire application, this data then becomes available to every component in the application (so you need to consider synchronizing access to the session and session data). The stored data is retrieved with the `getAttribute(String)` method. You can use the following methods with sessions to set and get data:

- `public Object getAttribute(String name)`: Gets the object with the given name from the session. If no object exists with that name, the method returns null.
- `public Enumeration getAttributeNames()`: Gets an enumeration of all the names used to store data in the session.
- `public void setAttribute(String name, Object value)`: Uses the given name to store the object in the session.
- `public void removeAttribute(String name)`: Removes the object with the given name from the session.

Creating and Managing a Session's Lifecycle

You can use the following methods to create sessions and manage a session's lifecycle:

- `public long getCreationTime()`: Returns the time that the session was created in milliseconds from January 1, 1970, 00:00:00 GMT.
- `public String getId()`: Gets the session ID.
- `public long getLastAccessedTime()`: Returns the last time in milliseconds from January 1, 1970, that the client sent a request associated with the session.
- `public boolean isNew()`: Returns `true` if the session was just created by a call to `getSession()` or `getSession(true)`. Also returns `true` if the client chooses not to join the session.
- `public void setMaxInactiveInterval(int interval)`: Sets the amount of time in seconds between requests that the session will remain active. After this amount of time, the server can invalidate the session. Passing a negative value indicates the session should never time out.
- `public int getMaxInactiveInterval()`: Returns the amount of time that the session will remain active between requests.
- `public void invalidate()`: Invalidates the session and all the objects stored in the session.

The `isNew()` method returns `true` when the client has refused the session (usually by rejecting the cookie with the session ID), or when the session has just been created and the session ID has not been sent to the client yet. The `setMaxInactiveInterval(int)` method is used to tell the Servlet container how long a session can be inactive before it is invalidated. When that time limit is reached without activity, the session is invalidated. Using a negative value for the argument tells the container never to expire a session. A session is considered active when a client makes a request and sends the session ID with the request. Finally, the Servlet can actively expire the session by calling the `invalidate()` method.

Additionally, the following method returns the `ServletContext` for the session:

```
public ServletContext getServletContext()
```

This method returns a reference to the `ServletContext` object associated with the web application.

Storing Login Credentials in a Session

In the first Servlet example in this chapter (Listing 6-1), we created a simple Login Servlet. Now we'll see how to have that Servlet store login credentials in a session. Modify the Login Servlet from Listing 6-1 as shown in Listing 6-10.

■ **Note** The original Login Servlet did not validate the user credentials, did not use a secure connection for receiving the username and password, and did not store the Login information. In a real application, the Servlet would probably do all these things.

Listing 6-10. *Login Servlet, Modified to Use Sessions*

```
package com.apress.servlet;

import javax.servlet.http.*;
import java.io.*;

public class Login extends HttpServlet {
  public void doPost(
    HttpServletRequest request,
    HttpServletResponse response)
  {
    String username = request.getParameter("username");
    String password = request.getParameter("password");
    HttpSession session = request.getSession(true);
    session.setAttribute("username", username);
    session.setAttribute("password", password);
    try {
      response.setContentType("text/html");
      PrintWriter writer = response.getWriter();
      writer.println("<html><body>");
      writer.println(
        "Thank you, " + username + ". You are now logged into the system");
      String newURL = response.encodeURL("GetSession");
      writer.println(
        "Click <a href=\"" + newURL + "\">here</a> for another servlet");
      writer.println("</body></html>");
      writer.close();
    } catch (Exception e) {
      e.printStackTrace();
    }
  }
}
```

The `Login` Servlet includes a link to another Servlet. This Servlet, `GetSession`, is shown in Listing 6-11.

Listing 6-11. *GetSession Servlet*

```
package com.apress.servlet;

import javax.servlet.http.*;
import java.io.*;
import java.util.*;

public class GetSession extends HttpServlet {
  public void doGet(HttpServletRequest request,
                    HttpServletResponse response)
  {
    HttpSession session = request.getSession(false);
    try {
      response.setContentType("text/html");
      PrintWriter writer = response.getWriter();
      writer.println("<html><body>");
      if (session == null) {
        writer.println("You are not logged in");
      } else {
        writer.println("Thank you, you are already logged in");
        writer.println("Here is the data in your session");
        Enumeration names = session.getAttributeNames();
        while (names.hasMoreElements()) {
          String name = (String) names.nextElement();
          Object value = session.getAttribute(name);
          writer.println("<p>name=" + name + " value=" + value);
        }
      }
      writer.println(
        "<p><a href=\"login.html\">Return" + "</a> to login page");
      writer.println("</body></html>");
      writer.close();
    } catch (Exception e) {
      e.printStackTrace();
    }
  }
}
```

Compile these Servlets. The `GetSession` Servlet includes a link to an HTML page named `login.html`. This is the same page shown in Listing 6-2 earlier in this chapter. The directory structure for this example is shown in Figure 6-17.

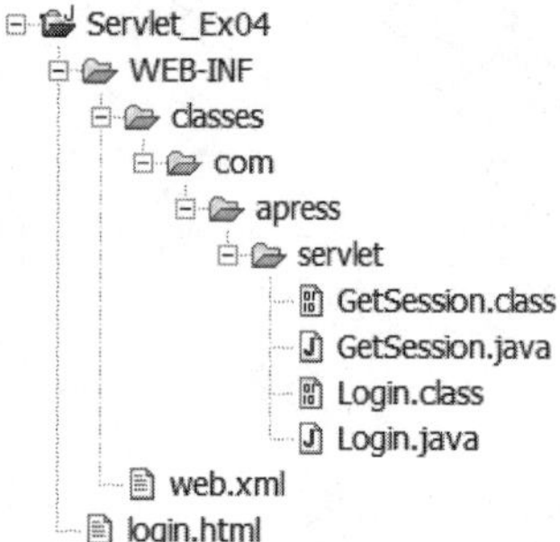

Figure 6-17. *The directory structure for Servlet_Ex04*

If you are using the Tomcat server, you will need a deployment descriptor. Listing 6-12 shows the deployment descriptor for this application. If you are using the Sun Application Server, the Deployment Tool will create the deployment descriptor for you.

Listing 6-12. *web.xml for Servlet_Ex03*

```
<?xml version='1.0' encoding='UTF-8'?>
<web-app
        version="2.5"
        xmlns="http://java.sun.com/xml/ns/javaee"
        xmlns:xsi="http://www.w3.org/2001/XMLSchema-instance"
        xsi:schemaLocation="http://java.sun.com/xml/ns/javaee ➥
                   http://java.sun.com/xml/ns/javaee/web-app_2_5.xsd">
    <display-name>Servlet_Ex04</display-name>
    <servlet>
        <display-name>GetSession</display-name>
        <servlet-name>GetSession</servlet-name>
        <servlet-class>
            com.apress.servlet.GetSession
        </servlet-class>
    </servlet>
    <servlet>
        <display-name>Login</display-name>
        <servlet-name>Login</servlet-name>
        <servlet-class>com.apress.servlet.Login</servlet-class>
    </servlet>
```

```
    <servlet-mapping>
        <servlet-name>GetSession</servlet-name>
        <url-pattern>/GetSession</url-pattern>
    </servlet-mapping>
    <servlet-mapping>
        <servlet-name>Login</servlet-name>
        <url-pattern>/Login</url-pattern>
    </servlet-mapping>
</web-app>
```

If you are using the Sun Application Server and Deployment Tool, create a web application named `Servlet_Ex04`. Use the New Web Application WAR Wizard (File ➤ New ➤ Web Component) to create components for both Servlets. Make sure that you add both Servlet `.class` files to the first WAR module, and for the second component, select Add to Existing WAR Module on the second wizard screen, instead of creating a new WAR module. Select each component in the left pane, and select the Aliases tab in the right pane to set the alias. The alias for the `GetSession` Servlet is `/GetSession`; the alias for the `Login` Servlet is `/Login`.

After deploying the application, open a browser and ensure that it is accepting cookies. Enter the URL `http://localhost:8080/Servlet_Ex04/GetSession` (assuming that you gave the name `Servlet_Ex04` to the web application). Because you do not have a session yet, this Servlet should respond with a page that tells you to go to the `login.html` page, as shown in Figure 6-18.

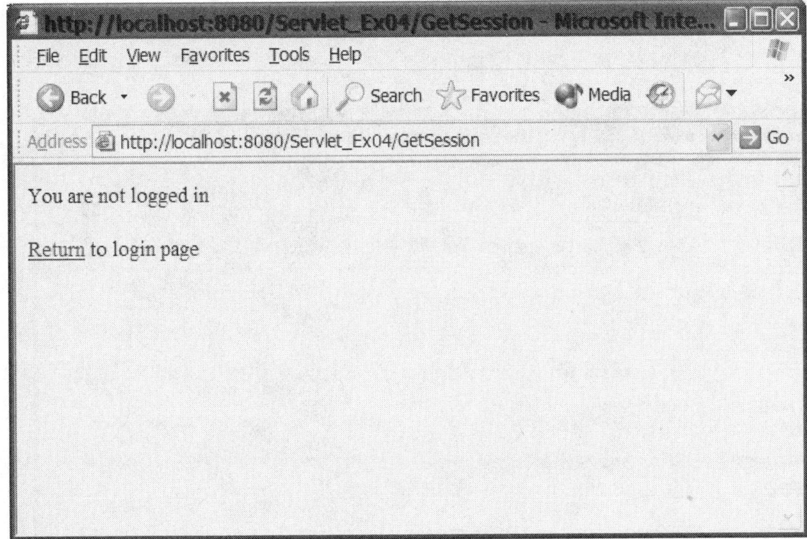

Figure 6-18. *Since there is no session yet, GetSession prints out a message and link to the login page.*

On the login page, enter a username and password, as shown in Figure 6-19, and click Submit.

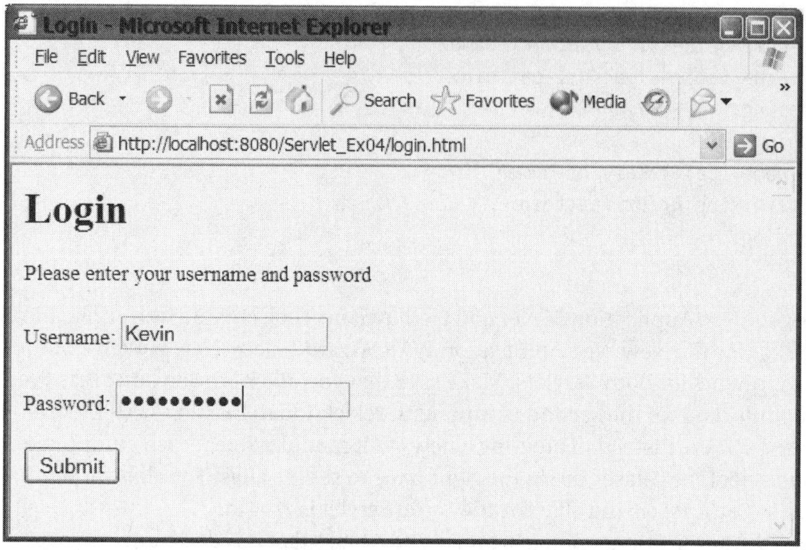

Figure 6-19. *Enter a username and password in the login page and click the Submit button.*

The next page prints a short message that includes a link to the `GetSession` Servlet. Click the link. Now that you have a session, the `GetSession` Servlet prints out the value of the attributes in your session. In Figure 6-20, you can also see the session ID has been appended to the URL.

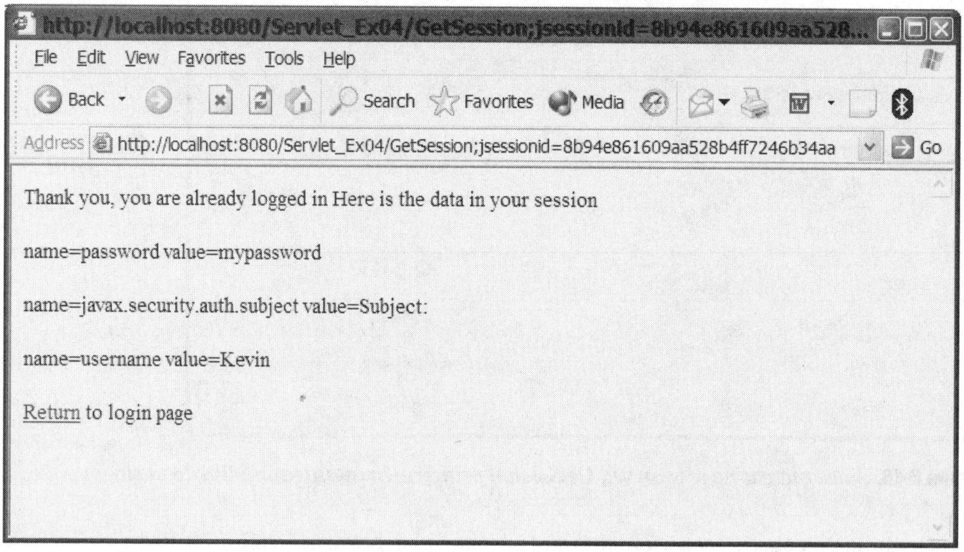

Figure 6-20. *GetSession prints out the request attributes when you have a session.*

When you first access the `GetSession` Servlet, there is no session. Since there is no session, the `GetSession` Servlet provides a link to the login page. At the login page, you can enter a username and password, and then submit the request to the `Login` Servlet.

This new version of the `Login` Servlet starts by trying to access an existing session by calling the `request.getSession()` method. Since we pass in `true` as the parameter, a new session will be created if one doesn't already exist. Once the Servlet has a `session` object, it stores the username and password in it.

A client does not have a session until the server creates a session for the client, the server has sent the session ID to the client, *and* the client has returned the session ID in a cookie or URL. Because the `Login` Servlet is the first web component to create the session, the session has not been joined when `Login` generates the page that has the link for the `GetSession` Servlet. The `Login` Servlet calls `encodeURL()` for the link, and since the client has not joined the session, the URL is rewritten to append the session ID. This is the session ID that appears in the browser address window for the page generated by `GetSession` Servlet. When you click the link that sends the request to `GetSession`, you have finally joined the session.

Using Cookies in Place of Sessions

Using the `session` object provided through the Servlet API is the preferred method for working with sessions. However, you can use another method for storing and retrieving information about the client in conjunction with, or in place of, `session` objects. That method is to use cookies.

Usually, information about the client's request is kept in a `session` object, and cookies are only used to pass the session ID between the client and server. Instead of storing information about a client's request in a `session` object, you could send all that information as a cookie to the client. For example, in an e-commerce application, you could store all the shopping cart information in cookies that are sent to the client.

The `session` object has two advantages over cookies:

- As mentioned earlier, clients can reject cookies sent by a server; however `session` objects live on the server, and can always be created, either by setting the session ID in a cookie or through URL rewriting.

- Cookies can store only text data, so you are limited to storing text information or information that can be represented by text. Using a `session` object, you can store any Java object in a session.

For these reasons, you should always use the Session API for session management. However, there is one place where cookies make sense.

Have you ever registered at a web site, and then the next time you went back to the site, the site logged you in automatically? This was probably accomplished by sending a cookie to your browser. The cookie was used as a mini-session to bootstrap your session on the server. The cookie contained an ID that the server could use to identify you. When your browser sends the request, it sends the cookie, and the server is able to identify you, retrieve your personalization information from some persistent store, and preload a `session` object with your data before your browser has actually joined the session.

Let's look briefly at how you might use a cookie to do this. Using the `Cookie` object in the Servlet API is straightforward. Cookie data comes in name/value pairs, so the `Cookie` constructor takes a name and a value:

```
Cookie(String name, String value)
```

You could then set a number of properties of the cookie. The following are the two property settings that you are most likely to use:

- `public void setMaxAge(int expiry)`: Specifies how long, in seconds, the cookie should be kept by the client. If you do not set a maximum age, the cookie is discarded when the client exits the browser.
- `public void setValue(String newValue)`: Allows you to change the value held by the cookie.

After creating a cookie, you can add it to the response using the `addCookie()` method of the `HttpServletResponse` class:

```
void addCookie(Cookie cookie)
```

Cookies are added to the header of the response message, so the Servlet must call the `addCookie()` method before any message body data is written to the response.

When a client sends a request to the Servlet, the Servlet can access the cookies using the `HttpServletRequest`'s `getCookies()` method:

```
Cookie[] getCookies()
```

This returns an array containing `Cookie` objects for all the cookies sent by the client. Note that the client sends only the name/value pairs of the cookies, and not any other information such as maximum age. The Servlet can access the names and values of each `Cookie` using the `Cookie` methods `getName()` and `getValue(String name)`.

Finally, even though we have discussed the `Cookie` object and its methods in terms of session management, cookies can be used to send any text data to the client browser, regardless of whether or not it is used for session management.

Filters

So, you've finished writing the Servlet for your application, and it's working great. You have a Servlet that handles user logins; when users submit their credentials, your code checks them against the user information stored by the application. The Servlet creates a session for the user, so that other components in the application know that the user has logged in properly and can get user data from the session.

Everything is fine—until the customer comes to you and asks you to make a log entry for each login attempt to the application server's log system. That's relatively simple, so you edit the Servlet code and redeploy it. Then the customer decides that login attempts should be logged to a database table. So, you edit the code and redeploy it again. Then the customer changes his mind again.

Pretty soon, your Servlet is filled with a lot of code that is useful but is outside the scope of the core job of a Servlet, which is receiving and responding to requests. There has got to be an easier way. The solution is to use filters.

Filters are a way to provide a plug-in capability to your web application. Using filters, you can encapsulate different behaviors needed to help process a request. Filters also make it easy to modify the functionality of a web application with just a change to the deployment descriptor.

The Javadoc for the Filter interface suggests a number of filter uses, including the following:

- Authentication filters
- Logging and auditing filters
- Data compression filters
- Encryption filters

The primary job of a Servlet is to accept requests and provide responses to clients. Anything outside that scope is the candidate for other classes. So, whether you need the functionality suggested by the list in the Javadoc or your application needs to provide some other functionality, filters offer an excellent solution. Furthermore, by encapsulating that functionality in a filter, the same filter can easily be used with several Servlets.

To implement a filter for your web application, you need to do two things: write a class that implements the Filter interface and modify the deployment descriptor to tell the container when to call the filter.

Implementing the Filter Interface

The Filter API consists of three interfaces: Filter, FilterChain, and FilterConfig. javax.servlet.Filter is the interface you will use to implement a filter. It has three methods:

- void init(FilterConfig filterConfig): Called by the web container to indicate to a filter that it is being placed into service.
- void doFilter(ServletRequest request, ServletResponse response, FilterChain chain): Called by the container each time a request/response pair is passed through the chain due to a client request for a resource at the end of the chain.
- void destroy(): Called by the web container to indicate to a filter that it is being taken out of service.

You can see that this interface is very similar to the Servlet interface. Based on this interface, you won't be surprised to learn that a filter lifecycle is very similar to a Servlet lifecycle. When the filter is created, the container will call the init() method. Inside the init() method, you can access init parameters through the FilterConfig interface. However, unlike with a Servlet, if you need to access the FilterConfig in the doFilter() method, you will need to save the reference yourself. To service requests, the container calls the doFilter() method. When the container needs to end the filter lifecycle, it will call the destroy() method.

The javax.servlet.FilterConfig interface is fairly straightforward and almost identical to ServletConfig. If you need to use init parameters or other features of the FilterConfig, you can get more details from the Javadoc.

The javax.servlet.FilterChain interface represents a chain of filters. It defines a method that each filter can use to call the next filter in the chain:

```
void doFilter(ServletRequest request, ServletResponse response)
```

This method causes the next filter in the chain to be invoked, or if the calling filter is the last filter in the chain, it causes the resource at the end of the chain to be invoked.

Notice that when a filter's doFilter() method is called, one of the arguments passed is a reference to a FilterChain. When the filter calls chain.doFilter(), the next filter in the chain is called. Code that is executed before the chain.doFilter() method call is executed prior to the Servlet processing. Thus, any processing that the filter needs to do to the request should occur prior to the call to chain.doFilter(). Code that is executed after the chain.doFilter() method call returns is executed after the Servlet, so that code performs processing on the response. If you need to do processing both before and after the Servlet, then you put code both before and after the chain.doFilter() call. On the other hand, if any of the filters needs to abort processing (think of a filter that provides user authentication), it can easily do this by not calling doFilter(). If all this sounds a little confusing, Figure 6-21 should make it clearer.

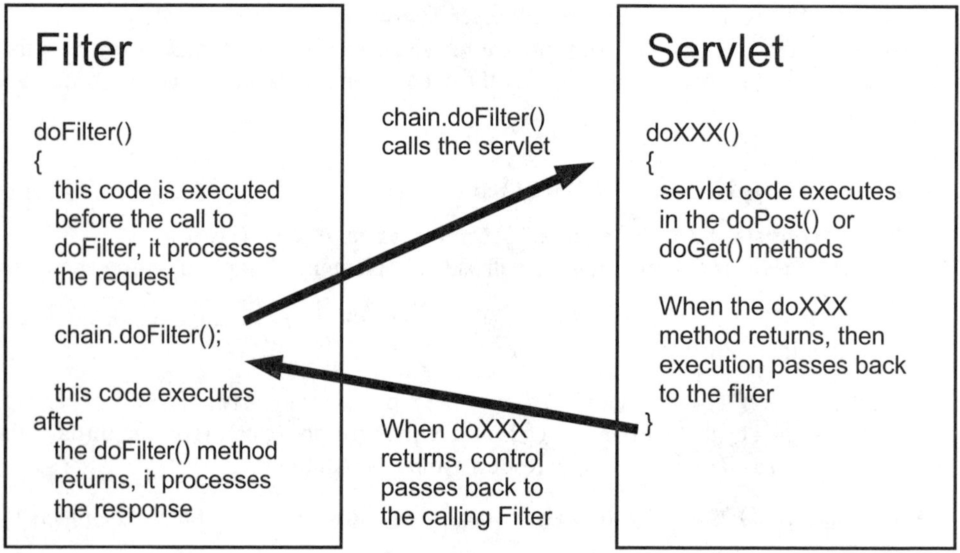

Figure 6-21. *Each filter in the chain calls the next filter until the Servlet is called. Then execution returns through each filter. Code that executes before a call to doFilter() acts on the request; code that executes after doFilter() acts on the response.*

Modifying the Deployment Descriptor to Use a Filter

You use the deployment descriptor to tell the container which, if any, filters to call for each Servlet in the application. Two tags within the deployment descriptor describe the filters and indicate to which Servlet requests the filters should be applied.

The first element is <filter>, which has several subelements:

```
<filter>
  <icon>path to an icon file</icon>
  <filter-name>the name of the filter for the application</filter-name>
  <display-name>named for use by management tool</display-name>
  <description>a description</description>
  <filter-class>fully qualified class name</filter-class>
  <init-param>
```

```
    <param-name>some_name</param-name>
    <param-value>a_value</param-value>
  </init-param>
</filter>
```

Only two of these subelements are required: <filter-name> and <filter-class>. If you use <init-param>, then <param-name> and <param-value> are required. These init values can be accessed through the FilterConfig object.

The second element is the <filter-mapping> element. It looks like this:

```
<filter-mapping>
  <filter-name>same name as filter-name in filter element</filter-name>
  <url-pattern>URL pattern that the filter applies to</url-pattern>
</filter-mapping>
```

or like this:

```
<filter-mapping>
  <filter-name>Same name as filter-name in filter element</filter-name>
  <servlet-name>Name of Servlet from servlet element</servlet-name>
</filter-mapping>
```

If multiple filters are needed for a request, then each filter is listed in separate <filter-mapping> elements. The filters are applied in the same order that the <filter-mapping> elements appear in the deployment descriptor. For example, suppose you had this series of <filter-mapping> elements in the deployment descriptor:

```
<filter-mapping>
  <filter-name>FilterD</filter-name>
  <servlet-name>Login</servlet-name>
</filter-mapping>

<filter-mapping>
  <filter-name>FilterA</filter-name>
  <servlet-name>Login</servlet-name>
</filter-mapping>

<filter-mapping>
  <filter-name>FilterW</filter-name>
  <servlet-name>Login</servlet-name>
</filter-mapping>
```

Then any request for the Login Servlet is first sent to FilterD, since the <filter-mapping> element for that filter appears first in the deployment descriptor. When FilterD calls chain.doFilter(), FilterA is called. After that, FilterW is called. Finally, when FilterW calls doFilter(), the Login Servlet is invoked.

Listing 6-13 is the first of two filters that show filter processing. It actually does nothing except print some output to the log and pass the request to the next filter.

Listing 6-13. *FilterA.class*

```
package com.apress.servlet;

import java.util.logging.Logger;

import javax.servlet.*;

public class FilterA implements Filter {
  private ServletContext context;
  public void init(FilterConfig filterConfig) {
    context = filterConfig.getServletContext();
  }

  public void doFilter(
    ServletRequest request,
    ServletResponse response,
    FilterChain chain) {
    Logger logger = Logger.getLogger("com.apress.beginjavaee");
    logger.info("Entered FilterA.doFilter()");
    logger.info("FilterA passing request to next filter");

    try {
      chain.doFilter(request, response);
    } catch (Exception e) {
      System.out.println("Exception on doFilter" + e.getMessage());
    }

    logger.info("Returned to FilterA.doFilter()");
    logger.info("FilterA is now processing the response");
  }

  public void destroy() {}
}
```

Listing 6-14 shows another filter, which reads some data from the request and logs it to the server log.

Listing 6-14. *FilterB.java*

```
package com.apress.servlet;

import java.util.logging.Logger;

import javax.servlet.*;
```

```
public class FilterB implements Filter {
  private ServletContext context;
  public void init(FilterConfig filterConfig) {
    context = filterConfig.getServletContext();
  }

  public void doFilter(
    ServletRequest request,
    ServletResponse response,
    FilterChain chain)
  {
  Logger logger = Logger.getLogger("com.apress.beginjavaee");
    logger.info("Entered LogB doFilter()");
    logger.info("protocol is " + request.getProtocol());
    logger.info("remote host is " + request.getRemoteHost());
    logger.info("content type is " + request.getContentType());
    logger.info("content length is " + request.getContentLength());
    logger.info("username is " + request.getParameter("username"));
    logger.info("FilterB passing request to next filter");

    try {
      chain.doFilter(request, response);
    } catch (Exception e) {
      e.printStackTrace();
    }
  logger.info("Returned to FilterB.doFilter()");
  logger.info("FilterB is now processing the response");
  }

  public void destroy() {}
}
```

Both of these classes use the `java.util.logging` API to log messages to the Servlet log. At the start of the `doFilter()` method, each class gets a reference to a named logger using the static `Logger.getLogger(String)` method.

Listing 6-15 shows the Servlet for this web application. This is a `Login` Servlet that is very similar to the first example in this chapter.

Listing 6-15. *Login.java*

```
package com.apress.servlet;

import javax.servlet.http.*;
import java.io.*;
import java.util.logging.Logger;
```

```
public class Login extends HttpServlet {
  public void doPost(HttpServletRequest request,
                     HttpServletResponse response)
  {
    Logger logger = Logger.getLogger("com.apress.beginjavaee");
    logger.info("Entered Login servlet doPost()");
    String username = request.getParameter("username");
    try {
      response.setContentType("text/html");
      PrintWriter writer = response.getWriter();
      writer.println("<html><body>");
      writer.println("Thank you, " + username +
                     ". You are now logged into the system.");
      writer.println("</body></html>");
      writer.close();
    } catch (Exception e) {
      e.printStackTrace();
    }
  logger.info("Login do Post finished processing");
  }
}
```

Finally, you will need a web client to call the Servlet. For this example, use the same `login.html` page shown in Listing 6-2.

Deploying the Login Servlet Using Filters to Tomcat

If you are using the Tomcat server, you will also need to create the deployment descriptor. Listing 6-16 shows the deployment descriptor for this example.

Listing 6-16. *web.xml for Servlet_Ex05*

```
<?xml version='1.0' encoding='UTF-8'?>
<web-app
        version="2.5"
        xmlns="http://java.sun.com/xml/ns/javaee"
        xmlns:xsi="http://www.w3.org/2001/XMLSchema-instance"
        xsi:schemaLocation="http://java.sun.com/xml/ns/javaee
         http://java.sun.com/xml/ns/javaee/web-app_2_5.xsd">
  <display-name>Servlet_Ex05</display-name>
  <filter>
    <filter-name>FilterA</filter-name>
    <filter-class>com.apress.servlet.FilterA</filter-class>
  </filter>
```

```
  <filter>
    <filter-name>FilterB</filter-name>
    <filter-class>com.apress.servlet.FilterB</filter-class>
  </filter>
  <filter-mapping>
    <filter-name>FilterA</filter-name>
    <url-pattern>/Login</url-pattern>
  </filter-mapping>
  <filter-mapping>
    <filter-name>FilterB</filter-name>
    <url-pattern>/Login</url-pattern>
  </filter-mapping>
  <servlet>
    <display-name>Login</display-name>
    <servlet-name>Login</servlet-name>
    <servlet-class>com.apress.servlet.Login</servlet-class>
  </servlet>
  <servlet-mapping>
    <servlet-name>Login</servlet-name>
    <url-pattern>/Login</url-pattern>
  </servlet-mapping>
  <welcome-file-list>
    <welcome-file>login.html</welcome-file>
  </welcome-file-list>
</web-app>
```

Figure 6-22 shows the directory structure for this example.

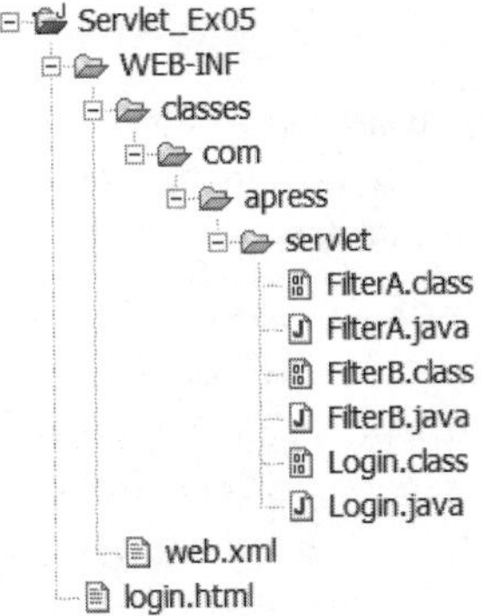

Figure 6-22. *The directory structure for Servlet_Ex05*

To deploy this application, create a WAR file and copy it to the Tomcat `webapps` directory.

Deploying the Login Servlet Using Filters to Java EE

If you are using the Sun Application Server, follow these steps to deploy the Servlet:

1. Run the Deployment Tool and create a web component using the `login.html`, `Login.class`, `FilterA.class`, and `FilterB.class` files. Name the WAR file `Servlet_Ex05`.
2. Select the `Login` web component in the folder view of the Deployment Tool, and create an alias of `/Login` in the Aliases tab, as shown in Figure 6-23.

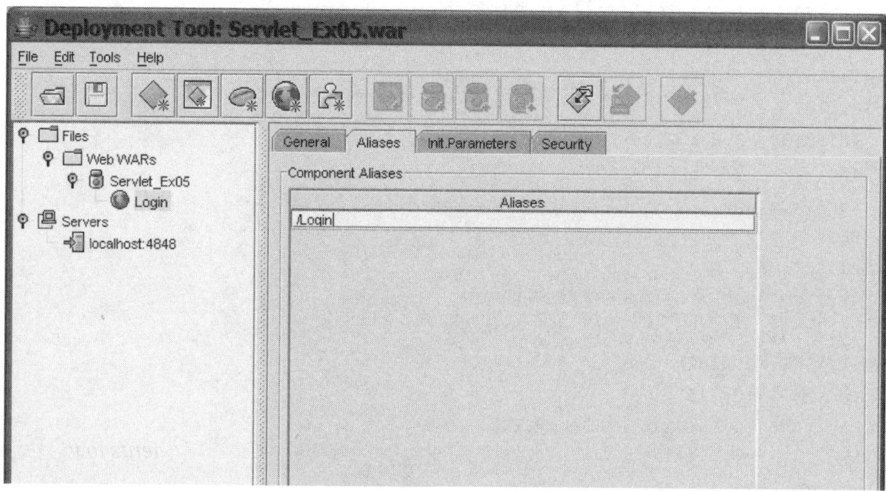

Figure 6-23. *The alias for the Servlet is /Login.*

3. Select the `Servlet_Ex05` WAR file in the folder view, and select the Filter Mappings tab in the left pane of the Deployment Tool.
4. Click the Edit Filter List button to bring up a dialog box that you can use to specify the available filter classes. Click the Add Filter button and add each of the filter classes, `FilterA` and `FilterB`, to the list, as shown in Figure 6-24. Then click OK.
5. When you are back in the main window, you can add filter mappings by clicking the Add button in the Filter Mapping tab. In the Add Servlet Filter Mapping dialog box, pick the filter name from a drop-down list, and then select the target by either entering a URL pattern or picking a Servlet name. In the Dispatcher Options section, you can further limit which types of request the filter applies to: forwards, includes, normal requests, or errors. If you select none of the options, the filter applies to all types; if you want the filter to apply to only certain types, select the check boxes for those types. Figure 6-25 shows the Add Servlet Filter Mapping dialog box for the `FilterA` filter.

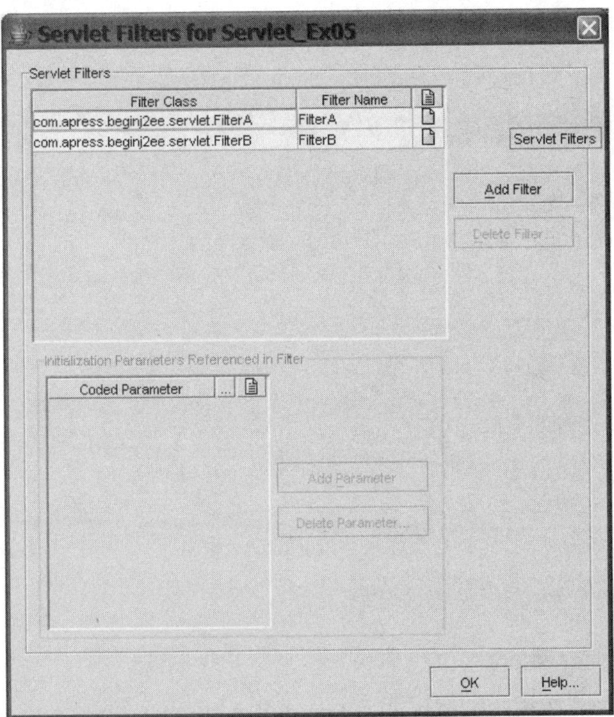

Figure 6-24. *The Servlet Filters dialog box is used to add filter elements to the web application.*

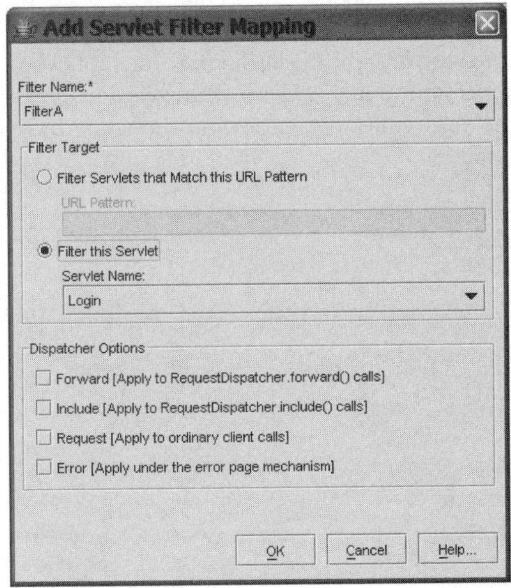

Figure 6-25. *The Add Servlet Filter Mapping dialog box is used to specify the filters and which actions and components they apply to.*

6. After you've added both filter mappings, the Filter Mapping tab should look like Figure 6-26.

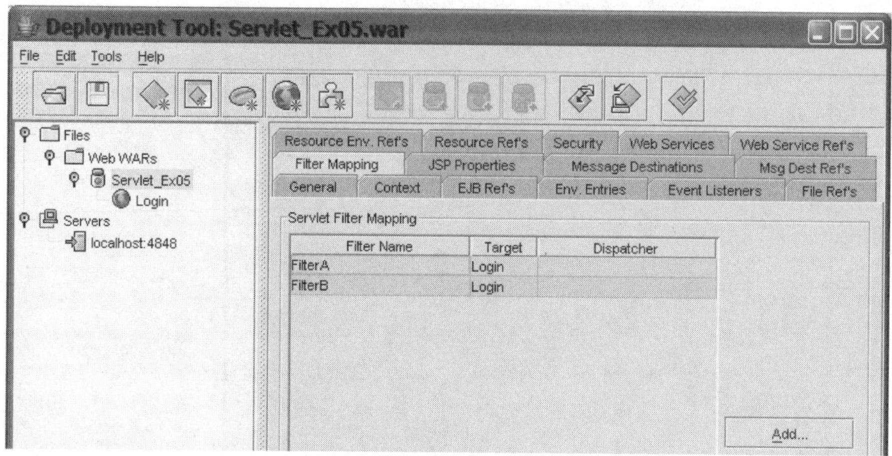

Figure 6-26. *The complete list of filter mappings*

Running the Login Servlet Using Filters

After the application is deployed, load the `login.html` page into a browser. Enter a username and password, and click the Submit button. Assuming the application is configured and deployed correctly, you will not see anything special about the page returned. It should look like Figure 6-9, shown earlier in this chapter. However, if you examine the server log, you should see entries in the log from each filter and from the Servlet.

To examine the server log, you will need to find the log file for your server. Tomcat's log file is `stdout.log` located in the Tomcat `/logs` directory. The log file for the Sun Application Server is `server.log` located in the `/logs` directory for the domain. Here are the relevant lines from the Sun Application Server log on our system. We've edited the entries for conciseness by removing the time tags and other extraneous information.

```
Entered FilterA.doFilter()
FilterA passing request to next filter
Entered LogB doFilter()
protocol is HTTP/1.1
remote host is 127.0.0.1
content type is application/x-www-form-urlencoded
content length is 24
username is Kevin
FilterB passing request to next filter
Entered Login servlet doPost()
Login do Post finished processing
Returned to FilterB.doFilter()
FilterB is now processing the response
Returned to FilterA.doFilter()
FilterA is now processing the response
```

If you examine the output, you can see that each `logger.info()` method call in the classes resulted in a log entry in the server log.

The `FilterA` filter, which was the first filter listed in the deployment descriptor, is called first. It makes some log entries, and then calls the `chain.doFilter()` method. This calls the next filter in the chain, `FilterB`. The `FilterB` filter reads some of the request headers and the request parameter from the request and prints them to the log. Then `FilterB` calls `chain.doFilter()`. Since it is the last filter in the chain, this calls the Servlet, which performs its processing of the request.

When the `doPost()` method of the Servlet completes, the thread of execution returns to the caller, which, in this case, is the `FilterB` filter. The thread of execution returns to the `doFilter()` method of `FilterB`. After `FilterB` makes a few more log entries, its `doFilter()` method completes, and execution returns to `FilterB`'s caller, `FilterA`. When the thread of execution returns to `FilterA`, execution continues after from the method call `chain.doFilter()`. Since there is code following that method call, it now executes. In a real filter, when the thread of execution returned to the filter, the filter could perform some processing on the response. In the example, all that the filter does is write some strings to the log.

The MVC Architecture

In the previous JSP chapters, and previously in this chapter, we used an architectural model known as Model 1. In a Model 1 architecture, HTTP requests are handled primarily by web components— Servlets or JSP pages—which process the request and then return a response to a client. In this architecture, a single web component (or small number of components) handles both the business logic and display logic.

A second model is also used for Java EE applications. Unsurprisingly, this model is known as *Model 2* or *Model-View-Controller* (MVC). In an MVC architecture, there is a division of functionality: the business data is separated from the display logic, and components that process the data do not manage the display of the data, and vice versa.

■ **Note** We use *MVC* to refer to the Model 2 architecture. Although both terms are used in the development world, we think MVC is more descriptive.

Model 1 vs. MVC

A Model 1 system mixes both application and business logic with display logic. While this is probably okay for small applications, it becomes more and more of a problem as your application grows. This model leads to JSP pages interspersed with a lot of Java code, or Servlets that have a lot of `print` statements that output HTML text to the client. While the examples we've used previously aren't too bad (the first `Login` Servlet example in this chapter had only three `println` statements), imagine an HTML-heavy application written entirely with Servlets, or a code-intensive application written with JSP pages. Your application will become less maintainable as changes to display logic affect business logic and vice versa.

You can solve this problem in various ways. For example, one approach, before the days of JSP, was to create template files for all the web pages in the application. The template files contained HTML with special place markers for request-specific data. When a Servlet needed to send a response to a client, it used a utility class that had methods for reading a template and replacing the markers with strings. The `toString()` method of the utility class returned a `String` that contained the entire HTML web page. Then it was just a simple matter of using one `println` statement to send the response to the client. While this solution is workable, it starts to break down when you have lists, tables, or combo boxes in the web page. You don't know ahead of time how many list items or table rows you might have. Thus, HTML strings start appearing in your Servlet code again.

MVC separates the display from the business logic in another way. In an MVC application, separate components handle the business logic and the display logic. As long as the interface between the two is stable and well defined, the business logic can be changed without affecting the view components, and vice versa.

The Components of MVC

In an MVC application, the components of the application are divided into three categories:

Model: The model includes both the data and the business logic components that operate on that data. Again, any class can act as a model component, and many web applications use only JSP pages or Servlets with regular (not Java EE API) classes providing business logic. As you will see from Chapter 9 onwards, EJBs make excellent components for the model category.

View: After the request is processed, the controller determines which view component should be used to display the data to the user. In simpler applications, the controller component may also act as the view component. In more complex systems, view and controller objects are separate. JSP pages tend to make good view components.

Controller: Components in this category receive the client requests, process the request, or forward the request to other components that process the data, and then direct the request to a view component. Any web application component—such as a JSP page, a Servlet, or an EJB—could be a controller component. However, Servlets tend to make good controllers due to their basic structure. A Servlet is intended to receive requests from clients and return responses to clients, and that matches the purpose of the controller.

Let's take a quick look at an example of a design that uses MVC. Imagine that we are working on an application that lists stock market analysts and the ratings they have made on certain stocks. In this example, we want to have a web page that shows the names of the stock market analysts, with actions to add or delete an analyst. We also want to have a page that shows the different stocks and the ratings given to them by an analyst, with an action to add a new rating. That's the view side of our simple application.

What about the controller side? For this application, we'll use a Servlet to be the controller. The primary job of the controller Servlet is to route requests to the appropriate JSP page or to another Servlet. The other Servlet in this application will be a Servlet that responds to the "add rating" request from a JSP page.

Finally, for the model side, in a real application, we would probably use a robust data persistence tier. This might include both a database and objects such as EJBs to access the data. Figure 6-27 shows a simple diagram illustrating what this application might look like.

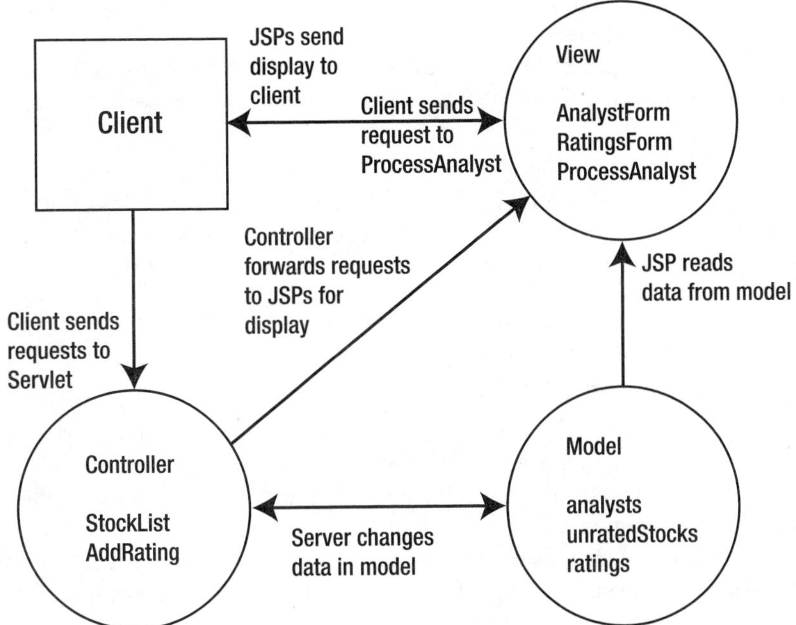

Figure 6-27. *An example of the MVC architecture*

Servlet Chaining

If a Servlet is going to be a controller in an MVC application, it needs some way to forward requests to the display components of the application, since the display components create the response back to the client. This is accomplished by getting an object called a `RequestDispatcher`. Through a request dispatcher, a Servlet can forward the request to another web component or include the response of another web component in the current response. This is the same as the JSP standard actions `<jsp:forward>` and `<jsp:include>`, which we looked at in Chapter 3.

Getting a RequestDispatcher

You can get a `RequestDispatcher` from the `ServletRequest` object or from the `ServletContext` object. The method signature for the `ServletRequest` method is as follows:

```
RequestDispatcher getRequestDispatcher(String path)
```

This method returns a `RequestDispatcher` for the web component at the given location. The `path` argument is the path to the web application resource. This path can be a relative path or an absolute path, as explained earlier in this chapter. Recall that the path to the `Login` Servlet earlier in the chapter was `/Login`. This path starts with a forward slash (`/`), so it is interpreted as an absolute path that is relative to the application context. For example, if the application context is `/Servlet_Ex06`, then `/Login` would be the resource at `/Servlet_Ex06/Login`. If the path does not start with a slash, it is a relative path that is interpreted relative to the current web component location. For example, if the web component were `/Servlet_Ex06/reports/DisplayReport`, then the path PrintReport would be the resource /Servlet_Ex06/reports/PrintReport. If the resource does not exist, the method returns null.

You can also get a RequestDispatcher using a ServletContext object. The GenericServlet class defines a method to get a reference to the ServletContext object for your Servlet:

```
ServletContext getServletContext()
```

Since your Servlet is a subclass of GenericServlet, you can just call this method directly from your Servlet. The ServletContext represents the application context in which the Servlet executes. Next, your Servlet can call one of two methods of the ServletContext to get a RequestDispatcher:

```
RequestDispatcher getNamedDispatcher(String name)
RequestDispatcher getRequestDispatcher(String path)
```

Either method can be used to return a RequestDispatcher for the resource at the given path or name. If the resource does not exist, the methods return null. The path argument for getRequestDispatcher(String) must begin with a slash (/), and is interpreted relative to the application context. The name argument for getNamedDispatcher(String) must be the same name used in the <servlet-name> subelement of <servlet-mapping> in the deployment descriptor. So, using the Login Servlet example again, the deployment descriptor for this Servlet had this entry:

```
<servlet-mapping>
    <servlet-name>Login</servlet-name>
    <url-pattern>/Login</url-pattern>
  </servlet-mapping>
```

The call to getNamedDispatcher("Login") would return a RequestDispatcher for the web resource /Servlet_Ex06/Login (remember that /Login is interpreted relative to the application context).

Forwarding or Including Requests Using a Request Dispatcher

Request dispatchers can be used either to forward a request to another resource or to include another resource's response in the current response. To forward a request, use this method:

```
void forward(ServletRequest request, ServletResponse response)
      throws ServletException, java.io.IOException
```

Since this method relies on another resource to generate the response output, the calling Servlet should not write any data to the response stream before calling this method. If response data is sent to the client before this method is called, this method will throw an exception. Also, since the response stream will be complete when the other resource is finished, the calling Servlet should not attempt to use the response object after the forward() method returns.

Alternatively, you can call another resource and include its response data in the current response. This is done with the following method:

```
void include(ServletRequest request, ServletResponse response)
      throws ServletException, java.io.IOException
```

Since this method includes another response in the current response, you can safely write response data to the client both before and after calling this method.

Adding Parameters to the Request

At times, you may need to add additional information to the request object that you use in a forward() or include() method call. The ServletRequest interface defines a number of methods for adding, getting, and removing data from the request object:

```
Object getAttribute(String name)
Enumeration getAttributeNames()
void setAttribute(String name, Object o)
void removeAttribute(String name)
```

The calling Servlet can add attributes to the request object using setAttribute(String name, Object o). Take care not to duplicate names already used for attributes; if you use a duplicate name, the new attribute will replace the previous attribute. The receiving Servlet will use the getAttribute(String name) method to get the attribute, using the same name that the calling Servlet used to set the attribute.

Creating an MVC Application

Let's take the simple stock market analysts and ratings design we introduced at the beginning of this section and turn it into a working web application. We will develop view and controller segments as described earlier. For the model layer, we will simply use some ArrayList and Vector objects to store the data.

We'll start with a view component that is a static HTML page, to serve as the entry point into the application. Listing 6-17 shows this file. Save the file into the /Servlet_Ex06 directory with the name index.html. This web page provides two links into the application.

Listing 6-17. *index.html for the StockList Application*

```
<html>
  <head>
    <title>Stocks and Analysts</title>
  </head>
  <body>
    <h1>Stocks and Analysts</h1>
    <p>
      <a href="StockList/AnalystForm">See all Analysts</a>
    <p>
      <a href="StockList/RatingsForm">See all Ratings</a>
    <hr>
  </body>
</html>
```

As you will see later, the link is simply StockList, which specifies the StockList Servlet. The additional path information of AnalystForm or RatingsForm will be used by the StockList Servlet. Now we'll create the controller for this application. Listing 6-18 shows this Servlet. Name this code StockListServlet.java. Save it into the /WEB-INF/classes/ directory, following the package structure for the subdirectories.

Listing 6-18. *StockListServlet*

```
package com.apress.servlet;

import javax.servlet.*;
import javax.servlet.http.*;
import java.util.*;

public class StockListServlet extends HttpServlet {
  static ArrayList analysts = new ArrayList();
  static ArrayList unratedStocks = new ArrayList();
  static ArrayList ratings = new ArrayList();

  public void init() {
    analysts.add("Fred");
    analysts.add("Leonard");
    analysts.add("Sarah");
    analysts.add("Nancy");
    unratedStocks.add("ABC");
    unratedStocks.add("DDBC");
    unratedStocks.add("DDC");
    unratedStocks.add("FBC");
    unratedStocks.add("INT");
    unratedStocks.add("JIM");
    unratedStocks.add("SRI");
    unratedStocks.add("SRU");
    unratedStocks.add("UDE");
    unratedStocks.add("ZAP");
    Vector v = new Vector();
    v.add("Fred");
    v.add("ZZZ");
    v.add("Smashing!");
    ratings.add(v);
  }

  public void doPost(HttpServletRequest request,
                     HttpServletResponse response)
  {
    doGet(request, response);
  }

  public void doGet(HttpServletRequest request,
                    HttpServletResponse response)
  {
    try {
      ArrayList data = null;
      RequestDispatcher dispatcher;
      ServletContext context = getServletContext();
```

```
      String name = request.getPathInfo();
      name = name.substring(1);

      if ("AnalystForm".equals(name)) {
        data = analysts;
        request.setAttribute("data", data);
      } else if ("RatingsForm".equals(name)) {
        request.setAttribute("data", ratings);
        request.setAttribute("analysts", analysts);
        request.setAttribute("unrated", unratedStocks);
      } else if ("AddRating".equals(name)) {
        request.setAttribute("data", ratings);
        request.setAttribute("analysts", analysts);
        request.setAttribute("unrated", unratedStocks);
      } else if ("ProcessAnalyst".equals(name)) {
        //no need to set any attributes for this resource
      } else {
        name = "Error";
      }

      dispatcher = context.getNamedDispatcher(name);
      if (dispatcher == null) {
        dispatcher = context.getNamedDispatcher("Error");
      }
      dispatcher.forward(request, response);
    } catch (Exception e) {
      log("Exception in StockListServlet.doGet()");
    }
  }
}
```

You're now ready for the first JSP view component. This is a page that will show all the analysts in the application. Listing 6-19 shows the file `AnalystForm.jsp`, which you should save into the `/Servlet_Ex06` directory.

Listing 6-19. *AnalystForm.jsp*

```
<html>
  <head>
    <title>Analyst Management</title>
  </head>
  <body>
    <%@ page import="java.util.*" %>
    <h1>Analyst Management Form</h1>
    <form action="ProcessAnalyst" method="POST">
      <table>
      <%
      ArrayList analysts = (ArrayList)request.getAttribute("data");
```

```
      if (analysts == null) {
      %>
        <h2> Attribute is null </h2>
      <%
      } else {
        for (int i = 0; i < analysts.size(); i++) {
          String analyst = (String)analysts.get(i);
      %>
        <tr>
          <td>
            <input type="checkbox" name="checkbox" value="<%= analyst %>"
          </td>
          <td>
            <%= analyst %>
          </td>
        </tr>
      <%
        }
      }
      %>
      </table>
      <input type="submit" value="Delete Selected" name="delete"><p>
      <input type="text" size="40" name="addname">
      <input type="submit" value="Add New Analyst" name="add">
    </form>
  </body>
</html>
```

When the user attempts to add or delete an analyst from `AnalystForm.jsp`, the request is sent directly to another JSP page. That JSP page is `ProcessAnalyst.jsp`, shown in Listing 6-20. You will see it does not really add or delete an analyst. Save this file into the `/Servlet_Ex06` directory, too.

Listing 6-20. *ProcessAnalyst.jsp*

```
<html>
  <head>
    <title>Process Analyst Request</title>
  </head>

  <body>
    <h1>Process Analyst Request</h1>
    Adding or deleting an analyst from the database is not currently
    implemented. Implementation of this feature is left as an exercise
    for the reader.
  </body>
</html>
```

The other functionality provided by this application is to show the ratings the analysts have given to certain stocks. This view of the data is handled by the `RatingsForm.jsp` shown in Listing 6-21. Again, since this is a JSP page, save it to the `/Servlet_Ex06` directory.

Listing 6-21. *RatingsForm.jsp*

```
<html>
  <head>
    <title>Stock Ratings</title>
  </head>

  <body>
    <h1>Stock Ratings</h1>

    <%@ page import="java.util.*" %>
    <%
    ArrayList stocks = (ArrayList) request.getAttribute("data");
    if (stocks != null && stocks.size() > 0) {
    %>
    <form action="AddRating" method="post">
      <table border="1">
          <tr>
            <th>Ticker</th>
            <th>Analyst</th>
            <th>Rating</th>
          </tr>
      <%
      for (int i = 0; i < stocks.size(); i++) {
        Vector v = (Vector) stocks.get(i);
        String ticker = (String)v.elementAt(0);
        String analyst = (String)v.elementAt(1);
        String rating = (String)v.elementAt(2);
      %>
      <tr>
        <td><%= ticker %></td>
        <td><%= analyst %></td>
        <td><%= rating %></td>
      </tr>
      <%
      }
      %>
     </table>
```

```
<table>
      <tr>
        <td>
          <select name="analysts">
            <%
            ArrayList analysts =
              (ArrayList) request.getAttribute("analysts");
            for (int i = 0; i < analysts.size(); i++) {
              String analyst = (String)analysts.get(i);
            %>
            <option value="<%= analyst %>">
              <%= analyst %>
              <%
              }
              %>
          </select>
        </td>
        <td>
          <select name="stocks">
            <%
            ArrayList unratedStocks =
              (ArrayList) request.getAttribute("unrated");
            for (int i = 0; i < unratedStocks.size(); i++) {
              String ticker = (String)unratedStocks.get(i);
            %>
            <option value="<%= ticker %>">
              <%= ticker %>
              <%
              }
              %>
          </select>
        </td>
        <td>
          <select name="ratings">
            <option value="Run away! Run away!">Run away! Run away!
            <option value="Could be worse!">Could be worse!
            <option value="A bit of OK!">A bit of OK!
            <option value="Take a chance!">Take a chance!
            <option value="Smashing!">Smashing!
          </select>
        </td>
      </tr>
      <tr>
        <td>
          <input type="submit" value="Submit Rating">
        </td>
      </tr>
```

```
    </table>
  </form>
  <%
  } else {
  %>
  No stock information found
  <%
  }
  %>
 </body>
</html>
```

Now, we need a Servlet to process the request to add a stock rating from an analyst. After adding the rating, the Servlet will send the request back to the `RatingsForm.jsp` to display the new model of the data. This Servlet is shown in Listing 6-22. Save it to the `/WEB-INF/classes` directory.

Listing 6-22. *AddRating Servlet*

```
package com.apress.servlet;

import javax.servlet.*;
import javax.servlet.http.*;
import java.util.*;

public class AddRating extends HttpServlet {
  public void doPost(HttpServletRequest request,
                     HttpServletResponse response)
  {
    try {
      String analyst = request.getParameter("analysts");
      String ticker = request.getParameter("stocks");
      String rating = request.getParameter("ratings");

      Vector v = new Vector();
      v.add(analyst);
      v.add(ticker);
      v.add(rating);

      ArrayList ratings = (ArrayList)request.getAttribute("data");
      ratings.add(v);

      ArrayList unratedStocks =
        (ArrayList)request.getAttribute("unrated");
      unratedStocks.remove(unratedStocks.indexOf(ticker));
```

```
      ServletContext context = getServletContext();
      RequestDispatcher dispatcher =
        context.getNamedDispatcher("RatingsForm");
      dispatcher.forward(request, response);
    } catch (Exception e) {
      log("Exception in AddRating.doPost()", e);
    }
  }
}
```

Last, if you plan to deploy this application to a Tomcat server, you need to create the deployment descriptor. The `web.xml` file we used is shown in Listing 6-23. Save this file into the `/WEB-INF` directory. If you are deploying this application to the Java EE server, you can skip this step (as you know, the Java EE Deployment Tool will create an appropriate deployment descriptor for you).

Listing 6-23. *web.xml for Servlet_Ex06*

```
<?xml version='1.0' encoding='UTF-8'?>
<web-app
        version="2.5"
        xmlns="http://java.sun.com/xml/ns/javaee"
        xmlns:xsi="http://www.w3.org/2001/XMLSchema-instance"
        xsi:schemaLocation="http://java.sun.com/xml/ns/javaee
         http://java.sun.com/xml/ns/javaee/web-app_2_5.xsd">
    <display-name>Servlet_Ex06</display-name>
    <servlet>
        <display-name>AnalystForm</display-name>
        <servlet-name>AnalystForm</servlet-name>
        <jsp-file>/AnalystForm.jsp</jsp-file>
    </servlet>
    <servlet>
        <display-name>ProcessAnalyst</display-name>
        <servlet-name>ProcessAnalyst</servlet-name>
        <jsp-file>/ProcessAnalyst.jsp</jsp-file>
    </servlet>
    <servlet>
        <display-name>AddRating</display-name>
        <servlet-name>AddRating</servlet-name>
        <servlet-class>com.apress.servlet.AddRating</servlet-class>
    </servlet>
    <servlet>
        <display-name>StockListServlet</display-name>
        <servlet-name>StockListServlet</servlet-name>
        <servlet-class>com.apress.servlet.StockListServlet</servlet-class>
    </servlet>
```

```
    <servlet>
        <display-name>RatingsForm</display-name>
        <servlet-name>RatingsForm</servlet-name>
        <jsp-file>/RatingsForm.jsp</jsp-file>
    </servlet>
    <servlet-mapping>
        <servlet-name>ProcessAnalyst</servlet-name>
        <url-pattern>/ProcessAnalyst</url-pattern>
    </servlet-mapping>
    <servlet-mapping>
        <servlet-name>StockListServlet</servlet-name>
        <url-pattern>/StockList/*</url-pattern>
    </servlet-mapping>
    <jsp-config>
    </jsp-config>
</web-app>
```

Compile the Servlet classes. The directory structure of your application should now look like Figure 6-28.

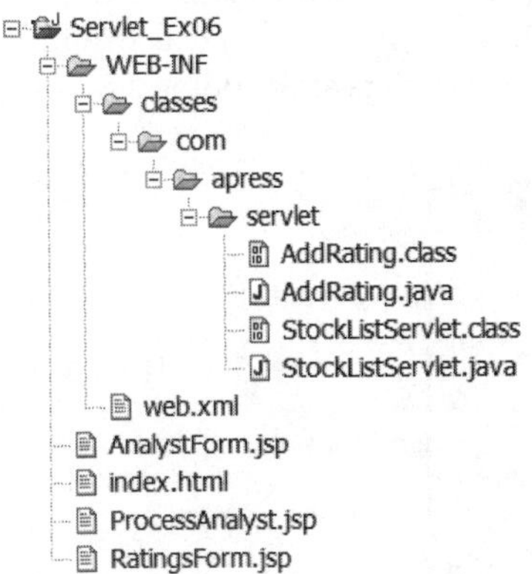

Figure 6-28. *The directory structure for Servlet_Ex06*

Finally, deploy the application.

If you're using the Sun Application Server, use the Java EE Deployment Tool, as you have for the other examples in this chapter. When you first create the web component, using the wizard, you can specify only a single Servlet or JSP to set up. You can create additional components by selecting File ➤ New ➤ Web Application War from the menu. Then, instead of creating a new WAR module, add the components to the existing WAR module. You also need to create two aliases. First, alias the `StockListServlet` to `/StockList/*`. Second, alias the `ProcessAnalyst` JSP to `/ProcessAnalyst`. When you are finished, the Deployment Tool will show five web components in the web application, as shown in Figure 6-29.

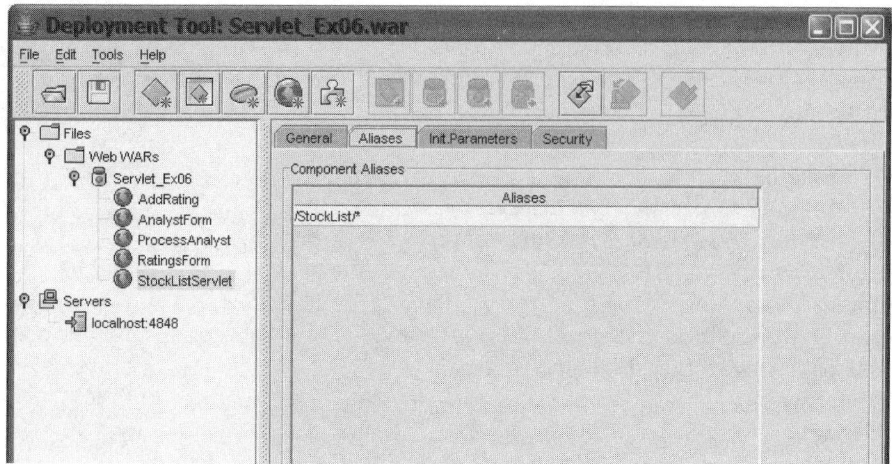

Figure 6-29. *The Stock application has five web components.*

If you're deploying to the Tomcat server, copy the entire directory structure into the /webapps directory of the Tomcat installation, or create the WAR file and copy it into the /webapps directory.

After you've deployed the application, fire up your browser and navigate to the URL `http://localhost:8080/Servlet_Ex06/index.html`. Use the links or buttons to navigate and try different requests. Figure 6-30 shows the `RatingsForm.jsp` web page after adding a rating.

Stock Ratings - Microsoft Internet Explorer

File Edit View Favorites Tools Help

Address http://localhost:8080/Servlet_Ex06/StockList/AddRating Go

Stock Ratings

Analyst	Ticker	Rating
Fred	ZZZ	Smashing!
Fred	ABC	Run away! Run away!

Fred DDBC Run away! Run away!

Submit Rating

Figure 6-30. *After adding a rating, the RatingsForm displays the ratings.*

Although this is a simple example, there is a lot of code here. Rather than go over each Servlet and JSP line by line, we'll cover some of the more interesting points of each.

The `index.html` static HTML page contains links that create two slightly different requests. Each link goes to the same Servlet, `StockListServlet`, but each link uses the additional path technique to pass information to the controller Servlet. In the first link, `/AnalystForm` is the additional path information; in the other link, it is `/RatingsForm`.

```
<a href="StockList/AnalystForm">See all Analysts</a>
<a href="StockList/RatingsForm">See all Ratings</a>
```

So, although `/StockList/AnalystForm` looks as though it should reference the `AnalystForm` JSP directly, it does not. The deployment descriptor creates a mapping that tells the Servlet container that any URL of the form `StockList/*` should be sent to the `StockList` Servlet. This Servlet reads the extra path information and forwards the request to the appropriate JSP page.

When `StockListServlet` is initialized, it populates the various `ArrayLists` and `Vectors` that are being used as the model in this MVC application. When it gets a request, it parses the extra path information using the `request.getPathInfo()` method. It uses this information to determine what model data to add to the request using the `setAttribute()` method. Then it uses the extra path information to forward the request to the appropriate view or other controller Servlet:

```
String name = request.getPathInfo();
//.....some code not shown
dispatcher = context.getNamedDispatcher(name);
//.....some code not shown
dispatcher.forward(request, response);
```

The dispatcher is obtained with a `getNamedDispatcher()` call. The name used to obtain the dispatcher is the same name assigned to the component in the deployment descriptor. Notice also that the `doPost()` method in this Servlet simply calls `doGet()`. This is a common technique when you want to support both `GET` and `POST` with the same processing. You could also have `doGet()` call `doPost()`.

The `AnalystForm.jsp` view component reads the data from the model and displays it to the user. The controller Servlet (`StockListServlet`) added the model data to the request with `setAttribute()`. The data is obtained in the JSP page by calling the `getAttribute()` method. The JSP page creates a form, and when the user clicks one of the buttons on the page, the controller Servlet sends the request to `ProcessAnalyst.jsp` (which does nothing in this example).

The `RatingsForm.jsp` view component displays the analyst, stock ticker, and rating for all stocks that currently have ratings. It gets the model data from the request by calling the `getAttribute()` method of the `request` object. Then it lists all the analysts, all unrated stocks, and the valid ratings. This allows the user to select a stock and assign it a rating. Clicking the Submit button sends the request to `StockListServlet`, which forwards the request to the `AddRating` Servlet.

`AddRating` is the controller Servlet that adds a rating to the model. The Servlet gets the model components from the request and calls a method to change their data. Notice that it does not need to add the model components back to the request. The request already holds a reference to the model; calling the `add()` or `remove()` methods of `ArrayList` does not change the reference held by the request—it changes only the state of the object. After changing the model, this Servlet forwards the request back to `RatingsForm.jsp`, so that it can display the new model.

You should now understand the basics of a simple MVC application. You would not want to use this example directly, though. For one thing, because the data is held in member variables in the Servlet, there is no persistence. As soon as the Servlet is destroyed, any changes to the model are lost. In later chapters, we will extend this example with a more robust model.

Summary

We've covered quite a lot of information in this chapter. After reading this chapter, you should know:

- Servers respond to requests, and specifically, web servers respond to HTTP requests such as `GET` and `POST`.
- Servlets extend a server's functionality by providing a server-side program that can respond to HTTP requests. `HttpServlets` live inside Servlet containers.
- A Servlet lifecycle consists of four phases: loading and creating, initialization, request handling, and end of life. For each of those phases, specific Servlet methods realize those phases. The Servlet will spend most of its lifecycle in the request-handling phase.
- You can make your Servlet thread-safe by using local variables for request data and using instance variables for constant data. If you need to change instance variables or outside resources, synchronize access to them. Making your Servlet implement `SingleThreadModel` does not guarantee that your server is thread-safe. Synchronizing `service()`, `doGet()`, or `doPost()` will make your Servlet thread-safe, but doing this is very impractical.
- You should always handle exceptions and never allow an exception to bypass the Servlet's response (unless it is an `IOException` that occurs during the response).
- The Servlet API facilitates session tracking, which allows you to create a web application that can keep track of a client's interactions with the application.
- Filters provide a pluggable architecture for processing requests and responses. They encapsulate processing that is outside the scope of the Servlet.
- The Model-View-Control (MVC) architecture can help create applications that are easier to maintain than Model 1 applications. Code is kept away from JSP pages; HTML is kept away from Servlets.

You should now be able to tackle most of the Servlet challenges that you will face as you begin to develop web applications. As usual, though, there is so much more that just could not be covered within the chapter. If you will be doing extensive work with Servlets, you may want to obtain a copy of *Java Servlet Programming, Second Edition*, by Jason Hunter (O'Reilly, 2001; ISBN 0-59600-040-5). In addition, there are several online forums that cover Servlet technology. Sun's developer forum hosts a Servlet forum at `http://forum.java.sun.com/`.

Exercises

1. In the "The response Object" section in this chapter, we very briefly outline the basic steps for using a Servlet to send binary data to a client. Create a Servlet that accepts a request from a client for an image file. The name of the image file can be passed as a form parameter, part of the URL, or as extra path information. Write the Servlet to load the named image into a byte array, set the content type for an image, set the content length (the number of bytes in the array), and write the image to the response.

2. Write a Servlet class with a synchronized `doGet()` or `doPost()` method. Put a `sleep()` method in the class. Open several browser windows and use them to submit several simultaneous requests to the Servlet. Record the response time for each request. Now remove the synchronization keyword from the `doGet()` or `doPost()` method. Submit the same number of simultaneous requests, and compare the response time of the unsynchronized Servlet to that of the synchronized Servlet.

3. In the session-tracking example (Listings 6-10 and 6-11), remove the code that performs the URL rewriting, set your browser to reject cookies, and experiment with the example to see how it behaves in this situation.

4. Expand the session-tracking example (Listings 6-10 and 6-11) to write a cookie with the user ID to the client browser. Use this cookie to "recognize" the user and initialize some session data.

5. If you have read Chapters 3 and 4, rewrite the final example in this chapter to use custom actions in the JSP pages.

6. Implement `ProcessAnalyst.jsp` (Listing 6-20) so that it can be used to add or delete an analyst.

CHAPTER 7

Working with Databases

Many Java EE applications that you work on will be dependent on a database. Search engines use databases to store information about web pages; e-commerce sites use databases to store information about products, customers, and orders; geo-imaging sites that provide photographic images of the world from space use databases to store images and information about those images; and the list goes on and on. Since your Java EE application, regardless of what service it performs, will likely use a database, we are going to spend the next two chapters looking at how to use databases with other Java EE components.

In this chapter, we will be using the PointBase database that comes with the Java EE SDK as our sample database. PointBase is an example of a relational database. Data in a relational database is stored in a set of tables. Each table consists of rows and columns. Each row is a set of data; each column in the row is a piece of data in that set. For example, you could use a table to store information about customers of an e-commerce web application. Each row in the table would represent a customer, and each column in the row would represent a particular piece of data about that customer, such as name or address. You might also have a separate table that records data about customer orders. Rather than repeating customer information in the orders table, the orders table would have a column that identifies the customer from the customer table. This creates a relationship between the two tables, and thus is why the database is called a relational database.

Note Don't worry if you are using some other database, such as Oracle, MySQL, or Sybase. Even though we use PointBase in this chapter, you should be able to easily modify the examples to work with your database. We will usually point out where you need to adapt the examples to your particular system or database.

Java has an API for working with databases, and this technology is known as JDBC. JDBC provides the developer with tools that allow clients to connect to databases and send commands to the database. These commands are written in the Structured Query Language, or SQL. (For more on SQL, see Appendix B.) Relational databases are not the only kind of database, although they are the most common. JDBC can be used with any kind of database. That is because JDBC abstracts common database functions into a set of common classes and methods, and database-specific code is contained in a code library, commonly called a *driver library*. If there is a driver library for a database, you can use the JDBC API to send commands to the database and extract data from the database.

This chapter will get you started connecting and using databases in the Java EE world. In the next chapter, we will look at some advanced topics that you will find useful as you begin to develop Java EE applications.

Here are the topics covered in this chapter:

- How to create a `DataSource` in the application server
- How to get a `Connection` in your client application from the `DataSource`
- How to use a `Statement` object to insert, update, and delete data from a database
- How to read the results of a query from a `ResultSet`

Connecting to Databases

The first step in being able to work with a database is to connect to that database. It's a process that's analogous to a web browser making a connection to a web server. The browser makes a network connection to a server, uses a specific protocol (HTTP) to send a specially formatted message to the server, and receives a formatted response (HTML) back from the server. When working with a database, your code will use the JDBC API to get a network connection to a database server, send a specially formatted message to the server, and receive a formatted response back from the server. As mentioned at the beginning of this chapter, the JDBC API is an abstraction, and it uses a database-specific code library to communicate with a particular database. A high-level diagram of that process is shown in Figure 7-1.

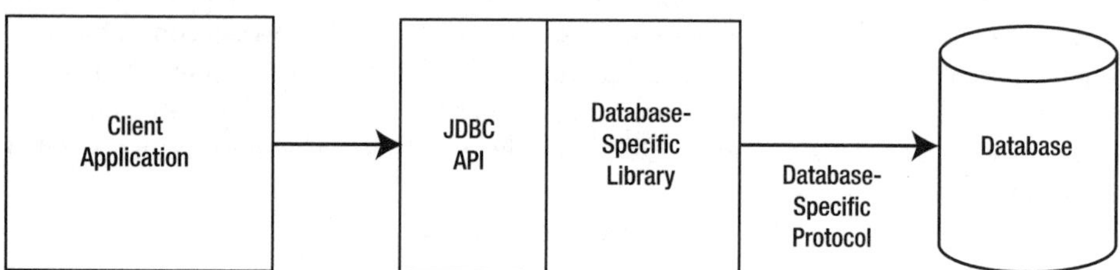

Figure 7-1. *A logical view of the connection between a client and a database*

To make a database connection, your code does not need to open any sockets or use any classes of the `java.net` package. As you may recall from Chapter 1, database connections are part of the "plumbing and wiring" infrastructure that is provided by the application server. In a Java EE environment, all the details of creating a connection are handled by the application server. The application server provides this connection through a class known as `DataSource`, which is part of the database-specific library shown in Figure 7-1.

Using Data Sources for Connections

Data sources were introduced as part of JDBC 2.0 and are currently the preferred means of getting a connection to persistent storage in Java EE applications. The `DataSource` interface provides a flexible architecture for creating and using database connections. As you will see, by using a `DataSource` object to obtain a connection, the database accessed by client code can be changed without impacting the client code. The `DataSource` hides the connection details so that you, as the client programmer, never need to worry about the connection parameters.

`DataSource` objects usually provide connections from a connection pool, which is a set of predefined database connections. This avoids the time-consuming activity of creating a new connection to a database each time a connection is requested. On the client side, there is no difference in how the connection is used. The difference lies in how the application server creates connections, hands out connections, and returns connections to the pool.

A `DataSource` is usually obtained by performing a lookup in a context. A very simple definition of a *context* is that it is just a means to associate a name with a resource. Within the application server, someone will create a `DataSource` instance, and then bind that instance to a name. *Binding* is the action that associates a resource to a name. For example, when you create a Java source code file in an editor and save that file to disk, you cause a collection of bytes to be written to the hard drive; at the same time, you tell the operating system to associate (or bind) that collection of bytes with some name. Thus, anyone who has access to the hard drive can get the collection of bytes by giving the correct name to the operating system. Similarly, a client can get a reference to a `DataSource` by giving the correct name to the application server.

Configuring a DataSource and Connection with Java EE

Before you, as the client programmer, can use a `DataSource`, someone needs to configure the `DataSource` in the application server. If you're lucky, that someone is a separate system administrator or database administrator. If you're on a small team, or learning Java EE on your own, that someone is you. So let's look at how to configure a `DataSource` and database connection in a Java EE application server. First, you'll see how to configure the `DataSource` in the Java EE reference implementation from Sun, and then in Tomcat. If you are using some other application server, you should be able to follow the same general procedure for your system (check your system documentation for specific procedures for your system).

1. Ensure that your Java EE application server is running, and then open a browser to the administration page. One way to get to the administration web page on Windows is to select Start menu ➤ All Programs ➤ Sun Microsystems ➤ Application Server ➤ Admin Console. On either Windows or Solaris, you can also open a web browser and manually enter the address `http://localhost:4848/` into your browser. (If the server is on a different machine or port, change `localhost` or `4848` to the appropriate value for your setup.) After entering the admin username and password, you will see the Sun Application Server administration web page, as shown in Figure 7-2.

Figure 7-2. *The Sun Application Server administration web page*

2. On the left side of the page is a tree view of various configurable items. There are nodes for applications, resources, and configuration. Under the Resources node, expand the JDBC node. You will see two nodes, labeled JDBC Resources and Connection Pools. With the Sun Application Server, the connection pool resource holds all the parameters for the database connection. Click the Connection Pools label, and a page that shows the connection pools will be loaded into a frame to the right side of the page, as shown in Figure 7-3. If you've just installed the Java EE server, or have never configured any connection pools, you will see that the server comes preconfigured with two connection pools. (You can see three connection pools in Figure 7-3. The one named `PointBaseExample` is the one we are adding in this set of steps.)

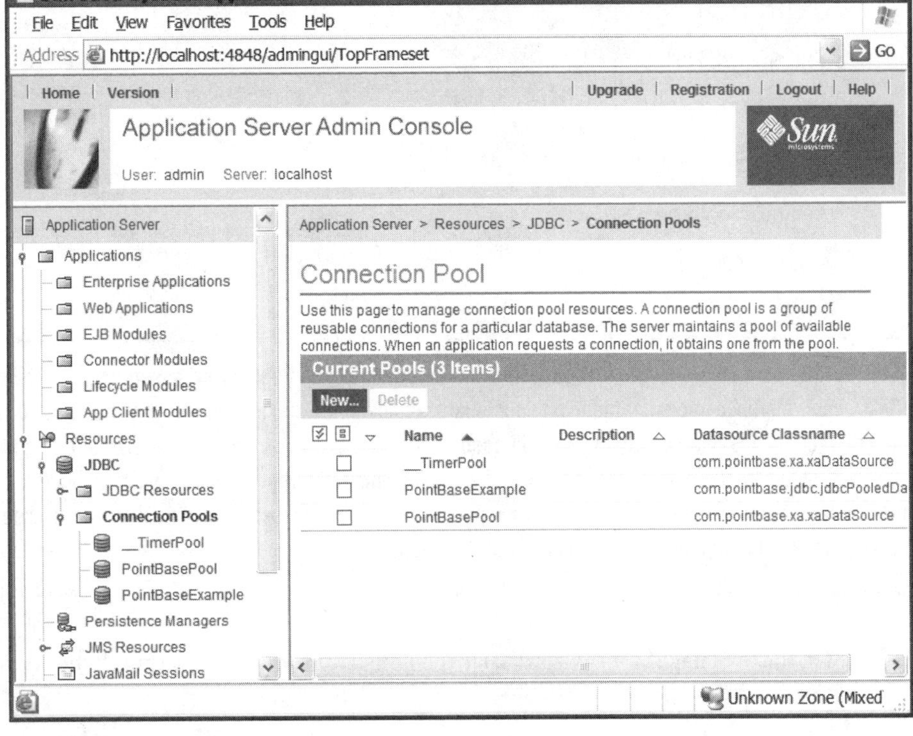

Figure 7-3. *The Connection Pools page shows the connection pools that are configured in the server.*

3. To create a new connection pool, click the New button on the page. This starts a wizard that collects information from you about the connection parameters.

4. On the first page of the Create Connection Pool wizard, enter the following information, and then click Next:

   - Name: `DataSourceExample`
   - Resource Type: `javax.sql.ConnectionPoolDataSource`
   - Database Vendor: PointBase

5. On the second page of the wizard, for the Datasource Classname, enter `com.pointbase.jdbc.jdbcPooledDataSource`. Then click Next.

6. On the third page of the wizard, scroll to bottom of page and enter the following. Then click Next:

   - Password: `PBPUBLIC`
   - ServerName: `localhost`
   - PortNumber: 9092
   - DatabaseName: `sample`
   - User: `PBPUBLIC`

Note The parameters on the last page of the Create Connection Pool wizard assume you have installed the Java EE reference implementation on your local machine. If the application server or database is installed on a different workstation or server, you will need to change `localhost` to the host name or IP address of the machine where the database is installed. If you are using a different database, you will need to change the parameters for your database. The various parameters are discussed in the "Reviewing the DataSource and Connection Parameters" section later in this chapter.

---

7. On the final page of the wizard, click the Finish button. A page listing all the connection pools, including the one you just created, will be displayed.

8. You can now test the connection pool you just created. Click the name of the new connection pool. This loads the Edit Connection Pool page. With your database running (select Start ➤ All Programs ➤ Sun Microsystems ➤ Application Server ➤ Start PointBase), click the Ping button. If the connection works, the page will reload with a message at the top that says, "Ping was Successful!" If the ping is not successful, you will need to do some troubleshooting. Check that the database is running, and also check that you entered the parameters correctly.

9. When the connection is working correctly, you now need to create a JDBC resource to use the connection pool. Click the JDBC Resources label on the left side of the administration page to load the JDBC Resources page. Click the New button to create a new resource. On the page that loads next, enter the JNDI Name as `jdbc/DataSourceExample`. For the Pool Name, enter `PointBaseExample`. Click the OK button to create the resource.

Note While not required, a common practice is to prefix the JNDI resource name with a short word that describes the resource. Database resources use the prefix `jdbc`. In the EJB chapters later in the book, you'll see that EJB resources use the prefix `ejb`.

WHAT IS JNDI?

On the JDBC Resources page of the Sun Application Server administration web page, you entered a value for JNDI Name. Just what is JNDI?

Directories, like databases, can be used to hold information. A phone book is a directory that binds names to phone numbers. A hard disk directory binds names to files. A domain name server binds domain names to an Internet address. If you have access to the directory, and you know a name, you can look up the resource that is bound to the name.

Just as JDBC provides a vendor-neutral interface to numerous databases, Java has provided a vendor-neutral interface to directory services: the Java Naming and Directory Interface (JNDI). This API provides a common set of functions for accessing directories. Your code uses the JNDI API to communicate with a directory. The details of talking to a particular directory are provided by directory-specific libraries, in a similar fashion to JDBC drivers. The JNDI API is provided by the `javax.naming` package.

With JNDI, a `Context` object provides the interface to the directory. When a resource is created, it is bound to a name using the `bind()` method call. When a resource is acquired, it is acquired using the `lookup()` method call.

Using a DataSource and Connection with a JSP

Now that a `DataSource` has been created in the application, components within the server can access the `DataSource` to get a connection to the database. In this section, we will create a JSP to act as the client to the database (see Listing 7-1). The JSP will perform a lookup of the `DataSource` using a coded name. The coded name that the JSP uses is `jdbc/DataSourceExample`. That name is the same name we used to bind the connection pool in the application server. However, with Sun's Application Server, you can use any name you wish as the coded name.

Listing 7-1. *DataSourceExample.jsp*

```
<%@ page import="java.sql.*, javax.sql.*, java.io.*, javax.naming.*" %>
<html>
  <head>
    <title>DataSource Example</title>
  </head>
  <body>
    <h1>DataSource Example</h1>
<%
    InitialContext context = new InitialContext();
    DataSource dataSource =
      (DataSource) context.lookup("java:comp/env/jdbc/DataSourceExample");
    Connection conn = null;
    Statement stmt = null;
    ResultSet rset = null;
```

```
    try {
      conn = dataSource.getConnection();
      stmt = conn.createStatement();
      rset = stmt.executeQuery("select * from CUSTOMER_TBL");
      if (rset.next()) {
%>
    <table width="100%" border="1">
      <tr align="left">
        <th>Customer Num</th><th>Name</th><th>email</th>
      </tr>
<%
        do {
%>
      <tr>
        <td><%= rset.getString("CUSTOMER_NUM") %></td>
        <td><%= rset.getString("NAME") %></td>
        <td><%= rset.getString("EMAIL") %></td>
      </tr>
<%
        } while (rset.next());
%>
    </table>
<%
      } else {
%>
    No results from query
<%
      }
    } catch (SQLException e) {
%>
    <%= e.getMessage() %>
<%
      e.printStackTrace();
    } finally {
      if (rset != null) { rset.close(); }
      if (stmt != null) { stmt.close(); }
      if (conn != null) { conn.close(); }
      if (context != null) { context.close(); }
    }
%>
  </body>
</html>
```

You use the Deployment Tool to create this JSP, just as you did for the JSPs we have deployed in previous chapters. However, there is one additional step you need to perform to ensure the DataSource is available to the JSP before deploying the web application. After creating the WAR, you must set up a Resource Reference for the web component. Here are the steps:

1. Create the JSP in Listing 7-1 and deploy it in a WAR file to the Sun Application Server.
2. Select the Resource Ref's tab in the web application, as shown in Figure 7-4. Click the Add button to add a Resource Reference.

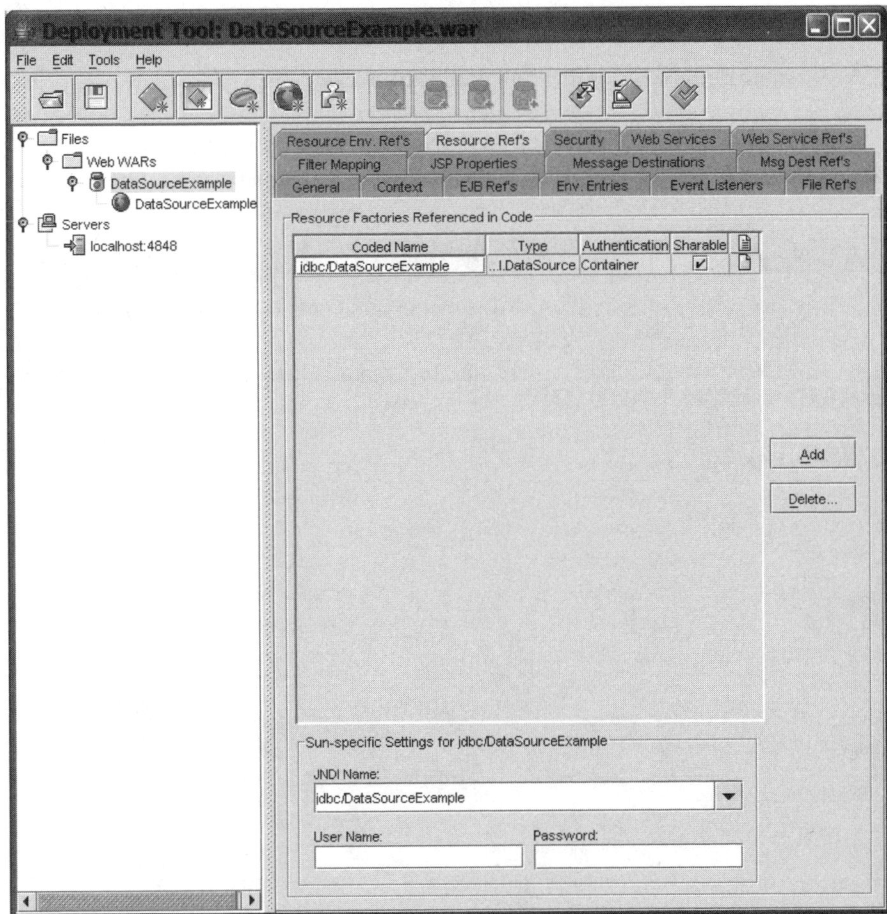

Figure 7-4. *Click the Add button on the Resource Ref's tab to configure a resource for the web component.*

3. Click in the Coded Name field and enter the coded name for the resource. The coded name of the resource must match the name used in the JSP source, which is `jdbc/DataSourceExample`. Select `javax.sql.DataSource` for the Type. You can use the default entries for the columns labeled Authentication and Sharable.
4. Next, you must relate the coded name to the JNDI name. In the JNDI Name field at the bottom of the screen, enter the JNDI name for the JDBC resource. That name should also be `jdbc/DataSourceExample`, which is the JNDI name you used when you created the JDBC resource in the application server.

Note Even though the example uses the same string in the JSP and for the JNDI name, you can use any name you desire in the JSP; it does not need to match the JNDI name. Because Sun provides a mapping between the coded name and the JNDI name, you can use any name in your code to access the JDBC resource.

---

5. Save and deploy the application to the Java EE server.

Assuming the database server is running, and your code is correctly deployed, you should see something similar to Figure 7-5 when you open the JSP in a browser.

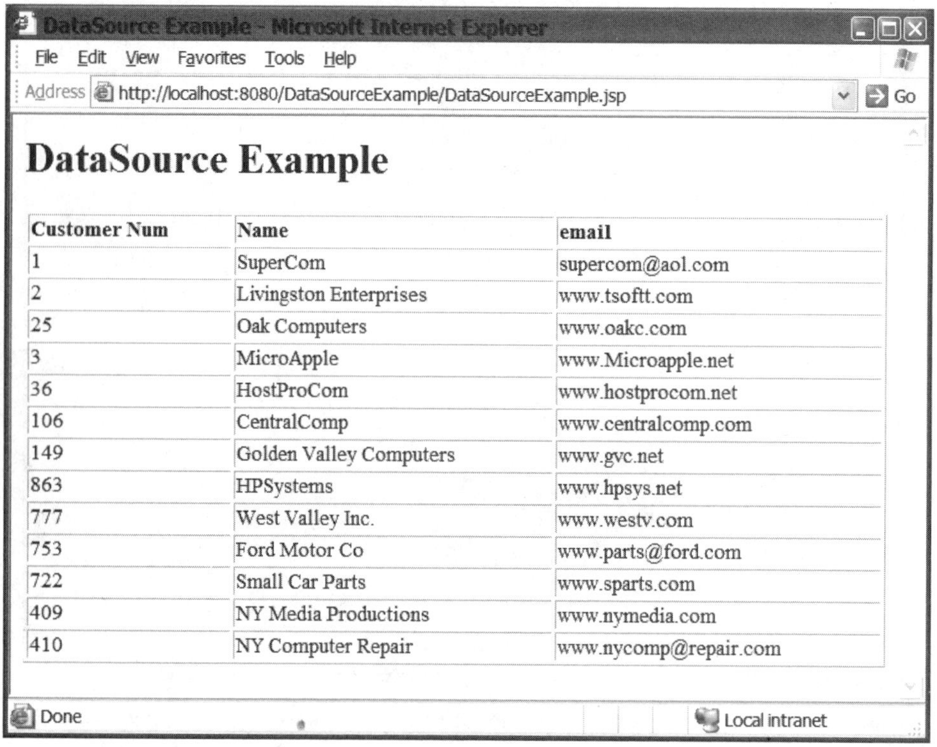

DataSource Example - Microsoft Internet Explorer

File Edit View Favorites Tools Help

Address http://localhost:8080/DataSourceExample/DataSourceExample.jsp Go

DataSource Example

Customer Num	Name	email
1	SuperCom	supercom@aol.com
2	Livingston Enterprises	www.tsoftt.com
25	Oak Computers	www.oakc.com
3	MicroApple	www.Microapple.net
36	HostProCom	www.hostprocom.net
106	CentralComp	www.centralcomp.com
149	Golden Valley Computers	www.gvc.net
863	HPSystems	www.hpsys.net
777	West Valley Inc.	www.westv.com
753	Ford Motor Co	www.parts@ford.com
722	Small Car Parts	www.sparts.com
409	NY Media Productions	www.nymedia.com
410	NY Computer Repair	www.nycomp@repair.com

Done Local intranet

Figure 7-5. *The output of the DataSourceExample.jsp*

The code for `DataSourceExample.jsp` (Listing 7-1) actually demonstrates a number of JDBC method calls. For the moment, you need to look at only the `DataSource` and `Connection` code. At the top of the JSP, you imported the packages needed for this example:

- `java.sql.*` is the `java` package for the `Connection`, `Statement`, and `ResultSet` objects. We will discuss these objects later in this chapter and in the next chapter.
- `javax.sql` is the `java` package for the `DataSource` object.
- `javax.naming` is the package for the `InitialContext` object.

The process of getting a connection starts when you create an instance of InitialContext:

```
InitialContext context = new InitialContext();
```

By using the default constructor, you get a reference to the default context for the application server.

Next, the context is used to perform a lookup:

```
DataSource dataSource =
    (DataSource) context.lookup("java:comp/env/jdbc/DataSourceExample");
```

Notice that in this example, the lookup name jdbc/DataSourceExample has additional information prefixed to it. The prefix java:comp/env is used when you are performing a lookup of resources provided by the server on which your component is running. Notice also that the lookup() method call returns a reference of type Object, so the Object reference is cast to the correct reference type of DataSource.

Also, for this example to work, you needed to map the coded name jdbc/DataSourceExample to the JNDI name jdbc/DataSourceExample in the Sun Application Server. This allows you to use any name in the JSP, as long as you map it to the correct JNDI name. Note that this won't necessarily work for other Java EE servers.

Using the DataSource, the JSP is then able to get a connection to the database:

```
conn = dataSource.getConnection();
```

Using this connection, the JSP was able to query the database for information in a table and receive the data returned by the database. We will look at how the JSP does this later in the chapter.

Reviewing the DataSource and Connection Parameters

Notice that the JSP did not use any database-specific information or parameters to get the connection. The only parameter you (as the client programmer) needed to know to connect to the database was the JNDI name of the database. This allows an almost total isolation between the presentation layer of your web application (the JSP) and the data layer (the database).

Any of the parameters for connecting to the database can change, and your JSP code is completely unaffected. If the database analysts in your company move the database to a different server, your code is unaffected. If the database analysts in your company use a different port, your code is unaffected. If the... well, you get the picture.

This is particularly useful when moving between development, test, and production environments. Rather than having different versions of the code or different configuration files for each environment, your code is always the same. When your code is deployed, it automatically gets whichever DataSource and Connection have been configured.

On the other hand, if you are responsible for configuring the DataSource and the Connection, as you did for the previous example, you do need to know the database connection parameters. Let's start with the easy ones first. Here are the parameters that were set through the Create Connection Pool wizard of the Sun Application Server:

- **ServerName:** The host name or IP address of the server where the database is running.
- **PortNumber:** The port that the database server listens to for connections. Different databases use different ports. In addition, this port is usually configurable. The default port for PointBase is 9092.

- **DatabaseName:** The name of the database used to access a set of tables and other resources. It is the name used when someone executed the SQL command `CREATE DATABASE` *name*. The Java EE server comes with two predefined databases (`sample`, and `sun-appserv-samples`); we used the one named `sample`.
- **User and Password:** The username and password of a user account in the database server. This user should also have the correct permissions to access the database. The Java EE server comes with a predefined user named `PBPUBLIC`.
- **Resource Type:** There are three different resource types that can be defined. The three types are identified by the fully qualified class name of a `DataSource` interface from the JDBC API. You use `javax.sql.XADataSource` when you need to have distributed transactions. We will look at distributed transactions in the next chapter. You use `javax.sql.ConnectionPoolDataSource` when you want connections to be pooled, as we did in the example. Pooled connections allow connections to be predefined and reused. Finally, you use javax.sql.DataSource when you don't need pooled connections or distributed transactions.
- **Datasource Classname:** This is the fully qualified class name of the database-specific class that provides and manages connections to the database. The best way to determine this class is to consult the database documentation for your database. The `DataSource` class name needs to be a class that implements the `javax.sql.DataSource` interface. PointBase's documentation lists three classes that implement the `DataSource` interface: `com.pointbase.jdbc.jdbcDataSource`, `com.pointbase.jdbc.jdbcPooledDataSource`, and `com.pointbase.xa.xaDataSource`. Since we wanted to use a connection pool, we chose the `jdbcPooledDataSource` class. In the next chapter, you'll see how to use the `xaDataSource` with distributed transactions.

■ **Note** Unfortunately, no PointBase documentation comes with the Java EE reference implementation, and the PointBase web site does not provide direct access to the documentation. To get access to the documentation from PointBase, you will need to register with PointBase (`www.pointbase.com`) and request access to the documentation. Alternatively, you can download an evaluation copy of the PointBase database server, which includes the documentation.

The class will be contained in a JAR file that is made available to the application server. When using the PointBase server with the Sun Application Server, the classpath of the server already includes the PointBase driver library. If you want to use a different database, you will need to provide the driver library to the server. This is done by copying the driver library (the JAR file that contains the driver) to the `lib` directory of the application server installation. If you are using a different application server, you will need to look at your documentation to determine the correct location for the library or the correct way to adjust the classpath to include the driver library.

Configuring a DataSource and Connection with Tomcat

Tomcat also provides a facility for defining `DataSource` objects that can be used by Java EE components. As with the Sun Application Server, Tomcat provides a web-based GUI for configuring the `DataSource`. As mentioned in the previous section, the database driver files need to be made available to the application server. With Tomcat, this is done by copying the JAR file to the Tomcat `common/lib` directory.

1. If you've installed the Sun Application Server, navigate to the PointBase `lib` directory (`C:\Sun\AppServer\pointbase\lib` is the default location for Windows) and copy the `pbclient.jar` file to the Tomcat `\common\lib` directory (for Windows, that will be a path similar to `C:\Program Files\Apache Software Foundation\Tomcat 5.028\common\lib`). Note that Tomcat imports only JAR files automatically, so the library must be a JAR file.

■ **Tip** If you don't have the Sun Application Server, your other option for obtaining the driver library is to download an evaluation copy of PointBase from `www.pointbase.com`. Not all driver libraries are this hard to obtain, however. Most database vendors make the driver libraries easily available to developers.

---

2. If Tomcat is already running, you need to restart it so that it can load the driver library. If Tomcat is not running, you can start it now.

3. If you created the JSP in Listing 7-1 and deployed it in a WAR file to the Sun Application Server, take that same WAR file and drop it into the Tomcat `webapps` directory. This causes the Tomcat server to deploy the web application in the WAR. If you did not create the JSP earlier, now is the time to enter and save the source code in Listing 7-1. In addition, if you did not use the Sun Deployment Tool earlier, you need to create the `web.xml` file shown in Listing 7-2. Then create a WAR file to hold the JSP and `web.xml` files. (Refer to Chapter 3 if you need to be refreshed on the structure of a WAR file.) After the WAR file is created, drop it into the Tomcat `webapps` directory.

Listing 7-2. *web.xml File for the Tomcat DataSource Example*

```
<?xml version="1.0" encoding="UTF-8"?>
<web-app version="2.5" xmlns="http://java.sun.com/xml/ns/javaee"
                 xmlns:xsi="http://www.w3.org/2001/XMLSchema-instance"
                 xsi:schemaLocation="http://java.sun.com/xml/ns/javaee
http://java.sun.com/xml/ns/javaee/web-app_2_5.xsd">
  <display-name>DataSourceExample</display-name>
  <servlet>
    <display-name>DataSourceExample</display-name>
    <servlet-name>DataSourceExample</servlet-name>
    <jsp-file>/DataSourceExample.jsp</jsp-file>
  </servlet>
```

```
    <resource-ref>
      <res-ref-name>jdbc/DataSourceExample</res-ref-name>
      <res-type>javax.sql.DataSource</res-type>
      <res-auth>Container</res-auth>
      <res-sharing-scope>Shareable</res-sharing-scope>
    </resource-ref>
  </web-app>
```

4. Open a web browser to the Tomcat administration page, either by opening the web browser to the Tomcat home page at `http://localhost:8080` and clicking the Tomcat Administration link or by going directly, using the address `http://localhost:8080/admin/`. If necessary, replace `localhost` and `8080` with the proper host name and port number for your system. At the administration home page, you will need to enter the admin username and password for your system.

5. After logging into the administration tool, you will see a web page similar to that shown in Figure 7-6. As with the Sun Application Server administration tool, the page shows a tree view of resources in the left frame. Clicking a node in the tree will either expand the node or load the details of a node into the right frame.

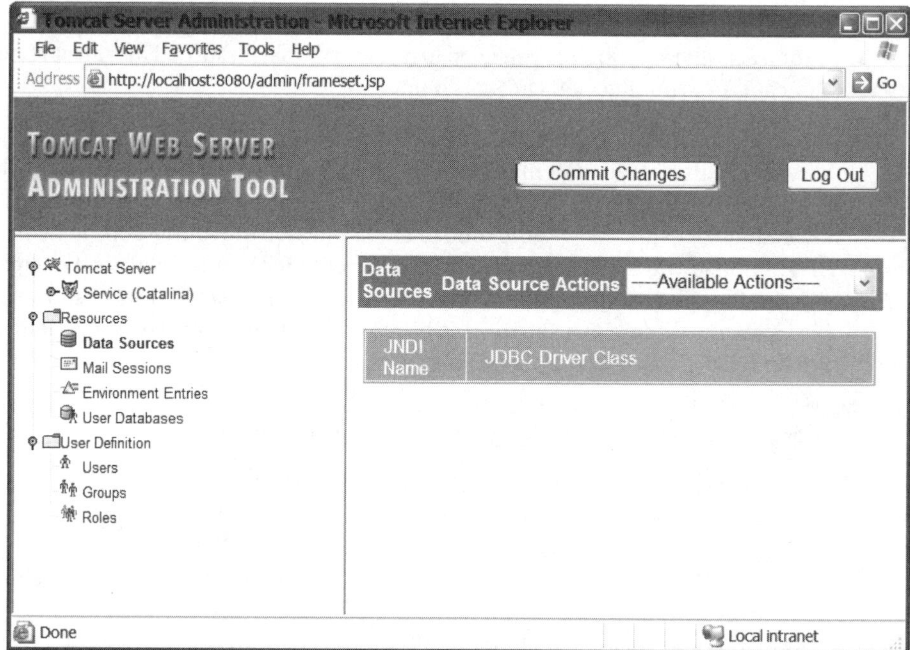

Figure 7-6. *The Tomcat administration web interface after selecting the DataSources node*

Tomcat allows you to configure a `DataSource` that is local to a web application or a global `DataSource` that can be used by all web applications. We'll first show you how to create a global `DataSource`, because the procedure for creating a local `DataSource` is simply a subset of the procedure for creating a global `DataSource`.

Creating a Global DataSource in Tomcat

Here is the procedure to create a global `DataSource`, continuing from the previous section:

1. Click the Data Sources node under the Resources node. In the right frame, select Create New Data Source from the Data Source Actions drop-down list. This loads the form shown in Figure 7-7.

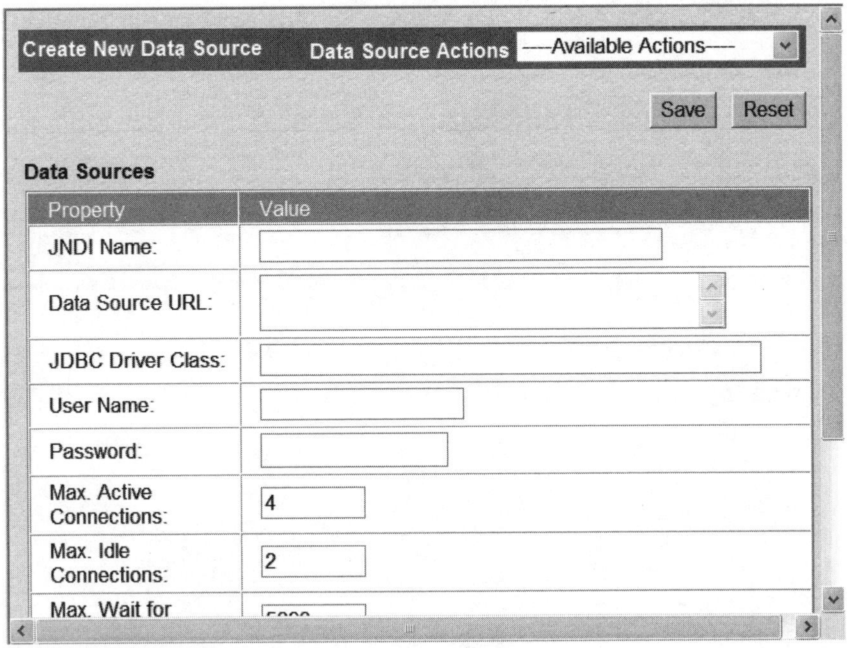

Figure 7-7. *The Create New Data Source form*

2. In the form, enter the following values for these fields:

   - JNDI Name: `jdbc/DataSourceExample`
   - Data Source URL: `jdbc:pointbase:server://localhost:9092/sample`
   - JDBC Driver Class: `com.pointbase.jdbc.jdbcUniversalDriver`
   - User Name: `PBPUBLIC`
   - Password: `PBPUBLIC`

   You can leave the other fields in the form with their default values. We'll review these parameters shortly.

3. Click the Save button to save the Data Source.

4. Now you need to make the DataSource available to the web application. Even though it is a global resource, it is not globally available until you create a link to the resource from each web application. In the left frame, expand the Service, Host, then Context nodes, as shown in Figure 7-8. If you've correctly deployed the WAR file, there will be a Context node for DataSourceExample JSP. Select the Resources, then Data Sources node for the DataSourceExample Context.

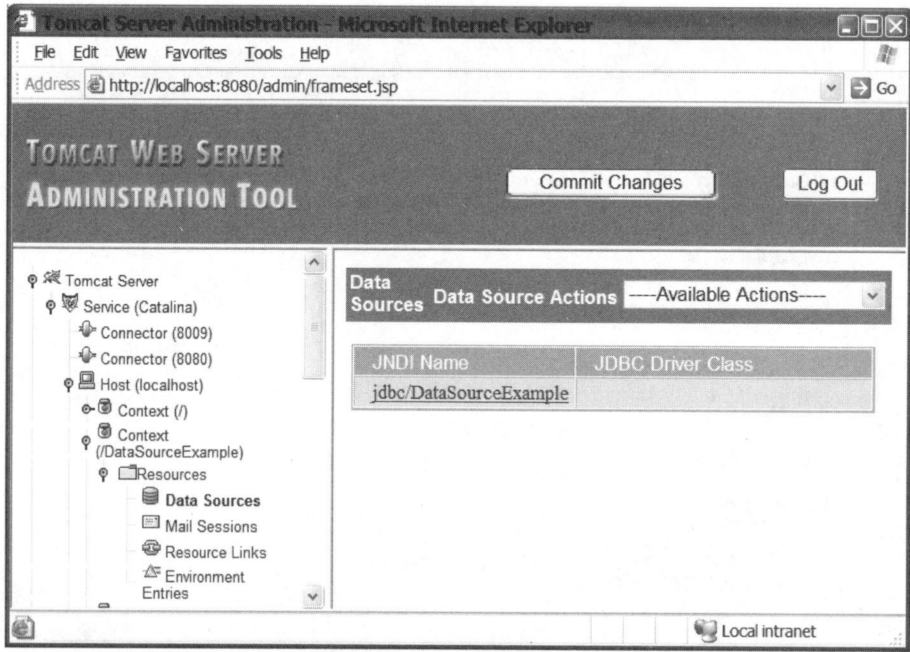

Figure 7-8. *The Data Sources page*

5. There will likely already be a JNDI entry for the Context Data Source. This is because Tomcat reads the web.xml file and automatically starts an entry for the DataSource. However, at the moment, we do not want to create an application DataSource, so select the Delete Data Sources action from the Data Source Action drop-down list in the right frame. Select the check box next to the JNDI name and click the Save button.

6. In the left frame, select the Resources node, then Resource Link node. This loads the Resource Link page in the right frame. Select the Create New Resource Link action in the Resource Link Actions drop-down list. This loads the page shown in Figure 7-9.

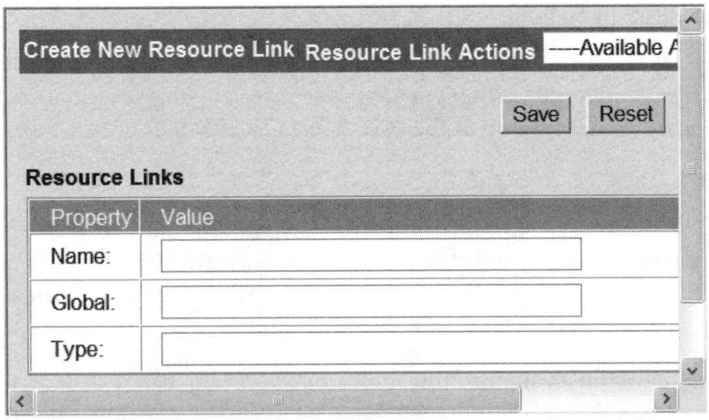

Figure 7-9. *The Create New Resource Link form*

7. Enter the following values in each field:

   • Name: `jdbc/DataSourceExample` (or whatever name you used in the JSP)

   • Global: `jdbc/DataSourceExample` (the name of the global resource)

   • Type: `javax.sql.DataSource`

Note When using a global `DataSource` resource and a web application with a link to the global resource, you can use any name you want for the JNDI name and any coded name in your JSP. That is because the Resource Link provides a mapping between the JSP coded name and the JNDI name.

---

8. Click the Save button to save the Resource Link.

9. Since your web application has already been loaded, it is still running in the old environment, which does not include the new `DataSource`. There are a couple of ways to get your web application executing with the new resources:

   • Click the Commit button at the top of the Tomcat administration interface. This causes the web application environment to be restarted, and it also makes any changes to the web resources permanent. The next time you restart Tomcat, the `DataSource` and Resource Link values will be reloaded.

   • Alternatively, go to the Tomcat Management page (`http://localhost:8080/manager/html`) and click the Reload link for the application. This causes the web application to be reloaded with the new environment. However, this does not make the `DataSource` and resource link permanent.

After the changes have been committed, or the application reloaded, you can load the JSP into your browser, and you should see the same page as shown earlier in Figure 7-5.

Creating a Local DataSource in Tomcat

Creating a `DataSource` that is local to a web application is almost exactly the same as creating a global data source. The only difference is that you do not need to create a resource link. Here are the steps, continuing from the last step in the "Configuring a DataSource and Connection with Tomcat" section.

1. In the left frame of the Tomcat administration tool, expand the Service, Host, then Context nodes, as shown earlier in Figure 7-8. If you've correctly deployed the WAR file, there will be a Context node for the `DataSourceExample` JSP. Select the Resources node, then Data Sources node for the DataSourceExample Context.
2. In the right frame, click the link in the table for the JNDI Name `jdbc/DataSourceExample`. This loads a form similar to the one shown earlier in Figure 7-7. The difference is that in this form, you cannot enter a value for the JNDI name, since it is already set.
3. In the form, enter the following values for these fields:
   - Data Source URL: `jdbc:pointbase:server://localhost:9092/sample`
   - JDBC Driver Class: `com.pointbase.jdbc.jdbcUniversalDriver`
   - User Name: `PBPUBLIC`
   - Password: `PBPUBLIC`

   You can leave the other fields in the form with their default values.
4. Click the Save button, and then click the Commit Changes button to save the `DataSource`.

When you next run the web component, it will have access to the `DataSource` local to the web application.

Reviewing the DataSource and Connection Parameters

Here are the parameters that were set through the GUI of the Tomcat administration tool:

- **JNDI Name:** This is the name used by the application server to identify the `DataSource`. We used `jdbc/DataSourceExample` in this example. This name can be anything you want it to be. You map the coded name used by the JSP to the name used by the application server.
- **Data Source URL:** The URL is a string that tells the driver how to access the database. The URL for each database will vary depending on the database and the driver. However, all URLs will have the general form `jdbc:`*<subprotocol>*`:`*<subname>*, with the *<subprotocol>* usually identifying the vendor, and *<subname>* identifying the database and providing additional information needed to make the connection. We used the URL `jdbc:pointbase:server://localhost:9092/sample`, where the subprotocol is `pointbase:server` and the subname is `//localhost:9092/sample`.

Note If you read the earlier section about configuring a `DataSource` with Java EE, the subname portion of the URL used with Tomcat may look somewhat familiar. These values are the same as those for the ServerName, PortNumber, and DatabaseName fields in the Sun Application Server configuration. However, different databases use different URLs. For example, the MySQL driver uses a URL that is similar to PointBase: `jdbc:mysql://locahost:3306/sample`. Oracle's is not so similar: `jdbc:oracle:thin:@localhost:1521:orcl`. If you are using a database other than PointBase, consult your JDBC driver documentation for the correct format for the URL.

- **JDBC Driver Class:** The Driver Class is the fully qualified class name of the database-specific class that provides and manages the database connections. We used `com.pointbase.jdbc.jdbcUniversalDriver`. Notice that for Tomcat, we are not using a class that implements the `DataSource` interface, but a class that implements the `java.sql.Driver` interface.
- **User Name and Password:** These are the username and password for the database user. We used `PBPUBLIC`.

JDBC DRIVERS

JDBC provides a database-neutral set of classes and interfaces that can be used by your Java class. The database-specific code is included in a driver library that is developed by the database vendor or third parties. The JDBC specification identifies four types of drivers that can be used to communicate with databases:

- **Type 1 Driver:** This driver provides a mapping between JDBC and a data access API known as ODBC. The ODBC API then calls a native ODBC library to complete the communication with the database.
- **Type 2 Driver:** This type of driver is similar to the Type 1 driver because it communicates with the database through a native API. However, because it makes calls directly to the native API and bypasses the additional data access layer, this type of driver tends to be more efficient than Type 1. Since they require a native API, you can use these drivers only where the API exists on all platforms, and you have the ability to install the API on all platforms.
- **Type 3 Driver:** This type of driver sends database calls to a middleware component running on another server. The middleware server then communicates with the database using a database-specific protocol.
- **Type 4 Driver:** This type of driver, also commonly known as a *thin driver*, is written completely in Java. It communicates directly with a database using the database's native protocol. The PointBase driver is a Type 4 driver. Since Type 4 drivers are Java-based, you can use them on any platform that supports Java.

For the most part, you do not need to worry about the driver type. Most drivers are Type 4 drivers. You will usually just use the default vendor driver without worrying which type it is. If you must choose, you will most often be making a choice between a Type 2 and a Type 4 driver. You might think that Type 2 drivers are faster because they use native code, or you might think Type 4 drivers are faster because they do not need to communicate through another layer. In fact, which driver is faster depends on many factors. Either may be a good choice for your system, and you should run tests with your production code to determine which driver is better.

Closing Connections

In the previous section, you saw how to get a database connection from a DataSource. Primarily, though, we showed you how to configure the DataSource, and then obtained the connection with this line of code:

```
conn = dataSource.getConnection();
```

and used the connection with this line of code:

```
stmt = conn.createStatement();
```

For now, this is about all that you need to know about connections. We will cover more methods of the Connection object when we discuss Statement objects later in this chapter and in the next chapter. We will also use the Connection object when we look at transactions in the next chapter. However, there is one aspect of connections that we need to cover here: they need to be closed properly.

The Connection class has a method for releasing the connection:

```
public void close() throws SQLException
```

Many beginners will try to use it like this:

```
Connection conn = dataSource.getConnection();
// Then some JDBC code that works with the database
conn.close();
```

This is a mistake! Almost all JDBC methods throw SQLExceptions (which are discussed in the "Handling Exceptions" section later in this chapter). If the JDBC code between the getConnection() method call and the close() method call throws a SQLException, the call to close() is completely skipped.

The correct way to use close(), is to put it inside the finally block of a try-catch-finally exception handler, as in Listing 7-1. Here it is again:

```
try {
  conn = dataSource.getConnection();
  //...a lot of JSP code
} catch (SQLException e) {
  //...
} finally {
  if (rset != null) { rset.close(); }
  if (stmt != null) { stmt.close(); }
  if (conn != null) { conn.close(); }
  if (context != null) { context.close(); }
}
```

Thus, you are assured that close() will be called, no matter what happens with the JDBC code. However, there's still a problem in the code in Listing 7-1, which we ignored for the example, but which you do need to know about. The close() method also throws a SQLException. So, in the first statement of the finally block, the rset.close() method call can throw a SQLException. If this occurs, the following statements in the finally block will be skipped.

To be safe, each call to close() should also be in a try-catch-finally handler. So, the JDBC code begins to look something like this:

```
try {
  conn = dataSource.getConnection();
  // Then some JDBC code that works with the database
} catch (SQLEXception e) {
  // Handle the exception
} finally {
  try {
    rset.close();
  } catch (SQLException e2) {
    // Usually this is ignored
  }
  try {
    stmt.close();
  } catch (SQLException e2) {
    // Usually this is ignored
  }
  try {
    conn.close();
  } catch (SQLException e2) {
    // Usually this is ignored
  }
}
```

And of course, this needs to be in every class that uses a connection. Pretty soon, you have finally blocks with enclosed try-catch-finally blocks all over the place, and things are starting to look pretty cluttered! Later in this chapter, in the "Using Statements to Insert Data into a Database" section, we'll look at a better way to close and release resources.

WHAT CAN GO WRONG WITH CONNECTIONS

I once worked on team developing a web application that locked up every time we stress-tested it with thousands of database transactions. We were getting very frustrated because we couldn't release the application to production until it could reliably handle thousands of transactions per hour.

The database vendor included a management utility for the system that showed how many database connections had been opened and how many had been released. Whenever we tested our application, the utility would show that the number of opened connections slowly but steadily diverged from the number of released connections. While the number of opened connections steadily increased, the number of closed connections increased faster. For various unrelated reasons, we didn't trust that the vendor's software was error-free, so even though the number seemed to be wrong, we figured as long as more connections were closed than were opened, we were okay. Still, we couldn't understand why the application always appeared to lock up.

Continued

Although I had the most JDBC experience on the team, I had not written the JDBC code. And because the JDBC code worked with small numbers of transactions, I had been concerned about the components I was working on, rather than the JDBC section of the application. Finally, the lockup problem became important enough that I decided I had to investigate the JDBC code.

When I inspected the JDBC code line by line, I discovered that the vendor's utility had been correct all along. It turned out that the developer who had written the JDBC code hadn't understood how to close connections properly. He had written many long methods inside a gigantic class (which wasn't a JSP, by the way), and all of these methods were opening connections at the top of a `try` block, and many hundreds of lines later closing them inside their own `try`...`catch` blocks. Sometimes the same connection would be closed several times, and sometimes connections were not being closed at all. The count of closed connections was greater than the count of opened connections because connections were being closed multiple times. But it was the connections that were not closed that were the bigger problem.

Connections that are not closed are not available to be reused from the pool. Whenever we tested the code, it didn't take long for the defects in the code to cause the system to be starved for connections. After enough time, the application just locked up, waiting for connections that were no longer available.

To fix this code, I went through the class line by line and made sure that every time a connection was opened inside a `try` block, there was a corresponding `finally` block that called the `close` method to close the connection. When we tested the new code, I paid a lot more attention to that system diagnostic that compared open and released connections. When the code was finally correct, the two numbers were always equal when all the transactions were completed. Next time we sent the code to test, the system did not lock up. Mission successful!

One other way we might have narrowed down the problem is by setting a login timeout. Our application appeared to lock up because the code was waiting for a connection that never became available. It waited and it waited... and it would have waited forever if we let it.

Setting the Login Timeout

There is a way to tell the `DataSource` to wait only a certain amount of time for a connection. To do this, the `DataSource` class provides the following method:

```
public static void setLoginTimeout(int)
```

The `int` parameter indicates the number of seconds that the driver manager should wait for a connection. If the driver does not return a connection in that amount of time, the manager throws a `SQLException`.

Handling Exceptions

Earlier, we mentioned that almost all JDBC methods declare that they throw `SQLExceptions`. In most respects, `SQLException` objects are the same as the other exception objects that you encounter in your Java code. Your web components that use JDBC code will need to either handle these exceptions in `try-catch-finally` blocks or let the `SQLException` be handled higher in the call chain.

Usually in web components, letting the exception pass out of the web component is a bad idea. While application servers are designed to handle exceptions thrown by web components, this usually results in an ugly error message being sent to the client, such as the one shown in

Figure 7-10. It won't take too many of these kinds of bad user experiences before your traffic drops to zero.

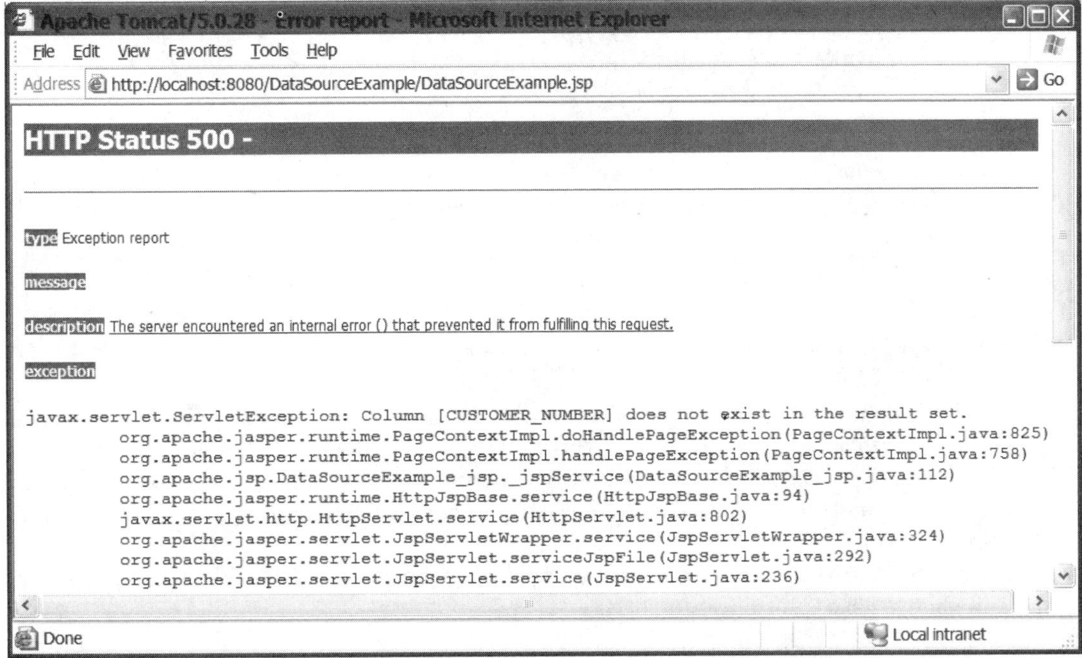

Figure 7-10. *This is the kind of error message you don't want your users to see.*

There are some ways, however, in which `SQLExceptions` are different from other exceptions. To enable you to better handle exceptions from the database, `SQLExceptions` add additional behavior to the `Exception` class. One additional feature is that they can be chained. What this means is that the `SQLException` you catch in your code may contain a reference to another `SQLException`, which, in turn, may contain a reference to another `SQLException`, and so on. It's a linked list of exceptions. The `SQLException` class adds a method for dealing with chained exceptions:

```
public SQLException getNextException()
```

Another difference is that the `SQLException` can contain additional information about the error that occurred inside the database. Databases have their own error codes that identify the problem that occurred. These error codes are returned inside the `SQLException` object, and you can get the error code with a call to this method:

```
public int getErrorCode()
```

Here is a small snippet of code showing these two methods:

```
try {
  // Some JDBC code
} catch (SQLException e) {
  while (e != null) {
    System.out.println("The error code is " + e.getErrorCode();
    e = e.getNextException();
  }
}
```

Inside the `while` loop, the error code from the database is printed, and then `getNextException()` is called. The reference returned by `getNextException()` is assigned back to the variable `e`. When the last exception is reached, `getNextException()` returns null and the `while` loop will terminate.

Logging with a DataSource

If you've done much Java coding, you've probably had many opportunities to use the poor man's debugging tool: `System.out.println()`. This prints directly to the console. You also probably know the problem that can happen with this. You'll have so many `System.out.println()` commands that what is printed scrolls right off the screen or is lost among the hundreds of lines of debugging information.

The `DataSource` class provides a method that can be used to redirect debug output and a method to get a `PrintWriter` for logging:

```
public static void setLogWriter(PrintWriter)
public static PrintWriter getLogWriter()
```

Using `setLogWriter(PrintWriter)`, you can direct the `DataSource` object's debug statements to an instance of `PrintWriter`. The `PrintWriter` can be a wrapper for any `Writer` or `OutputStream` (such as a file or a stream), or a `PipedWriter`. When the `DataSource` is first created, its `PrintWriter` reference is null, meaning that nothing is logged. Here is a snippet of code showing how we could have used this feature in the example shown earlier in Listing 7-1:

```
// At the top of the JSP
FileWriter fw = new FileWriter("mydebug.log");
PrintWriter pw = new PrintWriter(fw);
DriverManager.setLogWriter(pw);
// After getting the Connection
dataSource.write.("connection is " + conn);
```

Note that you would want to use this for database-specific logging. For general web component logging messages, you would want to use the normal logging provided by the web component. Recall that for JSPs and servlets, that would be a call to the `log()` method.

Creating and Using Statement Objects

Earlier in this chapter, you saw how to get a connection to a database. However, the connection does not provide any methods that allow you to do anything to the database. To actually create, retrieve, update, or delete data from the database, you need to use the `Statement` class.

`Statement` objects are your primary interface to the tables in a database. We will look at using statements to insert new rows into a table, update a row in a table, and delete a row from a table. In the next section on resultsets, you will see how to use a statement to query tables in a database.

`Statement` objects are created by calling the following methods of the `Connection` class:

- `public Statement createStatement()`: Creates a `Statement` object. If the statement is used for a query, the `ResultSet` returned by the `executeQuery()` method is a nonupdatable, nonscrollable `ResultSet`.
- `public Statement createStatement(int,int)`: Creates a `Statement` object. If the statement is used for a query, the two parameters determine whether the `ResultSet` returned by the `executeQuery()` method is updatable or scrollable.
- `public Statement createStatement(int,int,int)`: In JDBC 3.0, creates a `Statement` object. If the statement is used for a query, the first two parameters determine whether the `ResultSet` returned by the `executeQuery()` method is updatable or scrollable, and the third parameter determines holdability.

For now, don't worry what *updatable, scrollable,* and *holdable* mean. These apply to statements used to execute a SQL `SELECT` command. We will cover those topics in the section about resultsets. When executing any other SQL command, you only need a statement created with the `createStatement()` method that takes no parameters.

Once you have a `Statement` object, you use it to send SQL commands to the database. You can use the following methods to send SQL commands to the database:

- `public int executeUpdate(String)`: Used to any execute SQL that is not a query. Those will primarily be create, insert, update, and delete SQL operations.
- `public ResultSet executeQuery(String)`: Used for querying database tables.
- `public int[] executeBatch()`: Used for sending multiple SQL commands in a single operation.
- `public boolean execute(String)`: Used for executing unknown SQL or SQL that could return either an `int` value or a `ResultSet` object.

Here, we will look at the `executeUpdate(String)` and `executeBatch()` methods. We will look at `executeQuery(String)` in the section on `ResultSet` objects. The `execute(String)` method is used only in the rare situation when the SQL could return a `ResultSet` (as from a query), an `int` (as from some kind of update), or both, and you don't know which it will return. Since you are not likely to encounter this situation too often, we won't cover it in detail in this book. If you're interested in learning more, consider reading *JDBC API Tutorial and Reference, Third Edition,* by Maydene Fisher, et al (Addison-Wesley; ISBN: 0-32117-384-8).

Executing Single Statements

The `executeUpdate(String)` method is fairly straightforward. It is used to execute a single SQL command. The `String` parameter is the SQL command that you want to execute in the database. It can be any SQL command except for a query. The return value of the method is the number of rows affected by the SQL command. This value can range from 0 to the number of rows in the database table. The number of rows returned by various types of SQL commands is shown in Table 7-1.

Table 7-1. *Possible Return Values for executeUpdate(String)*

SQL Type	Number of Rows Affected
`CREATE`, `ALTER`, `DROP`, and other statements that affect tables, indexes, and so on	0
`INSERT` statements	1 to *n*, where *n* is any number
`DELETE` statements	0 to *n*, where *n* is the number of rows in the table
`UPDATE` statements	0 to *n*, where *n* is the number of rows in the table

If you attempt to execute a SQL query through the `executeUpdate(String)` method, a `SQLException` will be thrown.

Performing Batch Updates

One way that you can improve the performance of your JDBC application is to execute a number of SQL commands in a batch. With batch execution, you add any number of SQL commands to the statement. The statement holds these SQL commands in memory until you tell it that you are ready for the database to execute the SQL. When you call `executeBatch()`, the statement sends the entire batch of SQL in one network communication. In addition to the `executeBatch()` method, two other methods are needed for batch execution:

- `public void addBatch(String)`: Adds a SQL command to the current batch of commands for the `Statement` object.
- `public void clearBatch()`: Makes the set of commands in the current batch empty.

The use of batch updating is straightforward. You add SQL commands to the statement with the `addBatch(String)` command. When you are ready for the commands to be executed, you call the `executeBatch()` method. This causes the statement to send all the SQL commands to the database for execution. In code, it looks like this:

```
// The variable someSqlCommand in the method calls is a SQL command
stmt.addBatch(someSqlCommand);
stmt.addBatch(someSqlCommand);
stmt.addBatch(someSqlCommand);
stmt.addBatch(someSqlCommand);
int[] results = stmt.executeBatch();
```

As you can see in this snippet, the `executeBatch()` method returns an `int` array that contains the number of rows affected by each of the commands. The result of the first SQL command that was added to the statement is returned in the first element of the array, the result of the second SQL command is in the second element, and so on. Since the `executeBatch()` method returns an `int` array, the one type of SQL command that cannot be executed by batching is a SQL `SELECT` command, which returns a `ResultSet` object, not an `int`.

Releasing Statements

Just as with `Connection` objects, it is important to release `Statement` objects when you are finished with them. This does not mean that you must immediately release the statement after executing a SQL command; you can use the same `Statement` object to execute multiple SQL commands. However, when you no longer need the statement to execute SQL, you should release it. The `Statement` class has its own `close()` method.

If you're near a computer, take a moment to read the Javadoc for the `Statement` class (`http://java.sun.com/j2se/1.4.2/docs/api/`). You'll see that for the `close()` method, the Javadoc states, "Releases this Statement object's database and JDBC resources immediately instead of waiting for this to happen when it is automatically closed."

The reference to automatically closing the `Statement` object refers to the automatic closing of the object when it is garbage-collected or when the `Connection` used to create the `Statement` is closed. Garbage collection can occur when the `Statement` object goes out of scope or is otherwise no longer reachable and thus is eligible for garbage collection. When the object is garbage-collected, its resources can be released. However, there's always the possibility that objects that you think are out of scope are still reachable. In addition, even if an object is eligible for garbage collection, it may not be collected immediately.

■ **Note** Garbage collection of objects relies on the reachability of objects. An object is reachable if there is a chain of references that reach the object from some root reference. More information can be found at `http://java.sun.com/docs/books/performance/1st_edition/html/JPAppGC.fm.html`.

Similarly, even though closing a `Connection` will close any open `Statement` objects, you should not leave the `Statement` open, intending to let it be closed when the `Connection` is closed. Database resources are limited, and it's never a good idea to hold onto them longer than you need. That is why the Javadoc for `close()` also states, "It is generally good practice to release resources as soon as you are finished with them to avoid tying up database resources."

Just as with the `Connection` objects, the `close()` method call for `Statement` objects should be in a `finally` block, and since it also throws a `SQLException`, it needs to be wrapped inside a `try-catch` block. And since developers usually close the connection right after the statement, this usually leads to code that looks something like this:

```
try {
  //Some JDBC code
} finally {
  try {
    stmt.close();
    conn.close();
  } catch (Exception e) {
    //Recover from the exception
  }
}
```

If the `stmt.close()` method call does happen to throw a `SQLException`, the call to `conn.close()` will be skipped, and now your application has unclosed connections lying around. You can avoid that problem by wrapping each call in its own `try-catch` block:

```
try {
  //Some JDBC code
} finally {
  try {
    stmt.close();
  } catch (Exception e) {
    //Recover from the exception
  }
  try {
    conn.close();
  } catch (Exception e) {
    //Recover from the exception
  }
}
```

This is better from the point of view that an exception from `stmt.close()` will not cause the `conn.close()` method to be skipped. However, it's worse because you now have this code duplicated in every web component that uses the database. It also makes your code harder to understand because of the nested `try-catch` blocks. Code that is not easy to understand is not easy to maintain. In the next section, we'll look at one way to close statements and connections without cluttering your code with nested `try-catch` blocks.

Using Statements to Insert Data into a Database

The next example demonstrates one solution to the problem presented in the previous section. The solution is to create a separate class to manage `Connections` and `Statements`, as shown in Listing 7-3.

Listing 7-3. *JdbcManager.java*

```
package com.apress.jdbc;


import java.sql.*;
import javax.sql.*;
import javax.naming.*;

public class JdbcManager {
  private static InitialContext context = null;
  public static Connection getConnection()
    throws SQLException, NamingException {
    if (context == null) {
      context = new InitialContext();
    }
    DataSource dataSource =
      (DataSource) context.lookup("java:comp/env/jdbc/DataSourceExample");
    return dataSource.getConnection();
  }
  public static void close(Connection conn) {
    if (conn != null) {
      try {
        conn.close();
      } catch (Exception ignored) {}
    }
  }
  public static void close(Statement stmt) {
    if (stmt != null) {
      try {
        stmt.close();
      } catch (Exception ignored) {}
    }
  }
}
```

The `JdbcManager` class shown in Listing 7-3 does two things:

- It moves the lookup code out of the JSP and into this helper class. It is the same lookup code as in the first example of the chapter (`DataSourceExample.jsp`, shown in Listing 7-1), but now it's in one location that can be used by multiple components in your application. If you are going to have multiple web components in your application all accessing database resources, you don't need to duplicate the lookup code in every component.
- It provides a centralized location for closing database resources. Again, this is code that does not need to be duplicated in every web component that accesses the database. In addition, by putting the code here, you can wrap every `close()` method call in a `try-catch` block and avoid ugly `try-catch` blocks littering your web component code.

■ **Note** The `JdbcManager` code in Listing 7-3 catches the `SQLExceptions`, but then ignores them. This is fine for a sample program such as this one. However, in a production environment, you should never ignore exceptions. Admittedly, there is not much you can do if closing a connection causes an exception, but you should at least log this event, so you can be aware of problems in your system.

Listing 7-4 shows a JSP that uses the `JdbcManager` class.

Listing 7-4. *StatementExample.jsp*

```
<%@ page import="java.sql.*, com.apress.jdbc.*" %>
<html>
  <head>
    <title>Statement Example</title>
  </head>
  <body>
    <h1>Statement Example</h1>
<%
    Connection conn = null;
    Statement stmt = null;
    try {
      conn = JdbcManager.getConnection();
      stmt = conn.createStatement();
      String sqlcmd = "insert into stock_tbl values ('" +
        request.getParameter("symbol") + "', '" +
        request.getParameter("name") + "')";
      int result = stmt.executeUpdate(sqlcmd);

      if (result == 1) {
%>
Data sucessfully inserted into database
<%
      } else {
%>
Data was not inserted into database. Reason for failure is unknown
<%
      }
    } catch (SQLException e) {
%>
    <%= e.getMessage() %>
```

```
<%
      e.printStackTrace();
    } finally {
      JdbcManager.close(stmt);
      JdbcManager.close(conn);
    }
%>
  </body>
</html>
```

This JSP accepts an HTML request to insert data into the database. The data is entered into a web form, and then submitted to the JSP. The JSP gets a `Connection` object from the `JdbcManager` class and uses the `Connection` object to create a `Statement` object. It then constructs a SQL command using the parameters passed in the web request. This is a SQL `INSERT` command to insert a row of data into a database table. The JSP uses the `executeUpdate(String)` method to send the command to the database. If the method returns a 1, which is the expected value, the `INSERT` was successful. If the method returns a 0, the `INSERT` failed, although there is no information about why it failed. In the `finally` block at the end of the JSP, we use the new `JdbcManager` class to close the `Connection` and `Statement` objects.

Listing 7-5 shows the first piece of a stock market application. In this application, we want a table to hold information about a public company. In a real-world application, we would be storing a lot of information about companies. In this example, though, we're storing only two pieces of data: the stock symbol and the company name. The web page in Listing 7-5 collects those two pieces of information, as shown in Figure 7-11, and submits the data to the JSP in Listing 7-4. The JSP inserts the data into the database.

Listing 7-5. *StockEntryForm.html*

```
<html>
  <head>
    <title>Stock Entry Form</title>
  </head>
  <body>
    <h1>Enter a stock symbol and name</h1>
    <form action="PersistStock.jsp">
      <table>
        <tr><td>Symbol: </td>
            <td><input type="text" name="symbol"></td>
        </tr>
        <tr><td>Name: </td>
            <td><input type="text" name="name"></td>
        </tr>
        <tr><td><input type="submit" value="Submit"></td></tr>
      </table>
    </form>
  </body>
</html>
```

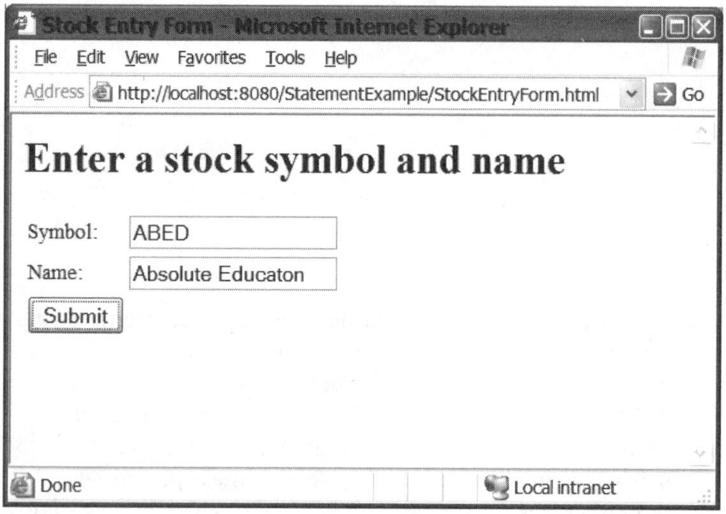

Figure 7-11. *The HTML form for collecting the stock symbol and stock name*

Creating a Table to Hold the Information

Before you deploy the sample application, you need to create a table in the PointBase server to hold the company information. PointBase provides two different tools for accessing the database: a command-line tool and a GUI tool.

Using the Command-Line Tool

You can start the command-line tool by running the `startcommander` script in the `\pointbase\tools\serveroption` directory within the Sun Application Server directory on your system (assuming you installed the application server on a Windows machine using the default settings, that location is `C:\Sun\AppServer\pointbase\tools\serveroption`). When you first start the tool, you will need to log in to the database.

The command-line tool presents the following prompts:

```
Do you wish to create a "New/Overwrite" Database? [default: N]:
Select product to connect with: Embedded (E), or Server (S)? [default: E]: S
Please enter the driver to use: [default: [com.pointbase.jdbc.jdbcUniversalDriver]:
Please enter the database URL to use: ➥
    [default: [jdbc:pointbase:server://localhost/sample]:
Username: [default: PBPUBLIC]:
Password: [default: PBPUBLIC]:
```

In each case, you can just press Enter to select the default value, except for the prompt for product, for which you want to enter `S` for server.

The tool then connects to the database and displays a `SQL>` prompt. Enter the following command at the command prompt:

```
SQL> create table stock_tbl (symbol varchar(10), name varchar(30));
```

Press Enter, and if you entered the command properly, the tool responds with this:

```
SQL>
OK
```

Using the GUI Tool

You can start the GUI tool by running the `startconsole` script in the `\pointbase\tools\serveroption` directory within the Sun Application Server directory on your system (assuming you installed the application server on a Windows machine using the default settings, that location is `C:\Sun\AppServer\pointbase\tools\serveroption`). When you first start the tool, you will see a form to enter login parameters, as shown in Figure 7-12.

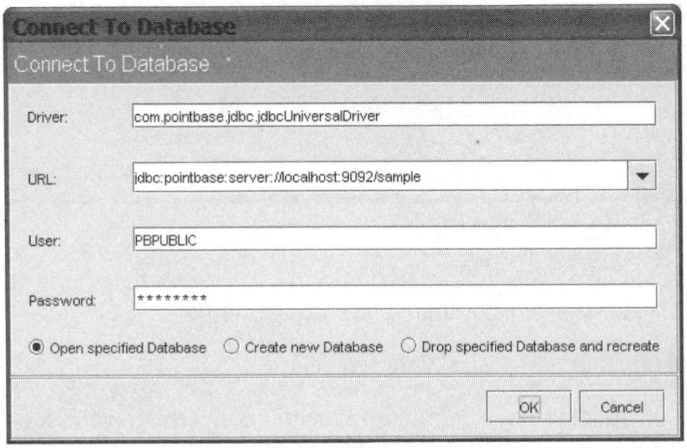

Figure 7-12. *The PointBase Console login form*

The form will have some default values already entered. Simply enter the password `PBPUBLIC` in the Password field and click the OK button to log in. If the login is successful, the status pane at the bottom of the tool will display this message:

```
Connecting to Database, jdbc:pointbase:server://localhost:9092/sample ➥
    *** PLEASE WAIT ***
OK Connected to Database: jdbc:pointbase:server://localhost:9092/sample, Ready
```

As shown in Figure 7-13, the PointBase Console tool has the standard menu and toolbar features found in many GUI applications. Three panes fill the center of the tool's window. To the left is a tree view of the database and its properties and objects. On the lower right is a pane where query results are displayed. On the upper right is a pane labeled Enter SQL Commands.

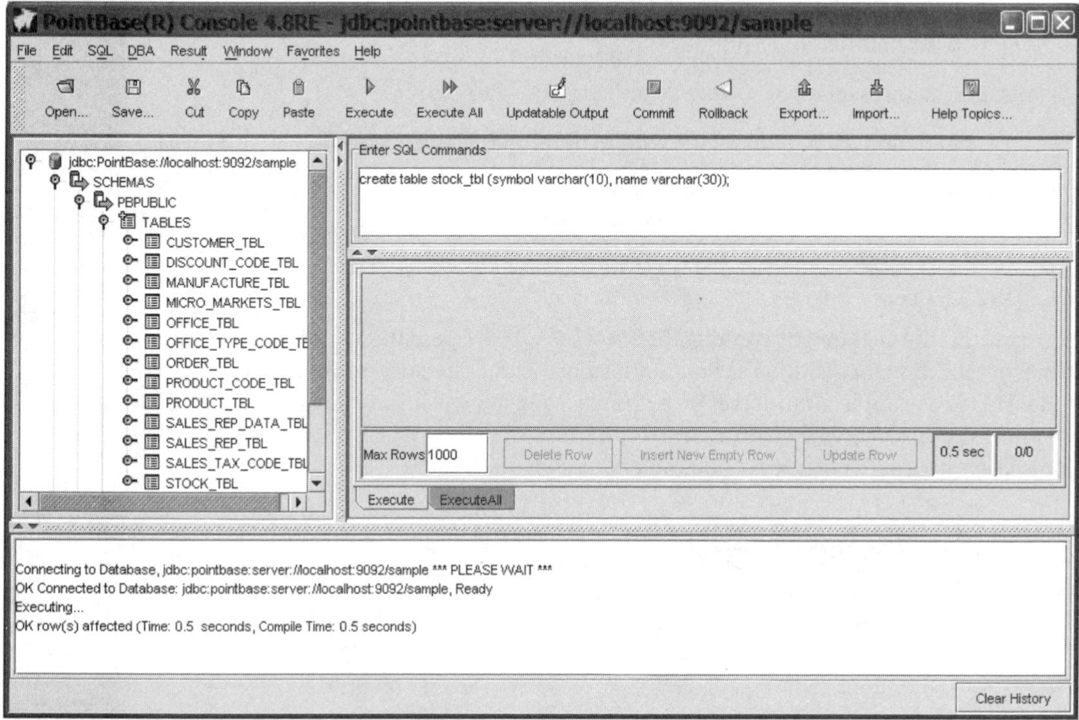

Figure 7-13. *The PointBase Console tool*

In the upper-right pane, enter the following command (see Figure 7-13):

```
create table stock_tbl (symbol varchar(10), name varchar(30));
```

Then click the Execute button in the toolbar. If the command executes correctly, you will see the following messages in the status pane at the bottom of the window:

```
Executing...
OK row(s) affected (Time: 0.172  seconds, Compile Time: 0.172 seconds)
```

You're now ready to deploy the application.

Deploying the Application to the Sun Application Server

If you are using the Sun Application Server Deployment Tool, create a new web component. Add the three files shown in Listings 7-3, 7-4, and 7-5 to the web component in the correct locations. The HTML and JSP files should be located in the root directory of the web component. The `JdbcManager` class file should be located in the correct package in the `WEB-INF\classes` directory of the web component.

Using the Deployment Tool, create a JDBC resource using the Resource Ref's tab, as described earlier in the chapter. If you did not work through that example, refer to the "Configuring a DataSource and Connection with Java EE" section to see how to set up a JDBC resource in the application server and how to configure the resource in the web component. Save the component and then deploy it to the application server.

Deploying the Application with Tomcat

If you are using Tomcat, you will need to create the web.xml file shown in Listing 7-6.

Listing 7-6. *web.xml file for the Tomcat Statement Example*

```
<?xml version="1.0" encoding="UTF-8"?>
<web-app version="2.5" xmlns="http://java.sun.com/xml/ns/javaee"
                 xmlns:xsi=http://www.w3.org/2001/XMLSchema-instance
                 xsi:schemaLocation="http://java.sun.com/xml/ns/javaee
 http://java.sun.com/xml/ns/javaee/web-app_2_5.xsd">
  <display-name>StatementExample</display-name>
  <servlet>
    <display-name>PersistStock</display-name>
    <servlet-name>PersistStock</servlet-name>
    <jsp-file>/PersistStock.jsp</jsp-file>
  </servlet>
  <resource-ref>
    <res-ref-name>jdbc/DataSourceExample</res-ref-name>
    <res-type>javax.sql.DataSource</res-type>
    <res-auth>Container</res-auth>
    <res-sharing-scope>Shareable</res-sharing-scope>
  </resource-ref>
</web-app>
```

Package the files shown in Listings 7-3, 7-4, 7-5, and 7-6 into a WAR file and deploy it to Tomcat. Then, using the Tomcat administration tool, create either a global JDBC resource and a resource link or a local JDBC resource, as described in the "Configuring a DataSource and Connection with Tomcat" section earlier in this chapter.

Running the Application

With the database and the application server running, start the application by loading the HTML form into your web browser (see Figure 7-11). Enter a stock symbol (it doesn't need to be a real one) into the first field and a stock name into the second field. Click the Submit button to call the JSP. If your application works correctly, you will see a web page that says the data was successfully inserted into the database. If the executeUpdate(String) method call returns a 0, the web page will say that the data was not inserted into the database. If an exception is thrown, the web page will print the error message from the SQLException object.

You can also check if the JSP worked by using either the PointBase command-line or GUI tool. Enter and execute the following SQL command:

```
select * from stock_tbl;
```

The tool will display the results of the query, as shown in Figure 7-14. If the JSP worked correctly, the results should include the data you entered in the web form.

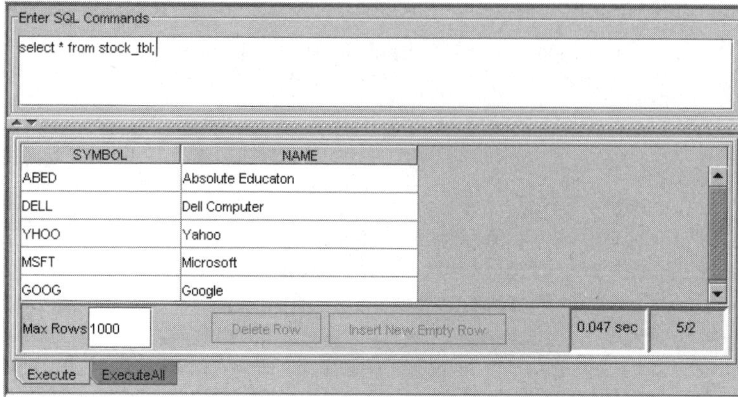

Figure 7-14. *A table showing data inserted by the StockEntry.jsp*

Using the ResultSet Class

When you perform a query of a table in a database, the results of the query are returned in a `ResultSet` object. The `ResultSet` object allows you to scroll through each row of the results and read the data from each column in the row. The first example in this chapter (Listing 7-1) used a `ResultSet` object to display data from the `customer_tbl` table in the PointBase `sample` database. In this section, we will look at the `ResultSet` in more detail.

Moving Through the ResultSet

The `ResultSet` interface defines a number of methods that can be used for moving through the results returned from a query (*resultsets*). However, not all methods are available for every `ResultSet`. Earlier in the chapter, you saw the methods of the `Connection` object that are used to create `Statement` objects. Here again are the three methods:

- `public Statement createStatement()`
- `public Statement createStatement(int, int)`
- `public Statement createStatement(int, int, int)`

Nonscrollable Resultsets

When you use the first method to create a `Statement` object (`createStatement()`), the `ResultSet` object that is returned by `executeQuery()` is a nonscrollable resultset, or one that is of type forward-only. This means that you can only move from the first row to the last row, and cannot scroll backward through the results. The following is the only method that you can use for moving through the `ResultSet` object:

```
public boolean next()
```

When you call the `executeQuery(String)` method, the method will always return a non-null `ResultSet`. It may or may not have any data, but it will always be non-null. When the `executeQuery()` method returns the `ResultSet`, the cursor is positioned prior to the first row of data.

Note *Cursor* is a database term. It generally refers to the set of rows returned by a query. When a cursor is positioned at a row, you are accessing a particular row in the set.

To get to the first row of data, you must call the `next()` method. Each time you need to get the following row of data, you call `next()` again. The `next()` method returns a `boolean` value. If there is another row of data, the cursor is positioned at that row, and the method returns `true`; if there are no more rows of data, the cursor is positioned after the last row, and the `next()` method returns `false`. If there are no results at all in the resultset, then `next()` will return `false` the first time it is called. If you use any of the other movement methods (which we will see shortly) with a nonscrollable resultset, the `ResultSet` class will throw a `SQLException`.

In Listing 7-1, the JSP called the `next()` method first to determine if any rows were in the `ResultSet`. When `next()` returns `true` to the JSP, the JSP reads and displays the rows in a `do-while` loop. The condition on the `while` statement is also a call to `next()`; as long as `next()` returns `true`, the loop continues to read rows from the `ResultSet`.

Scrollable Resultsets

Now, let's take a look at the other two forms of `createStatement()`. These two forms have method parameters. The first parameter sets the scrollability. The *scrollability* refers to whether you can move backward through the resultset. The second parameter defines whether you can update the table through the resultset. We'll talk about updatable `ResultSet` objects later in the chapter, in the "Using Updatable Resultsets" section. For the first parameter, you can pass one of these three arguments:

- `ResultSet.TYPE_SCROLL_SENSITIVE`
- `ResultSet.TYPE_SCROLL_INSENSITIVE`
- `ResultSet.TYPE_FORWARD_ONLY`

The arguments are constant values defined in the `ResultSet` class. The first two values create a scrollable resultset through which you can move forward or backward. If changes occur to the database while you are going through a resultset, `TYPE_SCROLL_SENSITIVE` means you will see those changes; `TYPE_SCROLL_INSENSITIVE` means you will not see the changes. The third value creates a nonscrollable resultset that does not see updates.

For scrollable resultsets, the `ResultSet` class provides the following methods for moving through the resultset:

```
boolean next()                 boolean previous()
boolean first()                boolean last()
void beforeFirst()             void afterLast()
boolean absolute(int)          boolean relative(int)
boolean isFirst()              boolean isBeforeFirst()
boolean isLast()               boolean isAfterLast()
void moveToInsertRow()         void moveToCurrentRow()
int getRow()
```

Because these methods are fairly self-explanatory, and since the use of these methods is documented in the Javadoc (`http://java.sun.com/j2se/1.4.2/docs/api/`), we will not cover them here. However, we will use them in the example shown later in Listing 7-7.

COUNTING THE ROWS IN A RESULTSET

A common problem when dealing with `ResultSet` objects is determining the number of rows in a resultset. Imagine that you are building some kind of search function into your web application. After performing a search, you want to tell the user how many results were returned by the search. In addition, you may want to page the results if there are a lot of results. Unfortunately, many developers pick the wrong way to determine the row count.

With JDBC 1.0, most developers did something like this:

1. Execute the query.
2. Execute `ResultSet next()`, add 1 to the count, and repeat until `next()` returns `false`.
3. Reexecute the query and present the result to the user.

It should be obvious why this is bad. First, you need to execute your query twice to present results to the user. Not only is it a waste to execute the same query twice, the results may change between the first and second queries, so you need to wrap both queries in a transaction. (Transactions are covered in the next chapter.) Second, if you have a very large `ResultSet`, it could take a long time to scroll through the results. Too much time means the user will not be visiting your web site anymore.

So, many developers rejoiced when JDBC 2.0 introduced scrollable `ResultSet` objects and the `getRow()` method. Now they could do this to get the row count and display results:

1. Execute the query.
2. Execute `last()` to move to the last row.
3. Execute `getRow()` to get the row number.
4. Execute `first()` to move to the first row.
5. Display the results to the user.

Continued

Unfortunately, this is not much better than the first solution. Sure, you are now executing the query only a single time, so you've eliminated that inefficiency. If you translate these steps into real code and test it with either of the sample databases that come with Sun's Java EE server (the `sample` or `sun-appserv-samples` database) in PointBase, the code should do what you want. The problem is that `sun-appserv-samples` is a toy database. Someday, you may be working with a real enterprise database, with tables that contain thousands or even millions of rows. If you try these steps with an enterprise database, your code will likely fail. Why? Because most drivers cache the rows in memory to provide scrollability. So, if you call `last()` on a `ResultSet` with a million rows of data, the driver is going to try to cache all those rows in memory as it scrolls to the last row. Guess who is going to run out of memory and crash the application.

So, what is the right way to determine the number of rows in a resultset. Here are two solutions (you may be able to think of others):

- Execute a query that counts the number of rows. Most databases support a syntax such as `count (*) from` *`table`* `where` *`conditions`*. If you are querying from multiple tables, and your database supports nested queries, you may need to `count (*) from select` *`columns`* `from` *`tables`* `where` *`conditions`*. This will return a `ResultSet` object with a single row and a single column containing the row count of the query. Then you can execute the real query and present the results to the user. To ensure that both queries are consistent, you should wrap them in a single transaction.
- Build your database so that most queries are precomputed. For example, suppose you have an address table that users can search by last name. You have a second table with a column for last name and count. For every unique last name in the first table, you have a row in the second table with the frequency count. When a user queries for last name, you can fetch the frequency count in the same query.

Obviously, this is a very simple example. If you are working with a real system, the queries can be much more complex than searching for a single column. In that case, you will need to consult with some real database experts to determine the best way to build the database to do what you need. This is just one example of why it is important to have experienced database analysts on your team if you are dealing with large amounts of data in enterprise databases.

Reading Data from Resultsets

The `ResultSet` class also contains a number of methods for reading the data in a query result. These methods allow you to reference the column by number or by name, and to retrieve just about any data type. Here are two examples:

```
double getDouble(int)
double getDouble(String)
```

These methods allow you to read a double from the current row of the `ResultSet`. The first method gets a double from the column with the index given by the `int` parameter. The second method gets the double from the column with the name given by the `String` parameter. There are `get`*`XXX`*`()` methods for every Java primitive and for numerous kinds of Java objects. These methods retrieve the column values from the current row in the `ResultSet`. (Consult the Javadoc for `ResultSet` for the complete list of available methods.)

Like the getDouble() methods, each getXXX() method comes in two overloaded forms:

- One form takes an int argument. The parameter you pass to the method is the column number of the column you wish to retrieve. Note that columns returned from a table are numbered starting from one, not zero. If you call one of these methods, and pass a zero as the argument or pass a column number that is too great, a SQLException is thrown.
- The second form takes a String parameter. The argument you pass the name of the column you wish to retrieve. If you pass an invalid name, a SQLException will be thrown.

Whether you use the int parameter or the String parameter depends on your application. Using the int parameter is more efficient. However, the String parameter is more flexible. This is because column indexes sometimes change, but column names rarely do. If you hard-code the column number into your code, you'll have problems as soon as the database analysts change the schema of the database tables so that the column numbers change.

Listing 7-7 shows a JSP that uses a few of the methods for moving through a ResultSet and reading data from a ResultSet. This JSP again connects to the PointBase sample database that comes with the Java EE reference implementation. It performs a query of the customer_tbl in the sample database, and then moves back and forth through the results.

Listing 7-7. *ResultSetExample.jsp*

```
<%@ page import="java.sql.*, com.apress.jdbc.*" %>
<html>
  <head>
    <title>ResultSet Example</title>
  </head>
  <body>
    <h1>ResultSet Example</h1>
<%
    Connection conn = null;
    Statement stmt = null;
    ResultSet rset = null;
    try {
      conn = JdbcManager.getConnection();
      stmt = conn.createStatement(ResultSet.TYPE_SCROLL_SENSITIVE,
        ResultSet.CONCUR_READ_ONLY);
      String sqlcmd = "select * from customer_tbl";
      rset = stmt.executeQuery(sqlcmd);
      if (rset.next()) {
%>
<p>On first row, expected value of isFirst() is true
<p>isFirst() = <%= rset.isFirst()%>
<p>Now calling next() twice, expected value of getRow() is 3
<% rset.next(); rset.next(); %>
<p>getRow() = <%= rset.getRow() %>
```

```
<p>Moving to row 4, customer num, name, and email are
<% rset.next(); %>
<p>Row <%= rset.getRow() %>:
<%= rset.getString("CUSTOMER_NUM") %>,
<%= rset.getString("NAME") %>,
<%= rset.getString("EMAIL") %>
<p>Now calling last() to move to last row, expected value of isLast() is true
<% rset.last(); %>
<p>isLast() = <%= rset.isLast() %>, row number is <%= rset.getRow() %>
<p>Now calling previous(), expected value of isLast() is false
<% rset.previous(); %>
<p>isLast() = <%= rset.isLast() %>, row number is <%= rset.getRow() %>
<p>Now calling beforeFirst()
<% rset.beforeFirst(); %>
<p>isBeforeFirst() = <%= rset.isBeforeFirst() %>,
   isFirst() = <%= rset.isFirst() %>
<%
      } else {
%>
No rows found by query
<%
      }
    } catch (SQLException e) {
%>
    <%= e.getMessage() %>
<%
      e.printStackTrace();
    } finally {
      JdbcManager.close(rset);
      JdbcManager.close(stmt);
      JdbcManager.close(conn);
    }
%>
  </body>
</html>
```

As with other JDBC resources, it is important that you close the ResultSet object when it is no longer needed. One important point to remember is that you must not close the Statement or Connection objects until after you are finished with the ResultSet object, since closing the Statement or Connection objects automatically closes the ResultSet object. Just as with Statement objects, though, you shouldn't rely on closing the Connection to close the ResultSet. You should close resources as soon as you are finished with them. This JSP closes the ResultSet in the finally block near the bottom of the listing. For this to work, you will need to add the appropriate method to the JdbcManager class from Listing 7-3. Listing 7-8 shows the method to be added to JdbcManager.

Listing 7-8. *close (ResultSet) Method to Add to JdbcManager.java*

```
public static void close(ResultSet rset) {
  if (rset != null) {
    try {
      rset.close();
    } catch (Exception ignored) {}
  }
}
```

If you are using the Sun Application Server, deploy this JSP using the Deployment Tool in the same manner as the previous examples in this chapter. Add the `ResultSetExample.jsp` and `JdbcManager.class` files (`JdbcManager.java` is shown in Listing 7-3, with the addition shown in Listing 7-8, and `ResultSetExample.jsp` is shown in Listing 7-7) to a web component, create a resource reference for the JDBC resource, and deploy the component to the server.

If you are using Tomcat, you will need to manually create a `web.xml` file similar to the one in Listing 7-6, changing it as needed for this JSP. Create a WAR file with the `ResultSetExample.jsp` (Listing 7-7), `JdbcManager.class` (Listing 7-3 with the addition shown in Listing 7-8), and `web.xml` files, and then deploy the WAR file to Tomcat. Using the Tomcat administration tool, create a JDBC resource for the web component.

Ensure that the application server and the database server are running, and then load the JSP into a browser. Your browser should display a page similar to that shown in Figure 7-15.

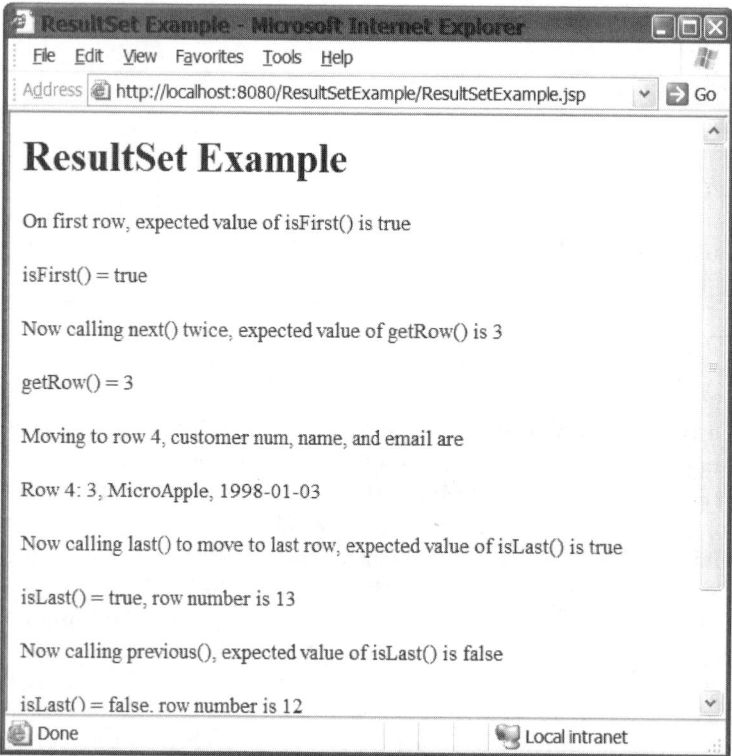

Figure 7-15. *The ResultSetExample.jsp*

Working with Null Values

NULL is a special value in the world of SQL. NULL is not the same thing as an empty string for text columns, nor is it the same thing as zero for a numeric field. NULL means that no data is defined for a column value within a relation. However, for primitive types and for Booleans, the JDBC driver cannot return a null. When the column data for a row is a primitive or Boolean type and the value is a SQL NULL, the `getXXX()` method returns a value that is appropriate for the return type. For `getXXX()` methods that return a Java primitive, a SQL NULL is returned as a 0. For the `getBoolean()` method, a SQL NULL is returned as a `false`.

This creates a potential problem. Suppose you call the `getDouble(int)` method and the return value is 0. How do you know if the column value is really 0 or NULL?

```
int result = rset.getDouble(1);
if (result == 0) {
  //is the result really 0 or is it NULL?
}
```

The `ResultSet` class provides a method that can give you this information. Here is its signature:

```
public boolean wasNull()
```

It does not take a column number or a column name. It provides its answer based on the most recently read column.

```
int result = rset.getDouble(1);
if (result == 0) {
  if (rset.wasNull()) {
    //double was really null
  } else {
    //double was really 0
  }
}
```

Note that this is not a problem for any method that returns an object. For example, the `ResultSet` class has a method that can return a `java.sql.Date` object for a database column of SQL `Date` type.

```
public Date getDate(int)
public Date getDate(String)
```

Since the reference to an object can be a Java null, the method will return a Java null when the column value is a SQL NULL.

Using Updatable Resultsets

The second parameter in the `createStatement(int, int)` and `createStatement(int, int, int)` methods determines whether you can update the database through the `ResultSet` object. Prior to JDBC 2.0, `ResultSet` objects could be used only to select data, move forward through the data, and read the data in each column. To update the data, you needed to execute another SQL command through a `Statement` object. JDBC 2.0 introduced the ability to update the data in the table directly through the ResultSet, so as you move through the data, you can call methods that insert, update, or delete the data.

To control the updatability of a ResultSet, you pass one of these two arguments as the second parameter in the createStatement() method call:

- ResultSet.CONCUR_READ_ONLY
- ResultSet.CONCUR_UPDATABLE

The arguments are constant values defined in the ResultSet class. The first value creates a ResultSet that can be used to read the column values but cannot be used to update the table. The second value creates a ResultSet that can be used to update the table. The following are the commonly used methods for updating a table through a ResultSet:

```
void updateRow()                      void cancelRowUpdates()
void moveToInsertRow()                void moveToCurrentRow()
void insertRow()                      void deleteRow()
void updateBoolean(int, boolean)      void updateBoolean(String, boolean)
void updateByte(int, byte)            void updateByte(String, byte)
void updateDate(int, Date)            void updateDate(String, Date)
void updateDouble(int, double)        void updateDouble(String, double)
void updateFloat(int, float)          void updateFloat(String, float)
void updateInt(int, int)              void updateInt(String, int)
void updateLong(int, long)            void updateLong(String, long)
void updateNull(int)                  void updateNull(String)
void updateString(int, String)        void updateString(String, String)
```

When you move through a resultset using the methods described in the previous sections, you can update whichever row you are currently positioned at. You update the data in the current row with the update*XXX*() methods. There is an update*XXX*() method for every data type supported by JDBC. (Consult the Javadoc for the full list of update methods.)

Each method comes in two overloaded versions. The first parameter of one version takes a String argument that gives the name of the column to be updated; the other version uses the column number of the column to be updated. The column number refers to the index of the column in the ResultSet, not the table. The column that is named first in the SELECT command is column 1, and so on. The second parameter in each method is the new value for the column.

■ **Note** Check your driver documentation for the requirements for updating a ResultSet. Some databases do not allow you to use SELECT * FROM *table* for an updatable ResultSet. You may need to explicitly name each column in the SELECT command.

After you have updated all the columns that you want to update, you call the updateRow() method to write the updated row to the table. The following code snippet shows how this could be accomplished for a fictional stock in the stock_tbl we created in the "Using Statements to Insert Data into a Database" section earlier in this chapter:

```
static String sqlQuery = "select SYMBOL, NAME from STOCK_TBL " +
                         "where SYMBOL='ABED' ";
rset = stmt.executeQuery(sqlQuery);
rset.next();

rset.updateString(2, 'Absolute Education');
rset.updateRow();
```

If, before you call updateRow(), you decide that you don't want to update the row, you can call cancelRowUpdates().

You can also insert a new row of data through the ResultSet. This is accomplished by moving to a special row in the ResultSet, known as the *insert row*. You move to the insert row by calling the following method:

```
rset.moveToInsertRow();
```

When you move to the insert row, the ResultSet remembers the position you were at, and this remembered position is known as the *current row*. Then, you update each column with the appropriate value using the update*XXX*() methods. When you are finished entering data for the new row, you call this method:

```
rset.insertRow();
```

After you have called insertRow(), the ResultSet is still positioned at the insert row. You can insert another row of data, or move back to the remembered position (the current row) in the ResultSet. You can move back to the current row by calling moveToCurrentRow(). You can also cancel an insert by calling moveToCurrentRow() before you call insertRow().

Finally, you can delete a row from the table and the ResultSet by calling the following method:

```
rset.deleteRow();
```

Keeping the ResultSet Open: ResultSet Holdability

When you execute another SQL command with a statement, any previously opened ResultSet objects are closed. Also, when commit() is called with a JDBC 2.0 or 1.0 driver, the ResultSet is closed. JDBC 3.0 adds a new ResultSet object feature called *holdability*, which refers to whether or not a ResultSet is closed when a new SQL command is executed by a statement or when commit() is called. JDBC 3.0 gives you the capability to keep the ResultSet open.

Two class constants were added to the ResultSet interface to provide parameters for the createStatement() method:

- ResultSet.HOLD_CURSORS_OVER_COMMIT specifies that the ResultSet object should not be closed when changes are committed.
- ResultSet.CLOSE_CURSORS_AT_COMMIT specifies that the driver can close the ResultSet object when changes are committed.

A new `createStatement()` method was added to the `Connection` class to support this feature:

```
createStatement(int resultSetType, int resultSetConcurrency, ➥
                    int resultSetHoldability)
```

As of the time this chapter was written, Sun listed almost three dozen drivers that support JDBC 3.0. Check your database documentation to see if it supports holdability functionality. PointBase does support holdability if you are using a JVM version 1.4 or later.

Summary

In this chapter, we looked at some of the ways you can communicate with databases. After finishing this chapter, you should know:

- How to create a `DataSource` in the Sun Application Server and the Tomcat server. You should also know how to get a connection from a `DataSource`.
- `Statement` objects are used to send SQL commands to the database. `Statement` objects are created by `Connection` objects. SQL commands are sent using either `executeUpdate(String)` or `executeQuery(String)`.
- `ResultSet` objects are used to read the data returned by a SQL query. `ResultSet` objects can be scrollable, updatable, and holdable. You move through a `ResultSet` using methods such as `next()`, `previous()`, `first()`, and `last()`. You read results using methods such as `getString(int)` and `getDouble(String)`.

This chapter has been an introduction to the basics of JDBC. If you are new to JDBC programming, this chapter provided you with enough information to get you started. However, this book is about Java EE applications. As a Java EE developer, you are going to quickly encounter some more complex situations. In the next chapter, we will look at some of the more advanced topics that you will need to know as a Java EE developer.

Exercises

1. All the examples in this chapter used the JDBC API and JDBC code statements in the JSPs to talk to the database. However, in the JSP chapters, we looked at ways to use standard actions and tag libraries to abstract code out of the JSP. The Java Standard Tag Library (JSTL) includes tags for adding SQL commands to a JSP. Using the JSTL, rewrite one or more JSP examples in this chapter to use the SQL tags rather than the JDBC API methods.

2. Update the `StatementExample` (Listing 7-4) presented in this chapter. Change the JSP so that after the symbol and name are submitted from the HTML page, the JSP queries the `stock_tbl` table for the symbol using an updatable `ResultSet`. If the symbol is found, the JSP uses the `ResultSet` to update the row with the submitted name; if the symbol is not found, the JSP uses the `ResultSet` to insert a new row. Display both the old row (if found) and the new row.

3. In the sidebar titled “Counting the Rows in a Resultset,” we discussed various ways to count the rows in a resultset. Find or create a table with at least 100,000 rows. Attempt to cause an `OutOfMemoryError` using a scrollable resultset to query the table. Document the row number at which the error occurs.

4. Create a `DataSource` that provides a pooled connection. Define another that creates and provides a regular, nonpooled connection. Run tests to measure the time it takes to obtain a pooled connection versus a nonpooled connection. Which is faster?

5. With a `Connection` object, you can obtain a reference to an object named `DatabaseMetaData`. Write a JSP that uses a `DatabaseMetaData` object to display information about your database. Details about how to use `DatabaseMetaData` can be found in the Javadoc.

6. With a `ResultSet` object, you can obtain a reference to an object named `ResultSetMetaData`. Write a JSP that uses a `ResultSetMetaData` object to display information about a table and the results in the `ResultSet`. Details about how to use `ResultSetMetaData` can be found in the Javadoc.

CHAPTER 8

■ ■ ■

Advanced Topics in JDBC

In the previous chapter, we looked at some basic features of JDBC: how to get a connection, how to query and update a database using `Statement` objects, and how to read the results of a query using a `ResultSet` object. Once you've gained an understanding of these fundamentals, you'll be able to write simple JDBC programs.

However, in the fast-paced world of web applications, you will soon find that you need more skills than those presented in the previous chapter. In this chapter, we will cover some advanced JDBC topics that you will find invaluable as a Java EE developer. We will also look at some problems you might encounter in a Java EE application and how to avoid them with well-designed JDBC code.

In this chapter, you will learn the following:

- How to use `PreparedStatement` objects to make your JDBC more efficient and to insert nonprimitive data types into a database
- What stored procedures are, why they are useful, and how you can call them with JDBC code
- How to ensure that your JDBC code takes the database from one valid and consistent state to another, so that the database does not contain corrupted data
- How to deal with the problem of multiple users trying to change data in the database at the same time

Prepared Statements

`PreparedStatement` objects are used to send SQL commands to the database. As you may recall from the previous chapter, `Statement` objects are also used to send SQL commands to the database. If both `Statement` and `PreparedStatement` objects are used to send commands to a database, how are they different? Let's first consider the situations where you would want to bother with prepared statements.

Reasons for Using Prepared Statements

PreparedStatement objects are useful in several situations:

- When you are working with different database systems
- When you are sending many SQL commands to the database, and only the data values are changing
- When you need to insert nonprimitive data into a table

Dealing with Database Differences

To demonstrate a common problem when you're dealing with different database systems, let's work through an example with PointBase, using its console (or command-line) tool. Navigate to the PointBase \tools\serveroption directory of your Java EE installation and run the startconsole or startcommander script file. When you first start either tool, you will need to log in to the database named sample (see Chapter 2 or Chapter 8 for details on how to do this).

After the tool starts up, enter the following SQL command at the SQL> prompt. If you are using the console tool, enter the SQL command in the SQL Command field and click the Execute button.

```
update customer_tbl set name="No Name";
```

If you are using the command-line tool, this is what you will see:

```
SQL> update customer_tbl set name="No Name";
SQL>                               ^
SQL>
SQL> Error Message:  Column "No Name" not found in table at position 29.
SQL> Error SQLState: ZD002
SQL> Error Code:     15004
```

If you are using the console tool, you will see the same error message, but it will be in an error dialog box.

The error message says that "No Name" is not a column in the table. That is quite obvious. Run describe customer_tbl at the command line, or expand the customer_tbl node in the console tool, as shown in Figure 8-1. You will see a description of all the columns, and none of them are named No Name. But the column you tried to update was the name column, and that is certainly one of the columns in the table.

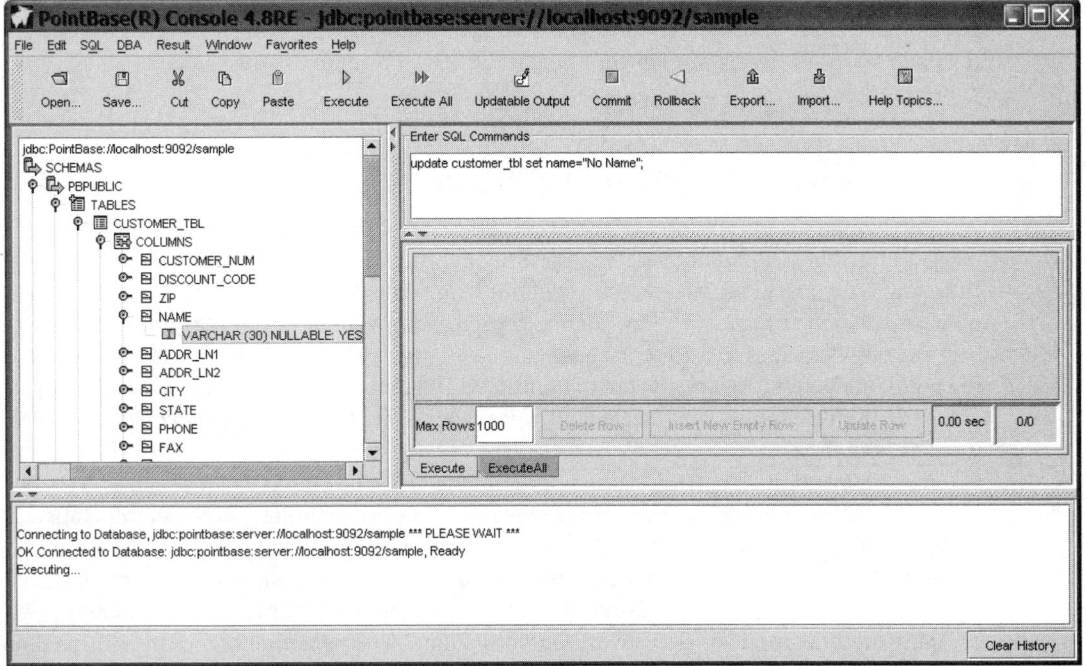

Figure 8-1. *Using the console tool, you can expand the tree in the left pane to see information about the database.*

So, the column name you are trying to use is correct, but PointBase is complaining about a column that doesn't exist. The SQL appears to be correct. It certainly follows the syntax for an UPDATE command. It has the following elements:

- `update`: The command itself
- `customer_tbl`: The table name
- `set`: Part of the syntax for an UPDATE command
- `name`: The correct column name
- `"No Name"`: The new `String` value for the column

Perhaps reviewing some code you executed earlier can help explain what is happening. You inserted string data into the database in the previous chapter in the `StatementExample.jsp` (Listing 7-4). Here are the lines of code where the SQL command is constructed:

```
String sqlcmd = "insert into stock_tbl values ('" +
  request.getParameter("symbol") + "', '" +
  request.getParameter("name") + "')";
```

Beyond the obvious difference that this is an `INSERT` command, and the command that failed was an `UPDATE` command, there is one other important difference between the commands. In Listing 7-4, you used single quotes to delimit string data. Most databases accept only single quotes to delimit strings, but a few, such as MySQL, accept single or double quotes.

The obvious solution is to replace the double quotes with single quotes. That would solve the problem that we just looked at with PointBase. But before you rush out and ensure that all your strings are delimited with single quotes, let's look at another problem you might see when working with JDBC.

A common question in JDBC discussion forums is, "How do I insert a name such as O'Grady into my database, since the apostrophe in the name acts as a delimiter?" The common answer to that question is to change the single quote in the name to two single quotes. Thus `O'Grady` becomes `O''Grady` (notice that it's not a double quote—it's two single quotes in a row). With MySQL, you can escape the single quotes, so `O'Grady` becomes `O\'Grady`. (Unfortunately, escaping the apostrophe does not work with other databases.) Another common solution that is recommended for this problem is to write a little method that searches for single quotes in the strings and changes them to whatever works for the database in question.

There is a better solution though. Rather than worrying about how to delimit strings, or how to change single quotes into pairs of single quotes, JDBC provides a class that can do all this work for you. That class is the `PreparedStatement` class. The `PreparedStatement` class (or more specifically, the database-specific class that implements the `PreparedStatement` interface) can insert strings into a database, and it will automatically use the correct delimiter and handle a string with embedded delimiters.

CHALLENGES OF INTEGRATING SYSTEMS

One of the projects I recently worked on involved three geographically separated teams. Each team was responsible for a system, and the three systems were supposed to work together to solve the user's problem. The team I was on was developing one of the systems, and we were also responsible for integrating the whole mess together. The project provides an excellent example of the platform-independence notion of Java and JDBC, but it also points out that there are differences between databases.

One of the teams was using MySQL (`http://www.mysql.com`) as its development database, but the final system was using Sybase as the production database. As soon as I tried integrating their code, their system threw a `SQLException`. The `SQLException` indicated that the problem was in one of the SQL commands in the JDBC code, but the code appeared to be correct. What made it even more frustrating is that the error message did not seem to have any relation to the problem.

It turned out that the code I got from the other team used double quotes to delimit strings, and as soon as I ran the code against Sybase, Sybase threw a `SQLException`. MySQL accepts double quotes to delimit strings, but Sybase does not. The problem was that JDBC is platform-independent, but the SQL command was not platform-independent.

Reusing SQL Commands

There is another often-mentioned reason for using a PreparedStatement object. Most databases keep previously executed SQL in a cache. If you send a SQL command that matches one in the cache, the database reuses the SQL from the cache because it has already been compiled and optimized. This improves performance. To reuse a command, the SQL command you send must match one in the cache exactly. Suppose you send these two SQL commands to a database:

```
insert into customer_tbl (name, state, zip) ➥
values ('Giordanos Pizza', 'Illinois;, '60611')
insert into customer_tbl (name, state, zip) ➥
values ('Independent Records', 'Illinois', '60611')
```

These commands enter values into three columns (name, state, and zip) in the customer_tbl table. You can easily see that these two SQL commands are essentially the same, except for the literal values for the customer data. For the database, however, these two SQL commands are entirely different. It cannot reuse the first SQL command when you send the second SQL command.

Suppose, however, you could pass the database a SQL command that had variables in it. Then the database could reuse the same SQL command any time you passed it new values for the variables. This is what the prepared statement does. A PreparedStatement object allows you to create a SQL command with variables that the database server can precompile. Then you just pass it the values, and the database executes the precompiled command with the values you passed. Pass another set of new values, and the command is executed again with the new values. This is why, for SQL commands that you execute many times, the PreparedStatement object provides a performance enhancement over SQL commands executed with a Statement object.

Inserting Nonprimitive Data

The third situation where PreparedStatement objects are useful is when you need to insert nonprimitive data into a database table.

When you need to insert a simple literal value into a table, it is quite easy. You just write the SQL command to include the literal. For example, the SQL command for inserting a string value is

```
INSERT INTO mytable (myStringColumn) VALUES ('This is a string literal');
```

Inserting a number into a table is just as simple:

```
INSERT INTO mytable (myNumberColumn) VALUES (42);
```

But Java is an object-based language, and inserting objects into a database table is a bit more tricky. How do you write a SQL command to insert an array? How do you write a SQL command to insert a binary object? The answer is by using the PreparedStatement object. A PreparedStatement object can accept Java objects of any type, and correctly insert them into a database table for you (assuming the database table has a column of the correct type for the object).

Now that we've seen some of the situations in which PreparedStatement objects are useful, the next section will demonstrate how to use a PreparedStatement object in these situations.

Creating a PreparedStatement

Creating a PreparedStatement object is similar to creating a Statement object. One difference is that with a prepared statement, you need to tell the database what SQL you intend to execute. You pass the SQL in the creation method, rather than in the execute method. You can use the following methods of the Connection class to create a PreparedStatement object:

- prepareStatement(String sql): Creates a prepared statement for the given SQL. If the prepared statement returns a ResultSet, the ResultSet has a type forward-only, is not updatable, and is not holdable.
- prepareStatement(String sql, int resultSetType, int resultSetConcurrency): Creates a prepared statement for the given SQL. If the prepared statement returns a ResultSet, the ResultSet has the given ResultSet type and concurrency and is not holdable.
- prepareStatement(String sql, int resultSetType, int resultSetConcurrency, int resultSetHoldability): In JDBC 3.0, creates a prepared statement for the given SQL. If the prepared statement returns a ResultSet, the ResultSet has the given ResultSet type, concurrency, and holdability.

The resultSetType parameter refers to whether a ResultSet is scrollable. The resultSetConcurrency parameter is the ability to update a ResultSet. The resultSetHoldability parameter refers to whether a ResultSet is closed when changes are committed. Refer to Chapter 7 for more information about these concepts.

The first argument in each method is a SQL string. The SQL string can have placeholders (variables) that represent data that will be set at a later time. The placeholder is represented by the question mark symbol (?).

Let's take the SQL command presented earlier and change it so that it could be used as part of a prepared statement. Earlier, in the "Reusing SQL Commands" section, we presented two commands that inserted some literal data into a customer table. By replacing the literal data with placeholders, we can create a SQL command that can be reused with different data values:

```
insert into customer_tbl (name, state, zip) values (?, ?, ?)
```

Placeholders are referred to by their index in the SQL command. Placeholders are consecutively indexed, starting with index 1 at the beginning of the SQL string. When the SQL in the prepared statement is sent to the database, the database compiles the SQL command. Before you execute a prepared statement, you must set the placeholders with data. The driver sends the data to the database when the prepared statement is executed, and the database executes the SQL command with the data.

■ **Note** A PreparedStatement object can be used with any SQL command, regardless of whether it has placeholders or not. Placeholders make it easy to reuse the command with different data values and to use the command with complex data. However, the PreparedStatement object can be used to execute any SQL command.

Using a Prepared Statement

After creating the PreparedStatement object, but before the SQL command can be executed, the placeholders in the command must be set. The PreparedStatement interface defines various methods for doing this. You can also use the PreparedStatement object for setting null values in a table. The other advantage of using a prepared statement is that the values you set do not need to be reset every time you want to execute the SQL command; that is, the values you set are persistent. Finally, you can perform batch updating with a prepared statement.

Setting Placeholders

The methods for setting placeholders take the form of set*XXX*(), where *XXX* is a string that identifies the kind of data being set. Here is the method for setting a String:

```
void setString(int parameterIndex, String x)
```

There are other set*XXX*() methods available, one for each Java primitive, and methods for many object types, such as Date and BigDecimal. You should consult the Javadoc for information about all the available methods.

The first argument in the set*XXX*() method will be the index of the placeholder in the SQL command. Each placeholder is referenced by its position in the SQL string. Starting from the beginning of the string, the first placeholder is at index 1, the second at 2, and so on.

The second argument is the data value that replaces the placeholder. So, using the same SQL INSERT statement from the previous example, here's how the data values would be set:

```
String sql = "insert into customer_tbl (name, state, zip) values (?, ?, ?)"
// Placeholder index:                                             1  2  3
PreparedStatement ps = conn.prepareStatement(sql);
ps.setString(1, "Giordano's Pizza");
ps.setString(2, "IL");
ps.setString(3, "60611");
ps.executeUpdate();
```

Caution If you do not set all the parameters before executing the SQL, the driver will throw a SQLException.

When the values have all been set, you execute the SQL command by calling the executeUpdate() method as shown here. If you call the executeQuery(String), executeUpdate(String), or execute(String) method, the driver will throw a SQLException. You must call the no-parameter versions of those methods with a prepared statement.

Setting Placeholders with Complex Data

Another advantage of PreparedStatement objects is that they can be used to insert and update complex data in the database. As you saw earlier, when you insert a string into a database table using a statement, you can simply delimit the string with single quotes, and the table accepts the string. What happens, however, when the table column is a date or timestamp type? Unless you work with that column type on a frequent basis, you'll always need to consult the documentation for the correct format: is it 2005/07/23, 23-Jul-05, or some other format? With a prepared statement, you never need to remember the correct format for complex types.

With a prepared statement, the `PreparedStatement` object handles any formatting to prepare the data for insertion into the database. In the case of dates, times, and timestamps, you simply create the correct `java.sql` object and pass it to the `setDate()` method, as shown here:

```
//Assume getSqlDate() returns a Date with the given date
java.sql.Date d = getSqlDate("23-Jul-05");
pstmt.setDate(1, d);
```

Now it doesn't matter what the correct database date format is, because the `PreparedStatement` object will take the `Date` object and perform the formatting for you.

If you look at the Javadoc for `PreparedStatement`, you will see that there are `setXXX()` methods for various types of complex data such as arrays, streams, dates, times, and so on. There is even a method for setting an arbitrary object: `setObject()`. In some enterprise databases, you can create complex column types. For example, you could create a column type called `address`, which contains street, city, state, and zip code data. You can then write a Java class that corresponds to these complex column types. The `setObject()` method is used to set the parameter data for a column with a complex type.

Setting Null Values

You might think that you can insert a null into a database table by not setting the placeholder that corresponds to the column that will have the null value. However, if you do not set all the parameters, the driver will throw a `SQLException`. Null values are inserted into the database by using one of the two `setNull()` methods:

```
void setNull(int parameterIndex, int sqlType)
void setNull(int parameterIndex, int sqlType, String typeName)
```

As with the other `setXXX()` methods, the first parameter is the index of the placeholder. The second parameter is defined in the Java class `java.sql.Types`. The `java.sql.Types` class contains `int` constants that correspond to every JDBC type. Thus, if you want to set a `String` column to null, you would pass `java.sql.Types.VARCHAR` (`VARCHAR` is the SQL equivalent to a string). If you want to set a `Date` column to null, you would pass `java.sql.Types.DATE`. You would pass the appropriate constant for the column you are setting to null.

The second form of the `setNull()` method has a third parameter. The `java.sql.Types` class defines a constant with the name `OBJECT`. When you use `java.sql.Types.OBJECT` as the second argument, the `typeName` parameter must be the fully qualified type name of the type being set to null. This method can be used for any type, but is provided primarily for user-named types and `REF` type parameters. Some databases support user-defined types. Inside the database, you can create a custom column type. You can then create a table with a column of that type. In your Java code, you create a class that corresponds to that type. In the `setNull(int, int, String)` method, you pass `java.sql.Types.OBJECT` as the `sqlType` parameter, and the fully qualified class name of the class as the `typeName` parameter.

■ **Tip** For more information about creating and mapping Java classes to database column types, see Section 3.6 of the advanced JDBC tutorial, at `http://developer.java.sun.com/developer/Books/JDBCTutorial/index.html`.

Reusing a Prepared Statement Object

Once a placeholder has been set with data, the data remains set for that placeholder until the code explicitly changes the value for the placeholder. In other words, you are not required to set every placeholder every time you want to execute some SQL using the same prepared statement. If you set the placeholder at some point in the code, and that value is reused in multiple rows, you need to set the placeholder only the first time.

For example, let's use the code snippets shown earlier where customer data was inserted into the `customer_tbl` table. You could create a JSP that accepts a state and zip code, and passes these values to a JSP that allows a user to enter customer names for that state and zip code. Here's a code snippet that shows how the Java code in that second JSP might look:

```
String sql = "insert into customer_tbl (name, state, zip) values (?, ?, ?)"
PreparedStatement ps = conn.prepareStatement(sql);
ps.setString(2, req.getParameter("state"));
ps.setString(3, req.getParameter("zip"));
String[] names = req.getParameterValues("names");
for (int i = 0; i < names.length; i++) {
  ps.setString(1, names[i]);
  int result = ps.executeUpdate();
}
```

Before the loop is entered, `setString()` is called to set the value for the second and third arguments. Inside the loop, you need to set the value of only the first argument. Since the loop never resets the values of the second and third arguments, the values are reused for every `executeUpdate()` method call.

As shown in this example, you can reset the value of a placeholder simply by calling one of the `set`*`XXX`*`()` methods with a new value. If you need to clear all the values in a prepared statement, that can be done by calling the `PreparedStatement` class's `clearParameters()` method.

Reusing a SQL Command

Earlier, we mentioned that using a prepared statement can provide a performance enhancement over using a statement. This enhancement occurs even if you use a new `PreparedStatement` object. In other words, if a component in your application uses a `PreparedStatement` object to execute a SQL command, some other component will get the advantage of the compiled SQL command on the database side. It doesn't matter whether the `PreparedStatement` object is the same; it only matters whether the SQL command is the same. This occurs because it is the database that stores the compiled SQL command in its cache. If the same SQL command is sent by any other client, the database can reuse the compiled SQL command.

Performing Batch Updates

Just as with a statement, you can use a prepared statement to perform batch updating. The difference is that before calling addBatch(), you must set each placeholder with the setXXX() methods as shown earlier. After you have set the placeholders, you call addBatch(). This adds the data values to the batch. After you have added all the rows you want, you call executeBatch(). This sends all the data values to the database for execution with the already stored SQL command. Rewriting the code snippet shown earlier to use batching looks like this:

```
String sql = "insert into customer_tbl (name, state, zip) values (?, ?, ?)"
PreparedStatement ps = conn.prepareStatement(sql);
ps.setString(2, req.getParameter("state"));
ps.setString(3, req.getParameter("zip"));
String[] names = req.getParameterValues("names");
for (int i = 0; i < names.length; i++) {
  ps.setString(1, names[i]);
  ps.addBatch();
}
int results[] = ps.executeBatch();
```

Listing 8-1 shows a JSP that uses some of the features of the PreparedStatement class. This JSP reuses the JdbcManager class from the previous chapter (see Listing 7-3 and Listing 7-8). The SaveRatings JSP is part of a hypothetical brokerage firm application. On a periodic basis, stock analysts in the firm will submit a rating for some set of stocks. The SaveRatings JSP reads data about stock ratings from a request (see Listing 8-2), and then inserts that data into a database table named stock (see Listing 8-3). It inserts the data using a PreparedStatement object. The request contains a parameter for stock analyst name, a list of stocks being rated, and a rating for each stock.

Listing 8-1. *SaveRatings.jsp*

```
<%@ page import="java.sql.*, com.apress.jdbc.*" %>
<html>
  <head>
    <title>Easy Street - Save Ratings</title>
  </head>
  <body>
    <h1>Save Ratings</h1>
<%
    Connection conn = null;
    PreparedStatement stmt = null;
    try {
      conn = JdbcManager.getConnection();
      String sqlcmd = "insert into stock (tickerSymbol, analyst, rating) " +
        "values (?,?,?)";
      stmt = conn.prepareStatement(sqlcmd);
      String analystName = request.getParameter("AnalystName");
      stmt.setString(2, analystName);
      String[] stockNames = request.getParameterValues("stockNames");
```

```
      for (int i = 0; i < stockNames.length; i++) {
        stmt.setString(1, stockNames[i]);
        String rating =  request.getParameter(stockNames[i]);
        if (rating.equals("No Rating")) {
          stmt.setNull(3, java.sql.Types.VARCHAR);
        } else {
          stmt.setString(3, request.getParameter(stockNames[i]));
        }
        stmt.addBatch();
      }
      int results[] = stmt.executeBatch();
      for (int i = 0; i < results.length; i++) {
        if (results[i] == 1) {
%>
          <p>Rating of &quot;<%=request.getParameter(stockNames[i])%>&quot;
          for <%= stockNames[i] %> was inserted successfully</p>
<%
        } else {
%>
          <p>Rating for <%= stockNames[i] %> was not inserted successfully</p>
<%
        }
      }
    } catch (SQLException e) {
%>
      <%= e.getMessage() %>
<%
      e.printStackTrace();
    } finally {
      JdbcManager.close(stmt);
      JdbcManager.close(conn);
    }
%>
  </body>
</html>
```

This JSP uses the JdbcManager class to get a connection. (Don't forget to create the JDBC resource when you deploy the application.) After the PreparedStatement object is created by the connection, the JSP reads the analyst name from the request, and sets the second parameter in the PreparedStatement with that value. Notice that this is the only time that the second parameter is set. The value is reused for every SQL command. Notice also that the second parameter is set before any other; the parameters can be set in any order, as long as they are all set.

Next, the JSP gets a String array from the request that contains the stock symbols. It uses this array in a loop. Inside the loop, the stock symbol becomes the name used to retrieve the request parameter that holds the rating for the stock. The JSP sets the stock symbol and rating parameters in the PreparedStatement; if the request contains a value of "No Rating" for a stock, the JSP sets the column to null (for no other reason than to demonstrate using the setNull() method). The JSP then calls addBatch() to add the values to the batch. After the loop completes, the code calls the executeBatch() method to send all the batched commands to the database for execution. It then runs through the result array to determine which commands succeeded.

Listing 8-2, EnterRatings.jsp, shows the JSP that submits the stock ratings to the SaveRatings JSP. This JSP uses an input field with the name "AnalystName" to accept an analyst name. It then creates a table consisting of the stock symbols and radio buttons for six possible ratings. In this JSP, we've hard-coded the symbol names. In a real application, you would probably read the symbols to be rated from a database. The JSP uses the String array of stock names to create the table. Each row in the table contains a field named stockSymbols with the symbol of one stock. When the form is submitted, the five symbols will be submitted together with the same name. This is what allows the SaveRatings JSP to get the symbols as a String array. Finally, each row contains a radio button. The name used for all radio button input tags in a row is the stock symbol.

Listing 8-2. *EnterRatings.jsp*

```
<%@ page import="java.sql.*, com.apress.jdbc.*" %>
<html>
  <head>
    <title>Easy Street - Enter Ratings</title>
  </head>
  <body>
    <h1>Stock Ratings</h1>
    <form action="SaveRatings.jsp">
      Enter your name:
      <input type="text"
             name="AnalystName"
             value=""/>
    <p>Here are the stocks to rate for this week:</p>
<%
    String[] stocks = new String[] {
      "DDC", "SRU", "SRI", "UDE", "ZAP"
    };
%>
      <table border="1">
<%
    for (int i = 0; i < stocks.length; i++) {
%>
        <tr>
          <td><input type="hidden" name="stockNames"
                     value="<%= stocks[i] %>"><%= stocks[i] %></td>
          <td><input type="radio" name="<%= stocks[i] %>"
                     value="Smashing">Smashing</td>
          <td><input type="radio" name="<%= stocks[i] %>"
                     value="Take a chance">Take a chance</td>
          <td><input type="radio" name="<%= stocks[i] %>"
                     value="It's OK">It's OK</td>
```

```
            <td><input type="radio" name="<%= stocks[i] %>"
                       value="Could be worse">Could be worse</td>
            <td><input type="radio" name="<%= stocks[i] %>"
                       value="Run away">Run away</td>
            <td><input type="radio" name="<%= stocks[i] %>"
                       value="No Rating">No Rating</td>
          </tr>
<%
    }
%>
        </table>
        <input type="submit" name="submit" value="Submit Ratings"/>
      </form>
    </body>
</html>
```

After creating the stock table (Listing 8-3) and deploying the application (remember to create a JDBC resource), you will start by loading the EnterRatings JSP into your browser. You should see a web page that looks like Figure 8-2. You can then enter a name and select ratings for each stock. Notice that in Figure 8-2, we've entered a name that includes embedded double quotes. Also, one of the ratings uses an embedded single quote. If you tried to insert this data using a Statement object, you would certainly have problems. However, as you will see in a moment, the PreparedStatement object handles this data without any problems.

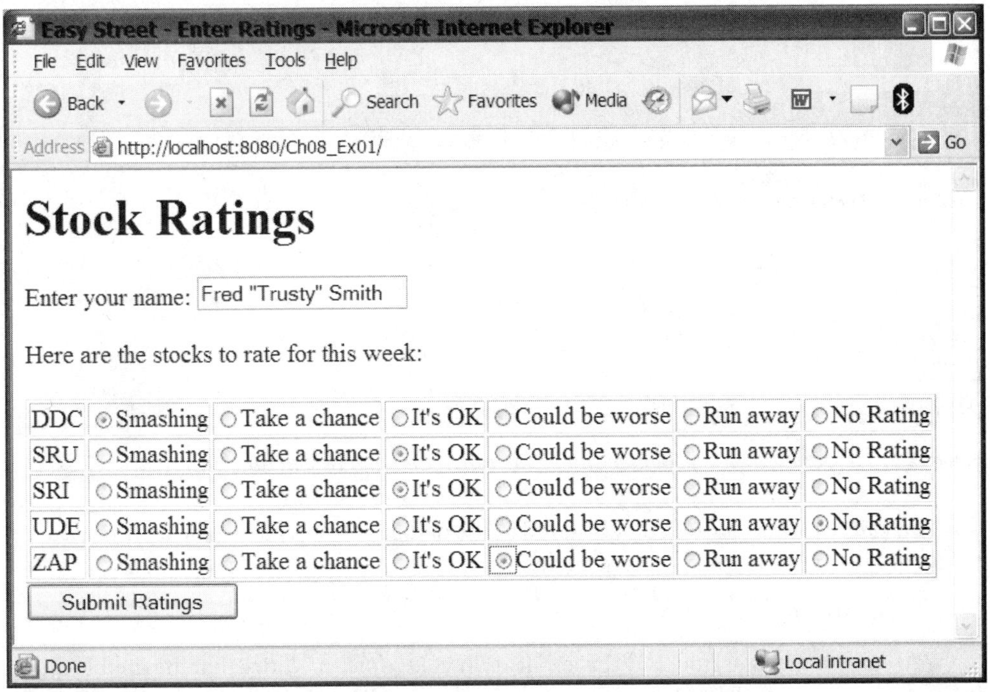

Figure 8-2. *The EnterRatings web page accepts an analyst name and ratings for each stock.*

Before you can run the application, however, you need to create a database table to hold the ratings. Using either the console or command tool, log in to the `sample` database using the `PBPUBLIC` username and password. Execute the command shown in Listing 8-3 to create the database table.

Listing 8-3. *SQL Command to Create the stock Table*

```
create table stock (
  tickerSymbol varchar(10),
  analyst varchar(30),
  rating varchar(30));
```

After you create the table, it will be empty. Load the `EnterRatings` JSP, enter some values, and submit the form. The `SaveRatings` JSP will read the data and insert it into the database. Assuming that there are no problems, you should see a web page similar to Figure 8-3.

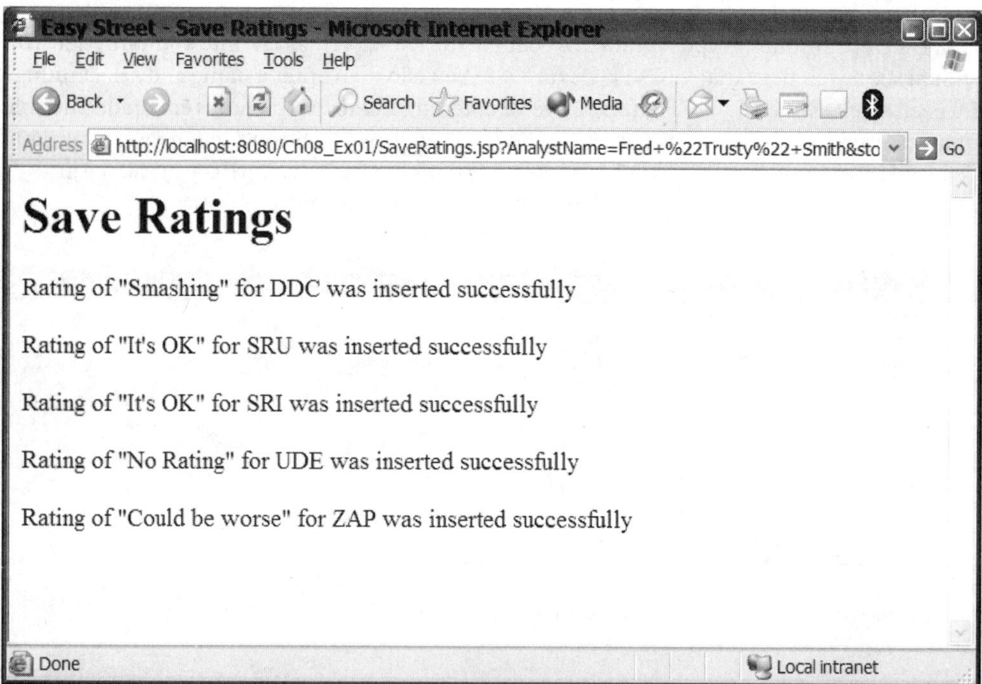

Figure 8-3. *The SaveRatings web page shows the result for each row of data inserted.*

You can also view the data that is stored in the database by executing the following command using one of the PointBase tools:

```
select * from stock;
```

You can see the data stored by the application in Figure 8-4. Notice that the double quote in the analyst name and the single quote in the rating "It's Okay" were both saved successfully.

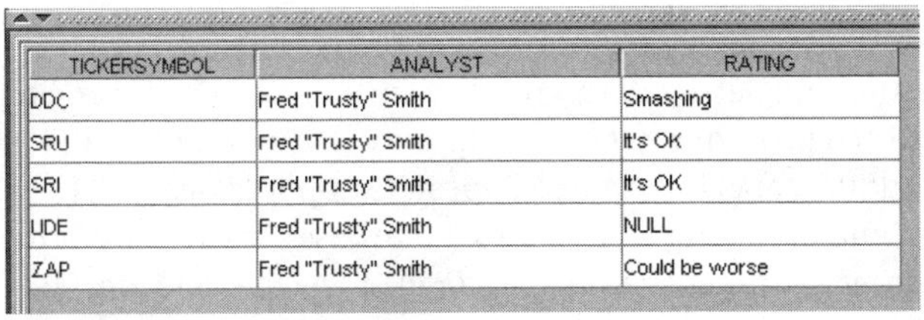

TICKERSYMBOL	ANALYST	RATING
DDC	Fred "Trusty" Smith	Smashing
SRU	Fred "Trusty" Smith	It's OK
SRI	Fred "Trusty" Smith	It's OK
UDE	Fred "Trusty" Smith	NULL
ZAP	Fred "Trusty" Smith	Could be worse

Figure 8-4. *The PreparedStatement correctly handled single quotes and double quotes submitted by the web application.*

Callable Statements

In many enterprise applications, the business logic for the application will be encapsulated in stored procedures, or *sprocs* for short, inside the database. Stored procedures are just like methods in your Java code. They have names, they can have parameter lists, they have a body (containing SQL and procedural commands) that performs some work, and they can return values. Your code can execute stored procedures in a database through the use of `java.sql.CallableStatement` objects.

In this section, the term *stored procedure* is used generically to refer to both procedures and functions. The main difference between the two is that a function can return one or more values and a procedure does not return a value. If your database supports storing procedural and SQL statements in the database for execution, but uses a different term, you should consider *stored procedure* to be a synonym for the term used by your database. For example, Sybase has different definitions for procedures and functions. In Sybase, a function can return only a single value (similar to a Java method), while a procedure can return any number of output parameters.

Reasons for Using Stored Procedures

There are many reasons why you would use stored procedures. Here are some of the benefits of stored procedures:

- A stored procedure can encapsulate a common set of SQL commands. A client can access this functionality without needing to make many different JDBC calls.
- You can reuse stored procedures that are already developed, rather than re-creating their functionality from scratch in JDBC.
- The stored procedure makes transaction control easier. We will look at transactions and transaction control in greater detail later in this chapter.
- Providing a given functionality in a stored procedure ensures that every part of the application that uses the functionality does so in the same way. If requirements change, only the procedure may need to be changed, and everyone who uses the procedure automatically gets the change.
- By having a procedure in a database, the code exists in one place only, yet is accessible to any client, Java or not, that can connect to the database.

Creating a CallableStatement

Even though they provide useful features, not all databases implement stored procedures. For example, MySQL does not support stored procedures. Other databases may provide similar functionality in a different manner. Cloudscape, for example, doesn't support storing SQL statements, but does support storing and executing Java classes. PointBase provides a hybrid solution: you can create stored procedures and functions, but the stored procedures and functions call external Java methods that you write.

JDBC code can call stored procedures using a `CallableStatement` object. A `CallableStatement` object is created in much the same way as the `PreparedStatement` object, by calling a method of the `Connection` object. The following are the `Connection` interface methods for creating a `CallableStatement` object:

- `prepareCall(String sql)`: Creates a `CallableStatement` object for the given SQL. If the `CallableStatement` returns a `ResultSet` object, the `ResultSet` has a type of forward-only, is not updatable, and is not holdable.
- `prepareCall(String sql, int resultSetType, int resultSetConcurrency)`: Creates a `CallableStatement` object for the given SQL. If the `CallableStatement` returns a `ResultSet`, the `ResultSet` has the given `ResultSet` type and concurrency, and is not holdable.
- `prepareCall(String sql, int resultSetType, int resultSetConcurrency, int resultSetHoldability)`: In JDBC 3.0, creates a `CallableStatement` object for the given SQL. If the `CallableStatement` returns a `ResultSet`, the `ResultSet` has the given `ResultSet` type, concurrency, and holdability.

The `resultSetType` parameter refers to whether a `ResultSet` is scrollable. The `resultSetConcurrency` parameter is the ability to update a `ResultSet`. The `resultSetHoldability` parameter refers to whether a `ResultSet` is closed when changes are committed. Refer to the previous chapter for more information about these concepts.

The first argument in each `prepareCall()` method is a SQL string. The SQL string for calling a stored procedure can take one of several forms. The most basic form is the SQL for calling a stored procedure that takes no parameters. The SQL string looks like this:

```
{ call procedure_name }
```

Common among all the forms is the SQL keyword `CALL` that appears before the procedure name, and the curly braces that surround the SQL. This syntax is known as JDBC *escape* syntax. This signals the JDBC driver that the SQL is not an ordinary SQL command and that the SQL must be converted into the correct form for calling a procedure in the target database.

For example, suppose the database had a stored procedure named `adjust_prices`, which took no parameters and returned no value. The code to create a `CallableStatement` object for this stored procedure would look like this:

```
String sql = "{ call adjust_prices }";
CallableStatement cs = connection.prepareCall(sql);
```

Setting Placeholders

When a procedure or function takes parameters, the SQL uses placeholders, just as with a prepared statement. Suppose the database had a stored procedure named `set_price` that took two parameters. The code to create a CallableStatement object for this stored procedure would look like this:

```
String sql = "{ call set_price(?, ?) }";
CallableStatement cs = connection.prepareCall(sql);
```

The set_price procedure takes two parameters and returns no value. Placeholders mark each parameter in the procedure call. The placeholders in a CallableStatement are set in the same way as placeholders in a PreparedStatement, as described earlier in this chapter.

Placeholders are also used when a function returns a value. If the database had a stored function named get_price that took one parameter and returned a value, the code to create a CallableStatement object for this stored function would look like this:

```
String sql = "{ ? = call get_price(?) }";
CallableStatement cs = connection.prepareCall(sql);
```

The return value of the function is marked by a placeholder, as is the parameter sent to the function. In the case of the return value, however, the CallableStatement provides additional methods for reading the return value.

As with the PreparedStatement object, the placeholders are numbered consecutively, starting with number 1 for the placeholder that appears in the leftmost position in the string. Moving from left to right, each placeholder is given the next number in sequence.

If a placeholder is used to pass an argument to a stored procedure, this parameter is known as an IN parameter. Its value must be set before the statement can be executed. If you fail to set one of the placeholders, the driver will throw a SQLException when you attempt to execute the SQL. The CallableStatement interface inherits the set*XXX*() methods of the PreparedStatement interface for doing this. In addition to the set*XXX*() methods inherited from PreparedStatement, CallableStatement adds some set*XXX*() methods that look similar to this method for setting a double:

```
void setDouble(String, double)
```

In the method call, the first parameter allows you to use a name to identify the parameter when a name has been set by the stored procedure.

■ Tip If you did not create the stored procedure yourself, you can determine if it has named parameters by calling the DatabaseMetaData.getProcedureColumns() method. This returns a ResultSet in which each row of the ResultSet describes a parameter of the procedure. One of the columns is the name of the parameter.

Registering Output Parameters

A stored procedure can also set an input parameter to a new value, and that value is passed back to the caller through the parameter list. For example, this SQL command has two parameters in the parameter list:

```
call set_price(?, ?)
```

If this were a Java method call, the method could set the value of either parameter inside the method, and that value would not be visible to the caller. However, if the argument in the Java method is an object reference, the state of the Java object could be changed inside the method, and that change would be visible to the caller.

With a SQL stored procedure, the parameters can be set or changed inside the procedure, and the new values are visible to the caller. If the placeholder is used to pass data to the stored procedure, and the stored procedure passes data back through the parameter, this is an INOUT parameter. A placeholder that is used only to pass data back, or that is a return value, is an OUT parameter.

If any of the parameters in the SQL command are INOUT or OUT parameters, the JDBC type of the placeholder must be registered before the call can be executed, or you will get a `SQLException`. To register parameters, use the following methods:

```
void registerOutParameter(int parameterIndex, int jdbcType)
void registerOutParameter(int parameterIndex, int jdbcType, int scale)
```

Unlike the `setXXX()` methods, the `registerOutParameter()` method has only two forms. The first parameter in the method is the position of the placeholder in the SQL string. The second parameter is one of the constants defined in the `java.sql.Types` class. The `Types` class defines a constant for each SQL type.

So, for example, if you were calling a stored procedure that passed a value through the second parameter in a parameter list, and the SQL type returned was a varchar (essentially a string), you would register the parameter like this:

```
cs.registerOutParameter(2, java.sql.Types.VARCHAR);
```

If the return value of a function were a double, you could use this:

```
cs.registerOutParameter(1, java.sql.Types.DOUBLE);
```

For the complete list of the available `java.sql.Types` constants, consult the Javadocs.

When registering a parameter that is one of the numeric types such as float, double, numeric, or decimal, you could also use the second form of the `registerOutParameter()` method. This method takes a third parameter that defines the scale of the returned value. For example, to register a return type that returned a number with two digits to the right of the decimal point, you could use this:

```
cs.registerOutParameter(1, java.sql.Types.DOUBLE, 2);
```

Note that if any of the placeholders is an INOUT parameter, the JDBC code must call both a `setXXX()` method and a `registerOutParameter()` method prior to executing the callable statement. If you fail to set the value or register the parameter, the driver will throw a `SQLException`.

As with the `PreparedStatement` object, once a placeholder has been set with data, that placeholder remains set until the code explicitly changes the placeholder. All the placeholders can be cleared by calling the method `clearParameters()`. The value of a placeholder is changed by calling one of the `setXXX()` or `registerOutParameter()` methods, again with the appropriate index.

Calling a Stored Procedure

After the data values are set, the code calls one of the execute methods—executeUpdate(), executeQuery(), or execute()—to tell the database to execute the stored procedure. Most often, you will call the execute() method. However, stored procedures can also return a ResultSet; in that case, you could use executeQuery(). If the stored procedure returned a row update count, you could use executeUpdate(). You should use executeUpdate() or executeQuery() only if you know the stored procedure returns a ResultSet or update count. For any other return value, or for procedures that do not return a value, call the stored procedure using the execute() method.

Caution If you call the executeQuery(String), executeUpdate(String), or execute(String) method, the driver will throw a SQLException. You must call the no-parameter versions of those methods with a CallableStatement.

After executing the stored procedure, the return values of any placeholders are retrieved with get*XXX*() methods of the CallableStatement, similar to those used to retrieve the column values from a row in a ResultSet. The get*XXX*() methods of CallableStatement have two forms: one that takes an int parameter and one that takes a String parameter.

```
returnType getXXX(int)
returnType getXXX(String)
```

The int parameter is the index of the placeholder in the callable statement. If the stored procedure has named parameters, you can use the String parameter to retrieve the value of the named parameter.

Listing 8-4 shows a code snippet that highlights some of the features discussed in this section. The code snippet extends the example shown in Listing 8-1. In this example, a hypothetical stored function named save_rating is called. This hypothetical function takes three parameters: a stock symbol, an analyst name, and a numerical stock rating from 1 to 5. The function has a return value that is the number of analysts who have rated the stock. It also uses the rating parameter to return the average rating for the stock.

Listing 8-4. *Code Snippet Illustrating CallableStatement*

```
String sql = "{ ? = save_rating(?, ?, ?) };
CallableStatement cs = connection.prepareCall(sql);

//Set the input parameters
cs.setString(2, "ZAP");  //the stock symbol is the second parameter
cs.setString(3, "Fred Smith");  //the analyst name is the third parameter
cs.setInt(4, 3);  //the numerical rating is the fourth parameter

//Register the out parameters
//the return value is the first placeholder
cs.registerOutParameter(1, java.sql.Types.INTEGER);
```

```
//and the fourth parameter is used as an INOUT parameter to return another value
cs.registerOutParameter(4, java.sql.Types.INTEGER);

//Execute the procedure and get the return values
cs.execute();
int ratingsCount = cs.getInt(1);
int avgRating = cs.getInt(4);
```

Transactions

So far in the examples in this chapter, every SQL command sent to the database was immediately executed, and the change was automatically made permanent in the database. In database terms, when the change is made permanent, we say that we *commit* the change, or that the change was *committed*. In an earlier example, you inserted a row into a table in the PointBase database, and as soon as the SQL was sent to the database, the change was committed. This commit is performed automatically by the JDBC driver. If you had done a query on the table, the new data would be returned by the query.

Suppose you were inserting 50 rows into that table, and each insertion was being automatically committed by the driver. Halfway through the 50 insertions, your workstation suffered a power failure. Rather than having a total failure, with no changes made to the database, the half of the rows that had been sent to the table before the power failure would be in the table. Only half of the work would be incomplete. There are times when this might be okay. Most times, however, a partial success would be bad and would make the table invalid.

Let's look at the canonical bank account transfer problem. In this example, a user wants to transfer money between accounts. The process debits one account and credits the second account (or vice versa: credit then debit) by some amount. If the database fails halfway through the transfer, the amount would be deducted from one account and not added to the other (or vice versa). The database is in an invalid state where it does not reflect the correct balances in either account. This is not a good situation for the customer (or the bank).

Or suppose you were working on an Internet stock trading application, and the "sell stock" process failed halfway through. The software may have deposited the funds, but not moved the stock, or vice versa. In either case, the database is in an invalid state: the client's account has both the proceeds and the stock, or neither the proceeds nor the stock.

In both examples, you want all the changes to be made to a database or none of the changes to be made.

This is the main purpose of *transactions* in the database: they take the database from one consistent state to the next. That is their job. When you commit work in the database, you are assured that all of your changes have been saved; if you roll back the work, none of the changes are saved.

Ending Transactions

In some SQL dialects, the code must explicitly tell the database that a transaction is beginning before it executes SQL commands. In Microsoft SQL Server, for example, the `BEGIN TRAN` command starts a transaction. JDBC does not require you to explicitly begin a transaction (and thus, does not provide any class or methods for you, the application programmer, to perform this action). The JDBC driver you are using will start a transaction for you automatically. The transaction can be ended automatically or manually.

Whether the transaction is ended automatically or manually is determined by the autocommit status of the connection. For JDBC, the default autocommit status is `true`; that is, transactions are automatically committed by the driver. That is why, in all the examples thus far, the SQL commands were automatically committed by the driver.

The point at which the transaction ends depends on what type of statement is being executed, as shown in Table 8-1.

Table 8-1. *Transaction Autocommit Rules*

Statement Type	When the Transaction Is Committed
SQL `INSERT`, `UPDATE`, or `DELETE`	The statement has finished executing, from the client's view, as soon as `executeUpdate()` or `execute()` returns.
SQL `SELECT`	All the rows in the `ResultSet` object have been retrieved, or a `Statement` object is used to execute a new SQL command on the same connection.

With autocommit enabled, the driver ends the transaction by automatically calling the commit method. Even with a SQL query, which has no changes to be saved, there is still a transaction. The driver still must signal the database that the transaction has ended.

When the autocommit status is `false`, it is the responsibility of the client to explicitly manage and end transactions.

Managing Transactions

When your code gets a connection from a data source, JDBC requires that the connection be in autocommit mode (autocommit enabled). When autocommit is enabled, each SQL command is treated as a transaction and the transaction is committed when the statement is complete, as shown in Table 8-1.

Having the driver in autocommit mode may be acceptable when you are learning JDBC or when you are using a single-user database. However, the fact that the JDBC API defaults to autocommit enabled is problematic for most real-world applications. Real-world database applications are almost always multiuser applications or applications that touch more than a single table to complete a given task. Thus, for almost any type of real-world application, the next method call after obtaining a connection should be a call to `setAutoCommit(boolean)`, as shown here:

```
Connection conn = dataSource.getConnection();
conn.setAutoCommit (false);   // Autocommit disabled
```

Now, all the control of the transaction resides with the client, which is where it belongs. The developer can code the transaction so that it includes all the queries, insertions, updates, and deletions to take the database from one consistent state to another, and commit only after all the statements have succeeded (or roll back if there are problems).

The Connection class provides several methods for managing transactions:

- void setAutoCommit(boolean): Sets the autocommit mode to true (commit transaction automatically, the default setting) or false (require explicit transaction commit).
- void commit(): Commits the current transaction. All changes made since the last commit or rollback are made permanent. Any database locks are released.
- void close(): Not explicitly part of transaction management. However, closing the Connection may cause a transaction to be committed. The exact behavior depends on the database; the JDBC specification does not require a particular behavior.
- void rollback(): Returns the database to the state that existed at the start of the current transaction.
- Savepoint setSavepoint(): Creates an unnamed savepoint in the current transaction and returns that Savepoint object.
- Savepoint setSavepoint(String): Creates a named savepoint in the current transaction and returns that Savepoint object.
- void releaseSavepoint(Savepoint): Removes the given savepoint from the current transaction.
- void rollback(Savepoint): Undoes all the changes that were performed after the given savepoint was created.

Committing and Rolling Back Transactions

When the autocommit mode is set to false, transaction management must now be performed explicitly by the code. SQL commands sent to the database will still be executed, but the transaction is not committed when the statement is complete. The transaction will be committed when the code calls the commit() method of the Connection object. Alternatively, the transaction could be rolled back if the code calls the rollback() method. Here is an example of code that shows how you might do this:

```
try {
  stmt = conn.createStatement();
  stmt.executeUpdate("delete from customer_tbl");
  conn.commit();
} catch (Exception e) {
  conn.rollback();
} finally {
  JdbcManager.close(stmt);
  JdbcManager.close(conn);
}
```

One example of when you would need to perform manual transaction management is where your application updates more than one table. If both updates need to occur for the database to remain consistent, you do not want to use autocommit. With autocommit, a failure that occurs between table updates would leave the database in an inconsistent state.

Listing 8-5 shows the SaveRatings.jsp file revised to update two tables as part of a single transaction. In this case, along with a rating, the analyst also submits a price target for the stock. For the purposes of this example, price targets will be stored in a separate table (see Listing 8-6). This JSP works much as it did in the earlier example (Listing 8-1). The main difference is that after using batch updating to insert all the ratings, another loop is executed that gets the price targets from the EnterRatings.jsp and inserts that data into the target table.

Listing 8-5. *SaveRatings.jsp*

```
<%@ page import="java.sql.*, com.apress.jdbc.*" %>
<html>
  <head>
    <title>Easy Street - Save Ratings</title>
  </head>
  <body>
    <h1>Save Ratings</h1>
<%
    Connection conn = null;
    PreparedStatement stmt1 = null;
    Statement stmt2 = null;
    try {
      conn = JdbcManager.getConnection();
      conn.setAutoCommit(false);
      String sqlcmd1 = "insert into stock (tickerSymbol, analyst, rating) " +
        "values (?,?,?)";
      stmt1 = conn.prepareStatement(sqlcmd1);
      String analystName = request.getParameter("AnalystName");
      stmt1.setString(2, analystName);
      String[] stockNames = request.getParameterValues("stockNames");
      for (int i = 0; i < stockNames.length; i++) {
        stmt1.setString(1, stockNames[i]);
        String rating =  request.getParameter(stockNames[i]);
        if (rating.equals("No Rating")) {
          stmt1.setNull(3, java.sql.Types.VARCHAR);
        } else {
          stmt1.setString(3, request.getParameter(stockNames[i]));
        }
        stmt1.addBatch();
      }
      int results[] = stmt1.executeBatch();

      boolean batchSucceeded = true;
      for (int i = 0; i < results.length; i++) {
        if (results[i] == 1) {
```

```
%>
          <p>Rating of &quot;<%=request.getParameter(stockNames[i])%>&quot;
          for <%= stockNames[i] %> was inserted successfully</p>
<%
        } else {
          batchSucceeded = false;
%>
          <p>Rating for <%= stockNames[i] %> was not inserted successfully</p>
<%
        }
      }

      for (int i = 0; i < stockNames.length; i++) {
        String sqlcmd2 = "insert into target (tickerSymbol, priceTarget) " +
          "values ('" + stockNames[i] + "', " +
            request.getParameter(stockNames[i] + "_target") + ")";
        stmt2 = conn.createStatement();
        stmt2.executeUpdate(sqlcmd2);
      }

      if (batchSucceeded) {
        out.write("<p>Batch succeeded, and all targets inserted, " +
          "committing data");
        conn.commit();
      } else {
        out.write("<p>Batch failed rolling back data");
        conn.rollback();
      }
    } catch (SQLException e) {
%>
      <%= e.getMessage() %>
<%
      e.printStackTrace();
      out.write("<p>Exception thrown, rolling back data");
      conn.rollback();
    } finally {
      JdbcManager.close(stmt2);
      JdbcManager.close(stmt1);
      JdbcManager.close(conn);
    }
%>
  </body>
</html>
```

After performing the batch update, the JSP checks the return value from the batch update. If any update row returned a value of zero, a Boolean is set to indicate that one of the batch updates failed. Later in the JSP, this value is checked to determine whether to roll back the transaction.

Additionally, after the batch update, the price targets are inserted into the `target` table. If any insertion fails here and a `SQLException` is thrown, the transaction is rolled back in the `catch` clause.

Before running this JSP, you need to create another table in the database in addition to the `stock` table created by the command in Listing 8-3. Using either the console or command tool, log in to the `sample` database using the `PBPUBLIC` username and password. Execute the command shown in Listing 8-6 to create the `target` table.

Listing 8-6. *SQL Command to Create the Target Table*

```
create table target (
  tickersymbol varchar(10),
  pricetarget decimal (10,2)
);
```

Finally, `EnterRatings.jsp` needs one additional input field in the table for the analyst to enter price targets. Listing 8-7 shows the JSP code for this additional column in the table.

Listing 8-7. *Additional Form Code in EnterRatings.jsp for the Price Target Field*

```
      <td><input type="radio" name="<%= stocks[i] %>"
                 value="No Rating">No Rating</td>
      <td><input type="text" name="<%= stocks[i] %>_target"></td>
    </tr>
```

This input field creates a text box for entering the price target. The `name` of the field is `stockSymbol_target`. For example, in the row of the table for the stock ZAP, the price target field will be named `ZAP_target`. This allows the `SaveRatings.jsp` to get the price target.

Deploy these components and the `JdbcManager` class to your application server. Remember to create or configure the `DataSource` for the application, as described in Chapter 7. When your code is deployed and configured, load the `EnterRatings.jsp` into the browser. Figure 8-5 shows this page with some ratings and price targets entered in the form.

When you click the Submit Ratings button, the `SaveRatings.jsp` will insert the ratings and price targets into the appropriate tables. If all the insertions are successful, the transaction will be committed. You should see a page similar to Figure 8-6. Using the console or command tool, you can log in to the database and verify that all the data was inserted and saved.

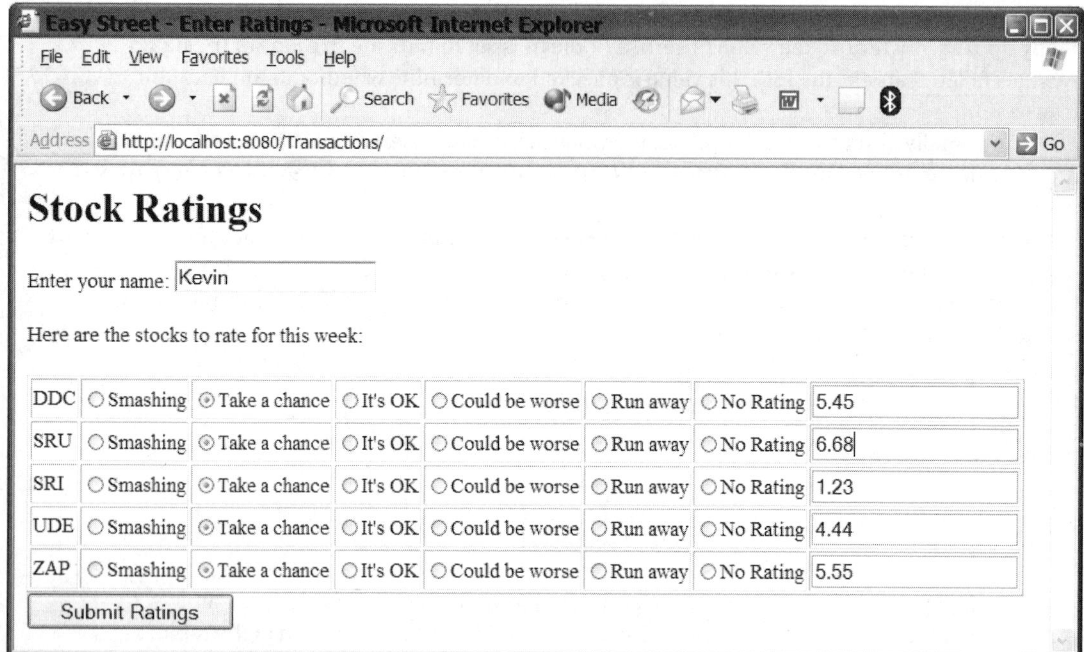

Figure 8-5. *The new EnterRatings.jsp with a price target field*

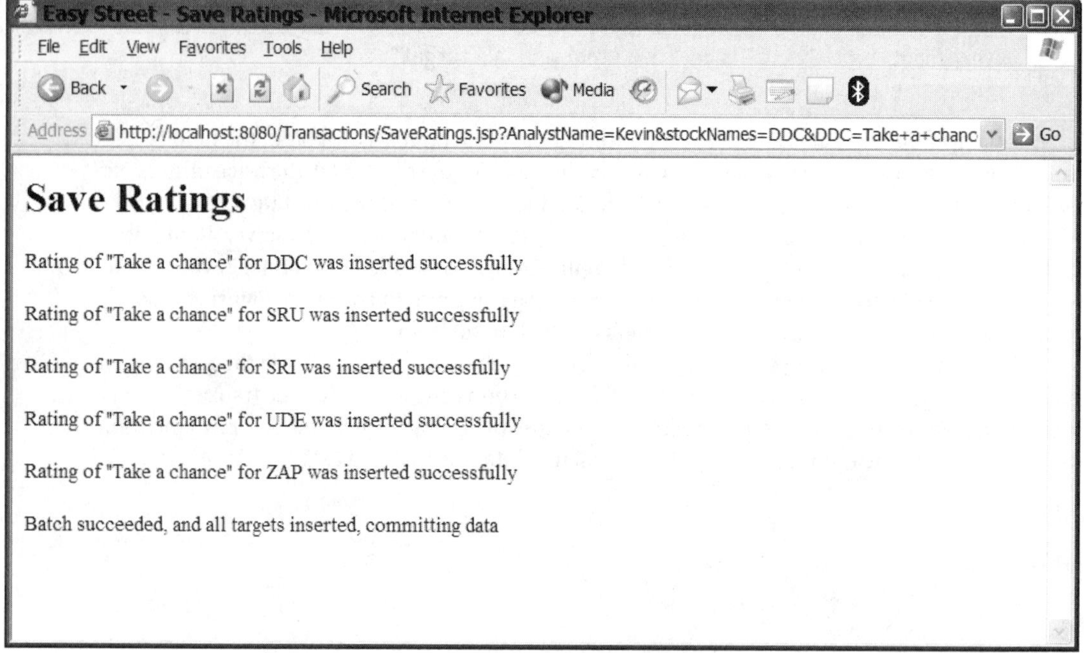

Figure 8-6. *The new SaveRatings.jsp tells you that all data was inserted and committed.*

Now, set one of the price target fields in the EnterRatings.jsp to be an invalid price. One way to do this is to enter a string instead of a number. For example, Figure 8-7 shows the result of setting one of the price targets to "six," and then submitting the page.

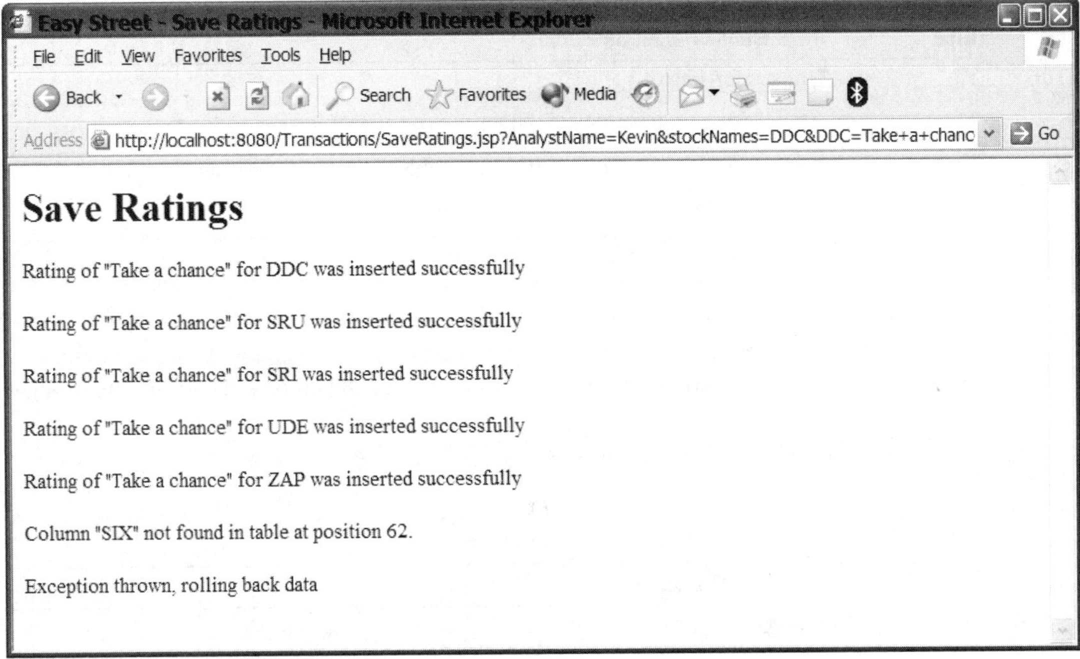

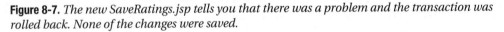

Figure 8-7. *The new SaveRatings.jsp tells you that there was a problem and the transaction was rolled back. None of the changes were saved.*

Every rating is properly inserted into the database. The return value of the batch update indicates that all the rows were inserted correctly into the stock table. But because autocommit is disabled, none of these insertions are made permanent yet. Then the JSP attempts to insert the price targets into the target table. Because "six" is not a valid decimal number, the statement throws an exception. In the catch block, the transaction is rolled back, and all of the changes to the stock and target tables are discarded.

Using Savepoints

In addition to commit() and rollback(), you might be able to control transactions with a feature known as a *savepoint*. Savepoints have been available in databases for some time, but they are a new feature for JDBC. They are part of the JDBC 3.0 specification, so they are not widely supported by drivers yet. Check your driver documentation to see if savepoints are supported.

Let's look at an example that shows how savepoints might be used. Suppose you have a transaction that manipulates data in two tables, A and B. If the changes to table A succeed, the database will be left in a consistent state, and the transaction could be committed at that point. However, for business reasons, the changes to table B are required to be part of the transaction. If the SQL for table A succeeds, but some or all of the SQL for table B fails, the database will be in an inconsistent state; if the transaction were committed, the database would contain bad data. Table 8-2 shows what this scenario might look like.

Table 8-2. *A Hypothetical Transaction Without Savepoints*

Time	Transaction Without Savepoint
T0	Transaction begins.
T1	SQL insert, update, or delete data into table A. SQL succeeds.
T2	SQL insert, update, or delete data into table B. Some SQL succeeds and some fails.
T3	Client must roll back. All changes to tables A and B are lost.

Without savepoints, all the changes in the transaction must be rolled back because there is no way to perform a partial rollback. Also, there is no easy way to know which parts of table B need to be fixed, so there is no way to recover from the table B failure and commit the changes to table A.

Table 8-3 shows the same example, but with savepoints.

Table 8-3. *A Hypothetical Transaction with Savepoints*

Time	Transaction with Savepoint
T0	Transaction begins.
T1	SQL insert, update, or delete data into table A. SQL succeeds.
T2	Savepoint s1 created.
T3	SQL insert, update, or delete data into table B. SQL fails.
T4	Client calls `rollback` to savepoint `s1`.
T5	Client performs additional SQL.
T6	Client commits transaction. Changes to table A are committed, but changes to table B are not committed.

With savepoints, the client is able to perform a partial rollback of data, do some additional work if needed to put the database into a consistent state, and then commit the transaction. Thus, some of the work performed in a transaction is not lost. Listing 8-8 shows an example of what this might look like in code. In Listing 8-8, `insertIntoTable1()` and `insertIntoTable2()` are methods that perform some database actions. If there is a problem, the methods will throw a `SQLException`. Based on whether or not an exception is thrown, and whether or not the savepoint is set, the code commits all the data, performs a partial rollback and commit, or does a complete rollback.

Listing 8-8. *Using Savepoints to Perform a Partial Rollback*

```
Savepoint sp1 = null;
try {
  insertIntoTable1();
  sp1 = conn.setSavepoint();
  insertIntoTable2();
  // No exceptions, so commit the changes
  conn.commit();
} catch (SQLException e) {
  // This exception means either insertIntoTable1()
  // or insertIntoTable2() failed
  try {
    // If Savepoint is NOT null, then insertIntoTable1() was good
    // but insertIntoTable2() failed, do partial rollback, then commit
    if (sp1 != null) {
      conn.rollback(sp1); conn.commit();
    } else {
      // insertIntoTable1() failed, do complete rollback
      connection.rollback();
    }
  } catch (SQLException e2) {
    e2.printStackTrace();
  }
} finally {
  JdbcManager.close(conn);
}
```

Here are some additional points that you need to be aware of when using savepoints:

- Calling `commit()` or `rollback()` invalidates all savepoints created since the transaction started.
- Calling `releaseSavepoint(Savepoint)` invalidates the given savepoint.
- Calling `rollback(Savepoint)` invalidates any savepoints that had been created after the given savepoint.

Using Transactions with Stored Procedures

As you've seen, transaction control belongs in the hands of the developer. The system requirements should provide information on the business rules for the application, and the developer can use those requirements to make the best decision on what sequence of SQL constitutes the transactions for the system, and when those transactions should be committed. Another way to provide this control is to put all the statements that constitute a transaction into a stored procedure.

Stored procedures are perhaps the easiest and most accessible method to ensure correct transactions. If you follow a programming paradigm that says, "A stored procedure call is a transaction," you'll have an easier time controlling your transactions and building new ones.

You could code stored procedures that receive all of the necessary inputs to perform the work, to take the database from one consistent state to the next. When you invoke this procedure, you wrap the procedure call in transaction-control statements, like this:

```
// Disable autocommit
connection.setAutoCommit(false);
String sql = "{ call MyProcedure }";
CallableStatement cs = connection.prepareCall(sql);
// Call procedure
cs.execute();
connection.commit();
```

Now, if `MyProcedure` completes successfully, you will commit all of the work it did. If it fails, you'll roll back the work (although that is not shown in the snippet). The reason you would not put the commit directly into `MyProcedure` itself is because, at some later date, you might need to combine two or three procedures into one transaction. By leaving transaction control to the client (which is where the choice belongs), you can assemble larger transactions as a collection of stored procedures.

Using Distributed Transactions

So far, we've been looking at transactions involving a single connection to a single database. In your work with Java EE applications, you may be faced with a situation where you need to use *distributed transactions*. Distributed transactions can include two or more databases, as illustrated in Figure 8-8, or can span multiple connections to the same data source, as shown in Figure 8-9. Just as for single connection transactions, all the changes made by each connection in the distributed transaction must be successful for the transaction to be committed.

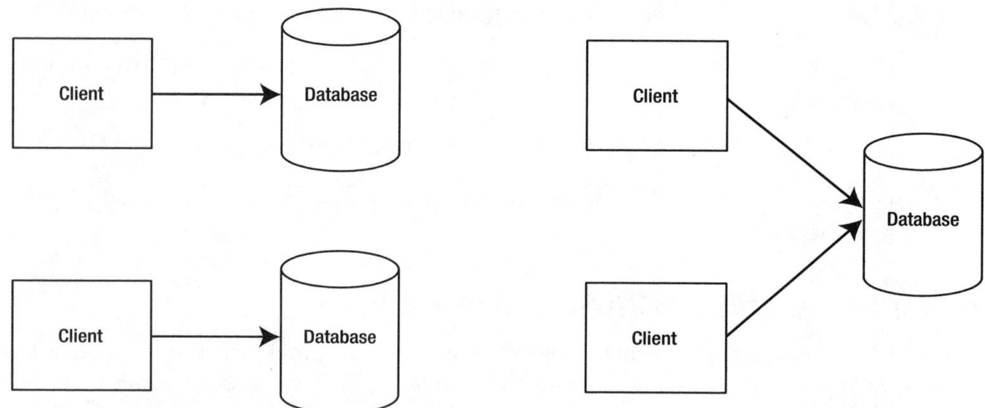

Figure 8-8. *A distributed transaction can be formed by two or more clients accessing one or more databases.*

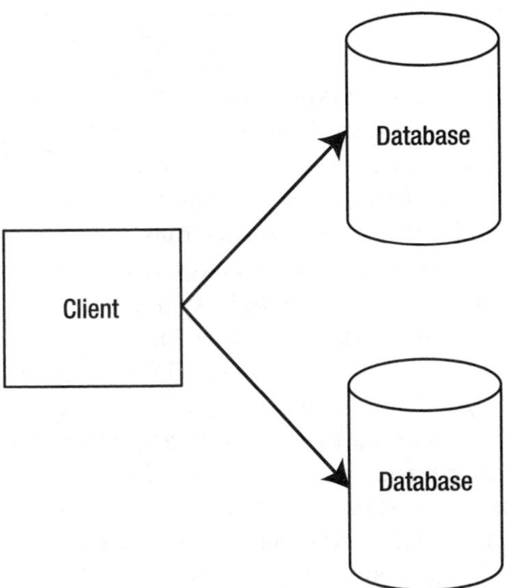

Figure 8-9. *A distributed transaction can be formed from a single client accessing databases over multiple connections.*

From the client's point of view, coding a distributed transaction is almost the same as coding for a single-connection transaction. Here, we will look at distributed transactions primarily from the client's perspective.

While you can use multiple data sources or connections within your JDBC application, the term *distributed transactions* usually applies to applications or classes that have distributed components. One place where you are likely to run into distributed applications is a Java EE application, where various Java EE components are combined to create an application and may execute on the same or different servers. You've seen some of these components already: JSPs, and Servlets. In the following chapters, we'll look at other Java EE components such as Enterprise JavaBeans (EJBs). Distributed transactions in EJBs are different from those in other Java EE components, so in this section, we will look at only distributed transactions in JSPs and Servlets.

When separate components provide part of a transaction, no single component can determine when or how to commit or roll back changes. This then becomes the responsibility of the transaction manager. Since we're working in the Java world, that manager will be an implementation of the Java Transaction API (JTA).

Major interfaces of the JTA include `javax.transaction.UserTransaction` and `javax.transaction.TransactionManager`. The `UserTransaction` is exposed to application components, while the underlying interaction between the Java EE server and the JTA `TransactionManager` is transparent to the application components. The `TransactionManager` implementation supports the server's control of container-demarcated transaction boundaries. The JTA `UserTransaction` and JDBC's transactional support are both available to Java EE application components. You can learn more about the JTA at `http://java.sun.com/products/jta`.

Getting a Connection for a Distributed Transaction

The application server will use a transaction manager to provide distributed transaction support to the components in a Java EE application. As part of providing transaction support, the application server will use special JDBC classes. Those classes will implement the XADataSource, XAConnection, and XAResource interfaces. The application server vendor or the database vendor will provide these classes. At least one of these classes might look vaguely familiar: the XAConnection. Its name is similar to Connection, but it has that XA bit on the front. As its name suggests, the XAConnection interface represents connections. However, in this case, it represents a connection that can be used in a distributed transaction. Similarly, XADataSource and XAResource represent data sources and resources used in distributed transactions.

However, the client does not need to use or be aware of these classes. At the client level, the code will use the same interfaces that you have seen throughout this and the previous chapter: Connection, Statement, and ResultSet. In earlier examples, the code created a reference of type java.sql.Connection. However, since java.sql.Connection is an interface, the underlying object returned by the DataSource was a concrete class that implements the interface. It was probably an object of type com.pointbase.jdbc.jdbcConnection, but the client simply used a reference of type java.sql.Connection. Similarly, even though the underlying object may be some object that implements javax.sql.XAConnection, the client will still use a reference of type Connection. The client code used to communicate with the database will not look very different from code you have seen previously in this chapter. For example, the code to get a connection might look like this:

```
Context context = new InitialContext();
DataSource dataSource = context.lookup("jdbc/DataSource");
Connection connection = dataSource.getConnection();
```

If you look at the examples earlier in this chapter and in the previous chapter, you will see that the code used to get a regular data source is essentially the same code used by an application involved in a distributed transaction. Under the covers, the application server will likely use an XAConnection implementation to get the connection that is passed to the client, but in the client, the object will be referenced as a Connection. After getting the Connection, the code would use one of the Statement objects to send SQL to the data source. The difference between a nondistributed and a distributed transaction is in how the transaction is committed or rolled back.

Committing or Rolling Back Distributed Transactions

Since the transaction is being controlled by a transaction manager outside the client, any class involved in a distributed transaction is prohibited from calling any of these methods:

- commit()
- rollback()
- setSavepoint()
- setAutoCommit(true)

Committing or rolling back a transaction is entirely under the control of the transaction manager. All the client needs to do is start the transaction and end the transaction. After all the components involved in the transaction have completed and the client ends the transaction, the transaction manager will commit or roll back the transaction.

This commit (or rollback) is called a *two-phase commit.* It has two phases because the transaction manager must poll all the data sources (phase 1) before deciding to commit or roll back (phase 2). As each data source is polled, it throws an exception if it cannot commit its changes. If no data source throws an exception in the polling phase, the transaction manager instructs the data sources to commit their changes. Suppose you have two clients involved in a distributed transaction. Table 8-4 shows a timeline of the actions in the two-phase commit process.

Table 8-4. *The Two-Phase Commit Process*

Time	Description
T0	Both clients have called `close()` to signal that they have completed their work.
T1	Transaction manager calls the `prepare()` method of `XAResource`. There is an `XAResource` for each data source.
T2	If neither `XAResource` throws an exception, then each is ready to commit.
T3	Transaction manager calls the `commit()` method of each `XAResource`. This message is passed to each data source, which then commits.

Note that all the tasks in Table 8-4 would occur outside the client code. It is entirely handled by the transaction manager. If no data sources throw an exception in the polling phase, the transaction manager tells all the data sources to commit their changes. If any data source throws an exception, all the data sources are notified to roll back the changes.

Using the UserTransaction Interface

So, the client needs to start and end the transaction, and the transaction manager handles the commit or rollback. The client starts and ends the transaction using the `javax.transaction.UserTransaction` interface. The following are some of methods of this interface:

- `void begin()`: Signals the start of a transaction.
- `void commit()`: Tells the transaction manager to commit the transaction.
- `void rollback()`: Tells the transaction manager to roll back the transaction.
- `void setRollbackOnly()`: Tells the transaction manager that the only valid action for the transaction is rolled back.

Listing 8-9 shows a code snippet demonstrating how you would use `UserTransaction` in a JSP or Servlet.

Listing 8-9. *Distributed Transaction in a JSP or Servlet*

```
Context context = new InitialContext();
UserTransaction utx = (UserTransaction) ctx.lookup("tnx/SampleUserTransaction");
utx.begin();

DataSource dataSource = (DataSource) context.lookup("jdbc/SampleDataSource");
Connection conn = dataSource.getConnection();
Statement stmt = conn.createStatement();
//… perform inserts, updates, or deletes to database
conn.close();

utx.commit();
```

This code snippet is very minimal. It doesn't show the `try-catch-finally` blocks and does not have any error checking. However, the intent is to show the important steps for the client to perform in a distributed transaction.

You can see that the code starts by performing a lookup to get a `UserTransaction` method. Just as with the `DataSource` that we've been using in this chapter and the previous chapter, a `UserTransaction` object must be configured in the application server. Once it is configured, any client can access the `UserTransaction` by performing a lookup with the correct name. In the code snippet shown here, the name is `tnx/SampleUserTransaction`. After obtaining a `UserTransaction`, the client begins the transaction by calling the `begin()` method.

Following this is the JDBC code. You can see that it looks exactly like JDBC code in a normal transaction. The client looks up a `DataSource` and gets a connection from that. It then performs its work and closes the connection. Notice that the client does not call the connection `commit()` or `rollback()` methods. It simply closes the connection when all the work is complete.

To actually commit the work, the client calls the `UserTransaction` `commit()` method. If there had been some error, the client would call the `UserTransaction` `rollback()` method or `setRollbackOnly()` method to roll back the transaction.

In this section, you've seen how to deal with situations where you are updating more than a single table. These are situations where you might be making numerous changes to a database, and all the changes must succeed for the database to be in a consistent state at the end of the transaction.

Often, though, in a web application, your client application will be only one of many that are trying to perform a transaction simultaneously. In the few minutes it took to write this paragraph, during the busy shopping season of December, Amazon.com just processed 1,324 transactions. That's 1,324 transactions potentially touching the same rows in the database. (Well, that's more likely for the top-ranked sellers.) Using transaction control will ensure that all of the changes in a transaction are committed or rolled back, but it says nothing about what happens when two or more transactions are dealing with the same data. That situation requires locking.

Locking and Isolation

In any application where you must be concerned with two or more clients interacting with the database (and that includes almost every Java EE application with a database), you need to be concerned with the problem of *concurrency*—how do you allow multiple users to interact with the database and yet prevent their actions from interfering with each other?

Databases handle this problem through *isolation* and some type of concurrency control that usually involves *locking* the data in the database. However, different databases handle isolation and locking differently. You can tell the database what level of isolation to use, and thus have some control over isolation. Locking, however, is totally under the control of the database. There is no way for you, as a JDBC developer, to tell the database how to lock the data. The database chooses to lock or not, based on the SQL commands you are executing. For this reason, we will not discuss the locking behavior of any particular database.

■ **Note** Locking is highly database-dependent. You must check the database documentation to determine how your database handles concurrency control and locking.

Setting Isolation Levels

Isolation refers to the degree to which actions taken in one transaction can be seen by other transactions. At the highest level of isolation, any actions taken in a transaction cannot be seen by any other transaction. This applies to both reads and writes; that is, if one transaction reads or writes a row or rows of data, no other transaction is impacted by the first transaction. At the lowest level of isolation (as defined by the SQL specification), everything done in any transaction whether committed or not, can be seen by any other transaction.

The ANSI/ISO SQL92 standard identifies three different types of interactions between transactions, listed here from the lowest to the highest level of isolation:

- **Dirty reads:** Changes made in one transaction can be seen in other transactions, whether or not they are committed.
- **Nonrepeatable reads:** Updates to existing rows, deletions, and insertions made in one transaction are seen by other transactions as soon as they are committed. Thus, multiple queries that are the same may retrieve different data within a single transaction.
- **Phantom reads:** Insertions to tables made in one transaction are seen by other transactions as soon as they are committed.

The transaction level you select will depend on the business requirements of your application. The SQL specification identifies the following four isolation levels that indicate which interactions are allowed or prevented:

- **Read uncommitted:** Lowest level, allows all interactions
- **Read committed:** Prevents dirty reads
- **Repeatable read:** Prevents nonrepeatable reads and dirty reads
- **Serializable:** Highest level, which prevents all interactions

Most databases have a default level of read committed, and this will be sufficient for most applications. You can select a higher level with the `setTransactionIsolation()` method from the `Connection` interface:

```
void setTransactionIsolation(int level)
```

This method is called before a transaction begins. You pass it one of the following four arguments, which are defined as constants in the `Connection` interface:

- `TRANSACTION_READ_UNCOMMITTED`
- `TRANSACTION_READ_COMMITTED`
- `TRANSACTION_REPEATABLE_READ`
- `TRANSACTION_SERIALIZABLE`

Listing 8-10 shows an example of how you might set the transaction isolation level for a transaction that temporarily needs a higher level of transaction isolation.

Listing 8-10. *Changing the Transaction Level for a Transaction*

```
Connection conn = JdbcManager.getConnection();
//Save the current isolation level
int transactionLevel = conn.getTransactionIsolation();
//Assume that for business reasons, this transaction must occur at highest level
conn.setTransactionIsolation(Connection.TRANSACTION_SERIALIZABLE);
conn.setAutocommit(false);
//...now the code executes some SQL commands
conn.commit();
//Now reset to the default isolation level
conn.setTransactionIsolation(transactionLevel);
```

A database may not support all levels of isolation. Check your database documentation to see which levels are supported.

Using Pessimistic and Optimistic Locking

Even though you cannot control how the database locks data, the SQL commands you execute and how you execute them can have a big impact on how separate concurrent transactions in a database interfere, or don't interfere, with each other.

Let's look at what might happen if two transactions attempt to modify the same data when the application is not properly designed for concurrency and isolation. Suppose that you are working on an online reservation system for a small bed-and-breakfast. A guest can log on to the site, see which rooms are available, and make reservations for an available room. Table 8-5 shows a sequence of SQL commands that might occur.

Table 8-5. *A Sequence of SQL Commands for Reserving a Room*

Time	Transaction A	Transaction B
T0	Beth logs on to the web site and queries the application for available rooms. The system reads from the database and shows that the Pikes Peak room is available.	Jennifer logs on to the web site and performs the same query. Again, the Pikes Peak room is shown as available.
T1		Jennifer makes a reservation for the Pikes Peak room. The application updates the database to show that the Pikes Peak room is reserved for Jennifer.
T2	Beth makes a reservation for the Pikes Peak room. The application updates the database, this time setting the data to show that the room is reserved for Beth.	

You can see that at T1, the database has been placed into a particular state. In this state, a table has been updated to show certain information. However, because transaction A was operating on the database based on its original view of the data, when it updates the same table, the updates from transaction B are overwritten or lost. This is known as a *lost update.*

Either transaction could have prevented this problem by the proper use of locking. If pessimistic locking had been used, then the first transaction to perform the original query would have locked that data, preventing the other transaction from modifying the data. If optimistic locking had been used, then the second transaction to attempt to update the table would have been prevented from doing so because it would have found that the table had changed since the original query. In the next two sections, we'll look at each type of locking in more detail.

Pessimistic Locking

Pessimistic locking is usually used when there is a high likelihood that other transactions might want to change the table between a query and an update. For example, in an online concert ticketing system, if the user selects a particular seat, there is an implicit promise that the user can buy that seat before any other user can purchase it. The application should give that user the option of completing the purchase; only if the user declines to purchase the ticket should it be offered to anyone else. Thus, the application should somehow lock that data at the time the seat is selected. This is called pessimistic locking because we are pessimistic about the chances of no one wanting to buy the same tickets (or access the same data) between the times the user checks the availability of seats and purchases the tickets. To use pessimistic locking, you must tell the database that you intend to update some data.

In SQL, you indicate that you intend to update some data using the `FOR UPDATE` clause of your `SELECT` statement. When you use `FOR UPDATE` with `SELECT`, it signals to the database that it should lock the data against other updates until your transaction is complete. Remember, however, that every database will do this differently.

Let's look at an example based on the sequence of actions in Table 8-5. Recall that this involved a hypothetical bed-and-breakfast reservation system. For this example to work, you need a database table to hold room information. The SQL command to create this table and fill it with one row of data is shown in Listing 8-11.

Listing 8-11. *SQL Command to Create the Reserve Table*

```
create table reserve (
  roomid varchar(5),
  res_date date,
  res_flag boolean,
  res_name varchar(30));
insert into reserve (roomid, res_date, res_flag)
  values ('PIKE', '2005-04-15', false);
```

Start up and log in to the Sybase database (or whichever database you are using) and execute the commands in Listing 8-11. If you are using Sybase, log in to the `sample` database. Note that if you use another database, you may need to change the syntax of the `INSERT` command so that the date and Boolean data are properly inserted.

The `res_flag` field in the table indicates whether a room is reserved. A value of `false` means the room is not reserved. Listing 8-12 shows an HTML page that is used to start the example. In a real application, there would be web components to search for available rooms and display those rooms to the user. In this example, there is only one row of data in the table, so all the page does is accept the username, and then call a JSP to reserve the one available room.

Listing 8-12. *The SearchRooms HTML Page*

```
<html>
  <head>
    <title>Search For Available Rooms</title>
  </head>
  <body>
    <h1>Available Rooms</h1>
    <form method="POST" action="ReserveRoom.jsp">
    <p>User name: <input type="text" name="UserName" /></p>
    <p><input type="Submit" value="Reserve Room"/></p>
    </form>
  </body>
</html>
```

The HTML page in Listing 8-12 submits to the `ReserveRoom.jsp` shown in Listing 8-13. The JSP selects the one row from the database using the `FOR UPDATE` syntax mentioned earlier. This tells the database that it should lock the row. After that, the JSP updates the row with the username and sets the reservation flag to `true`.

Listing 8-13. *ReserveRoom.jsp*

```
<%@ page import="java.sql.*, com.apress.jdbc.*" %>
<html>
  <head>
    <title>Reserve Room</title>
  </head>
  <body>
    <h1>Reserve Room</h1>
<%
    Connection conn = null;
    PreparedStatement stmt = null;
    ResultSet rset = null;
    try {
      conn = JdbcManager.getConnection();
      conn.setAutoCommit(false);

      //Select the row for update
      String sqlsel = "select roomid, res_date, res_flag, res_name " +
        "from reserve where res_flag=false for update";
      stmt = conn.prepareStatement(sqlsel);

      rset = stmt.executeQuery();
      if (rset.next()) {
        String roomId = rset.getString("roomid");
        Date date = rset.getDate("res_date");
        String name = request.getParameter("UserName");

        String sqlupd = "update reserve set res_flag=true, res_name=? " +
          "where roomid=? and res_date=?";
        stmt = conn.prepareStatement(sqlupd);
        stmt.setString(1, name);
        stmt.setString(2, roomId);
        stmt.setDate(3, date);

        try { Thread.sleep(5000); } catch (Exception ignored) {}
        int result = stmt.executeUpdate();
        conn.commit();
        out.write("Room reserved");
      } else {
        out.write("No available rooms");
      }
    } catch (SQLException e) {
%>
      <%= e.getMessage() %>
```

```
<%
      e.printStackTrace();
      conn.rollback();
    } finally {
      JdbcManager.close(rset);
      JdbcManager.close(stmt);
      JdbcManager.close(conn);
    }
%>
  </body>
</html>
```

This JSP uses the `JdbcManager` class to get a connection to the database, so when you deploy the application, you will need to create the `DataSource` as you have done for the other JDBC examples. The connection is set to autocommit disabled so that you can control the transaction.

After deploying the application, open two browser windows and navigate to the `SearchRooms.html` page (see Figure 8-10 for one such window). In each window, enter a different name, but do not click the Reserve Room button. After you have entered a name in both windows, click the Reserve Room button in each window.

Figure 8-10. *The SearchRooms.html page with a username entered*

When you click each Reserve Room button, a thread is created in the application server to service each request. When you click the first button, that page submits the username to the `ReserveRoom.jsp`, which queries the database for the row of data with the reserve flag set to `false`.

The `FOR UPDATE` clause tells the database that the transaction intends to update the table, and that the database should perform locking to ensure that no other transaction can modify the data until the first transaction is complete. However, notice that there is no way to tell the database how to lock the data. This is one of the features of a declarative language like SQL. You instruct the database to execute a command, such as `SELECT`, `INSERT`, or `UPDATE`, and the database determines how to execute the command.

After the first thread queries the table, the code saves the value of the roomid and res_date columns. Before executing the update, the code executes a Thread.sleep() method. This simulates the real-world behavior of some lag in time between when a user queries some data and submits new data for updating the database. It also provides a time gap in which the second thread can execute.

Like the first thread, the second thread executes a query that looks for rooms in the database that have not yet been reserved. If a row is found, the second thread attempts to reserve the room. However, the second thread's query is blocked, apparently because the database has locked the reserve table for update by the first thread.

After five seconds, the first thread wakes, and continues executing. The code performs a SQL UPDATE to reserve the room, and then commits the transaction. As Figure 8-11 shows, when the first thread completes, the row has been updated and the room reserved.

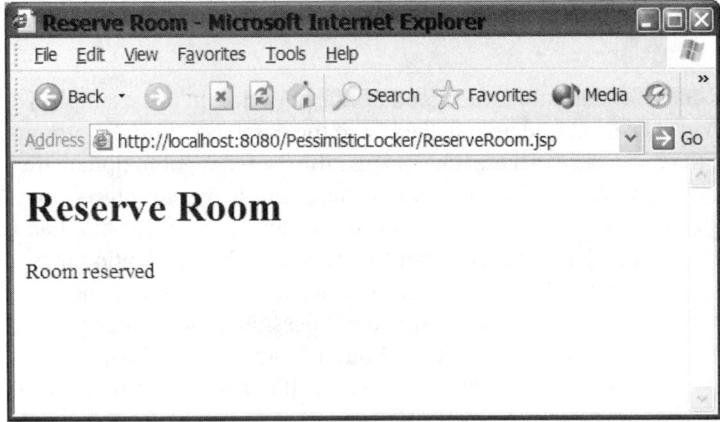

Figure 8-11. *The room has been reserved by the first thread to query the database.*

When the row is unlocked, the second thread's query then finds no rooms available. Figure 8-12 shows the page displayed for this thread. Thus, by using the FOR UPDATE syntax of the SELECT command, the first thread was able to ensure that its update to the database was not overwritten by some other thread. Using pessimistic locking has prevented a lost update.

To show that this really does prevent a lost update, you could modify the JSP to remove FOR UPDATE from the SQL SELECT command. After making this change and redeploying the JSP, submit two different usernames as you did previously. You will find that both submissions are able to reserve the room. After the first thread updates the table, the second thread overwrites the changes, causing a lost update.

However, there is one big disadvantage to pessimistic locking: because of the way Sybase locks the database, the second query thread is blocked until the first thread completes the update. For example, if it took two minutes to complete the update, the second thread would not complete for the same two minutes. This means that the user would be looking at an empty web browser with the progress icon spinning around for two minutes.

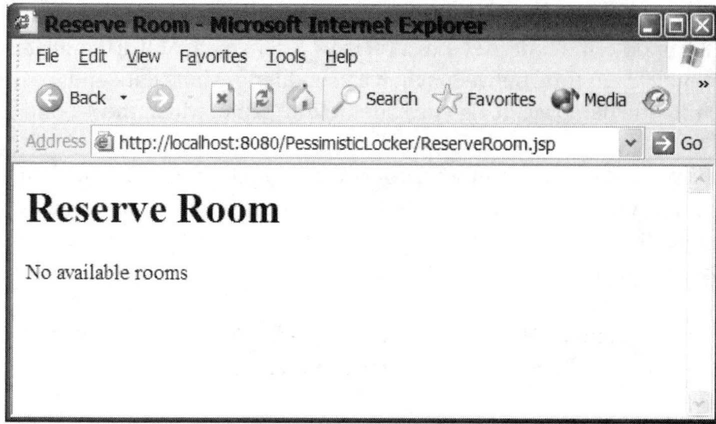

Figure 8-12. *No unreserved rooms are found by the second thread.*

As you can guess, this does not make for a very good user experience. In this example, we allowed one transaction to get access to and update data from the database. With the proper use of pessimistic locking, the first user to access the data was the user that got to update the data. However, that came at a cost. With the particular way this example was structured, any other user would be completely prevented from any access to the table. Suppose user A had walked away from her computer for 15 minutes, or even 15 hours. User B's application may have been frozen for that entire length of time. That's a heavy price to pay to ensure a good user experience (for user A, not user B). Thus, if you are going to use pessimistic locking to prevent lost updates, you need to be certain that there will be a minimal delay between the query and the update, so that the database does not hold a lock for too long. It's very important to stress, though, that other situations or other databases may not have prevented user B from querying the table. That's why it's so important for you to understand how your database handles this situation.

Note Locking is very dependent on the database. This example may or may not work with other databases. Even if it does work with different databases, the behavior you see may be different. Consult the database documentation to find out how locking works, so that you understand how the database deals with multiple users in the database and how to control their interactions

---

Optimistic Locking

Optimistic locking is usually used when there is a low likelihood that other transactions might want to change the table between a query and an update. In fact, unlike pessimistic locking, it really does not involve locking at all, but it still prevents the problem of lost updates. It is called *optimistic* because we are optimistic about the chances of no one wanting to access the same data (or reserve the same room) between the time the user queries the data and attempts to update the data.

To implement optimistic locking in your code, when your code performs a query, it keeps a local copy of all the data it retrieved. It then presents this data to the user for him to modify. Then when your code issues the UPDATE statement, it includes a WHERE clause in the SQL command, which checks that the data in the table still matches the data originally retrieved. If it does not, that means some other user has modified the data between your query and your update. Your UPDATE command fails, but the other user's update is not lost.

Listing 8-14 shows a modified version of the ReserveRoom.jsp that uses optimistic locking. This code is almost identical to the code in Listing 8-13. There are only two significant changes to the JSP, and two minor changes:

- The SQL SELECT command has been modified to remove FOR UPDATE:

  ```
  String sqlsel = "select roomid, res_date, res_flag, res_name " +
    "from reserve where res_flag=false";
  ```

- The SQL UPDATE command has been modified to include another condition in the WHERE clause:

  ```
  String sqlupd = "update reserve set res_flag=true, res_name=? " +
    "where roomid=? and res_date=? and res_flag=false";
  ```

- There is an additional line of code after the query to show that both queries do find the row of data for the available room:

  ```
  out.write("Found a room");
  ```

- There is the addition of code after the UPDATE command to check the return value of the executeUpdate() method:

  ```
  if (result == 1) {
    out.write("Room reserved");
  } else {
    out.write("Could not reserve room");
  }
  ```

Listing 8-14. *ReserveRoom.jsp Using Optimistic Locking*

```
<%@ page import="java.sql.*, com.apress.jdbc.*" %>
<html>
  <head>
    <title>Reserve Room</title>
  </head>
  <body>
    <h1>Reserve Room</h1>
<%
    Connection conn = null;
    PreparedStatement stmt = null;
    ResultSet rset = null;
    try {
      conn = JdbcManager.getConnection();
      conn.setAutoCommit(false);
```

```
        //Select the row for update
        String sqlsel = "select roomid, res_date, res_flag, res_name " +
          "from reserve where res_flag=false";
        stmt = conn.prepareStatement(sqlsel);

        rset = stmt.executeQuery();
        if (rset.next()) {
          out.write("Found a room");
          String roomId = rset.getString("roomid");
          Date date = rset.getDate("res_date");
          String name = request.getParameter("UserName");

          String sqlupd = "update reserve set res_flag=true, res_name=? " +
            "where roomid=? and res_date=? and res_flag=false";
          stmt = conn.prepareStatement(sqlupd);
          stmt.setString(1, name);
          stmt.setString(2, roomId);
          stmt.setDate(3, date);

          try { Thread.sleep(5000); } catch (Exception ignored) {}
          int result = stmt.executeUpdate();
          conn.commit();
          if (result == 1) {
            out.write("Room reserved");
          } else {
            out.write("Could not reserve room");
          }
        } else {
          out.write("No available rooms");
        }
      } catch (SQLException e) {
%>
        <%= e.getMessage() %>
<%
        e.printStackTrace();
        conn.rollback();
      } finally {
        JdbcManager.close(rset);
        JdbcManager.close(stmt);
        JdbcManager.close(conn);
      }
%>
  </body>
</html>
```

In this code, the JSP performs a query on the table, but does not use the `FOR UPDATE` syntax. This means that when each thread enters the JSP, both threads will find a room available for reservation. This is demonstrated by the line of code that prints "Found a room" after the `SELECT` query.

However, even though the `SELECT` command found a room for both threads, both threads will not be able to reserve the room. The additional condition in the `UPDATE` command means that the update will check the data in the table before attempting to update it. If the data is still the same as retrieved earlier by the `SELECT` command, then the data has not been updated and the thread can complete its update. If, however, another thread has updated the row, the second thread's `UPDATE` command will fail because the command will not be able to find a row that matches all the conditions in the `WHERE` clause.

This JSP accesses the same table as in the pessimistic locking example. You can find the code to create and populate the table in Listing 8-11. If you already ran the pessimistic locking example, all you need do is delete the old data from the table using this command:

```
delete from reserve;
```

Then you can repopulate the table using the `INSERT` command shown in Listing 8-11.

Deploy this JSP along with the `SearchRooms.html` page (Listing 8-12) and the `JdbcManager` class (Listing 7-3 and Listing 7-8). After deploying, remember to create a `DataSource` for the database connection, as described in Chapter 7.

Then, just as in the pessimistic locking example, open two browser windows to the `SearchRoom.html` page and enter a different name in each form. After you have entered names in both forms, click the Reserve Room button in each window. You will see that the first thread will find a room, and be able to reserve the room. The second thread will also find an available room, but it will not be able to reserve the room, as shown in Figure 8-13. This occurs because after the first thread has updated the row, the `UPDATE` command can no longer find a row that matches the row found by the `SELECT` command.

Figure 8-13. *The second thread is unable to reserve the room, even though it found the available room.*

This shows how proper use of optimistic locking can prevent lost updates. The first thread was able to update the table, and the second thread was prevented from overwriting the changes.

In this example, a single JSP handled both requests. Because both threads executed the same `sleep`, the first thread was able to execute the `UPDATE` before the second thread. However, in the real world, this is not always the case. In a real-world application, the query will most likely execute in a different request than the `UPDATE`. Then it will not be the order of queries that determines who gets to make the update; rather, it will be the client that makes the update request first that gets to update the table.

For a lost update to occur, all that needs to happen is for two or more users to query and attempt to change the same data: one user reads the data, a second user updates the data, the first user then attempts to update his view of the data, which no longer matches what is in the database. Without optimistic locking, the first update would be overwritten by the second update.

Notice also the differences between pessimistic locking and optimistic locking. With pessimistic locking, the first user to query the data gets to commit his changes. With optimistic locking, the first user to update the table gets to commit his changes. Pessimistic locking works better from the user's point of view. With optimistic locking, the user may expend significant effort to input all the changes he wants, only to be told that the update failed when he tries to submit the data. On the other hand, pessimistic locking ties up a database resource, and depending on the database, can prevent other users from working with the database. Which method you choose will depend on the business rules of your application and the type of locking supported by your database.

Summary

In this chapter, we've looked at some advanced topics in JDBC and how to use JDBC in a Java EE environment. If you are working in a real-world Java EE application, you will almost certainly find that you will be using at least some of the concepts covered in this chapter.

After finishing this chapter, you should know:

- `PreparedStatement` objects are used to send SQL commands to the database. `PreparedStatement` objects are useful when you are sending many SQL commands to the database, and only the data values are changing. Because the database caches the SQL command, `PreparedStatement` objects can be more efficient that `Statement` objects. Prepared statements are also useful when you need to insert nonprimitive data into a table. Prepared statements make it easy to insert dates, nulls, strings, and other objects, because the driver formats the data for you.

- `CallableStatement` objects are used to call stored procedures and functions (also called *sprocs*) in a database. Stored procedures have many advantages, so if your system contains sprocs, you should consider using them rather than re-creating their behavior in JDBC.

- Transactions are used to ensure that databases move from one consistent state to another. Properly using transactions can ensure that all the changes your code makes succeed or are all rolled back.

- A Java EE application needs to deal with problems of isolation and locking. Setting the proper isolation level can prevent one transaction from seeing changes made to the database by other transactions. Preventing two users from changing the same data such that one update is lost is usually done through pessimistic or optimistic locking.

If you find yourself deeply into database programming, you should explore some of the more advanced books that focus on the subject of databases and JDBC programming. Consider reading *Java Persistence for Relational Databases*, by Richard Sperko (Apress, 2003; ISBN 1-59059-071-6).

Exercises

1. If your database does support stored procedures, find an existing stored procedure, or create one of your own, and write JDBC code that calls the stored procedures.
2. Create a database table containing some number of columns of various types. Create a program that inserts to the table using a `Statement` and a `PreparedStatement`. Make timing measurements to determine the performance difference between the two.
3. If your database has multiple driver types (for example, you can use either a Type 2 or a Type 4), create a database table and perform various insertions, deletions, and updates to the rows. Make timing measurements to determine if one driver has a performance advantage.
4. Create a program that makes multiple insertions into a database table. Use the default autocommit setting and measure the performance of inserting data this way. Now set the autocommit setting to `false` and commit only after all data has been inserted. Measure the performance of this and compare it to autocommitting every insertion.

CHAPTER 9

EJB Fundamentals and Session Beans

So far, we've discussed the user interface, business logic, and database connection aspects of developing Java EE applications. The primary mechanism discussed to this point for expressing business logic has been JavaBeans accessed from JSP and Servlet code. Java EE has a powerful facility dedicated to expressing the business logic of an application and for accessing a database using a JavaBeans-like concept. That facility is *Enterprise JavaBeans*, known as EJBs for short.

In this chapter, we'll begin exploring the world of EJBs, which is a very important capability of the Java EE platform. EJBs provide infrastructure for developing and deploying mission-critical, enterprise applications. We'll first look at some EJB fundamentals, and then focus on one type of EJB: the session bean.

In this chapter, you will learn the following:

- The benefits of using EJBs
- The three kinds of EJBs: session, entity, and message-driven beans
- The makeup of session beans
- How to develop session beans
- Differences between stateful and stateless session beans

Understanding EJBs

Application architectures often consist of several tiers that each has its own responsibilities. One such architecture that consists of three tiers is illustrated in the Unified Modeling Language (UML) diagram shown in Figure 9-1.

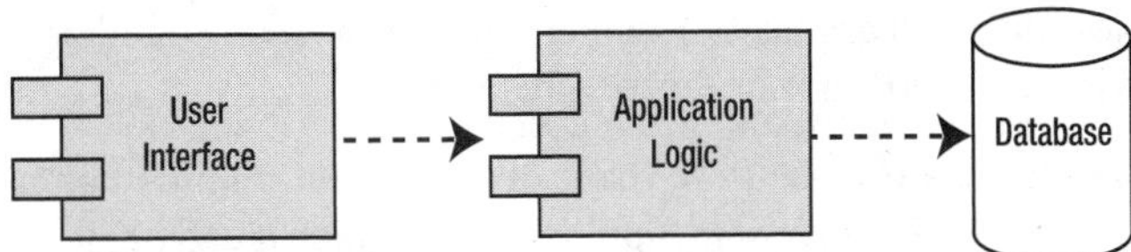

Figure 9-1. *The classic model of a multitiered, or layered, architecture*

The two elements on the left side of the diagram in Figure 9-1 are called *components* in the UML notation. Components represent software modules. The diagram describes what is called a *multitiered*, or *layered*, architecture. Multitiered architectures have many advantages, not the least of which is the ability to change any one of the layers without affecting all of the other layers. This is in contrast to a *single-tier* architecture, within which all aspects of the program design coexist in a single element. Changes or actions that affect one portion of the single-tier element also potentially affect the other members of that element.

Consider the three-layer architecture shown in Figure 9-1, consisting of user interface, application logic, and database layers. If the database layer is changed, only the application logic layer is affected. The application logic layer shields the user interface layer from changes to the database layer. This facilitates ongoing maintenance of the application, and also increases the application's ability to incorporate new technologies in its layers.

These layers provide an excellent model of how EJBs fit into your overall program design. EJBs provide an application logic layer and a JavaBeans-like abstraction of the database layer. The application logic layer is also known as the *middle tier*.

■ **Note** JavaBeans and Enterprise JavaBeans are two different things, but because of their similarities (and for marketing reasons), they share a common name. JavaBeans are components built in Java that can be used on any tier in an application. They are often thought of in relationship to Servlets, and as GUI components. Enterprise JavaBeans are special, server-based components, used for building the business logic and data-access functionality of an application.

Why Use EJBs?

Not too long ago, when system developers wanted to create an enterprise application, they would often start by "rolling their own" (or purchasing a proprietary) application server to support the functionality of the application logic layer. Some of the features of an application server include the following:

- **Client communication:** The client, which is often a user interface, must be able to call the methods of objects on the application server via agreed-upon protocols.
- **Session state management:** You'll recall our discussions on this topic in the context of JSP and Servlet development back in Chapter 6.
- **Transaction management:** Some operations, for example when updating data, must occur as a unit of work. If one update fails, they all should fail. Transactions were discussed in Chapter 8.
- **Database connection management:** An application server must connect to a database, often using pools of database connections for optimizing resources.
- **User authentication and role-based authorization:** Users of an application must often log in for security purposes. The functionality of an application to which a user is allowed access is often based on the role associated with a user ID.

- **Asynchronous messaging:** Applications often need to communicate with other systems in an asynchronous manner; that is, without waiting for the other system to respond. This requires an underlying messaging system that provides guaranteed delivery of these asynchronous messages.
- **Application server administration:** Application servers must be administered. For example, they need to be monitored and tuned.

The EJB Specification

The EJB specification defines a common architecture, which has prompted several vendors to build application servers that comply with this specification. Now developers can get off-the-shelf application servers that comply with a common standard, benefiting from the competition (in areas such as price, features, and performance) among those vendors.

Some of the more common commercial EJB application servers are WebLogic (BEA), Sun ONE (Sun), OC4J containers for Oracle Database 10g, and WebSphere (IBM). There are also some very good open-source entries in this market such as JBoss and JOnAS. The JBoss application server was used to develop, deploy, and test all the examples throughout the book. Sun also provides an open source Reference Implementation (Java EE SDK) of the Java EE 5 and EJB 3.0 specifications that developers can use to develop and test applications for compliance with those specifications. (The Reference Implementation may not, however, be used to deploy production systems.) Currently under development, the reference implementation is codenamed "Glassfish" and is available at `https://glassfish.dev.java.net/`. The platform provides a basic EJB 3.0 test platform; more details can be found on the website and in the related discussion forums. These application servers, in conjunction with the capabilities defined in the EJB specification, support all of the features listed here and many more.

The EJB specification was created by experienced members of the development community; such a body is called an *expert group*. In the EJB specification's expert group are members from such organizations as the JBoss group, Oracle, and Google. Thanks to them, we now have a standard, specifications-based way to develop and deploy enterprise-class systems. We are approaching the Java dream of developing an application that can run on any vendor platform as-is. This is in contrast to the vendor-specific way we used to develop, where each server had its own way of doing things, and where the developer was locked into the chosen platform once the first line of code was written!

The version of the EJB specification that is included with the Java EE 5.0 recommendation is 3.0, and this is the version we refer to in this book when discussing EJBs. The EJB 3.0 specification has added many improvements to its predecessor (version 2.1, which was a part of the J2EE 1.4 recommendation), including metadata annotations to simplify deployment concerns, a higher degree of control over bean persistence, and a much more simplified (but no less powerful) programming model for developing EJBs. For more information about the EJB specification, visit the `http://java.sun.com/products/ejb/docs.html` web site.

If your eyes glazed over when reading all this, don't worry. The next few chapters will tell you how to use all those cool features!

The Three Kinds of EJBs

There are actually three kinds of EJBs: session beans, entity beans, and message-driven beans. Here, we will present a brief introduction to each type of bean. The balance of this chapter will then focus on session beans.

■ **Note** When referring to EJBs in the general sense in this book, we'll use the term *EJBs*, *enterprise beans*, or simply *beans*.

Session Beans

One way to think about the application logic layer (middle tier) in the sample architecture shown in Figure 9-1 is as a set of objects that, together, implement the business logic of an application. Session beans are the construct in EJBs designed for this purpose. As shown in Figure 9-2, there may be multiple session beans in an application. Each handles a subset of the application's business logic.

A session bean tends to be responsible for a group of related functionality. For example, an application for an educational institution might have a session bean whose methods contain logic for handling student records. Another session bean might contain logic that maintains the lists of courses and programs available at that institution.

There are two types of session bean, which are defined by their use in a client interaction:

- **Stateless:** These beans do not declare any instance (class-level) variables, so that the methods contained within can act only on any local parameters. There is no way to maintain state across method calls.
- **Stateful:** These beans can hold client state across method invocations. This is possible with the use of instance variables declared in the class definition. The client will then set the values for these variables and use these values in other method calls.

There may be more work involved for the server to share stateful session beans than is required to share stateless beans. Storing the state of an EJB is a very resource-intensive process, so an application that uses stateful beans may not be easily scalable. Stateless session beans provide excellent scalability, because the EJB container does not need to keep track of their state across method calls. You'll see how to develop both stateless and stateful session beans later in this chapter.

All EJBs, session beans included, operate within the context of an EJB server, as shown in Figure 9-2. An EJB server contains constructs known as EJB containers, which are responsible for providing an operating environment for managing and providing services to the EJBs that are running within it.

In a typical scenario, the user interface (UI) of an application calls the methods of the session beans as it requires the functionality that they provide. Session beans can call other session beans and entity beans. Figure 9-2 illustrates typical interactions between the user interface, session beans, entity beans, and the database.

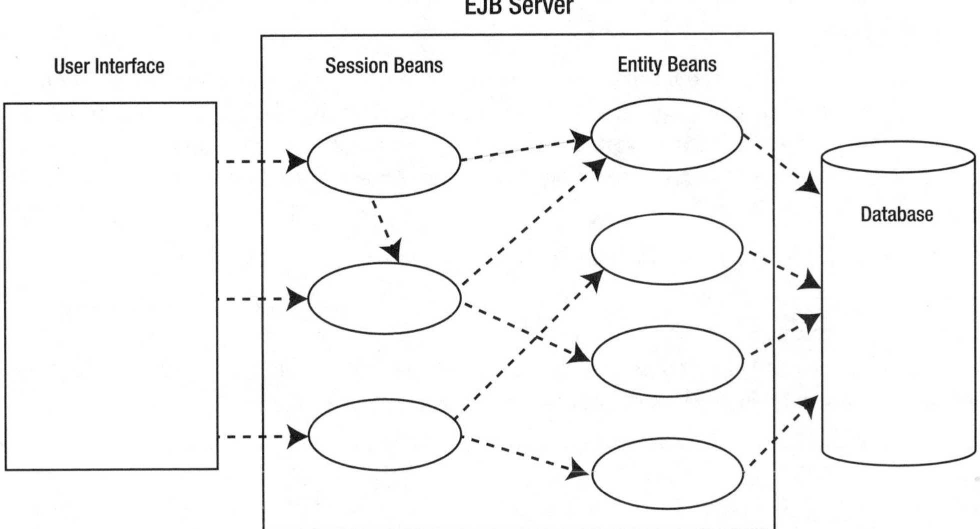

Figure 9-2. *Session and entity beans in an application*

Entity Beans

Before object orientation became popular, programs were usually written in procedural languages and often employed relational databases to hold the data. Because of the strengths and maturity of relational database technology, it is now often advantageous to develop object-oriented applications that use relational databases. The problem with this approach is that there is an inherent difference between object-oriented and relational database technologies, making it less than natural for them to coexist in one application. The use of entity beans is one way to get the best of both of these worlds, for the following reasons:

- Entity beans are objects, and they can be designed using object-oriented principles and used in applications as objects.
- The data in these entity bean objects are persisted in some data store, usually relational databases. All of the benefits of relational technologies—including maturity of products, speed, reliability, ability to recover, and ease of querying—can be leveraged.

In a typical EJB scenario, when a session bean needs to access data, it calls the methods of an entity bean. Entity beans represent the persistent data in an EJB application. For example, an application for an educational institution might have an entity bean named `Student` that has one instance for every student that is enrolled in an institution. Entity beans, often backed by a relational database, read and write to tables in the database. Because of this, they provide an object-oriented abstraction to some information store.

As shown in Figure 9-2, it is a good practice to call only session beans directly from the client, and to let the session beans call the entity beans. Here are some reasons for this:

- This practice doesn't circumvent the business logic contained in the session beans. Calling entity beans directly tends to push the business logic into the UI logic, which is usually a bad thing.

- The UI doesn't need to be as dependent on changes to the entity beans. The UI is shielded from these changes by the session beans.
- In order for a client to interact with a bean on the EJB server, there must be a remote reference to the bean, which takes resources. There tends to be far more (orders of magnitude) entity bean instances in an application than session bean instances. Restricting client access to session beans conserves server and network resources considerably.

We will cover entity beans in detail in the next chapter.

■ **Note** Developing entity beans does not require a business interface; in fact, message-driven beans are the only EJBs that must implement some business interface.

Message-Driven Beans

When an EJB-based application needs to receive asynchronous messages from other systems, it can leverage the power and convenience of message-driven beans. Asynchronous messages between systems can be analogous to the events that are fired from a UI component to an event handler in the same JVM. For example, in the business-to-business (B2B) domain, a wholesaler could have an EJB application that uses message-driven beans to listen for purchase orders issued electronically from retailers. We'll discuss message-driven beans in more detail in Chapter 13.

Which Type of EJB Should You Use?

So, how do you decide whether a given EJB should be a session bean, entity bean, or a message-driven-bean? Here are some guidelines for deciding:

- Session beans are great at implementing business logic, processes, and workflow. For example, a `StockTrader` bean with `buy()` and `sell()` methods, among others, would be a good fit for a session bean.
- Entity beans are the persistent data objects in an EJB application. In a stock trading application, a `Stock` bean with `setPrice()` and `getPrice()` methods would be an appropriate use of an entity bean. The `buy()` method of the previously mentioned `StockTrader` session bean would interact with instances of the `Stock` entity bean by calling their `getPrice()` methods, for example.
- Message-driven beans are used for the special purpose of receiving asynchronous messages from other systems, like a wholesaler application that listens for purchase orders.

Now that we've covered some basics concerning the three types of EJBs, we'll use the rest of this chapter to take a closer look at the first type mentioned: session beans.

The Anatomy of a Session Bean

Every session bean requires the presence of a bean interface and a bean class. A bean interface is the mechanism by which client code will interact with the bean internals, while the bean class is the implementation of those internals, as illustrated in Figure 9-3.

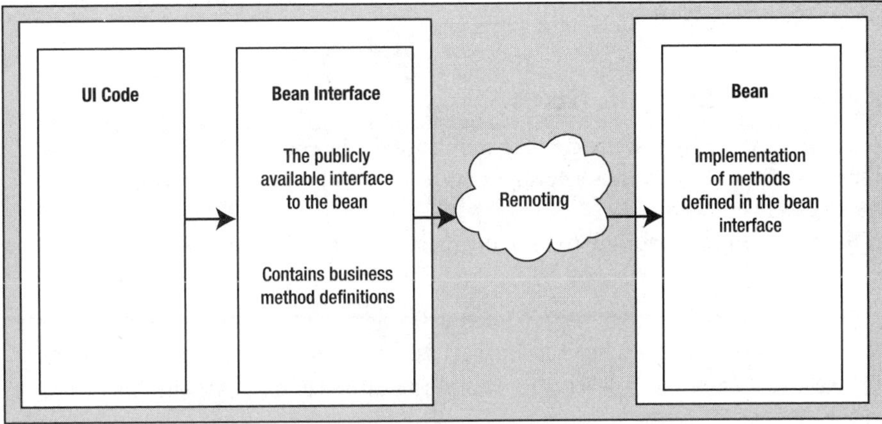

Figure 9-3. *Elements of a session bean*

The implementation of the business logic of a session bean is located in its bean class. The bean class of the session bean must either implement the `javax.ejb.SessionBean` interface or prefix its class definition with the metadata descriptor `@Stateless`.

■ **Note** *Metadata* is a new addition to the Java language with the introduction of J2SE 5.0. It effectively allows developers to elaborate on class definitions, adding further descriptive and behavioral information to the generation of the class file. The EJB 3.0 specification has used this facility to describe the majority of its workings. To learn more about this new addition to the Java language, read the official specification at `http://jcp.org/en/jsr/detail?id=175`.

The bean interface (or business interface, as some refer to it) that exposes the internals of the EJB to calling code may be implemented by the developer, or it can be generated automatically. The compiler will create a bean interface for you that is a map of the public methods available in the bean class.

As a naming convention for this book, we'll append the word `Bean` to the name of a bean to indicate that it is a bean class. For example, a session bean with the name `StockTrader` would have a bean class named `StockTraderBean`.

Developing Session Beans

It is now time to put all this theory into practice. In this section, we're going to develop our first session bean in an example that's on par with the traditional "Hello World!" sample program.

First, we'll walk through the bean-creation code in a good bit of detail, reinforcing concepts we just covered and introducing new ones. Then we'll explain how to compile the example. For this, we'll use the Java compiler that comes with the Java 2 SDK Standard Edition 5.0 (J2SE SDK 1.5). Finally, we'll deploy the example in JBoss.

Using a Stateless Session Bean

Since this is the first EJB example, we're going to walk through the code now and then run it later. There are three Java source files for this example: `SimpleSession.java`, `SimpleSessionBean.java`, and `SimpleSessionClient.java`.

Listing 9-1 shows the code for the remote business interface, `SimpleSession.java`.

■ **Note** The term *remote business interface* signifies that this interface is accessed and called by "remote" clients. Don't jump to conclusions! We'll define what exactly is meant by that statement when we explain this code later on in the chapter.

Listing 9-1. *SimpleSession.java*

```
package beans;

import javax.ejb.Remote;

@Remote
public interface SimpleSession
{
  public String getEchoString(String clientString);
}
```

Listing 9-2 shows the code for the actual bean implementation, `SimpleSessionBean.java`.

Listing 9-2. *SimpleSessionBean.java*

```
package beans;

import javax.ejb.Stateless;

@Stateless
public class SimpleSessionBean implements SimpleSession {
  public String getEchoString(String clientString) {
    return clientString + " - from session bean";
  }
}
```

Finally, Listing 9-3 shows the client code to test the session bean.

Listing 9-3. *SimpleSessionClient.java*

```
package client;

import beans.SimpleSession;
import javax.naming.InitialContext;

public class SimpleSessionClient {
  public static void main(String[] args) throws Exception
  {
    InitialContext ctx = new InitialContext();
    SimpleSession simpleSession
      = (SimpleSession) ctx.lookup(SimpleSession.class.getName());
    for (int i = 0; i < args.length; i++) {
      String returnedString = simpleSession.getEchoString(args[i]);
      System.out.println("sent string: " + args[i] +
                         ", received string: " + returnedString);
    }
  }
}
```

Organize the files in a directory called `SimpleSessionApp`, as shown in Figure 9-4.

Figure 9-4. *The structure of the sample session bean files*

Compiling the Simple Session Bean Application

After you've created and organized the sample session bean files as just described, follow these steps to compile the application:

1. Open a command prompt in the `SimpleSessionApp` directory.

2. Compile the classes, ensuring that the `CLASSPATH` is set to contain all the necessary JBoss libraries. These libraries contain all of the EJB functionality needed to make your code interact with the application server, so it is extremely important that you get this step right. At the command line, type the following (this should all be on one line!):

```
> set CLASSPATH=.;C:\jboss\lib\concurrent.jar; ➥
C:\jboss\lib\jboss-common.jar; ➥
c:\jboss\client\jboss-j2ee.jar;➥
c:\jboss\lib\commons-httpclient.jar;➥
C:\jboss\server\all\lib\jboss.jar; ➥
C:\jboss\server\all\lib\jboss-remoting.jar; ➥
C:\jboss\server\all\lib\jboss-transaction.jar;➥
C:\jboss\server\all\lib\jnpserver.jar; ➥
C:\jboss\server\all\deploy\ejb3.deployer\jboss-ejb3.jar; ➥
C:\jboss\server\all\deploy\ejb3.deployer\jboss-ejb3x.jar; ➥
C:\jboss\server\all\deploy\jboss-aop.deployer\➥
jboss-aop.jar; ➥
C:\jboss\server\all\deploy\jboss-aop.deployer\➥
jboss-aspect-library.jar
```

3. Within the SimpleSessionApp directory where the client and beans directories are located, execute the following commands from the command prompt:

```
> javac -d . client/*.java
> javac -d . beans/*.java
```

The -d option tells the Java compiler to place the class files in subdirectories matching their package structure, subordinate to the given directory. In this case, the given directory is the current directory, signified by the period. As a result, the Java class files should end up in the same directories as the source files.

Deploying the Simple Session Bean Application

Now we need to start the JBoss Server using the procedure described in Chapter 2. Once the JBoss Server is up and running, you can deploy your class files. In order to deploy your class files, you need to package your different application components together in a compressed JAR file. Make the extension of this file .ejb3, so that JBoss can deploy it.

To create the application EJB3 file, open a command prompt in the same directory that SimpleSessionApp resides in and type in the following command:

```
>jar cf SimpleSessionApp.ejb3 beans\*.java
```

Now copy the resulting EJB3 file to the %JBOSS_HOME%/server/all/deploy directory. If your JBoss installation is in C:\JBoss, for example, copy the file to C:\JBoss\server\all\deploy.

JBoss will automatically detect and deploy your code for you. The directory structure should now have the files shown in Figure 9-5.

Now for the last step: running your new bean!

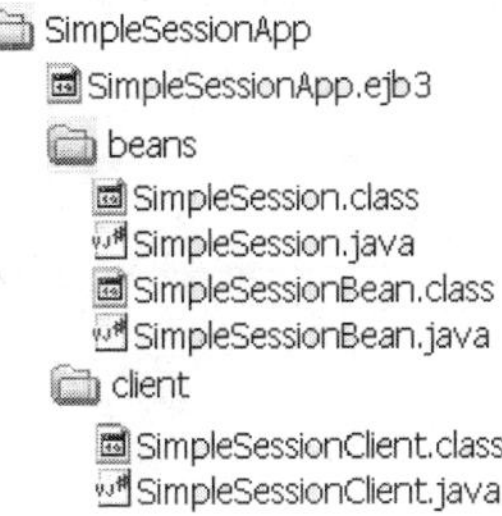

Figure 9-5. *Structure of the deployed session bean application*

Running the Simple Session Bean Application

To run the sample client, set the CLASSPATH to the same value you did earlier to compile the application.

On a default Java EE 5 SDK Windows installation, ensure the CLASSPATH is set correctly by using the following command:

```
> set CLASSPATH=.;C:\jboss\lib\concurrent.jar;➥
C:\jboss\lib\jboss-common.jar;➥
C:\jboss\server\all\lib\jboss.jar;➥
C:\jboss\server\all\lib\jboss-remoting.jar;➥
C:\jboss\server\all\lib\jboss-transaction.jar;➥
C:\jboss\server\all\lib\jnpserver.jar;➥
C:\jboss\server\all\deploy\ejb3.deployer\jboss-ejb3.jar;➥
C:\jboss\server\all\deploy\ejb3.deployer\jboss-ejb3x.jar;➥
C:\jboss\server\all\deploy\jboss-aop.deployer\jboss-aop.jar;➥
C:\jboss\server\all\deploy\jboss-aop.deployer\➥
jboss-aspect-library.jar
```

Next, with SimpleSessionApp as the current directory, execute the following command from the command prompt (remember that this is all one line):

```
> java➥
-Djava.naming.factory.initial=➥
org.jnp.interfaces.NamingContextFactory➥
-Djava.naming.factory.url.pkgs=➥
org.jboss.naming:org.jnp.interfaces ➥
-Djava.naming.provider.url=➥
localhost client.SimpleSessionClient ➥
Now is the time for all good men
```

When you run the SimpleSession client program, it will produce the following output:

```
sent string: Now, received string: Now
sent string: is, received string: is
sent string: the, received string: the
sent string: time, received string: time
sent string: for, received string: for
sent string: all, received string: all
sent string: good, received string: good
sent string: men, received string: men
```

It may not seem very practical, but it makes you unbelievably popular at parties.

Reviewing the Stateless Session Bean Source Code

We have three Java source files to walk through here. We'll start with the client and work our way back up to the session bean interface and class.

The main() method of the SimpleSession class kicks things off by using the JNDI to help us get a reference to the business interface of the session bean. JNDI provides a common interface to directory services (This includes LDAP, CORBA providers, and in this case, your local file-system). The directory that we're dealing with here is internal to the EJB server and holds the reference to the business interface of our session bean. That reference is accessed by providing the JNDI lookup with the bean interface's qualified name. We could also specify the bean's location by absolute JNDI pathname, passing the lookup() function the string literal ejb/beans.SimpleSession.

Once the lookup() function has returned an object for our use, we immediately cast it to the base interface SimpleSession. Pay special attention to our decision to acquire a JNDI reference by using the SimpleSession class name. By requesting a JNDI reference for an interface annotated by the @Remote metadata descriptor, we have implicitly stated the method that we wish to use to communicate with the bean—pretty cool, huh?

```
InitialContext ctx = new InitialContext();
    SimpleSession simpleSession
      = (SimpleSession) ctx.lookup(SimpleSession.class.getName());
```

The client code for this example, which follows, demonstrates that we can pass an argument to a method of a session bean that exists on the server, operate on the argument in the method, and return a different value to the client. More specifically, the code loops through the arguments that were passed to the client's main() method via the command line, and passes them one at a time to the getEchoString() method of the session bean class. This is accomplished by calling the getEchoString() method of the bean interface that exists on the client:

```
for (int i = 0; i < args.length; i++) {
      String returnedString = simpleSession.getEchoString(args[i]);
      System.out.println("sent string: " + args[i] +
                         ", received string: " + returnedString);
}
```

Note that invoking the getEchoString() method of the bean interface on the client invokes the getEchoString() method of the session bean class on the server. This is possible through the use of *remoting*, the mechanism by which method calls present on the server hosting the bean are remotely invocated.

The business method of our session bean that the client class calls takes a `String` argument passed in and returns that same string with a status message appended to it back to the calling client:

```
public String getEchoString(String clientString) {
    return clientString + " - from session bean";
}
```

This method is also defined in the bean interface specified in the `SimpleSession.java` code listing:

```
  public String getEchoString(String clientString);
```

The bean interface deserves a second look for one very important reason: metadata.

```
import javax.ejb.Remote;

@Remote
public interface SimpleSession
```

While the `@Remote` may not look like much, its presence is extremely relevant to the development of the session bean. This annotation tells the compiler and EJB container that the interface in question is to be made available to remote clients. The compiler will provide the interface with all the necessary functionality that is needed to let remote clients invoke methods from the EJB container directly, and all you needed to do was add an extra argument to your interface declaration. If it were any easier, the program would be coding itself.

Speaking of easy, take another look at the `SimpleSessionBean.java` file; take particular note of the `@Stateless` annotation.

```
package beans;

import javax.ejb.Stateless;

@Stateless
public class SimpleSessionBean implements SimpleSession
```

The `@Stateless` descriptor is an instruction to the compiler and EJB container, indicating that the class file in question should be deployed and managed as a stateless session bean. As discussed earlier in the chapter, this annotation is the primary method you'll use to develop your EJBs. In the following chapters, you'll learn how to extend bean annotations with extra configuration directives to enrich your object definitions.

In this `SimpleSessionApp` example, you learned how to develop a session bean, including how to deploy and start it in a Java EE application server. You also learned how to develop a client application that uses session beans. Because the `SimpleSessionApp` was deployed as a stateless session bean, it can't be counted on to retain data between method invocations. The next section will introduce the idea of a stateful session bean and compare these two types.

TROUBLESHOOTING THE DEPLOYMENT

We know that it's hard to believe, but occasionally your application may not deploy successfully on the first try. If you get an exception when placing your bean content in the deployment folder, obviously, you should first go back and verify that all the instructions were followed.

If you are still getting exceptions when deploying, then open a command prompt and enter the following command:

```
>%JBOSS_HOME%\bin\shutdown.bat -S
```

When you have done this, the JBoss Server window will close. Delete your bean file from the deployment directory and start the server once more. After JBoss has finished its startup procedure, copy your bean file into the deployment directory once again and monitor the JBoss Server output for any deployment exceptions. If it still doesn't deploy, then repeat the previous command, rebooting your machine after stopping the JBoss Server.

If it still doesn't deploy, then check your logs in `%JBOSS_HOME%\server\all\log`. You can find extra messages and information about the server's operation in these files.

Finally, if the application still won't deploy, then it seems reasonable that a step has been missed or incorrectly performed. Go back and check everything again.

Choosing Between Stateful and Stateless Session Beans

As mentioned previously, session beans are a great choice for implementing business logic, processes, and workflow. When you choose to use a session bean to implement that logic, you have yet another choice to make: whether to make that session bean stateful or stateless.

Consider a fictitious stock trading application where the client uses the `buy()` and `getTotalPrice()` methods of a `StockTrader` session bean. If the user has several different stocks to buy and wants to see the running total price on the tentative purchases, then that state needs to be stored somewhere. One place to store that kind of transient information is in the instance variables of the session bean itself. This requires that the session bean be defined as stateful by usage of the `@Stateful` bean class metadata descriptor.

There are advantages and disadvantages to making a session bean stateful. The following are some of the advantages:

- Transient information, such as that described in the stock trading scenario, can be stored easily in the instance variables of the session bean, as opposed to defining and using entity beans (or JDBC) to store it in a database.
- Since this transient information is stored in the session bean, the client doesn't need to store it and potentially waste bandwidth by sending the session bean the same information repeatedly with each call to a session bean method. This bandwidth issue is a big deal when the client is installed on a user's machine that invokes the session bean methods over a phone modem, for example. Bandwidth is also an issue when the data is very large or needs to be sent many times repeatedly.

The main disadvantage is that stateful session beans don't scale up as well on an EJB server, because they require more system resources than stateless session beans do. Not only do stateful session beans require memory to store the state, but they also can be swapped in and out of memory (activated and deactivated) as the EJB container deems necessary to manage server resources. The state gets stored in a more permanent form whenever a session bean is deactivated, and that state is loaded back in when the bean is activated.

■ **Note** The generic bean interface from which all EJBs derive defines several session bean lifecycle methods, including `ejbActivate()` and `ejbRemove()`. A stateful session bean class can implement these callback methods to cause special processing to occur when it is activated or removed (for that matter, so can the other beans we review in the upcoming chapters).

Using a Stateful Session Bean

Let's look at an example of using a stateful session bean in a generally familiar context: the common calculator. This example mimics some very simple calculator operations: adding, subtracting, and keeping a running total. (This may not be very impressive by today's standards, but you would have paid good money for a calculator with those functions in the early 1970s!) That "keeping a running total" part is what demonstrates the use of a stateful session bean. Figure 9-6 shows the GUI client for this example.

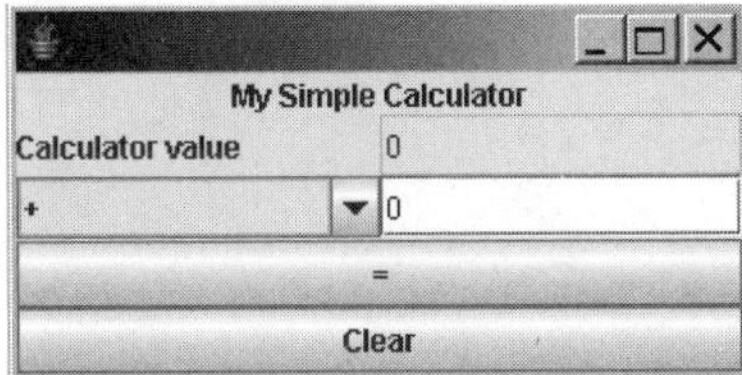

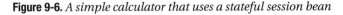

Figure 9-6. *A simple calculator that uses a stateful session bean*

There are three Java source files in this example: `Calculator.java` (in the `beans` package), `CalculatorBean.java` (in the `beans` package), and `CalculatorClient.java` (in the `client` package). Since `CalculatorClient.java` focuses primarily on presentation, we won't list it here. If you would like to examine the client code, you'll find it included with the book's downloadable code (available available in the Downloads section the Downloads section of the Apress web site, `www.apress.com`).

Listing 9-4 shows the code for the bean interface, `Calculator.java`. It defines the business method of the calculator.

Listing 9-4. *Calculator.java*

```
package beans;

import javax.ejb.Remote;

@Remote
public interface Calculator {
  public void clearIt();
  public void calculate(String operation, int value);
  public int getValue();
}
```

Listing 9-5 shows the code for the bean class, `CalculatorBean.java`.

Listing 9-5. *CalculatorBean.java*

```
package beans;

import javax.ejb.Stateful;

@Stateful
public class CalculatorBean implements Calculator {
  private int _value = 0;
  public void clearIt() {
    _value = 0;
  }
  public void calculate(String operation, int value) {
    if (operation.equals("+")) {
      _value = _value + value;
      return;
    }
    if (operation.equals("-")) {
      _value = _value - value;
      return;
    }
  }
  public int getValue() {
    return _value;
  }
}
```

Add these code files to a new application directory called `SimpleCalculatorApp`. Within the directory add `beans` and `client` subdirectories. Place `Calculator.java` and `CalculatorBean.java` in the `beans` directory, and `CalculatorClient.java` in the `client` directory.

Now compile the `.java` files following the same instructions as in the previous example. At the command-line, type the following (again, remember that this is all on one line):

```
> set CLASSPATH=.;C:\jboss\lib\concurrent.jar;C:\jboss\lib\jboss-common.jar; ➥
C:\jboss\server\all\lib\jboss.jar; ➥
C:\jboss\server\all\lib\jboss-remoting.jar; ➥
C:\jboss\server\all\lib\jboss-transaction.jar; ➥
C:\jboss\server\all\lib\jnpserver.jar; ➥
C:\jboss\server\all\deploy\ejb3.deployer\jboss-ejb3.jar; ➥
C:\jboss\server\all\deploy\ejb3.deployer\jboss-ejb3x.jar; ➥
C:\jboss\server\all\deploy\jboss-aop.deployer\ ➥
jboss-aop.jar; ➥
C:\jboss\server\all\deploy\jboss-aop.deployer\➥
jboss-aspect-library.jar
```

Next, within the `SimpleCalculatorApp` directory where the `client` and `beans` directories are located, execute the following commands from the command prompt:

```
> javac -d . client/*.java
> javac -d . beans/*.java
```

Now enter the following command at the prompt:

```
>jar cf SimpleCalculatorApp.ejb3 SimpleCalculatorApp
```

Then copy the resulting EJB3 file to your JBoss deployment directory:

```
%JBOSS_HOME%\server\all\deploy.
```

Running the Stateful Session Bean Application

After deploying the application, you can now run it. On a default Java EE 5 SDK/JBoss Windows installation, the `CLASSPATH` would be set correctly by using the following command:

```
> set CLASSPATH=.;C:\jboss\lib\concurrent.jar;➥
C:\jboss\lib\jboss-common.jar; ➥
C:\jboss\server\all\lib\jboss.jar;➥
C:\jboss\server\all\lib\jboss-remoting.jar;➥
C:\jboss\server\all\lib\jboss-transaction.jar;➥
C:\jboss\server\all\lib\jnpserver.jar;➥
C:\jboss\server\all\deploy\ejb3.deployer\jboss-ejb3.jar;➥
C:\jboss\server\all\deploy\ejb3.deployer\jboss-ejb3x.jar;➥
C:\jboss\server\all\deploy\jboss-aop.deployer\➥
jboss-aop.jar;➥
C:\jboss\server\all\deploy\jboss-aop.deployer\➥
jboss-aspect-library.jar
```

Next, with `SimpleCalculatorApp` as the current directory, execute the following command from the operating system prompt:

```
> java ➥
-Djava.naming.factory.initial=➥
org.jnp.interfaces.NamingContextFactory ➥
-Djava.naming.factory.url.pkgs=➥
org.jboss.naming:org.jnp.interfaces ➥
-Djava.naming.provider.url=➥
localhost client.CalculatorClient
```

The GUI of the client should appear, as shown earlier in Figure 9-6.

To operate the calculator, type a number into the text box, select an operation (+ or -) from the drop-down list, and click the = button. The running total will be displayed beside the Calculator value label.

Reviewing the Stateful Session Bean Source Code

To understand how this example works, we'll walk through some of the GUI client code contained in the `CalculatorClient.java` source file, and then we'll take a closer look at the EJB code.

■ **Note** In the code examples, you'll notice that some of the `import` statements are wildcards and some explicitly name the class or interface. For instructional purposes, we've chosen to be explicit on the imports that are relevant to Java EE, the subject of this book. We've chosen to be more frugal with lines of code by using wildcards for the more familiar ones that are relevant to J2SE.

The client is a standard Java Swing application, complete with GUI components and event-handler methods. The client needs to call methods of the stateful session bean, so as in the previous example, it gets a reference to the bean's remote interface and gets a reference to the session bean on the server. The code that performs this is in the `getCalculator()` method of the `CalculatorClient` class, which is called from the constructor:

```
private Calculator getCalculator() {
  Calculator calculator = null;
  try {
    // Get a naming context
    InitialContext ctx = new InitialContext();

    // Get a Calculator
    calculator
      = (Calculator) ctx.lookup(Calculator.class.getName());
  } catch(Exception e) {
    e.printStackTrace();
  }

  return calculator;
}
```

When the = button is clicked, two things are passed to the calculate() method of the calculator session bean: the operator (either + or -) and the value to be added or subtracted from the running total:

```
_calculator.calculate(oper, operVal);
```

Since it is a stateful session bean, it is able to store the running total in an instance variable. The client then calls the getValue() method of the calculator session bean to retrieve the running total and subsequently display it:

```
_topNumber.setText("" + _calculator.getValue());
```

When the user clicks the Clear button, the clearIt() method of the calculator session bean is called, which sets the running total to 0.

The implementations of the three calculator business methods of the CalculatorBean class follow. They manipulate the instance variable named _value, which holds the running total between invocations of any of these calculator session bean methods.

```
private int _value = 0;
public void clearIt() {
  _value = 0;
}
public void calculate(String operation, int value) {
  if (operation.equals("+")) {
    _value = _value + value;
    return;
  }
  if (operation.equals("-")) {
    _value = _value - value;
    return;
  }
}
public int getValue() {
  return _value;
}
```

The bean indicates its use by the presence of the @Stateful metadata descriptor, just as our earlier bean indicated it was stateless by the use of the @Stateless descriptor. This pattern will follow throughout much of Java EE 5. Much of the hard work present in earlier versions of Java EE has been abstracted into the implementation behind the metadata descriptors.

Keep in mind that a session bean that holds values in instance variables should never be configured as stateless, because the values of the instance variables are not predictable. This is because the EJB container has complete control over managing stateless (and stateful) session beans, including initializing the values of instance variables as the bean is shared among various clients. This is a common trap because sometimes the values are retained, giving a false indication that everything is okay, and then one day, you can't figure out why the program isn't working correctly. From personal experience, that's a fun one to diagnose!

Summary

In this chapter, we explained what EJBs are and built a case for using them. We touched on the three types of EJBs: session beans, entity beans, and message-driven beans.

The balance of this chapter was then devoted to session beans, and we started that discussion by explaining that session beans are made up of two parts: the bean interface and the bean class. After finishing this chapter, you should know:

- What EJBs are, the different types of EJB, and their general behavior.
- How to create stateful and stateless session beans using the `@Stateful` and `@Stateless` metadata descriptors. You should also know how to invoke your session bean from a remote client by using a remote bean interface annotated by the `@Remote` descriptor. Making your application accessible to client applications is best facilitated by using session beans, and will allow you to better focus your application's design by abstracting away the client concerns.
- The difference between stateful and stateless session beans. Stateful session beans are most suitable in situations where you must retain some information about the client's interaction with your application. Stateless session beans are best deployed when you need a very simple, low-overhead interface for your application's clients.
- How to deploy your EJB using the JBoss Server, and how to create a simple client application that will use the application server to invoke your EJB's functionality.

The topics we've covered thus far only brush the surface of using session beans powerfully in your design. This is a pattern that will be repeated over the next few chapters as we discuss the other types of EJBs. What you learn in this book will give you a strong grounding in the basics, but this is just the beginning of a thorough EJB education. When you feel comfortable with moving on to more advanced topics, check out J. Jeffrey Hanson's *Pro EJB 3* (Apress, 2005; ISBN 1-59059-473-8).

Now that we've explored session beans, in the next chapter we'll turn our attention to another type of enterprise bean: the entity bean.

Exercises

1. Write a stateless session bean that takes a word and returns it spelled backwards.
2. Write a stateful session bean that takes one word at a time and appends it to the previous words received to make a sentence. Return the entire sentence each time a word is added.
3. Modify the previous exercise, adding a stateless session bean with a method that counts the number of letters in a word. Call this method from the builder bean to count the number of letters in each word. Show this number in the returned string.

CHAPTER 10

EJB Entity Beans

The previous chapter introduced EJBs and provided an overview of three different types defined by the EJB specification: session beans, entity beans, and message-driven beans. We then looked at session bean development in detail. In this chapter and the following one, we'll focus on developing entity beans, which are the persistent data objects in an EJB application.

In this chapter, you will learn the following:

- How entity beans and session beans work together to provide server-side functionality
- The makeup of entity beans
- How to find an entity bean via its primary key
- How to develop container-managed persistence (CMP) and bean-managed persistence (BMP) entity beans
- How to find entity beans with the Enterprise JavaBeans Query Language (EJB QL)

How Entity Beans Work with Session Beans

As we mentioned in the previous chapter, entity beans can provide an object-oriented abstraction of a relational database. They are essentially JavaBeans that are backed by a persistent data store.

Note Throughout this chapter, you'll see terms like *persistent data storage* and *data store*. These terms are merely a fancy way to refer to a *relational database*, while remaining abstract enough to protect the authors' hides from the inevitable repurposing of EJB entity bean storage facilities that will arise in the future.

Entity beans work well with session beans in providing the server-side functionality of the application. Figure 10-1 depicts how session and entity beans work together for this purpose (this is the same diagram presented in Chapter 9, repeated here for easy reference).

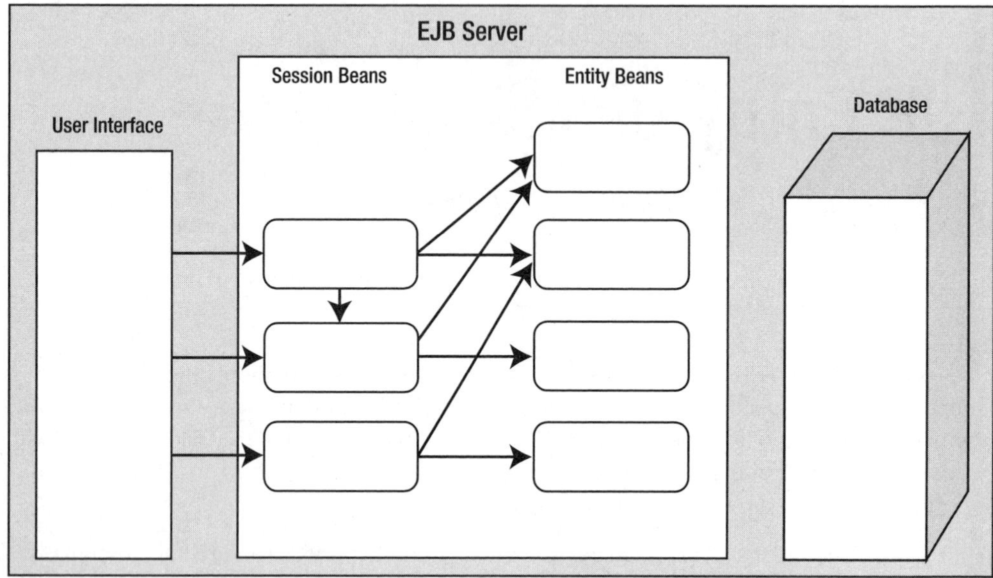

Figure 10-1. *The interaction between the client, the bean logic, and the database*

Session beans generally implement the business logic, processes, and workflow of an application, and entity beans are the persistent data objects. The differences between the two extend to the implementation as well. Session beans, which expose some functionality, are composed of a plain old Java interface and an object. Entity beans, which must act only as a data object, are composed of merely a plain old Java object. The two types are immediately complementary.

For example, in this chapter, we will build an application that manipulates stocks. We will create a session bean named `StockList` that implements the processes that a stockbroker might use for manipulating stocks. We will also create an entity bean named `Stock` whose instances represent individual stocks.

As noted in the previous chapter, it is good practice for the client to call session bean methods, and for session beans to manipulate the entity beans, for the following reasons:

- Calling entity bean methods directly circumvents the business logic contained in session beans and tends to push the business logic into the UI code.
- Session beans can protect the UI from changes to the entity beans.
- Restricting client access to session beans conserves server and network resources.

The Anatomy of an Entity Bean

As we noted in the previous section, entity beans are structurally dissimilar from session beans because they are not constructed with a bean interface. The construction of an entity bean at the most basic level is merely the creation of a serializable plain old Java object that is annotated by the `@Entity (javax.persistence.Entity)` descriptor. All of the instance fields described in the annotated class are persisted to the entity store, except for those fields annotated by the `@Transient (javax.persistence.Transient)` descriptor. Figure 10-2 illustrates the difference between the entity bean and session bean construction.

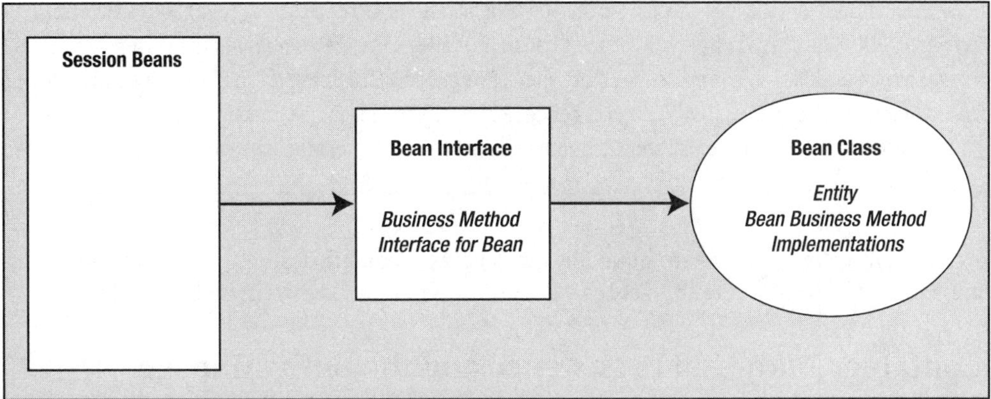

Figure 10-2. *Session beans accessing the information contained in entity beans*

Session beans may create and remove entity beans in the store by using the appropriate methods of the `EntityManager`. Entity beans are created in the store by passing them to the `persist()` method, and they are removed by passing them to the `remove()` method. Strictly speaking, other clients such as user interfaces and external systems could access entity beans directly, although as we stated previously, this is not usually the best practice. Querying the store to find, remove, and use an entity bean is facilitated through the use of the `javax.persistence.EntityManager` interface.

The Entity Bean Class

The entity bean class contains several types of methods:

Getter and setter methods for all persistent fields: For example, a `Stock` class might have a field named `tickerSymbol`, with a getter method named `getTickerSymbol()` and a setter method named `setTickerSymbol()`. We sometimes call entity bean fields *virtual fields*, because having a field in the entity bean actually named `tickerSymbol` is not required. The getter and setter method names just imply the name of a field, similar to JavaBean properties.

Methods that contain business logic: These methods typically access and manipulate the fields of the entity bean. For example, if you had an entity bean named `StockTransactionBean` with a `price` field and a `quantity` field, a method named `getTransactionAmount()` could be created to multiply the two fields and return the amount of the transaction.

Lifecycle methods that are called by the EJB container: For example, as with session beans, the method annotated by the `@PostConstruct` descriptor is called after the entity bean has finished its instantiation, but before any of its business methods are called. These callback methods can be overridden to pass in initialization values.

■ **Note** Bean lifecycle methods are called for nearly every significant bean event that you can imagine. Entity beans in particular receive a special set of lifecycle callback methods that are executed whenever an interaction occurs with the `EntityManager`. These callback methods are invoked before and after before and after persist, update, remove and load actions; the method annotations are `@PrePersist` (`javax.persistence.PrePersist`), `@PostPersist` (`javax.persistence.PostPersist`), `@PreRemove` (`javax.persistence.PreRemove`), `@PostRemove` (`javax.persistence.PostRemove`), `@PreUpdate` (`javax.persistence.PreUpdate`), `@PostUpdate` (`javax.persistence.PostUpdate`) and `@PostLoad` (`javax.persistence.PostLoad`). You can use these callbacks to more intelligently react to interactions with the persistent store.

The entity bean class is annotated by the `@Entity` metadata descriptor and must also implement the `java.io.Serializable` interface if it is to be used by remote interfaces.

Container-Managed Persistence and the EntityManager Interface

Entity beans are backed by some type of persistent data store, often a relational database. This persistence can be managed automatically by the EJB container, which is called *container-managed persistence* (CMP). Recall from the previous chapter that an EJB container is a facility within an EJB server that manages, and provides services to, the EJBs running within it. With CMP, an entity bean is mapped to a database table that is dedicated to the purpose of storing instances of that entity bean. For example, an entity bean named `Stock` might have a table named `stock`, `stock_table`, or perhaps `StockBeanTable` dedicated to it. Each record in the table would represent an instance of the entity bean.

The `EntityManager` (`javax.persistence.EntityManager`) interface allows you to create, remove, and find entity beans within the data store. This interface represents a program's abstracted view of the persistent data storage that facilitates an entity bean's existence. The `EntityManager` interface contains the following methods for querying and updating the data store:

- Calling the `persist()` method creates a new entity bean instance within the data store. It is important to note that the `persist()` method does not create a new instance of an entity bean; it creates an entity bean's associated entry in the store based on the entity bean instance you pass to it.

- Calling the `remove()` method deletes the specified entity bean from the data store.

- Calling the `find()` method finds the appropriate entity bean instances by their primary key. Primary keys are discussed in the next section.

- Calling the `createQuery()` method allows you to access the store in a more generalized manner, similar to using the SQL database query language.

■ **Note** The EJB Query Language (EJB QL) enables you to run queries against entity beans. EJB QL is, as the name suggests, a very close relative of SQL. Just like SQL, EJB QL features advanced database querying features such as aggregate functions and subqueries, as well as EJB-specific operations such as fetch queries. These queries are encapsulated in entity bean methods so that developers that use an entity bean can call methods instead of constructing SQL queries. EJB QL is described in the "The EJB Query Language" section later in this chapter and in Appendix B.

- Calling the getter and setter methods corresponding to the fields of the entity bean causes the fields of the database table to be read from and written to, respectively. These fields are often called *CMP fields*, as they are managed by the container. In the class we'll create in this chapter, the `Stock` entity bean has two CMP fields: `tickerSymbol` and `name`, as indicated by its getters and setters.

When using CMP, the schema of the database directly reflects the design of the entity beans. Figure 10-3 shows the relationship for the example we will develop in this chapter.

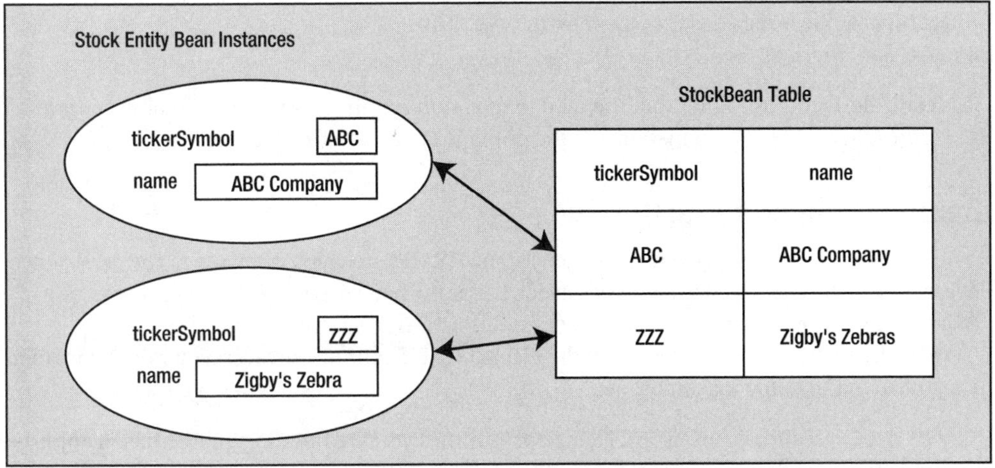

Figure 10-3. *The Stock entity bean instances with respect to their host table*

Like a relational database, entity beans have an abstract schema that defines the CMP fields of each entity bean and the container-managed relationships between entity beans. For each relationship, there are corresponding methods in the related entity beans that refer to each other. Container-managed relationships will be covered in more detail in the next chapter.

■ **Note** CMP fields are formally defined as those fields in your entity bean definition that are private members. You are restricted to using Java primitive types, the Java string class, serializable Java types, and other entity beans for single-valued persistent class members. Multivalued persistent class members (collections of values, such as an array) are restricted to those classes that derive from `java.util.Collection` or `java.util.Set`.

Primary Keys

A requirement of an entity bean is that one or more of its CMP fields must make it unique. This field (or combination of fields) is known as the *primary key*, which is useful in finding a particular entity bean. A primary key may be any serializable object, such as a `String` or an `Integer`. Primary keys also enable another nice feature of entity beans: the ability of the EJB container to manage the relationships between entity beans, which will be covered in the next chapter.

You can let the container do the work of maintaining your primary key for you by using the `@Id` (`javax.persistence.Id`) metadata descriptor to indicate how the uniqueness of the key is maintained:

```
@Id(generate=javax.persistence.GeneratorType.AUTO)
private int id;
```

This code alerts the container that the field in question requires some unique value generated for it automatically when an instance of the entity is created in the data store.

Bean-Managed Persistence

The alternative to CMP is bean-managed persistence (BMP), in which you write all the persistence logic yourself. This persistence logic goes inside the entity bean itself—all database connection, query, and update mechanisms will be contained within the entity bean.

BMP beans are not provided for in the EJB 3.0 specification. However, you might consider using BMP in the following situations:

- A database already exists in a legacy system, and you are building an EJB-based application on top of that database. If the design of the entity beans does not match the existing database schema, BMP will be required.
- There is no database, but rather, the entity beans are a wrapper for an external system. For example, you might be persisting the entity data as flat XML files to some WebDAV store, or mirroring the directory information provided by an LDAP server.
- The EJB server doesn't support CMP with the database that you are using. This could be in cases where the database in question lacks support for JDBC, or the means to interact with the database are sufficiently complex to warrant a custom solution.

Most of the entity bean discussions and examples in this book are of the CMP variety, and are in accordance with the EJB 3.0 specification. This chapter does include one BMP example, however, to give you an idea of how to develop this type of entity bean. Implementing BMP requires you to use the 2.1 specification to deploy the entity beans. Fortunately, this isn't difficult, since one of the goals of the EJB 3.0 working group is backward-compatibility with older versions of the specification.

Now that you have an idea of how entity beans work, let's see how to use them in your applications.

Developing CMP Entity Beans

CMP entity beans have their data persistence managed by the EJB container through the use of a database. Consequently, designing the entity beans in an application can be very much like designing the tables in a relational database, keeping in mind that entity beans are objects and therefore can have business methods as well as data.

During analysis, the entities, which are often "nouns" in a problem domain, are considered candidates for being represented as entity beans. For example, an application that helps students manage their education might have entity beans such as `Student`, `Institution`, `Counselor`, `Course`, and `Program`. Another logical step is to discover which persistent fields each entity bean should have. For example, the `Course` entity bean could have CMP fields for the name of the course and the course abstract.

■ **Caution** Plan carefully! The size of the information you decide to persist will dictate how much space is occupied in your data store and how much time it takes for the container to populate your entity with its persisted data.

Building the CMP Entity Bean Application

The example we'll work through in this section is a simple application in which the user can create, find, update, and delete stocks. This application uses two EJBs:

- An entity bean named `Stock` that holds information about stocks. There is one instance of this entity bean per stock.
- A session bean named `StockList` that uses the `Stock` beans and provides business methods to the UI that enables it to maintain the `Stock` beans.

Listing 10-1 shows the code for the entity bean, `Stock.java`.

Listing 10-1. *Stock.java*

```
package beans;

import javax.persistence.Entity;
import java.io.Serializable;
import javax.persistence.Id;

@Entity
public class Stock implements Serializable {
  // The persistent fields
  private String tickerSymbol;
  private String name;

  // Constructors
  public Stock() { }
  public Stock(String tickerSymbol, String name) {
    this.tickerSymbol = tickerSymbol;
    this.name = name;
  }

  // The access methods for persistent fields
  // tickerSymbol is the id
  @Id
  public String getTickerSymbol() {
    return tickerSymbol;
  }

  public void setTickerSymbol(String tickerSymbol) {
    this.tickerSymbol = tickerSymbol;
  }

  public String getName() {
    return name;
  }

  public void setName(String name) {
    this.name = name;
  }
}
```

Listings 10-2 and 10-3 show the source code files for the session bean, `StockList.java` and `StockListBean.java`.

Listing 10-2. *StockList.java*

```
package beans;

import javax.ejb.Remote;

@Remote
public interface StockList {
  // The public business methods on the StockList bean
  public String getStock(String ticker);
  public void addStock(String ticker, String name);
  public void updateStock(String ticker, String name);
  public void deleteStock(String ticker);
}
```

Listing 10-3. *StockListBean.java*

```
package beans;

import beans.Stock;
import javax.persistence.PersistenceContext;
import javax.ejb.Stateless;
import javax.persistence.EntityManager;

@Stateless
public class StockListBean implements StockList {

  // The reference to the entity manager
  @PersistenceContext
  private EntityManager _manager;

  // The public business methods. these must be coded in the
  // interface also.

  public String getStock(String ticker) {
    Stock stock = _manager.find(Stock.class, ticker);
    return stock.getName();
  }

  public void addStock(String ticker, String name) {
    _manager.persist(new Stock(ticker, name));
  }

  public void updateStock(String ticker, String name) {
    Stock stock = _manager.find(Stock.class, ticker);
    stock.setName(name);
  }
```

```
  public void deleteStock(String ticker) {
    Stock stock = _manager.find(Stock.class, ticker);
    _manager.remove(stock);
  }
}
```

Finally, Listing 10-4 shows the source code file that defines the user interface, `StockClient.java`.

Listing 10-4. *StockClient.java*

```
package client;

import beans.StockList;
import javax.naming.InitialContext;

// General imports
import java.awt.*;
import java.awt.event.*;
import javax.swing.*;

public class StockClient extends JFrame
implements ActionListener {
  private StockList _stockList;
  private JTextField _ticker = new JTextField();
  private JTextField _name = new JTextField();
  private JButton _get = new JButton("Get");
  private JButton _add = new JButton("Add");
  private JButton _update = new JButton("Update");
  private JButton _delete = new JButton("Delete");

  public StockClient() {
    // Get the stock lister
    _stockList = getStockList();

    // Add the title
    JLabel title = new JLabel("Stock List");
    title.setHorizontalAlignment(JLabel.CENTER);
    getContentPane().add(title, BorderLayout.NORTH);

    // Add the stock label panel
    JPanel stockLabelPanel = new JPanel(new GridLayout(2, 1));
    stockLabelPanel.add(new JLabel("Symbol"));
    stockLabelPanel.add(new JLabel("Name"));
    getContentPane().add(stockLabelPanel, BorderLayout.WEST);
```

```
    // Add the stock field panel
    JPanel stockFieldPanel = new JPanel(new GridLayout(2, 1));
    stockFieldPanel.add(_ticker);
    stockFieldPanel.add(_name);
    getContentPane().add(stockFieldPanel, BorderLayout.CENTER);

    // Add the buttons
    JPanel buttonPanel = new JPanel(new GridLayout(1, 4));
    _get.addActionListener(this);
    buttonPanel.add(_get);
    _add.addActionListener(this);
    buttonPanel.add(_add);
    _update.addActionListener(this);
    buttonPanel.add(_update);
    _delete.addActionListener(this);
    buttonPanel.add(_delete);
    getContentPane().add(buttonPanel, BorderLayout.SOUTH);
    addWindowListener(new WindowAdapter() {
      public void windowClosing(WindowEvent e) {
        System.exit(0);
      }
    });

    setSize(330, 130);
    setVisible(true);
  }

  private StockList getStockList() {
    StockList stockList = null;
    try {
      // Get a naming context
      InitialContext ctx = new InitialContext();

      // Get a StockList object
      stockList
        = (StockList) ctx.lookup(StockList.class.getName());
    } catch(Exception e) {
      e.printStackTrace();
    }

    return stockList;
  }
```

```
public void actionPerformed(ActionEvent ae) {
  // If get was clicked, get the stock
  if (ae.getSource() == _get) {
    getStock();
  }

  // If add was clicked, add the stock
  if (ae.getSource() == _add) {
    addStock();
  }

  // If update was clicked, update the stock
  if (ae.getSource() == _update) {
    updateStock();
  }

  // If delete was clicked, delete the stock
  if (ae.getSource() == _delete) {
    deleteStock();
  }
}

private void getStock() {
    // Get the ticker
  String ticker = _ticker.getText();
  if (ticker == null || ticker.trim().length() == 0) {
    JOptionPane.showMessageDialog(this, "Ticker is required");
    return;
  }

  // Get the stock
  try {
    String name = _stockList.getStock(ticker.trim());
    _name.setText(name);
  }
  catch (Exception e) {
    e.printStackTrace();
  }

}

private void addStock() {
    // Get the ticker
  String ticker = _ticker.getText();
  if (ticker == null || ticker.trim().length() == 0) {
    JOptionPane.showMessageDialog(this, "Ticker is required");
    return;
  }
```

```
    // Get the name
    String name = _name.getText();
    if (name == null || name.trim().length() == 0) {
      JOptionPane.showMessageDialog(this, "Name is required");
      return;
    }

    // Add the stock
    try {
      _stockList.addStock(ticker.trim(), name.trim());
      JOptionPane.showMessageDialog(this, "Stock added!");
    }
    catch (Exception e) {
      e.printStackTrace();
    }
  }

  private void updateStock() {
      // Get the ticker
    String ticker = _ticker.getText();
    if (ticker == null || ticker.trim().length() == 0) {
      JOptionPane.showMessageDialog(this, "Ticker is required");
      return;
    }

    // Get the name
    String name = _name.getText();
    if (name == null || name.trim().length() == 0) {
      JOptionPane.showMessageDialog(this, "Name is required");
      return;
    }

    // Update the stock
    try {
      _stockList.updateStock(ticker.trim(), name.trim());
      JOptionPane.showMessageDialog(this, "Stock updated!");
    }
    catch (Exception e) {
      e.printStackTrace();
    }
  }
```

```
  private void deleteStock() {
    // Get the ticker
    String ticker = _ticker.getText();
    if (ticker == null || ticker.trim().length() == 0) {
      JOptionPane.showMessageDialog(this, "Ticker is required");
      return;
    }

    // Delete the stock
    try {
      _stockList.deleteStock(ticker.trim());
      JOptionPane.showMessageDialog(this, "Stock deleted!");
    }
    catch (Exception e) {
      e.printStackTrace();
    }
  }

  public static void main(String[] args) {
    StockClient stockClient = new StockClient();
  }
}
```

Organize the files in the StockListApp application directory. The Stock.java, StockList.java, and StockListBean.java files (Listings 10-1, 10-2, and 10-3) go in the beans subfolder. The source file that defines the user interface, StockClient.java (Listing 10-4), goes in the client subfolder.

Compiling the CMP Entity Bean Application

To compile the source code for the application, open a command prompt in the StockListApp directory, ensure that the CLASSPATH is set correctly (shown here for a default Java EE SDK 5 Windows installation), and compile the classes:

```
>set CLASSPATH=.;➥
  c:\jboss\lib\concurrent.jar;➥
  c:\jboss\client\jboss-j2ee.jar;➥
  c:\jboss\lib\commons-httpclient.jar;➥
  c:\jboss\client\jbossall-client.jar;➥
  c:\jboss\lib\jboss-common.jar;➥
  c:\jboss\server\all\lib\jboss.jar;➥
  c:\jboss\server\all\lib\jboss-remoting.jar;➥
  c:\jboss\server\all\lib\jboss-transaction.jar;➥
  c:\jboss\server\all\lib\jnpserver.jar;➥
  c:\jboss\server\all\lib\javax.servlet.jar;➥
  c:\jboss\server\all\deploy\ejb3.deployer\jboss-ejb3.jar;➥
  c:\jboss\server\all\deploy\ejb3.deployer\jboss-ejb3x.jar;➥
  c:\jboss\server\all\deploy\ejb3.deployer\ejb3-persistence.jar;➥
```

```
c:\jboss\server\all\deploy\jboss-aop-jdk50.deployer\➥
    jboss-aop-jdk50.jar;➥
c:\jboss\server\all\deploy\jboss-aop-jdk50.deployer\➥
    jboss-aspect-library-jdk50.jar
```

Next, within the directory where the `client` and `beans` directories are located, execute the following commands from the command prompt:

```
> javac -d . client/*.java
> javac -d . beans/*.java
```

Deploying the CMP Entity Bean Application

To deploy the application, start the JBoss Server using the procedure described in Chapter 2.

To create the application EJB3 file that contains the `StockList` session and entity bean classes, open a command prompt in the same directory that `StockListApp` resides in, and then type the following command:

```
>jar cf StockListApp.ejb3 beans/*.class
```

Before deploying the application, you should make sure that no other applications are deployed. This is a good habit because some of these examples use the same JNDI name for a session bean, and you want the correct session bean reference to be found. Also, you want JBoss to be stable as long as possible. To verify that no other applications are deployed, open a web browser, visit `localhost:8080`, click on the JMX console link in the tree in the left panel, and click the Stop button for any listed applications that you deployed. Leave any applications that you didn't deploy alone.

Now you can deploy the application. Copy the EJB3 files for the `StockList` session bean to the *JBOSS_HOME*`\server\all\deploy` directory. If your JBoss installation is in `C:\JBoss`, for example, copy the file to `C:\JBoss\server\all\deploy`.

■ Note You may be wondering why no extra work was required to make allowances for the database back-end of your entity beans. Fortunately, the JBoss implementation of EJB 3.0 provides a lightweight Hypersonic SQL (HSQL) database that will provide your entity bean with persistent data. For more information about HSQL, visit `http://sourceforge.net/projects/hsqldb/`.

Running the CMP Entity Bean Application

To run the client that uses the beans you've built, enter the following command:

```
>java ➥
-Djava.naming.factory.initial=org.jnp.interfaces.NamingContextFactory➥
-Djava.naming.factory.url.pkgs=org.jboss.naming:org.jnp.interfaces ➥
-Djava.naming.provider.url=localhost client.StockClient
```

Figure 10-4 shows an example of adding an entry for Jukebox Sellers Incorporated stock to the `StockList` application.

Figure 10-4. *The StockList client with user input*

After at least one stock name has been added, you can enter a symbol and click the Get button, which causes the desired entity bean to be found and its name displayed. Changing the Name text field and clicking the Update button causes the CMP `name` field of the entity bean to be updated. Clicking the Delete button results in the entity bean being deleted.

Now that we've built, deployed, and run the application, let's see how it works. We're going to examine the code for this example from the inside out, beginning with the entity bean. For a diagram of these entity bean classes, see Figure 10-3, shown earlier in the chapter.

Reviewing the CMP Entity Bean

Let's first look at the entity bean class, `Stock.java` (Listing 10-1). Issues of rich object use aside, why do we expend the effort to have two constructors? The EJB specification requires that all entity beans provide at least one no-argument constructor to the EJB container. We provide the second constructor purely for functional purposes on the part of calling clients.

The following are a few other points worth mentioning about this entity bean:

- We implement the `java.io.Serializable` interface for our entity bean. We do this in order to make it available for use by remote interfaces (or more specifically, our `StockList` interface).
- We do not provide a generator type for the `@Id` annotation. This is because we are relying on a client-provided key to identify our `Stock` objects in the store, and we cannot easily automate making this key a unique value based on past entries to the store.
- We do not initialize any variables in our no-argument constructor. This is to avoid instantiating persistent variables with non-null (but not relevant) data that might be mistakenly persisted to the store.

Reviewing the Session Bean

Let's turn our attention to the session bean code. The `StockList` session bean (Listing 10-2) uses our entity bean. The four methods in that interface will be used by the client to carry out the get, add, update, and delete stock operations shown in the GUI client. The session bean class, `StockListBean.java` (Listing 10-3), supports this functionality with the `getStock()`, `addStock()`, `updateStock()`, and `deleteStock()` methods, respectively.

Each of these methods calls methods that belong to the `EntityManager` interface we discussed earlier, but how did we instantiate the class that implements `EntityManager`? If you're a perceptive reader (of course you are!), you'll notice the `@PersistenceContext` (`javax.persistence.PersistenceContext`) annotation preceding our declaration of the `EntityManager` member. What is `@PersistenceContext`?

The @PersistenceContext annotation notifies the compiler that the variable or property it annotates represents a value that will be assigned to it by the containing application—in this case, our EJB container. When our session bean is instantiated, the manager variable will be automatically set to the container's EntityManager interface, saving us the tedious work of writing a lot of housekeeping code to find and acquire the container's EntityManager instance.

```
public String getStock(String ticker) {
  Stock stock = _manager.find(Stock.class, ticker);
  return stock.getName();
}
```

The getStock() method calls the find() method of the EntityManager interface, passing in the class of the Stock entity bean and the desired ticker symbol. Why do we pass the class to the EntityManager? Remember that each entity bean is associated with some specific location in the store—in this case, a database table. Passing the class to the EntityManager is effectively letting it know which table it should be searching for. If it finds the table, it asks the Stock entity bean for the value held in its CMP name field, and returns the value as follows:

- The addStock() calls the EntityManager's persist() method, passing it a newly instantiated Stock entity.
- The updateStock() method uses the find() method to get the desired Stock entity bean reference, and it uses a CMP method to update the name field.
- The deleteStock() method uses the find() method to get the desired Stock entity bean reference. It then calls the remove() method of the EntityManager interface.

The StockClient class (Listing 10-4) gets a reference to a session bean:

```
private StockList getStockList() {
  StockList stockList = null;
  try {
    // Get a naming context
    InitialContext ctx = new InitialContext();
    stockList ➥
      = (StockList) ctx.lookup(StockList.class.getName());
  } catch(Exception e) {
    e.printStackTrace();
  }

  return stockList;
}
```

This example demonstrated the use of a CMP entity bean. In the next section, you'll learn how to develop entity beans that don't rely on the EJB container to provide persistence.

Developing BMP Entity Beans

As you learned earlier in this chapter, BMP entity beans must supply their own persistence mechanism. In this section, we'll develop an example that demonstrates this technique by converting the Stock entity bean used in the previous example from a CMP entity bean to a BMP entity bean.

As we noted earlier, the EJB 3.0 specification doesn't make allowances for BMP. However, it does require backward-compatibility with earlier versions of the EJB specification—earlier versions that include support for BMP, for example.

The majority of the bean implementation will reside in an EJB 2.1 entity bean called StockBean.java. StockBean.java will be accompanied by Stock.java and StockHome.java, which are StockBean's business interface and home interface, respectively. The client file, StockClient.java, references an instance of the home interface to make use of the bean. The resulting EJB 2.1 bean will be deployed separately from the EJB 3.0 session bean, and it will require some additional files that we'll discuss as we encounter them in the example.

Note The home interface of an entity bean is a relic of the EJB 2.1 specification. It's used by EJB clients to acquire a reference to the entity bean through some mechanism. Since the home interface's use has largely been eclipsed by the advent of the EJB 3.0 specification, we will deal with it in a summary fashion in this text. Should an older developer ever try to engage you in conversation about these relics, you are encouraged to make loud noises or mention something about an impending dinosaur stampede. If these ruses fail, or if you would like to learn more about the subject, you're encouraged to purchase a copy of the incredibly well-written *Beginning J2EE 1.4: From Novice to Professional* (Apress, 2004; ISBN 1-59059-341-3). It even looks attractive on a bookshelf.

Building the BMP Entity Bean Application

The process to build and run this example is almost the same as the previous example, and all of the Java source filenames are the same.

StockList.java is shown in Listing 10-5.

Listing 10-5. *StockList.java for the BMP Example*

```
package beans;

import javax.ejb.CreateException;
import javax.ejb.FinderException;
import javax.ejb.Remote;

@Remote
public interface StockList {
  // The public business methods on the Stock List bean
  public String getStock(String ticker)
    throws FinderException;
  public void addStock(String ticker, String name)
    throws CreateException;
  public void updateStock(String ticker, String name)
    throws FinderException;
```

```
  public void deleteStock(String ticker)
    throws FinderException;
}
```

Listing 10-6 shows `StockListBean.java`.

Listing 10-6. *StockListBean.java for the BMP Example*

```
package beans;

import beans_2x.Stock;
import beans_2x.StockHome;
import javax.ejb.CreateException;
import javax.ejb.FinderException;
import javax.ejb.SessionBean;
import javax.ejb.SessionContext;
import javax.ejb.Stateless;
import javax.naming.InitialContext;
import javax.naming.NamingException;
import javax.rmi.PortableRemoteObject;

@Stateless
public class StockListBean implements StockList {

  // The public business methods. these must be coded in the
  // remote interface also.

  public String getStock(String ticker)
    throws FinderException {
    try {
      StockHome stockHome = getStockHome();
      Stock stock = stockHome.findByPrimaryKey(ticker);
      return stock.getName();
    }
    catch (FinderException fe) {
      throw fe;
    }
    catch (Exception ex) {
      throw new RuntimeException(ex.getMessage());
    }
  }

  public void addStock(String ticker, String name)
    throws CreateException {
    try {
      StockHome stockHome = getStockHome();
      stockHome.create(ticker, name);
    }
```

```
    catch (CreateException ce) {
      throw ce;
    }
    catch (Exception ex) {
      throw new RuntimeException(ex.getMessage());
    }
  }

  public void updateStock(String ticker, String name)
   throws FinderException {
    try {
      StockHome stockHome = getStockHome();
      Stock stock = stockHome.findByPrimaryKey(ticker);
      stock.setName(name);
    }
    catch (FinderException fe) {
      throw fe;
    }
    catch (Exception ex) {
      throw new RuntimeException(ex.getMessage());
    }
   }

  public void deleteStock(String ticker)
    throws FinderException {
    try {
      StockHome stockHome = getStockHome();
      Stock stock = stockHome.findByPrimaryKey(ticker);
      stock.remove();
    }
    catch (FinderException fe) {
      throw fe;
    }
    catch (Exception ex) {
      throw new RuntimeException(ex.getMessage());
    }
  }

  private StockHome getStockHome() throws NamingException {
    // Get the initial context
    InitialContext initial = new InitialContext();

    // Get the object reference
    Object objref = initial.lookup("beans_2x.Stock");
    StockHome home = (StockHome)
      PortableRemoteObject.narrow(objref, StockHome.class);
    return home;
  }
```

```
  // Standard ejb methods
  public void ejbActivate() {}
  public void ejbPassivate() {}
  public void ejbRemove() {}
  public void ejbCreate() {}
  public void setSessionContext(SessionContext context) { }
}
```

The EJB 2.1 files are `Stock.java`, `StockBean.java`, and `StockHome.java`. Listing 10-7 shows `Stock.java`.

Listing 10-7. *Stock.java for the BMP Example*

```
package beans_2x;

import java.rmi.RemoteException;
import javax.ejb.EJBObject;

public interface Stock extends EJBObject  {
  // The public business methods on the Stock bean
  // these include the accessor methods from the bean

  // Get the ticker. Do not allow ticker to be set through the
  // interface because it is the primary key.
  public String getTickerSymbol() throws RemoteException;

  // Get and set the name
  public String getName() throws RemoteException;
  public void setName(String name) throws RemoteException;
}
```

Listing 10-8 shows `StockBean.java`.

Listing 10-8. *StockBean.java for the BMP Example*

```
package beans_2x;

import java.sql.Connection;
import java.sql.PreparedStatement;
import java.sql.ResultSet;
import java.sql.SQLException;
import javax.ejb.CreateException;
import javax.ejb.EJBException;
import javax.ejb.EntityBean;
import javax.ejb.EntityContext;
import javax.ejb.FinderException;
import javax.ejb.NoSuchEntityException;
import javax.ejb.ObjectNotFoundException;
```

```
import javax.naming.InitialContext;
import javax.naming.NamingException;
import javax.sql.DataSource;

public class StockBean implements EntityBean {

  // Persistent fields
  private String tickerSymbol;
  private String name;

  // Keeps the reference to the context
  private EntityContext context;

  // Keeps the reference to the db connection
  private Connection connection;

  // The access methods for persistent fields
  public String getTickerSymbol() {
    return tickerSymbol;
  }

  public String getName() {
    return name;
  }

  public void setName(String name) {
    this.name = name;
  }

  // Standard entity bean methods

  public String ejbFindByPrimaryKey(String primaryKey)
    throws FinderException {

    boolean result;

    try {
      String stmt =
        "select tickerSymbol " +
        "from stock where tickerSymbol = ? ";
      PreparedStatement pstmt =
        connection.prepareStatement(stmt);
      pstmt.setString(1, primaryKey);
```

```
      ResultSet rs = pstmt.executeQuery();
      result = rs.next();
      pstmt.close();
    }
    catch (SQLException ex) {
      throw new EJBException("ejbFindByPrimaryKey: " +
        ex.getMessage());
    }

    if (result) {
      return primaryKey;
    }
    else {
      throw new ObjectNotFoundException
        ("Ticker " + primaryKey + " not found.");
    }
  }

  public String ejbCreate(String tickerSymbol, String name)
    throws CreateException {

    try {
      String findstmt =
        "select tickerSymbol " +
        "from stock where tickerSymbol = ? ";
      PreparedStatement pfindstmt =
        connection.prepareStatement(findstmt);
      pfindstmt.setString(1, tickerSymbol);

      ResultSet rs = pfindstmt.executeQuery();
      boolean findresult = rs.next();
      if (findresult) {
        throw new CreateException("Ticker already exists!");
      }

      String stmt =
        "insert into stock values ( ? , ? )";
      PreparedStatement pstmt = connection.prepareStatement(stmt);

      pstmt.setString(1, tickerSymbol);
      pstmt.setString(2, name);

      pstmt.executeUpdate();
      pstmt.close();
    }
    catch (SQLException ex) {
      throw new EJBException("ejbCreate: " + ex.getMessage());
    }
```

```
    this.tickerSymbol = tickerSymbol;
    this.name = name;

    return tickerSymbol;
  }

  public void ejbPostCreate(String tickerSymbol, String name)
    throws CreateException { }

  public void ejbRemove() {
    try {
      String stmt =
        "delete from stock where tickerSymbol = ? ";
      PreparedStatement pstmt =
        connection.prepareStatement(stmt);

      pstmt.setString(1, tickerSymbol);
      pstmt.executeUpdate();
      pstmt.close();
    }
    catch (SQLException ex) {
      throw new EJBException("ejbRemove: " + ex.getMessage());
    }
  }

  public void ejbLoad() {
    try {
      String stmt =
        "select name from stock where tickerSymbol = ? ";
      PreparedStatement pstmt =
        connection.prepareStatement(stmt);

      pstmt.setString(1, tickerSymbol);

      ResultSet rs = pstmt.executeQuery();

      if (rs.next()) {
        this.name = rs.getString(1);
        pstmt.close();
      }
      else {
         pstmt.close();
         throw new NoSuchEntityException("Ticker: " +
           tickerSymbol + " not in database.");
      }
    }
```

```
    catch (SQLException ex) {
      throw new EJBException("ejbLoad: " + ex.getMessage());
    }
  }

  public void ejbStore() {
    try {
      String stmt =
            "update stock set name =  ? " +
            "where tickerSymbol = ?";
      PreparedStatement pstmt =
        connection.prepareStatement(stmt);

      pstmt.setString(1, name);
      pstmt.setString(2, tickerSymbol);
      int rowCount = pstmt.executeUpdate();
      pstmt.close();

      if (rowCount == 0) {
        throw new EJBException("Store for " +
          tickerSymbol + " failed.");
      }
    }
    catch (SQLException ex) {
      throw new EJBException("ejbStore: " + ex.getMessage());
    }
  }

  public void ejbPassivate() { }

  public void ejbActivate() { }

  public void setEntityContext(EntityContext ctx) {
    context = ctx;

    try {
      getDatabaseConnection();
    }
    catch (Exception ex) {
      throw new EJBException("Unable to connect to database. " +
      ex.getMessage());
    }
  }
```

```
  public void unsetEntityContext() {
    context = null;
    try {
      connection.close();
    }
    catch (SQLException ex) {
      throw new EJBException("unsetEntityContext: " +
        ex.getMessage());
    }
  }


  private void getDatabaseConnection()
    throws NamingException, SQLException {

    InitialContext ctx = new InitialContext();
    DataSource ds =
      (DataSource) ctx.lookup("java:comp/env/jdbc/StockDB");
    connection =  ds.getConnection();
  }
}
```

Listing 10-9 shows `StockHome.java`.

Listing 10-9. *StockHome.java*

```
package beans_2x;

import java.rmi.RemoteException;
import javax.ejb.CreateException;
import javax.ejb.EJBHome;
import javax.ejb.FinderException;

public interface StockHome extends EJBHome {
  // The create method for the Stock bean
  public Stock create(String ticker, String name)
    throws CreateException, RemoteException;

  // The find by primary key method for the Stock bean
  public Stock findByPrimaryKey(String ticker)
    throws FinderException, RemoteException;
}
```

Because we're using EJB 2.1 beans, we'll also need XML deployment descriptor files: `application.xml`, `ejb-jar.xml`, and `jboss.xml`. These files describe the operation of the EJB 2.1 entity bean to the JBoss Server.

■Note The EJB 3.0 specification also makes allowances for XML deployment descriptors for all EJBs; however, much of the functionality provided in the XML deployment files has been appropriated to the metadata descriptors used in this book.

Listing 10-10 shows Application.xml.

Listing 10-10. *Application.xml*

```
<?xml version="1.0" encoding="UTF-8"?>
<application xmlns="http://java.sun.com/xml/ns/javaee" version="5"
    xmlns:xsi="http://www.w3.org/2001/XMLSchema-instance"
    xsi:schemaLocation="http://java.sun.com /xml/ns/javaee ➥
http://java.sun.com/xml/ns/javaee/application_5.xsd">
    <display-name>StockListBmpApp</display-name>
    <description>Application description</description>
    <module>
        <ejb>StockList2xBmp.jar</ejb>
    </module>
</application>
```

Ejb-jar.xml is shown in Listing 10-11.

Listing 10-11. *Ejb-jar.xml*

```
<?xml version="1.0" encoding="UTF-8"?>
<ejb-jar xmlns="http://java.sun.com/xml/ns/javaee" version="3.0"
    xmlns:xsi="http://www.w3.org/2001/XMLSchema-instance"
    xsi:schemaLocation="http://java.sun.com/xml/ns/javaee ➥
http://java.sun.com/xml/ns/javaee/ejb-jar_3_0.xsd">
    <display-name>StockListBmpJar</display-name>
    <enterprise-beans>
        <entity>
            <ejb-name>StockEjb</ejb-name>
            <home>beans_2x.StockHome</home>
            <remote>beans_2x.Stock</remote>
            <ejb-class>beans_2x.StockBean</ejb-class>
            <persistence-type>Bean</persistence-type>
            <prim-key-class>java.lang.String</prim-key-class>
            <reentrant>false</reentrant>
            <resource-ref>
                <res-ref-name>jdbc/StockDB</res-ref-name>
                <res-type>javax.sql.DataSource</res-type>
                <res-auth>Container</res-auth>
                <res-sharing-scope>Shareable</res-sharing-scope>
            </resource-ref>
```

```
            <security-identity>
                <use-caller-identity/>
            </security-identity>
        </entity>
    </enterprise-beans>
    <assembly-descriptor>
        <container-transaction>
            <method>
                <ejb-name>StockEjb</ejb-name>
                <method-intf>Remote</method-intf>
                <method-name>setName</method-name>
                <method-params>
                    <method-param>java.lang.String</method-param>
                </method-params>
            </method>
            <trans-attribute>Required</trans-attribute>
        </container-transaction>
        <container-transaction>
            <method>
                <ejb-name>StockEjb</ejb-name>
                <method-intf>Remote</method-intf>
                <method-name>getName</method-name>
            </method>
            <trans-attribute>Required</trans-attribute>
        </container-transaction>
        <container-transaction>
            <method>
                <ejb-name>StockEjb</ejb-name>
                <method-intf>Remote</method-intf>
                <method-name>remove</method-name>
            </method>
            <trans-attribute>Required</trans-attribute>
        </container-transaction>
        <container-transaction>
            <method>
                <ejb-name>StockEjb</ejb-name>
                <method-intf>Remote</method-intf>
                <method-name>getTickerSymbol</method-name>
            </method>
            <trans-attribute>Required</trans-attribute>
        </container-transaction>
    </assembly-descriptor>
</ejb-jar>
```

Listing 10-12 shows `Jboss.xml`.

Listing 10-12. *Jboss.xml*

```
<!DOCTYPE jboss PUBLIC
          "-//JBoss//DTD JBOSS 4.0//EN"
          "http://www.jboss.org/javaee/dtd/jboss_4_0.dtd">
<jboss>
    <enterprise-beans>
        <entity>
            <ejb-name>StockEjb</ejb-name>
            <jndi-name>beans_2x.Stock</jndi-name>
            <resource-ref>
                <res-ref-name>jdbc/StockDB</res-ref-name>
                <jndi-name>java:/DefaultDS</jndi-name>
            </resource-ref>
        </entity>
    </enterprise-beans>
</jboss>
```

Finally, Listing 10-13 shows the implementation behind `StockClient.java`.

Listing 10-13. *StockClient.java for the BMP Example*

```
package client;

import beans.StockList;
import javax.ejb.CreateException;
import javax.ejb.FinderException;
import javax.naming.InitialContext;

// General imports
import java.awt.*;
import java.awt.event.*;
import javax.swing.*;

public class StockClient extends JFrame
  implements ActionListener {
  private StockList _stockList;
  private JTextField _ticker = new JTextField();
  private JTextField _name = new JTextField();
  private JButton _get = new JButton("Get");
  private JButton _add = new JButton("Add");
  private JButton _update = new JButton("Update");
  private JButton _delete = new JButton("Delete");

  public StockClient() {
    // Get the stock lister
    _stockList = getStockList();
```

```
    // Add the title
    JLabel title = new JLabel("Stock List");
    title.setHorizontalAlignment(JLabel.CENTER);
    getContentPane().add(title, BorderLayout.NORTH);

    // Add the stock label panel
    JPanel stockLabelPanel = new JPanel(new GridLayout(2, 1));
    stockLabelPanel.add(new JLabel("Symbol"));
    stockLabelPanel.add(new JLabel("Name"));
    getContentPane().add(stockLabelPanel, BorderLayout.WEST);

    // Add the stock field panel
    JPanel stockFieldPanel = new JPanel(new GridLayout(2, 1));
    stockFieldPanel.add(_ticker);
    stockFieldPanel.add(_name);
    getContentPane().add(stockFieldPanel, BorderLayout.CENTER);

    // Add the buttons
    JPanel buttonPanel = new JPanel(new GridLayout(1, 4));
    _get.addActionListener(this);
    buttonPanel.add(_get);
    _add.addActionListener(this);
    buttonPanel.add(_add);
    _update.addActionListener(this);
    buttonPanel.add(_update);
    _delete.addActionListener(this);
    buttonPanel.add(_delete);
    getContentPane().add(buttonPanel, BorderLayout.SOUTH);
    addWindowListener(new WindowAdapter() {
      public void windowClosing(WindowEvent e) {
        System.exit(0);
      }
    });

    setSize(330, 130);
    setVisible(true);
  }

  private StockList getStockList() {
    StockList stockList = null;
    try {
      // Get a naming context
      InitialContext ctx = new InitialContext();
```

```
      // Get a StockList object
      stockList
        = (StockList) ctx.lookup(StockList.class.getName());
    } catch(Exception e) {
      e.printStackTrace();
    }

    return stockList;
  }

  public void actionPerformed(ActionEvent ae) {
    // If get was clicked, get the stock
    if (ae.getSource() == _get) {
      getStock();
    }

    // If add was clicked, add the stock
    if (ae.getSource() == _add) {
      addStock();
    }

    // If update was clicked, update the stock
    if (ae.getSource() == _update) {
      updateStock();
    }

    // If delete was clicked, delete the stock
    if (ae.getSource() == _delete) {
      deleteStock();
    }
  }

  private void getStock() {
    // Get the ticker
    String ticker = _ticker.getText();
    if (ticker == null || ticker.length() == 0) {
      JOptionPane.showMessageDialog(this, "Ticker is required");
      return;
    }

    // Get the stock
    try {
      String name = _stockList.getStock(ticker);
      _name.setText(name);
    }
```

```
    catch (FinderException fe) {
      JOptionPane.showMessageDialog(this, "Not found!");
    }
    catch (Exception e) {
      e.printStackTrace();
    }
  }

  private void addStock() {
    // Get the ticker
    String ticker = _ticker.getText();
    if (ticker == null || ticker.length() == 0) {
      JOptionPane.showMessageDialog(this, "Ticker is required");
      return;
    }

    // Get the name
    String name = _name.getText();
    if (name == null || name.length() == 0) {
      JOptionPane.showMessageDialog(this, "Name is required");
      return;
    }

    // Add the stock
    try {
      _stockList.addStock(ticker, name);
      JOptionPane.showMessageDialog(this, "Stock added!");
    }
    catch (CreateException fe) {
      JOptionPane.showMessageDialog(this, "Already found!");
    }
    catch (Exception e) {
      e.printStackTrace();
    }
  }

  private void updateStock() {
    // Get the ticker
    String ticker = _ticker.getText();
    if (ticker == null || ticker.length() == 0) {
      JOptionPane.showMessageDialog(this, "Ticker is required");
      return;
    }
```

```
    // Get the name
    String name = _name.getText();
    if (name == null || name.length() == 0) {
      JOptionPane.showMessageDialog(this, "Name is required");
      return;
    }

    // Update the stock
    try {
      _stockList.updateStock(ticker, name);
      JOptionPane.showMessageDialog(this, "Stock updated!");
    }
    catch (FinderException fe) {
      JOptionPane.showMessageDialog(this, "Not found!");
    }
    catch (Exception e) {
      e.printStackTrace();
    }
  }

  private void deleteStock() {
    // Get the ticker
    String ticker = _ticker.getText();
    if (ticker == null || ticker.length() == 0) {
      JOptionPane.showMessageDialog(this, "Ticker is required");
      return;
    }

    // Delete the stock
    try {
      _stockList.deleteStock(ticker);
      JOptionPane.showMessageDialog(this, "Stock deleted!");
    }
    catch (FinderException fe) {
      JOptionPane.showMessageDialog(this, "Not found!");
    }
    catch (Exception e) {
      e.printStackTrace();
    }
  }

  public static void main(String[] args) {
    StockClient stockClient = new StockClient();
  }
}
```

Organize the files in a new application directory with beans, beans_2x, meta-inf and client subfolders. The StockList.java and StockListBean.java files (Listings 10-5 and 10-6) go in the beans subfolder. Stock.java, StockBean.java, and StockHome.java (Listings 10-7, 10-8, and 10-9) go in the beans_2x directory. The XML deployment descriptor files application.xml, ejb-jar.xml, and jboss.xml (Listings 10-10, 10-11, and 10-12) go in the meta-inf directory. The source file that defines the user interface, StockClient.java (Listing 10-13), goes in the client subfolder.

Deploying the BMP Entity Bean Application

To deploy the sample application, first change your CLASSPATH environment variable to reflect the location of the required classes for compilation.

```
>set CLASSPATH=.;➥
  c:\jboss\lib\concurrent.jar;➥
  c:\jboss\client\jboss-j2ee.jar;➥
  c:\jboss\lib\commons-httpclient.jar;➥
  c:\jboss\client\jbossall-client.jar;➥
  c:\jboss\lib\jboss-common.jar;➥
  c:\jboss\server\all\lib\jboss.jar;➥
  c:\jboss\server\all\lib\jboss-remoting.jar;➥
  c:\jboss\server\all\lib\jboss-transaction.jar;➥
  c:\jboss\server\all\lib\jnpserver.jar;➥
  c:\jboss\server\all\lib\javax.servlet.jar;➥
  c:\jboss\server\all\deploy\ejb3.deployer\jboss-ejb3.jar;➥
  c:\jboss\server\all\deploy\ejb3.deployer\jboss-ejb3x.jar;➥
  c:\jboss\server\all\deploy\ejb3.deployer\ejb3-persistence.jar;➥
  c:\jboss\server\all\deploy\jboss-aop-jdk50.deployer\➥
      jboss-aop-jdk50.jar;➥
  c:\jboss\server\all\deploy\jboss-aop-jdk50.deployer\➥
      jboss-aspect-library-jdk50.jar
```

Within the directory where the client, beans_2x, and beans directories are located, execute the following commands from the command prompt:

```
> javac -d . beans_2x/*.java
> javac -d . beans/*.java
> javac -d . client/*.java
```

Create and populate the EJB 2.1 bean JAR, using StockList2xBmp.jar as the JAR name.

```
>jar cf StockList2xBmp.jar META-INF/ejb-jar.xml ➥
META-INF/jboss.xml beans_2x/*.class
```

Next, package the EJB 2.1 bean JAR with its deployment files by creating an EAR file.

```
>jar cf StockListBmpApp.ear META-INF/application.xml ➥
StockList2xBmp.jar
```

Create the EJB 3.0 file for the session bean that invokes the entity bean.

```
>jar cf StockListApp.ejb3 beans/*.class
```

Now you'll need to populate the HSQL database that services the entity bean with a table to hold your BMP data. (Remember that since the bean itself is managing the data persistence, there is no guarantee that the table for the entity bean will be created automatically.) You can use the jmx console to start the Hypersonic Database Manager to add the table. Open a browser and go to http://localhost:8080/jmx-console. From there, find the link service=Hypersonic and click it. On the next page, scroll down to the startDatabaseManager section and click the Invoke button under the method name. The window for the database manager will appear shortly thereafter. Enter the following SQL query into large text box:

```
DROP TABLE stock if exists;

create table stock
(
  tickerSymbol VARCHAR(10),
  name VARCHAR(50),
   CONSTRAINT pk_stock PRIMARY KEY (tickerSymbol)
);
```

Then click the Execute SQL Statement button. Once the query has executed, choose Options ➤ Commit from the menu.

Deploy the application by first copying the EAR file, then the EJB3 file, to the JBoss deployment directory.

Running the BMP Entity Bean Application

Enter the following command to run the client that uses the beans we've built:

```
>java ➥
-Djava.naming.factory.initial=org.jnp.interfaces.NamingContextFactory ➥
-Djava.naming.factory.url.pkgs=org.jboss.naming:org.jnp.interfaces ➥
-Djava.naming.provider.url=localhost client.StockClient
```

The application will look the same as the CMP version.

Reviewing the BMP Entity Bean

Looking at the code for this BMP entity bean, you can begin to appreciate what the EJB container does for you when using CMP. In this example, as with CMP, a table in the database is dedicated to our BMP entity bean. Each row represents a bean instance.

The BMP entity bean must supply implementations for the persisted field's getter and setter methods. In our example, this consists of using instance variables to hold these values, as seen in the getTickerSymbol(), getName(), and setName() methods:

```
public String getTickerSymbol() {
  return tickerSymbol;
}

public String getName() {
  return name;
}

public void setName(String name) {
  this.name = name;
}
```

The implementation of the `find()` method declared in the home interface *must* be supplied. This is seen in the `ejbFindByPrimaryKey()` method. Notice that JDBC is used to enable this `find()` method.

```
public String ejbFindByPrimaryKey(String primaryKey)
  throws FinderException {

  boolean result;

  try {
    String stmt =
      "select tickerSymbol " + "from stock where tickerSymbol = ? ";
    PreparedStatement pstmt = connection.prepareStatement(stmt);
    pstmt.setString(1, primaryKey);

    ResultSet rs = pstmt.executeQuery();
    result = rs.next();
    pstmt.close();
  }
  catch (SQLException ex) {
    throw new EJBException("ejbFindByPrimaryKey: " +➥
ex.getMessage());
  }

  if (result) {
    return primaryKey;
  } else {
    throw new ObjectNotFoundException
      ("Ticker " + primaryKey + " not found.");
  }
}
```

The `ejbCreate()` method, rather than simply tucking away arguments into instance variables, uses JDBC to insert the corresponding row into the table.

```
public String ejbCreate(String tickerSymbol, String name)
  throws CreateException {

  try {
    String findstmt =
      "select tickerSymbol " +
      "from stock where tickerSymbol = ? ";
    PreparedStatement pfindstmt =
      connection.prepareStatement(findstmt);
    pfindstmt.setString(1, tickerSymbol);

    ResultSet rs = pfindstmt.executeQuery();
    boolean findresult = rs.next();
    if (findresult) {
      throw new CreateException("Ticker already exists!");
    }

    String stmt = "insert into stock values ( ? , ? )";
    PreparedStatement pstmt = connection.prepareStatement(stmt);

    pstmt.setString(1, tickerSymbol);
    pstmt.setString(2, name);

    pstmt.executeUpdate();
    pstmt.close();
  } catch (SQLException ex) {
    ex.printStackTrace();
    throw new EJBException("ejbCreate: " + ex.getMessage());
  }

  this.tickerSymbol = tickerSymbol;
  this.name = name;

  return tickerSymbol;
}
```

The ejbRemove() method is responsible for deleting the row that represents the entity bean's instance from the table.

```
public void ejbRemove() {
  try {
    String stmt = "delete from stock where tickerSymbol = ? ";
    PreparedStatement pstmt = connection.prepareStatement(stmt);
```

```
      pstmt.setString(1, tickerSymbol);
      pstmt.executeUpdate();
      pstmt.close();
    } catch (SQLException ex) {
      throw new EJBException("ejbRemove: " + ex.getMessage());
    }
  }
```

In a bean's lifecycle, the values of its fields are often changed by the application. For this reason, the EJB 2.1 container calls the `ejbLoad()` and `ejbStore()` methods when appropriate to keep the state of the entity bean in sync with the underlying data store. The BMP entity bean performs SQL `SELECT` and `UPDATE` statements via JDBC to implement these methods.

```
  public void ejbLoad() {
    try {
      String stmt = "select name from stock where tickerSymbol = ? ";
      PreparedStatement pstmt = connection.prepareStatement(stmt);

      pstmt.setString(1, tickerSymbol);
      ResultSet rs = pstmt.executeQuery();

      if (rs.next()) {
        this.name = rs.getString(1);
        pstmt.close();
      } else {
         pstmt.close();
         throw new NoSuchEntityException("Ticker: " +
           tickerSymbol + " not in database.");
      }
    } catch (SQLException ex) {
      throw new EJBException("ejbLoad: " + ex.getMessage());
    }
  }

  public void ejbStore() {
    try {
      String stmt =
            "update stock set name = ? " +
            "where tickerSymbol = ?";
      PreparedStatement pstmt = connection.prepareStatement(stmt);

      pstmt.setString(1, name);
      pstmt.setString(2, tickerSymbol);
      int rowCount = pstmt.executeUpdate();
      pstmt.close();
```

```
      if (rowCount == 0) {
        throw new EJBException("Store for " +
          tickerSymbol + " failed.");
      }
    } catch (SQLException ex) {
      throw new EJBException("ejbStore: " + ex.getMessage());
    }
  }
```

The setEntityContext() method is called by the EJB 2.1 container after an entity bean is created. Since this entity bean uses JDBC to manage its persistence, we take this opportunity to get a JDBC connection. This connection is obtained within the private getDatabaseConnection() method. We close the JDBC connection when the unsetEntityContext() method is called by the container.

```
  public void setEntityContext(EntityContext ctx) {
    context = ctx;

    try {
      getDatabaseConnection();
    } catch (Exception ex) {
      throw new EJBException("Unable to connect to database. " +
        ex.getMessage());
    }
  }

  public void unsetEntityContext() {
    context = null;
    try {
      connection.close();
    } catch (SQLException ex) {
      throw new EJBException("unsetEntityContext: " + ex.getMessage());
    }
  }

  private void getDatabaseConnection()
    throws NamingException, SQLException {

    InitialContext ctx = new InitialContext();
    DataSource ds =
      (DataSource) ctx.lookup("java:comp/env/jdbc/StockDB");
    connection =  ds.getConnection();
  }
}
```

The deployment XML files we created specify a number of different items, including the fully qualified names of the home and business interface classes. Pay special attention to the ejb-jar.xml file, which contains blocks such as this:

```
<container-transaction>
    <method>
        <ejb-name>StockEjb</ejb-name>
        <method-intf>Remote</method-intf>
        <method-name>setName</method-name>
        <method-params>
            <method-param>java.lang.String</method-param>
        </method-params>
    </method>
    <trans-attribute>Required</trans-attribute>
</container-transaction>
<container-transaction>
    <method>
        <ejb-name>StockEjb</ejb-name>
        <method-intf>Remote</method-intf>
        <method-name>getName</method-name>
    </method>
    <trans-attribute>Required</trans-attribute>
</container-transaction>
<container-transaction>
    <method>
        <ejb-name>StockEjb</ejb-name>
        <method-intf>Remote</method-intf>
        <method-name>remove</method-name>
    </method>
    <trans-attribute>Required</trans-attribute>
</container-transaction>
```

Comparing this implementation with the CMP bean example, you can see how many of the steps required in making the associations between the EJB and the application server are done automatically for you when you're using EJB 3.0. The EJB 3.0 specification saves you from needing to manually define EJB entry points and semantics outside your code. You can do so if you wish, but it is not required, as it is in the earlier versions of the EJB specification.

Now that you've experimented with both CMP and BMP entity beans, let's turn to another feature of entity beans: the use of the EJB Query Language (EJB QL).

The EJB Query Language

Entity beans provide an object-oriented abstraction to an underlying database, complete with the ability to create business methods that operate on the data contained in the entity beans. One problem with this is that the abstract schema can become quite complex, making it very tedious and slow to use Java code to do query-like operations that span multiple entity beans. EJB QL lets you embed queries with SQL-like syntax into entity beans that can be accessed via methods of the entity beans. The results of EJB QL queries are often entity bean references, which can be operated on directly, so you get the combined advantages of object orientation and SQL.

■ **Note** If you need a quick start guide to EJB QL, see Appendix B of this book. For more details, refer to the EJB QL chapter in the EJB specification, which provides a complete reference for EJB QL. To view it, download the EJB 3.0 specification from `http://java.sun.com/products/ejb/docs.html#specs`.

EJB QL Queries

EJB QL queries are issued by the `EntityManager` interface, typically under the auspices of the session beans that make use of the entity bean store in question. The `EntityManager` interface provides a `createQuery()` method that returns a `javax.persistence.Query` object for your use.

■ **Note** The `javax.persistence.Query` object is an abstraction of the EJB QL query you provided, allowing you to alter certain specific aspects of the query after issuing the query string but before receiving results. Its implementation provides you with the ability to set the maximum number of results returned, set query parameters and hints, change certain aspects of the query's execution behavior, and issue the command to the database, as well as return the results.

Consider a fictional astronomy application that has an entity bean named `Planet`. Your session beans that access `Planet` entities could query the `EntityManager` via EJB QL to return only the planets with a given number of moons. The EJB QL query behind it could be something like this:

```
SELECT p
  FROM Planet p
  WHERE p.numMoons = :1
```

This query will do the following:

- Take the argument passed into the method (in this case 0), which is represented by the `:1` portion of the query. This is the same concept as using SQL parameters.
- Find all of the entity bean instances with the abstract schema name of `Planet` whose `numMoons` field contains the value 0. This is indicated by the `WHERE p.numMoons = :1` portion of the code snippet.
- Return a `javax.persistence.Query` object that holds a collection of references to `Planet` entity beans.

The `SELECT` portion of the query snippet indicates that the result will be an entity bean reference or collection of references. The `(p)` indicates that the type of entity bean reference returned will be one with an abstract schema name of `Planet`. That association was indicated by the `Planet p` portion.

Queries can also return a single entity bean reference, rather than a `Collection`. In this case, the singular entity bean would be returned by the `fetchSingleResult()` method of the `Query` object, and the EJB QL query would be designed to return only one entity bean.

Building and Deploying the EJB QL Queries Application

Our next example highlights the development of EJB QL queries by adding two such queries to the `StockList` session bean from the CMP example. To demonstrate the functionality supplied by the find methods, we will change the `StockClient` application quite a bit. Figure 10-5 shows the user interface that we will be using for this modified application.

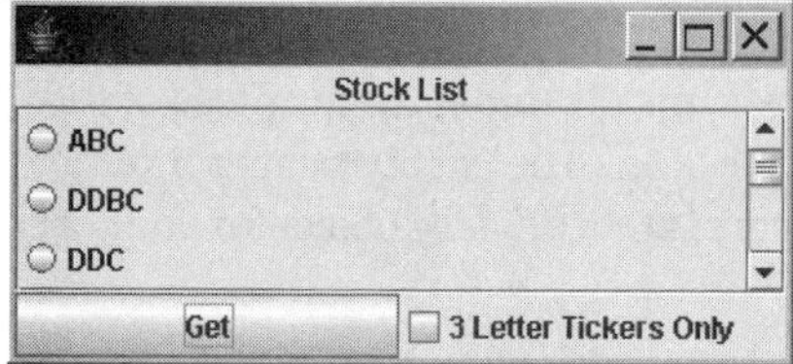

Figure 10-5. *The StockList application showing find method functionality*

When the client starts up, the scrolling panel is populated with radio buttons that represent all of the stock entity beans. If you select one of the stocks and click the Get button, a message dialog box appears with the ticker symbol and name of the stock. When you select the 3 Letter Tickers Only check box, only the stocks with three-letter ticker symbols appear in the scrolling panel.

For this example, the names of the source files are the same as in the CMP example (Listings 10-1 through 10-4), and the process of building, configuring, deploying, and running the example is nearly the same as well. Here are the steps:

1. Create a new application directory, and create the `beans` and `client` subfolders within it.
2. Copy the code files into their respective folders, and then compile them.

Note For this example, `StockList.java`, `StockListBean.java`, and `StockClient.java` are modified from the CMP example. As for all the examples in this book, each of the files for this application is available from the Downloads section of the Apress web site (`www.apress.com`). Because it's very lengthy, the `StockClient.java` file is not listed here, but we will look at its important changes.

---

3. Start the JBoss Server.
4. Create and deploy the entity beans as for the previous examples in this chapter.

When creating the entity bean, there are a couple of additional steps involved (as if there weren't enough already):

- Enter the EJB QL queries in your session bean.
- Load the database with CMP field data for the `Stock` entity beans.

Adding New Queries to the Session Bean

Let's add two methods to our session bean (and its interface) that demonstrate the functionality provided by EJB QL. We'll call the first method `getAllStocks` and the second `getSizeStocks`. The `getAllStocks()` method will quite magically find all stocks in the stocks entity table. The `getSizeStocks()` method will accept one parameter, which it uses to find only stocks whose ticker symbol exceeds some arbitrary length. Add the methods to the `StockListBean.java` file, as shown in Listing 10-14.

Listing 10-14. *StockListBean.java for the EJB QL Queries Example*

```
package beans;

import beans.Stock;
import javax.persistence.PersistenceContext;
import javax.ejb.Stateless;
import javax.persistence.EntityManager;
import javax.persistence.Query;
import java.util.*;

@Stateless
public class StockListBean implements StockList {
  // The reference to the entity manager
  @PersistenceContext
  private EntityManager _manager;

  // The public business methods. These must be coded in the
  // remote interface also.

  public String getStock(String ticker) {
    Stock stock = _manager.find(Stock.class, ticker);
    return stock.getName();
  }

  public void addStock(String ticker, String name) {
    _manager.persist(new Stock(ticker, name));
  }

  public void updateStock(String ticker, String name) {
    Stock stock = _manager.find(Stock.class, ticker);
    stock.setName(name);
  }

  public void deleteStock(String ticker) {
    Stock stock = _manager.find(Stock.class, ticker);
    _manager.remove(stock);
  }
```

```
  // The finder methods
  public String[] getAllStocks() {
    Query query =
      _manager.createQuery("SELECT s FROM Stock s " +
                           "ORDER BY s.tickerSymbol");
    List stockList = query.getResultList();
    String[] stocks = new String[stockList.size()];
    int j = 0;
    for (int i = 0; i < stockList.size(); i++) {
      Stock stock = (Stock) stockList.get(i);
      stocks[j++] = stock.getTickerSymbol();
    }
    return stocks;
  }

  public String[] getSizeStocks(int siz) {
    Query query =
      _manager.createQuery("SELECT s FROM Stock s " +
                           "WHERE LENGTH(s.tickerSymbol) = :len " +
                           "ORDER BY s.tickerSymbol");
    query.setParameter("len", siz);
    List stockList = query.getResultList();
    String[] stocks = new String[stockList.size()];
    int j = 0;
    for (int i = 0; i < stockList.size(); i++) {
      Stock stock = (Stock) stockList.get(i);
      stocks[j++] = stock.getTickerSymbol();
    }
    return stocks;
  }
}
```

Remember to add the associated method signatures to your `StockList.java` interface, as shown in Listing 10-15; otherwise, clients won't be able to use these tasty queries you've cooked up for them!

Listing 10-15. *StockList.java for the EJB QL Queries Example*

```
@Remote
public interface StockList {
  // The public business methods on the Stock List bean
  public void addStock(String ticker, String name);
  public void updateStock(String ticker, String name);
  public void deleteStock(String ticker);
  public String[] getSizeStocks(int siz);
  public String[] getAllStocks();
  public String getStock(String ticker);
}
```

Loading the Database with CMP Field Data for the Stock Entity Beans

To load the database, use the Hypersonic Database Manager as described earlier in this chapter, in the "Deploying the BMP Entity Bean Application" section, to invoke the following SQL commands:

```
insert into Stock values ('ABC', 'ABC Company');
insert into Stock values ('ZZZ', 'Zigby Zebras');
insert into Stock values ('ICS', 'Internet Corp of Slobovia');
insert into Stock values ('DDC', 'Digby Door Company');
insert into Stock values ('ZAP', 'Zelenarinski Ltd.');
insert into Stock values ('JIM', 'Jimco');
insert into Stock values ('SRU', 'Stocks R Us');
insert into Stock values ('SRI', 'Shelves and Radios Inc');
insert into Stock values ('FBC', 'Foo Bar Company');
insert into Stock values ('DDBC', 'Ding Dong Bell Company');
insert into Stock values ('UDE', 'Upn Down Elevator Company');
```

To run the client, set the CLASSPATH to use the client JAR. From the command prompt, enter the following:

```
>set CLASSPATH=.;➥
  c:\jboss\lib\concurrent.jar;➥
  c:\jboss\client\jboss-j2ee.jar;➥
  c:\jboss\lib\commons-httpclient.jar;➥
  c:\jboss\client\jbossall-client.jar;➥
  c:\jboss\lib\jboss-common.jar;➥
  c:\jboss\server\all\lib\jboss.jar;➥
  c:\jboss\server\all\lib\jboss-remoting.jar;➥
  c:\jboss\server\all\lib\jboss-transaction.jar;➥
  c:\jboss\server\all\lib\jnpserver.jar;➥
  c:\jboss\server\all\lib\javax.servlet.jar;➥
  c:\jboss\server\all\deploy\ejb3.deployer\jboss-ejb3.jar;➥
  c:\jboss\server\all\deploy\ejb3.deployer\jboss-ejb3x.jar;➥
  c:\jboss\server\all\deploy\ejb3.deployer\ejb3-persistence.jar;➥
  c:\jboss\server\all\deploy\jboss-aop-jdk50.deployer\➥
       jboss-aop-jdk50.jar;➥
  c:\jboss\server\all\deploy\jboss-aop-jdk50.deployer\➥
       jboss-aspect-library-jdk50.jar
```

Running the EJB QL Queries Application

You can enter the following command to run the client that uses the beans you've built:

```
>java ➥
-Djava.naming.factory.initial=➥
org.jnp.interfaces.NamingContextFactory ➥
-Djava.naming.factory.url.pkgs=➥
org.jboss.naming:org.jnp.interfaces ➥
```

```
-Djava.naming.provider.url=➥
localhost client.StockClient
```

Play with the client UI to see these EJB QL find methods in action.

Reviewing the Session Bean Find Methods

For this application, three Java source files changed from the last example: StockList.java, StockListBean.java, and StockClient.java. Quite appropriately, the Stock entity beans didn't change. Why? Because the changes we made were concerned with the *correct selection* of Stock entities, which has no effect on the actual composition of the Stock entity.

You'll notice that our new find methods are declared in the StockList session bean remote interface (Listing 10-15). The getAllStocks() method returns all of the Stock references. As expected, this interface declares the methods that will be called by the client application.

In the bean class for the StockList session bean, StockListBean.java (Listing 10-14), the getStock() method is the same as in the previous example. The getAllStocks() method calls the newly created getAllStocks() method we declared in the remote interface. The getAllStocks() method, you'll recall, returns a collection of ticker strings for the Stock entity beans. Calling clients can then iterate over those ticker names and access their data as necessary.

The getSizeStocks() method in StockListBean.java receives an integer value that it populates the query with using the setParameter() method of the Query object. You don't remember making the query able to be parameterized? Sure you do! Remember that odd little colon we put in the SQL query:

```
LENGTH(s.tickerSymbol) = :len
```

The :len indicates that we wish to make that particular segment of the query capable of being parameterized, which we take advantage of immediately afterwards by calling the setParameter method. Clients will then receive a String array of the results that match our conditional and use them as needed.

■ **Note** What if you returned an array of entity beans instead of strings? Should you worry about clients accidentally modifying persistent data that will be irrevocably changed in the store? The short answer is no. The entities that are returned are not considered managed. The concept of managed entities versus unmanaged entities is one that has its roots strongly tied to the EntityManager interface we have used throughout this chapter. When our remote interface passes the entities to a calling client, it detaches the entities from the persistence context of the EntityManager. At this point in the application flow, the entity beans have become snapshots of the data in the store; changing their fields will not change data in the store, and vice versa.

Let's turn our attention to the client, in the StockClient class. When you deselect the 3 Letter Tickers Only check box, the getAllStocks() method of the StockList session bean is called to provide the ticker symbols of all the Stock entity beans. When you select the check box, the getSizeStocks() of the session bean is called, passing in a value of 3, which returns a subset of the Stock entity bean's ticker symbols. This is shown in the stateChanged() method:

```
public void stateChanged(ChangeEvent ce) {
  try {
    if (_threeOnly.isSelected()) {
      String[] stocks = _stockList.getSizeStocks(3);
      populateStockPanel(stocks);
    } else {
      String[] stocks = _stockList.getAllStocks();
      populateStockPanel(stocks);
    }
  } catch (Exception e) {
    e.printStackTrace();
  }
```

Summary

This chapter was devoted to entity beans, which are the persistent data objects in an EJB application. You discovered that entity beans share a common anatomy with session beans, but that there are some basic differences between these EJB types.

After having read this chapter, you should know:

- By using CMP, an entity bean type is mapped to its own database table, and the data for each individual entity bean is stored in a row of that table. The EJB container handles all of the database persistence functionality for you. This saves a huge amount of time when developing applications, thereby increasing a developer's productivity.
- Each entity bean has a primary key that uniquely identifies it. The EntityManager has a method named find() that uses this primary key to return the corresponding entity bean.
- EJB QL queries are encapsulated in entity bean methods so that their functionality is available via a method call, using the createQuery() method of the EntityManager interface.

In the next chapter, we'll demonstrate how to create relationships among entity beans using container-managed relationships. In that context, you'll learn more about EJB QL queries. We'll also cover more EJB topics, such as using JDBC with EJBs and EJB timers, and implementing design patterns in EJB applications.

Exercises

1. Create an entity bean for a fictitious Audio CD Collection application named CompactDiscTitle. Attributes should be name (String, and it will be the primary key) and price (double). Write a stateless session bean that allows you to get, add, update, and remove a CD title. Write a client application to test the beans.
2. Modify the previous exercise to use local references for the CompactDiscTitle entity bean.

3. Modify the previous exercise to implement a finder that returns all CD titles in ascending order by name, and a finder that returns all CD titles within a certain price range in ascending order by name. Write a simple client application to test the new methods.

4. Modify the EJB QL stock list example presented at the end of this chapter to return a list of stock tickers that start with a string entered by the user. Order the list as ascending by ticker symbol.

CHAPTER 11

■ ■ ■

EJB Relationships, EJB QL, and JDBC

The previous chapter explored EJB entity beans, which are the persistent data objects in an EJB application. In this chapter, we will continue with EJB-related topics, including entity bean relationships, EJB QL queries, and JDBC with EJB applications.

In this chapter, you will learn the following:

- How to create relationships among entity beans
- How session beans can leverage EJB QL
- How to implement JDBC with EJBs

Entity Bean Relationships

As mentioned in the previous chapter, entity beans may have relationships to other entity beans. These relationships are defined by metadata that describes the reference to the related entity bean instance. The following are the entity bean relationship possibilities and their associated metadata descriptors:

- One-to-one, which is annotated by `@OneToOne` (`javax.persistence.OneToOne`)
- One-to-many, which is annotated by `@OneToMany` (`javax.persistence.OneToMany`)
- Many-to-one, which is annotated by `@ManyToOne` (`javax.persistence.ManyToOne`)
- Many-to-many, which is annotated by `@ManyToMany` (`javax.persistence.ManyToMany`)

As you have no doubt guessed, each of these associated metadata descriptors will be used to describe the point in an entity bean's class definition where a field or getter method provides some data that is related to the encapsulating entity. The relationship that results can (and must, in the case of `@OneToMany` and `@ManyToOne`) be bidirectional or unidirectional.

One-to-Many and Many-to-One Relationships

As an example, let's consider a fictitious application that manages a personal audio CD collection. In the music CD domain, the following might be some candidates for entity beans:

- `CompactDiscTitle`
- `SongTrack`
- `MusicalGenre`
- `Artist`
- `RecordLabel`

These entity beans have relationships with each other. For example, a `CompactDiscTitle` is published by one `RecordLabel`, and a `RecordLabel` has many `CompactDiscTitles`. Therefore, there is a *one-to-many relationship* from `RecordLabel` to `CompactDiscTitle` entity bean instances, and a *many-to-one* relationship from `CompactDiscTitle` to `RecordLabel`.

The term *navigate* is used to describe the process wherein a reference to a related entity bean is obtained from a given entity bean. To be able to navigate the relationships from one entity bean to another in this example, the following methods would be useful:

- A method of the `CompactDiscTitle` entity bean that would return the `RecordLabel` entity bean instance for a given `CompactDiscTitle`. A logical name for this would be `getRecordLabel()`.
- A method of the `RecordLabel` entity bean that would return all of the `CompactDiscTitle` entity bean instances published by a given `RecordLabel`. A good name for this would be `getCompactDiscTitles()`.

As you will soon see, the primary key of each entity bean (the class field or getter method annotated with `@Id`) helps establish these relationships with the other entity bean.

The crude beginning of an Audio CD Collection class diagram shown in Figure 11-1 illustrates the entity bean concepts presented so far. Note the multiplicity notation on the relationships in the diagram. For example, a `RecordLabel` can have 0 or more (0..n in the diagram) `CompactDiscTitles`, while a `CompactDiscTitle` can have only 1 `RecordLabel`. The container-managed relationship between the `CompactDiscTitle` and `RecordLabel` entity beans in the diagram is bidirectional. This is because there is a getter method in both entity beans (annotated by `@ManyToOne` in the case of `CompactDiscTitle`, and `@OneToMany` in the case of `RecordLabel`) that accesses the entity bean on the other side of the relationship. In a unidirectional relationship, only one of the entity beans would have an annotated getter method to access the other entity bean.

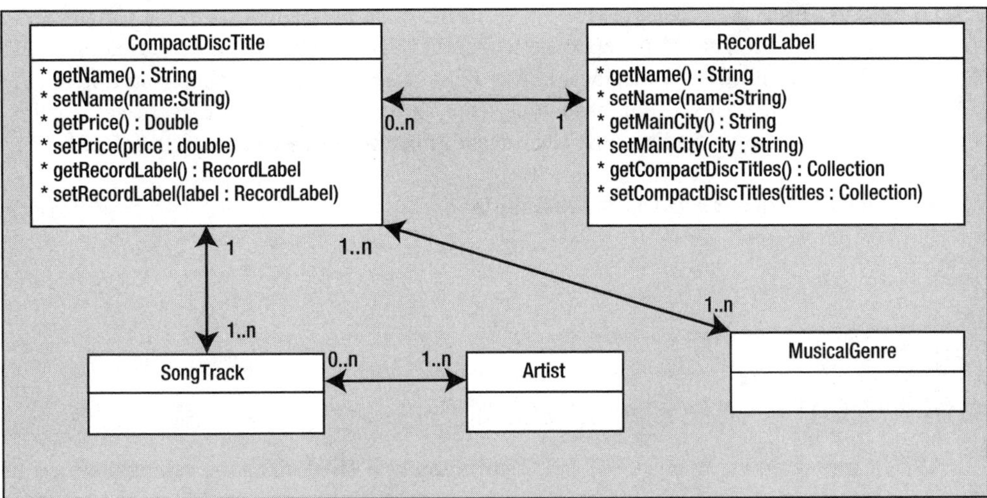

Figure 11-1. *The Audio CD Collection relationship model*

The persistent methods of the `RecordLabel` entity bean are `getName()`, `setName()`, `getMainCity()`, and `setMainCity()`. The `name` field is the name of the record company, and the `mainCity` field is where that record company is headquartered. The primary key of the `RecordLabel` entity bean will be the `name` field, so that field will be unique among the `RecordLabel` entity bean instances.

The methods of the `RecordLabel` entity bean that are affected by these entity bean relationships are `getCompactDiscTitles()` and `setCompactDiscTitles()`. Entity bean methods that interact with the many side of a relationship can use a `java.util.Collection` object to hold the bean interface references. For example, the `getCompactDiscTitles()` method returns a `Collection` of `CompactDiscTitle` bean interface references.

All relationships for entity beans are declared in the class definitions themselves. The `CompactDiscTitle` definition would look like this:

```
@Id
private String sku;
// Other code...
@ManyToOne
@JoinColumn(name="LABEL_ID")
private RecordLabel publishingLabel
```

You'll notice that we've annotated (with `@Id`) the string `sku` to be the primary key for `CompactDiscTitle`, so each bean instance will have a unique stock-keeping unit (SKU) number. The `@ManyToOne` annotation describes its relationship to `RecordLabel`.

The @JoinColumn (javax.persistence.JoinColumn) annotation signifies our desire to place the unique ID corresponding to the instance of RecordLabel in a database column named LABEL_ID. Our entity bean will store its persistence data in a database (or other permanent store), and the LABEL_ID column will be in the database table set aside for CompactDiscTitles. Its value will correspond to the primary key of some RecordLabel instance that our CompactDiscTitle belongs to.

Now, let's look at our RecordLabel definition:

```
@Id
private String name;
// Other code...
@OneToMany
@JoinColumn(name="LABEL_ID")
private Collection<CompactDiscTitle> publishedCDs;
```

We've annotated the string name to be the primary key. This will be the value that exists in the LABEL_ID column for all CompactDiscTitle instances that belong to the RecordLabel in question. The @OneToMany annotation describes its relationship to CompactDiscTitle.

Note that the name specified in the @JoinColumn annotation, LABEL_ID, is the same name we used in CompactDiscTitle. The nature of the relationship between the two objects (@OneToMany and @ManyToOne) indicates that there will probably be far more CompactDiscTitles than there are RecordLabels. The @JoinColumn used to further describe the @OneToMany inverts the relationship that CompactDiscTitle ascribed to RecordLabel, a far more efficient method than storing an indeterminate number of relation references for a single RecordLabel instance.

Assuming we were good Java programmers and made our respective getter and setter methods for the CompactDiscTitle and RecordLabel objects, the relationship we've defined will be persisted for us automatically. Creating a new RecordLabel object, populating its publishedCDs collection with a few CompactDiscTitles, and passing it to the create() method of the EntityManager will fill the tables for both RecordLabel and CompactDiscTitle.

Many-to-Many Relationships

With a many-to-many relationship, an additional database table exists that contains the primary keys from both of the entity beans in the relationship.

To demonstrate a many-to-many relationship, we'll alter the relationship in our example. Now our CompactDiscTitle may belong to multiple RecordLabels, which themselves may be related to any number of CompactDiscTitles—an orgiastic frenzy of CD publishing to be certain, but this is the type of thing that entity bean relationships handle easily.

Let's examine our revised CompactDiscTitle first:

```
@Id
private String sku;
// Other code...
@ManyToMany(cascade=CascadeType.CREATE,isInverse=true)
private Collection<RecordLabel> publishingLabels
```

Notice that we did not specify an @JoinColumn. The EJB implementation should automatically create a column to hold our foreign key (which is what a @JoinColumn is, effectively) for us. Note that some implementations may not honor this particular feature, so you will need to use the

@JoinColumn descriptor, as in the example presented in the "Container-Managed Relationships and EJB QL" section later in this chapter.

With the @ManyToMany tag, we used two attributes: cascade and isInverse. The cascade annotation attribute notifies the EJB implementation how persistence for the related entity beans should be affected when an object "above" them in the relationship hierarchy alters its persistence. CascadeType.CREATE (javax.persistence.CascadeType) implies that we wish to alter persistence only when the CompactDiscTitle in question is passed to the create() method of the EntityManager. Other possible values of CascadeType are MERGE, DELETE, and ALL (the default value). You may specify a particular cascade type for any relationship metadata descriptor (@ManyToOne, @OneToOne, and so on).

The isInverse metadata attribute is a Boolean value that notifies the EJB implementation that the relationship will be bidirectional. Any entity that is related to another may rely on the fact that the entity it's related to contains a relationship back to itself.

The RecordLabel definition looks much like the one for CompactDiscTitle:

```
@Id
private String name;
// Other code...
@ManyToMany(cascade=CascadeType.CREATE,isInverse=true)
private Collection<CompactDiscTitle> publishedCDs;
```

And you haven't even written any database code yet—not bad, huh?

An EJB QL Query to Acquire a Subset of Data

In many cases, you'll want to acquire some subset of related data from an entity bean. However, acquiring a subset of data by merely iterating over the collection of related objects becomes a costly exercise as the total number of related entity beans grows. This cost may be avoided by using EJB QL, which we introduced in Chapter 10.

Continuing with our Audio CD Collection application example, let's say that we want to know the names of the CD titles on record labels that have headquarters in a given city. To accomplish this, we could declare the following method in a MusicCollection session bean class:

```
public List<String> selectByRecordLabelCity(String city);
```

If this method were called with an argument having the value of Detroit, it would use the query() method of the EntityManager to return a query object whose execution provided a List of String values that contains titles such as Consume and White Blood Cells, by Plastikman and The White Stripes, respectively.

■ **Note** The Query (javax.persistence.Query) object returned by the query() method of EntityManager may be considered an abstraction of the EJB QL query you provided to the implementation. Once the Query has been returned, it may be executed by calling its method public List getResultList(). The Query object may also return only one result by calling the method public Object getSingleResult(). You can learn more about the Query object in Appendix B or in the official EJB 3.0 specification.

The EJB QL query that provides the functionality for this method would be something like this:

```
SELECT c.name
 FROM CompactDiscTitle c
 WHERE c.recordLabel.mainCity = :city
```

This query will take the argument passed into the method (in this case, `Detroit`), which is represented by the `:city` portion of the query. Then it will find all of the entity bean instances of `RecordLabel` whose `mainCity` field contains the value of `Detroit`. This is indicated by the `WHERE c.recordLabel.mainCity = :city` clause. The reason `recordLabel.mainCity` represents the `mainCity` field of the `RecordLabel` entity bean is that `c` represents the `CompactDiscTitle` entity bean, because of the `FROM` clause, and `c.recordLabel` represents the `RecordLabel` entity bean instance that is related to the `CompactDiscTitle` entity bean. It is like calling the `getRecordLabel()` method on the `CompactDiscTitle` bean. Finally, the query returns a collection of `String` values containing the `name` field of the related `CompactDiscTitle` entity beans.

■ **Caution** A caveat with using the dot operator to navigate between entity beans, as we do in this example, is that you cannot navigate to the many side of a relationship using it. You can use operators like `IN` and `MEMBER OF` for that kind of functionality. `IN` is a standard SQL operator, and `MEMBER OF` is an EJB QL operator. Notice that we used the dot notation to navigate through the one side of the relationship.

Now let's work through a more involved example that demonstrates both entity bean relationships and some methods that rely on EJB QL.

Container-Managed Relationships and EJB QL

To demonstrate the use of container-managed relationships (CMR) and EJB QL queries, we'll expand the `StockList` example from the previous chapter by adding an entity bean named `Analyst`. Each instance of the `Analyst` bean represents a stock analyst who assigns ratings to stocks. The `Analyst` entity bean and the `Stock` entity bean have a CMR that represents the stocks that a given analyst has rated. Figure 11-2 shows an example of the revised application after Fred the analyst rated the stock for the imaginatively named "ABC Company" and "Jimco".

Figure 11-3 shows a class diagram that depicts the enterprise beans involved in this application. Notice that the `Stock` and `Analyst` entity beans in the diagram represent all of their respective entity bean classes.

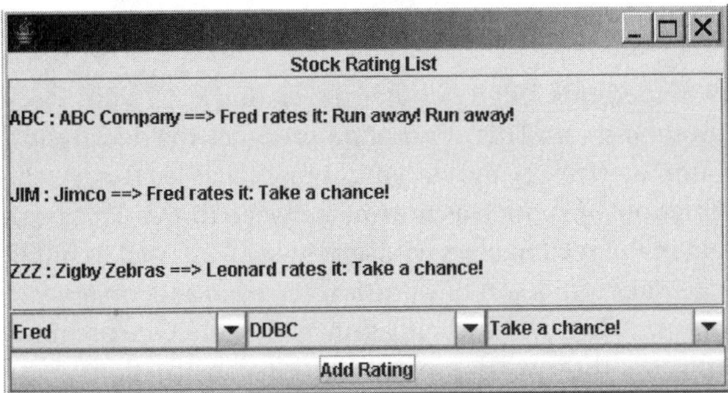

Figure 11-2. *The modified StockClient application*

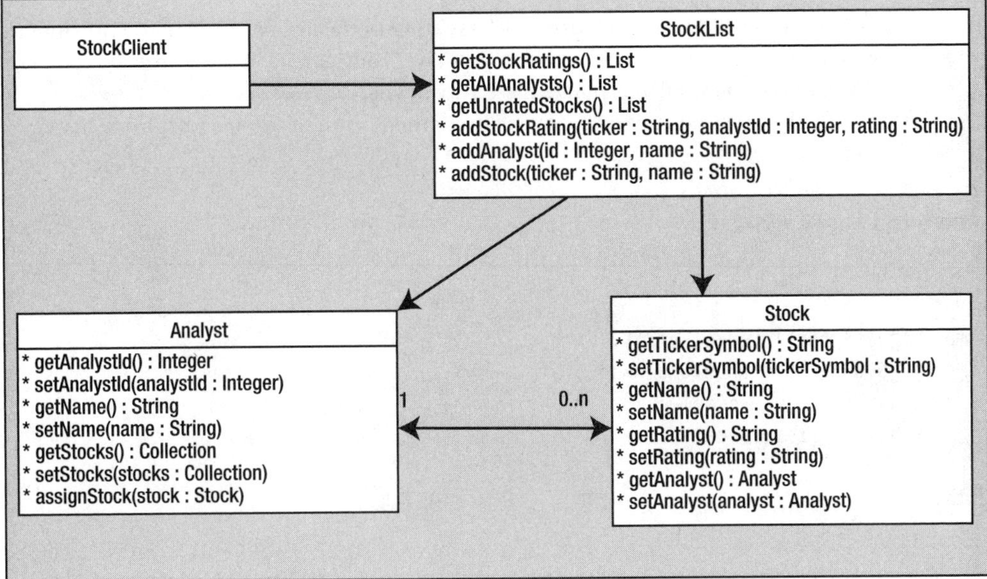

Figure 11-3. *The StockListCmrApp object model and relationship hierarchy*

Studying the diagram in Figure 11-3 in a bit more detail, you can see that the `StockClient` GUI uses methods of the `StockList` session bean to access and manipulate the `Stock` and `Analyst` entity beans. For example, to populate the drop-down list box that contains the analyst's names, it calls the `getAllAnalysts()` method of the session bean, which queries the entity store via EJB QL. When the user clicks the Add Rating button, the `addStockRating()` method of the session bean will be called on to create a relationship between the analyst and the stock being rated. That method will also set the value of the rating (for example, "Could be worse!" or "Take a chance!") into the `rating` field of the `Stock` bean.

The `Stock` bean contains an analyst getter and setter pair annotated by a relationship descriptor (`@ManyToOne`). These methods (named `getAnalyst()` and `setAnalyst()`) reflect the relationship to the `Analyst` bean. This relationship is facilitated by the existence of a primary key persistent field, `private String tickerSymbol`, whose public accessor is annotated by the

@Id descriptor. Also, the Stock bean has two other persistent fields (name and rating) made available by four accessor methods.

The Analyst bean has a similar set of methods, but it denotes its relationship to the Stock bean by the presence of the @OneToMany annotation. This annotation precedes the declaration of the stocks collection getter, and is parameterized by the statement mappedBy="analyst". The mappedBy attribute is used in two-way relationships, such as the one between the Analyst bean and the Stock bean, to describe the field in the related class whose value will be used to fulfill the relationship. In common database parlance, this sort of value is referred to as a *foreign key*.

Now we need to compile, configure, and deploy the application as we did in the previous chapter. The steps are basically the same, but there will be some additional instructions that pertain to CMR and EJB QL queries.

Building the Application with CMR

The names of the source files are the same as those used in the last example of the previous chapter, with the addition of the Analyst bean. Also, we'll add one Java program, StockListAdder.java, to initially populate the entity beans.

Listing 11-1 shows the source code for the implementation of the Analyst entity bean, Analyst.java.

Listing 11-1. *Analyst.java*

```
package beans;

import javax.persistence.Entity;
import javax.persistence.OneToMany;
import java.io.Serializable;
import javax.persistence.Id;

import java.util.*;

@Entity
public class Analyst implements Serializable {
  // The persistent fields
  private Integer analystId;
  private String name;
  // The cmr fields
  private Collection<Stock> stocks;

  // Constructors
  public Analyst() { }
  public Analyst(Integer analystId, String name) {
    this.analystId = analystId;
    this.name = name;
  }
```

```
  // The access methods for persistent fields
  @Id
  public Integer getAnalystId() {
    return analystId;
  }

  public void setAnalystId(Integer analystId) {
    this.analystId = analystId;
  }

  public String getName() {
    return name;
  }

  public void setName(String name) {
    this.name = name;
  }

  // The access methods for cmr fields
  @OneToMany(mappedBy="analyst")
  public Collection<Stock> getStocks()
  {
    return stocks;
  }

  public void setStocks(Collection<Stock> stocks)
  {
    this.stocks = stocks;
  }

  // Business methods
  public void assignStock(Stock stock) {
    if (stocks == null) {
      stocks = new ArrayList();
    }

    stock.setAnalyst(this);
    stocks.add(stock);
  }
}
```

Listing 11-2 shows the source code for the implementation of the `Stock` entity bean, `Stock.java`.

Listing 11-2. *Stock.java*

```
package beans;

import javax.persistence.Entity;
import javax.persistence.ManyToOne;
import java.io.Serializable;
import javax.persistence.Id;

@Entity
public class Stock implements Serializable {
  // The persistent fields
  private String tickerSymbol;
  private String name;
  private String rating;
  // The cmr fields
  private Analyst analyst;

  // Constructors
  public Stock() { }
  public Stock(String tickerSymbol, String name) {
    this.tickerSymbol = tickerSymbol;
    this.name = name;
    this.rating = null;
  }

  // The access methods for persistent fields
  // tickerSymbol is the id
  @Id
  public String getTickerSymbol() {
    return tickerSymbol;
  }

  public void setTickerSymbol(String tickerSymbol) {
    this.tickerSymbol = tickerSymbol;
  }

  public String getName() {
    return name;
  }

  public void setName(String name) {
    this.name = name;
  }
```

```
  public String getRating() {
    return rating;
  }

  public void setRating(String rating) {
    this.rating = rating;
  }

  // The access methods for cmr fields
  @ManyToOne
  public Analyst getAnalyst() {
    return analyst;
  }

  public void setAnalyst(Analyst analyst) {
    this.analyst = analyst;
  }
}
```

Listing 11-3 shows the source code for the remote interface of the `StockList` session bean, `StockList.java`.

Listing 11-3. *StockList.java*

```
package beans;

import javax.ejb.Remote;

// General imports
import java.util.*;

@Remote
public interface StockList {
  // The public business methods on the StockList bean
  public List getStockRatings();
  public List getAllAnalysts();
  public List getUnratedStocks();
  public void addStockRating(String ticker, Integer analystId,
    String rating);
  public void addAnalyst(Integer id, String name);
  public void addStock(String ticker, String name);
}
```

The `StockList` session bean, `StockListBean.java`, is shown in Listing 11-4.

Listing 11-4. *StockListBean.java*

```
package beans;

import javax.persistence.PersistenceContext;
import javax.ejb.Stateless;
import javax.persistence.EntityManager;
import javax.persistence.Query;

// General imports
import java.util.*;

@Stateless
public class StockListBean implements StockList {
  // The reference to the entity manager
  @PersistenceContext
  private EntityManager _manager;

  // The public business methods. these must be coded in the
  // remote interface also.

  public List getStockRatings() {
    List stkList = new ArrayList();
    Query query =
      _manager.createQuery("SELECT DISTINCT OBJECT(s) " +
                           "FROM Stock s " +
                           "WHERE s.analyst IS NOT NULL " +
                           "ORDER BY s.tickerSymbol");
    // Get the rated stocks
    List stocks = query.getResultList();
    for (int i = 0; i < stocks.size(); i++) {
        Stock stock = (Stock) stocks.get(i);
        String[] stockData = new String[4];
        stockData[0] = stock.getTickerSymbol();
        stockData[1] = stock.getName();
        stockData[2] = stock.getAnalyst().getName();
        stockData[3] = stock.getRating();
        stkList.add(stockData);
      }

      return stkList;
  }

  public List getAllAnalysts() {
    List analystList = new ArrayList();
    Query query =
      _manager.createQuery("SELECT Object(a) " +
                           "FROM Analyst a " +
                           "ORDER BY a.name");
```

```
    // Get the analysts
    List analysts = query.getResultList();
    for (int i = 0; i < analysts.size(); i++) {
      Analyst analyst = (Analyst) analysts.get(i);
      Object[] analystData = new Object[2];
      analystData[0] = analyst.getAnalystId();
      analystData[1] = analyst.getName();
      analystList.add(analystData);
    }

    return analystList;
  }

  public List getUnratedStocks() {
    List stkList = new ArrayList();
    Query query =
      _manager.createQuery("SELECT DISTINCT OBJECT(s) " +
                           "FROM Stock s " +
                           "WHERE s.analyst IS NULL " +
                           "ORDER BY s.tickerSymbol");
    // Get the unrated stocks
    List stocks = query.getResultList();
    for (int i = 0; i < stocks.size(); i++) {
      Stock stock = (Stock) stocks.get(i);
      stkList.add(stock.getTickerSymbol());
    }

    return stkList;
  }

  public void addStockRating(String ticker, Integer analystId,
    String rating) {
    Stock stock = _manager.find(Stock.class, ticker);
    Analyst analyst = _manager.find(Analyst.class, analystId);
    analyst.assignStock(stock);
    stock.setRating(rating);
  }

  public void addAnalyst(Integer id, String name) {
    _manager.persist(new Analyst(id, name));
  }

  public void addStock(String ticker, String name) {
    _manager.persist(new Stock(ticker, name));
  }
}
```

The StockClient class, StockClient.java, used to interface with the application is shown in Listing 11-5.

Listing 11-5. *StockClient.java*

```
package client;

import beans.StockList;
import javax.naming.InitialContext;

import java.util.*;

// General imports
import java.awt.*;
import java.awt.event.*;
import javax.swing.*;

public class StockClient extends JFrame
  implements ActionListener {
  private StockList _stockList;
  private Integer[] _analystIds;
  private JButton _get = new JButton("Add Rating");
  private JPanel _stockPanel = new JPanel();
  private JComboBox _analysts = new JComboBox();
  private JComboBox _tickers = new JComboBox();
  private JComboBox _ratings = new JComboBox();

  public StockClient() {
    // Get the stock lister
    _stockList = getStockList();

    // Add the title
    JLabel title = new JLabel("Stock Rating List");
    title.setHorizontalAlignment(JLabel.CENTER);
    getContentPane().add(title, BorderLayout.NORTH);

    JPanel activityPanel = new JPanel(new BorderLayout());
    try {
      // Add the stock list
      buildStockList();
      JScrollPane scroller = new JScrollPane(_stockPanel);
      activityPanel.add(scroller, BorderLayout.CENTER);

      // Add the rating panel
      JPanel ratingPanel = new JPanel(new GridLayout(1, 3));
      // add the analysts
      populateAnalysts();
      ratingPanel.add(_analysts);
```

```
      // Add the unrated stocks
      populateTickers();
      ratingPanel.add(_tickers);
      // Add the ratings to pick from
      _ratings.addItem("Run away! Run away!");
      _ratings.addItem("Could be worse!");
      _ratings.addItem("A bit of OK!");
      _ratings.addItem("Take a chance!");
      _ratings.addItem("Smashing!");
      ratingPanel.add(_ratings);
      activityPanel.add(ratingPanel, BorderLayout.SOUTH);

      getContentPane().add(activityPanel, BorderLayout.CENTER);
    }
    catch (Exception e) {
      e.printStackTrace();
    }

    // Add the buttons panel
    JPanel buttons = new JPanel(new GridLayout(1, 1));
    _get.addActionListener(this);
    buttons.add(_get);
    getContentPane().add(buttons, BorderLayout.SOUTH);

    addWindowListener(new WindowAdapter() {
      public void windowClosing(WindowEvent e) {
        System.exit(0);
      }
    });

    setSize(480, 250);
    setVisible(true);
  }

  private void buildStockList() throws Exception {
    java.util.List stoks = _stockList.getStockRatings();
    _stockPanel.removeAll();
    _stockPanel.setLayout(new GridLayout(stoks.size(), 1));
    for (int i = 0; i < stoks.size(); i++) {
      String[] stokInfo = (String[]) stoks.get(i);
      Box stokLine = Box.createHorizontalBox();
      String stokDesc = stokInfo[0] + " : " + stokInfo[1]
        + " ==> " + stokInfo[2] + " rates it: " + stokInfo[3];
      stokLine.add(new JLabel(stokDesc));
      _stockPanel.add(stokLine);
    }
```

```
    _stockPanel.invalidate();
    _stockPanel.validate();
  }

  private void populateAnalysts() throws Exception {
    java.util.List anlysts = _stockList.getAllAnalysts();
    _analystIds = new Integer[anlysts.size()];
    for (int i = 0; i < anlysts.size(); i++) {
      Object[] analystData = (Object[]) anlysts.get(i);
      _analystIds[i] = (Integer) analystData[0];
      _analysts.addItem((String) analystData[1]);
    }
  }

  private void populateTickers() throws Exception {
    _tickers.removeAllItems();
    java.util.List tkrs = _stockList.getUnratedStocks();
    for (int i = 0; i < tkrs.size(); i++) {
      String ticker = (String) tkrs.get(i);
      _tickers.addItem(ticker);
    }
    _tickers.invalidate();
    _tickers.validate();
  }

  private StockList getStockList() {
    StockList stockList = null;
    try {
      // Get a naming context
      InitialContext ctx = new InitialContext();

      // Get a StockList object
      stockList =
        (StockList) ctx.lookup(StockList.class.getName());
    } catch(Exception e) {
      e.printStackTrace();
    }

    return stockList;
  }

  public void actionPerformed(ActionEvent ae) {
    // get was clicked
    if (ae.getSource() == _get) {
      try {
        int anlystNo = _analysts.getSelectedIndex();
        if (anlystNo < 0) {
```

```
          JOptionPane.showMessageDialog(this, "No analyst selected!");
          return;
        }
        Integer aId = _analystIds[anlystNo];
        if (_tickers.getSelectedIndex() < 0) {
          JOptionPane.showMessageDialog(this, "No ticker selected!");
          return;
        }
        String tkr = (String) _tickers.getSelectedItem();
        if (_ratings.getSelectedIndex() < 0) {
          JOptionPane.showMessageDialog(this, "No rating selected!");
          return;
        }
        String rtg = (String) _ratings.getSelectedItem();
        _stockList.addStockRating(tkr, aId, rtg);
        buildStockList();
        populateTickers();
      }
      catch (Exception e) {
        e.printStackTrace();
      }
    }
  }

  public static void main(String[] args) {
    StockClient stockClient = new StockClient();
  }
}
```

Rather than using INSERT statements to populate the database, as we did in the previous chapter, we're going to use a Java program, StockListAdder.java. This program will use methods of the StockList session bean to create some Analyst and Stock entity beans. It will also use the StockList session bean to create a stock rating by associating a Stock entity bean with an Analyst entity bean and setting the rating field of the Stock entity bean. Listing 11-6 shows the source code for StockListAdder.java.

Listing 11-6. *StockListAdder.java*

```
package client;

import beans.StockList;
import javax.naming.InitialContext;

// General imports
import java.awt.*;
import java.awt.event.*;
import javax.swing.*;
import javax.swing.event.*;
```

```
public class StockListAdder {

  public static void main(String[] args) {
    try {
      InitialContext ctx = new InitialContext();

      // Get a StockList object
      StockList stockList =
        (StockList) ctx.lookup(StockList.class.getName());

      // Add analysts
      System.out.println("adding analysts");
      stockList.addAnalyst(new Integer(1), "Fred");
      stockList.addAnalyst(new Integer(2), "Leonard");
      stockList.addAnalyst(new Integer(3), "Sarah");
      stockList.addAnalyst(new Integer(4), "Nancy");
      System.out.println("analysts added");
    }
    catch (Exception e) {
      System.out.println("exception adding analysts");
      e.printStackTrace();
    }

    try {
      InitialContext ctx = new InitialContext();

      // Get a StockList object
      StockList stockList =
        (StockList) ctx.lookup(StockList.class.getName());

      // Add stocks
      System.out.println("adding stocks");
      stockList.addStock("ABC", "ABC Company");
      stockList.addStock("ZZZ", "Zigby Zebras");
      stockList.addStock("ICS", "Internet Corp of Slobovia");
      stockList.addStock("DDC", "Digby Door Company");
      stockList.addStock("ZAP", "Zapalopalorinski Ltd.");
      stockList.addStock("JIM", "Jimco");
      stockList.addStock("SRU", "Stocks R Us");
      stockList.addStock("SRI", "Shelves and Radios Inc");
      stockList.addStock("FBC", "Foo Bar Company");
      stockList.addStock("DDBC", "Ding Dong Bell Company");
      stockList.addStock("UDE", "Upn Down Elevator Company");
      System.out.println("stocks added");
    }
```

```
    catch (Exception e) {
      System.out.println("exception adding stocks");
      e.printStackTrace();
    }

    try {
      InitialContext ctx = new InitialContext();

      // Get a StockList object
      StockList stockList =
        (StockList) ctx.lookup(StockList.class.getName());

      // Add ratings
      System.out.println("adding ratings");
      stockList.addStockRating("ZZZ", new Integer(2),
        "Take a chance!");
      System.out.println("ratings added");
    }
    catch (Exception e) {
      System.out.println("exception adding stocks");
      e.printStackTrace();
    }
  }
}
```

Organize the files in the StockListCmrApp application directory. The Analyst.java, Stock.java, StockList.java, and StockListBean.java files (Listings 11-1 through 11-4) go in the beans subfolder. The StockClient.java (Listing 11-5) and StockListAdder.java (Listing 11-6) files go in the client subfolder.

Compiling the CMR Application

To compile the application, open a command prompt in the application directory (StockListCmrApp), set the CLASSPATH (shown here for a default JBoss Windows installation), and compile the classes:

```
> set CLASSPATH=.;➥
C:\jboss\lib\concurrent.jar; ➥
C:\jboss\lib\jboss-common.jar; ➥
c:\jboss\lib\commons-httpclient.jar;➥
C:\jboss\server\all\lib\jboss.jar; ➥
C:\jboss\server\all\lib\jboss-remoting.jar; ➥
C:\jboss\server\all\lib\jboss-transaction.jar; ➥
C:\jboss\server\all\lib\jnpserver.jar; ➥
C:\jboss\server\all\deploy\ejb3.deployer\jboss-ejb3.jar; ➥
C:\jboss\server\all\deploy\ejb3.deployer\jboss-ejb3x.jar; ➥
c:\jboss\client\jboss-j2ee.jar;➥
c:\jboss\server\all\deploy\ejb3.deployer\ejb3-persistence.jar;➥
C:\jboss\server\all\deploy\jboss-aop-jdk50.deployer\➥
jboss-aop-jdk50.jar; ➥
C:\jboss\server\all\deploy\jboss-aop-jdk50.deployer\➥
jboss-aspect-library-jdk50.jar
```

Within the StockListCmrApp directory, execute the following commands from the command prompt:

```
> javac -d . client/*.java
> javac -d . beans/*.java
```

Deploying the CMR Application

To deploy the application, start the JBoss Server (see Chapter 2 for details). Then create the application EJB3 file by executing the following command from the command prompt:

```
>jar cf StockListCmrApp.ejb3 beans/*.class
```

Copy the EJB3 file to the server's deployment directory, using a command like this:

```
>copy StockListCmrApp.ejb3 c:\jboss\server\all\deploy
```

Loading the Database

Run the StockListAdder.java application (Listing 11-6) to populate the beans by entering the following on the command line:

```
>java ➥
-Djava.naming.factory.initial=➥
org.jnp.interfaces.NamingContextFactory ➥
-Djava.naming.factory.url.pkgs=➥
org.jboss.naming:org.jnp.interfaces ➥
-Djava.naming.provider.url=➥
localhost client.StockListAdder
```

After running this command, you will see the following output displayed:

```
adding analysts
analysts added
adding stocks
stocks added
adding ratings
ratings added
```

Running the CMR Application

Now that the database is populated, run the client that uses the beans we've built by using the following command:

```
>java ➥
-Djava.naming.factory.initial=➥
org.jnp.interfaces.NamingContextFactory ➥
-Djava.naming.factory.url.pkgs=➥
org.jboss.naming:org.jnp.interfaces ➥
-Djava.naming.provider.url=➥
localhost client.StockClient
```

You should see a screen like the one shown in Figure 11-4.

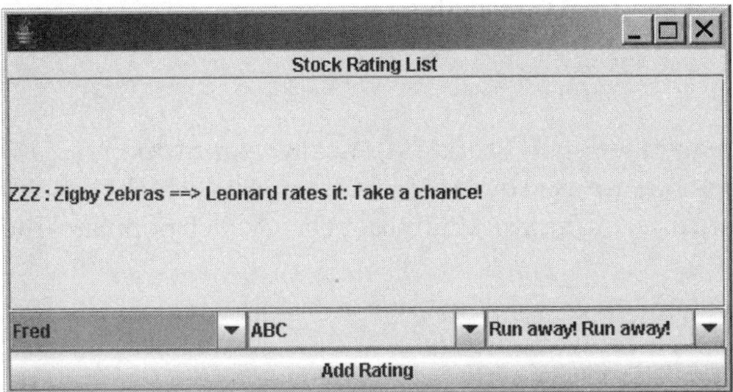

Figure 11-4. *Running the StockClient application*

Reviewing the CMR Application

Now, let's look at the new elements of our beans that pertain to CMR and EJB QL queries.

Analyst Entity Bean

In the `Analyst` entity bean, `Analyst.java` (Listing 11-1), the `stocks` CMR field is defined by the `getStocks()` and `setStocks()` methods. These methods return and take a `Collection` of `Stock` entity beans, respectively. The getter method is annotated by the `@OneToMany` descriptor in order to specify how the collection will be filled by the entity bean relationship. The `import java.util.*` statement is there because the `Collection` interface is in that package.

We've created a convenience method named `assignStock()` that adds a `Stock` entity bean to the many side of the relationship by performing the following steps:

- Check if the `stocks` object exists yet. If the field does not point to a valid object (one that implements the `java.util.Collection` interface), populate it with a new `ArrayList`.
- Add a new `stock` to the `stocks` collection after ensuring that the stock analyst reference points to `this`.

Since we've defined this relationship as bidirectional, the EJB container manages the other side of this relationship by using the `setAnalyst()` method of the `Stock` bean. Recall that we defined the relationship as bidirectional by annotating the fields that fulfilled this relationship with the dependent metadata descriptors `@OneToMany` and `@ManyToOne`.

This `assignStock()` method is called by the `StockList` session bean when assigning a `Stock` entity bean to an `Analyst` entity bean.

Stock Entity Bean

In our `Stock` entity bean, `Stock.java` (Listing 11-2), the `analyst` CMR field is defined by the `getAnalyst()` and `setAnalyst()` methods. As you might have noted while building this example, these methods return and take an `Analyst` bean reference, respectively. Recall that the relationship specified by the `@ManyToOne` metadata descriptor dictates that a stock can be rated by *only one* analyst, but an analyst can rate *many* stocks. Pay special attention to the fact that the relationship between the two classes is fulfilled automatically. The JBoss EJB container is able to intuit the correct fields enabling the data relationship based on the target of the @Id annotation in the related class. Other server containers may not fully provide such functionality; check your server documentation to see if support for that feature is provided.

StockList Session Bean

In the Java source code for the remote interface of the StockList session bean, StockList.java (Listing 11-3), the first four of these methods are used by the StockClient class, which provides the client UI. The last three methods are used by the StockListAdder class, which populates the entity beans initially.

In the source code for the implementation of the StockList session bean, StockListBean.java (Listing 11-4), the first method of interest is getStockRatings():

```
public List getStockRatings() {
  List stkList = new ArrayList();
  Query query =
    _manager.createQuery("SELECT DISTINCT OBJECT(s) " +
                         "FROM Stock s " +
                         "WHERE s.analyst IS NOT NULL " +
                         "ORDER BY s.tickerSymbol");
  // Get the rated stocks
  List stocks = query.getResultList();
  for (int i = 0; i < stocks.size(); i++) {
      Stock stock = (Stock) stocks.get(i);
      String[] stockData = new String[4];
      stockData[0] = stock.getTickerSymbol();
      stockData[1] = stock.getName();
      stockData[2] = stock.getAnalyst().getName();
      stockData[3] = stock.getRating();
      stkList.add(stockData);
    }

    return stkList;
}
```

This method creates a query object using the following EJB QL statement:

```
SELECT DISTINCT OBJECT(s)
                         FROM Stock s
                         WHERE s.analyst IS NOT NULL
                         ORDER BY s.tickerSymbol
```

The execution of this Query object returns a collection of Stock beans that have been rated. The getStockRatings() method then creates an ArrayList of String arrays. Each String array has four elements that contain the stock's ticker symbol, the stock's name, the name of the analyst that rated it, and the rating. The client UI uses the ArrayList returned from getStockRatings() each time it needs to display a current list of the stocks that have been rated.

Note In Chapter 12, you'll see how to move away from using `String` arrays to pass data between clients and session beans in favor of using classes that are modeled after the `Stock` and `Analyst` entity beans.

The `getAllAnalysts()` method similarly creates a `Query` object using an unqualified EJB QL query to get references to all of the `Analyst` beans:

```
public List getAllAnalysts() {
  List analystList = new ArrayList();
  Query query =
    _manager.createQuery("SELECT Object(a) " +
                         "FROM Analyst a " +
                         "ORDER BY a.name");
  // Get the analysts
  List analysts = query.getResultList();
  for (int i = 0; i < analysts.size(); i++) {
    Analyst analyst = (Analyst) analysts.get(i);
    Object[] analystData = new Object[2];
    analystData[0] = analyst.getAnalystId();
    analystData[1] = analyst.getName();
    analystList.add(analystData);
  }

  return analystList;
}
```

The `getAllAnalysts()` method returns the data contained in the `Analyst` beans via an `ArrayList` of `String` arrays. The client UI uses this method when it needs to populate the drop-down list that contains the names of the analysts.

The `getUnratedStocks()` method queries the entity store for all `Stock` objects whose relation field to `Analyst` objects is null:

```
public List getUnratedStocks() {
    List stkList = new ArrayList();
    Query query =
      _manager.createQuery("SELECT DISTINCT OBJECT(s) " +
                           "FROM Stock s " +
                           "WHERE s.analyst IS NULL " +
                           "ORDER BY s.tickerSymbol");
    // Get the unrated stocks
    List stocks = query.getResultList();
    for (int i = 0; i < stocks.size(); i++) {
      Stock stock = (Stock) stocks.get(i);
      stkList.add(stock.getTickerSymbol());
    }

    return stkList;
  }
```

The getUnratedStocks() method uses the collections returned from this query to identify the stocks that haven't been rated, and it returns an ArrayList of String values containing ticker symbols. The client UI uses this method when it needs to populate the drop-down list that contains the ticker symbols for stocks that haven't been rated.

Next is the addStockRating() method:

```
public void addStockRating(String ticker, ➥
    Integer analystId,➥
    String rating) {
  Stock stock = _manager.find(Stock.class, ticker);
  Analyst analyst = _manager.find(Analyst.class, analystId);
  analyst.assignStock(stock);
  stock.setRating(rating);
}
```

The addStockRating() method takes three arguments: the ticker symbol of the stock being rated, the ID number of the analyst rating the stock, and the rating value string. The first two arguments are the primary keys of the Stock and Analyst entity beans, respectively. This method uses these values to get references to a Stock bean and an Analyst bean. It then calls the assignStock() method of the Analyst bean, passing in the reference of the Stock bean being rated. The client UI uses this method when the user clicks the Add Rating button. The StockListAdder class uses this addStockRating() method as well to set up an initial stock rating.

Finally, let's look at the addAnalyst() and addStock() methods:

```
public void addAnalyst(Integer id, String name) {
  _manager.persist(new Analyst(id, name));
}

public void addStock(String ticker, String name) {
  _manager.persist(new Stock(ticker, name));
}
```

These methods take as arguments the values required for creating Analyst and Stock beans, respectively, after which they call the persist() method of the EntityManager interface. The StockListAdder class uses these methods to create entity beans, and the client UI (the StockClient class) does not use them at all.

Thus far in the chapter, our focus has been limited to EJB QL and CMR with entity beans. Using those technologies in concert will typically suffice for most applications where ease of development is of primary concern. However, there will be times when using JDBC as the method of access to entity information is preferable.

JDBC with EJB Entity Beans

As we've noted in this and previous chapters regarding entity beans, CMP is a method of transparently persisting data to some container-specified store. Enterprise application developers will find it an invaluable tool, as it allows them to avoid writing leagues of redundant database-access code. However, CMP is not a panacea for all data-aware object ills. Particularly, the use of CMP and EJB QL raises several concerns for you as the developer:

- CMP is another layer of abstraction between the application and the data, and must always be slower than a native JDBC solution. Efficient EJB implementations may provide a level of performance that operates imperceptibly slower than native access; a high level of performance cannot be guaranteed for all possible usage scenarios, however.
- Requesting large sets of CMP objects can be an expensive undertaking, on an order higher than retrieving a comparatively simple collection of data rows.
- Access to database-specific functionality is removed from the developer's immediate use. Special functions that perform operations such as XPath statements across an XML column or geospatial computations become unavailable through a standard `EntityManager` query. (Although you can issue native queries from `EntityManager`.)

Realize that even though there are pitfalls you should be aware of when using CMP in your application, this doesn't mean you must always adopt a custom JDBC-only object persistence layer. The minds behind the EJB specification have spent a significant amount of time making object persistence a near-painless task. However, when you need raw data fast and without extra semantics, it might be time to integrate JDBC into your application.

GOING REASONABLY NATIVE

The `EntityManager` interface exposes a method `public Query createNativeQuery(String sqlString)` that allows you to issue database queries directly to the underlying entity bean store. The method returns a `Query` object for your use, just as the `createQuery(String ejbqlString)` method does.

A good example of use for the `createNativeQuery()` method is the execution of a stored procedure in the database:

```
Query q = manager.createNativeQuery("exec sp_fetch_all_shoes()");
ArrayList<shoes> shoelist = q.getResultList();
```

It may seem as if there's hardly anything to the example. That is, of course, the exact point: having access to provider-specific stored procedures allows the application to gain the benefit of prepared rich data queries, while still having the ease of use provided by the CMP layer.

While having some facility to issue SQL queries directly to the database solves the problem of isolation from database-specific grammar, it does not concretely solve the problem of access efficiency. Passing the SQL through the `EntityManager` still demands at least one extra layer of execution, the presence of which may be unacceptable, depending on the query and application. Hard-coding SQL queries in code is a sure way to lose your credibility with other Java developers. Relying on a schema and database that is only as correct as of the last compilation is a practice directly in contrast with the "Java Philosophy," something that can only end in infamy, shame, and forced servitude in the spice mines.

Implementing JDBC with EJB Applications

Once you've decided to use JDBC in your EJB application, you need to address a bevy of questions in regard to implementation. Will your application be doing any `INSERT` or `UPDATE` operations using JDBC? Should all your queries be issued in transactions, or is the `COMMIT/ROLLBACK` approach unnecessary? These sorts of questions are necessary for the effective usage of JDBC within an EJB application.

For example, consider a video rental inventory application that consists of three types of entity beans—Renter, Video, and Rental—and one stateless session bean—InventoryViewBean. Renter and Video represent the details regarding the persons who rent out videos and the videos available in the store for rental, respectively. Rental is a representation of the transactions between the two; each Rental entity bean represents an instance where a customer has rented (and optionally, returned) a video from the store.

The previous sections in this chapter have shown how the relationships between the different entity beans may be formed. Rental has a @OneToMany relationship to both Renter and Video. Renter and Video, in turn, have a @ManyToOne relationship to Rental. However, suppose some sort of data is required in multiple instances that is transitive in nature. An example would be the likelihood of a particular individual returning her rented video on time. Such a value would be poorly represented as a persistent field when its value is derived from the state of its owner object and related objects at the time the value is requested. Furthermore, the singular nature of the value (in this case, a floating-point number) and the potentially expensive execution of the query seems to demand the low-overhead session with the database that you can obtain with JDBC.

To take the JDBC approach, since the value returned by the method reflects on the behavior of a Renter, it goes in the Renter class file. The method is declared static, to imply that the value gains its meaning outside the instanced data of all members of the Renter hierarchy. All that remains is the implementation:

```
public static float getRenterReliability(Renter r) {
  try {
    // Make the command
    String cmd = "{CALL ? := sp_computeReliability(?)}"
    Connection conn;
    // Get the db connection, statement and result
    CallableStatement stmt = conn.prepareCall(cmd);
    stmt.registerOutParameter(1,Types.FLOAT);
    stmt.SetInt(2,r.getId());
    stmt.Execute();
    float f=stmt.getFloat(2)
    conn.close();
    return f;
  }
  catch (Exception ex) {
    throw new RuntimeException(ex.getMessage());
  }
}
```

In short, all you've done is add a simple value fetcher to an EJB using JDBC. While this may seem trivial, it's important to note what you didn't do: you didn't use EJB QL to get your results, nor did you incur any extra overhead by interfacing with the object persistence layer. EJB QL and CMP are good enough to handle the tasks of persisting and iterating over the collection of video rental objects. As any good programmer will tell you, there's no sense reinventing the wheel unless the new wheel is cool enough to merit the time spent.

Using JDBC with the StockList Bean

To demonstrate using JDBC with an entity bean, we'll modify the previous example in this chapter to use JDBC to return a summary of analyst data. To accomplish this, we'll modify the `getAllAnalysts()` method of the `StockListBean` class that we walked through earlier in this chapter. This modification will entail removing the EJB QL call and executing a JDBC query instead. Other than this change to the `StockListBean.java` file, the rest of the previous example will remain the same.

Listing 11-7 shows the modified version of `StockListBean.java`.

Listing 11-7. *StockListBean.java for Use with JDBC*

```
package beans;

import java.sql.Connection;
import java.sql.ResultSet;
import java.sql.Statement;
import java.sql.SQLException;
import javax.persistence.PersistenceContext;
import javax.ejb.Stateless;
import javax.persistence.EntityManager;
import javax.persistence.Query;
import javax.naming.InitialContext;
import javax.naming.NamingException;
import javax.sql.DataSource;

// General imports
import java.util.*;

@Stateless
public class StockListBean implements StockList {
  // The reference to the entity manager
  @PersistenceContext
  private EntityManager _manager;

  // The public business methods. These must be coded in the
  // remote interface also.

  public List getStockRatings() {
    List stkList = new ArrayList();
    Query query =
      _manager.createQuery("SELECT DISTINCT OBJECT(s) " +
                           "FROM Stock s " +
                           "WHERE s.analyst IS NOT NULL " +
                           "ORDER BY s.tickerSymbol");
```

```
        // Get the rated stocks
        List stocks = query.getResultList();
        for (int i = 0; i < stocks.size(); i++) {
            Stock stock = (Stock) stocks.get(i);
            String[] stockData = new String[4];
            stockData[0] = stock.getTickerSymbol();
            stockData[1] = stock.getName();
            stockData[2] = stock.getAnalyst().getName();
            stockData[3] = stock.getRating();
            stkList.add(stockData);
          }

          return stkList;
      }

      public List getAllAnalysts() {
        try {
          // Make the sql
          StringBuffer sql = new StringBuffer();
          sql.append("SELECT analystId, name ");
          sql.append("FROM Analyst ");
          sql.append("ORDER BY name");

          // Get the db connection, statement and result set
          Connection conn = makeConnection();
          Statement stmt = conn.createStatement();
          ResultSet results = stmt.executeQuery(sql.toString());

          // Get the analysts
          List analystList = new ArrayList();
          while (results.next()) {
            Object[] analystData = new Object[2];
            analystData[0] = new Integer(results.getInt(1));
            analystData[1] = results.getString(2);
            analystList.add(analystData);
          }

          results.close();
          stmt.close();
          conn.close();

          return analystList;
        }
        catch (Exception ex) {
          throw new RuntimeException(ex.getMessage());
        }
      }
```

```
  public List getUnratedStocks() {
    List stkList = new ArrayList();
    Query query =
      _manager.createQuery("SELECT DISTINCT OBJECT(s) " +
                           "FROM Stock s " +
                           "WHERE s.analyst IS NULL " +
                           "ORDER BY s.tickerSymbol");
    // Get the unrated stocks
    List stocks = query.getResultList();
    for (int i = 0; i < stocks.size(); i++) {
      Stock stock = (Stock) stocks.get(i);
      stkList.add(stock.getTickerSymbol());
    }

    return stkList;
  }

  public void addStockRating(String ticker, Integer analystId,
    String rating) {
    Stock stock = _manager.find(Stock.class, ticker);
    Analyst analyst = _manager.find(Analyst.class, analystId);
    analyst.assignStock(stock);
    stock.setRating(rating);
  }

  public void addAnalyst(Integer id, String name) {
    _manager.persist(new Analyst(id, name));
  }

  public void addStock(String ticker, String name) {
    _manager.persist(new Stock(ticker, name));
  }

  private Connection makeConnection()
    throws NamingException, SQLException {

    InitialContext ic = new InitialContext();
    DataSource ds =
      (DataSource) ic.lookup("java:/DefaultDS");
    return ds.getConnection();
  }
}
```

StockListBean remains relatively unchanged, except for the presence of some JDBC connection code and the new getAllAnalysts() method. Examining the makeConnection() method, you can see that the DataSource that provides database connections to the entity store is obtained via the JNDI path java:/DefaultDS. This JNDI path refers to the default database maintained by

JBoss for entity beans. The getAllAnalysts() method remains functionally identical to its EJB QL predecessor, but now avoids the CMP overhead caused by issuing a query through EntityManager.

Organize the files in the StockListJDBCApp application directory. Put the StockListBean.java file (Listing 11-6), along with the Analyst.java, Stock.java, StockList.java, and StockListBean.java files (Listings 11-1 through 11-4) in the beans subfolder. Put StockClient.java (Listing 11-5) and StockListAdder.java (Listing 11-6) in the client subfolder.

To compile the application, open a command prompt in the StockListJDBCApp application directory, set the CLASSPATH, and deploy the classes (shown here for a default JBoss Windows installation):

```
> set CLASSPATH=.;➥
C:\jboss\lib\concurrent.jar; ➥
C:\jboss\lib\jboss-common.jar; ➥
c:\jboss\lib\commons-httpclient.jar;➥
c:\jboss\client\jboss-j2ee.jar;➥
c:\jboss\server\all\deploy\ejb3.deployer\ejb3-persistence.jar;➥
C:\jboss\server\all\lib\jboss.jar; ➥
C:\jboss\server\all\lib\jboss-remoting.jar; ➥
C:\jboss\server\all\lib\jboss-transaction.jar; ➥
C:\jboss\server\all\lib\jnpserver.jar; ➥
C:\jboss\server\all\deploy\ejb3.deployer\jboss-ejb3.jar; ➥
C:\jboss\server\all\deploy\ejb3.deployer\jboss-ejb3x.jar; ➥
C:\jboss\server\all\deploy\jboss-aop-jdk50.deployer\➥
jboss-aop-jdk50.jar; ➥
C:\jboss\server\all\deploy\jboss-aop-jdk50.deployer\➥
jboss-aspect-library-jdk50.jar
```

Next, within the StockListJDBCApp directory, execute the following commands from the command prompt:

```
> javac -d . client/*.java
> javac -d . beans/*.java
```

Start the JBoss Server and create the application EJB3 file by executing the following command from the command prompt:

```
>jar cf StockListJDBCApp.ejb3 beans/*.class
```

Copy the EJB3 file to the server's deployment directory:

```
>copy StockListJDBCApp.ejb3 c:\jboss\server\all\deploy
```

Populate the entity beans by running the StockListAdder.java application, as described in the "Loading the Database" section earlier in this last chapter.

Our better, faster, and 100 percent more JDBC Stock List application remains nearly identical to the implementation for the previous version. Although the speed and memory savings we mentioned at the beginning of this section are difficult to gauge at as focused a level as this example, you will find that in practice, such measures will prove a boon in resource-critical scenarios.

Summary

In this chapter, we continued the discussion of entity beans from the previous chapter, covering concepts such as entity bean relationships and using EJB QL to augment session beans. We also discussed the drawbacks of a CMP-only solution and the basic considerations that must be examined when integrating JDBC into your EJB application.

After having read this chapter, you should know:

- Entity bean relationships are a huge convenience to the developer, because the work in maintaining the relationships is performed by the EJB implementation. These relationships can be one to one, one to many, many to one, and many to many. In addition, each kind of relationship can be unidirectional or bidirectional.

- Associations do not need to be clumsily defined in some external table schema when using entity beans. Through accurate use of metadata, almost any relationship can be expressed.

- EJB QL shares the same basic pattern as SQL-92, and it's easy to translate your understanding of the one to the other. It is up to the developer to judge where such functionality might best be used, but with thoughtful deployment, the entity bean may provide a very rich set of functions to its dependent clients.

- JDBC and EJBs are not mutually exclusive. JDBC can provide fast, primitive data quickly to calling applications. EJBs can trivialize the task of maintaining an object schema separate from your table schema, as well as help the developer cut out unnecessary object mapping code. Learning the right instance to use either can be invaluable to your application.

In the next chapter, we'll cover implementing software design patterns in the context of EJBs.

Exercises

1. Using the class diagram of the fictitious Audio CD Collection application (Figure 11-1), implement the `CompactDiscTitle` and `RecordLabel` entity beans using local references, including the container-managed relationship. Implement a stateless session bean that allows you to add record labels and CD titles. Write a simple client application to test your beans.

2. Modify the previous exercise, adding a method to the session bean that uses JDBC to find all CD titles ordered by name. Change the client application to execute this method.

CHAPTER 12

Design Patterns and EJB

The previous chapter introduced EJB container-managed relationships (CMR) and the use of JDBC in session beans. Now, we move on to using design patterns with EJB applications.

In this chapter, you will learn the following:

- What design patterns are, and how they can be applied in EJB applications
- How to combine JSP and EJB technologies in one application

We begin by introducing design patterns and explain how they can facilitate the development and maintenance of EJB applications.

Better by Design

Back in Chapter 1, we talked about designing object-oriented software being analogous to building a house. Software objects are like some of the construction materials, or components, used to build the house. These components range in size and complexity, from a simple nail to a complete gas furnace.

Continuing this analogy, software *design patterns* are analogous to some of the concepts and styles used in house building. For example, when designing a house, an architect may specify that it have a gable roof, as opposed to, say, a hip roof or a gambrel (barn-style) roof. These well-known roofing styles, or patterns, can be used to facilitate the task of designing and building a house. The architect doesn't need to invent a roofing style each time she designs a house, and the builder is familiar with implementing the design pattern of a gable roof. (Not so coincidentally perhaps, roof trusses themselves are often built using a template, or pattern.)

Software design patterns describe solutions to specific software design problems. The following are some tasks developers can accomplish using design patterns:

- Design an application in such a way that the client UI doesn't need to worry about the architecture or location of the application logic layer of an application. We'll demonstrate shortly how you can use the Data Access Object (DAO), Delegate, and Transfer Object design patterns to address this design problem.
- Create an instance of a class that is vendor- or product-specific, in a generic way. We'll look at a very simple case of a pattern that enables this, known as the Factory pattern.
- Design a method in such a way that it will create and return the same instance of a class to any method that calls it. You'll see how the Singleton design pattern allows you to create such a method.

Note A given design pattern can be known by several names. For example, the Transfer Object pattern is also known as the Value Object pattern and the Data Transfer Object pattern. The Delegate pattern is often referred to as a the Façade pattern.

DESIGN PATTERN RESOURCES

The concept of software design patterns became well known as a result of a book published in 1994, titled *Design Patterns, Elements of Reusable Object-Oriented Software.* It was written by Erich Gamma, Richard Helm, Ralph Johnson, and John Vlissides (the "Gang of Four"), and it has a good starter set of software design patterns.

Other works have been created since then that offer additional design patterns for the general object-oriented software domain, as well as for specific domains such as Java EE applications. One such work is Sun Microsystems' Java BluePrints Patterns Catalog, which can be viewed from `http://java.sun.com/blueprints/patterns/catalog.html`. Books you may want to refer to include *Core J2EE Patterns: Best Practices and Design Strategies*, by Deepak Alur, John Crupi, and Dan Malks (Prentice Hall, 2003), *EJB Design Patterns*, by Floyd Marinescu (John Wiley & Sons, 2002), and *Holub on Patterns*, by Allen Holub (Apress, 2004). The last is notable in that it offers a running commentary on the implementation of the techniques presented in *Design Patterns*, complementing the designs with advice and Java code.

Applying Design Patterns

To demonstrate using design patterns with EJB applications, we'll build on the now familiar `StockList` example we've been using in the previous chapters, adding the Delegate, DAO, Transfer Object, Factory, and Singleton patterns.

Figure 12-1 shows the class diagram for the example. The dashed lines indicate dependencies between classes in the direction of the arrow. For example, methods of the `StockClient` class hold references to `StockTO` instances. We'll use the DAO pattern with the `Ejb3StockListDAO` class, which will provide an abstract means of fetching the entity data. `StockListDAO` will provide the interface for this class, new instances of which will be provided by the `StockListDAOFactory` class (appropriately using the Factory design pattern). Also, we'll implement a derivative of the DAO pattern to abstract the access to the `StockList` business method provider with the help of the `StockListDelegate` class. We'll employ the Singleton pattern in that class as well. We'll use the `StockTO` and `AnalystTO` classes to implement the Transfer Object pattern.

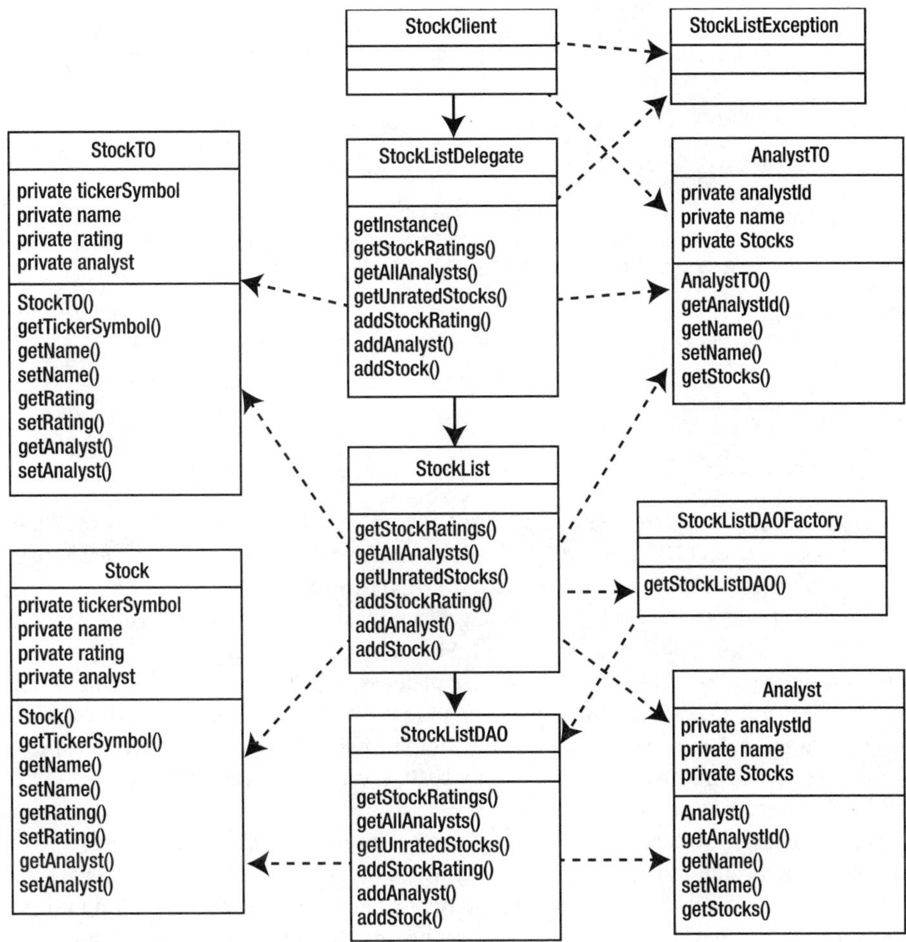

Figure 12-1. *The StockListAppPattern object model and relationship hierarchy*

This example includes ten new Java source files, as shown in Figure 12-1:

- `StockListDelegate.java`
- `StockListException.java`
- `AnalystTO.java`
- `StockTO.java`

- Ejb3StockListDAO.java
- Ejb3StockListDAOBean.java
- StockListDAO.java
- StockListDAOFactory.java
- Analyst.java and Stock.java in the dao package

In addition, four Java source files from the CMR example in Chapter 11 are modified:

- StockList.java
- StockListBean.java
- StockClient.java
- StockListAdder.java

To begin with, you'll create the main application folder, called StockListPatternsApp. The folder's contents will be based off the CMR example from Chapter 11, which will necessitate your copying the contents of that example to StockListPatternsApp.

You'll create six folders for the different packages: business, client, dao, delegate, entity, and transfer. The business package will hold your Session bean interface (StockList.java) and implementation (StockListBean.java). As you can guess, the client package will hold the client GUI (StockClient.java) and information entry class (StockListAdder.java). The dao package will contain the data access objects, which help provide data source anonymity; the classes you need to create in the package are AnalystDAO.java, Ejb3StockListDAO.java, Ejb3StockListDAOBean.java, StockDAO.java, StockListDAO.java, StockListDAOFactory.java, Analyst.java, and Stock.java. (Analyst.java and Stock.java are new files; they are not the entity beans of the same name.) The delegate package will contain the files StockListDelegate.java and StockListException.java, which are used by the client to make a connection to the session bean. The entity package folder will contain the now-familiar Analyst.java and Stock.java, which will act to provide data to the application. Finally, the transfer package will hold the transfer objects, a software design technique that helps to minimize the amount of data passed between objects.

Building the Application with Design Patterns

First, you need to type in the code (or download it from the Apress web site) for the StockListDelegate.java source file, shown in Listing 12-1, in which you can see many of the same method names and basic functionality that we've placed inside the session bean in previous examples.

Listing 12-1. *StockListDelegate.java*

```
package delegate;

import business.StockList;
import transfer.AnalystTO;
import transfer.StockTO;
```

```
import javax.naming.InitialContext;
// General imports
import java.util.*;

public class StockListDelegate {
  // Reference to singleton delegate
  private static StockListDelegate stockListDelegate;

  // The reference to the stocklist bean
  private StockList stockList;

  // private constructor - makes connection to session bean
  private StockListDelegate() throws StockListException {
    try {
      // Get a naming context
      InitialContext ctx = new InitialContext();

      // Get a StockList object
      stockList =
        (StockList) ctx.lookup(StockList.class.getName());
    } catch(Exception e) {
      throw new StockListException(e.getMessage());
    }
  }

  // The business methods. No exposure to actual implementation
  // on the server , and the communication method between client and
  // server is hidden to the client.

  public List getStockRatings() throws StockListException {
    try {
      List ratings = stockList.getStockRatings();
      return ratings;
    }
    catch (Exception re) {
      throw new StockListException(re.getMessage());
    }
  }

  public List getAllAnalysts() throws StockListException {
    try {
      List analysts = stockList.getAllAnalysts();
      return analysts;
    }
    catch (Exception re) {
      throw new StockListException(re.getMessage());
    }
  }
```

```
  public List getUnratedStocks() throws StockListException {
    try {
      List stocks = stockList.getUnratedStocks();
      return stocks;
    }
    catch (Exception re) {
      throw new StockListException(re.getMessage());
    }
  }

  public void addStockRating(StockTO stock)
    throws StockListException {
    try {
      stockList.addStockRating(stock);
    }
    catch (Exception re) {
      throw new StockListException(re.getMessage());
    }
  }

  public void addAnalyst(AnalystTO analyst)
    throws StockListException {
    try {
      stockList.addAnalyst(analyst);
    }
    catch (Exception re) {
      throw new StockListException(re.getMessage());
    }
  }

  public void addStock(StockTO stock) throws StockListException {
    try {
      stockList.addStock(stock);
    }
    catch (Exception re) {
      throw new StockListException(re.getMessage());
    }
  }

  public static StockListDelegate getInstance()
    throws StockListException {
    if (stockListDelegate == null) {
      stockListDelegate = new StockListDelegate();
    }

    return stockListDelegate;
  }
}
```

Next, enter the code for `StockListException.java`, shown in Listing 12-2.

Listing 12-2. *StockListException.java*

```
package delegate;

public class StockListException extends Exception {

  public StockListException(String msg) {
    super(msg);
  }
}
```

Now add the code for `AnalystTO.java`, shown in Listing 12-3.

Listing 12-3. *AnalystTO.java*

```
package transfer;

import java.io.Serializable;
import java.util.*;

public class AnalystTO implements Serializable {

  // Holds references to the attribute data
  private Integer analystId;
  private String name;

  // Holds references to the relationships
  private List stocks;

  public AnalystTO(Integer analystId, String name) {
    this.analystId = analystId;
    this.name = name;
    stocks = new ArrayList();
  }

  // Get analyst id. No setter because primary key
  public Integer getAnalystId() {
    return analystId;
  }

  // Get, set name
  public String getName() {
    return name;
  }
```

```
  public void setName(String name) {
    this.name = name;
  }

  // Get stocks
  public List getStocks() {
    return stocks;
  }
}
```

And, finally, enter StockTO.java, shown in Listing 12-4.

Listing 12-4. *StockTO.java*

```
package transfer;

import java.io.Serializable;
import java.util.*;

public class StockTO implements Serializable {

  // Holds references to the attribute data
  private String tickerSymbol;
  private String name;
  private String rating;

  // Holds references to the relationships
  private AnalystTO analyst;

  public StockTO(String tickerSymbol, String name, String rating) {
    this.tickerSymbol = tickerSymbol;
    this.name = name;
    this.rating = rating;
    analyst = null;
  }

  // Get ticker symbol. No setter because primary key
  public String getTickerSymbol() {
    return tickerSymbol;
  }

  // Get, set name
  public String getName() {
    return name;
  }
```

```
  public void setName(String name) {
    this.name = name;
  }

  // Get, set rating
  public String getRating() {
    return rating;
  }

  public void setRating(String rating) {
    this.rating = rating;
  }

  // Get, set analyst
  public AnalystTO getAnalyst() {
    return analyst;
  }

  public void setAnalyst(AnalystTO analyst) {
    this.analyst = analyst;
  }
}
```

Adding DAO Functionality

Now, you'll need to add the code that directly handles the entity beans (remember those?). This functionality is a part of the dao (Data Access Object) package, and looks remarkably like the session beans created in previous examples (because it *is* effectively identical to the session beans created in previous chapters). First, add the public interface for the dao bean, `StockListDAO.java`, as shown in Listing 12-5.

Listing 12-5. *StockListDAO.java*

```
package dao;

import java.util.List;

public interface StockListDAO {
  public List getRatedStocks();
  public List getAnalysts();
  public List getUnratedStocks();
  public void rateStock(String ticker, Integer analystId,
    String rating);
  public void addAnalyst(AnalystDAO analyst);
  public void addStock(StockDAO stock);
}
```

The implementation for the StockListDAO, as you might expect, is nearly identical to the previous StockList session bean implementation as well. In this particular case, it is simply named more appropriately for its function: Ejb3StockListDAO.java, shown in Listing 12-6, and its implementation, Ejb3StockListDAOBean.java, shown in Listing 12-7.

Listing 12-6. *Ejb3StockListDAO.java*

```
package dao;

import javax.ejb.Remote;

@Remote
public interface Ejb3StockListDAO extends StockListDAO { }
```

Listing 12-7. *Ejb3StockListDAOBean.java*

```
package dao;

import entity.Analyst;
import entity.Stock;
import javax.ejb.Stateless;
import javax.persistence.EntityManager;
import javax.persistence.PersistenceContext;
import javax.persistence.Query;

import java.util.*;

@Stateless
public class Ejb3StockListDAOBean implements Ejb3StockListDAO {
  // the reference to the entity manager
  @PersistenceContext
  private EntityManager _manager;

  public List getRatedStocks() {
    Query query =
      _manager.createQuery("SELECT DISTINCT OBJECT(s) " +
                           "FROM Stock s " +
                           "WHERE s.analyst IS NOT NULL " +
                           "ORDER BY s.tickerSymbol");
    // get the rated stocks
    List stocks = query.getResultList();
    List stockList = new ArrayList();
    for (int i = 0; i < stocks.size(); i++) {
      Stock stockBean = (Stock) stocks.get(i);
      StockDAO stock = new StockDAO();
      stock.setTickerSymbol(stockBean.getTickerSymbol());
      stock.setName(stockBean.getName());
      stock.setRating(stockBean.getRating());
```

```
      Analyst analystBean = stockBean.getAnalyst();
      AnalystDAO analyst = new AnalystDAO();
      analyst.setAnalystId(analystBean.getAnalystId());
      analyst.setName(analystBean.getName());
      stock.setAnalyst(analyst);
      stockList.add(stock);
    }

    return stockList;
  }

  public List getAnalysts() {
    Query query =
      _manager.createQuery("SELECT Object(a) " +
                           "FROM Analyst a " +
                           "ORDER BY a.name");
    // get the analysts
    List analysts = query.getResultList();
    List analystList = new ArrayList();
    for (int i = 0; i < analysts.size(); i++) {
      Analyst analystBean = (Analyst) analysts.get(i);
      AnalystDAO analyst = new AnalystDAO();
      analyst.setAnalystId(analystBean.getAnalystId());
      analyst.setName(analystBean.getName());
      analystList.add(analyst);
    }

    return analystList;
  }

  public List getUnratedStocks() {
    Query query =
      _manager.createQuery("SELECT DISTINCT OBJECT(s) " +
                               "FROM Stock s " +
                               "WHERE s.analyst IS NULL " +
                               "ORDER BY s.tickerSymbol");
    // get the unrated stocks
    List stocks = query.getResultList();
    List stockList = new ArrayList();
    for (int i = 0; i < stocks.size(); i++) {
      Stock stockBean = (Stock) stocks.get(i);
      StockDAO stock = new StockDAO();
      stock.setTickerSymbol(stockBean.getTickerSymbol());
      stock.setName(stockBean.getName());
      stockList.add(stock);
    }
```

```
    return stockList;
  }

  public void rateStock(String ticker, Integer analystId,
    String rating) {
    Stock stock = _manager.find(Stock.class, ticker);
    Analyst analyst = _manager.find(Analyst.class, analystId);
    analyst.assignStock(stock);
    stock.setRating(rating);
  }

  public void addAnalyst(AnalystDAO analyst) {
    _manager.persist(
      new Analyst(analyst.getAnalystId(), analyst.getName()));
  }

  public void addStock(StockDAO stock) {
    _manager.persist(
      new Stock(stock.getTickerSymbol(), stock.getName()));
  }
}
```

In this version, StockDAO or AnalystDAO objects are used for the method parameters of the business methods within the dao package, as opposed to the Stock and Analyst beans in the entity package. That is because the StockDAO and AnalystDAO classes merely act as placeholders for information immediately necessary in the creation of entity beans. Using entity beans as parameters for these method invocations would rob the application of its generality and incur a performance cost. We'll explain how this works in greater detail later, when we review the application, but for now, add the two files shown in Listings 12-8 and 12-9, AnalystDAO.java and StockDAO.java, to your dao package.

Listing 12-8. *AnalystDAO.java*

```
package dao;

import java.io.Serializable;

public class AnalystDAO implements Serializable {
  private Integer analystId;
  private String name;

  public Integer getAnalystId() {
    return analystId;
  }

  public void setAnalystId(Integer analystId) {
    this.analystId = analystId;
  }
```

```
  public String getName() {
    return name;
  }

  public void setName(String name) {
    this.name = name;
  }
}
```

Listing 12-9. *StockDAO.java*

```
package dao;

import java.io.Serializable;

public class StockDAO implements Serializable {
  private String tickerSymbol;
  private String name;
  private String rating;

  // Relationship attributes
  private Analyst analyst;

  public String getTickerSymbol() {
    return tickerSymbol;
  }

  public void setTickerSymbol(String tickerSymbol) {
    this.tickerSymbol = tickerSymbol;
  }

  public String getName() {
    return name;
  }

  public void setName(String name) {
    this.name = name;
  }

  public String getRating() {
    return rating;
  }

  public void setRating(String rating) {
    this.rating = rating;
  }
```

```
  public Analyst getAnalyst() {
    return analyst;
  }

  public void setAnalyst(Analyst analyst) {
    this.analyst = analyst;
  }
}
```

As a capstone for the DAO package, we'll create a factory class that exposes a single static method to obtain an instance of an initialized `Ejb3StockListDAO`. As shown in Listing 12-10, this file is named `StockListDAOFactory`. It is used by the actual client interface to obtain a specific data provider to the entity store. Again, we'll explain this in more detail in the upcoming review of the application.

Listing 12-10. *StockListDAOFactory.java*

```
package dao;

import javax.naming.InitialContext;

public class StockListDAOFactory {
  public static StockListDAO getStockListDAO() {
    // This is a simple implementation of a
    // factory. If other impementations of
    // the dao interface are needed, this
    // method can be changed to get the
    // appropriate implementation.
    try {
      // Get a naming context
      InitialContext ctx = new InitialContext();

      // Get a StockListDAO object
      StockListDAO stockListDAO =
        (StockListDAO) ctx.lookup(Ejb3StockListDAO.class.getName());
      return stockListDAO;
    } catch(Exception e) {
      throw new RuntimeException(e.getMessage());
    }
  }
}
```

Adding the Transfer Object Functionality

Next, we need to modify the source code for the `StockList` session bean so that it uses the transfer objects. Listing 12-11 shows the `StockList` session bean's remote interface, `StockList.java`.

Listing 12-11. *StockList.java*

```
package business;

import javax.ejb.Remote;
import transfer.AnalystTO;
import transfer.StockTO;

// General imports
import java.util.*;

@Remote
public interface StockList {
  // The public business methods on the StockList bean
  public List getStockRatings();
  public List getAllAnalysts();
  public List getUnratedStocks();
  public void addStockRating(StockTO stockTO);
  public void addAnalyst(AnalystTO analystTO);
  public void addStock(StockTO stockTO);
}
```

Every method in the interface shown in Listing 12-11 either takes transfer objects as an argument or returns transfer objects (actually in these cases, an `ArrayList` of them). So let's see how they are used by the new, transfer object-enabled version of the session bean's implementation class, `StockListBean.java`, shown in Listing 12-12.

Listing 12-12. *StockListBean.java*

```
package business;

import dao.AnalystDAO;
import dao.StockDAO;
import dao.StockListDAO;
import dao.StockListDAOFactory;
import transfer.AnalystTO;
import transfer.StockTO;
import javax.ejb.Stateless;

// general imports
import java.util.*;

@Stateless
public class StockListBean implements StockList {

  // the public business methods. these must be coded in the
  // interface also.
```

```
public List getStockRatings() {
  List stockList = new ArrayList();

  // get the rated stocks
  StockListDAO dao = StockListDAOFactory.getStockListDAO();
  List stocks = dao.getRatedStocks();
  for (int i = 0; i < stocks.size(); i++) {
    StockDAO stock = (StockDAO) stocks.get(i);
    StockTO stockTO = new StockTO(stock.getTickerSymbol(),
      stock.getName(), stock.getRating());
    AnalystDAO analyst = stock.getAnalyst();
    AnalystTO analystTO = new AnalystTO(analyst.getAnalystId(),
      analyst.getName());
    stockTO.setAnalyst(analystTO);
    stockList.add(stockTO);
  }

  return stockList;
}

public List getAllAnalysts() {
  List analystList = new ArrayList();

  // get the analysts
  StockListDAO dao = StockListDAOFactory.getStockListDAO();
  List analysts = dao.getAnalysts();
  for (int i = 0; i < analysts.size(); i++) {
    AnalystDAO analyst = (AnalystDAO) analysts.get(i);
    AnalystTO analystTO = new AnalystTO(analyst.getAnalystId(),
      analyst.getName());
    analystList.add(analystTO);
  }

  return analystList;
}

public List getUnratedStocks() {
  List stockList = new ArrayList();

  // get the unrated stocks
  StockListDAO dao = StockListDAOFactory.getStockListDAO();
  List stocks = dao.getUnratedStocks();
  for (int i = 0; i < stocks.size(); i++) {
    StockDAO stock = (StockDAO) stocks.get(i);
    StockTO stockTO = new StockTO(stock.getTickerSymbol(),
      stock.getName(), stock.getRating());
    stockList.add(stockTO);
```

```
    }

    return stockList;
  }

  public void addStockRating(StockTO stockTO) {
    StockListDAO dao = StockListDAOFactory.getStockListDAO();
    dao.rateStock(stockTO.getTickerSymbol(),
      stockTO.getAnalyst().getAnalystId(),
      stockTO.getRating());
  }

  public void addAnalyst(AnalystTO analystTO) {
    StockListDAO dao = StockListDAOFactory.getStockListDAO();
    AnalystDAO analyst = new AnalystDAO();
    analyst.setAnalystId(analystTO.getAnalystId());
    analyst.setName(analystTO.getName());
    dao.addAnalyst(analyst);
  }

  public void addStock(StockTO stockTO) {
    StockListDAO dao = StockListDAOFactory.getStockListDAO();
    StockDAO stock = new StockDAO();
    stock.setTickerSymbol(stockTO.getTickerSymbol());
    stock.setName(stockTO.getName());
    dao.addStock(stock);
  }
}
```

Let's take a look at the methods in this implementation class. In the `getStockRatings()` method in Listing 12-12, the following occurs:

- A call is made to the `getRatedStocks()` method of the `StockListDAO` interface obtained via the `StockListDAOFactory`. The method returns a `List` of `StockDAO` data access objects.
- We iterate over that `List` and create a `StockTO` instance from the fields of each data access object, populating an `ArrayList` with the `StockTO` references.
- Since the client UI is going to display information from the related `Analyst` entity bean, we use the `getAnalyst()` method of each `Stock` bean to get a reference to the `Analyst` bean. An `AnalystTO` instance is created from the fields of the `Analyst` bean, which is then associated with the `StockTO` instance via its `setAnalyst()` method.
- The `ArrayList` that contains `StockTO` references, each of which holds an `AnalystTO` reference, is serialized and streamed back to the caller. Recall that the caller in this case is the `StockListDelegate` class.

Caution If you decide to implement the idea of having methods in your value objects that mimic CMP methods, be careful not to carry the idea too far. You probably don't want to stream a graph of value objects back to the client in one method invocation that contains the data from all of the entity beans in the application, for example.

The other methods in Listing 12-12 that return an `ArrayList`—`getAllAnalysts()` and `getUnratedStocks()`—are similar in nature to the `getStockRatings()` method.

Turning our attention to the `addAnalyst()` method in Listing 12-12, we see that it takes an `AnalystTO` instance as its argument, which it passes to the DAO. In turn, the DAO handles the translation to its particular storage implementation—in this case, an `Analyst` entity bean. The `addStock()` method, at the end of the listing, is very similar in nature to the `addAnalyst()` method.

Notice how the flow of logic for the program implements the use of transfer objects. The session bean deals strictly in transfer objects in terms of input, but transforms them to plain placeholder objects when issuing them to the DAO. The DAO, in turn, accepts the presence of those plain placeholder objects as input and manages the entity bean transformation. This all happens in reverse as well, with entity beans being dealt with at the DAO level, plain object placeholders in use at the session bean level, and transfer objects being dealt with at the delegate level.

Next, we will take a brief look at the client classes, beginning with the `StockListAdder` class, in Listing 12-13, which initially loads the data into the entity beans via these value objects.

Listing 12-13. *StockListAdder.java*

```
package client;

import delegate.StockListDelegate;
import transfer.AnalystTO;
import transfer.StockTO;

public class StockListAdder {

  public static void main(String[] args) {
    try {
      StockListDelegate delegate = StockListDelegate.getInstance();

      // Add analysts
      System.out.println("adding analysts");

      delegate.addAnalyst(new AnalystTO(new Integer(1), "Fred"));
      delegate.addAnalyst(new AnalystTO(new Integer(2), "Leonard"));
      delegate.addAnalyst(new AnalystTO(new Integer(3), "Sarah"));
      delegate.addAnalyst(new AnalystTO(new Integer(4), "Nancy"));
      System.out.println("analysts added");
    }
```

```
    catch (Exception e) {
      System.out.println("exception adding analysts");
      e.printStackTrace();
    }

    try {
      StockListDelegate delegate = StockListDelegate.getInstance();

      // Add stocks
      System.out.println("adding stocks");
      delegate.addStock(new StockTO("ABC", "ABC Company", null));
      delegate.addStock(new StockTO("ZZZ", "Zigby Zebras", null));
      delegate.addStock(new StockTO("ICS", "Internet Corp of Slobovia", null));
      delegate.addStock(new StockTO("DDC", "Digby Door Company", null));
      delegate.addStock(new StockTO("ZAP", "Zapalopalorinski Ltd.", null));
      delegate.addStock(new StockTO("JIM", "Jimco", null));
      delegate.addStock(new StockTO("SRU", "Stocks R Us", null));
      delegate.addStock(new StockTO("SRI", "Shelves and Radios Inc", null));
      delegate.addStock(new StockTO("FBC", "Foo Bar Company", null));
      delegate.addStock(new StockTO("DDBC", "Ding Dong Bell Company", null));
      delegate.addStock(new StockTO("UDE", "Upn Down Elevator Company", null));
      System.out.println("stocks added");
    }
    catch (Exception e) {
      System.out.println("exception adding stocks");
      e.printStackTrace();
    }

    try {
      StockListDelegate delegate = StockListDelegate.getInstance();

      // Add ratings
      System.out.println("adding ratings");
      StockTO stockTO = new StockTO("ZZZ", null, "Take a chance!");
      stockTO.setAnalyst(new AnalystTO(new Integer(2), null));
      delegate.addStockRating(stockTO);
      System.out.println("ratings added");
    }
    catch (Exception e) {
      System.out.println("exception adding stocks");
      e.printStackTrace();
    }
  }
}
```

To create and populate an `Analyst` entity bean, for example, the desired data is passed into the constructor of the `AnalystTO` transfer object. The new `AnalystTO` object is then passed into the `addAnalyst()` method of the `StockListDelegate` class (the method's implementation is discussed after Listing 12-12). This is all performed in one method:

```
delegate.addAnalyst(new AnalystTO(new Integer(1), "Fred"));
```

The way that this client method got a reference to the `StockListDelegate` instance is in the statement shown here:

```
StockListDelegate delegate = StockListDelegate.getInstance();
```

Adding the Client

Finally, Listing 12-14 shows the Java source code for our new "transfer object-ized" version of the GUI client, `StockClient.java`.

Listing 12-14. *StockClient.java*

```
package client;

import delegate.StockListDelegate;
import transfer.AnalystTO;
import transfer.StockTO;

import java.util.*;

// General imports
import java.awt.*;
import java.awt.event.*;
import javax.swing.*;

public class StockClient extends JFrame
  implements ActionListener {
  private Integer[] _analystIds;
  private JButton _get = new JButton("Add Rating");
  private JPanel _stockPanel = new JPanel();
  private JComboBox _analysts = new JComboBox();
  private JComboBox _tickers = new JComboBox();
  private JComboBox _ratings = new JComboBox();

  public StockClient() {
    // Add the title
    JLabel title = new JLabel("Stock Rating List");
    title.setHorizontalAlignment(JLabel.CENTER);
    getContentPane().add(title, BorderLayout.NORTH);
```

```
    JPanel activityPanel = new JPanel(new BorderLayout());
    try {
      // Add the stock list
      buildStockList();
      JScrollPane scroller = new JScrollPane(_stockPanel);
      activityPanel.add(scroller, BorderLayout.CENTER);

      // Add the rating panel
      JPanel ratingPanel = new JPanel(new GridLayout(1, 3));
      // Add the analysts
      populateAnalysts();
      ratingPanel.add(_analysts);
      // Add the unrated stocks
      populateTickers();
      ratingPanel.add(_tickers);
      // Add the ratings to pick from
      _ratings.addItem("Run away! Run away!");
      _ratings.addItem("Could be worse!");
      _ratings.addItem("A bit of OK!");
      _ratings.addItem("Take a chance!");
      _ratings.addItem("Smashing!");
      ratingPanel.add(_ratings);
      activityPanel.add(ratingPanel, BorderLayout.SOUTH);

      getContentPane().add(activityPanel, BorderLayout.CENTER);
    }
    catch (Exception e) {
      e.printStackTrace();
    }

    // Add the buttons panel
    JPanel buttons = new JPanel(new GridLayout(1, 1));
    _get.addActionListener(this);
    buttons.add(_get);
    getContentPane().add(buttons, BorderLayout.SOUTH);

    addWindowListener(new WindowAdapter() {
      public void windowClosing(WindowEvent e) {
        System.exit(0);
      }
    });

    setSize(480, 250);
    setVisible(true);
  }
```

```
private void buildStockList() throws Exception {
  java.util.List stoks =
    StockListDelegate.getInstance().getStockRatings();
  _stockPanel.removeAll();
  _stockPanel.setLayout(new GridLayout(stoks.size(), 1));
  for (int i = 0; i < stoks.size(); i++) {
    StockTO stokInfo = (StockTO) stoks.get(i);
    Box stokLine = Box.createHorizontalBox();
    String stokDesc = stokInfo.getTickerSymbol() + " : " +
      stokInfo.getName() + " ==> " +
      stokInfo.getAnalyst().getName() + " rates it: " +
      stokInfo.getRating();
    stokLine.add(new JLabel(stokDesc));
    _stockPanel.add(stokLine);
  }
  _stockPanel.invalidate();
  _stockPanel.validate();
}

private void populateAnalysts() throws Exception {
  java.util.List anlysts =
    StockListDelegate.getInstance().getAllAnalysts();
  _analystIds = new Integer[anlysts.size()];
  for (int i = 0; i < anlysts.size(); i++) {
    AnalystTO analystData = (AnalystTO) anlysts.get(i);
    _analystIds[i] = analystData.getAnalystId();
    _analysts.addItem(analystData.getName());
  }
}

private void populateTickers() throws Exception {
  _tickers.removeAllItems();
  java.util.List tkrs =
    StockListDelegate.getInstance().getUnratedStocks();
  for (int i = 0; i < tkrs.size(); i++) {
    StockTO stockTO = (StockTO) tkrs.get(i);
    _tickers.addItem(stockTO.getTickerSymbol());
  }
  _tickers.invalidate();
  _tickers.validate();
}
```

```
  public void actionPerformed(ActionEvent ae) {
    // Get what was clicked
    if (ae.getSource() == _get) {
      try {
        int anlystNo = _analysts.getSelectedIndex();
        if (anlystNo < 0) {
          JOptionPane.showMessageDialog(this, "No analyst selected!");
          return;
        }
        Integer aId = _analystIds[anlystNo];
        if (_tickers.getSelectedIndex() < 0) {
          JOptionPane.showMessageDialog(this, "No ticker selected!");
          return;
        }
        String tkr = (String) _tickers.getSelectedItem();
        if (_ratings.getSelectedIndex() < 0) {
          JOptionPane.showMessageDialog(this, "No rating selected!");
          return;
        }
        String rtg = (String) _ratings.getSelectedItem();
        StockTO stockTO = new StockTO(tkr, null, rtg);
        stockTO.setAnalyst(new AnalystTO(aId, null));
        StockListDelegate.getInstance().addStockRating(stockTO);
        buildStockList();
        populateTickers();
      }
      catch (Exception e) {
        e.printStackTrace();
      }
    }
  }

  public static void main(String[] args) {
    StockClient stockClient = new StockClient();
  }
}
```

As you can see, the clients in an application that uses these design patterns can be well shielded from the realities of the application logic tier. The client's view of the rest of the application is the abstraction provided by the delegate and transfer objects.

Compiling and Running the Application with Design Patterns

Now you can compile the application, load the database, and run the example. We used `StockListPatternsApp.ejb3` for the EJB filename. The build process is nearly identical to the one that we have used for the examples in the previous chapters.

First, open a command window and change your directory to the location of the source files you've created. Then set the classpath by typing the following:

```
>set CLASSPATH=.;➥
C:\jboss\lib\concurrent.jar;➥
C:\jboss\lib\jboss-common.jar;➥
C:\jboss\lib\commons-httpclient.jar;➥
C:\jboss\client\jboss-j2ee.jar;➥
C:\jboss\server\all\lib\jboss.jar;➥
C:\jboss\server\all\lib\jboss-remoting.jar;➥
C:\jboss\server\all\lib\jboss-transaction.jar;➥
C:\jboss\server\all\lib\jnpserver.jar;➥
C:\jboss\server\all\deploy\ejb3.deployer\jboss-ejb3.jar;➥
C:\jboss\server\all\deploy\ejb3.deployer\jboss-ejb3x.jar;➥
C:\jboss\server\all\deploy\ejb3.deployer\ejb3-persistence.jar;➥
C:\jboss\server\all\deploy\jboss-aop-jdk50.deployer\jboss-aop-jdk50.jar;➥
C:\jboss\server\all\deploy\jboss-aop-jdk50.deployer\jboss-aspect-library-jdk50.jar
```

Next, compile the source files for the different packages by executing the following series of commands:

```
>javac -d . transfer/*.java

>javac -d . entity/*.java

>javac -d . dao/*.java

>javac -d . business/*.java

>javac -d . delegate/*.java

>javac -d . client/*.java
```

Create the application EJB3 file by typing the following in at the command line:

```
>jar cf StockListPatternsApp.ejb3➥
     transfer/*.class➥
     entity/*.class➥
     dao/*.class➥
     business/*.class
```

Copy the resultant EJB3 file to the JBoss deployment directory (for example, `C:\jboss\server\all\deploy`).

Next, load the tables with analysts and stocks by running `StockListAdder` from the command line:

```
>java ➥
-Djava.naming.factory.initial=➥
     org.jnp.interfaces.NamingContextFactory➥
-Djava.naming.factory.url.pkgs=➥
     org.jboss.naming:org.jnp.interfaces➥
-Djava.naming.provider.url=localhost➥
client.StockListAdder
```

Finally, just as in the previous chapters, run the application by executing the following at the command line:

```
java ➥
-Djava.naming.factory.initial=➥
     org.jnp.interfaces.NamingContextFactory~➥
-Djava.naming.factory.url.pkgs=➥
     org.jboss.naming:org.jnp.interfaces➥
-Djava.naming.provider.url=localhost➥
client.StockClient
```

As you can see, the differences are in the build, database loading, and execution process. The appearance and behavior of the client UI is the same as in both of the examples in the previous chapter.

Reviewing the Application's Design Patterns

Now that you've seen the design patterns in action, let's take a look at how they work. As we noted earlier, the application uses the Delegate, Singleton, Transfer Object, Factory, and DAO design patterns.

The Delegate Pattern

The Delegate pattern hides the server side of an application from the client with a thin veneer, or façade. As you can see in the class diagram shown earlier in Figure 12-1, the `StockClient` class is no longer directly dependent on the `StockList` session bean, but instead only knows about the `StockListDelegate` class. The client calls methods of the delegate class as if it were the application logic layer, and the delegate class (as its name suggests) invokes methods of the application logic layer (the `StockList` session bean in this case) as needed. This approach has several advantages, including the following:

- The location of the application logic layer of the application is hidden behind the delegate, so if its location changes, only the delegate needs to know about it.
- The client is insulated from changes to the application logic layer by the delegate. This tends to reduce maintenance by localizing the necessary changes to delegate classes, rather than scattered all over the UI.
- Data can be cached in the delegate. This is especially helpful in terms of optimization when the client and application logic layers are separated by a network. In this way, the delegate can maintain state for the UI.
- During development, the delegate methods can first be developed as stubs, mimicking the eventual functionality of the application tier methods. This facilitates simultaneous development of these tiers.

A disadvantage of using delegates is that by introducing a façade layer between the client and the application logic, data is passed from the client to the delegate, and then from the delegate to the application logic. Therefore, the data is passed one more time than necessary, but in our opinion, the advantages far outweigh this disadvantage.

When the constructor for the StockListDelegate class is called, it does the same thing that our client UIs have done in the past: gets a reference to a session bean. It stores that reference in an instance variable so that methods of the façade, when invoked by the client, can use the reference to call methods of the session bean. Of course, larger applications will typically contain multiple façades and session beans.

Notice that each of the methods of the StockListDelegate class throws a StockListException. The methods that call methods of the StockList session bean catch an exception and throw the StockListException, with the message of the original exception passed into the constructor. Using this technique allows the façade to further insulate the client from the implementation details of the application logic tier, so the client never needs to know about a RemoteException, for example.

The Singleton Pattern

The StockListDelegate class employs another design pattern as well: the Singleton pattern. Take a look at the getInstance() method, and you'll see that it is responsible for creating and returning an instance of a class. Notice, however, that if an instance already exists, it returns that instance. This is called the Singleton pattern because only a *single* instance of the returned class exists. This is useful in cases such as this façade example because multiple client UI classes may need a reference to a StockClientDelegate instance, but there is no need for more than one to exist. In fact, you wouldn't want more than one, because each instance would have a remote reference to the session bean, which would consume resources.

Note that in the case where the client is a Servlet or JSP, if you wanted the delegate to hold some state without having it shared by all the clients, you would use a modified Singleton pattern in conjunction with an HttpSession object. The getInstance() method would return the StockClientDelegate instance for a given session, creating one if it doesn't exist.

In addition to implementing the Singleton pattern, the getInstance() method implements a simple version of another design pattern known as the Factory pattern. This pattern is characterized by a method, typically static, that creates and returns an instance of a class. The method that creates the instance is called a *factory method*, and it returns an object that is guaranteed to be of some type. This type is often either an interface that the object implements or an abstract class of which the object's class is a subclass. This is preferable to directly using a constructor in some cases, because the returned class can be vendor-specific but created in a generic way. We'll look at the Factory pattern in more detail shortly, examining how it facilitates the creation of StockListDAO objects. As you saw in the StockClient.java code (Listing 12-13), the clients of this particular delegate class call StockListDelegate.getInstance() to obtain an instance of the StockListDelegate class.

The Transfer Object Pattern

As mentioned in Chapter 9, it is usually not good practice to allow clients to have remote references to entity beans, for the following reasons:

- Calling entity bean methods directly circumvents the business logic contained in session beans, and tends to push the business logic into the UI code.
- Session beans can protect the UI from changes to the entity beans.
- Restricting client access to session beans conserves server and network resources.

However, in the CMP example in Chapter 11, we needed to employ awkward mechanisms to compensate for the absence of these references. For example, ArrayLists of arrays of Strings were used to pass entity bean data between the client and the application logic tier. The Transfer Object design pattern addresses this problem by providing classes that are modeled after the entity beans. These classes are mainly used to carry entity bean data between tiers. The example employs two transfer object classes: the AnalystTO class represents the Analyst entity bean, and the StockTO class represents the Stock entity bean. To keep them separate from other classes, we've put them in their own package, named transfer.

The AnalystTO transfer object class contains an instance variable for each of the CMP fields of the Analyst entity bean. Its constructor takes all of these fields as arguments (although some value object implementations we've seen have only a no-argument constructor, and some have both forms of constructors). The AnalystTO transfer object also contains a getter and setter method for each of the nonprimary key fields. It has only a getter for the primary key field, because that field won't be changed.

Although not typical of Transfer Object pattern implementations, our transfer object also models CMR. To do this, it contains an instance variable that is capable of referencing an ArrayList of StockTO instances.

Since value objects are designed to carry data between tiers, they must implement the Serializable interface of the java.io package.

All of the things that were said about the AnalystTO class apply to this StockTO class as well. Due to the nature of the CMR in the Stock entity bean, the analogous methods in this transfer object return and take a single instance. If you take another look at the StockListDelegate class (Listing 12-1), you'll notice that these transfer object classes are passed into and returned by these methods, either as individual objects or inside ArrayList objects. The classes in this example that manipulate them most, however, are the ones associated with the StockList session bean and the client classes.

The Factory Pattern

Names like Transfer Object design pattern and Data Access Object design pattern may not make sense immediately. The Factory pattern, on the other hand, acts just as its title suggests: a developer may use methods of the factory class in order to "build" instances of some other class. The getStockListDAO() method of StockListDAOFactory illustrates this functionality in as direct a manner as possible: it simply returns objects inheriting the StockListDAO interface. This particular application contains only one implementation of the StockListDAO interface, but the strength of the Factory pattern lies in the flexibility with which implementations may be substituted for one another.

Imagine that you have another class implementing the functionality described in the StockListDAO interface. This class, which we'll call XMLStockListDAO, implements all the StockListDAO functions by accessing and searching XML documents on the filesystem. It still returns valid List objects filled with AnalystDAO and StockDAO objects, yet the method by which it acquires and alters them is radically different. All that is required on your part to make the switch from an EJB-dependent data provider to an XML flat-file provider completely transparent is changing the object's instantiation within the getStockListDAO() method.

The benefits provided by the Factory pattern are not limited to implementation hiding. The method that provides instances of the desired class can be used to perform certain initialization tasks on the object before it's returned to the invoker. Factory classes can also be used to limit the number of instances of the class in existence. Since the acquisition of class instances is done via the factory method, allocation tasks may be managed safely outside the definition of the implementations themselves.

The DAO Pattern

Referring again to the class diagram shown earlier in Figure 12-1, you can see two different points of business logic abstraction within the `StockListAppPattern` example. The first layer of abstraction, `StockListDelegate`, hides the minutia surrounding the client's access to the server-side business logic. The second layer of abstraction is provided via the `StockListDAO` object, which allows the server to abstract the method by which the `StockList` session bean obtains its data.

To understand why such an abstraction would be useful to a software designer, notice the different semantics attached to how the objects are received at each layer. The `StockListDelegate`, while mimicking `StockList` in method signatures, implements those method signatures in such a manner as to facilitate the client invoking methods from the `StockList` bean. The `StockListDAO` object, on the other hand, is itself invoked by the `StockList` bean to acquire the requested information from the necessary data store.

Do you recall the paragraph regarding the hypothetical `XMLStockListDAO` object in the preceding section about the Factory pattern? The `XMLStockListDAO` object implements the methods in the `StockListDAO` interface by accessing XML documents in the filesystem. You could just as easily write a `JDBCStockListDAO` that works directly with JDBC drivers and a database to return the required objects. You can see how you could write any number of classes that act as low-level interfaces to the data store, simply by inheriting the `StockListDAO` interface and returning their acquired data in `StockDAO` and `AnalystDAO` objects.

Applications that need to provide data from a variety of locations (such as document files, databases, and web services) benefit most from deft implementation of the DAO pattern.

Using JSP and Servlets with EJBs

All of the EJB examples shown up until this point have had clients that were either a simple command-line Java application or a Java Swing application. To tie things together, now we're going to demonstrate an example of an EJB application whose client UI consists of JSP pages and Servlets. To facilitate this, we'll use the patterns discussed in the previous section. In fact, all the code in this example is exactly the same as in the previous example, with one exception: instead of using the `StockClient` class as the client UI, we'll use a modified version of the JSP- and Servlets-based `StockList` example from Chapter 6.

Building the Modified JSP/Servlets Client

Since the EJB portion of the application is identical to the previous example in this chapter, you can use the same process to build and configure it. You can use the same process to build the JSP and Servlets portion of the application that you used to build it in Chapter 6. There is one additional step, however, which is to add the delegate and transfer object classes to the WAR file which is created in the deployment step of that example. These files are as follows:

- StockListDelegate.java
- StockListException.java

None of the source code changes for the session and entity beans, delegate, and transfer objects. The only source code that does change is JSP and Servlet code. Those changes are for the purpose of adapting the UI portion of the previous JSP- and Servlets-based StockList application to use the delegate and transfer objects. The following are the modified source files:

- StockListServlet.java
- RatingsForm.jsp
- AddRating.java
- AnalystForm.jsp

To combine the two examples, copy your StockListPatternsApp directory to a new directory called StockListJspPatterns. Copy the contents of the JSP/Servlet StockList examples from the JSP examples earlier in the book into this directory as well. Once you've done this, you should have a directory called StockListJspPatterns that contains the following package subdirectories: business, client, dao, delegate, entity, transfer, web, and web-deploy. The entry point into the StockList web application is this HTML page in the web-deploy package directory, index.html, shown in Listing 12-15.

Listing 12-15. *index.html for the Revised StockList Application*

```
<!DOCTYPE HTML PUBLIC "-//W3C//DTD HTML 4.01 Transitional//EN">
<html>
  <head>
    <title>Stocks and Analysts</title>
  </head>

  <body>
    <h1>Stocks and Analysts</h1>
    <p>
      <a href="/stock/servlet/StockList/AnalystForm">See all Analysts</a>
    <p>
      <a href="/stock/servlet/StockList/RatingsForm">See all Ratings</a>
    <hr>
  </body>
</html>
```

When you click one of the links, index.html submits a request to a Servlet called StockList, which is in StockListServlet.java (located in the web package), as shown in Listing 12-16.

Listing 12-16. *StockListServlet.java*

```
package web;

import javax.servlet.*;
import javax.servlet.http.*;
import java.io.*;
import java.util.*;
import delegate.*;

public class StockListServlet extends HttpServlet {
    public void doPost(HttpServletRequest request,
                       HttpServletResponse response)
    {
        doGet(request, response);
    }

    public void doGet(HttpServletRequest request,
                      HttpServletResponse response)
    {
        try {
            List data = null;
            RequestDispatcher dispatcher;
            ServletContext context = getServletContext();
            StockListDelegate delegate = StockListDelegate.getInstance();
            String name = request.getPathInfo();
            name = name.substring(1);
            System.out.println("name="+name);
            if ("AnalystForm".equals(name)) {
                data = delegate.getAllAnalysts();
                request.setAttribute("data", data);
            } else if ("RatingsForm".equals(name)) {
                data = delegate.getStockRatings();
                request.setAttribute("data", data);
                request.setAttribute("analysts", delegate.getAllAnalysts());
                request.setAttribute("unrated", delegate.getUnratedStocks());
            } else if ("AddRating".equals(name)) {
                //nothing to do here, just forward request
            } else {
                name = "Error";
            }

            dispatcher = context.getNamedDispatcher(name);
            if (dispatcher == null) {
                dispatcher = context.getNamedDispatcher("Error");
            }
            dispatcher.forward(request, response);
```

```
        } catch (Exception e) {
            e.printStackTrace();
        }
    }
}
```

Listing 12-17 shows the `RatingsForm.jsp` (located in `web-deploy`) source code.

Listing 12-17. *RatingsForm.jsp*

```
<!DOCTYPE HTML PUBLIC "-//W3C//DTD HTML 4.01 Transitional//EN">
<html>
  <head>
    <title>Stock Ratings</title>
  </head>
  <body>
    <h1>Stock Ratings</h1>
  <%@ page import="java.util.*, transfer.*" %>
<%
    ArrayList stocks = (ArrayList) request.getAttribute("data");
    if (stocks != null && stocks.size() > 0) {
%>
    <form action="/stock/servlet/StockList/AddRating" method="post">
    <table border="1">
        <tr>
          <th>Ticker</th>
          <th>Analyst</th>
          <th>Rating</th>
        </tr>
<%
      for (int i = 0; i < stocks.size(); i++) {
        StockTO stockInfo = (StockTO) stocks.get(i);
        String ticker = stockInfo.getTickerSymbol();
        String analyst = stockInfo.getAnalyst().getName();
        String rating = stockInfo.getRating();
%>
    <tr>
      <td><%= ticker %></td>
      <td><%= analyst %></td>
      <td><%= rating %></td>
    </tr>
<%
      }
```

```
%>
    </table>
    <table>
      <tr>
        <td>
          <select name="analysts">
<%
          ArrayList analysts = (ArrayList) request.getAttribute("analysts");
          for (int i = 0; i < analysts.size(); i++) {
            AnalystTO analyst = (AnalystTO) analysts.get(i);
%>
            <option value="<%= analyst.getAnalystId() %>">
              <%= analyst.getName() %>
<%
          }
%>
          </select>
        </td>
        <td>
          <select name="stocks">
<%
          ArrayList unratedStocks =
              (ArrayList) request.getAttribute("unrated");
          for (int i = 0; i < unratedStocks.size(); i++) {
            StockTO stock = (StockTO) unratedStocks.get(i);
%>
            <option value="<%= stock.getTickerSymbol() %>">
              <%= stock.getTickerSymbol() %>
<%
          }
%>
          </select>
        </td>
        <td>
          <select name="ratings">
            <option value="Run away! Run away!">Run away! Run away!
            <option value="Could be worse!">Could be worse!
            <option value="A bit of OK!">A bit of OK!
            <option value="Take a chance!">Take a chance!
            <option value="Smashing!">Smashing!
          </select>
        </td>
      </tr>
      <tr>
```

```
        <td>
          <input type="submit" value="Submit Rating">
        </td>
      </tr>
    </table>
    </form>
<%
    } else {
%>
    No stock information found
<%
    }
%>
    <hr>
    <address><a href="mailto:kmukhar@earthlink.net"></a></address>
  </body>
</html>
```

The `AddRating.java` source code (located in `web`) is shown in Listing 12-18.

Listing 12-18. *AddRating.java*

```
package web;

import javax.servlet.*;
import javax.servlet.http.*;
import delegate.*;
import transfer.*;

public class AddRating extends HttpServlet {
    public void doPost(HttpServletRequest request,
                       HttpServletResponse response)
    {
        try {
            String analyst = request.getParameter("analysts");
            Integer id = new Integer(analyst);
            String ticker = request.getParameter("stocks");
            String rating = request.getParameter("ratings");
            StockTO stockTO = new StockTO(ticker, null, rating);
            stockTO.setAnalyst(new AnalystTO(id, null));
            StockListDelegate delegate = StockListDelegate.getInstance();
            delegate.addStockRating(stockTO);
            request.setAttribute("data", delegate.getStockRatings());
            request.setAttribute("analysts", delegate.getAllAnalysts());
            request.setAttribute("unrated", delegate.getUnratedStocks());
            ServletContext context = getServletContext();
```

```
                RequestDispatcher dispatcher =
                    context.getNamedDispatcher("RatingsForm");
                dispatcher.forward(request, response);
            } catch (Exception e) {

            }
        }
    }
```

Like the StockList Servlet, the AddRating Servlet shown in Listing 12-18 uses the methods of the StockListDelegate class to access the services of the StockList session bean.

The other option available from the main page is the Analyst Management Form, whose UI logic is in the AnalystForm.jsp file (located in web-deploy), shown in Listing 12-19. Again, notice the use of the AnalystTO value object.

Listing 12-19. *AnalystForm.jsp*

```
<!DOCTYPE HTML PUBLIC "-//W3C//DTD HTML 4.01 Transitional//EN">
<html>
  <head>
    <title>Analyst Management</title>
  </head>
  <body>
    <%@ page import="java.util.*,transfer.*" %>
    <h1>Analyst Management Form</h1>
    <form action="/stock/servlet/ProcessAnalyst" method="POST">
      <table>
        <%
        ArrayList anlysts = (ArrayList) request.getAttribute("data");
        if (anlysts == null) {
        %>
          <h2> Attribute is null </h2>
        <%
        } else {
          for (int i = 0; i < anlysts.size(); i++) {
            AnalystTO analystData = (AnalystTO) anlysts.get(i);
        %>
          <tr>
            <td>
              <input type="checkbox" name="checkbox"
                     value="<%= analystData.getName() %>"
            </td>
            <td>
              <%= analystData.getName() %>
            </td>
          </tr>
        <%
          }
```

```
        }
        %>
      </table>
      <input type="submit" value="Delete Selected" name="delete">
      <p>
        <input type="text" size="40" name="addname">
        <input type="submit" value="Add New Analyst" name="add">
    </form>
    <hr>
    <address><a href="mailto:kmukhar@FIORE"></a></address>
  </body>
</html>
```

And that's all the code for this example. Once you've got all the code in the appropriate package directories, all that's left for you to do is compile and deploy. Open a command window and change your directory to the StockListPatternsApp directory.

1. Set your CLASSPATH variable to the following value:

```
>set CLASSPATH=.;➥
C:\jboss\lib\concurrent.jar;➥
C:\jboss\lib\jboss-common.jar;➥
C:\jboss\server\all\lib\jboss.jar;➥
C:\jboss\server\all\lib\javax.servlet.jar;➥
C:\jboss\server\all\lib\jboss-j2ee.jar;➥
C:\jboss\server\all\lib\jboss-remoting.jar;➥
C:\jboss\server\all\lib\jboss-transaction.jar;➥
C:\jboss\server\all\lib\jnpserver.jar;➥
C:\jboss\server\all\deploy\ejb3.deployer\jboss-ejb3.jar;➥
C:\jboss\server\all\deploy\ejb3.deployer\jboss-ejb3x.jar;➥
C:\jboss\server\all\deploy\ejb3.deployer\ejb3-persistence.jar;➥
C:\jboss\server\all\deploy\jboss-aop-jdk50.deployer\jboss-aop-jdk50.jar;➥
C:\jboss\server\all\deploy\jboss-aop-jdk50.deployer\jboss-aspect-library-➥
jdk50.jar;
```

2. Build and deploy the first portion of the application (using the instructions for the code taken from the first example in this chapter). You can just deploy the generated EJB3 file from that example as well, if you do not care to repeat your steps.

3. As indicated in the previous example, populate the data for the entity beans by running the StockListAdder application. You can run this application by executing the following command:

```
>java -Djava.naming.factory.initial=➥
     org.jnp.interfaces.NamingContextFactory ➥
-Djava.naming.factory.url.pkgs=➥
     org.jboss.naming:org.jnp.interfaces ➥
-Djava.naming.provider.url=➥
     localhost client.StockListAdder
```

4. Compile the servlet classes in the web package.

```
>javac -d . web/*.java
```

5. Copy the delegate directory to the web-deploy\WEB-INF\classes directory.

6. Copy the web directory to web-deploy\WEB-INF\classes.

7. Change your directory to the web-deploy directory and create the WAR file.

```
>cd web-deploy
>jar cf stock.war *.html *.jsp WEB-INF/web.xml ➥
    WEB-INF/classes/delegate/*.class WEB-INF/classes/web/*.class
```

8. Deploy the WAR file by copying it to %JBOSS_HOME%\server\all\deploy.

9. That's it! Test that the file is deployed correctly by visiting the URL http://localhost:8080/stock.

Figure 12-2 shows a page from this web application after Fred the Analyst rated the stock for the world's smallest tricycle infomercial company, Zapalopalorinski Ltd.

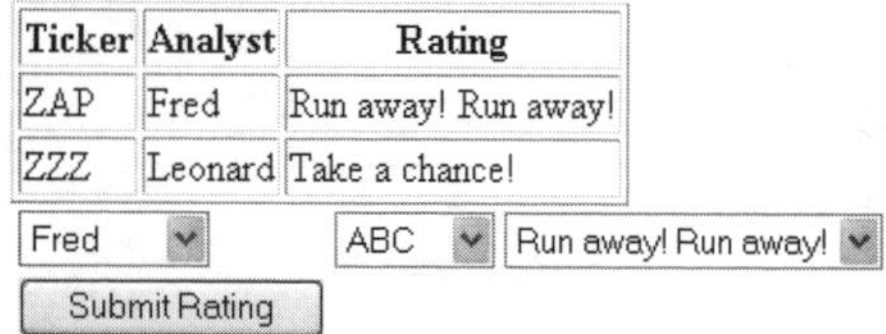

Stock Ratings
Ticker
Analyst
Rating
ZAP
Fred
Run away! Run away!
ZZZ
Leonard
Take a chance!
Fred
ABC
Run away! Run away!
Submit Rating

Figure 12-2. *Viewing stock ratings*

Reviewing the Modified JSP/Servlets Client

The StockList Servlet uses the static StockListDelegate.getInstance() method to get the singleton StockListDelegate instance, as shown in Listing 12-16. It uses that delegate reference to get the data, and then forwards the request to a JSP page for display. The request is forwarded based on the extra path information passed with the request:

- If getPathInfo() returns "AnalystForm", the request is forwarded to AnalystForm.jsp.
- If getpathInfo() returns "RatingsForm", the request is forwarded to RatingsForm.jsp.
- If getpathInfo() returns "AddRating", the request is forwarded to the AddRating Servlet.

The RatingsForm JSP creates a form that posts a request to the StockList Servlet. This request is forwarded to the AddRating Servlet. Take a moment to examine the use of value objects in the RatingsForm JSP shown in Listing 12-17. After adding the rating, the AddRating Servlet forwards the request to the RatingsForm JSP to display the new data.

This example again illustrates some of the advantages of using the Delegate and Transfer Object design patterns in your web application. JSP pages are primarily designed to provide a data visualization layer for a web application. Servlets are primarily designed to receive and respond to requests. By encapsulating the data-access details in the delegate and transfer objects, the JSP pages and Servlets don't need to worry about which EJB to access or how to access the EJBs. The JSP pages and Servlets don't even need to know that the data came from an EJB. The data could come directly from a database, from a flat file, or over the network.

Summary

In this chapter, we continued the discussion of EJBs from the previous chapter. After having read this chapter, you should know:

- How Java EE applications may benefit from the application of formally defined software designs to your code. Such patterns describe solutions to specific design problems and improve developer productivity by leveraging these solutions. There are many design patterns in use today, and new ones are continually being identified and documented by developers. The five patterns that we discussed were Delegate, Transfer Object, DAO, Factory, and Singleton.
- How to use JSP pages and Servlets with EJBs in an application. In this chapter, JSP pages and Servlets were shown in tandem with an EJB application, acting in the place of the rich GUI clients developed earlier in the book. The use of two different GUI methodologies in consuming your EJB application without any significant change in business logic on your part is both an incredible timesaver and a lofty application development goal.

In the next chapter, we'll take a look at two more EJB concepts: message-driven beans and EJB timers.

Exercises

1. Create a JSP/Servlet client for the `StockList` application detailed in this chapter. This JSP client will output only XML results of the different method calls to the `StockList` app, and can be consumed by other clients.
2. Modify the Ejb3StockListDAOBean to acquire Entity and Analyst beans from custom objects you'll create that obtain their data from XML files.

CHAPTER 13

Message-Driven Beans

As discussed in Chapter 9, in addition to session beans and entity beans is an EJB type known as *message-driven beans*. The question of accessing enterprise business logic was addressed by session beans, and the need to model the data used in that logic was filled by entity beans. So, what's left for message-driven beans, you ask? Consider that many large-scale enterprise applications must possess the ability to respond to some external event. Couple that with the requirement that the mechanism enabling such responses is both extensible and efficient, and you'll find that there does exist some need for a capable enterprise application tool to handle the task. Message-driven beans are the EJB 3.0 solution for such application scenarios.

In this chapter, you will learn the following:

- What message-driven beans are and what they're used for
- How message-driven beans interact with the Java Messaging Service (JMS)
- How to automatically invoke your message-driven bean based on some interval using the Timer service

Message-Driven Beans Overview

Message-driven beans (often abbreviated as *MDBs*, lest you find yourself wondering why a discussion of Microsoft Access has suddenly bloomed in the midst of a Java EE conversation) are the means by which EJB applications are able to respond to some external event (literally, a JMS message) without any extensive plumbing or hooks into external components. As stated previously, these messages are typically delivered via a JMS message producer; however, you may also use MDBs with other messaging frameworks—or even develop your own, so long as it delivers a JMS message.

MDBs exist for the purpose of receiving and processing asynchronous messages. These messages could be from external systems or from components of the same application. They are called *asynchronous* because they can arrive at any time, as opposed to being a direct result of a remote method invocation. Similar to the way that UI event-handling works, message-driven beans "listen" for asynchronous messages that have been sent to them. It is worth noting that, unlike calling a remote method, the sender of the asynchronous message doesn't block and wait for a response. The process of "blocking" can be equivocated with the idea of waiting, in this case: a process that blocked until a response was received would be similar to you pacing anxiously by the mailbox, waiting for a response to a letter you sent. In contrast, an asynchronous process would be similar to you sending a letter and then doing any number of other things until you receive a response to your letter.

So described generally, MDBs provide you with a simplified method to respond to asynchronous events. Due to the nature of the EJB container that brokers these messages to the MDB, you are saved from having to develop excessive thread-safety solutions or listener object maintenance. Each MDB you develop need only facilitate an `onMessage()` method that handles a message of the type you are expecting; the work of communicating that message through the application framework is handled for you.

MDBs are not only enabled by the EJB container, but also by a facility in Java EE known as the Java Message Service (JMS) API and external systems that are able to interact with a JMS system. Figure 13-1 shows the context in which the next example will operate, and it will serve as a basis for our discussion of the JMS API.

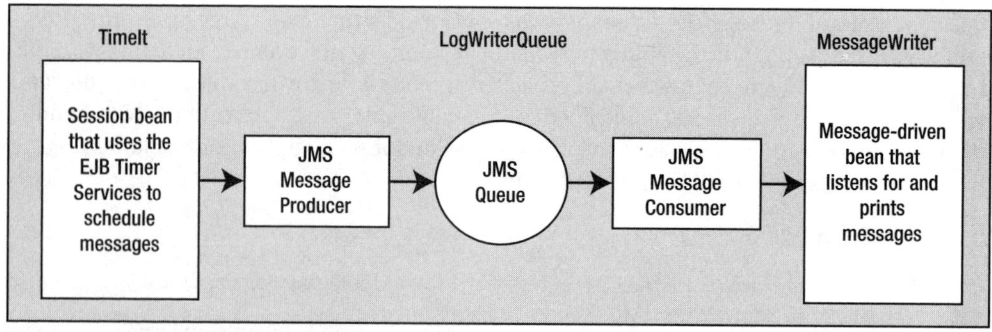

Figure 13-1. *The basic application layout for the MessageTimerApp example*

The functionality provided by MDBs—that is, responding to messages that arrive at some uncertain date, or not at all—should indicate to you the fact that MDBs are *stateless*. This term should not be new to you; you should have already encountered stateless session beans earlier, and you are likely now familiar with the core functionality present in a stateless object. That is to say, a stateless object does not maintain instance data across separate invocations. The MDB does not naturally store data from one message received to the next; if you need to ensure that repeated MDB invocations have access to data received from previous invocations, you'll need to store that data somewhere outside the bean.

Just like stateless session beans, MDBs are stateless, container-managed objects that respond to requests. The similarity is short-lived, however, as MDBs respond to JMS messages (`javax.jms.Message`) received from the container, whereas stateless session beans respond to client requests through the appropriate interface. The split is continued in that an MDB does not implement a local or remote interface, but instead implements the appropriate JMS messaging interface to describe its behavior. For our purposes, we will be implementing the `MessageListener` interface (`javax.jms.MessageListener`), which defines a very generic (and usable) MDB listening behavior. Other packages may describe more specialized behavior, such as the receipt of XML messages from clients.

MDBs are by no means just simple message response objects, however. MDBs have a rich programming model that includes support for higher-level concepts like message transactions (allowing message processing to be given a certain level of atomicity) and method interception.

Taking advantage of these tools provides your enterprise application a high level of functionality at a significantly low cost. Read on to learn how they might best benefit you.

Describing MDBs

Just as with all other bean types presented in the EJB 3.0 specification, MDBs are initially described by an annotation—in this case, @MessageDriven (javax.ejb.MessageDriven). This annotation is used by the container to determine certain behavioral traits about the bean (just as with entity beans and session beans), most notably the activation configuration. The activation configuration for a message driven bean can instruct the container for the appropriate messaging method to apply to the bean or what types of messages are allowed to be processed by the bean.

This excerpt from the code used later in this chapter will serve as an example of how an MDB is defined:

```
@MessageDriven(activateConfig =
  {
    @ActivationConfigProperty(propertyName="destinationType",
                              propertyValue="javax.jms.Queue"),
    @ActivationConfigProperty(propertyName="destination",
                              propertyValue="queue/LogWriter")
  })
public class MessageWriter implements MessageListener {
```

You can see here how the MDB has its activation configuration specified by an array of @ActivationConfigProperty (javax.ejb.ActivationConfigProperty) annotations. As you'll see later in the chapter, this particular segment alerts the EJB container as to where and how the messages received by this bean should be treated.

The MDB Context

Thankfully, MDBs provide more than just a simple message/response mechanism. The EJB specification has made provisions for MDBs to use transactions (whether provided by the EJB container or facilitated by the bean itself), special interceptor methods that enrich message-processing functionality, and access to a facility that allows for timed invocation of the bean. Access to transaction functionality and the timer service is provided by the MDB's MessageDrivenContext (javax.ejb.MessageDrivenContext) interface. This interface may be acquired through use of injection, a concept we originally discussed in Chapter 10.

Recall that injection is the means by which the container inserts a reference for the appropriate object automatically for the annotated member. Chapters 10 and 11 showed examples of injection such as the following:

```
@PersistenceContext
private EntityManager _manager;
```

The @PersistenceContext annotation performed a special sort of injection that was relative to the EntityManager interface it injected. The type of injection discussed here is a much more generic form of injection, called *resource injection*. Resource injection allows the container to insert the appropriate object based on your request. Consider the following code, for example:

```
@Resource
private MessageDrivenContext  _context;
```

The EJB container will set the member `_context` to reference the `MessageDrivenContext` valid for the currently loaded MDB. The member will be set automatically for you after the container has initialized the bean and before any messages are processed. As is often the case with the annotations described in the Java EE 5 specification, it's handy, isn't it?

MDB Transactions

As mentioned earlier, MDBs in EJB 3.0 are able to use transactions to allow a higher order of control over message processing. By using transactions, you may "roll back" the processing of a particular message if an action fails. This rollback feature cascades from the business method that initially required the transaction to the methods it invoked that support transaction processing. This functionality is semantically identical to the idea of transactions in databases, where entire sets of database operations may be rolled back or committed based on the success of individual instructions within the set.

In the sections that follow, we'll look at container-managed and user-defined transactions.

Container-Managed Transactions

As you might have guessed, the EJB specification has made provisions for containers to provide their own transaction functionality. This functionality can be added to an MDB merely by annotating the class name with the `@TransactionManagement` (`javax.ejb.TransactionManagement`) descriptor. Once the class is annotated, the business methods of the class must be annotated to specify how the container's transaction functionality will interpret their invocation. You can specify this behavior by using the `@TransactionAttribute` (`javax.ejb.TransactionAttribute`) annotation on business methods with either of the following two attributes: `REQUIRED` or `NOT_SUPPORTED`.

■ Note `@TransactionAttribute` can actually hold several different values to imply the transaction behavior: `MANDATORY`, `REQUIRED`, `REQUIRES_NEW`, `SUPPORTS`, `NOT_SUPPORTED`, and `NEVER`. MDBs may have business methods annotated with only `REQUIRED` or `NOT_SUPPORTED`, however.

`NOT_SUPPORTED` as a transaction type merely alerts the container that any previously existing transactions should be suspended as the MDB executes the method in question. Once the method has finished executing, the transaction is resumed and business continues as usual.

`REQUIRED` transactions, on the other hand, cascade the transaction functionality to the methods invoked within the original function. Therefore, if a simple SQL `INSERT` buried in the application fails, all methods invoked up to that point that use transactions are alerted to roll back, taking on their state before the error.

Thus, through some very simple-looking code such as the following:

```
@TransactionManagement
@MessageDriven (...)  // Simplified for this example
public class MyMDB {
     @TransactionAttribute(REQUIRED)
     public void onMessage(javax.jms.Message){
          ...
     }
}
```

some very functional logic may be achieved. Should a database operation triggered by a method in the onMessage() method cause a rollback in the current transaction, that rollback will cascade up to the MDB level. As you might guess, this is a handy way to make sure messages don't get processed until all the dependent logic executes successfully.

User-Defined Transactions

You are not required to stick with container-managed transactions. Simply add the parameter BEAN to the @TransactionManagement class annotation and the container will assume your MDB is handling all the finer details of transaction management. While the task of managing your own transactions is not an incredibly hard one, it does require a certain degree of vigilance in terms of adhering to coding standards.

The first step in managing the transactions manually for a particular class is obtaining it via (you guessed it) resource injection. The following line of code shows how to accomplish this:

```
@Resource javax.transaction.UserTransaction customTransaction;
```

Once you've added this to your MDB class definition, all you need to do is add the correct calls to the customTransaction object in your class. The following code presents a quick-and-dirty example:

```
@TransactionManagement(BEAN)
@MessageDriven (...)  // Simplified for this example
public class MyMDB {
     @Resource javax.transaction.UserTransaction customTransaction;
     public void onMessage(javax.jms.Message){
          customTransaction.update(); // Start the transaction
          ...
          customTransaction.commit(); // Assume transaction went well, commit
changes
     }
}
```

Invocation of an Interceptor

The aspect-oriented programming (AOP) model used in EJB 3.0 is a very simplistic form, wherein MDB and session bean business methods may be preceded or followed automatically by some "interceptor." These interceptors are called only before or after the execution of a bean business method; "true" AOP would allow you to actually attach to method calls within the business method itself.

■ **Note** AOP is a programming model wherein the invocation of a particular method may be "wrapped" by extra functionality automatically. Oft-quoted examples of AOP are adding caching or logging to existing frameworks. Imagine you have developed an entire application without any logging mechanism (bad developer!). Using an AOP framework, you could add extra configuration directives and a logging class to your application *without changing existing code* and log all calls to a particular method or any method at all.

You can indicate a particular method will "intercept" other business methods (such as `onMessage()`, in the case of MDBs) in its own bean by annotating it with the `@AroundInvoke` (`javax.ejb.AroundInvoke`) descriptor, for example:

```
@AroundInvoke
public Object messageFoo(InvocationContext ctx) throws Exception
{
   System.out.println("Method intercepted!");
   return ctx.proceed();
}
```

This particular method will be invoked prior to the execution of the business method. Upon encountering the call to `ctx.proceed()`, the container will check for any other intercepting methods. When it has exhausted its list of waiting interceptors, it will execute the business method itself.

You may also indicate a set of external objects that will act as interceptors through the use of the `@Interceptors` (`javax.ejb.Interceptors`) annotation:

```
@MessageDriven
@Interceptors({"util.logger","util.profiler","util.decompressor"})
public class GzipNetMessageActor{
// ...
}
```

The EJB container will wrap all business method calls to instances of `GzipNetMessageActor` with invocations of the methods annotated by `@AroundInvoke` in `util.logger`, `util.profiler`, and `util.decompressor` (in that order). This is a handy tool for quickly adding value to your application without modifying existing code. (Remember, you can also use interceptors in session beans.)

Java Message Service API

The JMS API is a Java API, located in the `javax.jms` package, that provides an interface for applications that require the services of a messaging system. A messaging system enables messages containing text, objects, and other message types to be sent and received *asynchronously*. This is in contrast with the remote procedure call (RPC) model that we've been using so far for EJBs, where interactions between components occur *synchronously*.

An implementation of a messaging system that complies with the JMS API is called a *JMS provider*. The JBoss application server has a JMS provider that we'll be using to enable the example in this section, and several vendors have commercial implementations available for use in enabling messaging in enterprise applications.

In Figure 13-1, the `TimeIt` session bean on the left sends asynchronous messages to the `MessageWriter` MDB on the right. Both of these beans have been created for this example (they aren't Java library classes). These `TimeIt` and `MessageWriter` beans are known as JMS clients because they are *clients* of the underlying messaging system.

Messaging systems enable asynchronous communication by providing a *destination* for messages to be held until they can be delivered to the recipient. The circle in the middle, `LogWriterQueue`, is the destination that holds messages from the `TimeIt` session bean that are bound for the `MessageWriter` MDB. There are two types of destinations in JMS:

- A *queue* is used to hold messages that are sent from one JMS client to be delivered to another. This model of messaging is known as *point-to-point*.
- A *topic* is used to hold messages that are sent from potentially many JMS clients to be delivered to potentially multiple JMS clients. This model of messaging is known as *publish/subscribe*.

The example we will look at later in this section uses a queue type destination, which is reflected in Figure 13-1. Also in Figure 13-1 are boxes for a JMS *message producer* and a JMS *message consumer*. These represent classes in a JMS provider that work on behalf of the JMS clients to send and receive messages. You don't have to create a JMS message consumer when working with MDBs, because the EJB container does that on the MDBs' behalf.

We'll have more to say about the JMS API when we walk through the example code, so let's turn our attention to another technology that will be used in the example: the EJB Timer Service.

EJB Timer Service

The EJB 2.1 specification introduced provisions for a service known as the *EJB Timer Service*. Its purpose in life is to register enterprise beans to receive timer callbacks after a specified elapsed time, or at specific intervals. This is useful, for example, if you want a session bean to initiate a process at 2:00 am every day to gather data from an external system.

■ Note The EJB Timer Service is not intended to act as a real-time process scheduler. In other words, don't expect nanosecond precision and high reliability; its primary intent is to serve as a model for application-level timing.

These events can be triggered as follows:

- At a particular time. Perhaps you could have your EJB notified at midnight on July 28, 2061 that it should do something special (to celebrate the next date that Haley's Comet will be closest to the sun).
- After a given elapsed time.
- On a recurring basis, after a given time interval.

These timer services are provided by the EJB container and are able to be obtained through much the same way as other container-level services. To obtain a TimerService object, you may

- Inject the TimerService into a class member using resource injection.

```
@Resource javax.ejb.TimerService myTimer
```

- Acquire an instance of the TimerService object through the getTimerService() method of your MessageDrivenContext or SessionContext object.

```
@Resource javax.ejb.MessageDrivenContext initialContext;
...
public void onMessage(javax.jms.Message){
     javax.ejb.TimerService ts=initialContext.getTimerService();
}
```

- Acquire an instance of the TimerService object through JNDI.

As you might expect, TimerService provides your EJB with timer objects that perform some action over a specified interval. To specify which action must take place, an EJB must annotate one of its methods with the @Timeout annotation.

Using MDBs, JMS, and the EJB Timer Service: Putting It All Together

In this section, we'll look at an example that demonstrates the technologies mentioned earlier in the chapter: MDBs, the JMS API, and the EJB Timer Service.

Figure 13-1 depicts the behavior of this example, which is as follows:

1. The TimeIt session bean uses the EJB Timer Service to be notified every ten seconds.
2. Each time the TimeIt bean is notified, it uses the JMS API to create a JMS message producer.
3. The TimeIt bean uses the JMS message producer to create and send a message that it wants delivered to the MessageWriter MDB. In our example, this is a text message that contains the date and time that the message was sent.
4. The JMS message producer sends the message to the LogWriter, which is an arbitrarily named JMS queue created for this example.
5. A JMS message consumer, which is created and managed by the EJB container, receives the text message.
6. The EJB container calls the onMessage() method of the MessageWriter MDB, passing the text message into the method.
7. The MessageWriter bean creates a String, concatenates the text message received, and sends it to System.out. Note that System.out is managed by the application server, so we'll start it up in a special way to see the output.

Creating the MessageTimerApp Example

To build the example, we'll create the following new .java files in the MessageTimerApp directory:

- TimeIt.java in the timer package
- TimeItBean.java in the client package
- TimeItTester.java in the timer package
- MessageWriter.java in the msg package
- timer-message-service.xml in the JMS deployment directory (c:\jboss\server\all\deploy\jms)

We'll implement the code involved in this example according to the flow of the message being sent. First, here's the remote interface of the TimeIt session bean, TimeIt.java:

```
package timer;

import javax.ejb.Remote;

@Remote
public interface TimeIt {
  // the public business method on the timer bean
  public void startTimer();
}
```

The remote interface has only one business method, startTimer(). This method will be invoked by the TimeItTester client application, seen in the following TimeItTester.java listing, just to get things started up:

```
package client;

import timer.TimeIt;
import javax.naming.InitialContext;

public class TimeItTester {
  public static void main(String[] args) throws Exception {
    // Get a naming context
    InitialContext ctx = new InitialContext();

    // Create a TimeIt object
    TimeIt timeIt =
      (TimeIt) ctx.lookup(TimeIt.class.getName());

    timeIt.startTimer();
  }
}
```

Now we'll get to the code at the heart of the example: using the EJB Timer Service. Here is the implementation of the TimeIt session bean contained in TimeItBean.java:

```
package timer;

import javax.annotation.Resource;
import javax.ejb.SessionContext;
import javax.ejb.Stateless;
import javax.ejb.Timeout;
import javax.ejb.Timer;
import javax.ejb.TimerService;
import javax.jms.Queue;
import javax.jms.Connection;
import javax.jms.ConnectionFactory;
import javax.jms.MessageProducer;
import javax.jms.Session;
import javax.jms.Session;
import javax.jms.TextMessage;

// General imports
import java.text.*;
import java.util.*;

@Stateless
public class TimeItBean implements TimeIt {
     private @Resource SessionContext ctx;
     private @Resource TimerService timer;
     private @Resource(name="ConnectionFactory")
     ConnectionFactory factory;
     private @Resource(name="queue/LogWriter")
     Queue queue;
     private SimpleDateFormat sdf =
          new SimpleDateFormat("yyyy.MM.dd 'at' HH:mm:ss.SSS");

  // Public business method to start the timer
  public void startTimer()
  {
    // After initial five seconds, then every ten seconds
    timer.createTimer(5000, 10000, "timer");
  }

  // Timer method - timer expires - send message to queue
  @Timeout
  public void timeoutHandler(Timer timer) {
    Connection connection = null;
    try {
      // Get a connection from the factory
      connection = factory.createConnection();
```

```
      // Create a session
      Session session =
        connection.createSession(false,
        Session.AUTO_ACKNOWLEDGE);
      // Create a sender for the session to the queue
      MessageProducer sender = session.createProducer(queue);
      // Create a text message
      TextMessage message = session.createTextMessage();
      // Set the text of the message
      message.setText
        ("log entry, the time is: " + sdf.format(new Date()));
      // Send the message
      sender.send(message);
    }
    catch (Exception e) {
      System.out.println("Exception in message: " + e.toString());
      e.printStackTrace();
    }
    finally {
      if (connection != null) {
        try {
          connection.close();
        }
        catch (Exception e) {}
      }
    }
  }
}
```

Here is the code for our MDB, `MessageWriter.java`. There aren't any bean interface listings to show because MDBs do not use them:

```
package msg;

import javax.ejb.ActivationConfigProperty;
import javax.ejb.MessageDriven;
import javax.jms.Message;
import javax.jms.MessageListener;
import javax.jms.TextMessage;

@MessageDriven(activateConfig =
  {
    @ActivationConfigProperty(propertyName="destinationType",
                              propertyValue="javax.jms.Queue"),
    @ActivationConfigProperty(propertyName="destination",
                              propertyValue="queue/LogWriter")
  })
```

```
public class MessageWriter implements MessageListener {
  // Must implement this method for MessageDriven
  public void onMessage(Message message) {
    TextMessage msg = null;

    try {
      if (message instanceof TextMessage) {
        msg = (TextMessage) message;
        System.out.println("Got message: " + msg.getText());
      }
      else {
        System.out.println("Got message of type: "
          + message.getClass().getName() + " ==> ignored!");
      }
    }
    catch (Throwable te) {
      te.printStackTrace();
    }
  }
}
```

Supporting the MDB is the JMS deployment XML file (`timer-message-service.xml`), which tells the JMS subsystem to create a message queue to be used by the MDB. Save this XML file in the JMS deployment directory of JBoss (`c:\jboss\server\all\deploy\jms`).

```
<?xml version="1.0" encoding="UTF-8" ?>
<server>
  <mbean code="org.jboss.mq.server.jmx.Queue"
        name="jboss.mq.destination:service=Queue,name=logQueue">
    <attribute name="JNDIName">queue/LogWriter</attribute>
    <depends optional-attribute-name="DestinationManager">
      jboss.mq:service=DestinationManager
    </depends>
  </mbean>
</server>
```

Building and Running MessageTimerApp

Now let's build and run the example.

1. Set your classpath as follows:

```
>set CLASSPATH=.;➥
C:\jboss\lib\concurrent.jar; ➥
C:\jboss\client\jboss-j2ee.jar; ➥
C:\jboss\lib\jboss-common.jar; ➥
c:\jboss\lib\commons-httpclient.jar;➥
C:\jboss\server\all\lib\jboss.jar; ➥
C:\jboss\server\all\lib\jboss-remoting.jar; ➥
C:\jboss\server\all\lib\jboss-transaction.jar; ➥
```

```
C:\jboss\server\all\lib\jnpserver.jar; ➥
C:\jboss\server\all\lib\javax.servlet.jar; ➥
C:\jboss\server\all\deploy\ejb3.deployer\jboss-ejb3.jar; ➥
C:\jboss\server\all\deploy\ejb3.deployer\jboss-ejb3x.jar; ➥
C:\jboss\server\all\deploy\jboss-aop-jdk50.deployer\jboss-aop-jdk50.jar; ➥
C:\jboss\server\all\deploy\jboss-aop-jdk50.deployer\➥
     jboss-aspect-library-jdk50.jar
```

2. You can use the following commands to compile these files:

```
>javac -d . msg/*.java
>javac -d . timer/*.java
>javac -d . client/*.java
```

3. Create a JAR file for the application named `MessageTimerApp.ejb3` by executing the following in the MessageTimerApp directory:

```
>jar cf MessageTimerApp.ejb3 msg/*.class timer/*.class
```

4. Copy the resulting EJB3 file to your JBoss deployment directory:

```
>copy MessageTimerApp.ejb3 c:\jboss\server\deploy
```

5. Now just start the client by typing the following from the command line:

```
>java -Djava.naming.factory.initial=org.jnp.interfaces.NamingContextFactory
-Djava.naming.factory.url.pkgs=org.jboss.naming:org.jnp.interfaces
-Djava.naming.provider.url=localhost client.TimeItTester
```

6. Once the application has started, you should see lines much like the following repeatedly appearing in the server's console output and any "info" logs.

```
05:54:25,672 INFO  [STDOUT] Got message: log entry, ➥
     the time is: 2005.07.27 at 05:54:25.657
05:54:35,672 INFO  [STDOUT] Got message: log entry, ➥
      the time is: 2005.07.27 at 05:54:35.657
05:54:45,672 INFO  [STDOUT] Got message: log entry, ➥
      the time is: 2005.07.27 at 05:54:45.657
05:54:55,672 INFO  [STDOUT] Got message: log entry, ➥
      the time is: 2005.07.27 at 05:54:55.672
```

Reviewing MessageTimerApp

Now that you've built and run the application, let's look at how these technologies work together (and why they're useful to you!). You'll first examine how the EJB Timer Service is implemented in the `TimeItBean` class.

The `@Resource SessionContext` directive in the session bean is fulfilled by the EJB container after the session bean is created:

```
private @Resource SessionContext ctx;
```

The container takes note of the @Resource directive (much like it did in Chapter 10, when we used @PersistenceContext to acquire an EntityManager in the session bean) and sets the value of the private member equal to the SessionContext object, which represents the EJB container context in which the session bean is running. As mentioned earlier in this chapter, such an act is called resource injection.

Resource injection is also used to acquire references to the JMS ConnectionFactory (javax.jms.ConnectionFactory), JMS message Queue (javax.jms.Queue), and EJB TimerService (javax.ejb.TimerService) objects. Note that by using the @Resource annotation to acquire these objects, you're saved any extra steps that might be required to use container services.

Once a reference to the TimerService object for the container has been obtained, you use it in the startTimer() method to create a timer object that executes over specific intervals. Specifically, the Timer (javax.ejb.Timer) object will expire, trigger, fire, go off—however you want to say it—in five seconds, and then every ten seconds thereafter:

```
public void startTimer()
{
  // After initial five seconds, then every ten seconds
  timer.createTimer(5000, 10000, "timer");
}
```

You might want to take a few moments at this point to examine the Java EE 5 SDK Java API documentation for the overloaded createTimer() methods of the TimerService class. These will familiarize you with how to create Timer objects with the different types of time-based logic (expiring at a specific time, elapsed time, or interval) described previously. By the way, one of the exercises at the end of this chapter specifies creating the different types of timers.

Whenever a timer fires, the method of the enterprise bean annotated with the descriptor @Timeout (javax.ejb.Timeout) gets invoked. In our example, this method (public void timeoutHandler(Timer timer)) uses the JMS API to send an asynchronous message to an MDB, so let's now turn our attention to that subject.

According to the diagram and description of this example's behavior given earlier, one thing that our method annotated by @Timeout needs to do is to create a JMS message producer that can send messages to the LogWriter queue. To do that, it will use the ConnectionFactory object acquired via the @Resource annotation to create a Session (javax.jms.Session) that communicates with MessageWriter. Note that both the ConnectionFactory and the Queue that the Session is connecting to are both considered to already be instantiated by the container.

```
private @Resource(name="ConnectionFactory")
ConnectionFactory factory;
private @Resource(name="queue/LogWriter")
Queue queue;
```

The name directive being passed to the @Resource annotation is instructing the container that it should populate the variable in question (factory or queue) with a reference to the instance that the container recognizes by that name. Remember the XML deployment file timer-message-service.xml? That particular file instructed the JMS subsystem to create a queue named (not at all coincidentally) queue/LogWriter. Here that JNDI name is referenced by the @Resource annotation to acquire it, where it is subsequently used by timeoutHandler(Timer timer):

```
Connection connection = null;
  try {
    // Get a connection from the factory
    connection = factory.createConnection();
    // Create a session
    Session session =
      connection.createSession(false,
      Session.AUTO_ACKNOWLEDGE);
    // Create a sender for the session to the queue
    MessageProducer sender = session.createProducer(queue);
    // Create a text message
    TextMessage message = session.createTextMessage();
    // Set the text of the message
    message.setText
      ("log entry, the time is: " + sdf.format(new Date()));
    // Send the message
    sender.send(message);
  }
```

The createProducer() method of the Session object is passed a reference to the Queue, and it creates a MessageProducer (javax.jms.MessageProducer) object that can send messages to that destination, as shown in the following code. The MessageProducer is represented by the JMS message producer in Figure 13-1.

```
// Create a sender for the session to the queue
MessageProducer sender = session.createProducer(queue);
```

Since a MessageProducer is useless without a message to produce, a TextMessage object is created by calling the createTextMessage() method of the Session object. This particular message type is a TextMessage, but you can look at javax.jms.Message (its superinterface) in the JMS API documentation to see a description of the other four message types available in JMS.

The String to be sent is built, placed into the TextMessage object, and sent to the destination (Queue):

```
// Create a text message
TextMessage message = session.createTextMessage();
// Set the text of the message
message.setText("log entry, the time is: " + sdf.format(new Date()));
// Send the message
sender.send(message);
```

You're not going to send any more messages until the next time the @Timeout annotated method is called, so you close the Connection, which closes the Session and MessageProducer created earlier. This all happens in the code located in the finally block of the example:

```
    finally {
      if (connection != null) {
        try {
          connection.close();
        }
        catch (Exception e) {}
      }
    }
```

Now it's up to the JMS provider to deliver the message to the LogWriter queue and on to the MessageWriter bean, which is an MDB. There aren't any bean interface listings to show because MDBs do not use them.

As shown in the listing for the MessageWriterBean class, MDBs must be annotated with the @MessageDriven (javax.ejb.MessageDriven) descriptor *and* implement the MessageListener interface. Take particular note of how the @MessageDriven declaration contains the relevant configuration information regarding the LogWriter queue:

```
@MessageDriven(activateConfig =
  {
    @ActivationConfigProperty(propertyName="destinationType",
                              propertyValue="javax.jms.Queue"),
    @ActivationConfigProperty(propertyName="destination",
                              propertyValue="queue/LogWriter")
  })
```

Note how array notation is used to fill the activateConfig parameter of the @MessageDriven annotation. The elements of this array are descriptors that inform the EJB container how certain parameters of the MessageDriven bean are to be set when the bean is invoked. The @ActivationConfigProperty (javax.ejb.ActivationConfigProperty) that sets the destination property equal to queue/LogWriter is of particular interest, as the container will use this to connect to the LogWriter queue specified in the JMS deployment XML for you. The destinationType property is used by the container to inform what object type the message destination will be.

In turn, the MessageListener interface grants possession of the onMessage() method. This method, called each time the MDB receives a message, is responsible for dispatching message information to your other components or taking some immediate action.

The onMessage() method of this example is expecting a TextMessage and will use the getText() method to obtain the String that was sent. Then, regardless of the message type received, you print something to System.out. Of particular note is the lack of interaction shown here between the onMessage() method and any other components within the EJB application. As you design your EJB applications around MDBs, be aware of the fact that your components will be acting upon response to messages and may be feasibly invoked at any time. While this may seem like an obvious fact, program designs that fail to take this into account during the development phase often add kludgy, inelegant constructs to help force their program execution to run correctly. In other words, remember this: MDBs are asynchronous—they can execute at any time!

MessageTimerApp Summary

Upon examining the previous application, although it may certainly seem like a nice trick to write something to the console every ten seconds, it certainly seems difficult to apply such usage to real-life scenarios. Applications for MDBs alone may seem obvious: objects receiving asynchronous messages from any number of clients fit quite nicely into the client/server model that most developers have become acclimated to in the past 20 years. Using message receivers to act upon time-based events, however, seems to be (at first glance) far more in the domain of a multithreaded application, where one or more threads execute at specific intervals, looking for work to do.

Such an approach isn't advised, however, for the shortsightedness it would show in respect to the EJB container resources. To say that spawning threads inside your EJB is an ill-advised practice is an understatement. Remember that all EJBs exist within the execution context of the EJB container; EJBs that do not treat resources in a predictable manner (an inevitable state in a multithreaded class) cannot be managed correctly by the container and may cause any number of unforeseen errors.

Summary

This chapter focused on the benefits and application of message-driven beans (MDBs). You saw how to use MDBs to initiate your application's logic based upon certain events. You also learned how MDBs integrate with the Java Message Service (JMS) API, a widely used messaging framework.

After having read this chapter, you should know:

- MDBs are a quick and easy method to plug your application into some greater event model. You can structure the internal business logic of your application without taking great pains to register with system events, abstracting such concerns away to any number of MDBs.
- The EJB 3.0 specification has provided for limited AOP functionality with the `@Interceptors` and `@AroundInvoke` descriptors. Using these annotations, you can enrich your application quickly without harming the overall application design.
- The JMS API provides you with a rich producer/consumer model that allows you to extend your application to handle any number of messages with ease. Using facilities already provided for your application, you can quickly register resources such as message queues for your MDBs, without excessive concern as to their management.

In the next chapter, we'll discuss the role of web services in Java EE 5.

Exercises

1. Write an MDB that takes a word and writes it to `System.out`. Write a simple application that writes to a message queue to test the message bean. Remember that `System.out` messages will go to the server log file.
2. Write a stateless session bean that implements the EJB Timer Service. Try using several of the different types of timers. Write an appropriate message to System.out to verify the timer is working.

CHAPTER 14

■ ■ ■

Web Services and JAX-WS

In the previous chapter we wrapped up the main part of our discussion about EJB. This chapter and the next focus on another mechanism used to enable distributed applications: web services.

In this chapter, you will learn the following:

- What web services are, why and when you should use them, and their fundamental concepts, including the web services protocol stack
- How to enable web services using SOAP and JAX-WS
- How to describe web services using WSDL
- Three ways a client can invoke web service methods

Note Before we continue, it is important to note that at the time of this writing, there are no full implementations of JSR-181 (Web Services Metadata for Java EE 5) and JAX-WS 2.0 (the second version of the specification formerly entitled JAX-RPC). The JBoss component that will provide JSR-181 functionality, JBossWS (`www.jboss.org/wiki/Wiki.jsp?page=JBossWS`), is still currently under development. This chapter provides instructions on how to obtain an in-development version of the components you need, but that version is not yet "complete."

Should you want to give other implementations of JSR-181 a shot, you can do so by downloading a simple reference implementation of the specification from BEA at `http://dev2dev.bea.com/webservices/jwsm.html`. You may choose to try out a more complex platform, Apache Beehive, which is an open source project jointly developed by volunteers at the Apache Software Foundation and BEA Systems, Inc. You can learn more about the Apache Beehive project from `http://incubator.apache.org/beehive/index.html` and from the book *Pro Apache Beehive*, by Kunal Mittal and Srinivas Kanchanavally (Apress, 2005; ISBN: 1-59059-515-7). You can also try out JAX-WS 2.0 by downloading the early release reference implementation from `https://jax-rpc.dev.java.net`. This reference implementation is currently valid only for the Sun Java EE Application Server.

Understanding Web Services

A *web service* consists of functionality available to applications via protocols associated with the Web. Example protocols commonly associated with the Web are HTTP (which, as you saw previously, is used for transmitting requests and responses between web clients, such as browsers and web servers), XML, and SOAP. (We'll look at XML and SOAP a little later on in this chapter.) Using these protocols, an application can make use of the functionality provided by a web service. For example, a bookseller named Apress might have a web service running on its web server that provides the ability to order books. We'll call this web service `ApressBookService`. An application could use this service when it needs to look up a price or order a book. This `ApressBookService` web service would have *operations*, each of which performs some functionality, for example:

- A `getPrice` operation could take the ISBN number of a book as input and return the price of the book.
- An `orderBook` operation could take an ISBN and a credit card number, and process an order for a book, including shipping instructions.

In the same way as the `ApressBookService` web service, organizations and individuals can offer services to applications over standard, ubiquitous protocols such as XML, SOAP, and HTTP. The availability of web services over such protocols makes them an attractive choice for developing distributed applications, which can be composed of web services offered by various divisions within a company or by other organizations.

Not sure yet? The concept of web services is a difficult one to grasp for some; the benefit of using them within your application may not seem readily apparent at first glance. By examining their usage as explained throughout this chapter, you will come to find that they are a flexible tool to be used by any developer. The act of making your business logic open and available to any client supporting the different web service layers grants your application a much higher overall value and functionality—all the more by virtue of the ease with which Java EE 5 allows you to create web services. In the sections that follow, we'll discuss the various web services standards and models, why you should consider using web services, and the protocols used in web services.

EXAMPLES OF WEB SERVICES

For examples of some of the web services currently available, check out `www.xmethods.com`. This site is one of several that allow developers to post information about a web service that they have developed, including a description of the service and instructions on how to use it. To give you a flavor of the kinds of web services being developed, the table that follows lists some interesting examples listed on the XMethods site at the time of this writing.

Web Service Name	Description
`BibleWebservice`	Retrieves biblical text
`Currency Exchange Rate`	Returns the exchange rate between two currencies
`Delayed Stock Quote`	Provides stock quotes delayed by 20 minutes
`DNS Server`	Provides name resolution services
`Fax Service`	Offers a commercial web service for sending faxes internationally
`FedEx - USPS - DHL Package Tracking`	Provides access to FedEx, USPS, and DHL package-tracking information
`Generate Bar Codes`	Generates (interleaved 2 of 5) bar code images
`Google Search API`	Provides the use of Google's search service for your own applications
`Image Converter`	Converts from one type of image to another
`Image Extractor`	Extracts the images from a given URL
`Shakespeare`	Takes a phrase from a William Shakespeare play and returns the associated speech, speaker, and play title
`StrikeIron Zip Code Information`	Retrieves the city, state, county, latitude, and longitude based on any U.S. zip code
`Weather - Temperature`	Returns the current temperature in a given U.S. region (by zip code)

Web Services Standards and Models

The ability for parts of a distributed application to communicate with each other and call each other's methods, as web services do, should be familiar to you from the EJB-related chapters earlier in this book. In fact, many standards have evolved that enable clients on one machine to invoke the operations or methods of a server on another machine, for example:

- **Remote Procedure Calls (RPCs)**: There are a few flavors of RPCs, including
    - Distributed Computing Environment (DCE) RPCs
    - Sun RPCs[1]
- **Common Object Request Broker Architecture (CORBA)**: This specification, adopted by Object Management Group (OMG), defines the interface and request model for a distributed set of objects. CORBA was originally proposed by a multicorporation group that included Sun Microsystems. It has compliant libraries and bindings for a multitude of programming languages and environments.

1. Interestingly enough, Sun was a pioneer of RPCs in the early 1980s.

- **Distributed Component Object Model (DCOM)**: This network-aware object acquisition technology is the successor to Component Object Model (COM). The COM technology was used widely throughout Microsoft Windows, but is gradually losing mindshare to the comparatively newer .NET Framework.
- **Java Remote Method Invocation (Java RMI)**: This technology enables EJBs.

All of these standards are excellent, but each is, to some degree, platform or programming-language dependent. To enable a future in which any application can invoke the methods of any other application (governed by security policies, of course), we need a standard that

- Is available with most of the popular programming languages
- Can be used on almost any hardware/operating system platform
- Uses communication protocols that are ubiquitous
- Encourages communication over ports that are not likely to have firewall issues

Web services promise to help us realize that future, as they meet all of the criteria just listed:

- Web services can be created in Java, C++, C#, Visual Basic, and many other programming languages.
- Web services can be used on most—if not all—major hardware operating system platforms. In addition, they typically run over TCP/IP and HTTP, both of which are ubiquitous.
- Because of the wide availability of web services, programmers can write applications that offer method-based services and can expect to be able to call the methods of applications that others have written.
- Web services applications can be deployed within the confines of a company's intranet and/or extranet, or on the Internet.

The *RPC model* is one way of implementing web services. In this model, a web service application makes an interface available to clients on the network; this is very similar to the EJB session bean model. Client programs can then find and invoke methods of this interface as if it were residing on the same machine. The data communicated between the client and the web service is expressed using Simple Object Access Protocol (SOAP) and XML.

The other way of implementing web services is using a *messaging model*. Each application can send SOAP messages to another, without expecting a return value as a caller of a method would. The applications communicate asynchronously, as did the components of the MDB example in the previous chapter. The web service will be initiated by a request call from the client, but the server will need to initiate its own response process, whether by signaling the client via some agreed-upon event interface or by attaching itself to an already known resource on the client.

We'll focus most of our attention in this book on the RPC model of web services.

Why Use Web Services?

The cross-platform nature of Java facilitates distributed applications running on multiple hardware and operating system platforms. If all of the components of a distributed application are written in Java, then using EJBs with Java RMI is a good choice. However, web services are a great choice for integrating applications that are written in various languages, because most major platforms have support for SOAP, which is the protocol used in web services for passing object data from one application to another. This enables, for example, an application developed in Java to use the web service operations of an application developed in Perl. Why should that differ from the previously mentioned methods of RPC communication, such as CORBA or RMI? Such mechanisms are considered "tightly bound" to the internals of your application, because your program must include at compile time certain artifacts that describe how the remote processes will behave. Should the remote process change its behavior, consuming applications must regenerate the required artifacts and be recompiled. Note that nearly all of the mechanisms mentioned provide runtime discovery and usage of data, but the method of doing so is clumsy when compared with the simplicity provided by web services.

A subtler advantage to web services is that they typically use HTTP as an underlying communication protocol. Because of this, they can easily and naturally be implemented over the TCP/IP ports most commonly open in firewalls: 80, 8080, and 443. Ports 80 and 8080 are used for standard browser-to-web server HTTP traffic, and port 443 is used for encrypted, secure HTTP traffic.

Because web services are so conducive to interoperability, legacy system vendors can expose functionality such that other systems can have access. For example, many banks provide customers with web access to their accounts, including the ability to perform transactions such as transferring money between accounts. But wouldn't it be nice if customers were able to use personal finance software to perform these transactions in real time, no matter what institutions hold those accounts? If every bank had a common set of secure web services that wrapped their account management systems, then that functionality could be a reality. Banks could easily massage their own internal data into the format specified, ensuring that their current customers would have access to the data, and also that they could use tools and software developed by other individuals (or other banks adhering to the same service format) with their own accounts. Banks wouldn't even need to drastically alter their own current account management software to gain these benefits; web services do not enforce a technology architecture change from current systems.

The use of web services in the area of personal finance brings up the important issue of security. Applications that share sensitive information with each other need to do so securely. This concern is addressed in web services in a similar manner to other web-based applications—that is, through the use of network traffic encryption and user authentication.

Let's now take a look at an architectural view of web services, in the form of a protocol stack.

Web Services Protocol Stack

Table 14-1 shows the protocols used in web services, from the highest to lowest level (reading from top to bottom). Note that we've omitted mention of layers lower than HTTP, notably the ones that employ TCP/IP and Ethernet technologies.

Table 14-1. *Web Service Protocols and Their Associated Layers*

Layer	Technology
Service discovery	UDDI
Service description	WSDL
Messaging	SOAP
Encoding	XML
Transport	HTTP

In the sections that follow, we'll cover these protocols in the reverse order from that shown in the table (i.e., from the bottom of the table up), and we'll briefly look at emerging layers as well.

Transport Layer

The typical transport layer is Hypertext Transfer Protocol (HTTP), the protocol over which most web traffic travels. As you may recall, HTTP was discussed in the context of Servlets and JSP pages in Chapter 5. Web services can also be carried over e-mail messages, using Simple Mail Transport Protocol (SMTP).

Encoding Layer

All web service traffic is expressed in Extensible Markup Language (XML). For information on XML, check out the resources mentioned in the "Summary" section at the end of this chapter or *XML Programming: Web Applications and Web Services with JSP and ASP* by Alexander Nakhimovsky and Tom Myers (Apress, 2002; ISBN 1-59059-003-1).

Messaging Layer

All application data sent via web services is enclosed in SOAP messages. SOAP is based entirely upon XML and contains structures such as the SOAP envelope, and within that, the SOAP header and SOAP body. The SOAP body, for example, contains all of the instance data of the objects that are being transported. The following example is a SOAP message for the `getPrice` operation of the fictional `ApressBookService`:

```
<SOAP-ENV:Envelope
  xmlns:SOAP-ENV="http://schemas.xmlsoap.org/soap/envelope/"
  <SOAP-ENV:Body>
    <m:getPrice xmlns:m="http://ws.apress.com">
      <isbn>1590593413</isbn>
    </m:getPrice>
  </SOAP-ENV:Body>
</SOAP-ENV:Envelope>
```

A Java application can use the API defined in SOAP with Attachments API for Java (SAAJ) to create, send, and receive SOAP messages. This API is contained in the `javax.xml.soap` package, which is included in the Java EE 5 SDK. As you'll see a little later, we'll use a facility known as

JAX-WS to develop a web service at a higher level of abstraction. JAX-WS uses the SAAJ API under the covers to produce and consume the SOAP message. You can learn more about SAAJ from the SAAJ 1.2 specification, which is available for download from `http://java.sun.com/xml/downloads/saaj.html`.

Service Description Layer

The functionality provided by a given web service is described by the Web Service Description Language (WSDL). When using JAX-WS (which we'll cover in more detail later in this chapter), web services are implemented in Java, with WSDL using XML to describe the interfaces, methods, arguments, return values, and the URL of a web service. Here are some terms you'll encounter when discussing WSDL:

- A WSDL *port* element is analogous to a Java *interface.*
- A WSDL *operation* element is analogous to a Java *method.*
- WSDL *part* elements (contained inside message elements) are analogous to Java *arguments* and *return values.*

You'll see an example of a WSDL file a little later in this chapter.

Service Discovery Layer

Web services can be registered for use and then discovered at runtime. For example, a client application seeking a web service that offers the functionality of a thesaurus could check to see which applicable web services are registered. This is known as Universal Description, Discovery, and Integration (UDDI). UDDI was originally a collaborative effort between Microsoft, IBM, and Ariba; the UDDI consortium now includes hundreds of members.

UDDI registries hold information about businesses and the web services they offer. These UDDI registries are hosted by various UDDI members and are available on the Internet, but they could also be located within a corporate intranet. You can find a list of UDDI registries available on the Internet and more information on UDDI at `www.uddi.org`.

There is also an API known as Java API for XML Registries (JAXR) that provides a uniform interface to registries such as UDDI. To learn more about UDDI and the JAXR API, please visit the URLs mentioned as resources in the "Summary" section of this chapter.

Emerging Layers

Some emerging layers of the web services stack deal with issues such as security, client identity, transaction coordination, web service user interfaces, and business process workflow. You can check out some of these emerging technologies with the Java Web Services Developer Pack (WSDP), available from Sun at `http://java.sun.com/webservices/index.jsp`. These new technologies are very important when using web services in mission-critical applications.

Developing a Web Service in Java

So far, you've learned the basics of web services and when and where to use them. In this section, you'll actually develop a web service in Java. We'll start off by introducing JAX-WS, the toolkit you'll use to develop the example, and then we'll install an early release version of the JBoss server that supports the Java EE 5 web service architecture. Once you've installed the server, we'll move on to create the example service.

Introducing JAX-WS

A number of toolkits may be used to develop web services in the Java programming language. One such toolkit is the very popular open source implementation of SOAP called Apache AXIS. AXIS is from the Apache Software Foundation (`http://ws.apache.org/axis`), an organization that provides support for open source projects.

Another such toolkit is the Java API for XML-based Web Services (JAX-WS), which provides a Java API for developing and implementing web services. JAX-WS handles all the details of the SOAP layer, enabling development in terms of simple method calls. JAX-WS is available in an early release reference implementation from `https://jax-rpc.dev.java.net`.

■ **Note** The JAX-WS implementation is not yet complete in the version of JBossWS available at the time of this writing. In this chapter, we'll use syntax defined in the predecessor of JAX-WS, JAX-RPC. You can follow the progress of the JAX-WS specification as it becomes finalized at `http://jcp.org/en/jsr/detail?id=224`. The API will still be referred to as JAX-WS throughout this chapter, in order to avoid confusion.

JAX-WS is an RPC-based programming model introduced in the J2EE 1.4 platform as JAX-RPC. The reasoning behind the name change from JAX-RPC to JAX-WS is to refocus the library's usage to a more web-service-centric model. Changing the name allowed the library developers to discontinue certain artifacts that no longer served a purpose in a web service model, and to more clearly define the purpose of the library. The drawback is that applications developed using the old version of the library must be changed in order to compile against the new version; the class hierarchy has changed drastically, removing any chance of binary compatibility.

JAX-WS's renewed purpose in life is to provide an API for Java applications to communicate with each other using the SOAP protocol. The programming model of JAX-WS is unique in that the client program will attempt to bind to a service (analogous to the WSDL `<service>` node) through the loading of a WSDL file or through reflection upon a class that has been annotated with the `@WebService` (`javax.jws.WebService`) descriptor. Upon acquiring a service, the program will request the specific `<port>` and call the method desired.

To better illustrate how a web service may be acquired and used by client programs, let's take the most obvious route and actually create a web service. Your first web service is going to be a very simple one (on par with a "Hello World!" application) named `SimpleService`. Unfortunately, you can't just jump into coding the service, due to the fact that the technology for the JBossWS libraries (the JBoss implementation of Java EE 5 web services) is not yet available in release form. You'll need to acquire a copy of the JBoss server currently in development, as described in the next section.

■ **Warning** You're about to download an in-development version of the JBoss Application Server. Although you should not experience any problems in downloading and compiling the development code, there's no 100-percent guarantee that it will all work. If you experience problems trying to run the server, are interested in seeing the development process of a high-profile software project, or would even like to try contributing your own time to the development of JBoss, you should visit the JBossWS forums at `www.jboss.com/?module=bb&op=viewforum&f=200`.

Downloading the CVS Tool

Remember back in the old days, when you were reading Chapter 2 and we were still just getting to know each other? Get ready to revisit those golden days of yore, as you'll need to acquire an entirely new version of the JBoss Server. This version features code still currently in development, which you'll acquire using a tool called Concurrent Versioning System (CVS). CVS is a tool that allows developers to archive and manage collections of source files. The CVS server tracks the changes made to files and allows developers to chart who made what changes to a file, what the changes were, and when the changes were made. As you'll see in just the next few paragraphs, CVS also allows different branches of source code to exist; different dependencies among source files may be registered to a particular branch, allowing you to obtain "snapshots" of the source tree upon request.

Your first step is to download CVS tools for your particular platform. Users of Windows NT/2000/XP and Red Hat Linux (or any RPM-aware system) will find CVS binaries at `www.march-hare.com/cvsnt`. If you're using a different system entirely, you can find the CVS source at `www.cvshome.org`. Windows users who are accustomed to GUI front-ends for command-line tools will be happy to know that both `www.wincvs.org` and `www.tortoisecvs.org` offer a more streamlined method to access CVS repositories. (One of this book's authors quite happily uses Tortoise CVS for both personal and professional tasks.)

Once you've downloaded a copy of the CVS tools for your system, run the installer (if you've downloaded a binary package), or compile the source and run the installation script. Open a command window (if you haven't done so already) and set the environmental variable `CVSROOT` equal to the following path:

```
:pserver:anonymous@anoncvs.forge.jboss.com:/cvsroot/jboss
```

Windows users will do so by typing the following:

```
>set CVSROOT=:pserver:anonymous@anoncvs.forge.jboss.com:/cvsroot/jboss
```

Users of Linux and BSD systems will use a different syntax:

```
>export CVSROOT=:pserver:anonymous@anoncvs.forge.jboss.com:/cvsroot/jboss
```

Once you've set the `CVSROOT` variable, the CVS tools will intuit the correct authentication protocol, username, CVS server, and initial path on the server to acquire source files from.

The following command tells the CVS tools that you wish to "check out" (`co`) the source code collection labeled `jboss-head`:

```
>cvs co -r JBossWS_1_0EA jboss-head
```

The parameter `-r JBossWS_1_0EA` (note that the `0` in question is a zero, not a letter) tells the CVS server you're interested in the branch of code labeled under `JBossWS_1_0EA`. In short, the branch of JBoss code that includes the JBossWS 1.0 "Early Access" libraries, allowing you to take the Java EE 5 web service implementation for a test drive. Note that this command downloads a fairly sizable collection of code, so having access to a fast connection and about 400MB of free space is a prerequisite to continue. (The directory will occupy about 355MB of space once you've compiled all the source files.)

Once the files have finished downloading, you'll need to compile them into a working JBoss Server. Change your directory to the source directory you just downloaded:

```
>cd jboss-head
```

and execute the compile script for your particular system. Windows users will type the following:

```
>build/build.bat
```

Linux and BSD users will type this:

```
>build/build.sh
```

The script you executed will use Ant (a Java tool that assists in complex compilation tasks; see `http://ant.apache.org`) to compile the entire package of source code you've downloaded. Once the script has completed successfully, you'll need to change your directory to the `webservices` directory:

```
>cd webservices
```

and run the Ant build script necessary to enable the JBossWS early access release:

```
>../tools/bin/ant deploy-jbossws
```

You've now compiled a fresh copy of the JBoss Application Server, complete with JBossWS 1.0 preview. All that remains is to start your server, which you can do by navigating to the directory `jboss-head/build/output/jboss-5.0.0alpha/bin` and executing the JBoss "run" script (as you've done throughout the book). You can now copy the directory `jboss-head/build/output/jboss-5.0.0alpha` to a more memorable location to ease the annoyance of working with unwieldy directory paths. Throughout the rest of the chapter, the directory containing this code will be referred to as `c:\jboss_cvs` to avoid any possible confusion.

Creating the Web Service

Because this is the first web services example, and you haven't learned to build and deploy web services yet, you're going to create your code files now and run them later. Create a directory called `JBossWSTest` for the project. You'll now create three Java source files for this example. These files are organized simply in two folders: one is named `client`, and the other is named `webservices`.

The first Java source file that you need to create is the service endpoint interface for this example. The filename is `SimpleService.java`, and it will be used by both the client and server:

```
package webservices;

import java.rmi.Remote;

public interface SimpleService extends Remote
{
String echo(String input);
}
```

The next file you need to create is the class that implements the web service interface, `SimpleServiceImpl.java`:

```
package webservices;


import org.jboss.annotation.ejb.RemoteBinding;
import org.jboss.ws.annotation.PortComponent;

import javax.jws.WebMethod;
import javax.jws.WebService;
import javax.ejb.Remote;
import javax.ejb.Stateless;

@WebService(name = "EndpointInterface", targetNamespace = "http://localhost",➥
      serviceName = "SimpleService")
@PortComponent(contextRoot="/jbosswstest ", urlPattern="/*")
@Remote(SimpleService.class)
@Stateless
public class SimpleServiceImpl implements SimpleService
{
   @WebMethod
   public String echo(String input)
   {
      return input;
   }
}
```

Now you need to create the file that will be the client you'll use to test the web service, `SimpleServiceClient.java`:

```
package client;

import webservices.SimpleService;
import javax.xml.rpc.ServiceFactory;
import javax.xml.rpc.Service;
import javax.xml.namespace.QName;
import java.net.URL;
```

```
public class SimpleServiceClient {
    private static final String _namespace="http://localhost";
    private static final String _service="SimpleService";
    private static final String _wsdl="http://localhost:8080/jbosswstest?wsdl";

    public static void main(String[] args) {
        try {
            URL defUrl=new URL(_wsdl);
            // Create the service factory
            ServiceFactory serviceFactory = ServiceFactory.newInstance();
            // Load the service implementation class
            Service remoteService=serviceFactory.createService(defUrl,➥
                new QName(_namespace,_service));
            // Load a proxy for our class
            SimpleService invoker = ➥
                (SimpleService)remoteService.getPort(SimpleService.class);
            // Invoke our interface for each argument
            for (int i = 0; i < args.length; i++) {
                String returnedString = invoker.echo(args[i]);
                System.out.println("sent string: " + args[i] ➥
                    + ", received string: " + returnedString);
            }
        } catch(Exception e) {
            e.printStackTrace();
        }
    }
}
```

This web service has one method, which takes a String as input. It concatenates the String "back at you!" to the input String and returns the resultant String. You'll build and run this example later in the chapter, but first you'll examine how it all works.

To recap, you now have three Java source files, which we'll walk through in the sections that follow, starting with the service endpoint interface. After that, we'll discuss the web service implementation class, followed by the web service client.

The Service Endpoint Interface

The interface defined in SimpleService is the service endpoint interface, which is used by both the client and server.

The server will use the interface as a remote interface to the stateless session bean SimpleServiceImpl. This relationship is specified by the annotation @Remote(SimpleService.class), which notifies the container that the type SimpleService is to be used just as if the interface itself were annotated with the @Remote designation. The server will also generate the WSDL document that describes SimpleService, based on the structure defined in the service endpoint interface.

The client will use SimpleService to request a "proxy" class to be generated for it that will transparently invoke the echo method on the server. You read that right: each invocation of echo(String s) will cause JAX-WS to issue a request to the server and return its response.

Appropriately, the service endpoint interface only defines one method:

```
String echo(String input);
```

This should be familiar enough to you by now. What may be new to you is the way in which the interface is defined:

```
public interface SimpleService extends Remote
```

The `Remote` interface `SimpleService` extends is not the familiar `javax.ejb.Remote` annotation used with session beans earlier in the book. This particular `Remote` interface, `java.rmi.Remote`, is used by JAX-WS to generate the appropriate implementation code when a client requests an instance of the interface to invoke methods on the server.

Notice that the `String echo(String input)` method takes a `String` as input and returns a `String`. In the "old" days (when JAX-RPC was used), you would find that the entirety of web service methods would receive and return primitive Java types. These web services arguments and return values were described by WSDL, and only those Java types that could be represented by WSDL were able to be used in the method signatures of a JAX-RPC–compliant application.

As noted at the beginning of this chapter, you're still required to use JAX-RPC to access your web services. Fortunately, the entirety of Java primitive types and their associated wrapper classes are supported. Table 14-2 lists these types and classes.

Table 14-2. *Supported Datatypes for JAX-RPC Parameters and Return Values*

Primitive Type	Wrapper Class (in java.lang)
`Byte`	Byte
`Short`	Short
`Int`	Integer
`Long`	Long
`Float`	Float
`Double`	Double
`Boolean`	Boolean

Additionally, the Java classes shown in Table 14-3 are supported, as well as many of the collection classes, such as `ArrayList` and `HashMap`.

Table 14-3. *Supported Nonprimitive Java Classes*

Package	Supported Class
`Java.lang`	`String`
`java.math`	`BigInteger` `BigDecimal`
`java.util`	`Date` `Calendar`

Arrays of the primitive types and classes listed in Table 14-2 are supported as well. Classes whose fields are composed exclusively of JAX-RPC–supported data types can also be supported. For more details on which types are supported by JAX-RPC, please consult the JAX-RPC specification, which you can download from `http://java.sun.com/xml/downloads/jaxrpc.html`.

Should the idea of adhering purely to primitive types push you to the edge, rest easy: as JAX-WS becomes more widely implemented, the options available to developers in terms of WSDL binding will increase. According to the current specification, JAX-WS will work in concert with Java API for XML Binding (JAXB) 2.0 to provide a richer, less limited model.

The Web Service Implementation Class

The implementation of the example web service is contained in `SimpleServiceImpl.java`, which implements the `SimpleService` interface. Take note of the bevy of annotations describing the class:

```
@WebService(name = "EndpointInterface", targetNamespace =➥
 "http://localhost", serviceName = "SimpleService")
@PortComponent(contextRoot="/jbosswstest ", urlPattern="/*")
@Remote(SimpleService.class)
@Stateless
public class SimpleServiceImpl implements SimpleService
```

The `@Stateless` annotation simply describes this class as a stateless session bean to the server container. You cannot simply annotate the class as a web service and expect the class to function correctly—by designating a class as a web service, you are "merely" exposing functionality already available in an existing class. In this particular case, you want to make certain that the class remains available to you and is managed by the server. Such functionality is best met by session beans.

As mentioned earlier, the `@Remote` annotation alerts the server container that the remote interface for this particular session bean is contained within a different class.

So far, so good, but of course there's a catch. Are you wondering what the following line means?

```
@PortComponent(contextRoot="/jbosswstest ", urlPattern="/*")
```

As you could probably intuit from the values given to the annotation parameters, this line instructs the server container how to deploy and make available the web service to clients. The web service will expose its functionality at a URL much like the following:

```
http://localhost:8080/jbosswstest
```

The `urlPattern` parameter simply instructs the JBossWS library to attempt to process any (*) request received in the `contextRoot` (`/jbosswstest`). What you might not be able to guess is the fact that this particular annotation is specific to the JBossWS library; users of other application servers may have similar functionality provided to them, but that is by no means guaranteed.

The `@WebService` annotation finishes the functionality that will be imparted to this class by identifying the names that this service will be available under. The value set to the `name` parameter will be assigned to the service's "port" (interface, remember!), while the `serviceName` parameter will be the name (predictably) given to the service itself. The `targetNamespace` directive further assists clients requesting your service, by assigning an arbitrary namespace to the WSDL that acts as a service map. In the case of your service, you'll assign it the suitably generic value `http://localhost`. Developers not familiar with the vagaries of XML (you've made it this far?) need not worry about placing some special code at `localhost`. The string will be used much like a package declaration is used in Java: to prevent identically named elements from somehow conflicting with each other.

Guess what—that's nearly all you need to do to expose a session bean to web service clients! The JAX-WS tools and server container do all the heavy lifting.

The Web Service Client

The client for your web service is the `SimpleServiceClient.java` code. The `main()` method takes an array of `String` arguments and loops through these arguments, calling the `echo()` web service method with each one.

As explained previously, a client communicates with a web service method via transparently generated proxy classes. The sample code instantiates a new `Service` object that provides the client with the needed methods to acquire a proxy instance of `SimpleService`. In order to do so, it passes the `serviceFactory` object the address to the autogenerated WSDL document for your web service and a `QName` object that will be used to search the WSDL document for the XML that describes the particulars of your web service.

■ **Tip** A `QName` is a "qualified name" used in specifying the exact name of a node within an XML document. It can specify a node name (`html`, as per the venerable `<html>`), a node name associated with a particular namespace (`<html xmlns="http://www.w3.org/1999/xhtml">`), and a node name with a namespace tied to a particular prefix (`<xhtml:html xmlns:xhtml="http://www.w3.org/1999/xhtml">`). Why are they being used here? The WSDL document is being autogenerated by the server container based off parameters specified in `SimpleServiceImpl`; to create objects that interface with a web service, JAX-WS will need to parse the WSDL document, searching for the nodes that match those same parameters. JAX-WS will use the `QName` objects you pass in to accurately pinpoint what elements of the WSDL document contain the information it needs to return a valid `Service` object to you.

"Wait a minute," you may be thinking. "I don't remember having autogenerated any WSDL document yet." You're absolutely right: the WSDL document for your web service has not been generated yet. Once you've compiled and successfully deployed the web service, however, the WSDL document will be made available at a URL following this pattern:

```
http://server.address:port/contextRoot?wsdl
```

Recall how the `contextRoot` specified in the `@WebService` annotation of `SimpleServiceImpl` was set to `/jbosswstest`; hence, the address to the WSDL document will be

```
http://localhost:8080/jbosswstest?wsdl
```

All that needs to be done once an instance of the web service is acquired is to request the appropriate "port," cast it to the `SimpleService` interface, and then process it as necessary:

```
// Load the service implementation class
Service remoteService=serviceFactory.createService(defUrl,➥
     new QName(_namespace,_service));
// Load a proxy for our class
SimpleService invoker =
      (SimpleService)remoteService.getPort(SimpleService.class);
```

Continuing on, the echo() method of the proxy class is then called, which communicates the argument via SOAP to the endpoint. This calls the web service implementation, which returns the value via the endpoint to the proxy, and then back to the client:

```
String returnedString = invoker.echo(args[i]);
```

The returned value ends up in the returnedString variable, which you print out just to prove that the round-trip to the web service was achieved:

```
System.out.println("sent string: " + args[i]
  + ", received string: " + returnedString);
```

Building, Testing, and Serving the Web Service

Now that you've gone through all those preparatory steps, it's time to build, test, and serve this application.

1. Open a command window and change your directory to the JBossWSTest folder you created for this project.

2. Set your CLASSPATH variable to the following libraries:

```
>set CLASSPATH=.;➥
c:\jboss_cvs\server\all\deploy\jbossws.sar\jbossws.jar;➥
c:\jboss_cvs\server\all\deploy\jbossws.sar\wsdl4j.jar;➥
c:\jboss_cvs\server\all\deploy\ejb3.deployer\jboss-ejb3x.jar;➥
c:\jboss_cvs\server\all\deploy\ejb3.deployer\jboss-ejb3.jar;➥
c:\jboss_cvs\client\jboss-jaxrpc.jar
```

3. Compile the webservices and client directories:

```
>javac -d . webservices\*.java
>javac -d . client\*.java
```

4. Make an EJB3 JAR file with the compiled classes in the webservices directory:

```
>jar cf SimpleService.ejb3 webservices\*.class
```

5. Copy SimpleService.ejb3 to your JBoss deployment directory:

```
>copy SimpleService.ejb3 c:\jboss_cvs\server\all\deploy\
```

6. You can now check to make certain that the service has been deployed correctly. Open a web browser and go to the following URL: http://localhost:8080/jbossws. You will see a page much like the one shown in Figure 14-1.

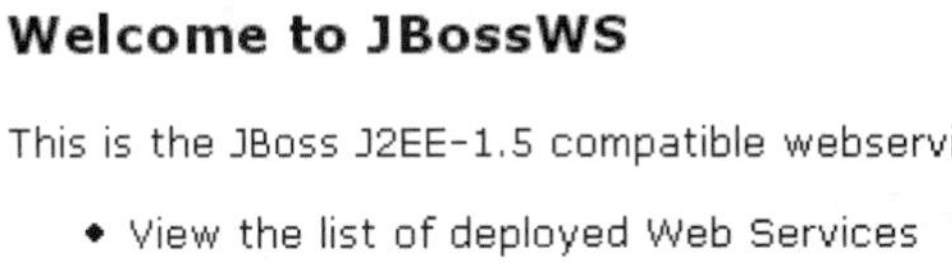

Welcome to JBossWS

This is the JBoss J2EE-1.5 compatible webservice implementation.

- View the list of deployed Web Services

Figure 14-1. *JBossWS deployment page*

Click the View link to display a list of currently deployed JBossWS web services. Your web service should appear much like the web service shown in Figure 14-2; if it does not, repeat the deployment process and watch the messages JBoss prints to your console screen as it attempts to deploy your web service. As mentioned earlier in the chapter, the version of JBoss you're using for this example is still in development, and isn't guaranteed to provide reliable results. Keep checking the JBoss website for more information regarding updated releases from the JBossWS subproject.

Registered Service Endpoints

ServiceEndpointID	ServiceEndpointAddress
SimpleService.ejb3#SimpleService/EndpointInterfacePort	http://prometheus:8080/jbosswstest?wsdl

Figure 14-2. *List of deployed web services*

Take note of the link under the Service Endpoint Address column. Recall that this link was mentioned in the `SimpleServiceClient` class:

```
private static final String _wsdl="http://localhost:8080/jbosswstest?wsdl";
```

Clicking this link displays the server-generated WSDL document for the `SimpleService` web service.

7. Once you've ensured that the web service has been deployed correctly, execute the client from the command line like so:

```
>java -classpath .;➥
c:\jboss_cvs\client\jboss-jaxrpc.jar;➥
c:\jboss_cvs\client\log4j.jar;➥
c:\jboss_cvs\client\logkit.jar;➥
c:\jboss_cvs\client\jbossws-client.jar;➥
c:\jboss_cvs\client\activation.jar;➥
c:\jboss_cvs\client\jboss-saaj.jar;➥
c:\jboss_cvs\client\mail.jar;➥
c:\jboss_cvs\client\wsdl4j.jar;➥
c:\jboss_cvs\lib\endorsed\xercesImpl.jar;➥
c:\jboss_cvs\client\jbossall-client.jar;➥
c:\jboss_cvs\server\default\lib\jboss-remoting.jar;➥
c:\jboss_cvs\server\default\lib\javax.servlet.jar ➥
client.SimpleServiceClient this is a test
```

Upon doing so, you should see the following output:

```
sent string: this, received string: this
sent string: is, received string: is
sent string: a, received string: a
sent string: test, received string: test
```

Congratulations! Add another notch to your Java programming belt, because you've written your first web service using Java EE 5.

Summary

In this chapter, you discovered that web services are a way to create distributed applications whose components communicate with each other over protocols associated with the Web. This application functionality can be offered via web services over the Internet or limited for use within a corporate intranet or extranet.

After reading this chapter, you should know:

- Web services promote the development of distributed applications whose components are written in various languages and deployed on various hardware and software platforms. This independence is enhanced by web services' ability to communicate over protocols and ports used on the Web.
- The availability of web services over the Internet makes security, in the form of data encryption and user authentication, an issue that developers should think about carefully before adopting them. Making business logic available online in any form requires serious consideration on the part of the developer.
- Web services protocol layers employ technologies such as HTTP, XML, SOAP, WSDL, and UDDI. You should also know that JAX-WS and its predecessor, JAX-RPC, are Java EE enabling technologies that allow you to forgo the work of navigating the different web service layers and concentrate on accessing the functionality you require.

Web services in Java EE 5 are still developing at the time of this writing. As the JSR-181 (Web Services Metadata for Java EE 5) and JAX-WS specifications become more fully implemented by vendors and development groups, we encourage you to visit this book's page on the Apress web site (`www.apress.com`) for corrections and elaborations upon the information provided here.

If you'd like to learn more about XML, we recommend visiting these web sites: `http://java.sun.com/xml/docs.html`, `www.xml.org`, and `www.xml.com`.

You can learn more about JAX-RPC from the JAX-RPC specification, which you can download from `http://java.sun.com/xml/downloads/jaxrpc.html`. You can read the JAX-WS specification as it is developed from its JCP page at `http://jcp.org/en/jsr/detail?id=224`, and you can download the SAAJ specification from `http://java.sun.com/xml/downloads/saaj.html`.

You can learn more about UDDI and the JAXR API from these web sites, respectively: `www.uddi.org` and `http://java.sun.com/xml/jaxr`.

Finally, the Java Web Services Developer Pack (WSDL) is available from Sun's Java web site at `http://java.sun.com/webservices/webservicespack.html`.

Exercises

1. Write a web service that takes a word and returns it spelled backward.
2. Write a web service that takes two numbers and a string operator value of + or -. Apply this operator to the numbers.

APPENDIX A

Tomcat: Who Needs Java EE 5?

Astute readers may have noticed that certain sections of this book contain phrases such as "this will be supported" or "pending final implementation of the specification." This is not merely an attempt to instill fear and uncertainty on the part of you, the enterprising reader. At the time of this writing, the Java EE 5 specification has not been fully approved. Application server providers are still in the process of developing compliant technology platforms for the specification, and even Sun has yet to provide a compatible reference implementation (RI) for public use.

Aside from JBoss, two other application server providers have made available "preview versions" of their product for developers to begin working on. The first, Oracle's 10*g* application server, is available at `www.oracle.com/technology/tech/java/ejb30.html` in preview form. The preview download focuses on the EJB 3.0 specification set down by the Java EE 5 specification. The second application server making obvious strides forward in Java EE 5 compliance is Caucho Resin (`www.caucho.com`). Resin also provides a rudimentary implementation of the EJB 3.0 section of the Java EE 5 specification.

Which brings us to Tomcat. (Not really, but by the time you've reached the appendixes, all the good segues have been used up.) Tomcat is an application server provided by the good folks at the Apache Software Foundation that you can install to give you basic Servlet and JSP support. Not at all coincidentally, JBoss itself uses Tomcat as a foundation.

What benefit does Tomcat give you, the application developer? Aside from running a lean, mean base from which to deploy your Servlets, you are given the opportunity to deploy individual components that meet the requirements set down by the component pieces of the Java EE 5 specification. You may also find components that provide alternative functionality that better serve your application domain. For example, the Hibernate (`www.hibernate.org`) library is one of many toolsets that provide an excellent alternative to the persistence features of EJB 3.0.

In this appendix, we discuss how to obtain, install, and run Tomcat.

Obtaining and Installing Tomcat

Tomcat is a part of the Apache Jakarta Project. You can get a copy of Tomcat from the Apache web site at `http://jakarta.apache.org/tomcat/index.html`. At the time of this writing, Tomcat version 5.5.9 was stable and provided support for the Servlet 2.4 specification and JSP 2.0 specification.

To download the Tomcat server, follow the Download links on the Tomcat web page to the page that contains the Tomcat 5.x files. The download files for Tomcat 5 will appear listed by version, then distribution format.

It is, of course, possible that these locations may have changed by the time you read this. If so, you can still access the download directories using the links on the Apache Jakarta web site. Whenever possible, make sure to use a mirror site to download your files.

If you are installing to Windows, you should download either the `.exe` or `.zip` files for the version you want. If you are installing to Linux, you can download a `.tar.gz` or a `.zip` file. Other Unix versions will use the `.tar.gz` file. We'll cover each installation in further detail in the sections that follow.

■ **Note** You can install and compile the source files of Tomcat if you are so inclined. However, this is not really necessary if all you want to do is use Tomcat as a server for JSP pages and Servlets. Since this book is about developing web applications, not developing servers, we will not cover the steps in building a Tomcat server from the source files. If you would like to explore this option, there are detailed instructions for Tomcat 5.5.x at `http://jakarta.apache.org/tomcat/tomcat-5.5-doc/building.html`.

Also, note that you will need a version of the Java JDK for Tomcat. We recommend using the Java 5 JDK. Check the Tomcat web page for the requirements for using earlier versions of the JDK. Ensure you have an environment variable named `JAVA_HOME` that points to your JDK installation on your machine.

Binary Installation to Windows

The simplest installation for Windows is to download the `.exe` distribution. This is an installation program that handles all of the installation tasks for you. Simply double-click the `.exe`, and the installer will run. The installer runs as a wizard, and for the most part you can simply accept the default options at each step. The installer will extract and copy all the files to their correct locations, and configure the environment variables for you. It will also create Start menu shortcuts for starting and stopping the server.

If you downloaded the zipped distribution file, start by extracting the files in the `.zip` archive to a directory. We recommend unzipping the files using the default directory name, `jakarta-tomcat-5.5.xx`, into the same location as your Java Standard and Enterprise development kit directories. For example, you might have the directory structure shown in Figure A-1 in the root of your C drive.

Name ▲	Size	Type	Date Modified
apache2		File Folder	7/5/2005 5:21 AM
Documents and Settings		File Folder	8/4/2005 8:47 PM
eclipse_workspace		File Folder	7/31/2005 4:54 PM
jakarta-tomcat-5.5.9		File Folder	8/4/2005 8:47 PM
java		File Folder	7/31/2005 4:19 PM
Program Files		File Folder	8/4/2005 8:47 PM
projects		File Folder	7/31/2005 3:45 PM
Windows		File Folder	8/4/2005 8:47 PM

Figure A-1. *Example filesystem contents*

After unzipping the files, you will need to set the environment variables yourself. You need to create an environment variable named `CATALINA_HOME`, which will point to the location of Tomcat. For example, if you installed Tomcat to the default directory as suggested, you will set `CATALINA_HOME` to `C:\jakarta-tomcat-5.5.9`. In Win9x and WinME, you will do this through the `autoexec.bat` file. For WinNT and Win2000, you can do this in the System dialog box, which you can access by selecting Start ➤ Settings ➤ Control Panel and choosing the System option. Then select the Advanced tab and click the Environment Variables button. Installing Tomcat this way does not create Start menu shortcuts, but you can access the `startup.bat` and `shutdown.bat` files for starting and stopping the server in the Tomcat `\bin` directory.

One other thing you need to do for Win9x and WinME is ensure there is enough environment memory. Navigate to the Tomcat `\bin` directory and right-click the `startup.bat` and `shutdown.bat` files, select Properties, click the Memory tab, and set the Initial Environment to 4096.

Binary Installation to Linux/Unix

If you downloaded the `.tar.gz` or `.zip` distribution file, start by creating a directory for the installation and extracting the files to that directory.

After installing the files, you will need to set an environment variable. The variable is named `CATALINA_HOME` and it will point to the location of Tomcat. For example, if you installed Tomcat to `/usr/local/tomcat`, you would set the variable with this command in the bash shell:

```
> CATALINA_HOME=/usr/local/tomcat
> export CATALINA_HOME
```

If you are using a different shell, use the command that is appropriate for that shell. The scripts for starting and stopping the server are in the Tomcat `/bin` directory.

Running Tomcat

After installing Tomcat, start the server using the Start menu, batch file, or script file for your system. When the server is running, you can open a browser to the Tomcat web page at `http://localhost:8080`. If the Tomcat installation is successful, you should see a web page like the one shown in Figure A-2.

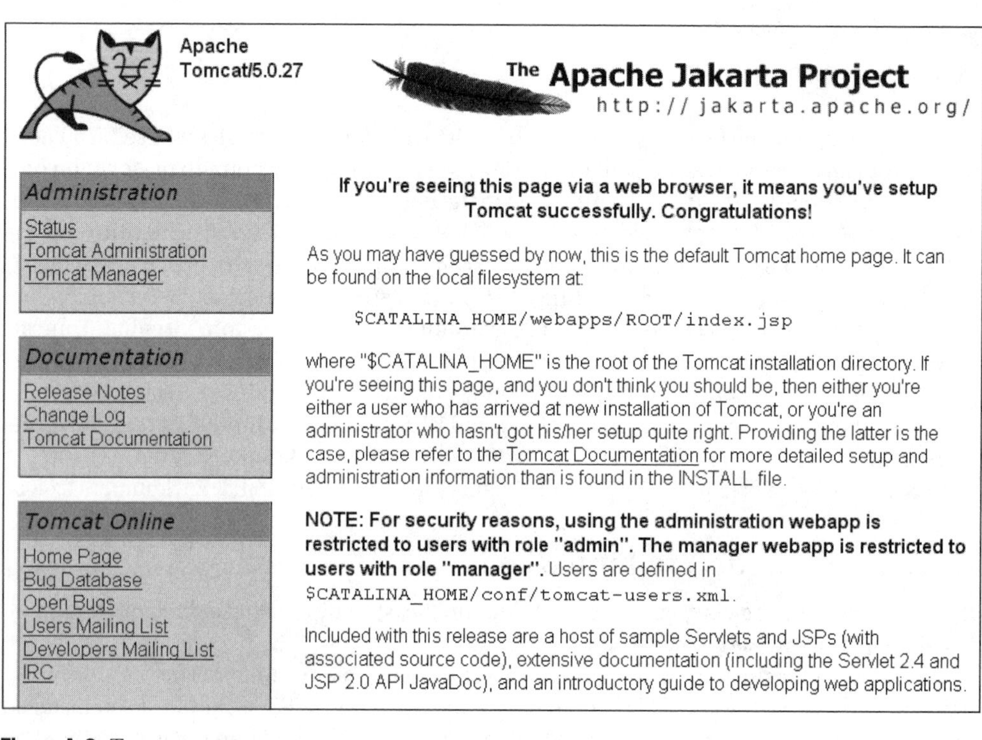

Figure A-2. *Tomcat startup page*

For the most part, if you follow these directions, you should have no problems installing Tomcat. If you do encounter any installation issues, check your Java installation and ensure that the JAVA_HOME and CATALINA_HOME environment variables are set. If you are using Win9x or WinME, ensure the environment memory space is set correctly, as explained earlier. If that doesn't help, check the Tomcat web page at `http://jakarta.apache.org/tomcat/index.html` for further information on installing, running, and troubleshooting Tomcat. You might also try posing a question with the specifics of your problem on one of the Tomcat mailing lists. At the time of this book's publication, subscription information for a couple of lists could be found here: `http://jakarta.apache.org/site/mail2.html#Tomcat`.

APPENDIX B

SQL and EJB QL

This appendix provides a brief introduction to the Structured Query Language (SQL) and the Enterprise JavaBeans Query Language (EJB QL), two techniques for accessing data that you can use in Java EE programming. SQL is relevant to data-access techniques using JDBC, discussed in Chapters 7, 8, and 11 of this book. EJB QL provides an alternative data-access methodology specific to entity EJBs, as described in Chapters 10 and 11.

Introduction to SQL

SQL is a standardized query language for retrieving and updating data held in a relational database management system (RDBMS). At the time of writing, the current version of SQL is SQL99, sometimes referred to as SQL3.

The SQL language is merely meant as an interface to the native fetch and update mechanisms of the RDBMS. To understand the SQL approach to an RDBMS, you need to know about the objects and relationships that, conceptually, make up an RDBMS.

SQL Objects

A relational database provides a logical framework to allow the storage of pieces of data. The relational model includes a hierarchy of the following objects:

- **Clusters**: A *cluster*, as described in the SQL99 specification, broadly corresponds to an RDBMS product and is a named set of catalogs available in a SQL session. The SQL99 specification indicates that access permissions may be controlled at the cluster level, but some database vendors implement permissions only at the catalog level and at lower levels of the hierarchy.
- **Catalogs**: A *catalog* is a uniquely named set of schemas. Some database products, for example Microsoft's SQL Server and Oracle, use the term *instance* to broadly correspond to a SQL99 catalog.
- **Schemas**: A *schema* is a uniquely named set of objects and data owned by an individual user.
- **Objects**: Most usage of SQL takes place at the object level and below. Objects include tables, views, modules, and routines.

- **Columns**: SQL objects consist of one or, usually, more columns. A typical database table will consist of several columns, each of which contains, for each row, a piece of data of a particular data type.
- **Domain-defined data types and user-defined data types**: Data types may be domain-defined, which are standard SQL-recognized data types, or may be defined by a user, which are user-defined data types. Each piece of data in a column must comply with the constraints on its possible values imposed by the specified data type.
- **Rules and assertions**: Data must sometimes conform to a rigid standard. SQL provides for the definition of those requirements, so that entered information is programmatically enforced to whatever standard necessary.

In this appendix, we will look primarily at how to use SQL to work with table objects and how to execute queries that select data from one or more columns in one or more tables. First, let's briefly look at the data types that are recognized in SQL99.

Note Many database management systems had proprietary methods of data retrieval and manipulation before SQL was disseminated, so database vendors provide somewhat variable support for SQL99. However, all the big-name databases provide significant SQL99 support. It is important, nonetheless, that you check which aspects of SQL99 are supported by the database management system that you plan to use.

CHARACTER CASE IN SQL CODE

RDBMS products differ in how they handle character case. Some products are case-sensitive; for example, they consider tables with the same names but different letter case as different objects. This means that code such as

```
SELECT * FROM presidents
```

and

```
SELECT * FROM Presidents
```

will work identically in a non-case-sensitive RDBMS but can cause difficult-to-diagnose problems in a case-sensitive RDBMS.

If there is any likelihood that you or your client will want to transfer data to another product at a future date, it is a good idea to have a consistent naming scheme for tables, columns, and so on. This will help you to avoid having different cases in names in different parts of your code, and thus avoid problems, and much wasted time, when you switch products.

Similarly, it is a good idea to adopt consistent use of case when writing SQL code. One convention is to use uppercase for all SQL commands and lowercase for table and column names. This is the style we use in this book. In addition, each clause of a SQL statement is expressed on a separate line, making the SQL code easier to read.

In practice, when working for a client, you will likely need to adopt the case convention already used in the existing databases and code.

SQL Data Types

SQL data types are essentially constraints on the types of data that may be stored in a column and on how that data is actually stored in the RDBMS. Careful consideration of which data types are appropriate is an important part of the analysis and design of a new database.

As with many aspects of RDBMS, the use of data types varies among RDBMS packages. Check the documentation to determine which data types it supports. Data types vary among vendors, but usually you will be able to identify their corresponding SQL99 data types.

String Data Types

String data is one of the most commonly used data types. String data of fixed length is specified using the `CHAR` keyword. For example, to declare the `last_name` column as accepting text of exactly 20 characters in length, use this code:

```
last_name CHAR(20)
```

Such declarations are used when creating columns for tables, as described in the next section. A `CHAR` declaration commonly is padded with spaces to the stated number of characters if the user-supplied string is shorter.

Commonly, a character string is declared to be of variable length. For example, to declare the `last_name` column as being a variable-length string up to 20 characters in length, use this code:

```
last_name VARCHAR(20)
```

A `VARCHAR` is stored more efficiently than a `CHAR` in terms of disk space, but performance during sorts of `VARCHAR` data is likely to be slower. Some database systems don't allow indexes to be created on `VARCHAR` data types, which further impacts performance. Some database packages use `LONG`, `TEXT`, or `MEMO` in place of `VARCHAR`.

In addition, the `NCHAR` and `NVARCHAR` data types support multibyte, or Unicode, characters.

■ **Note** All string data types, when referred to in SQL code, must be surrounded by paired apostrophes.

Numeric Data Types

At the risk of stating the obvious, numeric data types store numbers. Think carefully about the likely extreme values that may need to be stored when deciding among the list of data types in Table B-1.

In addition, many RDBMSs store a `MONEY` or `CURRENCY` data type.

Table B-1. *SQL Numeric Data Types*

Data Type	Description
BIT	Single-bit value, which can be 0 or 1.
DECIMAL	Floating-point values with specified level of precision. May also be DEC (Oracle, Postgres), FLOAT8 (Postgres), NUMERIC (SQL Server), or NUMBER (Oracle).
FLOAT	Floating-point values. May also be FLOAT4 (Postgres).
INT	Four-byte integer value. May also be INT4 (Postgres) or NUMBER (Oracle).
REAL	Four-byte floating-point value.
SMALLINT	Two-byte integer value. May also be INT2 (Postgres) or NUMBER (Oracle).
TINYINT	One-byte integer value.

Date and Time Data Types

Date and time data types vary among RDBMSs. Likely types include DATE, DATETIME, and SMALLDATETIME, which represent data in human-readable date and combined date/time formats. Each date type provides some different representation of the current time. For example, the omnipresent TIMESTAMP representation presents a value recording the number of seconds from the beginning of the Unix epoch (Midnight, January 1, 1970) to some arbitrary time. The more esoteric TIMESPAN (the Postgres RDBMS) and INTERVAL (the Oracle RDBMS) data types represent some interval of time.

Binary Data Types

Binary data types can be used to store data such as graphic images. Support may include BINARY, LONG RAW, RAW, and VARBINARY data types. It's a good idea to check the documentation of your RDBMS to confirm the allowable byte length.

Creating Tables

Creating and manipulating tables is a relatively infrequent but essential use of SQL, since typically a table will be created once, and then used with unchanged structure over extended periods of time. Changes to table structure, assuming that the database design has been well thought out, will be rare.

Since there are many objects in an RDBMS that "contain" some application value, the SQL specification provides for a general-purpose CREATE query that instructs the database to create some object. (A database object can be a table, a view, an index, a stored procedure and even a new database.) In SQL, a table is created using the CREATE TABLE statement. The general format for a simple CREATE TABLE statement is as follows:

```
CREATE TABLE tablename
(
 columnDefinitions
);
```

For example, to create a table called `presidents` with four columns—`last_name`, `first_name`, `birth_date`, and `gender`—use code like this:

```
CREATE TABLE presidents
(
  last_name VARCHAR(20) NOT NULL,
  first_name VARCHAR(20) NOT NULL,
  birth_date DATETIME NOT NULL,
  gender VARCHAR(6)
);
```

The `CREATE TABLE` statement causes an RDBMS to create a new table. The code in parentheses defines the columns to be created in that table. For each column, you declare the column name (note that we use the convention of all lowercase), its data type, the permitted number of characters, and then include a set of modifiers that specify some distinct behavior that the column will obey. The modifiers available to you depend on your RDBMS. The following are modifiers available in most RDBMSs:

- `AUTO_INCREMENT`: The database will automatically increment the value of the column by 1 for each new insertion. This modifier is typically used for the unique ID of the row, and it may be specified only in an integer column.
- `PRIMARY KEY`: The database will treat the column in question as the unique identifier for each inserted row and alter its storage of the information contained therein accordingly. This modifier is often used in conjunction with the `AUTO_INCREMENT` modifier, as it requires that each inserted row have a unique value in its `PRIMARY KEY` specified column.
- `INDEX`: The database will create an index on the specified column. Indices are most widely used to provide quick retrieval on those values that partially identify a row but are not flagged as the `PRIMARY KEY`.
- `NOT NULL`: The database will not allow a null or empty value to be assigned to the column in question.
- `DEFAULT`: The database will assign some default value to the column in question. `DEFAULT` is specified in the format `DEFAULT` *`defaultvalue`*, where *`defaultvalue`* is some literal value or function call.

There are many other common modifiers, as well as modifiers that are RDBMS-specific. The function of each modifier may imply database storage specifics, data type constraints, or relationships to other data.

Specifying Default Values

In some circumstances, you may find it useful to specify a default value for a column. For example, in a `presidents` table, you might want to acknowledge the historical situation and allow for future possibilities by including a `gender` column, with a default value of `Male`, as follows:

```
CREATE TABLE presidents
(
  last_name VARCHAR(20) NOT NULL,
  first_name VARCHAR(20) NOT NULL,
  birth_date DATETIME NOT NULL,
  gender VARCHAR(6)DEFAULT 'Male'
);
```

A default value can also be specified for columns that are marked as not accepting NULL values:

```
  gender VARCHAR(6) NOT NULL DEFAULT 'Male'
```

Updating the Structure of a Table

If you have designed your tables with enough careful thought, the need to alter the structure of a table should be an infrequent one. However, SQL provides an ALTER TABLE statement for such situations. For example, to add a death_date column to the presidents table, use the following code:

```
ALTER TABLE presidents
ADD death_date DATETIME
;
```

■ **Caution** Be aware that RDBMS products differ significantly in what alterations in structure they will allow. To avoid difficulties at a later date, it is good practice to take more care when designing the table structure when the data store is created.

Similarly, if you had created a column for death_date, and later decided you wanted to delete it, you could remove it using the following code:

```
ALTER TABLE presidents
DROP COLUMN death_date;
```

Deleting a column is not something you will do often, nor is it something to do lightly. If you don't have a backup, once you drop the column, that column and all of its data are gone forever, so be careful!

■ **Note** If you feel that you really want to carry out substantial restructuring of a table, it may be more appropriate to create a new table and use the INSERT SELECT statement to copy data from the existing table, verify that the desired data has copied, rename the original table, and then rename the new table to the name of the original table. You can expect to need to re-create any stored procedures, indexes, and so on.

Deleting Tables

Deleting, or dropping, a table is also not something to be done lightly, although it's simple to accomplish. The SQL syntax to drop the presidents table looks like this:

```
DROP TABLE presidents;
```

When you execute this statement, you probably won't see any confirmation dialog boxes, nor is there any way to undo the statement. Executing this statement will permanently remove the table and all of its data.

Handling Null Values

In a relational database, a value in a particular field (the intersection of a row and column) may contain a NULL value. A NULL value signifies an absent or unknown value. A NULL is *not* the same as an empty string, a sequence of space characters, or a value containing numeric zero. Most RDBMSs will set the value of a column to NULL by default when no other value has been specified.

When a column is created, it can be specified as allowing or disallowing NULL values. In a table called presidents, you might want to specify that the death_date column is allowed to contain a NULL value (the default situation), since not all United States presidents will have died at any selected time. On the other hand, you would likely want to specify that a last_name column and a first_name column are not allowed to contain NULL values (they should always contain data for each row in the database). You could achieve both desired constraints using the following code:

```
CREATE TABLE presidents
(
  last_name VARCHAR(20) NOT NULL,
  first_name VARCHAR(20) NOT NULL,
  birth_date DATETIME NOT NULL,
  death_date DATETIME
);
```

Selecting Data from Tables

Querying data in an existing table is likely to be the most common SQL task that you will perform. Such SQL queries are based on the SELECT statement. The simplest form of the SELECT statement is shown here:

```
SELECT * FROM presidents;
```

This selects all columns from the presidents table, as indicated by the * wildcard. Since there is no WHERE clause, all rows contained in the presidents table are retrieved.

If, as is more usual, you wish to retrieve selected columns from the presidents table, you use what is known as a *projection*. You simply replace the * wildcard with a comma-separated list of the columns you want to retrieve. Specifying selected columns is also likely to be a more efficient query than using the * wildcard. For example, to retrieve the last_name and first_name columns of the presidents table, use the following code:

```
SELECT last_name, first_name FROM presidents;
```

Filtering Data in Queries

In practice, it is unlikely that you will want to retrieve all rows from a table. In SQL, you can filter out unwanted rows by specifying those rows you do want to see using a WHERE clause in conjunction with a SELECT statement. For example, if you wanted to retrieve the rows that contained data concerning presidents Theodore Roosevelt and Franklin Roosevelt, you could use the following SQL:

```
SELECT * FROM presidents
WHERE last_name='Roosevelt';
```

The * wildcard signifies that all columns are retrieved from each row of the presidents table. The WHERE clause filters the results so that only those rows containing the value Roosevelt in the last_name column are retrieved.

The WHERE clause can use a number of operators in filtering data in addition to the = operator used in the preceding example. Table B-2 shows the operators that can be used in a WHERE clause.

Table B-2. *SQL Comparison Operators*

Operator	Description
=	Exact equality
<>	Inequality
!=	Inequality
<	Less than
<=	Less than or equal to
!<	Not less than
>	Greater than
>=	Greater than or equal to
!>	Not greater than
BETWEEN	Between two stated values (inclusive)
IS NULL	A NULL value

You will most probably have noticed that there is some duplication in the available operators. For example, you can use the !> or <= operator to signify that values less than or equal to a specified value are to be included. As you may have guessed, this is another area where vendors may differ in which SQL syntax they support. Again, you will want to check your RDBMS documentation carefully.

If you wanted to select information about all United States presidents except the two presidents named Roosevelt, you could use the following code:

```
SELECT last_name, first_name
FROM presidents
WHERE last_name <> 'Roosevelt'
;
```

Since the content of the last_name column is character data, you need to use paired apostrophes to delimit the value used in the WHERE clause. If the string value itself contains an apostrophe, then that will need to be escaped. The escape character varies between RDBMSs; for example, Microsoft SQL Server uses the apostrophe, and Oracle uses the backslash.

Similarly, if you wanted to retrieve information about presidents whose birth year was between 1800 and 1900 inclusive, you could use code like the following:

```
SELECT last_name, first_name
FROM presidents
WHERE birth_year BETWEEN 1800 AND 1900
;
```

In this case, the value contained in the birth_year column is numeric, so no delimiters are needed for the values to which the BETWEEN operator is applied. Notice the AND keyword, which is used in a WHERE clause of this type.

Sorting Data from Queries

Rows of data retrieved by a SQL query cannot be assumed to be in any particular order. If you want to sort the rows of data in a particular way, you must specify the criteria for ordering the data by using an ORDER BY clause in conjunction with a SELECT statement.

For example, to select all columns of information about all United States presidents from the presidents table and order them by last name, use the following code:

```
SELECT * FROM presidents
ORDER BY last_name
```

The ORDER BY clause can be used together with the WHERE clause. For example, if the year of appointment were stored in an appointment_year column, you could display the surname and first name with the year of appointment of all United States presidents whose surname begins with the letter *R* or later using the following:

```
SELECT last_name, first_name, appointment_year FROM presidents
WHERE last_name>'R'
ORDER BY appointment_year;
```

The list of presidents returned would be in order of earliest appointment to latest appointment (ascending format), but they could just as easily be returned in reverse (descending format). Simply add a DESC keyword to the end of the ORDER BY statement, like so:

```
ORDER BY appointment_year DESC
```

The list of presidents returned would be in series from latest appointment year to earliest. If you want to specify that you want ascending format (which the RDBMS should do as default), you can use the ASC keyword to do so.

If you want to sort the rows returned by a query by more than one criterion, you can do so by combining the two columns in the order needed. In this example, the rows are ordered alphabetically by last_name and then by the first_name:

```
SELECT last_name, first_name
FROM presidents
ORDER BY last_name, first_name;
```

Where there is more than one United States president with the same last name (the case for Adams, Roosevelt, and Bush), the ordering would be strictly alphabetical.

Using Wildcards and Regular Expressions

In addition to using the comparison operators described earlier, SQL provides facilities to allow you to retrieve data based on text patterns, similar to the pattern matching you can carry out using the regular expression support in Java.

The `LIKE` keyword allows text pattern searches. The `%` pattern matches zero or more text characters. (If your RDBMS supports it, you can also suffix the table name with * to indicate descendant tables are to be included in the search as well.) So, to retrieve data from the `presidents` table about presidents whose last name begins with the letter *B*, you could use the following code:

```
SELECT last_name, first_name
FROM presidents
WHERE last_name LIKE 'B%'
;
```

Notice that the text pattern is contained in paired apostrophes. The pattern `B%` matches any text string that begins with the uppercase *B* and that contains zero or more other characters. Therefore, when that pattern is used to match the `last_name` column, which contains presidential surnames, data on all presidents whose surname begins with *B* is retrieved.

If you did not want to retrieve data on President Buchanan, but only on those presidents whose surname begins with the characters *Bus*, you could refine the search like this:

```
SELECT last_name, first_name
FROM presidents
WHERE last_name LIKE 'Bus%'
;
```

Data on both presidents named Bush would be retrieved.

The underscore character used in text patterns matches exactly one character. So, using the following pattern retrieves the surname Bush:

```
SELECT last_name, first_name
FROM presidents
WHERE last_name LIKE 'Bu__'
;
```

If there were also a president named John Bull in the table, data on that fictional president would also be retrieved, since the pattern `Bu__` matches any string that is exactly four characters long and begins with the characters *Bu*.

■ **Note** If you plan to use the `LIKE` keyword, be aware that support for this keyword depends on the RDBMS package you use.

Some database management systems also explore fuller regular expression syntax, sometimes associated with the LIKE keyword and sometimes using the REGEXP keyword (with MySQL). For example, to retrieve data from a MySQL database on presidents whose surname begins with the letters *K* or *R*, use the following SQL code:

```
SELECT last_name, first_name
FROM presidents
WHERE last_name REGEXP "^[KR]."
;
```

Notice the REGEXP keyword and the text pattern contained in paired double quotes. The ^ character at the beginning of the pattern indicates that the text pattern matches the beginning of the data, and the square brackets indicate a character class. Any character in the character class that occurs at the beginning of the data in the column will match. The . metacharacter serves a similar function to the % character with the LIKE keyword.

■Note Regular expression support in your favorite database management system may not have the functionality that MySQL supports, or may use different metacharacters inside text patterns.

Adding Calculated Fields

Many pieces of data are reported exactly as they are held in the data store. However, sometimes you will want to retrieve data that combines data from more than one column. SQL provides calculated fields to achieve that functionality. Calculated fields can be created by combining string or numeric values.

■Note A *field* often means the same as a column, and does so in this case. Occasionally, in discussions of databases, *field* is used to refer to the intersection of a particular row and column. That is not the usage in the term *calculated field*.

For example, you might store address data in separate columns but want to display a city, regional code, and postal code together in an address. SQL code to achieve that might look like the following:

```
SELECT city+ ', ' + regional_code + ', ' + postal_code
FROM address
;
```

The + operator in the SELECT statement concatenates the string values contained in the city, regional_code, and postal_code columns.

Depending on the data type used to create the city, regional_code, and postal_code columns, you may want to trim out space characters contained as padding in the named columns, using the SQL RTRIM() function:

```
SELECT RTRIM(city)+ ', ' + RTRIM(regional_code) + ', ' + RTRIM(postal_code)
FROM address
;
```

If you declared the columns to be of type VARCHAR, there will be no padding space characters, and the RTRIM() function will be unnecessary.

Calculated fields also allow you to perform simple mathematical calculations to produce calculated fields. For example, you may want to display a product catalog with item price, tax rate, and tax rate information. In that case, you would want to use an alias for the calculated field. So, to fill the tax rate field, use code like this:

```
SELECT product_name, product_code,
item_price, tax_rate,
item_price * tax_rate AS taxed_price
FROM product_catalog
WHERE status = 'current'
;
```

Notice the AS keyword in the SELECT clause. In the third line of the SQL code, the value of the item_price and tax_rate columns are multiplied together to produce a calculated field with the alias of taxed_price.

Most database management systems will support standard mathematical operations of addition, subtraction, multiplication, and division using the standard mathematical operators, +, -, *, and /. Of course, Java provides the syntax to carry out these and more complex calculations. The choice of whether you use SQL or Java to achieve any desired calculations will depend on your level of comfort with the two languages, whether or not you wish the resource cost incurred by such calculations to be placed upon the database or the client, and the "correct" home of such calculations with respect to overall application design.

Using SQL Functions

A number of SQL functions are available to manipulate character, numeric, or date/time data. In the previous section, you saw the RTRIM() function, which can be used to remove padding space characters from character data columns of fixed width.

SQL functions can be used to extract part of a string (that is, a *substring*), to convert data types, return a number's ceiling, retrieve the current date, and so on. Unfortunately, the implementation and syntax of SQL functions varies greatly among database packages. If you are familiar with the corresponding Java functions, as you are likely to be if you are reading this book, it may well be more convenient to ignore the SQL functions in many situations where you are using JDBC. If you do decide to use SQL functions, be sure to carefully consult the documentation for the database management system in order to determine the appropriate syntax.

In practice, if you want your JDBC code to be portable, it is highly advisable to use the Java functions rather than the SQL functions. One exception to that general advice is SQL's aggregate functions, listed in Table B-3, which are fairly uniformly supported by popular database management systems. These SQL aggregate functions (defined officially in the SQL99 specification) avoid the need to retrieve, perhaps across a slow network, all rows in a table and perform the corresponding calculations in Java. The retrieval and calculation of data is likely to be much more efficiently carried out by the database management system.

Table B-3. *SQL Aggregate Functions*

Function	Description
AVG()	Returns the arithmetic mean value of a column
COUNT()	Returns the number of rows which contain a value in a named column
MAX()	Returns the largest value in a column
MIN()	Returns the smallest value in a column
SUM()	Returns the sum of the values in a named column

For example, to find the highest priced product in a product catalog, you might use code like the following:

```
SELECT MAX(product_price)
FROM product_catalog
WHERE status = 'current'
;
```

Many other retrieval techniques are possible in SQL, but those mentioned in the preceding sections will give you a start in how to use SQL syntax.

Modifying Table Data

As well as retrieving data, SQL can be used to insert new values in a database, update data, and delete data.

Inserting New Rows into a Table

The most straightforward technique to insert data into a table is to insert a completely new row. This is done using the INSERT statement. For example, to add information about the election of a president to the presidents table, with data for the last_name, first_name, and election_year columns, you might use the following code:

```
INSERT INTO presidents
(last_name, first_name, election_year)
VALUES ('Bush', 'George', 2000)
;
```

If you also wanted to store a middle name but weren't (at the time) aware of the newly elected president's middle name, to avoid ambiguity, use an explicit NULL value, like so:

```
INSERT INTO presidents
(last_name, first_name, middle_name, election_year)
VALUES ('Bush', 'George', NULL, 2000)
;
```

In the two preceding examples, each column was named. If you are totally confident of the ordering of column names, you can omit the column names, using code like the following:

```
INSERT INTO presidents
VALUES ('Bush', 'George', NULL, 2000)
;
```

Be aware that if you make even a slight error in the ordering of column data, an error will be generated unless all columns happen to have compatible data types. Omitting column names increases the likelihood of data values being swapped around.

Updating Data in Tables

If you need to correct a mistake in an existing row, you can do so using the UPDATE statement. When you use UPDATE statements, be very careful to include a WHERE clause, and also make sure that the WHERE clause is appropriately tightly defined. If you omit the WHERE clause, then every row in the chosen table will be updated in the way defined. For example, if you entered the following:

```
UPDATE presidents
SET middle_name = 'Walker'
;
```

this code would assign the middle name Walker to every United States president in the table, which is probably not what you intended. The existing data for middle name for all presidents, whether NULL or an actual value, would be overwritten. You have been warned! Mistakes of this type make you very glad that you have a recent backup of your valuable data. (You do have a recent, full backup, don't you?)

The WHERE clause is used to ensure that the UPDATE statement is appropriately applied. Thus, you could change the middle name of the president elected in 2000 using the following code:

```
UPDATE presidents
SET middle_name = 'Walker'
WHERE election_year = 2000
;
```

The preceding code makes the reasonable assumption that only one president was elected in the year 2000.

Deleting Data from a Table

You are unlikely to want to permanently delete information from a table like the presidents table, because it is of historical interest. However, in an e-commerce setting, you might choose to delete information about obsolete products. To achieve that, use the DELETE statement.

Be very, very careful not to omit the WHERE clause in a DELETE statement. Look at this example:

```
DELETE
FROM product_catalog
;
```

This code has potentially just deleted all the data in every row in your product_catalog table. If you don't have a very recent, usable backup, you may want to start writing your resignation letter.

Suppose you wanted to delete a product with product ID of ABC123. You could use the following code:

```
DELETE
FROM product_catalog
WHERE product_ID = 'ABC123'
;
```

The `WHERE` clause confines the deletion to the specified row in the table.

Constructing Joins

A *join* is the combination of results from more than one table in a query. This is a crucial technique for RDBMS systems for all but simple queries. Let's consider how this works by reviewing the basics of relationships in an RDBMS.

Relational database tables each have a *primary key*, which uniquely identifies each row in the table. Suppose you had several orders from one customer over a period of time. It would be inefficient and error-prone to enter customer address data into each order individually. If order data was held in an `orders` table, the corresponding customer data would be held in a `customers` table. A mechanism is needed to express the fact that a particular customer in the `customers` table is the customer for a particular order in the `orders` table. If the `customers` table contains a `customer_id` column that is the table's primary key, you can create a `customer_id` column in the `orders` table as a *foreign key*. This expresses the fact that a particular order is linked to a particular customer.

Suppose that you want to retrieve all orders for a particular customer. Let's assume that an order can be made up of only a single type of product, and that the `orders` table contains the following columns: `order_id`, `product_id`, `product_quantity`, `customer_id`, and `order_date`. Also, assume that the `customers` table consists of `customer_id`, `customer_name`, and `customer_address` columns (for simplicity). You can use a `SELECT` statement similar to the following to get the orders:

```
SELECT order_id, product_id, product_quantity, order_date, customer_name,
       customer_address
FROM orders, customers
WHERE orders.customer_id='ABC123'
AND orders.customer_id = customers.customer_id
;
```

This will retrieve all orders for the customer who has the ID of `'ABC123'`.

The `SELECT` statement in the join is similar to several you have seen earlier in this appendix, but notice that some of the columns are in the `orders` table, and some columns (`customer_name` and `customer_address`) are in the `customers` table. This is indicated by the `FROM` clause, which specifies both the `orders` and `customers` tables. You need to filter the retrieved rows, so you do that using a two-part `WHERE` clause. The first part of the `WHERE` clause specifies that you want data on the customer whose `customer_id` is `'ABC123'`. The second part specifies that all retrieved rows from the `customers` table must have a `customer_id` column equal to the `customer_id` column in the `orders` table. This uses notation that should look familiar: a `.` separates the name of the table object from the name of the column object:

```
orders.customer_id = customers.customers_id
```

Now suppose that you also want to retrieve price data, which is held in a separate prices table. You need a join that retrieves data from three tables. The following code will achieve that:

```
SELECT order_id, product_id, product_price, product_quantity, order_date,
       customer_name, customer_address
FROM orders, customers, prices
WHERE orders.customer_id='ABC123'
AND orders.customer_id = customers.customer_id
AND orders.product_id = prices.product_id
;
```

Notice the additional AND clause:

```
AND orders.product_id = prices.product_id
```

This clause means that you want to retrieve only products relevant to your query.

SQL allows you to construct joins from arbitrary numbers of tables.

As you probably realize, SQL is a topic that many entire books are devoted to. This appendix provided only a brief introduction. For more information, refer to a SQL reference, such as *The Programmer's Guide to SQL*, by Cristian Darie and Karli Watson (Apress; ISBN 1-59059-218-2).

Introduction to EJB QL

EJB QL is a relatively new method of data access, first introduced in the EJB 2.0 specification. In EJB 1.1, vendors provided their own, nonstandard query language for finder methods of entity EJBs, which meant that applications that used container-managed persistence needed to be partly rewritten if they were moved from one vendor's EJB container to another.

EJB QL is a query specification language for entity EJBs. EJB QL is used to define data queries for entity EJBs in a portable way. EJB QL is specified in the EJB specification (from EJB version 2.0 on); therefore, all EJB 3.0 implementations must conform to that specification. In that respect, EJB QL offers better portability than SQL, which, as mentioned in the preceding sections of this appendix, is implemented in significantly varying ways on different database management systems.

■ **Tip** The EJB 3.0 specification notes that EJB implementations may compile EJB QL queries into native SQL queries to fit their respective entity store. This type of transformation can provide a significant speed boost to your queries. Check your provider's documentation to see if this type of optimization is provided to your EJB applications.

EJB QL is confined to queries against in-memory objects, and thus, differs from SQL in that EJB QL cannot be used as a general-purpose query directly against a database.

Entity Bean References

An entity bean is a representation of data stored persistently in a database table. Data in an RDBMS is held in tables, and data in those tables can have relationships expressed using primary keys and foreign keys. Since entity beans represent data stored in database tables, it shouldn't be surprising that entity beans can similarly have corresponding relationships between them.

The relationships between entity EJBs are expressed either in metadata annotations in the class source file or in an XML deployment descriptor file. Typically, the EJB container will use the information acquired about entity bean relationships to create queries in a language such as SQL, which actually queries the data store. In the case of metadata annotations, this relationship is inferred via usage of one of the relationship descriptors (such as `@OneToMany`).

An EJB QL query references an entity bean by its name in the appropriate abstract schema. The mapping of abstract schema names to an entity bean is taken from the name acquired by usage of the `@Entity` annotation descriptor. This name can be generated for you automatically (in which case, it is the local name of the entity bean class), or it can be manually assigned in the descriptor:

```
@Entity(name="ElPresidente")
Public class President {
...
}
```

This block of code ensures that the abstract schema name for the `President` entity bean class is assigned to `ElPresidente`. Further queries against the entity store will then appear in the form:

```
SELECT variable FROM ElPresidente variable [query errata]
```

The javax.ejb.Query Object

EJB QL queries are issued to the persistence layer through the use of the `EntityManager` interface, which encapsulates them as `Query` objects. `Query` objects represent a high-level view of the query's execution and may be used to fine-tune the application's interaction with the entity bean store.

Assuming you've acquired a reference to the `EntityManager` in some session bean, an example of an interaction with the entity bean store would look something like this:

```
public List getAllPresidents(){
Query q=manager.createQuery("SELECT p FROM President p");
return q.getResultList();
}
```

This extremely simple example compiles an EJB QL query into a `Query` object and executes it, returning a `List` of `President` objects as a result.

The `Query` interface defines more than just the execution of a query. Its definition includes methods that set the maximum number of results returned, "hints" that specify operational parameters to the entity store, and parameter setting methods that allow you to generalize EJB QL queries across an application.

You can acquire `Query` objects from the `EntityManager` in both session beans and message-driven beans. EJB 3.0 entity beans will not be able to use `Query` objects, because `EntityManager` is unavailable for use in that context.

■ **Note** EJB QL functionality is made available to EJB 2.*x* entity beans through a feature called *finder methods*, wherein EJB QL queries defined in external deployment files are associated with class methods. This functionality is not available to EJB 3.0 annotated entity beans. For more information about the previous EJB specification, see *Beginning Java EE 1.4*, by Jim Crume, Kevin Mukhar, and James L. Weaver (Apress; ISBN 1-59059-341-3).

Building EJB Queries

An EJB QL query consists of the following:

- A `SELECT` clause, which specifies the type or values of objects to be selected.
- A `FROM` clause, which specifies the domain (or table) from which objects are to be selected.
- An optional `WHERE` clause, which is used to filter the results returned by the query.
- An optional `GROUP BY` clause, which is used to group the returned results so that aggregate functions may operate on them. This may be further classified by a `HAVING` clause, which further restricts the result groups based on some criterion.
- An optional `ORDER BY` clause, which is used to sort the data returned by the query.

If you have read through the section on SQL in this appendix, you will likely recognize that EJB QL syntax is similar to SQL syntax.

A common form of an EJB QL query is as follows:

```
SELECT variable
FROM abstractSchemaName [AS] variable
[WHERE value comparison value]
[GROUP BY ...]
[HAVING ...]
[ORDER BY ...]
```

The SELECT Clause

The `SELECT` clause may contain an identification variable, which is used to indicate the entity type requested. The `SELECT` clause can be filtered using a `WHERE` clause. For example, to retrieve data only for presidents whose surname is Bush, use the following EJB QL query:

```
SELECT p
FROM MyPresidentsSchema p
WHERE p.last_name = 'Bush'
```

Notice that the FROM clause associates the identifier variable p with the abstract schema name MyPresidentsSchema. The abstract schema name is specified in the deployment descriptor.

The WHERE clause filters the query results so that only those results that match the supplied parameter are returned to the client.

Navigation Operator

In EJB QL, the . operator is termed the *navigation operator*, and works in a similar manner to how objects are navigated in Java itself. The . operator allows you to navigate paths that are expressed in path expressions.

Input Parameters

You may use named input parameters in an EJB QL query. Each input parameter is indicated by a preceding literal :, followed by a string value naming the parameter. In other words, the parameter named "lastname" is expressed as :lastname.

In an earlier EJB QL example, you saw that a literal query could be constructed like this:

```
SELECT p
FROM MyPresidentsSchema p
WHERE p.last_name = 'Bush'
```

Using a named parameter, you can more flexibly construct the query as follows:

```
SELECT p
FROM MyPresidentsSchema p
WHERE p.last_name = :lastname
```

When an appropriate parameter is supplied, you can retrieve records for presidents with any specified surname using a method much like the following:

```
public List findPresidentBySurname(string surname){
Query q=manager.createQuery("SELECT p FROM~CCC
     MyPresidentsSchema p WHERE p.last_name=:surname");
q.setParameter("surname",surname);
return q.getResultList();
}
```

When there may be duplicate data, such as in the surnames of presidents, you can use multiple parameters as appropriate. To retrieve data on the younger George Bush, for example, use the following query (assuming appropriate declaration of a second parameter in the deployment descriptor):

```
SELECT p
FROM MyPresidentsSchema p
WHERE p.last_name = :surname AND p.election_year=:electyear
```

Wildcards

You may use the LIKE keyword together with the % and _ characters, as described for SQL in the "Using Wildcards and Regular Expressions" section earlier in this appendix. As a recap, the % character stands for zero or more characters, and the _ character stands for any single character.

Functions

EJB QL has string and numeric functions, which all EJB 3.0-conformant EJB containers will support. Table B-4 shows the EJB string functions, and Table B-5 shows the numeric functions.

Table B-4. *EJB String Functions*

Function	Description
`CONCAT(String, String)`	Concatenates two strings and returns a `String`
`SUBSTRING(String, start, length)`	Returns a `String`
`LOCATE(String, String [, start])`	Returns an `int`
`TRIM(String)`	Returns a string stripped of leading and trailing whitespace
`UPPER(String)`	Returns a string with all characters converted to uppercase
`LOWER(String)`	Returns a string with all characters converted to lowercase
`LENGTH(String)`	Returns an `int`

Table B-5. *EJB Numeric Functions*

Function	Description
`ABS(number)`	Returns an `int`, `float`, or `double` of the same data type as the argument to the function
`SQRT(double)`	Returns a `double`
`MOD(int, int)`	Returns an `int`

Subqueries

EJB QL includes the ability to issue subqueries within a `SELECT` query. The subquery may be present only in a `WHERE` or `HAVING` clause, and itself must be a simple `SELECT` query. For example, you could use a subquery to obtain a list of presidents whose total number of electoral votes exceeds the average of all electoral votes afforded to winning presidents, as follows:

```
SELECT p
FROM MyPresidentsSchema p
WHERE p.totalVotes > ( SELECT avg(po.totalVotes) FROM MyPresidentsSchema po )
```

Keep in mind that when a subquery is used as a value in an equality test, it must return some scalar value. Subqueries can return sets of values, but such scenarios are useful only when subjecting the returned set to some function or operation that acts on sets of returned values. If you wish to perform some equality test against a set of returned values, you must prefix the subquery with the `ALL` or `ANY` keyword. These keywords indicate that the comparison must hold true for `ALL` values returned by the query, or `ANY` of them.

Aggregate Functions

EJB QL has the following aggregate functions: AVG(), SUM(), COUNT(), MAX(), and MIN(). Refer to Table B-3 from earlier in this appendix for a good idea of the utility you can expect from each of these functions. The AVG() and SUM() functions must have a numeric argument. The other aggregate functions have an argument corresponding to the data type of the corresponding EJB field. These aggregate functions may be used only when grouping the returned results via the GROUP BY clause.

Values that contain NULL are eliminated before the aggregate functions are applied. The DISTINCT keyword can be used to eliminate duplicate values in conjunction with the EJB QL aggregate functions.

Using Relationships

You can use EJB QL to exploit relationships that are specified in the deployment descriptor. These relationships bear more than a striking resemblance to the JOIN syntax mentioned earlier in this appendix, which, quite without coincidence, is why EJB QL uses the same verbiage to indicate bean relationships.

For example, suppose you have an entity bean with the abstract schema name ActsSchema, which contains information about all acts passed by the United States Congress, including information about which president was in office at the time. You could construct the following query:

```
SELECT p
FROM MyPresidentsSchema p INNER JOIN p.ActsSchema a
WHERE a.president_surname = :surname
```

Notice the INNER JOIN clause, which includes the syntax p.ActsSchema expressing that there is a relationship between the MyPresidentsSchema, identified by the identifier variable p and the abstract schema ActsSchema. Of course, if this is to work, the necessary annotations for ActsSchema need to be present in the ActsSchema implementation.

Suppose that ActsSchema was itself related to another entity bean. Once you've acquired a reference to the entity bean of MyPresidentsSchema, you know you have a valid persistence reference to the ActsSchema object that it's related to; however, you do not have a guarantee that the persisted entity bean data in ActsSchema has been fetched. You can indicate to the persistence layer that you wish the entire persistence hierarchy to be fulfilled by using a different type of join syntax than what you've seen so far. This new join syntax adds the keyword FETCH to the query, like so:

```
SELECT p
FROM MyPresidentsSchema p INNER JOIN FETCH p.ActsSchema a
WHERE a.president_surname = :surname
```

Be aware that this type of functionality can be computationally expensive when used with complex entity relationship hierarchies.

There is much more to EJB QL than has been explained in this brief description. For further details on EJB QL, see the EJB 3.0 specification, which can be downloaded from the Sun web site at http://java.sun.com/products/ejb/docs.html.

APPENDIX C

■ ■ ■

Java EE Glossary

annotation

Definition: An addition to the Java language with the advent of J2SE 5. Annotations are used heavily throughout Java EE 5 and allow developers to include compile-time information with the different elements of an application. This information, termed *metadata*, allows a cleaner design and overall semantic.

Where used: In all J2SE 5 applications. Java applications written prior to the introduction of annotations may still take advantage of attributes by using a library called XDoclet (`http://xdoclet.sourceforge.net/xdoclet/index.html`) to annotate J2EE 1.4 components.

aspect-oriented programming (AOP)

Definition: A programming model that puts forth the idea of *aspects*, or elements of functionality that may be "weaved" into existing code at compile time or runtime, allowing developers to easily add functionality across the scope of an application without manually modifying all the affected code.

Where used: In a limited fashion with session bean and message-driven bean interceptors. The open source AspectJ compiler (`http://eclipse.org/aspectj`) provides a powerful AOP framework.

component

Definition: The building blocks of a Java EE application. Components are specific software units, supported by a container, and are configurable at deployment time. The four types of components defined within Java EE are EJBs, web components, applets, and application clients.

Where used: In all Java EE applications.

container

Definition: A software entity that provides services to components, including lifecycle management, security, deployment, and runtime services. A container of specific types of components, such as EJB, web, JSP, Servlet, applet, or application client, will provide the services its components need. For example, Servlet containers need to support HTTP as a protocol for requests and responses, whereas JSP containers need to provide the same services as Servlet containers, plus an engine to interpret and process JSP pages into Servlets.

Where used: In Java EE applications.

Common Object Request Broker Architecture (CORBA)

Definition: A standard architecture for distributed object systems, specified by the Object Management Group (OMG). This model allows a distributed, heterogeneous collection of objects to interoperate, regardless of platform or programming language.

Where used: In distributed object systems where language and platform independence is critical.

distributed application

Definition: An application composed of a variety of components running in separate runtime environments, often on different platforms, and connected over a network. Distributed application types include two-tier (client/server), three-tier (client/middleware/server), and multitier or n-tier (client/multiple middleware/multiple servers).

Where used: Wherever different components of an application need to be connected to each other over a network.

Enterprise JavaBeans (EJB)

Definition: A server-side component model for Java. EJB is a component architecture designed to enable developers to build and deploy scaleable, secure, multiplatform, business-critical applications that are object-oriented, reusable, and distributed. It allows enterprise developers to focus on writing business logic without the need to write code that handles such tasks as transactional behavior, security, connection pooling, or threading, since the architecture delegates these tasks to the server vendor.

Where used: In distributed business applications that will operate on any server that provides the EJB APIs.

EJB container

Definition: A container for EJB components that provides a scaleable, secure, transactional environment in which enterprise beans can operate. It is the container that handles the object lifecycle, including creating and destroying an object, as well as handling the state management of beans. When a bean is installed in a container, the container provides an implementation of the bean's remote interface. The container will also make the bean's interface available in the Java Naming and Directory Interface (JNDI). In addition, the container services requests for resource injection on the part of the bean. An EJB container is provided by an EJB or Java EE server.

Where used: In any distributed application that uses EJBs.

EJB server

Definition: A collection of services and resources needed to support an EJB installation. These services include management of distributed transactions, management of distributed objects, distributed invocations on these objects, and management of low-level system services. Since the Java EE architecture assumes that an EJB container is hosted by an EJB server from the same vendor, it does not specify the contract between these two entities. Each EJB server may host one or more EJB containers.

Where used: In distributed applications that employ one or more EJB containers.

eXtensible Markup Language (XML)

Definition: A universal syntax that allows developers to describe and structure data, independent of the application logic. Unlike HTML, which has fixed tags that deal mainly with style or presentation, XML tags are defined as needed. XML can be used to define unlimited languages for specific industries and applications. XML documents need to be transformed into a language with style tags under the control of a stylesheet before they can be presented by a browser or other presentation mechanism. Since XML and Java are both portable and extensible, they are an ideal combination for web applications.

Where used: In conjunction with Java EE technology, whenever an enterprise application needs to consume and generate information that is exchanged among different servers that run on varied system platforms.

injection

Definition: The process wherein a particular resource is automatically "injected" into an instance of an EJB by the EJB container. Injection can be specified on resources using the `@Resource` annotation, and it may also be specified for the special case of the `EntityManager` through use of the `@PersistenceContext` annotation.

Where used: In all EJB 3.0–compatible beans.

Java Enterprise Edition (Java EE)

Definition: A platform that creates an environment for developing and deploying multi-tiered web-based enterprise applications. Java EE allows developers to create standardized, modular components, and it provides those components with a complete set of services, APIs, and protocols that automatically handle many of the details of application behavior, without the need for complex programming. Java EE adds to the features of the Java Platform, Standard Edition (J2SE) by including full support for EJB components, Java Servlets API, JavaServer Pages (JSP), and XML. The library was previously known as "J2EE."

Where used: In distributed transactional enterprise applications in which the developer needs to reduce the costs and time of development, and use the speed, security, and reliability of server-side technology.

Java Interface Definition Language (Java IDL)

Definition: A technology for distributed objects, providing CORBA interoperability and connectivity capabilities for the Java EE platform. Similar to Remote Method Invocation (RMI), which supports distributed objects written entirely in the Java programming language, Java IDL enables objects to interact regardless of whether they're written in Java or another programming language. It uses CORBA's IDL to map Java to all other languages supported by CORBA.

Where used: In distributed applications in which objects written in Java will need to interact with objects that may be written in other programming languages.

Java Naming and Directory Interface (JNDI)

Definition: An API that enables Java applications to acquire named resources from a directory service. The resources in the directory service may be elaborated upon via attributes; these attributes may be used to locate and identify the resources requested by client applications. JNDI may work in concert with any number of directory service providers (LDAP, NDS, DNS, etc.) to provide these resources.

Where used: In scenarios where shared access to resources is necessary; any distributed application that must provide uniform access to a single store of resources.

JavaServer Pages (JSP)

Definition: A web technology that combines the tasks of page designing and programming. JSP pages use template data, custom elements, scripting languages, and server-side Java objects to return dynamic content to a client. Developers write the template data in HTML or XML, adding inline Java code within special tags to provide the dynamic content. These tags also allow JSP pages to interact with EJBs from a number of sources and display them. The beans can also be filled by using the input parameters of HTTP requests. Application servers compile JSP pages into Servlets.

Where used: In developing and maintaining dynamic web pages that leverage existing business systems.

Java Database Connectivity (JDBC)

Definition: An API that allows connectivity between Java EE applications and virtually any tabular data source. Typically, the data source is a SQL relational database management system (RDBMS), but the JDBC API also provides access to such data sources as flat files and spreadsheets.

Where used: Whenever a distributed application needs to access enterprise data.

Java Message Service (JMS)

Definition: An API for sending and receiving messages. JMS passes the received messages into a message store for listening applications to process. JMS may be extended to create a custom messaging API.

Where used: In message-driven beans.

module

Definition: A software unit that is the smallest deployable and usable unit of Java EE components. It consists of one or more components of the same container type and one deployment descriptor that contains meta-information about the components. The three types of modules are EJB, web, and application client. Modules can be deployed as standalone units, assembled as packages of related components, or assembled into a single application module.

Where used: Throughout all Java EE applications.

object-relational mapping (ORM)

Definition: The process wherein an object hierarchy is "mapped" to an information store. ORM is a technique used to persist object information beyond the lifetime of an application. Most often this information is persisted in a SQL database.

Where used: In the entity bean persistence of EJB 3.0. Alternative ORM and persistence frameworks include Hibernate (`www.hibernate.org`) and Java Data Objects (JDO) (`http://java.sun.com/products/jdo`).

resource manager

Definition: A Java EE component that manages the lifecycle of a resource type. This primarily involves providing access to a set of shared resources, including connection pooling, transaction support, and network communication. A resource manager provides and enforces the ACID (atomicity, consistency, isolation, durability) transaction properties for specific data and operations. An example of a resource manager is a relational database, which supports the persistent storage of relational data. The resource manager typically operates in a different address space or on a different machine from the clients that access it.

Where used: In enterprise applications where data and other operational resources require lifecycle management.

Remote Method Invocation (RMI)

Definition: A strictly Java-to-Java technology that allows an object running in one JVM to invoke methods on an object running in a different JVM. The JVMs can be on the same or different hosts. The object in the first program can make a call on a remote object in the second program once it has obtained a reference to the remote object.

Where used: Wherever distributed applications will involve only Java technology from end to end, or where provision is made, such as through RMI-IIOP, for Java technology to operate seamlessly with other languages.

Servlet

Definition: A component-based Java program that provides a simple, consistent mechanism for extending and enhancing the functionality of a web server and for accessing existing business systems. Servlets generate dynamic content and interact with web clients using a request/response paradigm. They have access to the entire family of Java APIs. Since Servlets are server and platform independent, they allow developers to select servers, platform, and tools of choice. Think of a Servlet as a GUI-less applet that runs on the server side.

Where used: In enhancing the functionality of a web server to access distributed enterprise systems.

Servlet container

Definition: A container that provides network services for sending requests and responses, as well as decoding requests, and formatting responses. Servlet containers are required to support HTTP as a protocol for requests and responses, but may additionally support other request/response protocols such as HTTPS.

Where used: Wherever Servlets are part of a distributed application.

Secure Sockets Layer (SSL)

Definition: A security protocol designed to enable private communications over a nonprivate network such as the Internet. SSL uses public key encryption and digital certificates to establish a secure connection between a client (such as a web browser) and a web server, to prevent eavesdropping or tampering with communications within and between distributed applications. Servers are always authenticated and clients are optionally authenticated. Web pages that are secured with SSL will likely display a "closed padlock" icon or other symbol to indicate that SSL has been enabled. By convention, such web site addresses will start with `https://` rather than the usual `http://`.

Where used: In virtually all distributed enterprise applications, especially those in which communications include private or sensitive material.

transaction

Definition: An indivisible unit of work that modifies data while ensuring its integrity. A transaction encloses one or more program statements, all of which must either complete (a commit) or be rolled back, ensuring that the data always remains in a consistent state. When a transaction commits, the data modifications made by its statements are saved. If any of the statements within a transaction fail, the transaction rolls back, undoing the effects of all statements in the transaction. Transactions control the concurrent access of data by multiple users.

Where used: In any application in which data is modified.

web application

Definition: An application written to be deployed over the Internet. This includes not only those built with Java technologies such as JSP and Servlets, but also those built with non-Java technologies such as CGI and Perl. Distributable web applications use Java EE technology, written to be deployed in web containers distributed across multiple JVMs running on the same host or different hosts.

Where used: Whenever a distributed application will be deployed over the Internet.

web container

Definition: A container that provides a runtime environment for web components, including security, concurrency, lifecycle management, transaction, deployment, and other services. A web container provides the same services as a JSP container, plus a federated view of the Java EE platform APIs. A web container is provided by a web or Java EE server. A distributed web container is one that can run a web application tagged as distributable and that executes across multiple JVMs running on the same host or on different hosts.

Where used: In any distributed application that includes web components.

web server

Definition: Software that provides a collection of services and resources for accessing the Internet, an intranet, or an extranet. A web server hosts web sites, provides support for HTTP and other protocols, and executes server-side programs. Within the Java EE architecture, a web server provides services, such as HTTP message handling, to a web container. Since the Java EE architecture assumes that a web container is hosted by a web server from the same vendor, it does not specify the contract between these two entities. Each web server may host one or more web containers.

Where used: Whenever web containers form part of an application—essentially, whenever any part of the application involves a network.

Index

Symbols

A

D

E

F

G

N

S

T